Lecture Notes in Computer Science 14142

Founding Editors

Gerhard Goos

Juris Hartmanis

The series Lecture Notes in Computer Science (LNCS), including its subseries Lecture Notes in Artificial Intelligence (LNAI) and Lecture Notes in Bioinformatics (LNBI), has established itself as a medium for the publication of new developments in computer science and information technology research, teaching, and education.

LNCS enjoys close cooperation with the computer science R & D community, the series counts many renowned academics among its volume editors and paper authors, and collaborates with prestigious societies. Its mission is to serve this international community by providing an invaluable service, mainly focused on the publication of conference and workshop proceedings and postproceedings. LNCS commenced publication in 1973.

José Abdelnour Nocera ·
Marta Kristín Lárusdóttir · Helen Petrie ·
Antonio Piccinno · Marco Winckler
Editors

Human-Computer Interaction – INTERACT 2023

19th IFIP TC13 International Conference
York, UK, August 28 – September 1, 2023
Proceedings, Part I

 Springer

Editors
José Abdelnour Nocera ⓘ
University of West London
London, UK

Helen Petrie ⓘ
University of York
York, UK

Marco Winckler ⓘ
Université Côte d'Azur
Sophia Antipolis Cedex, France

Marta Kristín Lárusdóttir ⓘ
Reykjavik University
Reykjavik, Iceland

Antonio Piccinno ⓘ
University of Bari Aldo Moro
Bari, Italy

ISSN 0302-9743   ISSN 1611-3349 (electronic)
Lecture Notes in Computer Science
ISBN 978-3-031-42279-9   ISBN 978-3-031-42280-5 (eBook)
https://doi.org/10.1007/978-3-031-42280-5

This Springer imprint is published by the registered company Springer Nature Switzerland AG
The registered company address is: Gewerbestrasse 11, 6330 Cham, Switzerland

Foreword

INTERACT 2023 is the 19th International Conference of Technical Committee 13 (Human-Computer Interaction) of IFIP (International Federation for Information Processing). IFIP was created in 1960 under the auspices of UNESCO. The IFIP Technical Committee 13 (TC13) aims at developing the science and technology of human-computer interaction (HCI). TC13 started the series of INTERACT conferences in 1984. These conferences have been an important showcase for researchers and practitioners in the field of HCI. Situated under the open, inclusive umbrella of IFIP, INTERACT has been truly international in its spirit and has attracted researchers from several countries and cultures. The venues of the INTERACT conferences over the years bear testimony to this inclusiveness.

INTERACT 2023 was held from August 28th to September 1st 2023 at the University of York, York, United Kingdom. The INTERACT Conference is held every two years, and is one of the longest-running conferences on Human-Computer Interaction. The INTERACT 2023 Conference was held both in-person and online. It was collocated with the British Computer Society HCI 2023 Conference.

The theme of the 19th conference was "Design for Equality and Justice". Increasingly computer science as a discipline is becoming concerned about issues of justice and equality – from fake news to rights for robots, from the ethics of driverless vehicles to the Gamergate controversy. The HCI community is surely well placed to be at the leading edge of such discussions within the wider computer science community and in the dialogue between computer science and the broader society. Justice and equality are particularly important concepts both for the City of York and for the University of York. The City of York has a long history of working for justice and equality, from the Quakers and their philanthropic chocolate companies, to current initiatives. The City of York is the UK's first Human Rights City, encouraging organizations and citizens to "increasingly think about human rights, talk about human rights issues and stand up for rights whether that's at work, school or home". The City of York has also launched "One Planet York", a network of organizations working towards a more sustainable, resilient and collaborative "one planet" future. York is now working to become the first "Zero emissions" city centre, with much of the medieval centre already car free.

Finally, great research is the heart of a good conference. Like its predecessors, INTERACT 2023 aimed to bring together high-quality research. As a multidisciplinary field, HCI requires interaction and discussion among diverse people with different interests and background. We thank all the authors who chose INTERACT 2023 as the venue to publish their research.

We received a total of 375 submissions distributed in 2 peer-reviewed tracks, 4 curated tracks, and 3 juried tracks. Of these, the following contributions were accepted:

- 71 Full Papers (peer reviewed)
- 58 Short Papers (peer reviewed)
- 6 Courses (curated)

- 2 Industrial Experience papers (curated)
- 10 Interactive Demonstrations (curated)
- 44 Interactive Posters (juried)
- 2 Panels (curated)
- 16 Workshops (juried)
- 15 Doctoral Consortium (juried)

The acceptance rate for contributions received in the peer-reviewed tracks was 32% for full papers and 31% for short papers. In addition to full papers and short papers, the present proceedings feature contributions accepted in the form of industrial experiences, courses, interactive demonstrations, interactive posters, panels, invited keynote papers, and descriptions of accepted workshops. The contributions submitted to workshops were published as an independent post-proceedings volume.

The reviewing process was primary carried out by a panel of international experts organized in subcommittees. Each subcommittee had a chair and a set of associated chairs, who were in charge of coordinating a double-blind reviewing process. Each paper received at least 2 reviews of associated chairs and two reviews from external experts in the HCI field. Hereafter we list the twelve subcommittees of INTERACT 2023:

- Accessibility and assistive technologies
- Design for business and safety/critical interactive systems
- Design of interactive entertainment systems
- HCI Education and Curriculum
- HCI for Justice and Equality
- Human-AI interaction
- Information visualization
- Interaction design for culture and development
- Interactive systems technologies and engineering
- Methodologies for HCI
- Social and ubiquitous Interaction
- Understanding users and human behaviour

The final decision on acceptance or rejection of full papers was taken in a Programme Committee meeting held in London, United Kingdom in March 2023. The full papers chairs, the subcommittee chairs, and the associate chairs participated in this meeting. The meeting discussed a consistent set of criteria to deal with inevitable differences among the large number of reviewers. The final decisions on other tracks were made by the corresponding track chairs and reviewers, often after electronic meetings and discussions.

INTERACT 2023 was made possible by the persistent efforts across several months by 12 subcommittee chairs, 86 associated chairs, 28 track chairs, and 407 reviewers. We thank them all.

September 2023

José Abdelnour Nocera
Helen Petrie
Marco Winckler

IFIP TC13 – http://ifip-tc13.org/

Established in 1989, the International Federation for Information Processing Technical Committee on Human–Computer Interaction (IFIP TC13) is an international committee of 37 IFIP Member national societies and 10 Working Groups, representing specialists of the various disciplines contributing to the field of human-computer interaction (HCI). This field includes, among others, human factors, ergonomics, cognitive science, computer science and design. INTERACT is the flagship conference of IFIP TC13, staged biennially in different countries in the world. The first INTERACT conference was held in 1984, at first running triennially and becoming a biennial event in 1993.

IFIP TC13 aims to develop the science, technology and societal aspects of HCI by encouraging empirical research promoting the use of knowledge and methods from the human sciences in design and evaluation of computing technology systems; promoting better understanding of the relation between formal design methods and system usability and acceptability; developing guidelines, models and methods by which designers may provide better human-oriented computing technology systems; and, cooperating with other groups, inside and outside IFIP, to promote user-orientation and humanization in system design. Thus, TC13 seeks to improve interactions between people and computing technology, to encourage the growth of HCI research and its practice in industry and to disseminate these benefits worldwide.

The main orientation is to place the users at the centre of the development process. Areas of study include: the problems people face when interacting with computing technology; the impact of technology deployment on people in individual and organisational contexts; the determinants of utility, usability, acceptability and user experience; the appropriate allocation of tasks between computing technology and users, especially in the case of autonomous and closed-loop systems; modelling the user, their tasks and the interactive system to aid better system design; and harmonizing the computing technology to user characteristics and needs.

While the scope is thus set wide, with a tendency toward general principles rather than particular systems, it is recognised that progress will only be achieved through both general studies to advance theoretical understanding and specific studies on practical issues (e.g., interface design standards, software system resilience, documentation, training material, appropriateness of alternative interaction technologies, guidelines, the problems of integrating multimedia systems to match system needs and organisational practices, etc.).

IFIP TC13 also stimulates working events and activities through its Working Groups (WGs). The WGs consist of HCI experts from around the world, who seek to expand knowledge and find solutions to HCI issues and concerns within their domains. The list of current TC13 WGs and their area of interest is given below:

- WG 13.1 (Education in HCI and HCI Curricula) aims to improve HCI education at all levels of higher education, coordinate and unite efforts to develop HCI curricula and promote HCI teaching.

- WG 13.2 (Methodology for User-Centred System Design) aims to foster research, dissemination of information and good practice in the methodical application of HCI to software engineering.
- WG 13.3 (Human Computer Interaction, Disability and Aging) aims to make HCI designers aware of the needs of people with disabilities and older people and encourage development of information systems and tools permitting adaptation of interfaces to specific users.
- WG 13.4/WG2.7 (User Interface Engineering) investigates the nature, concepts and construction of user interfaces for software systems, using a framework for reasoning about interactive systems and an engineering model for developing user interfaces.
- WG 13.5 (Resilience, Reliability, Safety and Human Error in System Development) seeks a framework for studying human factors relating to systems failure, develops leading-edge techniques in hazard analysis and safety engineering of computer-based systems, and guides international accreditation activities for safety-critical systems.
- WG 13.6 (Human-Work Interaction Design) aims at establishing relationships between extensive empirical work-domain studies and HCI design. It will promote the use of knowledge, concepts, methods and techniques that enable user studies to procure a better apprehension of the complex interplay between individual, social and organisational contexts and thereby a better understanding of how and why people work in the ways that they do.
- WG 13.7 (Human–Computer Interaction and Visualization) aims to establish a study and research program that will combine both scientific work and practical applications in the fields of Human–Computer Interaction and Visualization. It will integrate several additional aspects of further research areas, such as scientific visualization, data mining, information design, computer graphics, cognition sciences, perception theory, or psychology into this approach.
- WG 13.8 (Interaction Design and International Development) aims to support and develop the research, practice and education capabilities of HCI in institutions and organisations based around the world taking into account their diverse local needs and cultural perspectives.
- WG 13.9 (Interaction Design and Children) aims to support practitioners, regulators and researchers to develop the study of interaction design and children across international contexts.
- WG 13.10 (Human-Centred Technology for Sustainability) aims to promote research, design, development, evaluation, and deployment of human-centred technology to encourage sustainable use of resources in various domains.

IFIP TC13 recognises contributions to HCI through both its Pioneer in HCI Award and various paper awards associated with each INTERACT conference. Since the processes to decide the various awards take place after papers are sent to the publisher for publication, the recipients of the awards are not identified in the proceedings.

The IFIP TC13 Pioneer in Human-Computer Interaction Award recognises the contributions and achievements of pioneers in HCI. An IFIP TC13 Pioneer is one who, through active participation in IFIP Technical Committees or related IFIP groups, has made outstanding contributions to the educational, theoretical, technical, commercial, or professional aspects of analysis, design, construction, evaluation, and use of interactive systems. The IFIP TC13 Pioneer Awards are presented during an awards ceremony at each INTERACT conference.

In 1999, TC13 initiated a special IFIP Award, the Brian Shackel Award, for the most outstanding contribution in the form of a refereed paper submitted to and delivered at each INTERACT Conference, which draws attention to the need for a comprehensive human-centred approach in the design and use of information technology in which the human and social implications have been considered. The IFIP TC13 Accessibility Award, launched in 2007 by IFIP WG 13.3, recognises the most outstanding contribution with international impact in the field of ageing, disability, and inclusive design in the form of a refereed paper submitted to and delivered at the INTERACT Conference. The IFIP TC13 Interaction Design for International Development Award, launched in 2013 by IFIP WG 13.8, recognises the most outstanding contribution to the application of interactive systems for social and economic development of people around the world taking into account their diverse local needs and cultural perspectives. The IFIP TC13 Pioneers' Award for Best Doctoral Student Paper at INTERACT, first awarded in 2019, is selected by the past recipients of the IFIP TC13 Pioneer title. The award is made to the best research paper accepted to the INTERACT Conference which is based on the doctoral research of the student and authored and presented by the student.

In 2015, TC13 approved the creation of a steering committee for the INTERACT conference. The Steering Committee (SC) is currently chaired by Marco Winckler and is responsible for:

- Promoting and maintaining the INTERACT conference as the premiere venue for researchers and practitioners interested in the topics of the conference (this requires a refinement of the topics above).
- Ensuring the highest quality for the contents of the event.
- Setting up the bidding process to handle future INTERACT conferences. Decision is made up at TC13 level.
- Providing advice to the current and future chairs and organizers of the INTERACT conference.
- Providing data, tools, and documents about previous conferences to future conference organizers.
- Selecting the reviewing system to be used throughout the conference (as this impacts the entire set of reviewers).
- Resolving general issues involved with the INTERACT conference.
- Capitalizing on history (good and bad practices).

Further information is available at the IFIP TC13 website: http://ifip-tc13.org/.

IFIP TC13 Members

Officers

Chair

Paula Kotzé, South Africa

Vice-chair for Conferences

Marco Winckler, France

**Vice-chair for Equity
and Development**

José Abdelnour-Nocera, UK

**Vice-chair for Media
and Communications**

Helen Petrie, UK

**Vice-chair for Membership
and Collaboration**

Philippe Palanque, France

Vice-chair for Working Groups

Simone D. J. Barbosa, Brazil

Vice-chair for Finance (Treasurer)

Regina Bernhaupt, The Netherlands

Secretary

Janet Wesson, South Africa

INTERACT Steering Committee Chair

Marco Winckler, France

Country Representatives

Australia

Henry B. L. Duh
Australian Computer Society

Austria

Christopher Frauenberger
Austrian Computer Society

Belgium

Bruno Dumas
IMEC – Interuniversity
Micro-Electronics Center

Brazil

André Freire
Simone D. J. Barbosa (section b)
Sociedade Brasileira de Computação
(SBC)

Bulgaria

Petia Koprinkova-Hristova
Bulgarian Academy of Sciences

Croatia

Andrina Granić
Croatian Information Technology
Association (CITA)

Cyprus

Panayiotis Zaphiris
Cyprus Computer Society

Czech Republic

Zdeněk Míkovec
Czech Society for Cybernetics and
Informatics

Denmark

Jan Stage
Danish Federation for Information
Processing (DANFIP)

Finland

Virpi Roto
Finnish Information Processing
Association

France

Philippe Palanque
Marco Winckler (section b)
Société informatique de France (SIF)

Germany

Tom Gross
Gesellschaft fur Informatik e.V.

Ireland

Liam J. Bannon
Irish Computer Society

Italy

Fabio Paternò
Associazione Italiana per l' Informatica ed
il Calcolo Automatico (AICA)

Japan

Yoshifumi Kitamura
Information Processing Society of Japan

Netherlands

Regina Bernhaupt
Koninklijke Nederlandse Vereniging
van Informatieprofessionals (KNVI)

New Zealand

Mark Apperley
Institute of IT Professionals New Zealand

Norway

Frode Eika Sandnes
Norwegian Computer Society

Poland

Marcin Sikorski
Polish Academy of Sciences (PAS)

Portugal

Pedro Filipe Pereira Campos
Associacão Portuguesa para o
Desenvolvimento da Sociedade da
Informação (APDSI)

Serbia

Aleksandar Jevremovic
Informatics Association of Serbia (IAS)

Singapore

Shengdong Zhao
Singapore Computer Society

Slovakia

Wanda Benešová
Slovak Society for Computer Science

Slovenia

Matjaž Kljun
Slovenian Computer Society
INFORMATIKA

South Africa

Janet L. Wesson
Paula Kotzé (section b)
Institute of Information Technology
Professionals South Africa (IITPSA)

Sri Lanka

Thilina Halloluwa
Computer Society of Sri Lanka (CSSL)

Sweden

Jan Gulliksen
Swedish Interdisciplinary Society for
Human-Computer Interaction
Dataföreningen i Sverige

Switzerland

Denis Lalanne
Schweizer Informatik Gesellschaft (SI)

United Kingdom

José Luis Abdelnour Nocera
Helen Petrie (section b)
British Computer Society (BCS),
Chartered Institute for IT

International Members at Large Representatives

ACM

Gerrit van der Veer
Association for Computing
Machinery

CLEI

César Collazos
Centro Latinoamericano de Estudios en
Informatica

Expert Members

Anirudha Joshi, India
Constantinos Coursaris, Canada
Carmelo Ardito, Italy
Daniel Orwa Ochieng, Kenya
David Lamas, Estonia
Dorian Gorgan, Romania
Eunice Sari, Australia/Indonesia
Fernando Loizides, UK/Cyprus
Geraldine Fitzpatrick, Austria

Ivan Burmistrov, Russia
Julio Abascal, Spain
Kaveh Bazargan, Iran
Marta Kristin Lárusdóttir, Iceland
Nikolaos Avouris, Greece
Peter Forbrig, Germany
Torkil Clemmensen, Denmark
Zhengjie Liu, China

Working Group Chairpersons

WG 13.1 (Education in HCI and HCI Curricula)

Konrad Baumann, Austria

WG 13.2 (Methodologies for User-Centered System Design)

Regina Bernhaupt, Netherlands

WG 13.3 (HCI, Disability and Aging)

Helen Petrie, UK

WG 13.4/2.7 (User Interface Engineering)

Davide Spano, Italy

WG 13.5 (Human Error, Resilience, Reliability, Safety and System Development)

Tilo Mentler, Germany

WG13.6 (Human-Work Interaction Design)

Barbara Rita Barricelli, Italy

WG13.7 (HCI and Visualization)

Gerrit van der Veer, Netherlands

WG 13.8 (Interaction Design and International Development)

José Adbelnour Nocera, UK

WG 13.9 (Interaction Design and Children)

Gavin Sim, UK

WG 13.10 (Human-Centred Technology for Sustainability)

Masood Masoodian, Finland

Organization

General Chairs

Helen Petrie   University of York, UK
Jose Abdelnour-Nocera   University of West London, UK and ITI/Larsys,
         Portugal

Technical Program Chair

Marco Winckler   Université Côte d'Azur, France

Full Papers Chairs

Antonio Piccinno   University of Bari Aldo Moro, Italy
Marta Kristin Lárusdóttir   Reykjavik University, Iceland

Short Papers Chairs

Marta Rey-Babarro   Zillow, USA
Frode Eika Sandnes   Oslo Metropolitan University, Norway
Grace Eden   University of York, UK

Poster Chairs

Alena Denisova   University of York, UK
Burak Merdenyan   University of York, UK

Workshops Chairs

Jan Stage   Aalborg University, Denmark
Anna Bramwell-Dicks   University of York, UK

Panels Chairs

Effie Lai-Chong Law   Durham University, UK
Massimo Zancanaro   University of Trento, Italy

Student Volunteers Chairs

Sanjit Samaddar   University of York, UK
Daniel Lock   University of York, UK

Interactive Demonstrations Chairs

Barbara Rita Barricelli   University of Brescia, Italy
Jainendra Shukla   Indraprastha Institute of Information Technology,
                             India

Courses Chairs

Nikos Avouris   University of Patras, Greece
André Freire   Federal University of Lavras, Brazil

Doctoral Consortium Chairs

David Lamas   Tallinn University, Estonia
Geraldine Fitzpatrick   TU Wien, Austria
Tariq Zaman   University of Technology Sarawak, Malaysia

Industrial Experiences Chairs

Helen Petrie   University of York, UK
Jose Abdelnour-Nocera   University of West London, UK and ITI/Larsys,
                             Portugal

Publicity Chairs

Delvin Varghese   Monash University, Australia
Lourdes Moreno   Universidad Carlos III de Madrid, Spain

Advisors

Marco Winckler	University of the Côte d'Azur, France
Fernando Loizides	Cardiff University, UK
Carmelo Ardito	LUM Giuseppe Degennaro University, Italy

Web Master

Edmund Wei	University of York, UK

INTERACT Subcommittee Chairs

Anirudha Joshi	Industrial Design Centre, IIT Bombay, India
Célia Martinie	IRIT, Université Toulouse III - Paul Sabatier, France
Fabio Paternò	CNR-ISTI, Pisa, Italy
Frank Steinicke	Universität Hamburg, Germany
Gerhard Weber	TU Dresden, Germany
Helen Petrie	University of York, UK
José Campos	University of Minho, Portugal
Nikolaos Avouris	University of Patras, Greece
Philippe Palanque	IRIT, Université Toulouse III - Paul Sabatier, France
Rosa Lanzilotti	University of Bari, Italy
Rosella Gennari	Free University of Bozen-Bolzano, Switzerland
Simone Barbosa	PUC-Rio, Brazil
Torkil Clemmensen	Copenhagen Business School, Denmark
Yngve Dahl	Norwegian University of Science and Technology, Norway

INTERACT Steering Committee

Anirudha Joshi	Industrial Design Centre, IIT Bombay, India
Antonio Piccinno	University of Bari, Italy
Carmelo Arditto	University of Bari, Italy
Fernando Loizides	University of Cardiff, UK
Frode Sandnes	Oslo Metropolitan University, Norway
Helen Petrie	University of York, UK
Janet Wesson	Nelson Mandela University, South Africa
Marco Winckler (Chair)	Université Côte d'Azur, France
Marta Lárusdóttir	Reykjavik University, Iceland

Paolo Buono   University of Bari, Italy
Paula Kotzé   University of Pretoria, South Africa
Philippe Palanque   IRIT, Université Toulouse III - Paul Sabatier,
                                    France
Raquel Oliveira Prates   Universidade Federal de Minas Gerais, Brazil
Tom Gross   University of Bamberg, Germany

Program Committee

Alan Chamberlain   University of Nottingham, UK
Alessandra Melonio   Ca' Foscari University of Venice, Italy
Alessandro Pagano   University of Bari, Italy
Andrea Marrella   Sapienza Università di Roma, Italy
Andrés Lucero   Aalto University, Finland
Anna Sigríður Islind   Reykjavik University, Iceland
Antonio Piccinno   University of Bari, Italy
Ashley Colley   University of Lapland, Finland
Aurora Constantin   University of Edinburgh, UK
Barbara Rita Barricelli   Università degli Studi di Brescia, Italy
Bridget Kane   Karlstad University Business School, Sweden
Bruno Dumas   University of Namur, Belgium
Carla Dal Sasso Freitas   Federal University of Rio Grande do Sul, Brazil
Célia Martinie   Université Toulouse III - Paul Sabatier, France
Chi Vi   University of Sussex, UK
Christopher Power   University of Prince Edward Island, Canada
Christopher Clarke   University of Bath, UK
Cristian Bogdan   KTH, EECS, HCT, Sweden
Cristina Gena   Università di Torino, Italy
Dan Fitton   University of Central Lancashire, UK
Daniela Fogli   University of Brescia, Italy
Daniela Trevisan   Universidade Federal Fluminense, Brazil
Denis Lalanne   University of Fribourg, Switzerland
Dipanjan Chakraborty   BITS Pilani, Hyderabad Campus, India
Fabio Buttussi   University of Udine, Italy
Federico Cabitza   University of Milano-Bicocca, Italy
Fernando Loizides   Cardiff University, UK
Frode Eika Sandnes   Oslo Metropolitan University, Norway
Gerd Bruder   University of Central Florida, USA
Gerhard Weber   TU Dresden, Germany
Giuliana Vitiello   Università di Salerno, Italy
Giuseppe Desolda   University of Bari Aldo Moro, Italy

Helen Petrie	University of York, UK
Jan Van den Bergh	UHasselt - tUL - Flanders Make, Belgium
Jan Gulliksen	KTH Royal Institute of Technology, Sweden
Janet Wesson	Nelson Mandela University, South Africa
Janet Read	University of Central Lancashire, UK
Jens Gerken	Westphalian University of Applied Sciences, Germany
Jo Lumsden	Aston University, UK
Jolanta Mizera-Pietraszko	Military University of Land Forces, Poland
Jonna Häkkilä	University of Lapland, Finland
José Abdelnour Nocera	University of West London, UK
Judy Bowen	University of Waikato, New Zealand
Karen Renaud	University of Strathclyde, UK
Kaveh Bazargan	Allameh Tabataba'i University, Islamic Republic of Iran
Kris Luyten	Hasselt University - tUL - Flanders Make, Belgium
Kshitij Sharma	NTNU, Norway
Lara Piccolo	Open University, UK
Lene Nielsen	IT University of Copenhagen, Denmark
Lucio Davide Spano	University of Cagliari, Italy
Luigi De Russis	Politecnico di Torino, Italy
Manjiri Joshi	Swansea University, UK
Marco Winckler	Université Côte d'Azur, France
Maristella Matera	Politecnico di Milano, Italy
Mark Apperley	University of Waikato, New Zealand
Marta Lárusdóttir	Reykjavik University, Iceland
Netta Iivari	University of Oulu, Finland
Oliver Korn	Offenburg University, Germany
Paloma Diaz	University Carlos III of Madrid, Spain
Paolo Bottoni	Sapienza University of Rome, Italy
Paolo Buono	University of Bari Aldo Moro, Italy
Paula Kotzé	University of Pretoria, South Africa
Pedro Campos	ITI/LARSyS, Portugal
Peter Forbrig	University of Rostock, Germany
Raquel O. Prates	Universidade Federal de Minas Gerais, Brazil
Renaud Blanch	Université Grenoble Alpes, France
Sandy Claes	LUCA School of Arts, Belgium
Sayan Sarcar	Birmingham City University, UK
Shaun Macdonald	University of Glasgow, UK
Simone Kriglstein	Masaryk University, Czech Republic
Sophie Dupuy-Chessa	Université Grenoble Alpes, France

Sumita Sharma	University of Oulu, Finland
Sven Mayer	LMU Munich, Germany
Tania Di Mascio	Università dell'Aquila, Italy
Theodoros Georgiou	Heriot-Watt University, UK
Thilina Halloluwa	University of Colombo, Sri Lanka
Tilo Mentler	Trier University of Applied Sciences, Germany
Timothy Merritt	Aalborg University, Denmark
Tom Gross	University of Bamberg, Germany
Valentin Schwind	Frankfurt University of Applied Sciences, Germany
Virpi Roto	Aalto University, Finland
Vita Santa Barletta	University of Bari Aldo Moro, Italy
Vivian Genaro Motti	George Mason University, USA
Wricha Mishra	MIT Institute of Design, India
Zdeněk Míkovec	Czech Technical University Prague, Czech Republic
Zeynep Yildiz	Koç University, Turkey

Additional Reviewers

Abhishek Shrivastava
Adalberto Simeone
Aditya Prakash Kulkarni
Adrien Chaffangeon Caillet
Adrien Coppens
Aekaterini Mavri
Ahmad Samer Wazan
Aidan Slingsby
Aimee Code
Aizal Yusrina Idris
Akihisa Shitara
Aku Visuri
Alberto Monge Roffarello
Alessandro Forgiarini
Alessio Malizia
Alex Binh Vinh Duc Nguyen
Alex Chen
Alexander Maedche
Alexander Meschtscherjakov
Alexander Wachtel
Alexandra Voit
Alexandre Canny
Ali Gheitasy

Aline Menin
Alisson Puska
Alma Cantu
Amy Melniczuk
An Jacobs
Ana Serrano
Anderson Maciel
André Freire
Andre Salgado
Andre Suslik Spritzer
Andrea Antonio Cantone
Andrea Bellucci
Andrea Esposito
Andreas Fender
Andreas Mallas
Andreas Sonderegger
Andres Santos-Torres
Ángel Cuevas
Angela Locoro
Angus Addlesee
Angus Marshall
Anicia Peters
Anirudh Nagraj

Ankica Barisic
Anna Spagnolli
Annika Schulz
Anthony Perritano
Antigoni Parmaxi
Antje Jacobs
Antonella Varesano
Antonio Bucchiarone
Antonio Piccinno
Anupriya Tuli
Argenis Ramirez Gomez
Arminda Lopes
Arnaud Blouin
Ashwin Singh
Ashwin T. S.
Asim Evren Yantac
Axel Carayon
Aykut Coşkun
Azra Ismail
Barsha Mitra
Basmah Almekhled
Beat Signer
Beenish Chaudhry
Behnaz Norouzi
Benjamin Schnitzer
Benjamin Tag
Benjamin Weyers
Berardina De Carolis
Bharatwaja Namatherdhala
Bhumika Walia
Biju Thankachan
Bram van Deurzen
Çağlar Genç
Canlin Zhang
Carolyn Holter
Céline Coutrix
Chameera De Silva
Charlotte Magnusson
Chiara Ceccarini
Chiara Natali
Chikodi Chima
Christian Frisson
Christophe Kolski
Christopher Frauenberger
Christos Katsanos

Christos Sintoris
Cléber Corrêa
Cleidson de Souza
Daisuke Sato
Damianos Dumi Sigalas
Damon Horowitz
Dan Fitton
Daniel Görlich
Daniel Zielasko
Danielle Langlois
Daphne Chang
Dario Bertero
David Gollasch
David Navarre
Davide D'Adamo
Davide Mulfari
Davide Spallazzo
Debjani Roy
Diana Korka
Diego Morra
Dilrukshi Gamage
Diogo Cabral
Dixie Ching
Domenico Gigante
Dominic Potts
Donald McMillan
Edwige Pissaloux
Edy Portmann
Effie Law
Eike Schneiders
Elisa Mekler
Elise Grevet
Elizabeth Buie
Elodie Bouzbib
Emanuele Pucci
Enes Yigitbas
Eric Barboni
Estela Peralta
Euan Freeman
Evangelia Chrysikou
Evelyn Eika
Fabiana Vernero
Fabio Cassano
Fabrizio Balducci
Fanny Vainionpää

Fausto Medola
Favour Aladesuru
Federica Cena
Federico Botella
Florian Gnadlinger
Francesco Cauteruccio
Francesco Chiossi
Francesco Ferrise
Francesco Greco
Francisco Iniesto
Francisco Maria Calisto
Frank Beruscha
Frank Fischer
Frank Nack
Frida Milella
Funmi Adebesin
Gavin Sim
George Adrian Stoica
George Raptis
Georgios Papadoulis
Gianluca Schiavo
Girish Dalvi
Grischa Liebel
Guanhua Zhang
Guilherme Schardong
Gustavo Rovelo Ruiz
Hanne Sørum
Heidi Hartikainen
Himanshu Verma
Holger Regenbrecht
Hsin-Jou Lin
Hui-Yin Wu
Ikram Ur Rehman
Isabela Gasparini
Ivo Malý
Jack Jamieson
James Simpson
Jan Leusmann
Jana Jost
Jannes Peeters
Jari Kangas
Jayden Khakurel
Jean Hallewell Haslwanter
Jemma König
Jermaine Marshall

Jeroen Ceyssens
Jesper Gaarsdal
Jessica Sehrt
Jiaying Liu
Job Timmermans
Joe Cutting
Jonas Moll
Jonathan Hook
Joni Salminen
Joongi Shin
Jorge Wagner
José Campos
Joseph O'Hagan
Judith Borghouts
Julia Hertel
Julio Reis
Kajetan Enge
Kasper Rodil
Kate Rogers
Katerina Cerna
Katherine Seyama
Kathia Oliveira
Kathrin Gerling
Khyati Priya
Konstantin Biriukov
Kostantinos Moustakas
Krishna Venkatasubramanian
Laden Husamaldin
Lars Lischke
Lars Oestreicher
Laura Helsby
Leena Ventä-Olkkonen
Lele Sha
Leonardo Sandoval
Lorena Riol-Blanco
Lorenzo Torrez
Louise Barkhuus
Luis Leiva
Luis Teran
M. Cristina Vannini
Maälis Lefebvre
Magdaléna Kejstová
Malay Dhamelia
Manik Gupta
Manuel J. Fonseca

Marco de Gemmis
Marco Manca
Marco Romano
Margarita Anastassova
Margault Sacré
Margherita Andrao
Mari Karhu
Maria Fernanda Antunes
María Óskarsdóttir
Marianna Di Gregorio
Marika Jonsson
Marios Constantinides
Mark Apperley
Mark Lochrie
Marko Tkalcic
Markus Löchtefeld
Markus Tatzgern
Marta Serafini
Martin Hedlund
Martin Kocur
Massimo Zancanaro
Mateusz Dubiel
Matthias Baldauf
Matthias Heintz
Max Birk
Maxime Savary-Leblanc
Maximiliano Jeanneret Medina
Mehdi Rizvi
Mengyu Chen
Michael Burch
Michael Rohs
Michalis Xenos
Mihail Terenti
Min Zhang
Mireia Ribera
Mirko De Vincentiis
Miroslav Macík
Mohd Kamal Othman
Monica Divitini
Monisha Pattanaik
Mrim Alnfiai
Murali Balusu
Nada Attar
Nadine Flegel
Nadine Vigouroux

Nadir Weibel
Nahal Norouzi
Najla Aldaraani
Nancy Alajarmeh
Nicholas Vanderschantz
Nicoletta Adamo
Niels van Berkel
Nikolaos Avouris
Nils Beese
Nivan Ferreira
Nurha Yingta
Ohoud Alharbi
Omar Al Hashimi
Pallabi Bhowmick
Pallavi Rao Gadahad
Panayiotis Koutsabasis
Paolo Massa
Parisa Saadati
Pascal Lessel
Patricia Arias-Cabarcos
Paula Alexandra Silva
Pavel Slavik
Peter Bago
Philippe Truillet
Pinar Simsek Caglar
Po-Ming Law
Prabodh Sakhardande
Pranjal Protim Borah
Quynh Nguyen
Radovan Madleňák
Ragad Allwihan
Rahat Jahangir Rony
Rajni Sachdeo
Razan Bamoallem
Rekha Sugandhi
Rishi Vanukuru
Rogério Bordini
Rohan Gaikwad
Romane Dubus
Rosella Gennari
Rui José
Sabrina Burtscher
Sabrina Lakhdhir
Sahar Mirhadi
Saif Hadj Sassi

Salvatore Andolina
Salvatore Sorce
Samangi Wadinambi Arachchi
Sanika Doolani
Sanjit Samaddar
Sara Capecchi
Sarah Hodge
Saumya Pareek
Scott MacKenzie
Scott Trent
Sebastian Feger
Sebastian Günther
Sebastian Weiß
Sébastien Scannella
Shah Rukh Humayoun
Shunyao Wu
Siddharth Gulati
Siiri Paananen
Silvia Espada
Silvia Gabrielli
Simon Ruffieux
Simon Voelker
Simone Barbosa
Siti Haris
Sónia Brito-Costa
Sophie Dupuy-Chessa
Sophie Lepreux
Soraia M. Alarcão
Srishti Gupta
Stefan Johansson
Stéphanie Fleck
Stine Johansen
Subrata Tikadar
Suzanna Schmeelk
Sybille Caffiau
Sylvain Malacria
Taejun Kim
Tahani Alahmadi
Tahani Albalawi
Takumi Yamamoto
Tariq Zaman
Tathagata Ray
Telmo Zarraonandia
Teresa Onorati
Tero Jokela
Theodoros Georgiou

Thomas Kosch
Tilman Dingler
Tom Veuskens
Tomas Alves
Tomáš Pagáč
Tomi Heimonen
Tommaso Turchi
Tong Wu
Tzu-Yang Wang
Valentino Artizzu
Vanessa Cesário
Vanessa Maike
Vania Neris
Vasiliki Mylonopoulou
Vera Memmesheimer
Vickie Nguyen
Victor Adriel de Jesus Oliveira
Vidushani Dhanawansa
Vikas Upadhyay
Vincent Zakka
Vincenzo Dentamaro
Vincenzo Gattulli
Vinitha Gadiraju
Vit Rusnak
Vittoria Frau
Vivek Kant
Way Kiat Bong
Weiqin Chen
Wenchen Guo
William Delamare
Xiying Wang
Yann Savoye
Yao Chen
Yaoli Mao
Yaxiong Lei
Yilin Liu
Ying Ma
Yingying Zhao
Yong-Joon Thoo
Yoselyn Walsh
Yosra Rekik
Yuan Chen
Yubo Kou
Zhiyuan Wang
Zi Wang

Sponsors and Partners

Sponsors

UNIVERSITY OF
WEST LONDON

Partners

International Federation for Information Processing

In-cooperation with ACM

In-cooperation with SIGCHI

Contents – Part I

3D Interaction

AHO-Guide: Automatically Guiding the Head Orientation of a Local User
in Augmented Reality to Realign the Field of View with Remote Users 3
Lucas Pometti, Charles Bailly, and Julien Castet

Point- and Volume-Based Multi-object Acquisition in VR 20
Zhiqing Wu, Difeng Yu, and Jorge Goncalves

Using Mid-Air Haptics to Guide Mid-Air Interactions 43
*Timothy Neate, Sergio Alvares Maffra, William Frier, Zihao You,
and Stephanie Wilson*

Accessibility

Brilliance and Resilience: A New Perspective to the Challenges, Practices
and Needs of University Students with Visual Impairments in India 67
*Tigmanshu Bhatnagar, Vikas Upadhyay, P. V. Madhusudhan Rao,
Nicolai Marquardt, Mark Miodownik, and Catherine Holloway*

Mapping Virtual Reality Controls to Inform Design of Accessible User
Experiences 89
Christopher Power, Paul Cairns, and Triskal DeHaven

WAM-Studio: A Web-Based Digital Audio Workstation to Empower
Cochlear Implant Users 101
Michel Buffa, Antoine Vidal-Mazuy, Lloyd May, and Marco Winckler

Web Accessibility in Higher Education in Norway: To What Extent are
University Websites Accessible? 111
Yavuz Inal and Anne Britt Torkildsby

Wesee: Digital Cultural Heritage Interpretation for Blind and Low Vision
People 123
*Yalan Luo, Weiyue Lin, Yuhan Liu, Xiaomei Nie, Xiang Qian,
and Hanyu Guo*

Accessibility and Aging

Accessibility Inspections of Mobile Applications by Professionals
with Different Expertise Levels: An Empirical Study Comparing with User
Evaluations   135
    Delvani Antônio Mateus, Simone Bacellar Leal Ferreira,
    Maurício Ronny de Almeida Souza, and André Pimenta Freire

Evaluating the Acceptance of a Software Application Designed to Assist
Communication for People with Parkinson's Disease   155
    Julia Greenfield, Káthia Marçal de Oliveira, Véronique Delcroix,
    Sophie Lepreux, Christophe Kolski, and Anne Blanchard-Dauphin

"The Relief is Amazing": An In-situ Short Field Evaluation of a Personal
Voice Assistive Technology for a User Living with Dementia   165
    Ana-Maria Salai, Glenda Cook, and Lars Erik Holmquist

Towards an Automatic Easy-to-Read Adaptation of Morphological
Features in Spanish Texts   176
    Mari Carmen Suárez-Figueroa, Isam Diab, Álvaro González,
    and Jesica Rivero-Espinosa

Accessibility for Auditory/Hearing Disabilities

Challenges Faced by the Employed Indian DHH Community   201
    Advaith Sridhar, Roshni Poddar, Mohit Jain, and Pratyush Kumar

Haptic Auditory Feedback for Enhanced Image Description: A Study
of User Preferences and Performance   224
    Mallak Alkhathlan, M. L. Tlachac, and Elke A. Rundensteiner

Using Colour and Brightness for Sound Zone Feedback   247
    Stine S. Johansen, Peter Axel Nielsen, Kashmiri Stec,
    and Jesper Kjeldskov

Co-design

Common Objects for Programming Workshops in Non-Formal Learning
Contexts   275
    Nathalie Bressa, Susanne Bødker, Clemens N. Klokmose,
    and Eva Eriksson

Engaging a Project Consortium in Ethics-Aware Design and Research   297
    Päivi Heikkilä, Hanna Lammi, and Susanna Aromaa

Exploring Emotions: Study of Five Design Workshops for Generating
Ideas for Emotional Self-report Interfaces 307
   Carla Nave, Francisco Nunes, Teresa Romão, and Nuno Correia

Moving Away from the Blocks: Evaluating the Usability of EduBlocks
for Supporting Children to Transition from Block-Based Programming 317
   *Gavin Sim, Mark Lochrie, Misbahu S. Zubair, Oliver Kerr,
   and Matthew Bates*

Cybersecurity and Trust

Dark Finance: Exploring Deceptive Design in Investment Apps 339
   Ivana Rakovic and Yavuz Inal

Elements that Influence Transparency in Artificial Intelligent Systems -
A Survey 349
   *Deepa Muralidhar, Rafik Belloum, Kathia Marçal de Oliveira,
   and Ashwin Ashok*

Empowering Users: Leveraging Interface Cues to Enhance Password
Security 359
   *Yasmeen Abdrabou, Marco Asbeck, Ken Pfeuffer, Yomna Abdelrahman,
   Mariam Hassib, and Florian Alt*

Friendly Folk Advice: Exploring Cybersecurity Information Sharing
in Nigeria 369
   *James Nicholson, Opeyemi Dele Ajayi, Kemi Fasae,
   and Boniface Kayode Alese*

Trust in Facial Recognition Systems: A Perspective from the Users 379
   Gabriela Beltrão, Sonia Sousa, and David Lamas

Data Physicalisation and Cross-Device

Comparing Screen-Based Version Control to Augmented Artifact Version
Control for Physical Objects 391
   Maximilian Letter, Marco Kurzweg, and Katrin Wolf

EmoClock: Communicating Real-Time Emotional States Through Data
Physicalizations 416
   *Dennis Peeters, Champika Ranasinghe, Auriol Degbelo,
   and Faizan Ahmed*

Extending User Interaction with Mixed Reality Through
a Smartphone-Based Controller 426
  Georgios Papadoulis, Christos Sintoris, Christos Fidas,
  and Nikolaos Avouris

Fitts' Throughput Vs Empirical Throughput: A Comparative Study 436
  Khyati Priya and Anirudha Joshi

Eye-Free, Gesture Interaction and Sign Language

Developing and Evaluating a Novel Gamified Virtual Learning
Environment for ASL 459
  Jindi Wang, Ioannis Ivrissimtzis, Zhaoxing Li, Yunzhan Zhou, and Lei Shi

Effects of Moving Speed and Phone Location on Eyes-Free Gesture Input
with Mobile Devices 469
  Milad Jamalzadeh, Yosra Rekik, Laurent Grisoni, Radu-Daniel Vatavu,
  Gualtiero Volpe, and Alexandru Dancu

Hap2Gest: An Eyes-Free Interaction Concept with Smartphones Using
Gestures and Haptic Feedback 479
  Milad Jamalzadeh, Yosra Rekik, Alexandru Dancu, and Laurent Grisoni

User-Centered Evaluation of Different Configurations of a Touchless
Gestural Interface for Interactive Displays 501
  Vito Gentile, Habiba Farzand, Simona Bonaccorso, Davide Rocchesso,
  Alessio Malizia, Mohamed Khamis, and Salvatore Sorce

Haptic Interaction

Assignment of a Vibration to a Graphical Object Induced by Resonant
Frequency 523
  Marco Kurzweg, Simon Linke, Yannick Weiss, Maximilian Letter,
  Albrecht Schmidt, and Katrin Wolf

GuidingBand: A Precise Tactile Hand Guidance System to Aid Visual
Perception 546
  Atish Waghwase and Anirudha Joshi

Mid-air Haptic Cursor for Physical Objects 563
  Miroslav Macík and Meinhardt Branig

Stress Embodied: Developing Multi-sensory Experiences for VR Police
Training 573
    Jakob Carl Uhl, Georg Regal, Michael Gafert, Markus Murtinger,
    and Manfred Tscheligi

Healthcare Applications and Self-Monitoring

Co-designing an eHealth Solution to Support Fibromyalgia
Self-Management 587
    Pedro Albuquerque Santos, Rui Neves Madeira, Hugo Ferreira,
    and Carmen Caeiro

Designing Remote Patient Monitoring Technologies for Post-operative
Home Cancer Recovery: The Role of Reassurance 598
    Constantinos Timinis, Jeremy Opie, Simon Watt, Pramit Khetrapal,
    John Kelly, Manolis Mavrikis, Yvonne Rogers, and Ivana Drobnjak

SELFI: Evaluation of Techniques to Reduce Self-report Fatigue by Using
Facial Expression of Emotion 620
    Salma Mandi, Surjya Ghosh, Pradipta De, and Bivas Mitra

Usability and Clinical Evaluation of a Wearable TENS Device for Pain
Management in Patients with Osteoarthritis of the Knee 641
    Fatma Layas, Billy Woods, and Sean Jenkins

Author Index 651

3D Interaction

AHO-Guide: Automatically Guiding the Head Orientation of a Local User in Augmented Reality to Realign the Field of View with Remote Users

Lucas Pometti[(✉)] [iD], Charles Bailly[iD], and Julien Castet[iD]

Immersion SA, Bordeaux, France
{lucas.pometti,charles.bailly,julien.castet}@immersion.fr

Abstract. Augmented Reality (AR) offer significant benefits for remote collaboration scenarios. However, when using a Head-Mounted Display (HMD), remote users do not always see exactly what local users are looking at. This happens when there is a spatial offset between the center of the Field of View (FoV) of the HMD's cameras and the center of the FoV of the user. Such an offset can limit the ability of remote users to see objects of interest, creating confusion and impeding the collaboration. To address this issue, we propose the AHO-Guide techniques. AHO-Guide techniques are Automated Head Orientation Guidance techniques in AR with a HMD. Their goal is to encourage a local HMD user to adjust their head orientation to let remote users have the appropriate FoV of the scene. This paper presents the conception and evaluation of the AHO-Guide techniques. We then propose a set of recommendations from the encouraging results of our experimental study.

Keywords: Augmented Reality · Mixed Reality · Remote collaboration · Guidance · Field-of-View

1 Introduction

Seeing what other users see, do and in which context are key features for collaboration [29,35]. This is even more crucial when users are not collocated, for instance in remote assistance scenarios [10,17]. Many approaches have been explored to let users share a viewpoint from their workspace, from mobile devices [9] to robotic systems with cameras [10]. In this paper, we focus on Augmented Reality (AR) with Head-Mounted Displays (HMDs). Most HMDs are equipped with cameras and leave the hands of the user free. Turning the head around is enough to show to remote users the local workspace from a first-person perspective.

Supplementary Information The online version contains supplementary material available at https://doi.org/10.1007/978-3-031-42280-5_1.

J. Abdelnour Nocera et al. (Eds.): INTERACT 2023, LNCS 14142, pp. 3–19, 2023.
https://doi.org/10.1007/978-3-031-42280-5_1

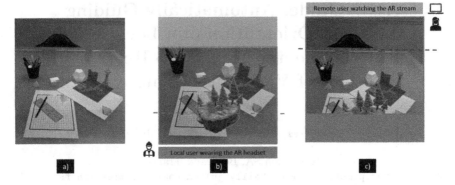

Fig. 1. Example of Field of View miss-alignment in a collaborative setting with an Augmented Reality HMD. a) Overview of the complete workspace. b) Vision of the local user wearing the HMD. c) Vision of the remote user seeing the headset video stream. The Field of View is vertically shifted, partially masking the augmented scene.

However, that does not mean that remote users see exactly the same view than the HMD wearer. As illustrated in Fig. 1, there can be a non-negligible gap between the two. This is for instance the case with the Hololens 2 HMD from Microsoft: the center of the Field of View (FoV) of the HMD's cameras is higher than the center of the HMD wearer's FoV. The result is a shifted view for remote users, who see only partially the main object of interest. This phenomenon can create confusion and harm the collaboration between users. While it may not have a significant impact in some application contexts, slowing down the collaboration and creating misunderstandings can be very problematic in critical contexts like industrial remote assistance [10] or augmented surgery [3,8]. One solution could be to let remote users ask the HMD wearer to re-orient the head so that they better see the scene. This may slow down the collaboration and force remote users to guide the HMD wearer towards a more suitable viewpoint. Another approach could be to let HMD wearers visualize what remote users can see so that they can adjust their FoV as needed. Nonetheless, this puts the burden of monitoring and adapting the FoV on the HMD wearer's shoulders. While acceptable for simple tasks, this additional burden is not suitable for mentally-demanding tasks like surgery [3]. Instead of relying on user actions, we explore in this paper an automated approach. The AHO-Guide techniques we propose are AR techniques designed to automatically encourage users wearing the HMD to adjust their head orientation. This way, remote users can see the salient part of the scene correctly. Our goal is to investigate the following research questions:

- Does an automatic detection and guidance approach can facilitate the work of the local user wearing the HMD? What are the impacts of the automation compared to letting users fully handle FoV adjustments?
- To what extend an automatic approach is distracting users? What level of intrusion and visual occlusion is acceptable to encourage the HMD wearer to quickly adjust the FoV without impacting too much the main task to be performed?

This paper contributes to explore these questions. We first detail the design of the 3 AHO-Guide techniques. Then, we evaluate these techniques through an experimental study. We use the results of this study to propose a set of recommendations about the automatic detection of shifted FoV and guidance techniques to correct this shift. These recommendations focus on 1) cognitive load considerations and 2) distraction and visual occlusion considerations.

2   Related Work

AHO-Guide techniques are inspired by previous studies about remote collaboration scenarios in Augmented Reality (AR). The following sections summarize recent advances on AR with an HMD for remote collaboration. We also consider attention guiding techniques and shared activity cues that could encourage a local user to adjust their FoV for remote users.

2.1   Seeing the Local Workspace

There is a large panel of literature investigating collaborative AR for many applications domains, including medicine [8], remote assistance in industrial contexts [10] or even education [25]. But independently of the application domain, conversational cues like voice and gestures are often not enough to support efficiently remote collaboration. The system should also provide to remote users a way to perceive the local workspace [35]. Some authors like Gauglitz et al. explored using mobile devices to offer a first-person view of the scene to remote users [9]. However, this approach forces the local users to hold the device with one or two hands, which is not suitable in many contexts like augmented surgery [8] or manufacturing [23]. Head-mounted displays (HMDs) and body-worn devices [27] allow to share a first-person view of the workspace while letting the wearer's hands free. For instance, Lee et al. proposed a system where a 360° camera in mounted on top of a HMD [19]. Such a system allows the remote helper to explore the whole scene panorama, even if the origin of the viewpoint is still linked to the local user's head. To avoid this issue, Gurevich et al. proposed a system based on a wheeled platform with cameras to let a remote user remotely explore the workspace [10]. This TeleAdvisor system is nonetheless design to offer an external and independent viewpoint of the scene. It may be difficult to get the exact first-person view of the local user ("through the eyes" view) due to the platform size.

Positioning of Our Study: In our work, we want remote users to have this exact view from the local user. We thus focus on HMDs streaming in real-time the mixed reality scene.

2.2   Explicitly Guiding the HMD Wearer

If remote users cannot see exactly what they want, they could simply guide the local user towards a more suitable viewpoint. Many previous studies investigated guidance techniques for this kind of scenario. Huang et al. divided explicit guidance cues into 4 main categories: pointer-based techniques, sketches and annotations, hand gestures and object-model techniques [13]. The 3 first categories are quite common, especially annotations [8,10]. However, object-model techniques are less frequent. Huang et al. regrouped in this category studies where a virtual model of task objects where shared with the local user to illustrate complex steps [13]. For instance, Oda et al. proposed to use virtual replicas of engine parts to facilitate assembly tasks [22]. Beyond these four categories, another distinction can be made: the intention of 1) guiding the attention towards a specific target (for instance, an object) or 2) encouraging the local user to adopt a given scene viewpoint. Many studies investigated AR techniques and visualizations to guide the attention towards an object [30,31] or location [33]. Some techniques also focus on offscreen targets to compensate the limited FoV of AR devices [24]. On the contrary, some previous studies worked on techniques to guide to another viewpoint. For instance, LeChenechal et al. proposed an AR system with virtual stretchable arms to help the HMD wearer to be correctly positioned in the workspace [5]. Sukan et al. proposed *ParaFrustrum*, a visualization technique to guide a user to a constrained set of positions and orientations [32].

Independently of these categorizations, it is important to keep in mind cognitive aspects related to explicit guidance techniques. For instance, Harada et al. observed that the direction of guidance could have an influence on the interaction and participants' cognitive load [11]. Markov et al. investigated the influence of spatial reference on visual attention and workload and observed that egocentric viewpoint guidance can be more efficient than allocentric guidance [20].

Positioning of Our Study: We hypothesize that letting remote users explicitly guide the local user to adjust the FoV slows down the collaboration and increase cognitive load. Instead, we want to investigate automatic techniques, without input from remote users. Besides, we focus on egocentric guidance only.

2.3   Implicitly Sharing Activity Cues

To avoid explicit input from remote users, previous studies have explored implicit cues [13]. Sharing activity cues may help the HMD wearer to realize when to adjust the FoV to the current point of attention of their collaborator. Many studies considered eye-gaze as a promising implicit cue to communicate activity and intentions [1,16,18,28]. For instance, Akkil et al. studied shared eye-gaze and the influence of the remote user's awareness of the eye-gaze sharing [1]. Blattgerste et al. compared eye-gaze and head-gaze [2] while Piumsomboon et al. also compared them with a FoV cue [26]. While head-gaze may be slower than eye-gaze [2], it can also be judged as more useful, easier to use and less confusing [26]. Other authors explored the combination of modalities, like Wang et al. with a system based on shared 2.5D gestures and eye-gaze [34].

Positioning of Our Study: Implicit cues require the HMD wearer to monitor them to keep track of the activity of remote users. We hypothesize that it may cause distraction and increase the HMD wearer's cognitive load. Our goal is to offload this work to the system. This way, we hope that the HMD wearer can better focus on the task and only adjust the FoV when needed instead of monitoring the activity of collaborators.

3 Proposed AHO-Guide Techniques

The main factor which influenced the conception of AHO-Guide techniques was the trade-off between user attention and the emergency of the FoV shift. We wanted the HMD wearer to be able to adjust the FoV quickly and precisely when needed. However, creating visual occlusion and drawing the user's attention could significantly impact the task currently performed. The first factor we wanted to explore was the level of distraction the technique could create for users. To do so, we chose to focus on visual occlusion, which particularly matters in AR due to the limited size of augmented FoV. The second axis we considered was the different spatial reference of guidance cues. On the one hand, visual cues anchored on the HMD FoV (hereafter noted *FoV-anchored*) are always visible for the user but can quickly create visual clutter. On the other hand, *World-anchored* cues are spatially anchored within the scene, but may be outside of the augmented FoV of the HMD.

By combining our two axes, we conceived three AHO-Guide techniques: *TargetZone*, *HeadAvatar* and *Mask*. These techniques are illustrated in Fig. 2.

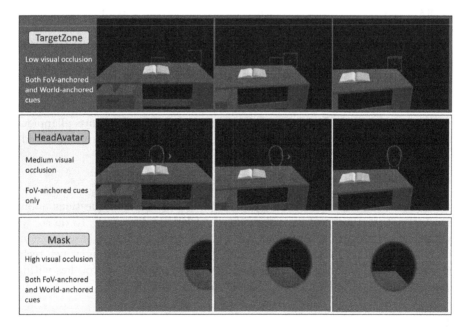

Fig. 2. Overview of the proposed AHO-Guide techniques. Example where the local user needs to realign the FoV to the right for remote users to better view the scene.

TargetZone: The goal of the TargetZone technique is to limit visual occlusion. When a FoV shift is necessary, a red empty square and a blue arrow appear in the center of the user's FoV (FoV-anchored cues). The blue arrow indicates the direction of the FoV shift to be made and points towards a blue visor in the scene (World-anchored cue). The user simply has to align the red square (similarly to a 2D homing task) with the visor to reach a viewpoint suitable for remote users. Upon reaching this viewpoint, the visual cues disappear.

HeadAvatar: This technique consists in displaying a virtual head model facing the user (FoV-anchored cue). The orientation of the head cue and a blue arrow indicate which movement should be performed to reach a suitable head orientation. Both these cues are adapted in real time based on the movements of the user. There is no World-anchored cue in this technique. Nonetheless, we hypothesized that showing a head model could be more explicit and clear than abstract cues like in TargetZone, which may help users despite the higher level of intrusion.

Mask: We designed the Mask technique to explore how we could constraint users to adjust the FoV as soon as possible. To do so, we hide nearly all the augmented FoV with an opaque orange mask when the technique triggers. Only a circular area centered on the target viewpoint is visible (World-anchored Cue). If the user is far from this viewpoint (area outside of the HMD FoV), then a small circular area on the side is left visible to indicate in which direction the user should turn the head (FoV-anchored cue). To limit creating too much distraction, the mask appears progressively. Besides, we chose a dark orange color to find an acceptable compromise between opacity and brightness.

An important aspect of AHO-Guide techniques is the automated trigger of these techniques. Determining the current object of interest for users and if remote users have a suitable view of it is a complex task. Performing this detection robustly and in real-time is out of the scope of the current study. Nonetheless, it is possible to obtain an approximation using activity cues like the HMD wearer's eye gaze [28]. Besides, each HMD affected by the FoV miss-alignment has a fixed offset which can be computed or at least empirically approximated.

4   Experimental Protocol

We conducted an experimental study to explore our research questions about impact of automatic detection and guidance of FoV realignment. To do so, we designed a AR task to compare our AHO-Guide techniques to a baseline, non-automated technique described below. Our goal is not to determine which technique is the best. Instead, we investigate a diverse panel of approaches within these techniques to find which factors seem the most impactful.

4.1   Task

Our goal was to create a collaboration scenario where the HMD wearer would have to realign their FoV. We also wanted to engage participants in different visual tasks to investigate the impact of the techniques on task distraction and visual occlusion. To do so, participants were playing the role of a shepherd in an AR game with asymmetric collaboration. Their goal was to protect a sheep enclosure from the attacks of wolves. They were helped by a remote player called hereafter the hunter, interpreted by an experimentor in the same room. An overview of the setup and AR game is available in Fig. 3.

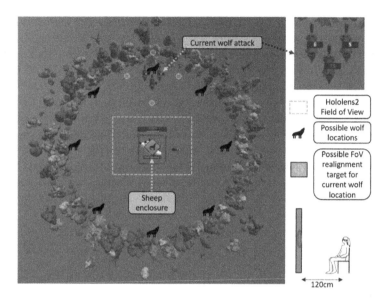

Fig. 3. Overview of the AR shepherd game used as experimental task.

Overall, the task was divided into 4 phases:

1. *Watch the sheep.* Participants seated and started by looking at a forest clearing with a virtual sheep enclosure displayed in front of them. Upon pressing a virtual button to start the trial, a number appeared in the enclosure to show the number of sheep present inside the enclosure. They had three seconds to memorize this number.
2. *Find attacking wolves.* After the three seconds, a wolf alert was triggered and the sheep number disappeared. Participants had to look around the woods nearby the enclosure to find the attacking wolves.
3. *Evaluate the threat and help the hunter.* Upon finding the attack location, participants had to addition the number displayed near each wolf to evaluate the pack threat. Red wolves threat had to be doubled. In parallel, they also had to help the hunter scare the wolves. Two seconds after locating the wolves, the current technique was triggered in a random direction to encourage participants to re-align their FoV. Once the hunter's FOV was correctly centered on wolves, the hunter could release a shepherd dog towards the wolves to make them flee.

4. *Decide if the sheep should be sheltered for the night.* Once the wolves were gone, participants could resume their counting task if needed (the numbers stayed visible). Then, they had to go back to the sheep enclosure and decide if the sheep should be sheltered for the night (wolf threat > sheep number) or if the sheep could stay in the enclosure (wolf threat < sheep number). A correct decision was awarded with +10 points (+0 for a wrong decision), then participants could start another trial.

The task was inspired by an ISO pointing task design [15] and Wizard of Oz techniques [6]. Wolf attacks were evenly split across 8 locations forming a circular pattern centered on the sheep enclosure. The sheep number and wolf threat assessment were designed to add memorization and calculus to the task in order to increase participant's cognitive load [4,12,14]. Our goal was to reflect occupied real users who do not focus only on re-align their FoV for remote users. When a FOV re-alignment technique was triggered, a sound notification was played to notify participants (in addition to the visual feedback depending on the technique). FOV re-alignement was associated with a direction (North, West, South or East) because different HMDs may have different spatial offsets between the cameras and wearer's point of view. Besides, we also wanted to take into account the fact that human attention can be biased among spatial directions [11].

4.2   Participants and Apparatus

16 participants from 22 to 44 years old ($sd = 6.9$) were recruited for this study from nearby universities and companies. As illustrated in Fig. 4, only 4 of them were using AR on a regular basis (at least several times per month). Participants were seated in a calm room and wore the Hololens 2 headset [21]. The real-time video stream from the Hololens was sent to a nearby laptop running the Windows Device Portal application. This allowed the experimentor seated in the same room to follow the AR scene and play the role of the hunter.

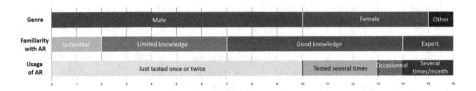

Fig. 4. Demographic data about participants recruited for the study.

4.3   Selected Techniques

In addition to the three *AHO-Guide* techniques, we selected a reference techniques without automation. *SharedCursor* was designed to be a continuous visual feedback reflecting the activity of the remote user. Directly after starting a trial, participants could see a virtual white cursor representing the head cursor of the hunter. This cursor was placed to match the order of magnitude of the Hololens 2 offset between the first-person view and the camera view sent to the hunter. **No additional reminder or cue was given to encourage participants to re-align their FoV.** In other words, the HMD wearer had to remember that they needed to re-align the FoV to help the hunter before they could give their answer about sheltering the sheep. On the contrary, we simulate automated techniques (as detailed at end of Sect. 3). Still, with AHO-Guide techniques participants do not have to remember or monitor implicit or explicit input from remote users to re-align their FOV correctly.

4.4 Study Design

After initial explanations, participants performed 4 sets of trials (1 set per interaction technique). Each set began with 4 training trials followed by 8 recorded trials. In addition to the technique currently tested, we considered two factors: the wolves locations (8 possible locations, each visited once during recorded trials) and the direction of the FOV re-alignment (4 possibilities, balanced random order). Upon finishing the recorded trials for a given technique, participants could take a short break before answering to an SUS questionnaire. Overall, participants performed a total of 32 recorded trials (4 sets of 8 trials each). The experiment took 45 min on average and the order of techniques was balanced between participants using a Latin-square design.

4.5 Measures

We recorded all relevant time measurements during trials. This included but was not limited to total trial times, times to find wolves locations and times to realign the FOV, as shown in Fig. 5. SUS questionnaires were also given to participants after each technique. Finally, for qualitative measures, we organized semi-structured interviews at the end of the experiment. Questions included ranking all techniques according to several criteria: easiness, speed, precision, feeling of distraction and overall preference.

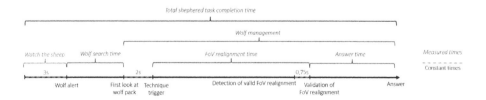

Fig. 5. Times measurements taken during trials.

4.6   Data Analysis

We conducted statistical analysis using Repeated-measures ANOVA (with $\alpha = 0.05$) followed by post hoc tests (pairwise t-tests) with Bonferroni corrections. When a non-parametric test was more suitable (ANOVA assumptions not respected or discrete data like number of errors), we employed a Friedman test instead followed by a Wilcoxon post hoc test with Bonferonni corrections. As suggested by Dragicevic [7], we aim at limiting as much as possible binary interpretations of results. To do so, we put emphasis on confidence intervals, effect sizes and nuanced language. In all Figures, error bars are 95% Confidence Intervals (CI).

5   Results

5.1   Quantitative Results

We observed good evidence of difference between the 4 interaction techniques in terms of total task completion time $((F(3,45) = 2.5, p = 0.07)$. Participants needed an average of 21.2 s with *TargetZone* to perform a shepherd task, 22.7 s with *Mask*, 23.7 s with *SharedCursor* and 25.0 s with *HeadAvatar*. Overall, there was thus a difference of 3.8 s on average between the quickest and the slowest technique. Post-hoc analysis highlighted a strong evidence of difference between *TargetZone* and *HeadAvatar* ($p = 0.009$). To better understand this phenomenon, we analysed each step of the task. As expected, we found no evidence of difference for step 1 (Watch the sheep, constant time of 3 s) and step 2 (Find attacking wolves, identical for each technique). However, we observed good evidence of difference for FoV realignment times, i.e. times between the trigger of the technique and its end $(F(3,45) = 5.8, p = 0.002)$. More precisely, we observed a strong evidence of difference between *TargetZone* (3.8 s on average) and *HeadAvatar* (7.1 s on average) with $p = 0.001$. We also found good evidence of difference between *Mask* (4.4 s on average) and *HeadAvatar* ($p = 0.06$). This phenomenon is illustrated in Fig. 6.

No other evidence of difference was found about time measurements, wolf location, technique direction or about the number of errors for each technique. Nonetheless, we observed evidence of difference on the average SUS score. On the one hand, *TargetZone* reached a high usability score of 87.1. On the other hand, the three remaining techniques reached a lower average usability score: 71.2 for *SharedCursor*, 68.2 for *HeadAvatar* and 68.5 for *Mask*.

5.2   Qualitative Results

Results from the final questionnaire given to participant support the SUS scores. 12/16 participants ranked *TargetZone* as their favourite technique overall (see Fig. 7). It was also perceived as a quick (ranked first by 11/16 participants), precise (ranked first by 10/16 participants) and intuitive technique. Four participants mentioned that *TargetZone* was similar to a video-game mechanism, in

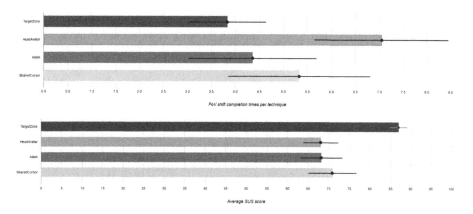

Fig. 6. Average FoV shift completion times and average SUS score per technique. Error bars are 95% CI.

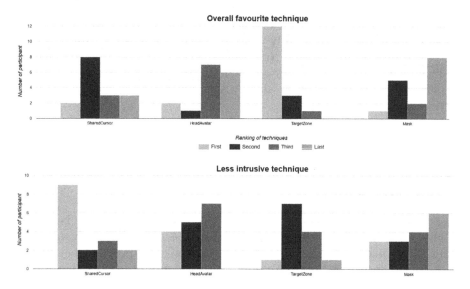

Fig. 7. Overview of technique ranking made by participants at the end of the study.

either a negative way or a positive way. For instance, P9 declared that it "may not be appropriate for all professional contexts".

SharedCursor was ranked as second favourite by half of the participants. 9/16 participants ranked *SharedCursor* as the least intrusive technique. Participants found that having a cursor was not visually disturbing and allowed to be precise. P9 mentioned that the cursor could even be bigger without being visually disturbing. Interestingly, we noticed of the video stream that 8/16 participants forgot once to three times to realign the FoV during trials. After computing the wolf pack strength, they directly went back to the sheep enclosure to give their answer. Upon seeing that the answer buttons were not yet displayed, they remembered that they had to help the hunter and went back to the wolves to realign the FoV.

A majority of participants judged that *HeadAvatar* was not precise enough (12/16 ranked it last in terms of precision). 7/16 participants reported they used only arrows to find the appropriate viewpoint, and 2/16 reported using both arrows and the head cue. We also noted that despite the lack of precision, half of participants found the technique intuitive and suitable for a tutorial or beginner; 3/8 explained that they particularly appreciated the aesthetic quality of this technique. Besides, 4/16 participants mentioned that *HeadAvatar* could be useful when large head movements are required to realign the FoV.

Finally, opinions were mixed about the *Mask* technique. It was perceived as an intrusive technique, which imposes a constraint (7/16 participants). For instance, P14 mentioned: "I feel constrained more than assisted by it". Nonetheless, 3 of these 7 participants also saw this constraint as a positive way, feeling more guided since they had no choice other than realigning the FoV first. P9 found the technique "simple, not distracting because it's quick and it allows to switch to something else efficiently". Only P13 reported trying to still count the wolves despite the orange mask. Nonetheless, after a few trials, this participant finally decided to change strategy and started realigning the FoV first. Overall, we did not observe any feedback about visual, physical or mental fatigue from participants.

6   Lessons Learned

6.1   Participants Preferred Having a Precise Indicator of Where to Turn the Head

Overall, the *TargetZone* is the AHO-Guide technique which led to the best compromise between visual occlusion, speed and precision. To achieve the latter, it seems that a majority of users preferred seeing the exact position they had to reach when turning the head. We observed this despite the facts that 1) the head movement amplitude was limited in our study and 2) participants did not need a high level of precision to validate a FoV realignment (the hidden targets we used for head ray-casting had a comfortable size). In our study, nearly all participants who ranked HeadAvatar as their least favorite technique mentioned a feeling of lack of precision. When choosing between using World-anchored and FoV-anchored cues, we thus recommend designers to consider how to precisely convey the location of the optimal head position.

6.2   Without Adapted Feedback, Participants Can Forget FoV Realignment

The non-automated baseline technique *SharedCursor* led to a good performances and feeling of precision while minimizing the level of intrusion. However, this last aspect can be a double-edged sword as half of participants forgot once or several times to realign their FoV during trials. Such an observation suggests that a passive cue based on implicit input from the remote user can sometimes not be enough. If the local user's cognitive load is high enough, the FoV realignment may be forgotten. On the contrary, we did not observe any oversight with the three AHO-Guide techniques. Of course, these three techniques created more visual occlusion and made appear visual cues at the center of the FoV. Many factors can influence to which extend a visual cue will draw user's attention. This includes visual cue size, placement, timing of trigger and visibility/contrast. Overall, we thus encourage designers to consider all these factors instead of only relying on classical passive cues linked to implicit input from remote users. Automated techniques and momentary visual occlusion can be better to let remote users fully view the salient part of the scene and facilitate the cooperation.

6.3   Forcing Immediate FoV Realignment Can Be Acceptable

Our study also suggests that it is possible to force an immediate FoV realignment. With the *Mask* technique, all participants ended up realigning as soon as possible their FoV. Of course, this approach forces users to interrupt their task and partially hides their surroundings. Nonetheless, despite the extreme visual occlusion, the constraint imposed by *Mask* was not always perceived negatively by participants. Leaving no choice can sometimes be perceived as more simple. We hypothesize that simply encouraging a FoV shift may leave more freedom to users, but also more cognitive load since they have to determine themselves the balance between their ongoing task and the need to help remote users to see the scene. Automation can thus be applied at two stages: 1) the detection of the FoV realignment need and 2) the immediate constraint to perform this realignment. Depending on the context, task and user profile, forcing an immediate realignment could thus be considered as a suitable option.

7   Limitations and Future Work

As a first exploration of the potential of AHO-Guide techniques, our study has several limitations. First, our experimental evaluation included limited collaboration between a participant and an experimentor. Secondly, we also considered only limited amplitudes for FoV realignment to reflect the offset we initially observed in the Hololens 2 HMD. Finally, we conceived a simple AR game with arithmetic and memorization as the main study task. It would be interesting to investigate further in more realistic contexts with a more complex task. Our current goal is to investigate further cognitive load aspects of the interaction in a more ecological collaboration context. In particular, we would like to quantify the benefits of AHO-technique in terms of cognitive load compared to 1) a technique based on implicit input but active cues and 2) the baseline technique of letting the remote user ask for a FoV realignment.

8   Conclusion

This paper contributes to exploring how to encourage a local user in AR with a HMD to realign their FoV with remote users. To do so, we proposed three AHO-Guide technique. Experimental results suggest that AHO-Guide techniques like *TargetZone* can reach high level of usability, user preference and feeling of precision. Besides, our techniques can prevent users from forgetting to adjust their FoV, which is not always the case for techniques directly based on implicit cues from remote users. Finally, we observed that forcing immediate FoV realignment is possible and not always perceived as a negative constraint despite a significant visual occlusion. The next step of our exploratory work will consist in investigating further cognitive load aspects in a remote assistance context.

Acknowledgements. This paper was made with the frame of the PI5G project, funded by the France Relance plan with the support of BPI France.

References

1. Akkil, D., Thankachan, B., Isokoski, P.: I see what you see: gaze awareness in mobile video collaboration. In: Proceedings of the 2018 ACM Symposium on Eye Tracking Research & Applications, Warsaw, Poland, pp. 1–9. ACM (2018). https://doi.org/10.1145/3204493.3204542. https://dl.acm.org/doi/10.1145/3204493.3204542

2. Blattgerste, J., Renner, P., Pfeiffer, T.: Advantages of eye-gaze over head-gaze-based selection in virtual and augmented reality under varying field of views. In: Proceedings of the Workshop on Communication by Gaze Interaction, COGAIN 2018, pp. 1–9. Association for Computing Machinery, New York (2018). https://doi.org/10.1145/3206343.3206349

3. Cassell, J.: On control, certitude, and the "paranoia" of surgeons. Cult. Med. Psychiatry **11**(2), 229–249 (1987). https://doi.org/10.1007/BF00122565

4. Chen, S., Epps, J., Chen, F.: A comparison of four methods for cognitive load measurement. In: Proceedings of the 23rd Australian Computer-Human Interaction Conference, OzCHI 2011, pp. 76–79. Association for Computing Machinery (2011). https://doi.org/10.1145/2071536.2071547

5. Chénéchal, M.L., Duval, T., Gouranton, V., Royan, J., Arnaldi, B.: The stretchable arms for collaborative remote guiding. In: ICAT-EGVE 2015 - International Conference on Artificial Reality and Telexistence and Eurographics Symposium on Virtual Environments, p. 4. The Eurographics Association (2015). https://doi.org/10.2312/EGVE.20151322. https://diglib.eg.org/handle/10.2312/egve20151322. ISBN 9783905674842

6. Dow, S., Lee, J., Oezbek, C., MacIntyre, B., Bolter, J.D., Gandy, M.: Wizard of OZ interfaces for mixed reality applications. In: CHI 2005 Extended Abstracts on Human Factors in Computing Systems, CHI EA 2005, pp. 1339–1342. Association for Computing Machinery (2005). https://doi.org/10.1145/1056808.1056911

7. Dragicevic, P.: Fair statistical communication in HCI. In: Robertson, J., Kaptein, M. (eds.) Modern Statistical Methods for HCI. HIS, pp. 291–330. Springer, Cham (2016). https://doi.org/10.1007/978-3-319-26633-6_13

8. Gasques, D., et al.: ARTEMIS: a collaborative mixed-reality system for immersive surgical telementoring. In: Proceedings of the 2021 CHI Conference on Human Factors in Computing Systems, CHI 2021, pp. 1–14. Association for Computing Machinery, New York (2021). https://doi.org/10.1145/3411764.3445576

9. Gauglitz, S., Nuernberger, B., Turk, M., Höllerer, T.: In touch with the remote world: remote collaboration with augmented reality drawings and virtual navigation. In: Proceedings of the 20th ACM Symposium on Virtual Reality Software and Technology - VRST 2014, Edinburgh, Scotland, pp. 197–205. ACM Press (2014). https://doi.org/10.1145/2671015.2671016. http://dl.acm.org/citation.cfm?doid=2671015.2671016

10. Gurevich, P., Lanir, J., Cohen, B.: Design and implementation of TeleAdvisor: a projection-based augmented reality system for remote collaboration. Comput. Support. Coop. Work (CSCW) **24**(6), 527–562 (2015). https://doi.org/10.1007/s10606-015-9232-7

11. Harada, Y., Ohyama, J.: Quantitative evaluation of visual guidance effects for 360-degree directions. Virtual Reality **26**(2), 759–770 (2022). https://doi.org/10.1007/s10055-021-00574-7

12. Hart, S.G., Staveland, L.E.: Development of NASA-TLX (task load index): results of empirical and theoretical research. In: Hancock, P.A., Meshkati, N. (eds.) Advances in Psychology, Human Mental Workload, vol. 52, pp. 139–183. North-Holland (1988). https://doi.org/10.1016/S0166-4115(08)62386-9. https://www.sciencedirect.com/science/article/pii/S0166411508623869

13. Huang, W., Wakefield, M., Rasmussen, T.A., Kim, S., Billinghurst, M.: A review on communication cues for augmented reality based remote guidance. J. Multimodal User Interfaces **16**(2), 239–256 (2022). https://doi.org/10.1007/s12193-022-00387-1

14. Iqbal, S.T., Zheng, X.S., Bailey, B.P.: Task-evoked pupillary response to mental workload in human-computer interaction. In: CHI 2004 Extended Abstracts on Human Factors in Computing Systems, CHI EA 2004, pp. 1477–1480. Association for Computing Machinery (2004). https://doi.org/10.1145/985921.986094

15. ISO: ISO 9241-400:2007. https://www.iso.org/standard/38896.html

16. Labrie, A., Mok, T., Tang, A., Lui, M., Oehlberg, L., Poretski, L.: Toward video-conferencing tools for hands-on activities in online teaching. Proc. ACM Hum.-Comput. Interact. **6**(GROUP), 10:1–10:22 (2022). https://doi.org/10.1145/3492829

17. Lanir, J., Stone, R., Cohen, B., Gurevich, P.: Ownership and control of point of view in remote assistance. In: Proceedings of the SIGCHI Conference on Human Factors in Computing Systems, CHI 2013, pp. 2243–2252. Association for Computing Machinery, New York (2013). https://doi.org/10.1145/2470654.2481309

18. Lee, G.A., et al.: Improving collaboration in augmented video conference using mutually shared gaze. In: ICAT-EGVE 2017 - International Conference on Artificial Reality and Telexistence and Eurographics Symposium on Virtual Environments, p. 8 pages. The Eurographics Association (2017). https://doi.org/10.2312/EGVE.20171359. https://diglib.eg.org/handle/10.2312/egve20171359. ISBN 9783038680383

19. Lee, G.A., Teo, T., Kim, S., Billinghurst, M.: A user study on MR remote collaboration using live 360 video. In: 2018 IEEE International Symposium on Mixed and Augmented Reality (ISMAR), Munich, Germany, pp. 153–164. IEEE (2018). https://doi.org/10.1109/ISMAR.2018.00051. https://ieeexplore.ieee.org/document/8613761/

20. Markov-Vetter, D., Luboschik, M., Islam, A.T., Gauger, P., Staadt, O.: The effect of spatial reference on visual attention and workload during viewpoint guidance in augmented reality. In: Symposium on Spatial User Interaction, SUI 2020, pp. 1–10. Association for Computing Machinery, New York (2020). https://doi.org/10.1145/3385959.3418449

21. Microsoft: HoloLens 2 - Présentation, Fonctions et Spécifications — Microsoft HoloLens (2022). https://www.microsoft.com/fr-fr/hololens/hardware

22. Oda, O., Elvezio, C., Sukan, M., Feiner, S., Tversky, B.: Virtual replicas for remote assistance in virtual and augmented reality. In: Proceedings of the 28th Annual ACM Symposium on User Interface Software & Technology, UIST 2015, pp. 405–415. Association for Computing Machinery, New York (2015). https://doi.org/10.1145/2807442.2807497

23. Ong, S.K., Yuan, M.L., Nee, A.Y.C.: Augmented reality applications in manufacturing: a survey. Int. J. Prod. Res. 46(10), 2707–2742 (2008). https://doi.org/10.1080/00207540601064773

24. Perea, P., Morand, D., Nigay, L.: Spotlight on off-screen points of interest in handheld augmented reality: halo-based techniques. In: Proceedings of the 2019 ACM International Conference on Interactive Surfaces and Spaces, ISS 2019, pp. 43–54. Association for Computing Machinery, New York (2019). https://doi.org/10.1145/3343055.3359719

25. Phon, D.N.E., Ali, M.B., Halim, N.D.A.: Collaborative augmented reality in education: a review. In: 2014 International Conference on Teaching and Learning in Computing and Engineering, Kuching, Malaysia, pp. 78–83. IEEE (2014). https://doi.org/10.1109/LaTiCE.2014.23. http://ieeexplore.ieee.org/document/6821833/

26. Piumsomboon, T., Dey, A., Ens, B., Lee, G., Billinghurst, M.: The effects of sharing awareness cues in collaborative mixed reality. Front. Robot. AI 6 (2019). https://www.frontiersin.org/articles/10.3389/frobt.2019.00005

27. Piumsomboon, T., Lee, G.A., Irlitti, A., Ens, B., Thomas, B.H., Billinghurst, M.: On the shoulder of the giant: a multi-scale mixed reality collaboration with 360 video sharing and tangible interaction. In: Proceedings of the 2019 CHI Conference on Human Factors in Computing Systems, Glasgow, Scotland UK, pp. 1–17. ACM (2019). https://doi.org/10.1145/3290605.3300458. https://dl.acm.org/doi/10.1145/3290605.3300458

28. Plopski, A., Hirzle, T., Norouzi, N., Qian, L., Bruder, G., Langlotz, T.: The eye in extended reality: a survey on gaze interaction and eye tracking in head-worn extended reality. ACM Comput. Surv. 55(3), 53:1–53:39 (2022). https://doi.org/10.1145/3491207

29. Radu, I., Joy, T., Bowman, Y., Bott, I., Schneider, B.: A survey of needs and features for augmented reality collaborations in collocated spaces. Proc. ACM Hum.-Comput. Interact. 5(CSCW1), 1–21 (2021). https://doi.org/10.1145/3449243. https://dl.acm.org/doi/10.1145/3449243

30. Renner, P., Pfeiffer, T.: Attention guiding techniques using peripheral vision and eye tracking for feedback in augmented-reality-based assistance systems. In: 2017 IEEE Symposium on 3D User Interfaces (3DUI), Los Angeles, CA, USA, pp. 186–194. IEEE (2017). https://doi.org/10.1109/3DUI.2017.7893338. http://ieeexplore.ieee.org/document/7893338/

31. Renner, P., Pfeiffer, T.: Attention guiding using augmented reality in complex environments. In: 2018 IEEE Conference on Virtual Reality and 3D User Interfaces (VR), pp. 771–772 (2018). https://doi.org/10.1109/VR.2018.8446396

32. Sukan, M., Elvezio, C., Oda, O., Feiner, S., Tversky, B.: ParaFrustum: visualization techniques for guiding a user to a constrained set of viewing positions and orientations. In: Proceedings of the 27th Annual ACM Symposium on User Interface Software and Technology, Honolulu, Hawaii, USA, pp. 331–340. ACM (2014). https://doi.org/10.1145/2642918.2647417. https://dl.acm.org/doi/10.1145/2642918.2647417

33. Sutton, J., Langlotz, T., Plopski, A., Zollmann, S., Itoh, Y., Regenbrecht, H.: Look over there! Investigating saliency modulation for visual guidance with augmented reality glasses. In: Proceedings of the 35th Annual ACM Symposium on User Interface Software and Technology, UIST 2022, pp. 1–15. Association for Computing Machinery, New York (2022). https://doi.org/10.1145/3526113.3545633

34. Wang, Y., Wang, P., Luo, Z., Yan, Y.: A novel AR remote collaborative platform for sharing 2.5D gestures and gaze. Int. J. Adv. Manuf. Technol. **119**(9–10), 6413–6421 (2022). https://doi.org/10.1007/s00170-022-08747-7

35. Young, J., Langlotz, T., Cook, M., Mills, S., Regenbrecht, H.: Immersive telepresence and remote collaboration using mobile and wearable devices. IEEE Trans. Visual. Comput. Graph. **25**(5), 1908–1918 (2019). https://doi.org/10.1109/TVCG.2019.2898737

Point- and Volume-Based Multi-object Acquisition in VR

Zhiqing Wu[1,2], Difeng Yu[1,3(✉)], and Jorge Goncalves[1]

[1] University of Melbourne, Melbourne, Australia
difengy@student.unimelb.edu.au
[2] Hong Kong University of Science and Technology (Guangzhou), Guangzhou, China
[3] University of Copenhagen, Copenhagen, Denmark

Abstract. Multi-object acquisition is indispensable for many VR applications. Commonly, users select a group of objects of interest to perform further transformation or analysis. In this paper, we present three multi-object selection techniques that were derived based on a two-dimensional design space. The primary design dimension concerns whether a technique acquires targets through point-based methods (selecting one object at a time) or volume-based methods (selecting a set of objects within a selection volume). The secondary design dimension examines the mechanisms of selection and deselection (cancel the selection of unwanted objects). We compared these techniques through a user study, emphasizing on scenarios with more randomly distributed objects. We discovered, for example, that the point-based technique was more efficient and robust than the volume-based techniques in environments where the targets did not follow a specific layout. We also found that users applied the deselection mechanism mostly for error correction. We provide an in-depth discussion of our findings and further distill design implications for future applications that leverage multi-object acquisition techniques in VR.

Keywords: Multiple targets · Object selection · Virtual Reality

1 Introduction

The rapid development of virtual reality (VR) systems shows great potential for its use in practice, such as in industrial design, data exploration, and professional training [7,17,18]. Many of these application scenarios require the acquisition of multiple targets altogether. For example, as shown in Fig. 1, a user wants to pick up all the bottles in a virtual chemistry lab or acquire data points with certain features in a 3D data cloud for further analysis.

To satisfy this particular need, many off-the-shelf VR applications, including Google Blocks, Tilt Brush, Tvori, Microsoft Maquette, and Gravity Sketch,

Supplementary Information The online version contains supplementary material available at https://doi.org/10.1007/978-3-031-42280-5_2.

Fig. 1. Example scenarios of multi-object acquisition in VR. Left: a user is trying to select all the bottles in a virtual chemistry lab. Right: a user is attempting to acquire all the green data points in a data cloud for further investigation. (Color figure online)

have released a diverse range of multi-object acquisition techniques [25]. Some techniques require users to select multiple targets by "touching" each one of them (point-based selection), others allow the creation of a selection volume that collects all of the objects inside (volume-based selection). These different approaches indicate that there is still no consensus on which technique is the most efficient and effective, thus highlighting the importance of investigating the design space of multi-object acquisition in VR.

We highlight two design factors of VR multi-object acquisition that are still underexplored in the existing literature. First, while volume-based selection techniques have been proven to be useful in structured environments [16,28], further research is needed to verify their performance in more randomized scenarios. In these randomized scenarios, the position of targets does not follow a specific layout and is difficult to predict (e.g., Fig. 1). Second, the effect of deselection, the mechanism that helps users remove unwanted selections, remains unclear in multi-object acquisition tasks. In such tasks where there are many interactable objects, no matter whether they are desired or undesired, it is likely that users will accidentally include unwanted objects in their initial selection. Thus, the deselection technique allows them to correct their errors. It may even enable new strategies for acquiring desired objects. For example, in a condition where the majority of the objects are targets, users may prefer selecting a whole volume of objects with a volume-based selection technique first and then remove unwanted objects with a deselection mechanism.

Our research, therefore, aims to explore how the choice of point-based and volume-based selection techniques, especially under randomized environments, and how the adoption of a deselection mechanism may affect user performance and experience. To achieve this, we first define a two-dimensional design space that considers point-/volume-based techniques and selection/deselection mechanisms. We implemented three techniques based on the design space and evaluated them in a user study that contains both randomized and structured scenarios. We found that a point-based technique was more robust in randomized scenarios, while a volume-based technique can perform particularly well in more structured, target-dense scenarios. We also found users rarely applied the deselection mechanism and mostly used them for error correction. Based on our findings, we provide implications that can inspire future designs of VR multi-object acquisition techniques.

2   Related Work

2.1   Object Acquisition in VR

Virtual pointing and virtual hand are the most common techniques for object acquisition in current VR systems [20,23,35,41]. Virtual pointing selects an object that intersects with a selection ray, while virtual hand selects an object that is "grabbed" by a user's hand. Many techniques have been proposed to overcome the limitation of virtual pointing and virtual hands (see reviews [1,14]). For example, because acquiring out-of-reach objects with a virtual hand is challenging, Poupyrev et al. [24] have proposed Go-Go which leverages a non-linear mapping function between real and virtual hands to extend the user's reach. More recent work proposed Ninja Hands which uses many hands to further extend the interactable area [26]. Baloup et al. [3] and Yu et al. [38] aimed to tackle the selection of small or even occluded targets, which are challenging scenarios for virtual pointing because of hand tremors and visual occlusion. Wagner et al. [32], on the other hand, tried to combine both virtual pointing and virtual hands to allow the technique to be adaptable to more complicated scenarios. However, most of these selection techniques were designed for selecting a single target, while being limited in selecting multiple targets as a user can only perform the selection serially (i.e., one target at a time).

2.2   Multi-object Acquisition

Multi-object acquisition is a frequent task for both 2D interfaces (e.g., desktop, tablet) and 3D interfaces (e.g., VR). Dedicated techniques have been proposed in the literature for such a task, which can be roughly categorized into two main approaches: selecting targets point-by-point (serially, one-by-one) or group-by-group.

2D Interfaces. There are several common interaction scenarios that require tools for multi-object acquisition on 2D interfaces. A user may want to select a subset of items for coloring, transformation, removal, or other further operations. One option is to select the targets one by one [28] by holding an additional button (e.g., the Ctrl button). Another common option is to use a rectangle lasso (i.e., a selection volume) to select a group of targets. For example, users can select files by creating a rectangle area that encloses the desired files [34]. Mizobuchi and Yasumura's work evaluated the performance of lasso selection and found it was efficient in selecting targets that are aligned with high cohesiveness [21]. Another multi-object acquisition strategy is to automatically select similar objects altogether based on certain algorithms that calculate a similarity score (e.g., pixel-wise correlation) [8]. However, performance results from 2D multi-object acquisition techniques may not be easily transferred to 3D because of the additional depth dimension.

3D Interfaces. Lucas et al. were the first to present a taxonomy of 3D multi-object acquisition [16]. One design dimension was concurrency, which means that a technique can enable the selection of either one object per operation (serial selection) or a group of objects at once (parallel selection). The authors conducted a user study to evaluate serial and parallel selection techniques, and analyzed their selection performance within a structured environment where all objects were placed on a grid. The authors found that the parallel selection technique outperformed the serial technique when objects are placed on a highly cohesive layout and when the number of target objects is large.

Ulinski et al. [29,30] also investigated techniques that select a group of objects within a created box (cube). Specifically, three bimanual box creation methods were evaluated, which were Two Corners (TC), Hand-on-Corner (HOC), and Hand-in-Middle (HIM). The authors found that TC outperformed the two other methods regarding both completion time and accuracy but can introduce more arm strain. Other researchers have also investigated methods that create various shapes of selection volumes. For example, Kang et al.'s technique [13] allowed the creation of selection volumes with customizable shapes by performing different hand gestures. Although this seemed to provide a handy way of fitting the layout of the targets, it was shown to have lower efficiency when users wanted to adjust the volume to a desired shape, and it was difficult for users to remember the gesture set. Worm Selector [9] leveraged an easier method to create 3D volume by auto-connecting multiple 2D surfaces to form a 3D worm-like volume. Although this technique can be intuitive and efficient to use, it does not provide further support on editing the selected volumes.

Physically-Based Volumetric Selection [4] allowed users to manipulate the position of objects before making a selection so that they can cluster the desired objects first and then apply a selection volume. This mimics how people would manipulate multiple objects in the physical world. However, this technique lacks efficiency since it takes time to translate objects. Magic Wand [28] leveraged a grouping mechanism that automatically selects objects based on their local proximity to other objects. The technique was shown to be highly efficient and easy to use when the object layout followed certain structures. Slicing-Volume [22] used a tablet to map 3D data points onto 2D surfaces and enabled group-based selection by using a controller and a pen metaphor. Balloon [5] uses a 2D interface to control the selection in 3D environments through a balloon metaphor. The size of the position of the selection volume (i.e., the balloon) was controlled by a user's fingers.

Existing research has also investigated point-based selection techniques that can be applied for selecting multiple objects serially in 3D interfaces. Brushing mechanisms [12] select objects that intersect with the trajectory of the virtual hand or end-point of the ray. Sewing [15] selects an object by penetrating its surfaces which simulates the real-life action of sewing with a needle and fabric.

Summary. We have identified two gaps in the literature. First, while most previous studies focus on applying volume-based selection techniques for more structured environments, it is unclear if they are still beneficial compared to point-based selection in randomized target layouts where the location of the targets can be difficult to predict [18,25]. Second, while previous research focuses on the selection phase of the acquisition process, the effect of object deselection (removing unwanted objects) has not been investigated. The ability of deselection can influence the overall selection strategies (e.g., selecting a large volume of objects that may include distractors and then trimming them off via deselection methods).

3 Technique Design

3.1 Design Space

We divided the design space into two dimensions. In the first design dimension, we separated a multi-object acquisition task into two action phases: selection and deselection. Selection represents the process of acquiring or identifying a particular subset of objects from the entire set of objects available [14]. Deselection represents the process of removing a subset of objects from the selected set of objects. In the second design dimension, we had point-based and volume-based techniques. A point-based method selects/deselects objects one by one while a volume-based method enables the selection/deselection of objects group by group. We used volume-based techniques because our literature review showed that it was the most prevalent for selecting multiple targets at once. Therefore, the design space leads to four combinations of techniques as shown in Fig. 2. Among the four combinations, we deemed that point-based selection + volume-based deselection to be counter-intuitive because users rarely select a series of wrong objects individually and then deselect all of them. We thus removed it from further exploration.

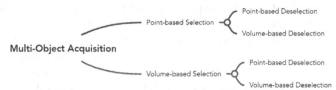

Fig. 2. Our design space resulted in four combinations of multi-object acquisition techniques.

3.2 Techniques

Based on the design space, we derived three techniques for multi-object acquisition. We made the following design factors consistent across all the techniques so that we could compare them through an experiment. All techniques leveraged game controllers rendered in the virtual environment as an indicator of the hand position. The techniques could be used with either one of the hands. There was consistent visual and audio feedback when object selection or deselection was triggered. Additionally, we rendered an outline to an object if it was selected and removed it once it was deselected.

PSPD (Point Selection + Point Deselection). With PSPD, a user can select an object by touching the object with the controller and pressing the trigger button (see Fig. 3). A group of objects can be selected by triggering the selection of each object serially. One can deselect an object by touching the selected object and pressing the trigger. Deselection of a group of objects also happens serially. This technique is similar to virtual hands [23] but applied in the context of multi-object acquisition.

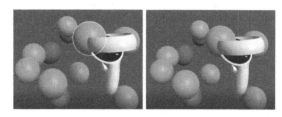

Fig. 3. With PSPD (Point Selection + Point Deselection), a user can select/deselect an object by touching the object with the controller and pressing the trigger button.

VSVD (Volume Selection + Volume Deselection). With VSVD, a user can select/deselect a group of objects with a volume-based selection mechanism. A user starts the process by creating a box-shape volume. Once the user presses the trigger of a controller, a box corner is initiated and fixed at the same position. The diagonal corner of the box updates as the position of the controller updates, so that the size of the box increases or decreases based on a user's action (see Fig. 4). Once the user releases the trigger, all objects within the box volume will be selected, and the selection box disappears. The same process is applied to the deselection phase.

A user can switch between selection and deselection mode by pressing the primary button of a controller. The mode was set to selection mode by default while entering a task. An indication of mode was attached to the center of the virtual controller, with a "+" sign representing the selection mode and the "-" representing the deselection mode. Unlike PSPD, we explicitly separated the two modes because we found it could cause user confusion if the two modes were combined during our pilot test.

We chose a box-shape selection volume to mimic the Two Corner technique proposed by Ulinski et al. [29,30], where the creation of a box was defined by the positions of two diagonal corners. However, unlike the Two Corner technique, which used both hands to manipulate the corners, our technique leveraged a single hand to create the cube to be consistent with the PSPD technique. The selection volume for both modes is semi-transparent, which was deemed as an effective representation of a fix-shaped selection box [37,40]. We distinguished the two modes further by using a green box to represent the selection box and a yellow box to represent the deselection box.

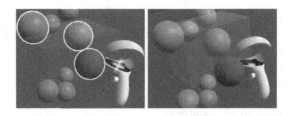

Fig. 4. With VSVD (Volume Selection + Volume Deselection), a user can select/deselect a group of object at once by creating a selection/deselection volume.

VSPD (Volume Selection + Point Deselection). With VSPD, a user can select a group of objects with a box-shape selection volume, like VSVD. The user can deselect one object at a time with the point-based mechanism, as in PSPD. The technique also has two explicit modes for selection and deselection, which requires a button click to switch between the different modes (Fig. 5).

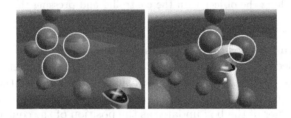

Fig. 5. With VSPD (Volume Selection + Point Deselection), a user can select a group of objects through a selection volume and deselect one object at a time.

4   User Study

4.1   Participants and Apparatus

We recruited 12 participants (5 women, 7 men) between the ages of 19 to 27 (mean = 22.83). Participants self-reported their familiarity with VR, and all of them had rather limited knowledge of VR (mean = 2.08, on a 5-point Likert scale). The system was implemented in Unity and the study was conducted on an Oculus Quest 2 headset.

4.2   Task Scenarios

We employed two types of task scenarios: randomized scenarios and structured scenarios. As we wanted to test whether volume-based selection would still be beneficial if the target layout was randomized and evaluate how selection and deselection mechanisms affect user performance, we leveraged a controlled scenario with randomly generated target layouts. Furthermore, as we also wanted to verify previous findings in more structured layouts, we also composed two structured scenarios.

For both task scenarios, there were targets and distractors, and all of them were selectable. While objects may be represented by different shapes in each task (e.g., a sphere, a book, molecules), the targets were always set in red to make them consistent across the tasks. All the tasks were in the primary working space [36] where objects were all in front of the user and were within arm-reach distance. We deemed that further manipulation of the objects normally happens within this space.

Randomized Scenarios. In the randomized scenarios, all objects were generated in a random position within the region of $100\,cm \times 50\,cm \times 50\,cm$. The objects were all spheres with a fixed diameter of $7.5\,cm$, representing a relatively easier selection of each target as seen in previous work [2]. These scenarios were designed to assess the techniques' performance with more randomized target layouts, such as selecting some data points for further analysis in an immersive analytics scenario and acquiring certain items from a messy workspace, where the target positions may not follow a particular structure. Programmatically, we generated the objects with the built-in `Random.Range` function in Unity within a bounding box. The targets could overlap with each other. Since the overlapping could happen in all conditions, it is quite unlikely to be a confounding factor.

We varied two independent variables in the randomized scenarios: TASK DIF-FICULTY and TARGET MAJORITY. With TASK DIFFICULTY, we varied the total number of each scenario, with a total of 15 objects in the simple condition and a total of 40 in the difficult condition. The choice of these numbers was inspired by the result of a previous study [16], which showed that the volume-based selection techniques started to show a significant advantage over the point-based techniques when the target number was large (around 30). With TARGET MAJOR-ITY, we varied the proportion of the targets among all the objects. In the target minority condition, the total number of target objects was approximately 1/3 of the total number of objects, while in the target majority condition, the target objects were 2/3 of the total objects. With this variable, we aimed to investigate whether the proportion of the targets would affect a user's strategy of using selection and deselection methods (Fig. 6).

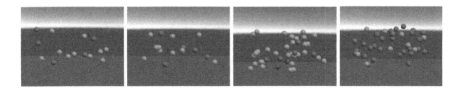

Fig. 6. Example conditions in the randomized scenarios.

Structured Scenarios. We designed two application scenarios to verify findings from previous research that volume-based selection techniques may have a better performance when the layout of objects were more structured.

The first was a bookshelf scenario where participants were supposed to select books from a bookshelf. There were a total number of 30 books (24 targets), and all of them were in the size of 15 cm × 5 cm × 20 cm. There were a total of 4 layers on the bookshelf, where each layer contained 7 or 8 books (see Fig. 7, left). The targets were always next to each other and the selection of targets was predetermined. The second scenario was to select certain atoms from a molecule. There were 28 atoms in the molecule and all of them had a diameter of 7 cm. There were 6 non-target atoms inside the molecule, which were placed together and were not in red. The two structured scenarios gave different layouts where all objects were placed at the same depth in the bookshelf scenario and the objects were placed at different depths in the molecule scenario. The parameters (i.e., target size, the number of targets) were fixed. The target number for both scenarios was larger than 20, with which the volume-based techniques were more likely to excel [16].

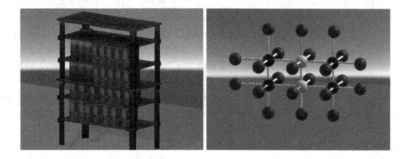

Fig. 7. Structured scenarios: the bookshelf scenario (left) and the molecule scenario (right).

In sum, we studied 6 scenarios (= 4 randomized scenarios + 2 structured scenarios). The randomized scenarios were composed of 2 TASK DIFFICULTY × 2 TARGET MAJORITY, whereas the structured scenario consisted of 1 bookshelf scenario (2D arrangement) and 1 molecule scenario (3D arrangement).

4.3 Evaluation Metrics

Performance Measures. To evaluate the techniques' performance, we employed the following two measures:

- *Selection time*: the time taken to complete the task for each trial.
- *Error rate*: the number of incorrect objects selected/not selected (i.e., false positives and false negatives) in relation to the total number of objects. The errors were recorded at the end of each trial, which was determined by participants pressing a finishing button on the controller.

Hand Movement Measures. We were interested in investigating how the techniques influence hand movement distance, which can correlate with arm fatigue [36,39].

- *Hand movement distance*: the aggregation of the hand movement distance by accumulating the displacement of hand per frame.

Subjective Measures. We further measured participants' subjective experience of using the techniques.

- *User Experience Questionnaires - short version (UEQ-S)* [27]: a questionnaire on 7-point scales regarding user experience.

Strategy Measures. We were interested in participants' strategies to solve the multi-object acquisition task, particularly in volume-based selection methods (e.g., performing multiple separate selections or selecting a large volume of objects and then teasing out unwanted objects). The following two measures were used as indicators of users' strategies.

- *Number of operations*: the number of selections/deselections have been made for each task trial.
- *Objects per operation*: the averaged number of selected/deselected objects in each operation of selection or deselection. If there is no such operation in a trial, the value is set to zero.

4.4   Design and Procedure

The study employed a 3×6 (techniques $\times$ scenarios) within-subject design. The techniques and scenarios have been introduced in previous sections. For each condition, we provided 7 repetitive trials to balance the stability of the results and user engagement in the study. Different trials had different targets and positions (i.e., re-randomized). The 4 randomized scenarios and 3 techniques were counterbalanced for 12 participants, and the structured scenarios appeared after the randomized conditions.

Before the experiment, participants were briefly introduced to this study and were asked to fill out a pre-test demographic questionnaire. Participants were instructed on how to use the VR system and the techniques and had enough time to practice before the start of each session. We did not prime participants on different selection strategies to simulate how the techniques would be used in real-world scenarios. During the experiment, participants remained seated, with no physical obstacles within arm-reach distance. They were also asked to complete the task as quickly and accurately as possible. User feedback was collected with UEQ-S after participants completed a technique in each scenario. Participants were asked to take a break before starting a new technique. After they completed all the tasks, participants were asked to rank the techniques and provide oral feedback regarding the experience of using each technique. The experiment lasted around 45 min in total for each participant.

4.5 Hypotheses

We were specifically interested in verifying the following three hypotheses via our user study.

- *H1.* The point-based selection technique (PSPD) will outperform the volume-based selection techniques (VSVD and VSPD) in randomized scenarios where the majority of the objects are distractors. Because the number of targets is not high in those cases, selecting objects in groups may make less sense with a randomized layout.
- *H2.* The volume-based selection techniques (VSVD and VSPD) will outperform the point-based selection technique (PSPD) in randomized scenarios where the majority of the objects are target objects, as it might be easier for users to make a large group selection and remove unwanted objects rather than selecting the targets additively.
- *H3.* The volume-based selection techniques (VSVD and VSPD) will outperform the point-based selection technique (PSPD) in the structured scenarios because the two volume-based techniques can select multiple clustered objects at once.

5   Results

We collected 1512 trials of data (12 participants × 3 techniques × 6 scenarios × 7 repetition) from the within-subject experiment. The trials that had time and error rates greater than three deviations from the mean value had been discarded in each condition (30 trials, 3% in the randomized scenarios; 18 trials, 3.6% in the structured scenarios). After removing the outliers, we performed Shapiro-Wilk normality tests. The results indicated that the data were not normally distributed. Hence, we used Aligned Rank Transform [33] to pre-process the data in both scenarios. We further conducted repeated-measures ANOVA (RM-ANOVA) and ART-based pairwise comparisons [10] to evaluate the performance and user experience of different techniques. In the following sections, we focus on main effects and two-way interaction effects that are related to the TECHNIQUE factor, because our main goal was to explore the difference in techniques under various conditions. We present the raw statistical results in the supplementary material.

5.1   Randomized Scenarios

Selection Time. RM-ANOVA showed that TECHNIQUE had a significant impact on task completion time ($F_{2,954} = 103.50, p < .001, \eta_p^2 = 0.18$). On average, the point-based selection technique (PSPD) took the least amount of time while VSPD took the longest (see Fig. 8 left). An interaction effect between TECHNIQUE and TARGET MAJORITY on complete time was identified ($F_{2,954} = 18.98, p < .001, \eta_p^2 = 0.04$)—the influence of the majority of target-major or distractor-major on the two volume-based selection techniques (VSVD and VSPD) was significantly larger than on the point-based selection technique (PSPD), as shown in Fig. 8 right. In the target minority scenario, the difference between VSVD and PSPD was not as large as in the target majority scenario.

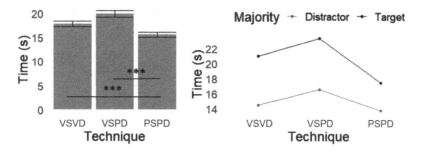

Fig. 8. Left: Average selection time ($\pm 1S.E.$) of the techniques in the randomized scenarios. Right: interaction effect between Technique and Target Majority.

Error Rate. RM-ANOVA showed that TECHNIQUE had a significant main effect on error rate ($F_{2,954} = 13.74, p < .001, \eta_p^2 = 0.03$). Interactions between TECHNIQUE × TARGET MAJORITY ($F_{2,954} = 27.84, p < .001, \eta_p^2 = 0.06$) and TECHNIQUE × TASK DIFFICULTY ($F_{2,954} = 18.06, p < .001, \eta_p^2 = 0.04$) were also identified. Pairwise comparisons showed that PSPD had a lower error rate than VSVD ($p = .024$), while VSVD led to lower error rate than VSPD ($p = .031$). However, the overall error rates of the techniques were very low (PSPD: 0.97%; VSVD: 1.15%; VSPD: 1.19%;).

Hand Movement Distance. RM-ANOVA indicated that TECHNIQUE had a significant main effect on hand movement distance ($F_{2,954} = 56.84, p < .001, \eta_p^2 = 0.11$). As in Fig. 9 left, the two volume-based techniques led to longer hand movement distance than the point-based technique (both $p < .001$). An interaction between TECHNIQUE and TARGET MAJORITY was also identified ($F_{2,954} = 8.79, p < .001, \eta_p^2 = 0.02$). While the hand movement distance increased when the majority of the objects became targets, as indicated in Fig. 9 right, the influence of TARGET MAJORITY was much larger on the volume-based techniques than on the point-based technique. We also observed that the hand movement distance of the three techniques did not differ significantly in the target minority condition.

Number of Operations. For the number of selection operations, RM-ANOVA indicated that TECHNIQUE had a significant main effect ($F_{2,954} = 797.99, p < .001, \eta_p^2 = 0.63$). Interaction effects of TECHNIQUE × TARGET MAJORITY ($F_{2,954} = 268.29, p < .001, \eta_p^2 = 0.36$) and TECHNIQUE × TASK DIFFICULTY ($F_{2,954} = 518.24, p < .001, \eta_p^2 = 0.52$) were also identified. As shown in Fig. 10 left, the point-based technique (PSPD) required significantly more operations

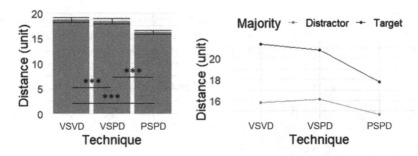

Fig. 9. Left: Average hand movement distance ($\pm 1S.E.$) of the techniques in the randomized scenarios. Right: an interaction effect between Technique and Target Majority.

than the other two volume-based techniques (VSVD and VSPD) when the target number was high in the difficult condition. Also, the number of selection operations of the three techniques was quite similar in the other three conditions.

For the number of deselection operations, RM-ANOVA suggested that TECHNIQUE had a significant main effect ($F_{2,954} = 98.30, p < .001, \eta_p^2 = 0.17$). Interaction effects of TECHNIQUE × TARGET MAJORITY ($F_{2,954} = 4.10, p = .017, \eta_p^2 = 0.01$) and TECHNIQUE × TASK DIFFICULTY ($F_{2,954} = 42.97, p < .001, \eta_p^2 = 0.08$) were also identified. Overall, as shown in Fig. 10 right, the number of deselection operations was quite low (i.e., less than 1.15 on average). The number for the difficulty-target major condition was slightly higher for all techniques than for the other conditions.

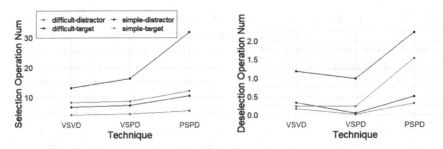

Fig. 10. Average number of (de-)selection operations in the randomized conditions.

Objects per Operation. For the number of objects per selection operation, RM-ANOVA indicated that TECHNIQUE had a significant main effect ($F_{2,954} = 438.78, p < .001, \eta_p^2 = 0.48$). Interaction effects of TECHNIQUE × TARGET MAJORITY ($F_{2,954} = 154.05, p < .001, \eta_p^2 = 0.24$) and TECHNIQUE × TASK DIFFICULTY ($F_{2,954} = 130.46, \eta_p^2 = 0.21$) were also identified. As shown in

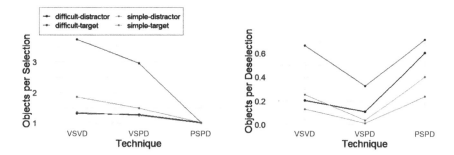

Fig. 11. Average number of (de-)selected objects per operation in the randomized conditions.

Table 1. Summary of the statistical main effects of Technique on the evaluation metrics in the structured scenarios.

Dependent Variable	Bookshelf			Molecule		
	F-value	p-value	η_p^2	F-value	p-value	η_p^2
Selection time	38.06	<.001	0.25	1.50	0.224	0.01
Error rate	3.35	0.037	0.03	1.74	0.176	0.02
Distance	14.92	<.001	0.11	3.94	0.021	0.03
Selection operation num	378.28	<.001	0.77	325.02	<.001	0.74
Deselection operation num	66.52	<.001	0.37	5.54	.004	0.05
Objects per selection	436.07	<.001	0.79	376.65	<.001	0.77
Objects per deselection	36.91	<.001	0.24	4.09	.018	0.03

Fig. 11, the number of selected object per operation was higher in the difficult-target majority condition for both volume-based selection techniques (VSVD and VSPD).

For the number of objects per deselection operation, RM-ANOVA indicated that TECHNIQUE had a significant main effect ($F_{2,954} = 77.84, p < .001, \eta_p^2 = 0.14$). An interaction effect of TECHNIQUE × TASK DIFFICULTY ($F_{2,954} = 25.12, p < .001, \eta_p^2 = 0.05$) was also identified. Very limited objects were getting deselected per operation (i.e., lower than 1 on average) for all the techniques.

5.2 Structured Scenarios

We summarize the statistical main effects of TECHNIQUE on different evaluation metrics in Table 1 and the average results of the techniques in Fig. 12. More details on the ART-based RM-ANOVAs and pairwise comparisons can be found in the provided supplementary material.

In the bookshelf scenario, overall, the volume-based techniques (VSVD and VSPD) were significantly faster than the point-based technique (PSPD), while

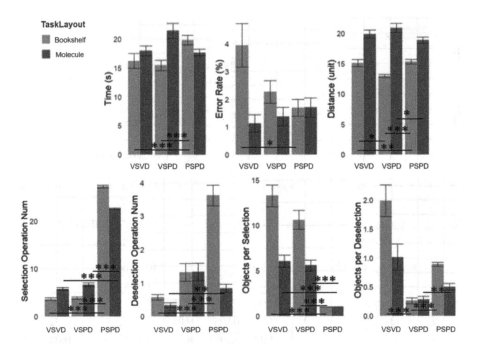

Fig. 12. Average selection time, error rate, hand movement distance, number of selection/deselection operations, and number of selected/deselected object per operation for both of the structured scenarios. Error bar indicates one standard error.

all of them maintained a relatively low error rate (<4%) throughout. VSPD led to the lowest movement distance, while PSPD was the highest. The selection operations were significantly lower for the volume-based techniques (VSVD and VSPD) than PSPD, and correspondingly, the objects per selection of these techniques were significantly higher. The number of deselection operations was significantly lower for VSVD and VSPD. The objects per deselection of VSPD was the lowest while VSVD was the highest.

In the molecule scenario, overall, the performance difference in terms of selection time and error rate among the three techniques was not identified to be significant. However, the hand movement distance while using VSPD was found to be significantly higher than PSPD. Similar to the bookshelf scenario, we also found that the volume-based techniques led to a much lower number of selection operations and a higher object number per selection. VSVD led to significantly lower deselection operations than PSPD, and VSPD led to a significantly lower number of objects per deselection as compared to PSPD. We infer group selection led to higher accuracy during the selection phase in structured scenarios, so there was less need to deselect objects.

5.3   User Experience

The UEQ-S results are summarized in Table 2. Overall, the PSPD led to the highest pragmatic value, while the VSVD and VSPD were more interesting to use. VSVD led to slightly higher overall quality than PSPD.

Table 2. UEQ-S results of each technique (the higher the better).

Technique	Pragmatic	Hedonic	Overall
PSPD	2.31 (Excellent)	-0.04 (Bad)	1.14 (> Average)
VSVD	1.35 (> Average)	1.13 (> Average)	1.24 (> Average)
VSPD	1.18 (> Average)	0.5 (< Average)	0.84 (< Average)

5.4   Observations and Subjective Feedback

We observed that most participants tended to select the objects one by one rather than creating selection volumes in the randomized environment even with the volume-based selection techniques. One participant mentioned the reason behind this behavior: the volume-based selection techniques were used as the point-based selection technique by instantiating very small cubes, and that was an easier way for this participant to complete the task in the randomized scenarios. In fact, seven of the participants self-reported that they preferred to make multiple separated selection operations rather than creating a large selection volume and then make deselections to remove unwanted objects. Half of the participants did not realize the later strategy, and the others felt the interaction of deselection to be overly complicated in randomized scenarios.

We also observed that participants moved the controller forward and backward repetitively to try to include or remove objects when creating a selection volume. Two of the participants commented that they had to make a few attempts to resize the selection volume to know how far they have reached.

When asking participants to rank the techniques, PSPD was the most favorite in general (10/12). Most preferred to use the volume-based selection techniques in the structured scenarios and the point-based selection technique in the randomized scenarios. Two of them further commented that VSVD was the most useful in the structured scenarios since it could cancel the selection of more than one object per operation.

6   Discussion

In the following, we compare and discuss the techniques based on our design dimensions: point- vs. volume-based technique and selection vs. deselection. We also examine the effect of different environmental factors (i.e., randomized vs. structured scenarios, task difficulties, and target/distractor majority) on technique performance.

6.1   Point- vs. Volume-Based Selection

Overall, when the target locations did not follow a certain layout (i.e., in the randomized scenarios), we found that the point-based technique (PSPD) led to significantly lower selection time and shorter movement distance as compared to the volume-based techniques (VSVD and VSPD). The difference between the techniques was larger in scenarios where the majority of the objects were targets. This contradicted our initial hypothesis (*H2*) that the volume-based techniques would outperform the point-based technique because of their convenience in selecting a large group of objects. *H1* was partially supported because the point-based technique led to, on average, lower selection time when the majority of the objects were distractors.

We identified two potential reasons why the volume-based techniques led to worse performance than the point-based technique in randomized scenarios. First, volume-based selection techniques might not be suitable for randomized scenarios. Indeed, both participants' comments and selected objects per operation indicated that they preferred to use the volume-based techniques similar to how they use the point-based technique by making small, additive selections (i.e., selecting a small number of objects per operation). It might also be the chaotic nature of the randomized environment that made the participants believe that it might not be beneficial to select a large group of objects altogether.

Second, based on our observation and participants' feedback, the difficulty of depth perception might also be one reason for delaying the task completion of the volume-based techniques. For example, participants were found to move the controller forward and backward repetitively to try to gauge how far they have reached and whether they would be able to include or remove particular objects. These findings are in line with Ulinski et al.'s work [29,30], where participants also had difficulty in creating volumes since the depth information was not clear enough in a monitor. Our immersive 3D VR setting, which allowed participants to observe the selection volumes from different perspectives, did not seem to alleviate this issue of depth perception. Notably, we have provided proper depth cues for objects in the 3D environment. For example, strong depth cues like shading, occlusion, and relative object sizes were given. One issue might be because the selection volume was rendered in a monotonous color [19,31].

In the (structured) bookshelf scenario, both volume-based techniques outperformed the point-based technique in terms of selection time while maintaining a relatively low error rate ($<4\%$). However, in the (structured) molecule scenario, the performance difference among the three techniques was not significant. In both cases, the volume-based techniques led to a significantly lower number of selection operations and thus higher object number per selection. These findings partially confirmed *H3* and indicated that participants were more willing to apply the group-based selection mechanism when objects were structured (e.g., on average >10 objects per selection in the bookshelf scenario and >5 objects per selection in the molecule scenario).

In both scenarios, the volume-based selection techniques did result in less number of selection operations (thus higher object number per selection) in a more complex condition (i.e., difficult-target majority in the randomized scenarios). This indicates that volume-based selection activities did happen when the targets were clustered together, but it was not more efficient to do so.

6.2 Selection vs. Deselection

According to the selection and deselection operation numbers, we found that, overall, participants applied selection more frequently while rarely using the deselection mechanism. We also found that few participants seek to use a new strategy multi-object acquisition as proposed in *H2*, where we assumed that users would select a large group of objects and then remove unwanted objects. They preferred selecting objects additively by making several separate selections, even with the volume-based selection techniques.

6.3 The Effect of Environmental Factors

We found changing Task Difficulty in randomized scenarios led to a somewhat more consistent impact on the performance of different techniques (all of them suffered similarly in more challenging scenarios [1,14]). In contrast, when switching from distractor majority to target majority conditions, both volume-based techniques were more severely impacted as compared to the point-based technique—there was a more significant increase in selection time and hand movement distance for the volume-based techniques.

Overall, our results suggest that the point-based technique (i.e., PSPD) was more robust under different environmental factors which resulted in its highest pragmatic value in UEQ-S [27]. The volume-based technique (i.e., VSVD and VSPD) can reduce the number of operations across different environments, and may perform especially well in more structured, target-dense scenarios.

6.4 Design Implications

Based on the study results and our discussions, we distilled the following design implications.

– When the target locations do not follow a specific layout (i.e., with more randomized, hard-to-predict object locations), we recommend choosing the point-based selection technique (PSPD) among the three techniques (PSPD, VSVD, and VSPD). Our results suggest that the point-based technique (PSPD) is not only more efficient than the volume-based techniques (VSVD and VSPD) but is also more robust across different environmental conditions (e.g., the majority of objects are targets or distractors).
– When the targets are structured or clustered, we recommend considering applying a volume-based technique (either VSVD or VSPD). Our results suggest that VSVD and VSPD tend to perform well on structured layouts. Furthermore, VSVD and VSPD led to a significantly lower number of selection operations in those scenarios.

- We recommend enabling the deselection mechanism (i.e., allowing users to remove unwanted selections). However, be mindful that users may only use this function occasionally to correct their errors and may not switch their acquisition strategies depending on enabling/disabling this function.
- To further improve our volume-based selection techniques (VSVD and VSPD), we recommend focusing on providing a better depth perception of the selection volume. Unlike 2D group-based selection techniques used in computers (i.e., a 2D rectangle selection volume), in a 3D VR environment, we might want to apply extensive depth cues for the selection volume itself (not a transparent box with a monotonous color). Providing additional depth cues like color/texture gradients is likely to be beneficial.

6.5   Limitations and Future Work

We have identified several limitations of this research. First, we only evaluated one type of volume-based selection mechanism (i.e., a cube selection volume [29, 30]), which seemed to be a good approximation of the rectangle lasso selection in PCs. We acknowledge that there are other types of strategies in VR, like using spherical selection volume or applying bimanual selection volume creation methods [25]. The choice of the volume-based selection mechanism can influence the technique's performance.

Second, we only evaluated one parameter level of the structured scenarios (i.e., the bookshelf and molecule scenarios). We did this because we wanted to focus on the randomized scenarios as they were less explored in previous research. While we were interested in verifying previous findings on structured scenarios, we did not want to put too much emphasis on these conditions considering the workload of the participants according to our pilot study (the experiment already lasted about 45 min). Also concerning the participant workload, we did not examine the effect of other factors such as target disparity, spread of targets, and target intersection and occlusion [1, 6, 11, 38] while kept them the same across conditions. Future research may scrutinize their effects and potential interactions in different application scenarios.

Third, all the participants in this study were novice users that only had limited experience in using VR. Future studies could include expert users to reduce the potential novelty effect [6]. Also, expert users who have experienced other off-the-shelf multiple interaction techniques in VR might provide interesting insights.

7   Conclusion

In this research, we investigated point-based and volume-based multi-object acquisition in VR. Specifically, we leveraged a two-dimensional design space that considered (1) point- or volume-based operation and (2) selection and deselection mechanisms. We derived three techniques based on the design space, and explored the performance and usability of these techniques under both randomized and structured scenarios. We found that point-based techniques are more efficient in randomized scenarios, while volume-based techniques are better suited for structured scenarios. We also found that users rarely applied the deselection mechanism and mostly used them for error correction. Based on our results, we discuss potential reasons behind technique performance under different conditions, and provided design implications that can aid the future design of similar techniques. We believe this research provides valuable lessons for designers to both optimize their interaction techniques and adopt deselection mechanisms in VR multi-object acquisition tasks.

References

1. Argelaguet, F., Andujar, C.: A survey of 3D object selection techniques for virtual environments. Comput. Graph. **37**(3), 121–136 (2013). https://doi.org/10.1016/j.cag.2012.12.003
2. Ariza, O., Bruder, G., Katzakis, N., Steinicke, F.: Analysis of proximity-based multimodal feedback for 3D selection in immersive virtual environments. In: 2018 IEEE Conference on Virtual Reality and 3D User Interfaces (VR), pp. 327–334. IEEE (2018). https://doi.org/10.1109/VR.2018.8446317
3. Baloup, M., Pietrzak, T., Casiez, G.: Raycursor: a 3D pointing facilitation technique based on raycasting. In: Proceedings of the 2019 CHI Conference on Human Factors in Computing Systems, CHI 2019, pp. 1–12. Association for Computing Machinery, New York (2019). https://doi.org/10.1145/3290605.3300331
4. Benavides, A., Khadka, R., Banic, A.: Physically-based bimanual volumetric selection for immersive visualizations. In: Chen, J.Y.C., Fragomeni, G. (eds.) HCII 2019. LNCS, vol. 11574, pp. 183–195. Springer, Cham (2019). https://doi.org/10.1007/978-3-030-21607-8_14
5. Benko, H., Feiner, S.: Balloon selection: a multi-finger technique for accurate low-fatigue 3D selection. In: 2007 IEEE Symposium on 3D User Interfaces, Charlotte, NC, USA, p. 4142849. IEEE (2007). https://doi.org/10.1109/3DUI.2007.340778
6. Bergström, J., Dalsgaard, T.S., Alexander, J., Hornbæk, K.: How to evaluate object selection and manipulation in VR? guidelines from 20 years of studies. In: Proceedings of the 2021 CHI Conference on Human Factors in Computing Systems, Yokohama, Japan, pp. 1–20. ACM (2021). https://doi.org/10.1145/3411764.3445193
7. Bowman, D.A. (ed.): 3D User Interfaces: Theory and Practice. Addison-Wesley, Boston (2005)
8. Dehmeshki, H., Stuerzlinger, W.: Design and evaluation of a perceptual-based object group selection technique. In: Proceedings of the 24th BCS Interaction Specialist Group Conference, BCS 2010, pp. 365–373. BCS Learning & Development Ltd., Swindon, GBR (2010)
9. Dubois, E., Hamelin, A.: Worm selector: volume selection in a 3D point cloud through adaptive modelling. Int. J. Virtual Reality **17**(1), 1–20 (2017). https://doi.org/10.20870/IJVR.2017.17.1.2884
10. Elkin, L.A., Kay, M., Higgins, J.J., Wobbrock, J.O.: An aligned rank transform procedure for multifactor contrast tests. In: The 34th Annual ACM Symposium on User Interface Software and Technology, pp. 754–768 (2021). https://doi.org/10.1145/3472749.3474784

11. Elmqvist, N., Tsigas, P.: A taxonomy of 3D occlusion management techniques. In: 2007 IEEE Virtual Reality Conference, pp. 51–58. IEEE (2007). https://doi.org/10.1109/VR.2007.352463

12. Hurter, C., Riche, N.H., Drucker, S.M., Cordeil, M., Alligier, R., Vuillemot, R.: FiberClay: sculpting three dimensional trajectories to reveal structural insights. IEEE Trans. Visual Comput. Graphics **25**(1), 704–714 (2019). https://doi.org/10.1109/TVCG.2018.2865191

13. Kang, J., Zhong, K., Qin, S., Wang, H., Wright, D.: Instant 3D design concept generation and visualization by real-time hand gesture recognition. Comput. Ind. **64**(7), 785–797 (2013). https://doi.org/10.1016/j.compind.2013.04.012

14. LaViola, J.J., Jr., Kruijff, E., McMahan, R.P., Bowman, D., Poupyrev, I.P.: 3D User Interfaces: Theory and Practice. Addison-Wesley Professional, Boston (2017)

15. Li, Y., Sarcar, S., Kim, K., Tu, H., Ren, X.: Designing successive target selection in virtual reality via penetrating the intangible interface with handheld controllers. Int. J. Hum. Comput. Stud. **165**, 102835 (2022). https://doi.org/10.1016/j.ijhcs.2022.102835

16. Lucas, J., Bowman, D., Chen, J., Wingrave, C.: Design and Evaluation of 3D Multiple Object Selection Techniques (2005)

17. Göbel, M.: Industrial applications of VEs. IEEE Comput. Graph. Appl. **16**(01), 10–13 (1996). https://doi.org/10.1109/MCG.1996.10005

18. Marriott, K., et al.: Immersive Analytics, vol. 11190. Springer, Cham (2018). https://doi.org/10.1007/978-3-030-01388-2

19. Matatko, A., Bollmann, J., Müller, A.: Depth perception in virtual reality. In: Advances in 3D Geo-Information Sciences, pp. 115–129 (2011). https://doi.org/10.1007/978-3-642-12670-3_7

20. Mine, M.R.: Virtual environment interaction techniques. Technical report, University of North Carolina at Chapel Hill, USA (1995)

21. Mizobuchi, S., Yasumura, M.: Tapping vs. circling selections on pen-based devices: evidence for different performance-shaping factors. In: Proceedings of the SIGCHI Conference on Human Factors in Computing Systems, CHI 2004, pp. 607–614. Association for Computing Machinery, New York (2004). https://doi.org/10.1145/985692.985769

22. Montano-Murillo, R.A., Nguyen, C., Kazi, R.H., Subramanian, S., DiVerdi, S., Martinez-Plasencia, D.: Slicing-volume: hybrid 3D/2D multi-target selection technique for dense virtual environments. In: 2020 IEEE Conference on Virtual Reality and 3D User Interfaces (VR), Atlanta, GA, USA, pp. 53–62. IEEE (2020). https://doi.org/10.1109/VR46266.2020.00023

23. Poupyrev, I., Ichikawa, T., Weghorst, S., Billinghurst, M.: Egocentric object manipulation in virtual environments: empirical evaluation of interaction techniques. Comput. Graph. Forum **17**(3), 41–52 (1998). https://doi.org/10.1111/1467-8659.00252

24. Poupyrev, I., Billinghurst, M., Weghorst, S., Ichikawa, T.: The go-go interaction technique: non-linear mapping for direct manipulation in VR. In: Proceedings of the 9th Annual ACM Symposium on User Interface Software and Technology - UIST 1996, Seattle, Washington, United States, pp. 79–80. ACM Press (1996). https://doi.org/10.1145/237091.237102

25. Romagnoli, G.: Best multi-object selection methods for virtual reality (2021). https://bootcamp.uxdesign.cc/best-multi-object-selection-methods-for-virtual-reality-97027160f584

26. Schjerlund, J., Hornbæk, K., Bergström, J.: Ninja hands: using many hands to improve target selection in VR. In: Proceedings of the 2021 CHI Conference on Human Factors in Computing Systems, CHI 2021. Association for Computing Machinery, New York (2021). https://doi.org/10.1145/3411764.3445759

27. Schrepp, M., Hinderks, A., Thomaschewski, J.: Design and evaluation of a short version of the user experience questionnaire (UEQ-S). Int. J. Interact. Multimedia Artif. Intell. **4**(6), 103–108 (2017). https://doi.org/10.9781/ijimai.2017.09.001

28. Stenholt, R.: Efficient selection of multiple objects on a large scale. In: Proceedings of the 18th ACM Symposium on Virtual Reality Software and Technology - VRST 2012, Toronto, Ontario, Canada, p. 105. ACM Press (2012). https://doi.org/10.1145/2407336.2407357

29. Ulinski, A., Wartell, Z., Hodges, L.F.: Bimanual task division preferences for volume selection. In: Proceedings of the 2007 ACM Symposium on Virtual Reality Software and Technology - VRST 2007, Newport Beach, California, p. 217. ACM Press (2007). https://doi.org/10.1145/1315184.1315228

30. Ulinski, A., Zanbaka, C., Wartell, Z., Goolkasian, P., Hodges, L.F.: Two handed selection techniques for volumetric data. In: 2007 IEEE Symposium on 3D User Interfaces, Charlotte, NC, USA, p. 4142853. IEEE (2007). https://doi.org/10.1109/3DUI.2007.340782

31. Vienne, C., Masfrand, S., Bourdin, C., Vercher, J.L.: Depth perception in virtual reality systems: effect of screen distance, environment richness and display factors. IEEE Access **8**, 29099–29110 (2020). https://doi.org/10.1109/ACCESS.2020.2972122

32. Wagner, J., Stuerzlinger, W., Nedel, L.: Comparing and combining virtual hand and virtual ray pointer interactions for data manipulation in immersive analytics. IEEE Trans. Visual Comput. Graphics **27**(5), 2513–2523 (2021). https://doi.org/10.1109/TVCG.2021.3067759

33. Wobbrock, J.O., Findlater, L., Gergle, D., Higgins, J.J.: The aligned rank transform for nonparametric factorial analyses using only anova procedures. In: Proceedings of the SIGCHI Conference on Human Factors in Computing Systems, Vancouver, BC, Canada, pp. 143–146. ACM (2011). https://doi.org/10.1145/1978942.1978963

34. Yamanaka, S., Stuerzlinger, W.: Modeling fully and partially constrained lasso movements in a grid of icons. In: Proceedings of the 2019 CHI Conference on Human Factors in Computing Systems, CHI 2019, pp. 1–12. Association for Computing Machinery, New York (2019). https://doi.org/10.1145/3290605.3300350

35. Yu, D., Liang, H.N., Lu, F., Nanjappan, V., Papangelis, K., Wang, W., et al.: Target selection in head-mounted display virtual reality environments. J. Univers. Comput. Sci. **24**(9), 1217–1243 (2018). https://doi.org/10.3217/jucs-024-09-1217

36. Yu, D., et al.: Gaze-supported 3D object manipulation in virtual reality. In: Proceedings of the 2021 CHI Conference on Human Factors in Computing Systems, pp. 1–13 (2021). https://doi.org/10.1145/3411764.3445343

37. Yu, D., Zhou, Q., Dingler, T., Velloso, E., Goncalves, J.: Blending on-body and mid-air interaction in virtual reality. In: 2022 IEEE International Symposium on Mixed and Augmented Reality (ISMAR), pp. 637–646. IEEE (2022). https://doi.org/10.1109/ISMAR55827.2022.00081

38. Yu, D., Zhou, Q., Newn, J., Dingler, T., Velloso, E., Goncalves, J.: Fully-occluded target selection in virtual reality. IEEE Trans. Visual Comput. Graphics **26**(12), 3402–3413 (2020). https://doi.org/10.1109/TVCG.2020.3023606

39. Yu, D., Zhou, Q., Tag, B., Dingler, T., Velloso, E., Goncalves, J.: Engaging participants during selection studies in virtual reality. In: 2020 IEEE Conference on Virtual Reality and 3D User Interfaces (VR), pp. 500–509 (2020). https://doi.org/10.1109/VR46266.2020.00071

40. Zhai, S.: Human performance in six degree of freedom input control [microform]. (1995)

41. Zhou, Q., Yu, D., Reinoso, M.N., Newn, J., Goncalves, J., Velloso, E.: Eyes-free target acquisition during walking in immersive mixed reality. IEEE Trans. Visual Comput. Graphics **26**(12), 3423–3433 (2020). https://doi.org/10.1109/TVCG.2020.3023570

Using Mid-Air Haptics to Guide Mid-Air Interactions

Timothy Neate[1]([✉]), Sergio Alvares Maffra[2], William Frier[3], Zihao You[1], and Stephanie Wilson[4]

[1] Department of Informatics, King's College London, London, UK
timothy.neate@kcl.ac.uk
[2] Department of Mathematics, King's College London, London, UK
[3] Ultraleap Ltd., Bristol, UK
[4] Centre for HCI Design, City, University of London, London, UK

Abstract. When users interact with mid-air gesture-based interfaces, it is not always clear what interactions are available, or how they might be executed. Mid-air interfaces offer no tactile affordances, pushing systems to rely on other modalities (e.g. visual) to guide users regarding how to interact with the interface. However, these alternative modalities are not always appropriate or feasible (e.g. eyes-free interactions), meaning that they are not easy to learn from touch alone. Despite the possibility of conveying contactless haptic information in mid-air through ultrasound phased arrays, this technology has been limited to providing feedback on user interactions. In this paper, we explore the feasibility of using mid-air haptics to guide gestures in mid-air. Specifically, we present approaches to guide the user's hand in cardinal directions, execute a hand gesture and navigate a 2D mid-air plane, which we tested with 27 participants. After, reporting encouraging results which suggest good accuracy and relatively low workload, we reflect on the feasibility and challenges of using haptic guidance mechanisms in mid-air.

Keywords: Mid-air haptics · guidance · gesture · mid-air interfaces

1 Introduction

Mid-air, touchless, gesture-based interfaces are increasingly common [29]. They are a means for users to interact with augmented and virtual reality (AR/VR) [70], vehicles [61], home environments [60] and public displays [49]. Research has considered how complex interactions, such as continuous control with interface elements [30] and text input [45], can be done in mid-air. This is often a challenge because mid-air interactions provide no tactile feedback, and visual and auditory feedback is often undesirable or insufficient (e.g. when driving [61,62] or flying [26]). In response to this, researchers have turned to mid-air haptics. Mid-air haptic devices provide tactile sensations on the user's skin, without the need for physical connection with a user's body [11,36,53]. This is commonly accomplished by focusing ultrasound – sound > 20 kHz and beyond the human hearing

J. Abdelnour Nocera et al. (Eds.): INTERACT 2023, LNCS 14142, pp. 43–64, 2023.
https://doi.org/10.1007/978-3-031-42280-5_3

range – onto a user's hand [53]. Mid-air haptics have been used to provide feedback on mid-air, eyes-free control tasks when driving [32,38], and in situations where it is unhygienic to touch a device physically, e.g. medical settings [54] or public displays [34,40].

A remaining challenge with mid-air interfaces is their lack of explicit information on how to use them as they are not, as Delamare et al. put it, *self-revealing* [14]. Mid-air interactions are innately ambiguous as they have no visual or physical representation. The available interactions, and how they should be executed, are not clear [56]. Currently, no work has considered how these cues might be provided through mid-air haptics, which are increasingly considered as an output modality for mid-air interactions. In this paper, we suggest that information about how to interact with a mid-air interface might be provided by mid-air haptics, addressing the potential ambiguity of mid-air interfaces. We explore how mid-air haptic sensations can be used to guide users in specific interactions, namely directional movement, hand gestures and path-based interactions. Our key contributions are:

1. Methods for mid-air haptics that guide directional movement, hand gestures and path-based interaction from users
2. An investigation of the efficacy and user experience of the proposed methods

2   Background

2.1   Mid-Air Interactions and Guidance

A key challenge for touchless mid-air interactions is the lack of tactile information as users complete gestures or control tasks. It is therefore not clear what gestural interactions are available to a user, or how successfully they are interacting. Information about possible interactions, or the user's ongoing interactions can be provided in visual form. However, this can add cognitive load to the interaction and is undesirable in many eyes-free contexts (e.g. driving [32]).

A common method for supporting users in understanding the ways they might interact with a mid-air interface is to tell them explicitly what interactions are available. For instance, some systems provide textual or spoken instructions about the relation between gestures and outcomes [62]. Others provide training for learning gestural input [2], or methods to simply suggest that mid-air interaction is possible in the first place [27]. Explicit tuition and feedback on gestures has also been considered in language therapy [55], but with the goal of communicating with others gesturally, rather than with a system. A body of research has also investigated what gestures are intuitive to people. Elicitation studies (see [66] for a systematic review), where participants respond via gesture to a given stimulus and preferences are aggregated, have been used to understand expected gestures in various contexts [16,68,72]. Research has also considered how we might best inform users when their interactions are out of the range of a sensor system. For instance, Morrison et al. [50] use audio to inform users when their body is out of range of a computer vision system.

Research has also been conducted to explore the notion of providing *guides* for users to support their interactions – e.g. giving information about the path which the user must traverse to complete a gesture. All prior approaches we are aware of are visual or offer only binary haptic feedback (e.g. off/on). OctoPocus [5] provides 2D visual indicators of the next steps in a given path to show where the user should move their gesture next in 2D space. Similarly, Delamare et al. [15] consider how these approaches might support interactions in 3D space. Anderson et al. [4] considered, through their 'YouMove' system, how users might record and then learn custom gestures for full-body interaction with augmented reality mirrors. Visual information has also been used to support users in continuous mid-air interactions by showing the next points in a gesture path in AR [10]. Freeman et al. [19] explored a feedforward method for conveying what interactions are possible with a mid-air interface via wrist-worn rhythmic vibration information and light displays. Finally, Lopes et al. [42] considered the concept of dynamic affordance, i.e. providing feedback on possible interactions to users via muscle stimulation.

Freeman et al. [20] augmented a mid-air haptic device with LEDs. The authors then showed that the combination of mid-air haptic and visual cues could help guide the user to a given position above the device. Van den Bogaert et al. [6] argued that using mid-air alone could convey information to the users *before* they executed an action. For instance, they suggested using mid-air haptics to produce a "force field" around potentially harmful home appliances (e.g. a hot oven). However, this idea was neither implemented nor tested. Taking the idea one step further, Brown et al. [9] showed that associations between patterns and given meanings could be conveyed through mid-air haptic patterns, which suggests the feasibility of employing mid-air haptics as a guidance mechanism. However, the guidance itself is something that remains to be implemented and tested – an endeavour that we undertake with the present study.

2.2   Mid-Air Haptics

Mid-air haptics have been considered as a means for providing tactile feedback without the need for physical contact with an interface. This has involved the use of air jets [64], electric arcs [63] and focused ultrasound [24,36]. Focused ultrasound approaches have been commercialised, based on the work of Carter et al. [11], in the form of Ultraleap (formerly Ultrahaptics). Typically, these systems use optical hand-tracking and an array of ultrasonic transducers to produce focused ultrasound on the user's palm, which induces a tactile sensation. Localisation and movement of such induced haptic stimuli have been demonstrated [71]. Building on this, modulation techniques have been developed to render 2D planar patterns [22,31,57], as well as 3D objects [37,41,47].

Due to its relative maturity in this field, we consider focused ultrasound as a means to convey mid-air haptic stimuli in the remainder of this section and in our work. Several researchers have explored the possibilities and limitations of mid-air haptics using ultrasound. Wilson et al. [71] reported that participants could localise mid-air haptics focus points on their hand within 8.5mm accuracy, finding motion perception best when the focus point travelled longer distances across the hand. Further studies [39,52] investigated oblique motion (e.g. diagonally across the hand), finding that it was easier to recognise cardinal (i.e. left/right/up/down) rather than oblique motion. Hajas et al. [31] showed that tracing a given 2D pattern with a slowly moving focal point on a user's hand produced better recognition performance than tracing the pattern rapidly and repeatedly [22], or with several focal points [57].

Applications of ultrasound mid-air haptics are diverse. For instance, the technology has been used for in-vehicle infotainment systems [25,32,38], to add haptic properties to objects in VR/AR [43,54], for interaction with public displays [40], and to augment audiovisual media [1]. In all these scenarios, mid-air haptics are employed as feedback mechanisms, using haptic information to convey the state of the interface following user actions. The presence of a feedback mechanism improves the user's perception of control in their action (i.e. sense of agency) [12,17]. However, it remains unclear whether mid-air haptics could help users in planning or learning a given action. Indeed, using mid-air haptics as a *guidance* mechanism has received little attention within HCI and haptic communities.

3   Mid-Air Haptic Guidance Stimuli Development

In this paper, we consider the use of mid-air haptics to guide users or suggest given actions. In doing this, we focused on two main types of interaction with mid-air interfaces:

- **Directional movement** in a 2D plane, which is common for the control of cursor-like elements and mid-air widgets – e.g. sliders, knobs;
- **Gestures**, due to the large number of mid-air interfaces which use gestures as input.

We began with the assumption that there is a finite number of directions and gestures that the user can use with a system. In future studies, larger and more complex sets of gestures might be considered via approaches such as elicitation (see [73] and Sect. 6). We developed mid-air haptic stimuli for conveying a limited number of directional, gestural and path-based interactions through 3 rounds of piloting with 8 researchers and students in City, University of London (4 male, 4 female), along with various intermediary piloting to tune parameters, also including self-piloting (by the authors of this paper). All mid-air haptic stimuli were developed using the Ultrahaptics Evaluation Kit (UHEV1) developed by Ultraleap (formerly Ultrahaptics). We also developed a custom Python front-end that would allow us to change the parameters of the stimuli for piloting, which linked to the Ultrahaptics SDK for driving the ultrasonic array (as in Fig. 3). The Python front-end, and usage instructions, can be found here.

3.1 Mid-Air Haptic Stimuli to Convey Direction

We started with the aim of investigating how to suggest a notion of direction to a user – i.e. that they should move their hand in a specific direction. This is analogous to the visual guides provided in prior work [4,5,14]. Lerusso et al. [39,52] have shown that motion is better perceived in cardinal directions, rather than oblique directions. We, therefore, considered cardinal direction as an initial focus. Building upon research such as [31,71], we chose to explore stimuli which traverse the whole hand as this research, and our initial piloting, found that larger movement differences are perceived better than smaller. Through piloting we also found that to convey a given direction, it was better to move the stimuli in the direction of intention – e.g. to convey 'left' it was better to move from right to left. This is analogous to 'default' rather than 'inverted in videogame controls' [23] and reverse scrolling, rather than natural, with a computer mouse. This is also similar to the methods used in similar work on (visual) guides [4,5,14], e.g. showing visual movement in the direction that the user should travel. The speed of the focus point's traversal and its frequency were also piloted until we found a good 'average match' for the population. We began with traversal values around 100 ms, up to around 1000 ms (maxima and minima from [71]), finding 500 ms to be the best fit overall. For modulation frequency, we arrived at 200 Hz. The final stimuli are shown in Fig. 1.

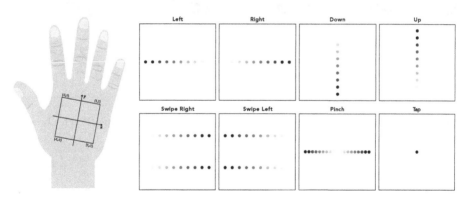

Fig. 1. All stimuli used in the experiment relative to a users' right hand. The mid-air sensation interpolated across all points on the user's palm – e.g. 'Left' interpolates from [1, 0] to [−1, 0]. Parameters set after piloting were: sensation duration of 500ms; modulation frequency of 200 Hz; a distance of 50 mm (most effective distance travelled on the palm from piloting – we did not fit 'per participant'). Darker dots indicate later in time (e.g. left goes from centre to far left).

3.2 Mid-Air Haptic Stimuli to Convey Gesture

We then explored specific gestures. Our aim here was to understand if we could convey the gestures available to a user, given some known qualities of the interface and its interactions – e.g. cardinal direction to convey translation (movement of a UI element in a given direction). In addition, we saw the potential for not just suggesting gestures available but using guidance information as a way to train a user in completing specific physical motions. This might be applied to learning a new mid-air interface and its inputs, but also in other digital, or remote learning environments – for instance guiding a user towards the correct note on a piano (e.g. extending [35]'s mid-air piano), or for specifically *training gestures*. A motivator for this work was also the importance of gestures in functional communication for people with complex communication needs. Gesture is a vital pathway for people who face challenges with verbal output. Augmented communication technologies should consider this, but currently do not [13]. Finally, on training gestural response for access needs, Marshall et al. [46] and Roper et al. [55] have also considered how technology can train gestures for those with complex communication needs.

We selected four commonplace gestures – "Swipe Left", "Swipe Right", "Tap", "Pinch" – based on their frequency of use in mid-air interactions literature – including those shortlisted by Van den Bogaert et al. [7] in their elicitation study, and those explored by Ameur et al. [3] and Marin et al. [44]. The final gestures are shown in Fig. 2. Guidance stimuli for these gestures were based on the Ultraleap Sensation Editor demos. Again, these stimuli were fine-tuned through piloting with participants. Stimuli are shown in Fig. 1.

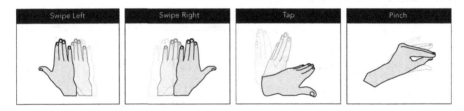

Fig. 2. Gestures used in the study – 'Swipe Left', 'Swipe Right', 'Tap', 'Pinch'. Images use 'motion blur' to indicate movement.

3.3   Mid-Air Haptic Stimuli to Convey Paths

Finally, we investigated conveying 2D paths to users as a form of guidance (i.e. the computer continuously 'controlling' a user in space). This is analogous to Burny et al. [10]'s work – previously discussed – who use visual information to support users in completing paths. We also sought to understand if we might use this strategy to position users anywhere above a mid-air haptic board (in 2D space) so that they can begin interactions – this might be useful, for instance, for positioning a user's hand correctly to interact with a specific part of the mid-air UI. As discussed in the Background section, previous work has considered how to position the user's hand in the centre of the board and at the correct height for stimulation with static mid-air haptics and light-based information [20], however, we saw this as an opportunity for positioning the user at *any* point (in a 2D plane) above the board. In piloting, we explored how we might support users in navigating paths. We found that a fruitful approach was to use the same stimuli as for cardinal direction to move a user across a discretized (3×3) grid (as shown in Fig. 3). We implemented it so that the cardinal direction stimuli discussed previously were linked to the keyboard – up to the 'up' key, down to the 'down' key, etc. – and controlled by a researcher. The directional stimuli played repeatedly and looped when the keys were held down, then stopped immediately (e.g. half-way through a stimuli) as soon as the key was released. We chose to use a human-controlled interaction to explore this proof of concept, rather than implement a control algorithm to guide the user on the path. We accept that this might have introduced a human-based bias into the interaction, but chose to do this after finding that error handling (e.g. a user straying from the path) introduced confounds beyond the scope of our present. We also chose to do this to explore human-in-the-loop dynamics for remote interaction (further delineated in the discussion).

4   Study Method

We undertook a study to determine the potential of our prototype mid-air stimuli for guidance addressing the following research questions:

RQ1 How intuitive are the mid-air haptic stimuli for guiding *directional movement*?

    RQ1.1 How accurately can we guide users with mid-air haptic stimuli in specific directions *without prior experience*?

    RQ1.2 How accurately can we guide users with mid-air haptic stimuli in specific directions *with prior experience* of the stimuli?

    RQ1.3 What is the user's *subjective experience* when guided in directions using mid-air haptics?

RQ2 How intuitive are the mid-air haptic stimuli for guiding *gestural responses*?

    RQ2.1 How accurately can we guide users with mid-air haptic stimuli to perform specific gestures *without prior experience*?

    RQ2.2 How accurately can we guide users with mid-air haptic stimuli in performing specific gestures *with experience* of the stimuli?

    RQ2.3 What is the user's *subjective experience* of being guided to perform specific gestures with mid-air haptic stimuli?

RQ3 How effective are the developed stimuli for *continuous, real-time guidance* along a given path?

    RQ3.1 How accurately can users *follow a given mid-air path* when guided by the developed mid-air haptic stimuli?

    RQ3.2 What is the *subjective experience* of being guided along a mid-air path with guidance from the mid-air haptic stimuli?

4.1   Participants

We recruited a convenience-based student sample of 27 participants. No participants had been involved in the earlier piloting stages. All participants self-reported good or corrected visual acuity and no challenges with experiencing sensations in their hands. 19 identified as male and 8 as female. Ages ranged from 20—33 (average = 25.4; SD = 4.0). All participants, except one, were confident with technology – agreeing or strongly agreeing with the statement "*I am technologically proficient - e.g. I use tablets, smartphones, computers regularly*". Only 2/27 participants had experience with mid-air haptics before the study.

4.2 Study Procedure

The study was conducted in a usability testing room at King's College London (Fig. 3). The study was run by one experimenter who had practised using the developed stimuli (discussed in the previous section), and the experimental technique, through piloting as described previously at City, University of London. Participants were consented by the experiment coordinator on the day through an informed consent procedure in line with our ethical approval process, with authorisation from the ethics committee at King's College London.

We used the Evaluation Kit developed by Ultraleap – an ultrasound phased array which provides tactile sensations in mid air (pictured top left, Fig. 3). Participants sat in front of the ultrasound phased array board with a large TV display (Samsung QM55R-B) directly in front of them for visual information when required. Each participant was instructed to place their hand 20cm above the board. Stimuli were played from a laptop (Lenovo IdeaPad 3) connected to the board, through a custom front-end interface built in Python. Participants were positioned so that they had no view of the experiment coordinator's laptop display. The experiment coordinator also used the directional keys on the laptop, again linked to the stimuli. Response data were collected via a spreadsheet by the experiment coordinator (on a separate laptop – a MacBook Pro) and subjective data were captured via an iPad. Pauses were introduced between trials and participants were free to rest when they wanted to mitigate fatigue.

Part 1.1: Conveying Directional Movement: No Prior Experience with Developed Stimuli. To answer RQ1, in Part 1 of the study, we aimed to find out if participants could determine cardinal direction from the developed mid-air haptic stimuli, with no prior experience with the stimuli (RQ1.1). We explained to participants that the device would produce a sensation and they should respond in the way they saw appropriate. On the display, we provided a visual aid showing the four possible responses the device was trying to convey to them – 4 videos of a hand moving in the given directions (up/down/left/right). Each participant received all four direction stimuli once (i.e. 4 trials), but in a random order. After each sensation was played, the participant was asked to respond by moving their hand in the direction they thought the stimuli was conveying, and verbally confirming the direction – e.g. "*up*". The experimental coordinator then entered the response into the spreadsheet.

Part 1.2: Conveying Directional Movement: With Knowledge of Developed Stimuli. After completing Study Part 1.1, regardless of success

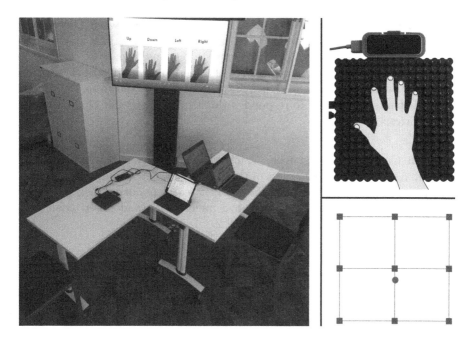

Fig. 3. Study setup shown left. Participants were seated on the left chair, the experiment coordinator on the right. Top right shows the UltraLeap UHEV1 board (later referred to as 'the board') used in the study, with example of hand position overlaid. Bottom right shows the UI for guiding the participant in Part 3 of the study – the nine grey points correspond to points in 2D space above the board – top left being the top left corner, for instance. The red point shows the position of the centre of the participant's hand. (Color figure online)

in determining the stimuli, participants were instructed with the 'correct' correspondence between given stimuli and intended response: they were given the chance to experience each stimulus again and the experiment coordinator told them its correspondence. To answer RQ1.2, participants then undertook 10 trials in which they were tasked with determining the cardinal direction from a given stimulus. Stimuli were played randomly across the four cardinal directions. As in Part 1.1, participants gave their response through movement and verbal confirmation.

Part 1.3: Subjective Response to Conveying Directional Movement.
To answer RQ1.3 – the users' subjective experience – we administered a NASA TLX to understand workload, and asked participants to rate how hard/easy they found it to understand each cardinal direction on a 5-point Likert scale, ranging from *Strongly Disagree* to *Strongly Agree* – e.g. *I found it easy to understand when the device was indicating to go 'up'.*

Part 2.1: Conveying Gestures: No Prior Experience with Developed Stimuli. To answer RQ2.1 we adopted the same strategy as was employed in Part 1.1, but this time we asked participants to respond from a set of common gestural responses (rather than from a set of directions). Again, the chosen four gestures – 'Swipe Left', 'Swipe Right', 'Tap', 'Pinch' were shown on the display and participants were asked to respond without prior knowledge of the gesture-stimuli correspondence.

Part 2.2: Conveying Gestures: With Prior Experience of Developed Stimuli. As in Part 1.2, regardless of their success in determining the gestures, participants were instructed with the 'correct' correspondence between given stimuli and intended gestures. We then conducted 10 randomised trials in a manner similar to Part 1.2 to answer RQ2.2.

Part 2.3: Subjective Response to Conveying Gestures. As before, subjective response (RQ2.3) was determined via NASA TLX and a Likert questionnaire with 5-point Likert scale questions to understand the ease of identifying each gesture.

Part 3.1: Path Tracing. We created four paths in a 2D plane across 9 points. Paths were analogous to a pattern unlock screen and the task analogous to teaching a user how to unlock a mid-air interface. Four paths, to be given to all participants, were chosen by choosing a random start and end coordinate four times (using a random number generator). Final generated paths are shown in Fig. 8.

To address RQ3.1, the experiment coordinator 'guided' the participant around each of the four paths indicated in Fig. 8. The experimental coordinator viewed the participant's hand position on their laptop screen (see Fig. 3, bottom right) and then used the mid-air haptic stimuli to guide the users' hand in the four cardinal directions, towards a target. The experiment coordinator operated the stimuli with the arrow keys which corresponded to the intended direction of travel. The stimuli were the same as in Part 1 (e.g. focus point traversing from right to left to indicate left travel), however, they were repeated as long as one of the arrow keys was held down. If the participant deviated from the path, the experiment coordinator aimed to bring the participant back to the point from which they diverged. Analysis was conducted by plotting each path and classifying it as 'correct' (all edges and points followed), 'partially correct' (over 50% of edges followed with correct start/end points) or incorrect (anything else), with 2 independent coders classifying the data. Plots of combined paths (i.e. all participants) were also made for aggregated analysis.

Part 3.2: Subjective Response to Path Tracing. As with the previous parts of the study, we administered a NASA TLX and a 5-point Likert questionnaire, asking about the ease of following the path, after the four paths were completed.

5   Results

5.1   Part 1.1: Conveying Directional Movement: No Prior Experience

As shown in Fig. 4, given no prior experience of cardinal direction stimuli, participants were able to correctly identify the stimuli-direction correspondence in a total of 95 out of the 108 trials (4 × 27) – 88% accuracy, with 2 no movement or a negative verbal response (accounting for the rows of Fig. 4 not summing to 100%). A confusion matrix is shown in Fig. 4 (left) – suggesting the most common confusion was right/left and up/down.

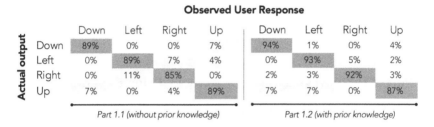

Observed User Response

Actual output	Down	Left	Right	Up	Down	Left	Right	Up
Down	89%	0%	0%	7%	94%	1%	0%	4%
Left	0%	89%	7%	4%	0%	93%	5%	2%
Right	0%	11%	85%	0%	2%	3%	92%	3%
Up	7%	0%	4%	89%	7%	7%	0%	87%

Part 1.1 (without prior knowledge)   Part 1.2 (with prior knowledge)

Fig. 4. Results of Parts 1.1 and 1.2, comparing the mid-air haptic stimuli for cardinal direction and user responses.

A χ^2 test of independence was conducted to determine the relationship between stimuli and observed user response to stimuli without prior experience. There was a significant relationship – Pearson-χ^2 (9, N = 106 = 240.125, p < 0.001), with a strong effect size ($\Phi = 1.50$) suggesting that users could identify the stimuli for cardinal directions significantly better than chance.

5.2   Part 1.2: Conveying Directional Movement: With Experience

With experience about how the stimuli related to the cardinal directions, participants were able to correctly determine the correspondence in 247 out of a total of 270 trials (10 × 27) – i.e. 91% accuracy). The random seed generated 'Down' 72 times, 'Up' 76 times, 'Left' 59 times and 'Right' 63 times. A confusion matrix is shown in Fig. 4 (right). A χ^2 test of independence was conducted to determine the relationship between stimuli and user response *with* experience of the stimuli. There was a significant relationship (Pearson-χ^2 (9, N = 270 = 639.784, p < 0.001), with a strong effect size ($\Phi = 1.54$), suggesting users could determine the correct response significantly better than chance.

Part 1.3: Subjective Response. Post-Part 1 Likert data results are shown in pink in Fig. 6. The cardinal directions were universally perceived as *"easy to understand"* – all with a median value of four. A Friedman test across the four

Observed User Response

	Pinch	Swipe Left	Swipe Right	Tap	Pinch	Swipe Left	Swipe Right	Tap
Pinch	58%	12%	4%	27%	73%	10%	3%	13%
Swipe Left	7%	74%	11%	7%	4%	88%	3%	5%
Swipe Right	0%	11%	85%	4%	4%	8%	80%	7%
Tap	28%	12%	0%	60%	23%	3%	2%	72%

Actual output (left label, vertical)

Part 2.1 (without prior knowledge)   *Part 2.2 (with prior knowledge)*

Fig. 5. Confusion matrix for Parts 2.1 and 2.2. of the study, comparing the mid-air stimuli for gestures and the user responses.

conditions suggests no significant difference in reported ease between cardinal directions: $\chi^2(3) = 1.0$, p = 0.80. As shown in Fig. 7 NASA TLX for this was 29.2.

5.3 Part 2.1: Conveying Gesture Without Prior Experience

For the response to gesture-based stimuli, with no prior experience participants correctly determined the relationship between the stimuli and the intended gesture in 73 out of 105 trials (3 missing datapoints where participants responded that they did not know) – a total accuracy of 68%. A confusion matrix is presented in Fig. 5. The most common mismatch was between the 'Tap' and 'Pinch' gestures. As with Part 1.1, a χ^2 test of independence was detected to determine if participant could determine stimuli without prior information better than chance. A significant relationship was (Pearson-χ^2 (9, N = 105 = 123.61, p < 0.001), with a strong effect size ($\Phi = 1.09$).

5.4 Part 2.2: Conveying Gesture with Prior Experience

With experience about how the stimuli related to the intended gestures, the participants' response accuracy increased to 79% – 212 out of 270 trials, with 2 missing data points. The random seed generated 'Swipe Left' 77 times, 'Swipe Right' 71 times, 'Pinch' 60 times and 'Tap' 62 times. Again, as shown in Fig. 5, the most common confusion was 'Tap'–'Pinch' (23%), however, this was smaller for 'Pinch'–'Tap' (13%). There was a significant relationship (Pearson-χ^2 (9, N = 268 = 425.9, p < 0.001), with a strong effect size ($\Phi = 1.26$), showing that participants could determine the gestures substantially better than chance.

5.5 Part 2.3: Subjective Experience of Gestural Response

Results of Part 2.3 are shown in Fig. 6. 'Swipe Left' and 'Swipe Right' gestures were generally perceived as easy to understand, with median ratings of 4. 'Pinch' and 'Tap' gestures were perceived as more challenging, with medians at 2, with only 5 ('Tap') and 4 ('Pinch') participants agreeing that this was easy. The four

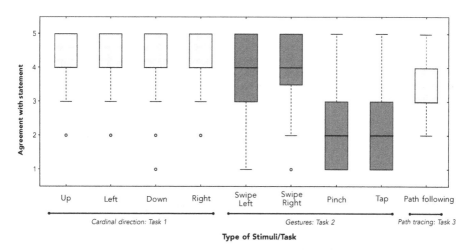

Fig. 6. Agreement with the statement *"I found it easy to understand when the device was indicating given [direction/gesture/path]"*, where 1 is "Strongly Disagree" and 5 is "Strongly Agree".

stimuli were compared via Friedman test, with a significant difference across the four gestures – $\chi^2(3) = 44.08$, p < 0.001. Post-hoc Wilcoxon Signed-Rank tests to determine differences in understanding between gestures were conducted. 'Tap' was perceived as significantly harder to understand than a 'Swipe Left' (Z = −3.643, p < 0.001) and 'Swipe Right' (Z = −3.885, p < 0.001). Similarly, 'Pinch' was significantly harder to understand than 'Swipe Left' (Z = −4.016, p < 0.001) and 'Swipe Right' (Z = 4.274, p < 0.001). There was no significant difference when comparing 'Pinch' and 'Tap' (Z = − 0.711 p = 0.477), and also no significant difference between 'Swipe Left' and 'Swipe Right' (Z = −1.134 p = 0.257). As shown in Fig. 7, NASA TLX for gestural stimuli was 40.37 – a higher workload than for the cardinal directions in Part 1 of the study.

NASA-TLX Average

	Mental Demand	Physical Demand	Temporal Demand	Performance	Effort	Frustration	Average
Part 1: Cardinal Direction	31.3	33.5	29.4	29.6	30.6	20.6	29.2
Part 2: Gesture	45.4	31.3	26.7	52.8	49.3	36.9	40.4
Part 3: Path Tracing	37.8	40.9	35.0	34.4	43.0	31.5	37.1

Fig. 7. Combined NASA-TLX averages for all 27 participants.

5.6 Part 3.1: Path Tracing

Success of path completion was determined by two coders. Coder agreement was high (96.4%). Inter-rater Reliability (IRR) was calculated (Cohen's $\kappa = 0.85$, p < 0.001) – i.e. 'almost perfect' agreement. The outcomes are shown in Table 1. Overall, the coders deemed that 75% of paths were completed correctly, 14.8% of paths were partially correct and 10.2% of paths were incorrect.

Table 1. Time to complete and the standard deviations are shown, along with the correctness of the paths overall.

	Path 1	Path 2	Path 3	Path 4	Overall
Time (seconds)	26.1	9.5	37.4	15.1	22.0
Time (Standard Deviation)	15.9	15.9	16.1	16.1	16.0
Correct (%)	66.7	77.8	74.1	81.5	75.0
Partially correct (%)	22.2	3.7	25.9	7.4	14.8
Incorrect (%)	11.1	18.5	0.0	11.1	10.2

5.7   Part 3.2: Subjective Experience of Path Tracing

As shown in Fig. 6, the path tracing task was judged as more challenging than determining cardinal directions in Part 1, but less challenging than determining non-directional gestures ('Tap', "Swipe") in Part 2. This is also the same for the TLX score which, as seen in Table 7, falls between the two, with an overall score of 37.1.

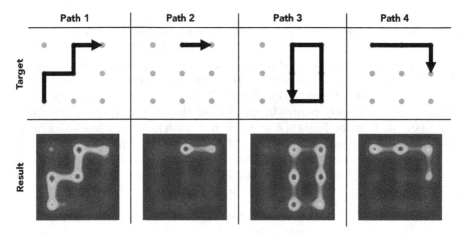

Fig. 8. Top shows the four target paths. Bottom shows combined paths of 27 participants as a heatmap for each path.

6   Discussion, Applications and Limitations

6.1   Discussion of Directional Guidance

Regarding RQ1, while the use of mid-air haptic stimuli to guide directional movement has not been reported in the literature, the results of Part 1 suggest that this is possible and feasible. Participants were able to determine which direction the system was guiding them to move in without prior experience of the relationship between stimuli and direction (RQ1.1). Then, after experiencing the relationships between stimuli and directions, this accuracy increased (RQ1.2) – indicating that training is effective. As discussed in the Background section of this paper, Wilson et al. [71] conducted a study of directional recall – e.g. which direction users believed the *haptic sensation* was moving in. Importantly, we differentiate our work from this by considering which direction the stimuli is indicating the user *should* move in – analogous to the visual guidance approaches previously discussed (c.f. [4, 5, 14]). Given that our results are broadly comparable – although with varying setups – suggests that using mid-air haptics for directional guidance is reasonably intuitive to a user. In comparison with other work which has considered the determination of cardinal direction, our accuracy figures were higher than studies using finger-based sensations (e.g. [59]), likely due to the larger surface area of the whole hand, and prior work which found that larger distances of movement of sensation across the hand result in more accurate recall [71]. Our findings slightly contrast with Wilson et al.'s [71] who, when asking users to differentiate between longitudinal (up/down) and transverse motion (left/right), found that transverse was more accurately recalled. We found no significant difference with our methods.

Considering perceived workload and user experience (RQ1.3), our NASA TLX data suggest that workload for cardinal direction is relatively low compared to other computer-based tasks, and in the bottom 20% of all tasks measured by TLX [28]. To build upon our work, future studies might consider expanding mid-air haptic guidance to support users in learning gestures/inputs which incorporate oblique and curved motion, as in [39]. Our approaches could support users in learning potential ways to interact and which interactions might be available, rather than relying entirely on visual or auditory representations of gestures. This might be important UIs where eyes-free interactions are important – e.g. automotive UI [25, 32, 62]. Beyond supporting the guidance of directional movement-based interactions, these forms of mid-air haptic stimuli might be used to support other interaction paradigms such as error handling. Consider a scenario such as a user scrolling through a horizontal list (e.g. of songs) in an automotive UI through mid-air hand movements. When the user reaches the end of the list, we might go beyond considering just feedback methods (e.g. vibrating to tell the user there are no more interactions they can perform), to consider how we might design feedforward-based guidance interactions. We might, for instance, suggest what the user could do to *remedy their situation* – e.g. suggest an 'escape gesture' or that they should go in a given direction. We might also provide users with information about how much there is in each direction before the scroll – analogous to [8]'s sonically enhanced scrollbars. This might be implemented by varying the intensity of the stimuli – e.g. by changing the frequency of the modulation, or by using movement speed as a proxy for intensity, as explored by Freeman et al. [21].

6.2   Discussion of Gestural Guidance

Regarding RQ2, guidance of gestural response via mid-air haptics has not been considered in the literature. Our study suggests that while directional gesture stimuli ('Swipe Left', 'Swipe Right') were effective, 'Pinch' and 'Tap' were less successful, yet still mostly determined correctly and significantly better than chance. When trained, this improved substantially – indicating that training is effective. There could be a number of reasons for this confusion. One reason is that the 'average' point of the stimuli was similar – and while 'Pinch' involved transverse motion (away from the centre), users were less able to make this differentiation. This might also relate to the *primacy effect*, a psychological effect where the first stimuli is remembered most prominently. In our case, as the starting points (in time) of the pinch and tap stimuli (see Fig. 1) are the same (the centre), it means that these are most prominently felt and remembered at the end of the stimuli. This concords with research by Wang et al. [69], who report a similar effect for haptic stimuli. Generally, this might mean that we consider avoiding stimuli with similar average points across the duration of the stimuli or similar beginning/end points when using haptic stimuli to convey gestural responses to users. However, more studies are needed to make conclusive recommendations. The workload, as measured by NASA TLX, was higher for gestures than for cardinal directions and path tracing. However, it was well within the lower 50% of workload for computer tasks, and in the lower 30% of tasks generally – again, suggesting promise in terms of general user experience and feasibility.

In future work, our gesture stimuli might be improved by offering a greater diversity of duration and frequency. Future stimuli might be designed through elicitation studies similar to Vogiatzidakis and Koutsabasis [67], except that the *referent* – i.e. the stimuli the user must respond to [73] – would be the mid-air haptic stimuli and the users' responses would be the basis for the analysis. Related to this, to complement use cases such as the training of gesture for people with severe language impairments (e.g. [46,55]), more stimuli are needed, with more considered design. For instance, to support the 30 pantomimic gestures used in Marshall et al. [46] would require diverse stimuli. Moreover, some gestures would be challenging to support without more flexibility of the apparatus – gestures such as 'Camera' (see [46]) require a user to hold their hand to their face, with their thumb and index in front of their eye. Keeping one's hand fixed in a 2D plane 20 cm above the board makes this impractical. Moreover, mid-air haptics is limited by its planarity – present implementations (e.g. the board used in this study) affect a 2D plane; we cannot affect the top of the hand from below, or indeed closed elements (e.g. when the user closes their hands by connecting their thumb to fingers). To overcome these obstacles, we might consider approaches such as Howard et al. [33], who consider the physical actuation of mid-air haptic boards, or approaches with transducer arrays above and below a user's hand (as in acoustic levitation work [48]).

6.3 Discussion of Path Tracing Guidance

The data suggest that our stimuli could guide users along a specified path. When guided by another user (the experiment coordinator) this was done with high accuracy, following the exact path 75% of the time and only failing in about 10%

of cases. Our work, therefore, could extend approaches such as Freeman et al. [19] – we might not only be able to guide a user to the 'sweet spot' on a mid-air haptic board, but indeed any spot. This might support users in discovering UI elements – for instance, encouraging users to move towards a slider/knob to begin a control task. Moreover, we might be able to indicate affordances to the user while completing this control task – e.g. that a slider is 'slidable' – an interaction that could be relevant to in-car settings such as [32]. Considering workload, it was higher for the path tracing task than for the simple cardinal direction, but lower than for gestures. Contrasting this with other TLX studies, it would be within the lowest 30% of tasks in general [28] – suggesting feasibility. We do acknowledge the limitation, however, that participants' experiences from Part 1 of this study might have supported them in completing the path-tracing tasks as the stimuli were similar and they had become more accustomed to the mid-air haptic stimuli. It is also notable that Physical Demand for path following was the highest recorded TLX dimension of all. This was likely caused by the fact that the paths required more time to complete and therefore required the user to elevate their hand for longer – resulting in greater physical demand. This is supported by the fact that 'Temporal Demand' was also the highest for this task.

Our work also shows that, beyond guiding a user to a specific point, we can move them along a specific path. Practically, this might have benefits such as supporting users in avoiding UI elements in mid-air interfaces, or guiding/teaching users to complete specific path-based interactions. For example, a mid-air unlock screen, or mid-air motions for teaching dancing, surgery, or even games that use mid-air control. Finally, we envision scenarios like the ones explored in this paper, where a user is being guided by another person (the experiment coordinator in this case). In some ways, this was a limitation to our study – control algorithms might have been used to guide the user along a path, or to a point. For example, in future implementations, one could envision that a recogniser, such as the $1 uni-stroke recognizer [74], could be used to provide instant feedback on whether the user has performed the correct path/gesture. Human-driven control via our approaches, however, are also scenarios we might envision. For instance, we might imagine using mid-air haptics for remote physicality – e.g. work such as [65], which considers how remote physical contact might be embodied through technology, or Neate et al. [51] who express the importance of tangibility in accessible communication (and indeed its loss during the pandemic for those who require it most). Finally, we might consider how mid-air haptics could be used for the remote control of objects (e.g. similar to [48,58]) – for remote presence and remote manipulation tasks such as those discussed by Follmer et al. [18] through actuation of objects in their inFORM project.

6.4   Limitations

Despite the general efficacy of our mid-air haptic approach to mid-air guidance, we acknowledge limitations in our work. One limitation is the convenience sample used for the study. As we recruited from a student population, our sample was biased towards a younger, 'tech-savvy' demographic. Moreover, the sample was skewed towards males in the main study (but with an equal male/female split in the piloting). Future work seeking to build on our proof of concept should ensure a more diverse sample of participants. Another limitation is the low number of stimuli explored for conveying gestures – this is a somewhat constrained discoverability task, with a small number of potential interactions. Further stimuli might result in more challenges in the disambiguation of gestures. Finally – as discussed in the background – we are constrained by the limitations of the Ultraleap board. While these have progressed since the UHEV1 board used in the study, further technical innovations in mid-air haptics (e.g. resolution, tactile sensation strength), and other future haptic approaches might make our approaches more feasible.

7   Conclusion

Mid-air interactions are increasingly commonplace, and are more frequently augmented by mid-air haptics. This paper has explored how we might leverage mid-air haptics to address one of the key challenges with mid-air interfaces – the lack of knowledge about how we might interact with them. We iteratively developed stimuli to guide users and to provide information about how they might interact. Our methods resulted in relatively low mental workload – suggesting the approach is feasible. While our stimuli set was limited, and providing guidance for the increasing set of interactions available with mid-air interfaces will be a major challenge, we have presented what we believe to be an interesting approach for supporting users with more intuitive mid-air interfaces. We invite future researchers to consider new guidance approaches to interactions with mid-air haptics, and to consider how they might be integrated into interaction scenarios and complement other modalities to make mid-air interactions more intuitive.

Acknowledgements. We would like to thank the participants for their involvement in the study and the anonymous reviewers of this work for their detailed feedback. We acknowledge funding from City, University of London's Research Development Fund's Pump Priming Scheme.

Authorship Statement

TN led the work with input from SAM, WF and SW. TN, WF, SAM and SW envisioned the experimental design. SAM built the Python front-end experimental apparatus, with input from TN and WF. ZY carried out the study with guidance from TN. The analysis was undertaken by TN, with support from WF, ZY and SAM. The paper writing was led by TN, with input from all authors.

References

1. Ablart, D., Velasco, C., Obrist, M.: Integrating mid-air haptics into movie experiences. In: ACM TVX (2017)
2. Ackad, C., Clayphan, A., Tomitsch, M., Kay, J.: An in-the-wild study of learning mid-air gestures to browse hierarchical information at a large interactive public display. ACM (2015)
3. Ameur, S., Khalifa, A.B., Bouhlel, M.S.: Hand-gesture-based touchless exploration of medical images with leap motion controller. In: Proceedings of SSD. IEEE (2020)
4. Anderson, F., Grossman, T., Matejka, J., Fitzmaurice, G.: YouMove: enhancing movement training with an augmented reality mirror. In: Proceedings of UIST (2013)
5. Bau, O., Mackay, W.E.: OctoPocus: a dynamic guide for learning gesture-based command sets. In: Proceedings of UIST, pp. 37–46. Association for Computing Machinery, New York (2008)
6. Van den Bogaert, L., Geerts, D., Rutten, I.: Grasping the future: identifying potential applications for mid-air haptics in the home. In: Extended Abstracts of ACM CHI. ACM (2019)
7. Van den Bogaert, L., Geerts, D.: User-defined mid-air haptic sensations for interacting with an AR menu environment. In: Nisky, I., Hartcher-O'Brien, J., Wiertlewski, M., Smeets, J. (eds.) EuroHaptics 2020. LNCS, vol. 12272, pp. 25–32. Springer, Cham (2020). https://doi.org/10.1007/978-3-030-58147-3_3
8. Brewster, S.A.: Using non-speech sound to overcome information overload. Displays **17**(3–4), 179–189 (1997)
9. Brown, E., Large, D., Limerick, H., Frier, W., Burnett, G.: Validating the salience of haptic icons for automotive mid-air haptic gesture interfaces (2021)
10. Burny, N., et al.: Feedup, feedback, and feedforward in curve mid-air 3d gestures (2018)
11. Carter, T., Seah, S.A., Long, B., Drinkwater, B., Subramanian, S.: UltraHaptics: multi-point mid-air haptic feedback for touch surfaces. In: Proceedings of UIST (2013)
12. Cornelio Martinez, P.I., De Pirro, S., Vi, C.T., Subramanian, S.: Agency in mid-air interfaces. In: Proceedings of ACM CHI (2017)
13. Curtis, H., You, Z., Deary, W., Tudoreanu, M.I., Neate, T.: Envisioning the (in)visibility of discreet and wearable AAC devices. In: Proceedings of ACM CHI (2023)
14. Delamare, W., Coutrix, C., Nigay, L.: Designing guiding systems for gesture-based interaction. In: Proceedings of EICS, EICS 2015, New York, NY, USA (2015)
15. Delamare, W., Janssoone, T., Coutrix, C., Nigay, L.: Designing 3d gesture guidance: visual feedback and feedforward design options. In: Proceedings of AVI (2016)
16. Dim, N.K., Silpasuwanchai, C., Sarcar, S., Ren, X.: Designing mid-air TV gestures for blind people using user- and choice-based elicitation approaches. In: Proceedings of ACM DIS (2016)
17. Evangelou, G., Limerick, H., Moore, J.: I feel it in my fingers! Sense of agency with mid-air haptics. In: Proceedings of IEEE WHC (2021)
18. Follmer, S., Leithinger, D., Olwal, A., Hogge, A., Ishii, H.: Inform: dynamic physical affordances and constraints through shape and object actuation (2013)
19. Freeman, E., Brewster, S., Lantz, V.: Do that, there: an interaction technique for addressing in-air gesture systems. ACM (2016)

20. Freeman, E., Vo, D.B., Brewster, S.: HaptiGlow: helping users position their hands for better mid-air gestures and ultrasound haptic feedback. In: Proceedings of IEEE WHC (2019)
21. Freeman, E., Wilson, G.: Perception of ultrasound haptic focal point motion. In: Proceedings of ICMI, ICMI 2021, pp. 697–701 (2021)
22. Frier, W., et al.: Using spatiotemporal modulation to draw tactile patterns in mid-air. In: Prattichizzo, D., Shinoda, H., Tan, H.Z., Ruffaldi, E., Frisoli, A. (eds.) EuroHaptics 2018. LNCS, vol. 10893, pp. 270–281. Springer, Cham (2018). https://doi.org/10.1007/978-3-319-93445-7_24
23. Frischmann, T.B., Mouloua, M., Procci, K.: 3-d gaming environment preferences: inversion of the y-axis. Ergonomics 58(11), 1792–1799 (2015)
24. Gavrilov, L.R.: The possibility of generating focal regions of complex configurations in application to the problems of stimulation of human receptor structures by focused ultrasound. Acoust. Phys. 54(2), 269–278 (2008)
25. Georgiou, O., et al.: Haptic in-vehicle gesture controls. In: Proceedings of AutomotiveUI (2017)
26. Girdler, A., Georgiou, O.: Mid-air haptics in aviation-creating the sensation of touch where there is nothing but thin air. arXiv preprint arXiv:2001.01445 (2020)
27. Grace, K., et al.: Conveying interactivity at an interactive public information display. In: Proceedings of PerDis (2013)
28. Grier, R.A.: How high is high? A meta-analysis of NASA-TLX global workload scores. In: Proceedings of HFES. SAGE Publications Sage, Los Angeles (2015)
29. Groenewald, C., Anslow, C., Islam, J., Rooney, C., Passmore, P., Wong, W.: Understanding 3d mid-air hand gestures with interactive surfaces and displays: a systematic literature review. In: Proceedings of BCS. HCI 2016 (2016)
30. Gupta, A., Pietrzak, T., Yau, C., Roussel, N., Balakrishnan, R.: Summon and select: rapid interaction with interface controls in mid-air. In: Proceedings ACM ISS (2017)
31. Hajas, D., Ablart, D., Schneider, O., Obrist, M.: I can feel it moving: science communicators talking about the potential of mid-air haptics. Front. Comput. Sci. 2, 534974 (2020)
32. Harrington, K., Large, D.R., Burnett, G., Georgiou, O.: Exploring the use of mid-air ultrasonic feedback to enhance automotive user interfaces. In: Proceedings of AutomotiveUI (2018)
33. Howard, T., Marchal, M., Lécuyer, A., Pacchierotti, C.: PUMAH: Pan-tilt ultrasound mid-air haptics for larger interaction workspace in virtual reality. IEEE Trans. Haptics 13, 38–44 (2020)
34. Huang, S., Ranganathan, S.P.B., Parsons, I.: To touch or not to touch? Comparing touch, mid-air gesture, mid-air haptics for public display in post COVID-19 society. In: SIGGRAPH Asia 2020 Posters (2020)
35. Hwang, I., Son, H., Kim, J.R.: AirPiano: enhancing music playing experience in virtual reality with mid-air haptic feedback. In: Proceedings of IEEE WHC (2017)
36. Iwamoto, T., Tatezono, M., Shinoda, H.: Non-contact method for producing tactile sensation using airborne ultrasound. In: Ferre, M. (ed.) EuroHaptics 2008. LNCS, vol. 5024, pp. 504–513. Springer, Heidelberg (2008). https://doi.org/10.1007/978-3-540-69057-3_64
37. Kovács, P.T., Balogh, T., Nagy, Z., Barsi, A., Bordács, L., Balogh, G.: Tangible holographic 3d objects with virtual touch. In: Proceedings of ITS (2015)
38. Large, D.R., Harrington, K., Burnett, G., Georgiou, O.: Feel the noise: mid-air ultrasound haptics as a novel human-vehicle interaction paradigm. Appl. Ergon. 81, 102909 (2019)

39. Lerusso, J., Rusanov, K., Perquin, M., Han, Y.j., Rossiter, H.E., Kolasinski, J.: Searching for the oblique effect in whole-hand tactile perception. Cortex (2019)
40. Limerick, H., Hayden, R., Beattie, D., Georgiou, O., Müller, J.: User engagement for mid-air haptic interactions with digital signage. In: PerDis 2019 (2019)
41. Long, B., Seah, S.A., Carter, T., Subramanian, S.: Rendering volumetric haptic shapes in mid-air using ultrasound. ACM TOG **33**(6), 1–10 (2014)
42. Lopes, P., Jonell, P., Baudisch, P.: Affordance++: allowing objects to communicate dynamic use. In: Proceedings of ACM CHI (2015)
43. Marchal, M., Gallagher, G., Lécuyer, A., Pacchierotti, C.: Can stiffness sensations be rendered in virtual reality using mid-air ultrasound haptic technologies? In: Nisky, I., Hartcher-O'Brien, J., Wiertlewski, M., Smeets, J. (eds.) EuroHaptics 2020. LNCS, vol. 12272, pp. 297–306. Springer, Cham (2020). https://doi.org/10. 1007/978-3-030-58147-3_33
44. Marin, G., Dominio, F., Zanuttigh, P.: Hand gesture recognition with leap motion and kinect devices. In: IEEE ICIP. IEEE (2014)
45. Markussen, A., Jakobsen, M.R., Hornbæk, K.: Vulture: a mid-air word-gesture keyboard. In: Proceedings of ACM CHI (2014)
46. Marshall, J., et al.: Computer delivery of gesture therapy for people with severe aphasia. Aphasiology **27**(9), 1128–1146 (2013)
47. Martinez, J., Harwood, A., Limerick, H., Clark, R., Georgiou, O.: Mid-air haptic algorithms for rendering 3d shapes. In: IEEE HAVE (2019)
48. Marzo, A., Seah, S.A., Drinkwater, B.W., Sahoo, D.R., Long, B., Subramanian, S.: Holographic acoustic elements for manipulation of levitated objects. Nat. Commun. **6**(1), 1–7 (2015)
49. Michelis, D., Müller, J.: The audience funnel: observations of gesture based interaction with multiple large displays in a city center. Intl. J. Hum.-Comput. Interact. **27**(6), 562–579 (2011)
50. Morrison, C., Smyth, N., Corish, R., O'Hara, K., Sellen, A.: Collaborating with computer vision systems: an exploration of audio feedback. In: Proceedings of DIS (2014)
51. Neate, T., Kladouchou, V., Wilson, S., Shams, S.: "Just not together": the experience of videoconferencing for people with aphasia during the COVID-19 pandemic. In: Proceedings of ACM CHI (2022)
52. Perquin, M., Taylor, M., Lorusso, J., Kolasinski, J.: Directional biases in whole hand motion perception revealed by mid-air tactile stimulation. Cortex J. Devoted Study Nervous Syst. Behav. **142**, 221–236 (2021)
53. Rakkolainen, I., Freeman, E., Sand, A., Raisamo, R., Brewster, S.: A survey of mid-air ultrasound haptics and its applications. IEEE Trans. Haptics **14**(1), 2–19 (2020)
54. Romanus, T., Frish, S., Maksymenko, M., Frier, W., Corenthy, L., Georgiou, O.: Mid-air haptic bio-holograms in mixed reality. In: IEEE ISMAR-Adjunct (2019)
55. Roper, A., Marshall, J., Wilson, S.: Benefits and limitations of computer gesture therapy for the rehabilitation of severe aphasia. Front. Hum. Neurosci. **10**, 595 (2016)
56. Rovelo, G., Degraen, D., Vanacken, D., Luyten, K., Coninx, K.: Gestu-Wan - an intelligible mid-air gesture guidance system for walk-up-and-use displays. In: Abascal, J., Barbosa, S., Fetter, M., Gross, T., Palanque, P., Winckler, M. (eds.) Gestu-wan-an intelligible mid-air gesture guidance system for walk-up-and-use displays. LNCS, vol. 9297, pp. 368–386. Springer, Cham (2015). https://doi.org/10.1007/ 978-3-319-22668-2_28

57. Rutten, I., Frier, W., Van den Bogaert, L., Geerts, D.: Invisible touch: how identifiable are mid-air haptic shapes? In: Proceedings of ACM CHI Adjunct (2019)
58. Sahoo, D.R., Nakamura, T., Marzo, A., Omirou, T., Asakawa, M., Subramanian, S.: JOLED: a mid-air display based on electrostatic rotation of levitated Janus objects. In: Proceedings of UIST (2016)
59. Sahoo, D.R., et al.: Tangible drops: a visio-tactile display using actuated liquid-metal droplets. In: Proceedings of ACM CHI (2018)
60. Samimi, N., von der Au, S., Weidner, F., Broll, W.: AR in TV: design and evaluation of mid-air gestures for moderators to control augmented reality applications in TV. In: Proceedings of MUM (2021)
61. Shakeri, G., Williamson, J.H., Brewster, S.: Novel multimodal feedback techniques for in-car mid-air gesture interaction. ACM (2017)
62. Shakeri, G., Williamson, J.H., Brewster, S.: May the force be with you: ultrasound haptic feedback for mid-air gesture interaction in cars. In: Proceedings of AutomotiveUI (2018)
63. Spelmezan, D., Sahoo, D.R., Subramanian, S.: Sparkle: Hover feedback with touchable electric arcs. ACM (2017)
64. Tsalamlal, M.Y., Issartel, P., Ouarti, N., Ammi, M.: Hair: haptic feedback with a mobile air jet. In: IEEE ICRA (2014)
65. Tsetserukou, D.: HaptiHug: a novel haptic display for communication of hug over a distance. In: Kappers, A.M.L., van Erp, J.B.F., Bergmann Tiest, W.M., van der Helm, F.C.T. (eds.) EuroHaptics 2010. LNCS, vol. 6191, pp. 340–347. Springer, Heidelberg (2010). https://doi.org/10.1007/978-3-642-14064-8_49
66. Villarreal-Narvaez, S., Vanderdonckt, J., Vatavu, R.D., Wobbrock, J.O.: A systematic review of gesture elicitation studies: what can we learn from 216 studies? In: Proceedings of DIS (2020)
67. Vogiatzidakis, P., Koutsabasis, P.: Gesture elicitation studies for mid-air interaction: a review. Multimodal Technol. Interact. **2**(4), 65 (2018)
68. Vogiatzidakis, P., Koutsabasis, P.: Frame-based elicitation of mid-air gestures for a smart home device ecosystem. Informatics **6**(2), 23 (2019)
69. Wang, C., Deng, H., Dong, Y., Zhang, X., Wang, D.H.: The capacity and cognitive processing of vibrotactile working memory for frequency. Current Psychol., 1–11 (2021)
70. Williams, A.S., Ortega, F.R.: Understanding gesture and speech multimodal interactions for manipulation tasks in augmented reality using unconstrained elicitation. Proc. ACM Hum.-Comput. Interact. 4, 1–21 (2020)
71. Wilson, G., Carter, T., Subramanian, S., Brewster, S.A.: Perception of ultrasonic haptic feedback on the hand: localisation and apparent motion. In: Proceedings of ACM CHI (2014)
72. Wittorf, M.L., Jakobsen, M.R.: Eliciting mid-air gestures for wall-display interaction. In: Proceedings of NordiCHI (2016)
73. Wobbrock, J.O., Aung, H.H., Rothrock, B., Myers, B.A.: Maximizing the guessability of symbolic input. In: Proceedings of ACM CHI Adjunct (2005)
74. Wobbrock, J.O., Wilson, A.D., Li, Y.: Gestures without libraries, toolkits or training: a $1 recognizer for user interface prototypes. In: Proceedings of UIST (2007)

Accessibility

Brilliance and Resilience: A New Perspective to the Challenges, Practices and Needs of University Students with Visual Impairments in India

Tigmanshu Bhatnagar[1,2(✉)] ⓘ, Vikas Upadhyay[3] ⓘ, P. V. Madhusudhan Rao[4] ⓘ, Nicolai Marquardt[1,5] ⓘ, Mark Miodownik[6] ⓘ, and Catherine Holloway[1,2] ⓘ

[1] UCL Interaction Centre, University College London, London WC1E6EA, UK
{t.bhatnagar.18,n.marquardt,c.holloway}@ucl.ac.uk
[2] Global Disability Innovation Hub, London E20 2AF, UK
[3] School of Information Technology, IIT Delhi, New Delhi 110016, India
vikas.upadhyay@cse.iitd.ac.in
[4] Department of Design, IIT Delhi, New Delhi 110016, India
pvmrao@design.iitd.ac.in
[5] Microsoft Research, Redmond 98052, USA
[6] UCL Mechanical Engineering, University College London, London WC1E7JE, UK
m.miodownik@ucl.ac.uk

Abstract. People with visual impairments in India have low literacy rates and only a few pursue higher education at the country's top universities. We present an insight into the educational experiences of these few university students with visual impairment based on the Frame of Interdependence. We found that educational challenges arise when interdependence fails due to restricted or misfitted assistance from social relations and ableist social interactions. Analysis of practices to overcome these challenges from the lens of Resilience Theory revealed that students develop a sense of self-confidence through successful academic experiences, internalise external stressors into intrinsic motivation, and find ways to navigate inaccessibility with the available social resources. In addition, students express the need to increase the integration of assistive technologies in education and facilitate social integration. Finally, we discuss the implications of these findings for equitable and inclusive education practices.

Keywords: Visual Impairment · Education · Assistive Technologies · Global South · Interdependence · Resilience · Interview Study

1 Introduction

Nearly a quarter of a million children with visual impairments live in India, where visual impairment (VI) is one of the most feared health problems [1]. Children born with a visual impairment who lose sight at a young age face emotional, social, and economic challenges over a lifetime [2]. The implementation and utilisation of public health programs and overall socioeconomic development have decreased the prevalence of childhood visual impairment in India [3]. On the one hand, it is imperative to reduce vision loss in children by managing preventable and treatable visual impairment. At the same time, it is important to support children with visual impairments to become independent, integrated and contributing individuals to their society.

Education is the single greatest tool for achieving social justice and equality. But the literacy rate for students with visual impairments (SVIs) in India is significantly lower than the overall literacy rate of the country [4]. Despite having one of the most progressive policy frameworks in the Global South towards the education of people with disabilities, there remain considerable gaps in implementation. Issues still need to be addressed in providing science and math education, teacher support and training, braille book access, assistive technologies, tactile displays, and training for screen readers. Attitudinal barriers and an apathetic approach to curriculum adaptation for SVIs also create a challenging environment to succeed [5, 6].

Some universities have implemented policies to support the enrolment of SVIs and provide accommodations to support learning. However, the specific number of SVIs in higher education is hard to find as enrolment is relatively low. A few students overcome significant challenges to attain higher education in competitive subjects from the country's top universities. Previous work has provided a good understanding of the barriers to the education of SVIs. However, it is unclear how social interdependencies play a role in the education of SVIs and how challenges are overcome. Likely, the combination of intrinsic motivation, problem-solving skills, a supportive social network, and the availability of assistive technologies influences overcoming challenges. Understanding the challenges and how SVIs are overcoming them is instrumental for designers and HCI practitioners to create products and services that facilitate more students to *make it*. Therefore, in this paper, we contribute a thematic analysis of the educational challenges of university students from India through the lens of the Interdependence Framework for Assistive Technology [7] and the strategies students use to overcome challenges with reference to the Resilience Theory [8]. We also identify and interpret the most pressing needs of students considering the above findings.

2   Related Work

2.1   Education of Students with Visual Impairments

In diverse and complex societies, experiences with disabilities intersect with sociocultural issues of class, gender and traditional beliefs [9]. The general understanding of disability exacerbates stigmatisation, and gender differences marginalise females with disabilities [10]. A significant proportion of people with disabilities with low income also have limited access to healthcare, education, and stable employment [11]. In India, for instance, less than 0.5% of the total number of students in university education are disabled [12], 9.65% of disabled people in India receive higher education [13] out of which 32.13% are visually impaired [14]. The Constitution of India cites the Right to Education as a fundamental right for free and compulsory education for all children aged six to fourteen years [15]. The National Education Policy (NEP) 2020 mandates that 'children with disabilities will be enabled to fully participate in the regular schooling process from the foundational stage to higher education' [16]. There are schemes to provide accessible content, teaching aids, transport allowance and teacher training. Still, a lack of support for training teachers in integrated schools [17], limited guidance and bureaucratic delays create challenges in obtaining the allocated funds to procure assistive technologies [18, 19].

Similar barriers in other countries have made teaching SVIs a neglected area. Borah and Sorathia [20], Sahasrabudhe and Palvia [21], Lamichhane [22] and Dey et al. [23] illustrates SVIs in India and Nepal's limited access to educational tools and report the consequences of limited assistive technology, for instance, being unable to take up math or science in higher education [5]. Wong and Cohen [24] describe the disconnection in the knowledge of assistive technology and ICT skills among teachers in Singapore. In their book Ableism in Academia, Brown and Leigh [27] theorise contemporary academia's ableist context, challenges and practices in the UK, while Baker et al. [25] explained reflections and barriers for visually impaired programmers from Europe and North America through surveys and follow-up interviews. They reported that barriers permeate all parts of SVI's education, from accessing material and doing homework, which increases isolation and decreases motivation.

As we can see, the education of blind students globally has many barriers and challenges. However, the community in SVIs is not behind in technology adoption and use. Due to the shortage of tactile content, students turn to audiobooks to access educational materials and freely share content with peers [26]. Pal and Lakshmanan [27] presented a rich narrative picture based on the voices of visually impaired employees in India and their increased use of assistive technologies at the workplace. India et al. [28] have shown that visually impaired students in an inclusive setting actively participate in play through tangible interfaces to understand basic math concepts and computational thinking without explicit instructions. It shows that students and teachers are keen to learn, provided there are ways to make education accessible, such as using games aligned with the educational curriculum [29]. An improved understanding of the challenges SVIs in higher education face in India, their voices, and leveraging the enhanced frameworks to understand ableism and inclusion will provide valuable insight for disability innovation [30, 31] and pathways towards a more accessible and inclusive society.

2.2 Disability and HCI

Mankoff et al. [32] brought learnings from disability studies to the domain of HCI. They argued that 'by exploring individual, cultural, societal and theoretical foundations of assistance, one can expand the view of Assistive Technology (AT) and its place in the complex world of disability'. From there on, particularly the social and biopsychosocial (BPS) model of disability has been used to understand and design for the diverse needs of users with disabilities, such as designing self-tracking devices for patients with chronic illness [33]. Applying the BPS models in the context of HCI resonates with Interdependence Framework for AT devices suggested by Bennett et al. [7]. The authors emphasise that an individual's relationship with the environment is mediated by ATs and relationships with people who collectively work to create access. It challenges the traditional ability-centric understanding and highlights the importance of considering the interactions between the user's impairment, technology, and the environment in which it is used. For example, through autoethnography, Jain et al. [34] explains in-situ coping strategies and how they go beyond technology. The authors, who themselves are disabled, realised that proactive customisations by social network, collaboration, and participation must go hand in hand to solve the in-situ need. Gadiraju et al. [35], through observations and interviews, brought in teachers' expectations of technology and found that introducing an element of play, including parents, and increasing collaborative skills can enhance education. Shinohara et al. [36] also reports that the inaccessibility of research tools adds time and effort but increases social and collaborative relationships.

However, despite being a practical framework for HCI and approximately one-third of the work published in HCI about accessibility relates to visual impairment [37], the use of the Interdependence Framework as a lens to understand the educational experiences of people with visual impairments, mainly where technology use is limited is at a nascent stage. Therefore, our study analyses the educational experiences and challenges of SVIs in India through the lens of the Interdependence Frame.

2.3 Resilience and Visual Impairment

Adverse events due to visual impairment life can be understood as a perturbation to which the person must adapt. This trait of Resilience has been previously used to analyse the coping process among visually impaired individuals. Resilience explains how a system recovers from adversity, sustains itself, and thrives. Ungar and Theron [8] describe resilience as the 'process of multiple biological, psychological, social and ecological systems interacting in ways that help individuals regain, sustain or improve their mental wellbeing when challenged by one or more risk factors'.

People can cope with visual impairment through self-awareness and adaptation, facing circumstances, and through positive reinforcement processes [38]. Pathways to resilience are also formed by independence, allowing people with visual impairments to understand their self-identity, create social connections, and engage in recreational activities [39]. For people with visual impairments in low-income contexts, mobile interactions with technologies are mediated through existing social infrastructure support that influences the use and experience of technology and, therefore, the perception of self [40]. It is also evident that to holistically support individuals with disabilities in India, crosscutting health issues, caste, religion, gender, and hierarchy must be considered alongside fostering resilience [11]. Our study uses theories of Resilience [41, 42] to identify the promotive, protective factors and processes that help overcome the difficulties faced in the education of SVIs in India.

3 Methods

The study aimed to learn about the challenges faced by students who made it to top universities in India, understand how they overcame the challenges in the journey, and identify the most pressing unmet needs. Data collection took place through a focus group discussion with SVIs who were at the time studying at some of the best universities in

Delhi. A focus group was suitable for this research question because it could discuss the topic in-depth. Furthermore, education and its challenges are relatable to every participant in the group, and there may be many overlapping experiences. The group discussion will bring forward prevalent challenges and differences, leading to sharing practices and strategies to address some issues. The Research Ethics Committee from UCL (UCL REC 18925/001) and Institute Ethics Committee from IIT Delhi (IEC P-086) provided the ethical clearance to conduct this study.

3.1 Participants

Table 1. Participants for the study

Participant	Age	Current Educational Degree	Visual Impairment	Background
P1	20	Bachelors in computer science	Congenital Blindness	Urban
P2	20	Bachelors in computer science	Congenital Blindness	Rural
P3	32	PhD in Political Science	Congenital Blindness	Urban
P4	27	MSc in Economics	Congenital Blindness	Rural
P5	28	PhD in English Literature	Congenital Visual Impairment (Light perception)	Rural
P6	21	Bachelor's in Political Science	Congenital Visual Impairment (Light perception)	Urban
P7	20	Bachelors in economics	Congenital Blindness	Urban

Seven university students with visual impairments participated in the study (Table 1). All the participants have been visually impaired since birth. The mean age of the participants was 24 (SD = 4.93). The recruitment took place using convenience sampling through personal communication with three participants in direct contact with the first author. They were requested to identify more volunteers for the study, which resulted in four more participants being a part of the study. Remuneration in the form of food and travel expenses was provided to the participants.

We balanced the group composition to include participants from urban and rural backgrounds. Three participants (P2, P4 and P5) were from rural backgrounds where awareness and understanding of disability are low, social stigmatisation against people with visual impairment is high, and schools are not adequately equipped with the required

AT [5]. Their recalled experiences of not having access to appropriate braille books in inclusive schools and being dependent on listening to teachers and friends. The remaining four participants (P1, P3, P6 and P7) were from an urban background and had studied at a special school for the blind. They had access to a bespoke education ecosystem where learning materials were available in braille, and special educators taught subjects like math and science. Despite a better education environment, there were still challenges at a social level and in integrating into an inclusive university.

The group represented a community of exceptionally educated young, congenitally visually impaired students of India who went through competitive exams to get admitted to one of the top institutions in the country. These exams included the Joint Entrance Exam for Engineers (JEE), JNU PhD Entrance Exam and Joint Admission Test for Masters (JAM). Everyone was comfortable in using digital technologies and social media and worked with laptops and smartphones daily.

3.2 The Procedure of the Focus Group Discussion

The focus group discussion was conducted in person in a well-ventilated room. It started with an icebreaker that warmed the participants to share their thoughts and ideas with the group. The focus group guide to conducting the data collection enquired about their motivations to pursue education, the difficulties they faced in the educational context, the general challenges in society and how they were overcome. The discussion also discussed the ideal vision in 25 years that the participants would like for future SVIs in India. The final questions of the discussion enquired about the most pressing unmet needs of the participants at present. The entire discussion happened in English and Hindi according to the participant's preference. The conversation was audio recorded, translated into English as needed and transcribed for analysis.

The discussion lasted for just over two hours, during which participants showed energy and engagement, leading to a natural flow of the conversation. Participants shared anecdotes, observations, and thoughts about their educational experiences, their perception of their societal attitudes, how they overcame challenges, and their expectations for the future.

3.3 Analysis of the Focus Group Discussion

Transcripts were analysed through a thematic analysis process through a hybrid reflexive approach [43]. Bennet et al. [7], with their Frame of Interdependence, proposed that the frame allows us to see how people and things are connected to create access. We used the frame to identify where things are disconnected and create inaccessibility. Therefore, the transcripts were coded by two researchers to find instances when the tenet of interdependence fails due to failing social relations, lack of assistance, ableist hierarchies and notions towards the achievements of the participants. These codes were clustered and combined to identify themes for challenges. Previous research has cited difficulties accessing suitable content and inadequate teaching practices [5, 11, 17, 20, 22]. Our findings highlight interactions between people and the environment that are restricted, misfitting or motivated by ableist notions. Therefore, with the frame of inter-dependence, we provide a new perspective on ecosystem problems beyond the more commonly reported financial, instructional, and technological barriers.

It is important to note that more is presented in literature about difficulties in educational experiences than factors that show how the difficulties are overcome. Therefore, from the data, we identified practices illustrating how the participants overcame the difficulties. Two researchers again coded practices from the data and used the principles of the Resilience Theory [8, 41] to interpret how students overcome challenges. Based on this data reflection, we contribute the themes of self-confidence, internalising extrinsic stressors and navigation with social resources to overcome difficulties.

For the speculative inquiry about the ideal future and critical reflection on the most pressing need, the seven participants one-by-one shared their vision and then the most pressing needs and challenges in the context of education. During the discussion, statements from each participant were enriched by comments, discussions, and anecdotes from other group participants. The discussions were noted on sticky notes. The notes were analysed through an affinity mapping exercise with the participants on the spot. Through this process, the group co-identified two significant themes – integrating assistive technologies and integrating disabled people in society.

4 Challenges

Participants in this research study were academically exceptional but shared several challenges in the educational context to achieve their accolades. Challenges arise when interdependence is broken, and this happens in two thematic ways:

4.1 Restricted and Misfitting Assistance in Learning

This thematic group entails scenarios where SVIs are keen to attain education, but social relations could be more cooperative, and technologies are unavailable to create the required access. The participants narrated many incidences in which they struggled to get essential attention because SVIs are considered an *extra burden*. Due to this perception, the needs of SVIs are entirely neglected, especially in an inclusive setting. For example, when P4 took what is often referred to as PCMB (Physics, Chemistry, Mathematics, and Biology) and made it into the 11th Std class, which is the first of two senior secondary education years in India, they faced discrimination:

"When I was in school, I took PCMB. I somehow managed 11th, but the schoolteachers were in a psychologically damaged mindset. Their first reaction towards me was, it's a government school, [and] they have the result as a liability or accountability, so from the principal to all the teachers, they were like the result will be bad only. Out of 20, this one will fail. He [P4] has come to this school, but our 5% result is gone, so out of that 95%, let us see how many students we can pass." – P4.

This resulted in actions such as:

"They [teachers] will come to the class, teach, and go without caring that I am there. There was a shortage of reading material there as well. I used to record their lecture, listen to them repeatedly." – P4.

This outright denial shows how the social environment may not take the necessary steps to create a relationship with SVI. It is not restricted to the school environment but is also prevalent in university education. Considering the mandates from a policy perspective, this social attitude creates a tokenistic approach toward people with disabilities. Rather than providing a more active environment with the support of assistive technologies, the social ecology in educational contexts is static and, to an extent, unwilling to support SVI's education. P6 explains this with an example:

"You see, there are a lot of [SVI] students enrolled in XXX University, and there has been an awareness [of disability] in the university for a long time. Once, it happened to me when our political lecture was going on, and I requested my professor to record his lecture, to which he refused directly, saying, 'No, you can't record my lecture'. Then I had to write an email to the principal and meet her. Further, she made my professor understand that we have such students, so you must conduct yourself needfully. Forcefully, I must work on such things, and then get the required returns." – P6.

This attitude also creeps to the top, where policies and directives get established. Misinformed perceptions about the capabilities of SVIs and the lack of awareness of assistive technologies limit opportunities for learning by creating barriers citing a lack of AT. It is likely because the voices of people with visual impairments in decision-making panels are also tokenistic. P5 shared his experience at a high-level meeting with government officials:

"I was invited to a high-level meeting with government secretaries, as a case was in the XXX Court, and they had to give feedback on what should be done to improve accessibility. They had a draft with them in which it was written that PPTs could not be provided, and another clause mentioned those sign language interpreters couldn't be provided." – P5.

To this attitude, P5 responded:

"I mean, how can you [secretaries] conclude in advance that such things can't be provided? It would help if you tried it first." - P5.

The negative perceptions about the capabilities of SVIs limit curriculum that disallows them to pursue specific subjects. For example, the omission of math from the curriculum of students with visual impairments in educational boards creates barriers for those who understand math and wish to pursue it in future. P1 explained this:

"One major problem is that after Std. 7[th,] the school will not let you study Math. Schools say that you will have to study the same math you studied in classes 5th, 6th, 7th, 8th, 9th, and 10th. So, because of this, it is hard to get Math in std. 11th & 12th." – P1.

Some narratives in the discussion appreciated attempts made by social relations in the educational context to bridge the access gap. Unfortunately, due to a lack of awareness of fit-for-purpose solutions and a casual approach to implementation, the bridge often does not fit. Social relations attempt to assist in education, but due to various reasons, the support needs to be aligned and complete. Such misfitting relations can happen when the mediative AT is inappropriate due to unawareness of dedicated AT solutions or their non-availability. It can also occur when the social environment attempts to create workarounds to communicate but at the cost of increased workload and poor management. For example, P4 shares:

"Professors wanted to help. They wanted to provide accessible material and work harder but had no ideas or knowledge. There were few things that they used to do at their personal level such as Latex typing and rather than sending us a scanned image and would be willing to type the equations and make the ppt."– P4.

This shows that there needs to be more awareness in general about best practices for inclusive education. Previous research also suggests that few learning resources and training are available for tutors in an integrated learning environment [44]. We found that institutions have created some form of accessible learning methods, which were in response to the demands of previous SVIs. However, even if tutors are cooperative, additional effort takes time to create accessible content that can be restrictive for the students. A lack of awareness about the importance of inclusion and weak enforcement of accessibility in education is also evident through these procrastinated and reactive attitudes to create an accessible solution for SVIs.

"The coding/programming course I was talking about had teaching assistants. So, whatever teachers have written on the blackboard, they have typed and given to me, but after the 1st lecture, they would give it to me after 15 days or a month later." – P2.

4.2 Ableist Social Interactions

From a social perspective, building relations with peers can often be challenging due to the need for more awareness and sensitisation about visual impairment. Lack of communication can cause stigma about disability and leads to the formation of *social bubbles*. P7 shared his discovery of this social phenomenon while in conversation with one of his sighted friends.

"I was talking to a sighted friend, and she made a very good point that many people, even in my university, are in their bubble. Someone in the 'normalcy bubble' wants to stay in that bubble. They may ask you [SVI] out of curiosity but don't want to leave their comfort zone. They don't want to go out of the way and understand our angle and things related to it." – P7.

People in these bubbles assert caution and hesitance when speaking to SVIs. P3 reflected that if people with visual impairments are part of society, then communication should be accessible and natural, be it about disability or anything else. However, suppose a person with visual impairment is not part of society. In that case, communication will be confounded with presumptions that may cause fear of sounding offensive. Such presumptions emerge when society fails to consider a person with a disability a part of society. Fear of speaking about disability by stepping out from the bubble of normalcy is created by the fact that a disabled person is perceived as not normal or as unfortunate and in need of charity.

"Most people consider us as an object of charity, people who need help, as if we are victims and we only need help and people owe a sympathy perception, but this is something we don't want now." – P1.

Directly talking to people with visual impairments about their disability appears to be discomforting, and people generally prefer to be in a bubble of misperceptions. It highlights deeply engrained attitudes that lead to ability-based hierarchies in which people with visual impairments must prove their capabilities more than others. Often SVIs are not considered productive or contributing group members and cannot be treated equally. Such notions often lead to social situations in which people with visual impairments are alienated despite being part of a group.

"Imagine there is a group of four friends. Amongst them, there is one friend's birthday is sighted. For his birthday, everyone will contribute except the VI one; no one will ask the visually impaired person." – P2.

On the contrary, in scenarios where the person does well in life, for example, lands a competitive job or clears a difficult public exam, society considers a person with a visual impairment to be a person with superpowers and gets subjected to inspiration porn [45].

"Recently, I visited my village where a lot of people say sir, you must have a super-intelligent mind'. I reply I have the same level of brain as you, it's just that I try to utilise it." – P4.

The examples show that the contributions from SVIs are not recognised due to the traditional ableist notions of disability. Hard work and persistence are misinterpreted to be superpowers. A general lack of participation and visibility of SVIs in education leads to these ableist notions. In conclusion, the participation of people with disabilities is promoted through inclusive policies, but the emergent social relations are not equitable. Assistance through these relations happens reactively and can be tokenistic, casual or procrastinated.

5   Overcoming Challenges

While speaking of the above challenges, participants also narrated how they overcame them. These practices reflected an understanding of themselves and the underpinning reasons for the motivation for education. The following three themes illustrate the personal and social factors that foster students' resilience in an educational environment.

5.1 Developing Self-confidence

Self-confidence is an individual's attribute concerned with the belief that a judgement is accurate. It is also considered an individual's ability to be sure about their abilities. For resilience, belief in one's abilities is crucial [41]. Positive educational experiences created a sense of self-confidence that motivated the participants to push ahead through limitations and difficulties. With increased self-confidence, SVIs develop a resilient mindset and a strong acceptance of their visual impairment. For instance, P5 had extremely few resources during his schooling, but positive experiences in learning created excitement to learn more.

> "When I was in school in rural XXX, I did not have books. I requested other people to narrate, yet I saw that I was performing much better than others by listening. I saw that despite my difficulties, I am doing good. I started enjoying this and wanted to take this further and try different things. It's becoming my personal journey by pushing through my limitations." – P5.

Social ecology plays a crucial role in building a positive sense of self and confidence in one's actions, for instance, bridging the access divide was enough for P5 to see his capabilities and build his confidence. Repeated positive experiences build autonomy, allowing students to experiment, try and explore to identify and navigate resources that sustain and improve well-being. Students demand more from the social environment to provide resources in the form of ATs and social support, which P7 explained:

> "I want to be successful and stand out from the crowd. Technology is there, I have a laptop and mobile phone in my hand, of course, limitations are there, but technology is there. I must focus, and developing my skills can't be limited. For that, I do a lot of experiments. I fail, but that's okay. This was one of the main reasons to pursue Liberals Arts and Sciences." – P7.

A positive mindset about self also helps build personal coping strategies to adapt to adverse situations. As explained in Sect. 4.1, restricted and misfitted interdependencies create adversities. Due to a positive self-identity and confidence in one's ability, SVIs identify workarounds in such scenarios and continue to excel. For instance, P4 developed his method to understand mathematical derivations that had missing steps due to inaccessible class notes.

> "We all are surviving because of being outstanding. We must get out of the box. For a sighted student, all the resources are available but for us reading material isn't there, you can't seek help from a book and the internet is not accessible. So, I used to read the logic step by step and imagine ways the sequences used to be formed to fill in the gaps in notes and then I used to check if it matched the result. But can every student [SVI] do this?" – P4.

As highlighted above, a strong personal belief is critical to overcoming adversities. The previous examples also showed that positive self-identity is necessary to build this resilience developed through successful experiences and increased autonomy to identify and create the resources needed to support well-being.

5.2 Internalising Extrinsic Stressors to Intrinsic Motivation

It was interesting to note that some participants had transformed extrinsic factors and events into intrinsic motivation. Reflecting on these behaviours from the theory of self-determination proposed by Deci and Rayn [42], social factors have created an intrinsic desire to achieve to give a response either to social injustices or become valued in the eyes of society. For example, P3 faced many social situations that motivated him to show people they were wrong in thinking about him and his mother.

> "As I was VI by birth, the first VI in my family, my mother faced societal taunts. So, when I was 3–4 years old, I often wondered why these people were saying such things to my mother. No one used to speak to me; instead, they talked with someone who used to accompany me. This was a strange societal problem as well. So, I wanted to become independent and have my own identity that people talk to me." - P3

Some stories revealed the years of discrimination and suppression that the participants faced due to their visual impairments. Responding appropriately to the stigma motivated the participants to attain a good education from a reputable place and acquire high-paying jobs. In this way, they believed society would respect them and their capabilities rather than doubt their abilities and potential for life. For example, for P4, his perceived image in the community he came from was important to him, and increasing his social value within this community motivated him:

> "I come from a rural background where educated people are highly valued. If, along with education, you get a permanent job, people *literally* worship you, so that's the kind of value you get there. So, for me that was a huge motivation to get a better education and get back to my region where I can get valued there." – P4

P6 was motivated by a more personal factor – his grandfather's job in the government service. The esteem and privilege that his grandfather's employment bestowed had motivated him to gain similar employment that would enable him to contribute to society's development, and in turn, he would be viewed as a contributing member of society.

> "Someone close told me that if I get educated, I will be a big man, so the words 'to be a big man' attracted me. My grandfather had a government job and was highly respected because of that. He was a big man. So, I wanted to be a big man." – P6

The above examples describe the internalization of social factors to create the intrinsic motivation to be educated. Social relations also facilitate access to missing information which we describe ahead in greater detail.

5.3 Navigating with Social Resources

In recent years, Resilience Theory has been used extensively to study social ecology's effect on an individual's ability to cope with adversities [8]. Many of the narratives described before highlight the role of empathetic teachers, peers, and friends to support and provide the access required for education. We use the term empathetic because these activities are not generally standardised and are invented by social relations in bespoke ways to create access. These include teachers who understand the needs of students and are willing to put in the required efforts to help them understand the subjects. It requires additional time from their end, increased workload, and creative effort to develop interfaces that are accessible to the students and help them learn about a concept. For example, for P6, learning Math was a challenge until a new teacher worked closely with him and changed his perspective and self-confidence toward learning.

"A new teacher had come; she didn't know how to teach well. I was very weak in Math. You can say that I used to fail in Math. But then we had another new teacher. He worked on me a lot and pushed me to the point that I could pass my Std.10th. Otherwise, I had no hope of passing." – P6.

P2 and P7 shared that teachers who provide special attention to students are highly appreciated. They can make learning more enjoyable and improve their educational experience.

"There used to be one teacher who supported me in English, Math, Science. I couldn't see much; there were no books. I was partially sighted, so we used to sit under the bright sun, and the teacher used to write big letters on the board from either a sketch pen or write big letters on the copy and teach Math. He used to teach me separately." – P5.

However, special attention can only reach some. It also means that education depends on the motivation and intelligence of the special educator. A good teacher can build confidence and capabilities; however, a bad teacher can severely damage the SVI's personal resilience and problem-solving ability. Teachers may also be unable to find ways to teach students with visual impairments at the same level as their sighted peers. In such scenarios, students tend towards friends and family members.

We identified many situations in which friends and family helped with reading, writing, and explaining a topic. Beyond access to education, these practices promote social inclusion and the formation of new relations and begin to include SVIs as part of the group. For example, when the teacher of P1 could not provide access in a needed way, he turned to friends, which increased his social integration within the university.

"My professor used to write code on boards rather than laptops. This used to be his problem. Many times, I told him to explain whatever he wrote, but he used to say it was my habit and used to say that he would do it next time, but he never did. So, I reached out to my friends and studied with them." – P1.

This highlights how SVIs and their community organise themselves to create pathways to access education. Better AT to promote and support such social relations can also improve inclusion and learning experiences. However, the ATs must promote the right attitudes towards people with visual impairments because existing perceptions may still be constrained within the ableist hierarchical structure. SVIs in social scenarios can still be perceived as an object of ill-health, as a student who is less productive, not equal, and in need of help.

6 Unmet Needs

Having understood the challenges SVIs face in education and how they overcome them, this section focuses on needs that still need to be met.

6.1 Integration of Assistive Technologies

Participants agreed that educational resources need to be improved for independent education, and access to graphs and diagrams is a significant issue. Specifically, the lack of accessibility to graphical data was highlighted, creating challenges for students to pursue math and science subjects to survive the challenges posed by the subject. Not being able to understand the subject due to a lack of resources is damaging as they may not understand and deliver to their fullest expectations.

> "If diagrams are unavailable and friends are not always available to help, how will a student survive at a university level? It will be very problematic. If one is interested in the field and cannot learn 100% in the field or give his 100%, then he will get demotivated." – P7.

Two participants strongly advocated that all visual media must be made accessible for students with visual impairments to understand the subject through tactile graphics or automated means to provide text-based descriptions of the graphics. This raises the need for a tactile display interface that is visualised by one of the participants in the following comment:

> "At the initial stages in school, during 9th and 10th, the tactile diagrams are available, but what after that? In college, there are not a finite number of problems. Making diagrams for everything is not possible. So, in this case, there needs to be a device, like a braille display, something that we connect to the laptop or smartphone and just like the braille text, we can see the diagram." – P1.

Enquiring further about tactile displays, it was surprising to note that none of the participants had purchased a tactile display. Two participants were given a refreshable braille display from the university, while one borrowed a display from a friend. The remaining participants have just seen such devices or never felt the need to buy one. Despite the need for tactile interactions expressed in academic literature and the amount of research and development in this field, people still are unsatisfied with the available products or at least need to perceive a sufficient benefit to purchasing. Another participant mentioned that finding a good scribe who can understand the answers and translate them to write in exams is a significant burden and can be eliminated by introducing computers as a medium for exams. Deliberating on this thought, the group discussed that it is possible only if computers are introduced in early education and with software solutions that require minimum human intervention. Accessing academic books through audio and appearing in exams through computers can solve many challenges that SVIs face.

"If we make computers accessible and available at an early school level, where the subjects are also confined, that will give more students a better education who may also take up technical fields. They will demand more and will create the need for better and more accessible materials." – P7.

Previous research has also pointed to increasing access to tactile media and introducing computer interfaces at an early school level. Doing so will provide SVIs with an opportunity for independent learning, increasing personal resilience and improving autonomy and problem-solving ability.

6.2 Integration in Society

Fostering personal resilience covers half of the factors necessary for a better educational experience. Two participants from the group (P4 and P2) strongly felt that the most pressing challenge is the lack of awareness and negative societal attitudes towards people with disabilities. The group regarded this issue as the root of the other challenges, as can be seen in the comment from P4:

"My biggest challenge is the lack of awareness of teaching and non-teaching staff. They don't know how to help or treat." – P4.

Participants shared that all educational institutions should treat an SVI like a regular student, not a special student with special needs. Participants agree that ATs discussed earlier will make people's lives easier and more productive. However, how society changes to include and value people with visual impairments at par with sighted people was still concerning.

"New technologies will keep coming, but how far the mindset of people will change, we don't know." – P2.

The group felt that attitudinal changes in society go much slower than technological advances. The availability of technology would surely facilitate the change in levels of accessibility. Still, it will create a gap between places where technological accessibility is available and where it does not exist.

"Attitude change is obviously at a very slow pace. Because of this, there would be a huge gap, which would be the most negative side because some institutes like private institutes will provide, and some will not." – P7.

Discussing this point further, P3 shared that the empowerment of people with technology will make them more independent and successful. As dependence on society decreases, society's negative attitude can be easily ignored or improved through better participation of SVIs. Hence, technological advances must also aim to change societal perceptions and attitudes toward disability. Society creates greater barriers for people because of its procrastinated, burdensome attitude toward accessibility and inclusion. The bubble of normalcy is so comfortable that people are happy to stay in the shadows of misinformation, away from reality and need for proper accessibility, equitable opportunities, and relevant support so that the motivation that drives SVIs is facilitated. Participants share this attitudinal concern concerning their social integration.

"Because of technology, we will get empowered. The technological shift will be there, but change will be at our level only. The attitudinal level changes at a slower pace. With AT, disabled people can do everything independently but won't have self-satisfaction with society. They will be educated and have everything but still will not get valued. Suppose you are doing a good job and still you face delays for your marriage." – P2

7   Discussion

This paper attempts to understand the challenges, practices, and needs of SVIs who make it to competitive universities in India based on the Framework of Interdependence and the Resilience Theory. We found that educational challenges arise when the tenants of interdependence break and the social environment around an SVI fails to take the necessary steps towards access. A lack of awareness about assistive technologies solidifies the ableist bubble of normalcy. Further, it hinders the development of social relations, while a lack of communication causes misperceptions about the capabilities of SVIs.

We also found that overcoming challenges requires self-confidence fostered by academic success. Many participants had also developed a method to internalise extrinsic social stressors into intrinsic motivation to succeed in education and navigate the challenges of inaccessibility with whatever is available in their ecology. Finally, we found that in terms of technology, there is still a dire need to increase the availability of tactile media and computers in education, with which students can learn independently and build their autonomy and command over the subjects of their choice. It is also important to note the need to facilitate social integration in the ecosystem to abolish ableist hierarchies and establish equitable interactions and collaborations.

7.1   Rethinking Education to Facilitate Independence and Interdependence

Existing education policies and practices can be critiqued to promote ableism and tokenism. It focuses on adapting SVIs to the education system, citing differences in abilities and accepting that visual impairment is a problem that requires special adjustments to be fixed. For example, it motivated the curricular adaptations that limit choices for students, and its implementation without appropriate teacher training limits the support SVIs get in schools. The policy allows students to use screen reading software to appear for exams and use computers in schooling; however, schools or the board have no mandate to provide software or hardware support [18, 19]. The lack of access to AT creates dependencies, and with inappropriate support, surviving the educational environment becomes challenging.

Therefore, on the one hand, the education system needs to empower students with AT to develop autonomy over their experience and develop more command by having the opportunity to learn independently. At the same time, the system needs to be empowered to identify ways that facilitate better and deeper relations with their social ecosystem. Empowerment through assistive technology in employment [27] and peer effects in learning [26] have been discussed before. Our findings extend these works by showing the impact of makeshift AT by interdependent actors in the educational ecosystem that creates access to information. Previous research also highlights the challenges in learning math at high schools [20, 22, 23]. Still, participants opted for math in our study. Our findings highlight how some exceptional students can internalise the challenge and develop bespoke methods to visualise and access mathematic information. We also found teachers overcoming the disconnection in AT knowledge and using ICT skills [24] but with the perception of an extra burden.

Therefore, there is more that needs to be done beyond access to affordable AT [46], better teaching practices [47], and putting people with diverse abilities together in an integrated classroom [16]. The ability-based design framework [48] proposes designing systems focusing on users' abilities. The Frame of Interdependence allows us to see these social relations, relations with AT, and the contributions of people with disabilities [7]. The Disability Interactions framework brings in the value of co-design and co-creation that acknowledges participation and power balances [49]. These frameworks and co-designing educational tools that increase independence and foster interdependence will be necessary for inclusive education. We aim to explore solutions at the intersection of these frameworks in future work.

7.2 From Assistive Education to Inclusive Education

Previous research has shown that due to a lack of tactile tools [20], accessible information [21, 23, 26, 27] and appropriate teaching practices [22], students find it difficult to pursue education. Our research highlights that assistive education was realised through makeshift tech by teachers in the educational ecosystem (such as Latex files) and through peers that collaborate to create access to information. In practice, these actions were considered an extra or a special effort to support a few capable and outstanding students; not every SVI can have that entitlement. Therefore, education as a human right needs to move away from the disability-centric bespoke approaches that have been reported to cause an invisible burden to the person with a visual impairment and their social environment [50] to widely available inclusive practices that every student can engage using their respective abilities.

Project Torino is an excellent example of an AT that can provide an equal collaborative learning experience not determined by the visual impairment [29, 51]. Its implementation has shown that students with diverse abilities actively participate in play through tangible interfaces to understand basic computational thinking concepts without explicit instructions [28]. Another tool called Tip-Toy uses tangible blocks with QR codes that allow students with diverse visual abilities to learn basic computing [52]. Play-based approaches have been used to co-design inclusive games that promote engagement between disabled and non-disabled players. The games used multisensory feedback and a tactile crafting process that engaged children in an engaged and collaborative behaviour [53]. However, despite the improved learning experience provided by tangible interfaces, their practical implementation in contexts where technology use has not been a traditional way of teaching requires developing ways for manageable adoption. In such cases, more mature technologies such as Alexa are paving the way to facilitate inclusion [54].

7.3 Limitations of the Study

While we contribute a qualitative rich insight into the challenges, practices and needs of SVIs in India that compliments research from around the world, the study has some limitations. Although the participants have diverse backgrounds and provide a good representation of challenges, the small sample size of seven participants needs to be improved in how SVIs create creative ways to overcome challenges. Second, all the study participants were male because very few people with visual impairments in top universities, and the number of female students is even less. From our sampling, finding more participants in the given was not feasible. However, this study is part of a longer ongoing research within which we hope to further develop our understanding through different genders, stakeholders of the educational system and cities. Third, using the frame of Interdependence and Resilience Theory to understand challenges and ways of overcoming them is just one of the many ways this data can be reflected. Furthermore, these are evolving conceptual frameworks; hence, we can identify richer and more detailed insights in future work as the frameworks evolve.

8 Conclusion

In this paper, we report findings from a focus group study that explored the educational experiences of university students with visual impairments in India. To improve educational experiences, significant steps are required. A lack of understanding about inclusion and a casual approach creates restricted or misfitted assistance and ableist social interactions. Students overcome these challenges through self-confidence, intrinsic motivation, and honing the ability to navigate accessibility through available social resources. We emphasise the need to empower SVIs through the necessary AT to support independent learning, foster social interdependence, and for the education system and practices to move from assisted education to inclusive education.

Acknowledgements. We want to thank all the participants for their time and support. UK FCDO AT2030 Life-changing Access to Assistive Technologies GB-GOV-1-300815 and UCL Graduate Research Scholarship supported this research.

References

1. Giridhar, P., Dandona, R., Prasad, M.N., Kovai, V., Dandona, L.: Fear of Blindness and Perceptions about Blind People. The Andhra Pradesh Eye Disease Study. Indian Journal of Ophthalmology [Internet]. 2002 [cited 2023 Jan 23]; 50:239. https://journals.lww.com/ijo/Fulltext/2002/50030/Fear_of_Blindness_and_Perceptions_about_Blind.18.aspx
2. Gilbert, C., Foster, A.: The Childhood blindness in the context of VISION 2020 — the right to sight right to sight. Bull. World Health Organ. **2001**, 6 (2020)
3. Wadhwani, M., Vashist, P., Singh, S.S., Gupta, V., Gupta, N., Saxena, R.: Prevalence and causes of childhood blindness in India: a systematic review. Indian J. Ophthalmol. **68**(2), 311 (2020). https://doi.org/10.4103/ijo.IJO_2076_18
4. Education of children with disabilities in India - UNESCO Digital Library [Internet]. https://unesdoc.unesco.org/ark:/48223/pf0000186611. Accessed 18 Jan 2023

5. Palan, R.: I seriously wanted to opt for science, but they said no: visual impairment and higher education in India. Disabil. Soc. [Internet]. **36**, 202–25 (2021). https://doi.org/10.1080/096 87599.2020.1739624

6. Senjam, S.S., Foster, A., Bascaran, C.: Barriers to using assistive technology among students with visual disability in schools for the blind in Delhi, India. Disabil. Rehabil. Assist. Technol [Internet]. **16**, 802–806 (2021). https://doi.org/10.1080/17483107.2020.1738566

7. Bennett, C.L., Brady, E., Branham, S.M.: Interdependence as a frame for assistive technology research and design. In: Proceedings of the 20th International ACM SIGACCESS Conference on Computers and Accessibility [Internet], pp. 161–73. ACM, Galway, Ireland (2018). https://doi.org/10.1145/3234695.3236348. Accessed 17 Sep 2020

8. Ungar, M., Theron, L.: Resilience and mental health: how multisystemic processes contribute to positive outcomes. The Lancet Psychiatry **7**(5), 441–448 (2020). https://doi.org/10.1016/S2215-0366(19)30434-1

9. Rao, S., Kalyanpur, M.: South Asia and Disability Studies: Redefining Boundaries and Extending Horizons. Peter Lang (2013)

10. Chatzitheochari, S., Butler-Rees, A.: Disability, social class and stigma: an intersectional analysis of disabled young people's school experiences. Sociology [Internet], 00380385221133710 (2022). https://doi.org/10.1177/00380385221133710

11. Kayama, M., Johnstone, C., Limaye, S.: The experiences of disability in sociocultural contexts of India: Stigmatization and resilience. Int. Soc. Work [Internet]. **64**, 596–610 (2021). https://doi.org/10.1177/0020872819828781

12. All India Survey on Higher Education 2018–19 | VOCEDplus, the international tertiary education and research database [Internet]. https://www.voced.edu.au/content/ngv:85633. Accessed 20 Jan 2023

13. Pattnaik, S., Murmu, J., Agrawal, R., Rehman, T., Kanungo, S., Pati, S.: Prevalence, pattern and determinants of disabilities in India: Insights from NFHS-5 (2019–21). Front. Public Health **11**, 1036499 (2023). https://doi.org/10.3389/fpubh.2023.1036499

14. Reports & Publications – National Centre for Promotion of Employment for Disabled People [Internet]. https://ncpedp.org/reports-publications/. Accessed 20 Jan 2023

15. Right to Education | Ministry of Education, GoI [Internet]. https://dsel.education.gov.in/rte. Accessed 1 Feb 2023

16. New Education Policy | Government of India, Ministry of Education [Internet]. https://www.education.gov.in/en/nep-new. Accessed 20 Jan 2023

17. Asamoah, E., Ofori-Dua, K., Cudjoe, E., Abdullah, A., Nyarko, J.A.: Inclusive Education: Perception of Visually Impaired Students, Students Without Disability, and Teachers in Ghana. SAGE Open [Internet]. **8**, 2158244018807791 (2018).https://doi.org/10.1177/2158244018807791

18. Sharma, M.: Evaluation of Implementation of IEDSS scheme in Himachal Pradesh. Research Paper [Internet]. https://www.academia.edu/43709320/Evaluation_of_Implementation_of_I EDSS_scheme_in_Himachal_Pradesh. Accessed 20 Jan 2023

19. Rethinking Disability in India [Internet]. Routledge India (2019). https://doi.org/10.4324/978 1315734064/rethinking-disability-india-anita-ghai. Accessed 20 Jan 2023

20. Borah, P.P., Sorathia, K.: Learning and creating mathematical diagrams: findings of a retrospective study conducted with users with blindness or low vision. India HCI 2021 [Internet], pp. 105–109. Association for Computing Machinery, New York, NY, USA (2022). https://doi.org/10.1145/3506469.3506486. Accessed 17 Dec 2022

21. Sahasrabudhe, S., Palvia, P.C.: Academic Challenges of Blind Students and Their Mitigation Strategies | Research-in-Progress. 2013. https://www.semanticscholar.org/paper/Academic-Challenges-of-Blind-Students-and-Their-1-Sahasrabudhe-Palvia/d5f04ff6e5f591b0990db 9bcb0627ec49ea3d612. Accessed 12 June 2023

22. Lamichhane, K.: Teaching students with visual impairments in an inclusive educational setting: a case from Nepal. Int. J. Incl. Educ. **21**, 1–13 (2017). https://doi.org/10.1080/13603116.2016.1184323

23. Dey, S., Bhushan, S., Neerukonda, M., Prakash, A.: Creating an accessible technology ecosystem for learning science and math: a case of visually impaired children in Indian schools (2018)

24. Wong, M.E., Cohen, L.: School, family and other influences on assistive technology use: Access and challenges for students with visual impairment in Singapore. Br. J. Visual Impair. **29**, 130–144 (2011). https://doi.org/10.1177/0264619611402759

25. Baker, C.M., Bennett, C.L., Ladner, R.E.: Educational Experiences of blind programmers. In: Proceedings of the 50th ACM Technical Symposium on Computer Science Education, pp. 759–65. Association for Computing Machinery, New York, NY, USA (2019)https://doi.org/10.1145/3287324.3287410. Accessed 7 June 2023

26. Vashistha, A., Brady, E., Thies, W., Cutrell, E.: Educational content creation and sharing by low-income visually impaired people in India. In: Proceedings of the Fifth ACM Symposium on Computing for Development [Internet], pp. 63–72. Association for Computing Machinery, New York, NY, USA (2014). https://doi.org/10.1145/2674377.2674385. Accessed 1 May 2022

27. Pal, J., Lakshmanan, M.: Assistive technology and the employment of people with vision impairments in India. In: Proceedings of the Fifth International Conference on Information and Communication Technologies and Development, pp. 307–17. Association for Computing Machinery, New York, NY, USA (2012). https://doi.org/10.1145/2160673.2160711. Accessed 17 Aug 2022

28. India, G., Ramakrishna, G., Pal, J., Swaminathan, M.: Conceptual learning through accessible play: project Torino and computational thinking for blind children in India. In: Proceedings of the 2020 International Conference on Information and Communication Technologies and Development, pp. 1–11. Association for Computing Machinery; New York, NY, USA (2022). https://doi.org/10.1145/3392561.3394634. Accessed 29 Aug 2022

29. India, G., Diwakar, N., Jain, M., Vashistha, A., et al.: Teachers' perceptions around digital games for children in low-resource schools for the blind. In: Proceedings of the 2021 CHI Conference on Human Factors in Computing Systems, pp. 1–17. Association for Computing Machinery, New York, NY, USA (2021). https://doi.org/10.1145/3411764.3445194. Accessed 6 June 2023

30. Parthasarathy, B., Dey, S., Gupta, P.: Overcoming wicked problems and institutional voids for social innovation: University-NGO partnerships in the Global South. Technol. Forecast. Soc. Change **173**, 121104 (2021). https://doi.org/10.1016/j.techfore.2021.121104

31. Holloway, C.: Disability interaction (DIX): a manifesto. Interactions **26**, 44–49 (2019). https://doi.org/10.1145/3310322

32. Mankoff, J., Hayes, G.R., Kasnitz, D.: Disability studies as a source of critical inquiry for the field of assistive technology. In: Proceedings of the 12th international ACM SIGACCESS conference on Computers and accessibility, pp. 3–10. Association for Computing Machinery, New York, NY, USA (2010). https://doi.org/10.1145/1878803.1878807. Accessed 20 Jan 2010

33. Heiselberg, K.: Designing self-tracking devices for vulnerable chronic Ill. Companion Publication of the 2019 on Designing Interactive Systems Conference 2019 Companion, pp. 89–92. Association for Computing Machinery, New York, NY, USA (2019). https://doi.org/10.1145/3301019.3324876. Accessed 20 Jan 2023

34. Jain, D., Potluri, V., Sharif, A.: Navigating graduate school with a disability. In: Proceedings of the 22nd International ACM SIGACCESS Conference on Computers and Accessibility, pp. 1–11. Association for Computing Machinery, New York, NY, USA (2020). https://doi.org/10.1145/3373625.3416986. Accessed 25 Jan 2023

35. Gadiraju, V., Doyle, O., Kane, S.: Exploring technology design for students with vision impairment in the classroom and remotely. In: Proceedings of the 2021 CHI Conference on Human Factors in Computing Systems, pp. 1–13. Association for Computing Machinery, New York, NY, USA (2021). https://doi.org/10.1145/3411764.3445755. Accessed 25 Jan 2023

36. Shinohara, K., Tamjeed, M., McQuaid, M., Barkins, D.A.: Usability, accessibility and social entanglements in advanced tool use by vision impaired graduate students. Proc. ACM Human-Comput. Interact. 6(CSCW2), 1–21 (2022). https://doi.org/10.1145/3555609

37. Colley, M., Kränzle, T., Rukzio, E.: Accessibility-related publication distribution in HCI based on a meta-analysis. In: 2022 CHI Conference on Human Factors in Computing Systems, pp. 1–28. Association for Computing Machinery, New York, NY, USA (2022). https://doi.org/10.1145/3491101.3519701. Accessed 20 Jan 2023

38. Sim, I.O.: Analysis of the coping process among visually impaired individuals, using interpretative phenomenological analysis (IPA). Int. J. Environ. Res. Publ. Health 17(8), 2819 (2020). https://doi.org/10.3390/ijerph17082819

39. Porcelli, P., Ungar, M., Liebenberg, L., Trépanier, N.: (Micro)mobility, disability and resilience: exploring well-being among youth with physical disabilities. Disabil. Soc. 29, 863–876 (2014). https://doi.org/10.1080/09687599.2014.902360

40. Barbareschi, G., Holloway, C., Arnold, K., Magomere, G., Wetende, W.A., Ngare, G., et al.: The social network: how people with visual impairment use mobile phones in Kibera, Kenya. In: Proceedings of the 2020 CHI Conference on Human Factors in Computing Systems, pp. 1–15. Association for Computing Machinery, New York, NY, USA (2020). https://doi.org/10.1145/3313831.3376658. Accessed 17 Sep 2023

41. Masten, A.S.: Ordinary magic. Resilience process in development. Am. Psychol. 56, 227–238 (2001)

42. Deci, E.L., Ryan, R.M.: Self-determination theory. In: Van Lange, P., Arie Kruglanski, E. (eds.) Handbook of Theories of Social Psychology: Volume 1, pp. 416–437. SAGE Publications Ltd, London (2012). https://doi.org/10.4135/9781446249215.n21

43. Demonstrating Rigor Using Thematic Analysis: A Hybrid Approach of Inductive and Deductive Coding and Theme Development - Jennifer Fereday, Eimear Muir-Cochrane, 2006. https://doi.org/10.1177/160940690600500107. Accessed 17 Sep 2023

44. Das, A.K., Kuyini, A.B., Desai, I.P.: Inclusive education in India: are the teachers prepared? Int. J. Special Educ. 28, 27–36 (2013). https://eric.ed.gov/?id=EJ1013694

45. Grue, J.: The problem with inspiration porn: a tentative definition and a provisional critique. Disabil. Soc. 31, 838–849 (2016).https://doi.org/10.1080/09687599.2016.1205473

46. Education of Blind and Visually Impaired Children in India. https://doi.org/10.1177/0145482X8908300106. Accessed 17 Dec 2022

47. Yusof, Y., Chan, C.C., Hillaluddin, A.H., Ahmad Ramli, F.Z., Mat Saad, Z.: Improving inclusion of students with disabilities in Malaysian higher education. Disabil. Soc. 35, 1145–1170 (2020). https://doi.org/10.1080/09687599.2019.1667304

48. Wobbrock, J.O., Kane, S.K., Gajos, K.Z., Harada, S., Froehlich, J.: Ability-based design: concept, principles and examples. ACM Trans. Access. Comput. 3(3), 1–27 (2011). https://doi.org/10.1145/1952383.1952384

49. Holloway, C., Barbareschi, G.: The disability interaction (DIX) approach. In: Holloway, C., Barbareschi, G. (eds.) Disability Interactions: Creating Inclusive Innovations, pp. 27–70. Springer International Publishing, Cham (2022). https://doi.org/10.1007/978-3-031-03759-7_3

50. Branham, S.M., Kane, S.K.: The invisible work of accessibility: how blind employees manage accessibility in mixed-ability workplaces. In: Proceedings of the 17th International ACM SIGACCESS Conference on Computers & Accessibility [Internet], pp. 163–71. Association for Computing Machinery, New York, NY, USA (2015)]. https://doi.org/10.1145/2700648.2809864. Accessed 2023 Jan 30

51. Morrison, C., Villar, N.,Thieme, A., Ashktorab, Z., Taysom, E, Salandin, O, et al.: Torino: a tangible programming language inclusive of children with visual disabilities. Human Comput. Interact. **35**, 191–239 (2020). https://doi.org/10.1080/07370024.2018.1512413

52. Barbareschi, G., Costanza, E., Holloway, C.: TIP-Toy: a tactile, open-source computational toolkit to support learning across visual abilities. In: Proceedings of the 22nd International ACM SIGACCESS Conference on Computers and Accessibility, pp. 1–14. Association for Computing Machinery, New York, NY, USA (2020). https://doi.org/10.1145/3373625.341 7005. Accessed 30 Jan 2023

53. Metatla, O., Bardot, S., Cullen, C., Serrano, M., Jouffrais, C.: Robots for Inclusive play: co-designing an educational game with visually impaired and sighted children. In: Proceedings of the 2020 CHI Conference on Human Factors in Computing Systems, pp. 1–13. Association for Computing Machinery, New York, NY, USA (2020). https://doi.org/10.1145/3313831.337 6270

54. With Alexa, Amir found a friend and vision for future. About Amazon India. 2022 https://www.aboutamazon.in/news/devices/with-alexa-amir-found-a-friend-and-vision-for-future. Accessed 30 Jan 2023

Mapping Virtual Reality Controls to Inform Design of Accessible User Experiences

Christopher Power[1,3]([✉]), Paul Cairns[2,3], and Triskal DeHaven[2]

[1] SMCS, University of Prince Edward Island, Charlottetown, PE C1A 4P3, Canada
cdspower@upei.ca
[2] Department of Computer Science, University of York, York, UK
paul.cairns@york.ac.uk
[3] The AbleGamers Charity, Kearneysville, WV 25436, USA

Abstract. A lack of accessible controls remains a barrier to disabled users engaging in virtual reality experiences. This paper presents a modified cognitive walkthrough of 120 virtual reality applications to identify 2,284 pairs of operant and resultant actions and creates an inventory of domain objects and their operant and resultant actions in the virtual space. This inventory captures both the form and prevalence of interactions that are expected of users in current virtual reality design. An analysis of this inventory reveals that while many barriers could be addressed by existing solutions, those options currently are not often present in current designs. Further, there are a set of barriers related to embodied controls that represent opportunities and challenges for new and innovative designs in virtual reality.

Keywords: Virtual reality · accessibility · input · controls

1 Introduction

Virtual reality (VR) is a platform for users to escape inside incredible virtual worlds, socialize with their friends and family, and to play games. Unfortunately, much of virtual reality, even at the very basic access level [20] of interaction remains inaccessible to disabled people[1] [7,9,27].

---

[1] In this paper we have chosen identity first language over people first language which is consistent with some communities. We acknowledge that language around disability is evolving and have made this choice for consistency within the paper.

We acknowledge the support of the Natural Sciences and Engineering Research Council of Canada (NSERC), grant RGPIN-2020-05570.

Supplementary Information The online version contains supplementary material available at https://doi.org/10.1007/978-3-031-42280-5_5.

© The Author(s), under exclusive license to Springer Nature Switzerland AG 2023
J. Abdelnour Nocera et al. (Eds.): INTERACT 2023, LNCS 14142, pp. 89–100, 2023.
https://doi.org/10.1007/978-3-031-42280-5_5

While there is an increasing amount of information about the barriers to users in VR, we have very little information about the design space in VR that leads to those barriers. For example, while we know that controllers and controls in VR can be a barrier, we do not know what specific designs that are being used that are causing the mismatch between users and the technology. Therefore, the goals of the research presented in this paper are to: analyse existing VR applications to identify the range of different controls available, analyze where there is the potential for barriers to disabled users, and where there are opportunities for innovation in design.

2   Literature Review

VR is often presented as a new and emerging technology. While it is true that the fidelity and commercialization of these technologies are ever advancing [16], the challenges of making VR accessible are not new. Indeed, accessibility research of VR applications emerged in the late 1990s s with some early VR devices. At that time, VR was being used in a range of innovative areas including: telepresence in medical consultations, exploratory virtual archaeology, and in providing an alternative venue for educational journeys for students [2, 12, 23].

The introduction of these early VR devices also coincided with the emergence of the dominant philosophies in accessibility and inclusion [5], which resulted in an increased interest in first-wave [11] research looking at the perceptual, motor and cognitive aspects of VR.

The devices that were available during this period of VR research provided opportunities to explore multi-modality in the virtual reality for both input and output. At that time, the most prevalent research was in accessibility for people with sensory disabilities, focused on modalities for presenting information in virtual spaces. Research with this generation of hardware investigated how blind and low vision users interpreted virtual objects, how different textures and shapes are perceived on surfaces in virtual space, and even how variations in the type of device and its mapping to VR changed perception [6, 15, 18, 19]. Research into interactions of blind and low vision users in virtual reality continue today [7].

Most of these studies worked with devices that had limited controls. In most cases, they consisted of a thimble or pen interface providing 6 degrees of movement in a virtual space and 1 or 2 buttons. In comparison, modern VR devices have one or more handheld controllers with many buttons and/or joysticks available to users. While these controls are immensely powerful, they are grounded in many assumptions about people having physical abilities that are similar to the average population [16, 17, 27] or what Gerling and Spiel refer to as the *corporeal standard body* [10]. For example, many recent VR devices assume users have two hands and two arms with full range of motion and motor control. A recent interview study by Mott *et al.* [17] found 7 broad barriers, many of which focused on the hardware and controls, with participants describing issues relating to reach of buttons or hand and arm strength to hold controllers, with no ability to replace the controller with something they can use, despite calls for this feature from users [27].

Beyond the controllers themselves, there is often need to adapt the mappings of the controller activations into the virtual space. Zhang *et al.* [28] undertook research on the actions related to locomotion within virtual spaces, and examined several different types of control variants. Authors ap Cenydd and Headland [1] provide a model of locomotion that describes the physicality and freedom of different types of control schemes. This model proposes four different types of movement and demonstrates the applicability of their model to a single application. However, both papers focus on a single interaction type: locomotion. While these papers can inform the design and evaluation of variety of locomotion controls, they do not provide any insight into what is a broad range of other interactions that can happen in VR space. Further, while Gerling *et al.* [9] indicates that remapping is a highly desired option within VR, we broadly lack a comprehensive examination of what controls exist and the form they take in VR in order to be able to propose that type of remapping or other forms of accessible design.

To address this gap in knowledge, we undertook an analytical study of existing VR applications to answer the following questions:

1. What is the form and function of interactions that users have in VR spaces?
2. How does the form of these VR interactions contribute to accessibility barriers?
3. Given the form of VR interactions, what are existing accessible design solutions for barriers to disabled users?

By answering these questions, we can understand the where there are solutions, and where there need for new designs for more accessible VR controls.

This paper presents the methodology, results, and analysis of a systematic review of 120 VR applications with 2,284 interactions that users can take in those applications. These interactions were analyzed to create a descriptive inventory of interactions in VR apps including both the physical actions that users undertake and how they map to the virtual world.

3   Methodology

In this study, VR applications were analyzed regarding the *objects* that users interacted with in the virtual world. The interactions with these objects were broken down into *operant actions*, that is the actions taken in the physical world undertaken by users, and the *resultant actions* that occur in the virtual space. This section details the systematic approach that was taken to identify the dimensions of users' interactions in VR.

3.1   Devices

Three virtual reality devices were chosen for the study as an opportunity sample of what was available on the market at the time of the study. The three devices represented different levels of complexity input devices including the Oculus Go [8] with a single handset, the Sony PlayStation Virtual Reality [24] with its wand controller or game controller and the HTC Vive [14] which had dual handsets.

3.2 Application Sample

For each platform, an opportunity sample of applications were selected for review on each of the 3 platforms. The sampling method for each platform was as follows:

1. Applications on each platform's online store were ranked by popularity.
2. The list was filtered for the applications were free.
3. Up to 40 applications were selected from that list.

The exception to the above was a small number of pre-purchased VR titles that were already available to the researchers on the PlayStation VR system.

This resulted in a set of 120 applications. Within the sample there were 5 broad categories of applications: single player games, multi-user social spaces, walking simulators, virtual tours and 360° video archives.

The complete list of applications chosen for this study are provided in the Appendix of this paper.

3.3 Data Collection

For each application, a modified version of the cognitive walkthrough inspection method was used to systematically record the operant and resultant actions that are applied by users [25, 26].

After installation of each application, a researcher reviewed the application for the key tasks users undertake in the application until saturation was reached and no new tasks were discovered. Each task was decomposed by the researchers into its most atomic tasks[2]. Then, researchers documented the path from where users would identify an action, perform it on a controller (the *operant action*), and then receive feedback from that action from VR (*the resultant action*).

For example, in many games there was the need to attack a target with a handheld projectile weapon. The task of firing the weapon was broken down into facing the target with the camera, aiming the weapon, and then firing the weapon via a virtual trigger mapped to a button. When using the PlayStation VR, this task resulted in the operant and resultant actions listed in Table 1. In cases where there were multiple possible operant actions for a single resultant action, all discovered alternative operant actions were recorded.

3.4 Data Analysis

After reviewing all of the applications, a content analysis using open coding was undertaken on the complete set of pairings of operant and resultant actions [13]. One researcher undertook the coding and a second researcher performed independent checks on the codes to ensure consistency and clarity of the coding scheme. This produced codes for a set of domain objects in virtual space that users interact with and a set of codes for both operant and resultant actions.

---

[2] For those familiar with hierarchical task analysis, these atomic tasks correspond to the leaves of the task tree.

Table 1. Example mapping of firing a weapon in a game to operant actions and resultant actions.

Task	Operant Action	Resultant Action
Firing Weapon	Aim with Head	Camera Turn Left/Right
	Aim with Controller	Aim Weapon
	Hold Up on D Pad	Aim Weapon
	Press X	Fire Weapon

4 Results

There were 2,284 pairs of operant and resultant actions collected from the applications.

There were 5 domain objects identified on which users interacted with operant/resultant pairs. These objects included: *Avatars* representing the user in virtual space regardless its form (e.g. person versus vehicle); *Camera*: a viewport to the world; *Combat Objects*: melee and range weaponry; *Environmental Objects*: items user may interact with in virtual space for a task, such as a tool, door, or box; and *User Interface Objects*: the user interface components that are included in the heads-up display (HUD).

For each object, there were groups of resultant actions that commonly occurred together. For example, all the controls in Table 1 labelled *Aim Weapon* in their resultant actions were put into a group: *Aim*, whereas *Fire Weapon* was grouped under *Attack* with other aggressive actions, and the *Camera Turn Left/Right* was grouped under *Smooth Camera Movement*. Table 2 shows the relationship between domain objects, groups and resultant actions.

Many applications encourage the manipulation of objects in diverse ways (173) and the movement of objects within the VR space (192). Similarly, when an Avatar is present in VR, movement along the horizontal plane (x/y axis), such as walking or driving, is common (189). In comparison, Avatar movement along the z-axis is seldom used (31).

Codes for operant actions included *Embodied Upper Limb Movement* and *Embodied Head Movement* which are actions that have a direct mapping between motions in the physical world and in the virtual one. There were four codes identified for actions through conventional button and joystick controls, one for a *Single Button* press and release, one for when users press and *Hold* a button or joystick for an extended period of time and one for repeated *Rapid* activations of a button connected to a single operant action. Finally, there was a code for *Complex* activations which combined two or more of the above. Table 3 presents the resultant groups mapped to the operant actions.

Embodied Head Movement is the most consistently mapped and used operant action. The movement of the head to target the camera was present in every app (720), with each using the full range of motion, which is consistent with the unique selling point of VR of being immersed in a completely virtual world.

Table 2. Number of unique instances of each resultant action grouped by domain objects.

Domain Object	Resultant Group	Resultant Action	Instances
Avatar	Control Velocity	Accelerate, Boost, Brake, Stop Movement, Stop Acceleration	30
	Horizontal Movement	Forward, Back, Left, Right, Move to Highlighted Area	189
	Vertical Movement	Hover, Jump, Land, Wall Climb, Wall Walking, Crouch, Stand, Dash, Dodge	31
Camera	Calibration	Calibration	11
	Hold Camera	Lock camera on target	3
	Smooth Camera Movement	Up, Down, Left, Right, Forward, Backward	750
	Still Camera Capture	Take Picture	2
	Tile Camera Movement	Up, Down, Left, Right, Reverse	46
	Viewpoint Change	Change Viewpoint (Front Facing, Panoramic, First Person View, Third Person View) Zoom-in, Zoom-out, Move Object View (Up, Down)	30
Combat	Aim	Up, Down, Left, Right	112
	Attack	Melee Attack, Throw Object, Fire Weapon, Rapid Fire Weapon, Use Ability, Stop Firing,	135
	Modifiers	Charge Attack, Increase Power, Prepare Weapon, Swap Weapon, Reload, Cancel Action	39
Environmental	Change Environment	Change Game Speed, Change Time of Day, Spawn Item	13
	Object Manipulation	Aim Tool (Up, Down, Left, Right), Use Tool, Highlight Object, Select Highlighted Object, Use Object, Interact with Object, Release Object, Shake Object, Change Gears	173
	Object Movement	Rotate Object (Up, Down, Left, Right), Use Object, Use Tool, Stop, Grab Object, Hold Object, Movement of Object (Up, Down, Left, Right)	192
User Interface	Control Application	Pause, Unpause, Exit, Skip Cutscene	70
	Menu Manipulation	Up, Down, Left Right, Forward, Back	295
	Move Menus	Drag UI	5
	Navigate Menu	Highlight Menu Option, Select Highlighted Menu Option, Close Menu, Open Menu, Grab/Release Menu, Drag Menu, Game Specific Menu, Yes	158

Embodied Upper Limb Movement in VR is a common activation when conducting an Aim related action on a combat weapon (72) and, surprisingly, in horizontal movement (65). For example, a user may point with their arm where they want to go while flying like Superman. Aim resultant actions were also used heavily in the user interfaces components of VR with the need to have users extend, wave, or hold their arms to target menu items within the display (82).

Predominantly, single button presses are seen in object manipulation (117) and menu manipulation (165). However, for movement of an avatar in the horizontal plane (60), movement of objects (51) and attacking in combat (37) there is a prevalence of users having to hold controls for an extended period. Holding an activation was often used as an alternative for embodied movement in the horizontal or vertical planes, making holding a surprisingly prevalent activation across the data set.

Most of the applications have a small number of one or two alternative operant action options. In cases where there was more, it was almost always isolated

Table 3. Cross-tabulation of the number of instances of each operant action within each resultant action group.

Resultant Group	Complex	Embodied Head Movement	Embodied Upper Limb Movement	Hold	Rapid	Single Button	Total
Aim	20	12	72	2	-	6	112
Attack	21	2	3	37	6	66	135
Calibration	3	-	2	3	-	3	11
Change Environment	4	-	1	1	1	6	13
Control Velocity	-	-	-	13	-	17	30
Control Application	-	-	-	3	-	67	70
Hold Camera	-	-	-	-	-	3	3
Horizontal Movement	21	7	65	60	9	27	189
Menu Manipulation	7	16	82	24	1	165	295
Modifiers	3	2	-	17	-	17	39
Move Menus	1	-	-	2	2	-	5
Navigate Menu	12	-	1	2	39	104	158
Object Manipulation	9	12	20	9	6	117	173
Object Movement	72	-	35	51	4	30	192
Smooth Camera Movement	6	720	4	17	3	-	750
Still Camera Capture	-	-	-	-	-	2	2
Tile Camera Movement	1	-	-	2	6	37	46
Vertical Movement	6	-	-	3	2	20	31
Viewpoint Change	7	-	1	6	2	14	30

to a specific group of actions. For example, some apps allowed alternative controls for movement in the horizontal plane for all directions but had no alternatives for other controls. A few applications had alternatives for camera movement, or firing weapons, or for grabbing/releasing objects. Finally, there was one consistent place where there were there were multiple operant actions, and this was in access to menus in the User Interface resultant group. For example, selecting highlighted menus had the largest number of apps that afforded operant control alternatives for that single resultant action (23).

5   Limitations

In this study we have undertaken a review of 120 applications, and while care was taken to select a wide variety of application types, there is a selection bias due to the focus on primarily free tier or low-cost applications. Even though this was an opportunity sample, we have representative applications from across the industry from commercial titles, to educational services such as museums, to games, meaning the applications sample is robust at least in terms of its variety of types of interactions that users are likely to have with VR. However, we cannot make any generalizations about control schemes in particular applications.

Finally, this data was gathered towards the end of 2019, meaning that the results are true for that time. With VR being a fast-moving field, these platforms are now being surpassed by the next generation of devices. However, given that we used three platforms from the very simple in the Oculus Go [8], to the very complex with the HTC Vive [14], we feel that the inventory produced in this study is representative of at least the minimum of what current platforms can do. Validation with current platforms will help increase the external validity of the results.

6 Discussion

While there are a variety of different virtual spaces that users will encounter in VR applications the things that they interact with can be categorized into 5 coherent domain objects whose resultant actions fall into 19 different categories. Moreover, there were 5 distinct categories of operant actions that map into all of those different resultant actions. These results can inform accessible design of VR by giving us a means to identify where we already have solutions and where we have difficult research problems to address.

Many of the operant actions require people to press buttons for activation in different ways, often with many individual actions being needed in a single application. As identified in existing literature, this will create barriers to people who are unable to use standard controllers due to disabilities related to dexterity or fine motor control, as well as those who can only use specific fingers or one hand. There are well understood techniques from a variety of computing environments about how to provide the much desired feature of remapping one button to another [3,9,21]. However, these options were rare in the applications we surveyed.

One of the most common control activations in VR was where users were required to hold controls when they are undertaking movement of cameras, avatars and objects. This type of hold for controls for extended periods of time can impact individuals who have strength related disabilities in their hands or where users fatigue quickly. Similarly, these same users will often encounter barriers to technology use when they have to conduct rapid repeated pressing of controls. However, there are good patterns and examples in domains such as digital games of how to toggle these controls to provide alternatives for users, meaning addressing this issue should be relatively straight-forward for VR designers.

In contrast, it is the embodied interactions that present the biggest opportunities and challenge for control research and innovation in VR. Whether operant actions are an embodied movement on their own, or if they are combined with one of the many button presses, simple remapping is unlikely to solve the accessibility barriers. In addition to users who have disabilities discussed above anyone with disabilities related to strength, motor control, or movement of their arms have the potential to encounter barriers.

For example, consider the fishing game Bait! [22]. Users must face the direction they want to cast, then press a button and hold it, swing their arm backward and then forward and release the button in time with the forward swing. In order to appropriately account for everything in this action, at a minimum designers would need a control scheme that can move in two dimensions for the head, a control that can move in one dimension for the arm, and a button, and yet be accessible to users where the original control scheme creates barriers.

7 Conclusion

In this paper, an analysis of 2,284 controls in VR has identified a variety of sources of barriers to disabled users. In some cases, the source of the barriers is the number or location of controls required for an application, which are barriers that can be addressed by existing solutions such as providing control remapping on existing controllers or to users' own custom controllers as is seen in other domains [21]. In other cases, such as holding buttons or rapid repeated presses of buttons, alternative ways of toggling controls or control reduction are well understood.

However, within VR there are a variety of embodied movements that are used for control. These controls create barriers to disabled users where there are no obvious pre-existing solutions. Given that there is a substantial number of key actions in VR that are linked to these types of embodied controls, expedited research and design is needed to create new alternatives that encompass the many dimensions these controls use to manipulate the virtual world.

Any alternative control solutions would fundamentally change the way a user engages with VR in comparison to the original controls. Beyond the question of how to implement new control schemes, there is the more important question of: how do adaptations alter the experience of users? There are studies in gaming that indicate that control changes can change experiences that are key to VR [4]. If this holds in VR, it means that disabled users will get a different experience from their non-disabled peers. Thus, we also need to understand the experiential goals of disabled users in virtual reality and whether or not the altered experiences delivered through adapted interfaces are acceptable and meet those goals.

Appendix: Application Sample

Table 4. Sample applications used in this study.

HTC Vive	Oculus Go	PlayStation Virtual Reality
1 2 3 Bugle	A Dead Body Drops	Allumette - Move Controllers
A Beautiful Anywhere	AltSpace VR	Ancient Amuletor Demo - Move Controllers
AD 2047 Demo	Amaze: Interactive Movies	Animal Force Demo - Move Controllers
BE THE HERO : Prototype	Bait	Aquishies Demo - Move Controllers
Blobby Tennis	Break a Leg	Astro Bot Rescue Mission Demo - PS4 Controller
Budget Cuts - Premature Demo Edition	Coco VR	Batman VR - PS4 Controller
Cast Demo	Conflict0: Shattered	Battle Zone - PS4 Controller
Chromatic Shift VR	Dark Corners	Bound Demo - PS4 Controller
Circaian Rhythm	Dead and Buried	Cyber Danganronpa VR - PS4 Controller
Cosmic-Attack VR Demo	DEO VR - Video Player	Dark Eclipse - Move Contollers
Cube Dancer	Epic Roller Coasters	Dino Frontier - Move Contollers
Domino Craft	Face Your Fears	Driveclub VR Demo - PS4 Controller
Exogen	Facebook 360	Eden Tomorro - PS4 Controller
Fairyland	Facebook Watch	Eve Valkerie - PS4 Controller
Finnair Virtual Flight	Fail Factory Demo	Far Point - PS4 Controller
Google earth VR	Gala 360 - Travel and Relax	Grand Turismo Sport - PS4 Controller
Guns'n'Stories: Preface VR	Galavi Shows	Harmonix Music VR - Move Contollers
Heart of the Eberstone: Coliseum	Guide Meditation VR	Head Master Demo - PS4 Controller
HyperVisor	Henry	Here They Lie Demo - PS4 Controller
Incane: Solo Training	Jurassic Park: Blue	Hustle Kings VR - Move Contollers
Invasion	Jurassic World: Apatosaurus	Job Simulator - Move Controllers
MermaidVR Video Player	Laura Croft	Moss Demo - PS4 Controller
Netflix VR	Maze VR	Playroom
PROGHET: A VR EXPERIENCE - Demo	Merry Snowballs	Prision Boss VR Demo - Move Contollers
Proze Prologue	Mission ISS	Raw Data Demo - Move Contollers
Ready Player One: Oasis beta	Oculus Browser	Rez Infinite - PS4 Controller
Sinister Halloween Demo	Oculus Rooms	Rigs - PS4 Controller
Spiderman Far From Home	Oculus TV	Skyrim VR - PS4 Controller
Spiderman Homecoming	Pet Lab	Star Child - PS4 Controller
Spirit Warrior VR	Play With Me	Superhot VR Demo - Move Controllers
Taphouse VR	PolyRunner VR	Tethered Demo - PS4 Controller
The Bellows	Project Rampage VR	The Last Guardian VR - PS4 Controller
The Body VR	Rilix Coaster	The Persistence Demo - PS4 Controller
The Last Day Defense	Shooting Showdown 2	Thumper Demo - PS4 Controller
USS Eisenhower Virtual Reality	Space Time	Tiny Trax - PS4 Controller
VIVEPORT VR	Star Wars: Droid Repair Bay	Tom Grennan - PS4 Controller
VR Aquarium	Temple Run	TumbleVR Demo - Move Controllers
VR Dino War	VeeR: Video, Movie, and Photo Platform	Until Dawn: Rush of Blood Demo - Move Controllers
Weapons Master	Wonderglade	VR Worlds - Move Controllers AND PS4 Controller
Weather God	Wonders of the World	Wayward Sky Demo - PS4 Controller

References

1. Ap Cenydd, L., Headleand, C.J.: Movement modalities in virtual reality: a case study from ocean rift examining the best practices in accessibility, comfort, and immersion. IEEE Consum. Electron. Mag. **8**(1), 30–35 (2018)
2. Barceló, J.A., Forte, M., Sanders, D.H.: Virtual reality in archaeology. Archaeopress Oxford (2000)
3. Beeston, J., Power, C., Cairns, P., Barlet, M.: Accessible player experiences (APX): the players. In: International Conference On Computers Helping People with Special Needs, pp. 245–253 (2018)

4. Cairns, P., Li, J., Wang, W., Nordin, A.I.: The influence of controllers on immersion in mobile games. In: Proceedings of the SIGCHI Conference on Human Factors in Computing Systems, pp. 371–380. CHI 2014, Association for Computing Machinery, New York, NY, USA (2014)

5. Clarkson, P.J., Coleman, R.: History of inclusive design in the UK. Appl. Ergon. **46**, 235–247 (2015)

6. Colwell, C., Petrie, H., Kornbrot, D., Hardwick, A., Furner, S.: Haptic virtual reality for blind computer users. In: Proceedings of the Third International ACM Conference on Assistive Technologies, pp. 92–99 (1998)

7. Façanha, A.R., Darin, T., Viana, W., Sánchez, J.: O&M indoor virtual environments for people who are blind: a systematic literature review. ACM Trans. Access. Comput. (TACCESS) **13**(2), 1–42 (2020)

8. Facebook Technologies: Oculus Go Overview (2021). https://www.oculus.com/go/. April 2023

9. Gerling, K., Dickinson, P., Hicks, K., Mason, L., Simeone, A.L., Spiel, K.: Virtual reality games for people using wheelchairs. In: Proceedings of the 2020 CHI Conference on Human Factors in Computing Systems, pp. 1–11 (2020)

10. Gerling, K., Spiel, K.: A critical examination of virtual reality technology in the context of the minority body. In: Proceedings of the 2021 CHI Conference on Human Factors in Computing Systems. Association for Computing Machinery, New York, NY, USA. ACM (2021)

11. Harrison, S., Sengers, P., Tatar, D.: Making epistemological trouble: third-paradigm HCI as successor science. Interact. Comput. **23**(5), 385–392 (2011)

12. Hoffman, H., Vu, D.: Virtual reality: teaching tool of the twenty-first century? Acad. Med. J. Assoc. Am. Med. Colleges **72**(12), 1076–1081 (1997)

13. Hsieh, H.F., Shannon, S.E.: Three approaches to qualitative content analysis. Qual. Health Res. **15**(9), 1277–1288 (2005)

14. HTC Corporation: Vive Hardware (2019). https://www.vive.com/uk/product/. April 2023

15. Kornbrot, D., Penn, P., Petrie, H., Furner, S., Hardwick, A.: Roughness perception in haptic virtual reality for sighted and blind people. Percept. Psychophys. **69**(4), 502–512 (2007)

16. Mott, M., et al.: Accessible by design: an opportunity for virtual reality. In: 2019 IEEE International Symposium on Mixed and Augmented Reality Adjunct (ISMAR-Adjunct), pp. 451–454. IEEE (2019)

17. Mott, M., Tang, J., Kane, S., Cutrell, E., Ringel Morris, M.: I just went into it assuming that I wouldn't be able to have the full experience. Understanding the Accessibility of Virtual Reality for People with Limited Mobility. In: The 22nd International ACM SIGACCESS Conference on Computers and Accessibility, pp. 1–13 (2020)

18. Penn, P., Petrie, H., Colwell, C., Kornbrot, D., Furner, S., Hardwick, A.: The perception of texture, object size and angularity by touch in virtual environments with two haptic devices. In: Proceedings of the 1st International Workshop on Haptic Human Computer Interaction (University of Glasgow, 2000-8-31 to 9–1) (2000)

19. Petrie, H., Penn, P., Kornbrot, D.: Haptic virtual environments for blind people: further explorations with the phantom device. In: Proceedings of the 3rd International Conference on Disability, Virtual Reality & Assistive Technology (ICD-VRAT), pp. 39–44 (2000)

20. Power, C., Cairns, P., Barlet, M.: Inclusion in the third wave: access to experience. In: Filimowicz, M., Tzankova, V. (eds.) New Directions in Third Wave Human-Computer Interaction: Volume 1 - Technologies, pp. 163–181. Springer International Publishing, Cham (2018)
21. Power, C., Cairns, P., Barlet, M., Haynes, G., Beeston, J., DeHaven, T.: Validation and prioritization of design options for accessible player experiences. Interact. Comput. **33**(6), 641–656 (2022). https://doi.org/10.1093/iwc/iwac017
22. Revolution Games: Bait (2016). https://www.resolutiongames.com/bait/. April 2023
23. Satava, R.M.: Medical applications of virtual reality. J. Med. Syst. **19**(3), 275–280 (1995)
24. Sony Interactive Entertainment Europe Limited.: PS VR in Detail: Technical specifications - CUH-ZVR1 model (2021). https://www.playstation.com/en-gb/explore/playstation-vr/buy-now/
25. Spencer, R.: The streamlined cognitive walkthrough method, working around social constraints encountered in a software development company. In: Proceedings of the SIGCHI Conference on Human Factors in Computing Systems, pp. 353–359. CHI 2000, Association for Computing Machinery, New York, NY, USA (2000)
26. Wharton, C., Rieman, J., Lewis, C., Polson, P.: The Cognitive Walkthrough Method: A Practitioner's Guide, pp. 105–140. John Wiley & Sons Inc., USA (1994)
27. Wong, A., Gillis, H., Peck, B.: VR accessibility: survey for people with disabilities. In: Disability Visibility Project & ILMxLAB (2018)
28. Zhang, Y., Huang, Z., Quigley, K., Sankar, R., Yang, A.: A user experience study of locomotion design in virtual reality between adult and minor users. In: 2019 IEEE International Symposium on Mixed and Augmented Reality Adjunct (ISMAR-Adjunct), pp. 47–51. IEEE (2019)

WAM-Studio: A Web-Based Digital Audio Workstation to Empower Cochlear Implant Users

Michel Buffa[1] , Antoine Vidal-Mazuy[1](✉), Lloyd May[2] ,
and Marco Winckler[1]

[1] University Côte d'Azur, CNRS, INRIA, Nice, France
{michel.buffa,antoine.vidal-mazuy,marco.winckler}@univ-cotedazur.fr
[2] Stanford University, Stanford, USA
lloydmay@stanford.edu

Abstract. This paper introduces *WAM-Studio*, an online Digital Audio Workstation (DAW) for recording, mixing, producing, and playing multitrack music. WAM-Studio advances music development by proposing a web-based environment based on a visual programming paradigm of end-user programming (EUP). In this paper, we describe how users can associate individual tracks with real-time audio processing plugins that can then be customized to produce a desired audio effect. Moreover, we describe how users can visually create macros to control multiple plugin parameters at once. While programming macro controls and customizing track parameters might have many applications in the music industry, they also present an opportunity to afford Hard-of-Hearing users greater control over their music listening. To illustrate the potential of WAM-Studio, we present a case study illustrating how this tool could be used by Hard-of-Hearing users to modify individual musical elements in a multitrack listening context to create a more enjoyable listening experience.

Keywords: Web Audio · DAWs · plugin architecture · Web standards

1 Introduction

The advent of synthesizers, samplers, and sequencers completely changed the paradigm in the music creation process [4]. Computer-assisted music production is a rapidly evolving field that utilizes computers to record, edit, and produce music. Many musicians embrace the use of Digital Audio Workstations (DAWs) for creating and manipulating digital audio and MIDI content to create music.

A DAW is a feature-rich software, resulting in a notably high complexity of use. It allows musicians to create multi-track songs by: (1) using audio samples directly (e.g., by incorporating an audio file into a track or recording from a microphone or sound card input), (2) synthesizing audio using virtual instruments (e.g., a software recreation of a piano), (3) mixing various audio tracks

J. Abdelnour Nocera et al. (Eds.): INTERACT 2023, LNCS 14142, pp. 101–110, 2023.
https://doi.org/10.1007/978-3-031-42280-5_6

together, and (4) applying sound effects to each track (e.g., reverb, frequency equalization, or auto-tune on vocals).

The four DAWs with the lion-share of the market (Logic Audio, Ableton, Pro Tools, Cubase)[1], are all large standalone software applications that must be installed. The first online DAWs appeared in 2008, using Flash technology, while the first DAWs using HTML5 and the Web Audio API for audio processing only appeared between 2015 and 2016 [3]. Online DAWs present distinct advantages over conventional DAWs such as lower barriers to entry and the ability to easily share and access projects from any device with an internet connection. A large variety of audio plugins (a kind of software module) extends the functionality of DAWs, offering users greater flexibility and control over their music production [2]. Since 1997, a significant market has developed for third-party plugin developers offering thousands of plugins that are compatible with all major DAWs.

A DAW is a complex application. A variety of individually adjustable parameters are available on each track, including volume, stereo panning, plugins, and their associated parameters, as well as the plugin order. Finally the "master track" sums all individual tracks together and presents an additional opportunity for plugin use and parameter tweaking. Given the amount of customization and complexity present in DAWs, they can be daunting applications for many users to engage with [4]. However, previous work has shown that even basic DAW controls can effectively be used to empower cochlear implant (CI) users to customize their music listening experience [7]. This is largely due to the reduced frequency resolution and speech-focused nature of CI processing.

Previous work has illustrated the similarities between end-user programming (EUP) tools and music composition tools such as DAWs [6,11,15]. EUP aims to solve the mismatch between end users' high expectations and specific domain knowledge but limited programming expertise [14]. Current practice shows that computer musicians become a kind of end-user programmer who face challenges that are similar to their professional counterparts in software engineering [8,12]. The difference is that DAWs aim to enable end users (musicians) to design, tailor, and customize audio. We suggest that some of the difficulties might be a result of the choice of programming paradigm. The user's ability to negotiate the constraints of the tool and assimilate its particular language is crucial in either case, whether engaging with visual metaphors or learning system-specific languages to build highly determined musical processes.

In this paper, we present a new Web-based digital audio workstation, WAM-Studio, that employs the visual programming paradigm for creating and editing multitrack audio. Section 2 introduces the main features of WAM-Studio and highlights how WAM-Studio enables users to create macro controls for adjusting many plugin parameters simultaneously (Sect. 2.4). Section 3 describes the overall tasks orchestration, demonstrating how the macro manager of WAM-Studio helps to simplify the process of adjusting various parameters at the same time. Apart from its conventional application in the music industry, we have discovered a potential utilization of the macro control feature to empower Hard-of-Hearing

---

[1] https://tinyurl.com/s4tbjzew.

users to customize their multi-track listening experience, as detailed in Sect. 4. The remaining sections compare WAM-Studio (Sect. 5) with similar tools before presenting conclusions and future work.

2 WAM-Studio's Main Features

Figure 1 shows WAM-Studio's user interface. This includes multiple tracks, their associated audio waveform, and a selection of available effect plugins (located inside the window titled *WAM2 Pedalboard* on the right-hand side) that can also be uniquely assigned and configured to each track.

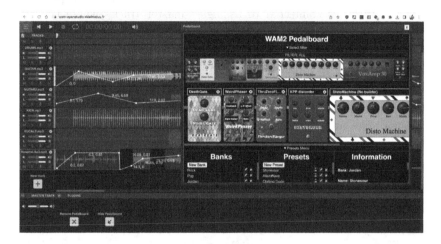

Fig. 1. Overview of WAM-Studio, featuring a set of tracks (on the left-side) and the associated effect plugins (the WAM2 Pedalboard window to the right-side).

2.1 Overview of Tracks

A track is a container for audio-related data that comes with an interactive display of these data, editing, and processing facilities as well as basic control parameters such as volume and left/right panning. WAM-Studio supports two types of tracks: **audio tracks** and **MIDI tracks**. Audio tracks contain recorded audio, such as a vocal take, a guitar recording, or any other type of audio signal, that is generally rendered graphically as waveforms. These audio tracks can be edited, processed, and mixed by copying, cutting, and pasting audio samples in the audio buffer associated with the track. The audio track's output can be further processed by a chain of audio effects, or plugins. As the name suggests, MIDI tracks do not contain audio information but rather MIDI data (the pitch of notes, velocity, and duration), which is used to control virtual instruments such as synthesizers. Figure 2 shows an isolated audio track with the waveform display of the associated audio buffer, and the default track controls/parameters on the left side (mute/solo, volume, stereo panning).

Fig. 2. A track in WAW-Studio.

Tracks can be added or removed from WAM-Studio, played in isolation, or with other tracks. They can also be armed for recording, allowing the armed track to record selected incoming audio while all other tracks can play along. Each track output is connected to a single "master track" where the global volume and panning of the final mix can be adjusted. It is also possible to apply audio effect plugins to the master track, allowing for a final adjustment of dynamics, frequency balancing, etc. A plugin, or multiple, can be applied to individual tracks, as shown in Fig. 3, to apply audio effects or synthesize audio (in the case of virtual instruments).

All audio effects and virtual instruments are plugins in the WAM-Studio. This design gives an extensive degree of control and adaptability and enables users to blend and manipulate the sound of each track with high precision and sophistication, thus making it easier to create intricate audio productions. So that, when one presses the play button of the DAW, all the tracks are rendered simultaneously, resulting in the final output signal, i.e. "the mix".

Fig. 3. Selecting a track and associating it to a chain of plugins.

2.2   Managing Plugin Chains

To apply a chain of effect plugins, WAM-Studio provides a special plugin, called *Pedalboard* [2], that acts as a central host for all other plugins, as illustrated by Fig. 3. The Pedalboard connects to a plugin server that sends back the list of plugins available as a JSON array of URIs. From this list of URIs, the Pedalboard plugin retrieves the descriptors and initializes the plugins to be displayed (upper part of Fig. 3). To create a chain of effects, plugins can be moved to the bottom part of the window in Fig. 3, re-ordered, and have their parameters set to create special effects.

Any configuration can be saved as a named preset (e.g. "guitar crunch 1"). Presets can be organized into banks ("rock", "funk", etc.). Naming and management of banks of presets is a task of the Pedalboard plugin. The parameters exposed correspond to the entire set of parameters of the active preset, with this whole process able to be automatad [3]. When a project is saved, the state of each track is saved, along with the state of the plugin configurations.

2.3   Recording, Dealing with Latency, Other Features

Recording in a DAW is one of the most delicate features to implement correctly. For instance, when recording a guitar track with real-time effects plugins, and playing over drum and bass tracks, it is crucial to ensure that the latency during recording is not noticeable as the musician must be able to play comfortably. Additionally, input latency is introduced as the time between a signal being emitted from a physical instrument and the time it is actually digitally recorded is non-trivial. This time depends on the sound card, operating system, drivers, audio buffer size, etc. The recorded audio must then be shifted back in time so that during playback, it is perfectly synchronized with the other tracks. There are many strategies to deal with latency issues [3] and WAM-Studio is able to automatically select the best strategy according to the context of use.

2.4   Macro Control for Synchronous Multi-track Management

A macro is a customized control that allows users to adjust a variety of settings at once, making it easier to manipulate sounds and effects in real-time, as illustrated in Fig. 4. A macro control refers to a way of controlling multiple parameters belonging to a plugin (effect or instrument) using a single knob, slider, or button. Therefore, when a parameter is assigned to a macro, a mapping is created that associates it to a specific range of values. When the macro is adjusted, the associated parameters change accordingly. For example, one might assign the filter cutoff, resonance, and envelope amount of a synth to a macro, so that it is possible to adjust all of these settings at once using a single knob called "timbre". Overall, macros are a powerful tool in WAM-Studio that can help streamline the workflow of sound production. WAM-Studio's macros are inspired by the system available in the *Ableton Live* DAW[2].

---

[2] https://www.youtube.com/watch?v=NOufylM_AEA&t=177s.

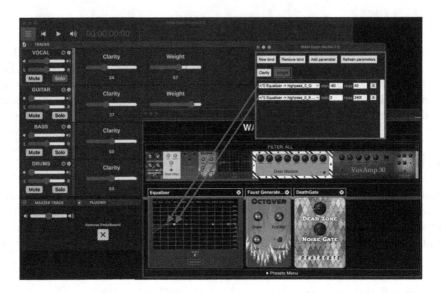

Fig. 4. Editing Macros in WAM-Studio: macro editor above the plugin chain.

Macros can be created, loaded, and saved dynamically within the WAM-Studio macro manager. They can be saved as presets, allowing custom settings to be quickly recalled and reused in future projects. When a project is saved, the current state and configuration of macros are saved as well.

3   Tasks for Creating a Multitrack Song in a Nutshell

The process of recording and mixing a new song is often iterative. Here are the different main tasks involved:

- **Hardware and instrument set-up:** Connect the computer, sound card, instruments, MIDI controllers, etc. and calibrate latency[3].
- **Create a new track:** For each audio element being recorded or played back;
- **Add plugins:** As needed on a track-by-track basis, such as audio effects for voice or virtual instrument to synthesise MIDI data, and adjust parameters;
- **Arm the track and record:** Record the desired section of audio and, if other tracks are present, recording is made while playing back other tracks in time.
- **Mix:** Adjust the volume and stereo panning of each track, and refine the sound by adjusting the plugin parameters of each track, including the master track.

All these steps are time-consuming, and require a certain amount of expertise and knowledge about each plugin. Macros play an important role in simplifying

---

[3] See at [3] details about why gear setup is required for every new hardware connected and security constraints prevent hardware discovery.

the often complicated process of plugin parameter adjustment, especially for users unfamiliar with audio processing. Unlike most existing DAWs, the WAM-Studio is a web application so that projects can be shared via simple http links, allowing remote collaborators to record and tweak settings. Therefore, macros play an additional role as they allow collaborators to create and share macros easily among collaborators, or even to the entire community of users.

4   Using Macro Controls to Customize Multi-track Listening for Cochlear Implant Users

More than 1 in 5 people worldwide are D/deaf or Heard-of-Hearing (DHH)[4], with many of them experiencing a large quality of life improvements through the use of hearing assistive technologies, such as hearing aids or cochlear implants (CIs) [18]. CIs are electronic devices that convert acoustic sound signals into electrical ones that are used to stimulate the cochlea. Currently, the internal audio processing on CIs is optimized for speech, resulting in the perceptual experiences of music and other complex auditory stimuli varying greatly among CI users [10,16]. CI users experience a maximum dynamic range that is reduced from 40–80 dB and a frequency resolution approximately 10–20 times lower than people with traditional hearing [5,19]. Therefore, CI users' perceptions of certain musical features, such as rhythm and tempo, are comparable to those with traditional hearing; however, the perception of timbral, harmonic, and melodic information differs greatly [9].

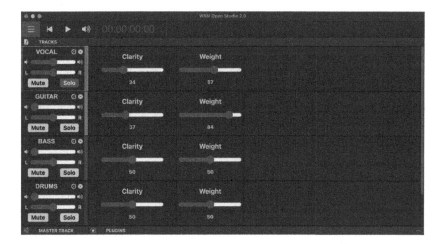

Fig. 5. Simplified view of WAM-Studio allowing DHH users to adjust sound properties.

---

[4] DHH is an expansive term for people with hearing loss or are otherwise aurally diverse, including those who identify as culturally Deaf and may use a signed language as their primary language.

Whilst the target users of WAM-Studio are musicians, we have found that macro controls could be useful for Hard-of-Hearing (HH) users. 10 CI users provided feedback and rated various mixes using a mix of qualitative and quantitative metrics, allowing us to determine mixing strategies and plug-in combinations that were often used in highly-rated mixes. Using WAM-Studio's macro controls to adjust certain sound parameters may increase CI user's enjoyment of listening to recorded music. In order to make the use of controls more easier to users, we have created a simplified view of macro controllers for HH users shown in as shown in Fig. 5. The first simplification is the replacement of the audio buffer waveform associated with the track by relevant macro sliders.

As we shall see in Fig. 5, the macro controllers are generated through previous research and given non-technical labels, such as "clarity", "punch", or "weight", allowing users to granularly adjust multiple settings of a plug-in chain using a single slider. A series of macros have been developed to be used on multiple instruments of varying genres. This includes macros tailored to both genre and instrumentation, for example:

- **"Clarity (Pop Vocal)"**: Increasing this macro increases the amount of 2kHz and 5kHz present in the signal, increases the wet/dry mix of a de-esser, and adds a medium-attack, slow-release compressor.
- **"Punch (Rock Drums)"**: Increases the compression ratio and wet/dry mix of a compressor with medium-fast attack and fast release, increasing the wet/dry mix on a sub-octave pitch-shifter, as well as the wet/dry mix on a saturation plug-in.
- **"Shine (Country Guitar)"**: This reduces the amount of sub-250 Hz information, increases the wet/dry mix on a one-octave-above pitch-shifter, and increases the ratio and wet/dry on a slow-attack slow-release compressor.

Several plugins have been developed specifically for HH users, such as an octaver and a tracking-EQ which boosts the fundamental frequency of the signal. The macros controls for HH users were created by the research team and advanced users using the WAM-plugin macro creator. The macro created can be exported for use in the simplified view that is aimed to reach a large audience of CI's users.

5   Related Work

In [17] a comparison of an online DAW (*Soundtrap*) with two native-based solutions (*Avid Cloud Collaboration* and *VST Transit*) showed that web-based DAWs "have the potential for widespread adoption and may even surpass the usage of the existing paradigms in professional audio mixing practice in future". Additionally, the use of a custom DAW for empowering HH users to customize multitrack listening is an original contribution to the field. Current approaches to enhance music enjoyment for CI users include adjustments to the internal signal processing on the CI itself, the creation of music composed specifically for CI users, and algorithmic pre-processing [13]. These approaches certainly have merits, but they fail to recognize the enormous diversity and variance in auditory perception and aesthetic preferences among CI users. Additionally, these processes assume a passive CI listener with a limited desire to play an active role in their listening experience.

WAM-Studio is an ongoing work, nevertheless, it is the only web-based DAW that features a macro system, that is open source, and that supports third-party-plugins. A survey of online DAWs can be found in [3] and a comparison with collaborative solutions based on native DAWs in [17].

6   Discussion and Future Work

In this paper, we have presented the design details and various features of WAM-Studio. Whilst the target users of WAM-Studio are musicians, we have found that some of its features (in particular the macro controls for multi-track management) could be useful for HH users. We illustrated how some macros can be created to help to adjust multitrack music using a simplified view of the WAM-Studio. This unexpected use of WAM-Studio presents an exciting opportunity to research questions of practical and theoretical importance about the uses of tools for creating sounds and customizing listening experiences. Of particular interest are CI users, as this user population is largely under-designed for, despite there being over 736K registered CI users (as of December 2019) [1]. CI users are additionally extremely heterogenous, potentially being well served by the level of customization and personalization offered by WAM-Studio.

It is worthy of notice that all tools described in this paper use recent Web technologies: W3C APIs WebAudio, WebMidi, Web Components, WebAssembly and have been developed as an open source demonstrator of what can be done on the web today in real time audio processing. WAM-Studio is readily available at http://annonymousURL.

Future work should include user testing with both versions of the tools including musicians and Hard-of-Hearing users, as well as additional focused user-testing and co-design sessions with CI users to adjust the mapping of various macros and further tailor the UI to increase the ease of use of the customized multitrack music player.

References

1. NIDCD fact sheet: Cochlear implants. National Institute of Deafness and Other Communication Disorders, March 2021
2. Buffa, M., Kouyoumdjian, P., Beauchet, Q., Forner, Y., Marynowic, M.: Making a guitar rack plugin -WebAudio Modules 2.0. In: Web Audio Conference 2022, Cannes, France, July 2022. https://hal.inria.fr/hal-03812948
3. Buffa, M., Vidal-Mazuy, A.: WAM-studio, a digital audio workstation (DAW) for the web. In: The Web Conference 2023 - DevTrack, Austin, Texas, USA (2023)
4. Burlet, G., Hindle, A.: An empirical study of end-user programmers in the computer music community. In: 2015 IEEE/ACM 12th Working Conference on Mining Software Repositories, pp. 292–302 (2015). https://doi.org/10.1109/MSR.2015.34

5. Hartmann, R., Kral, A.: Central responses to electrical stimulation. In: Zeng, F.G., Popper, A.N., Fay, R.R. (eds.) Cochlear Implants: Auditory Prostheses and Electric Hearing, vol. 20, pp. 213–285. Springer, New York (2004). https://doi.org/10.1007/978-0-387-22585-2_6

6. Hillerson, T.: In: Programming Sound with Pure Data, p. 196. The Pragmatic Bookshelf (2014)

7. Hwa, T.P., et al.: Novel web-based music re-engineering software for enhancement of music enjoyment among cochlear implantees. Otol. Neurotol. **42**(9), 1347–1354 (2021)

8. Ko, A.J., et al.: The state of the art in end-user software engineering. ACM Comput. Surv. **43**(3) (2011). https://doi.org/10.1145/1922649.1922658

9. Limb, C.J., Roy, A.T.: Technological, biological, and acoustical constraints to music perception in cochlear implant users. Hear. Res. **308**, 13–26 (2014)

10. Maarefvand, M., Marozeau, J., Blamey, P.J.: A cochlear implant user with exceptional musical hearing ability. Int. J. Audiol. **52**(6), 424–432 (2013)

11. Nash, C.: Manhattan: end-user programming for music. In: Proceedings of the International Conference on New Interfaces for Musical Expression, pp. 221–226. Zenodo, June 2014. https://doi.org/10.5281/zenodo.1178891

12. Nishino, H.: Cognitive issues in computer music programming. In: Proceedings of the International Conference on New Interfaces for Musical Expression, pp. 499–502. Zenodo, June 2011. https://doi.org/10.5281/zenodo.1178123

13. Nogueira, W., Nagathil, A., Martin, R.: Making music more accessible for cochlear implant listeners: recent developments. IEEE Signal Process. Mag. **36**(1), 115–127 (2018)

14. Paternò, F., Wulf, V. (eds.): New Perspectives in End-User Development. Springer, Cham (2017). https://doi.org/10.1007/978-3-319-60291-2

15. Sarkar, A.: In: Proceedings of the 27th Annual Conference of the Psychology of Programming Interest Group (PPIG 2016)

16. Spangmose, S., Hjortkjær, J., Marozeau, J.: Perception of musical tension in cochlear implant listeners. Front. Neurosci. **13**, 987 (2019)

17. Stickland, S., Athauda, R., Scott, N.: A new audio mixing paradigm: evaluation from professional practitioners' perspectives. Creat. Ind. J., 1–49 (2022)

18. WorldHealthOrganization: Deafness and hearing loss fact sheet, February 2023. https://www.who.int/news-room/fact-sheets/detail/deafness-and-hearing-loss

19. Zeng, F.G., Tang, Q., Lu, T.: Abnormal pitch perception produced by cochlear implant stimulation. PLoS ONE **9**(2), e88662 (2014)

Web Accessibility in Higher Education in Norway: To What Extent are University Websites Accessible?

Yavuz Inal[✉] and Anne Britt Torkildsby

Department of Design, Norwegian University of Science and Technology, Gjøvik, Norway
yavuz.inal@ntnu.no

Abstract. University websites should be accessible and easy to navigate for all users, regardless of their ability or disability. However, many university websites still have inaccessible features, even in countries where web accessibility is a legal requirement for public organizations. This study aims to investigate the accessibility of Norwegian university websites using both manual and tool-based evaluation methods. The results reveal significant accessibility violations in 6 of 10 websites, despite the implementation of regulatory frameworks since 2013. The most common violations include an absence of alternative text and very low contrast. Other frequent violations are a lack of keyboard support, lengthy navigation, empty buttons, missing form labels, empty links, and empty headings. These issues are considered critical and need to be addressed urgently because incorrect design elements and navigation problems can cause confusion and loss of control for users, particularly those relying on screen readers. The study indicates that the above-mentioned violations result from insufficient awareness and understanding of the accessibility prerequisites of individuals with a wide variety of characteristics.

Keywords: Web Accessibility · Accessibility Evaluation · Manual Evaluation · Tool-based Evaluation · Higher Education for All · University Websites

1 Introduction

University websites serve a multifaceted function, acting as a central information hub for students, providing access to everything from course materials to campus events and resources. With the increasing reliance on digital services, students with disabilities have a greater desire to access and engage with online information and services [14], i.e., they require assistive technologies adapted to their specific needs. Therefore, it is essential for universities to provide universally designed websites and thus meet the needs of "all people to the greatest extent possible, without the need for adaptation or specialized design" [23]. In the context of higher education, web accessibility aims to ensure inclusive learning by enabling all current and prospective students to access, perceive, navigate, and interact with university websites effectively, efficiently, and satisfactorily.

© The Author(s), under exclusive license to Springer Nature Switzerland AG 2023
J. Abdelnour Nocera et al. (Eds.): INTERACT 2023, LNCS 14142, pp. 111–122, 2023.
https://doi.org/10.1007/978-3-031-42280-5_7

To support academic success for all students, universities must guarantee that necessary information, announcements, course content, and online services are accessible with ease. By prioritizing web accessibility, universities can promote inclusive lifelong learning and create a positive learning environment, especially for those at risk of being excluded [12, 16, 18].

The World Wide Web Consortium (W3C) is recognized as the leading advocate for web accessibility and recommends accessibility guidelines for websites and equal access [28]. The guidelines include essential features that must be incorporated and are supported by technical specifications and educational materials to promote the development of accessible websites. However, despite regulatory frameworks for public and private organizations implemented for years in many countries [29], unmet accessibility guidelines - and thereby inaccessible features on university websites continue to hinder access, hence segregating and stigmatizing users. For instance, Laamanen et al. [17] explored the accessibility of all Finnish higher education institutions' homepages. The study revealed that the evaluated websites did not meet current accessibility requirements, there were in fact significant variations among the institutions regarding accessibility compliance. A more comprehensive study conducted by Acosta-Vargas et al. [1] on higher education institutions in Latin America found that the evaluated websites violated many checkpoints in the accessibility guidelines, especially the one for alternative text. Similarly, Alim [3] evaluated the web accessibility of the top research-intensive universities in the United Kingdom and found that the most common violations were related to insufficient text alternatives for non-textual content, contrast problems, and the ability of webpages to work with upcoming technologies and tools.

Ismailova and Inal [12] tested the web accessibility of top universities in Kyrgyzstan, Kazakhstan, Azerbaijan, and Turkey and discovered that most websites failed to meet the guidelines. The distribution of errors revealed that they mostly stemmed from failing to adhere to success criteria pertaining to non-text elements and modifying text sizes. In 2007, 2008, and 2009, Espadinha et al. [7] tested the accessibility of all Portuguese public university websites' landing pages aiming to detect the difference in accessibility compliance. Although the universities showed significant progress during the assessment period, the overall accessibility results were not at an acceptable level. In fact, only 12.5% of the universities supported services to students with a wide variety of characteristics. In another longitudinal study, Thompson et al. [22] assessed the accessibility of college and university websites in the United States over a five-year period. The findings revealed a noticeable improvement in accessibility according to certain measures. However, other measures demonstrated a deterioration in accessibility, such as full keyboard support.

The Norwegian government has shown a significant commitment to improving the quality of university websites by implementing regulatory frameworks for web accessibility. In 2013, Norway introduced legislation to force public and private sectors to meet accessibility guidelines [29]; and as of February 2023, all organizations must have an accessibility statement in place on their websites [25]. Nevertheless, previous research has consistently shown that professionals in general have low awareness of the field [8], and, moreover, the websites have significant accessibility issues [10, 19, 21]. This goes against national regulations and must be fixed to offer fully accessible online services to everyone in society. Since universities have the primary responsibility to provide information for all prospective and current students - no matter their skills or abilities, it is crucial to explore to what extent they have designed their websites to ensure accessibility, usability, and inclusion. Thus, in this study, ten Norwegian university websites were evaluated by performing manual and tool-based evaluations.

2 Methods

By conducting manual and automated tests, ten Norwegian universities - owned by the Ministry of Education and Research - were assessed regarding their compliance with WCAG 2.1 level AA [30]. The list of universities was obtained from the website of the Directorate for Higher Education and Skills [20], and all tests were conducted in February 2023. The names of the universities are the Norwegian University of Science and Technology (NTNU), Norwegian University of Life Sciences (NMBU), University of Bergen (UiB), University of Oslo (UiO), University of Stavanger (UiS), University of Tromsø - The Arctic University of Norway (UiT), University of Agder (UiA), Nord University (Nord), University of South-Eastern Norway (USN), Oslo Metropolitan University (OsloMet).

The regulations say that public websites must provide complete keyboard support and be compatible with assistive technologies, such as screen readers, to ensure easy access and navigation for individuals who are blind, visually impaired, or otherwise rely on a keyboard. In this regard, a manual evaluation was conducted using a screen reader to identify accessibility violations in detail - combined with a commonly used online evaluation tool called WAVE [31]. By performing both manual and tool-based assessments, we aimed to identify as many accessibility violations as possible based on the WCAG guidelines.

2.1 Scope of the Evaluation

To ensure a practical evaluation framework, representative samples of pages were selected from each university website rather than testing all pages. This is common practice, followed by many researchers when evaluating website accessibility. Therefore, ten representative homepages from each university website were evaluated, including the homepages for the university, library, faculty, department, staff, admission for a bachelor's program, admission for a master's program, admission for a Ph.D. program, exchange agreement, and student life, respectively. Homepages are most often the visitors' first point of contact before navigating to other pages; thus, they must comply with the accessibility guidelines. Likewise, inaccessible homepages, whether partially or completely, can cause difficulties when trying to access other website pages. Furthermore, accessibility violations are often repeated when two pages have the same layout and structure [10], i.e., selected homepages from each university have their unique layout, structure, menu design, and content flow, thereby representing many subpages on the respective university website. Please note that these representative pages were deemed essential by current and prospective students seeking information about a university.

2.2 Measures

Online tools have been employed to evaluate website accessibility for years and provide useful feedback on the identified accessibility violations and help developers in rectifying the detected issues. WAVE (Web Accessibility Evaluation) has been extensively used in several accessibility studies [10, 15, 33] and was utilized to evaluate accessibility compliance in this study. The tool generates proposals to fix errors and alerts based on WCAG compliance and offers comprehensive accessibility evaluation information such as errors, contrast errors, alerts, features, structural elements, and ARIA (accessible rich internet applications). To conduct this research, we established the evaluation criteria to identify the number of errors on evaluated pages that compromise WCAG 2.1 conformance level AA.

However, previous research demonstrates that less than half of the available accessibility errors are detected by online tools [13, 27]. Therefore, elucidating the outcomes of accessibility evaluation derived from online tools requires vigilant scrutiny. For example, online evaluation tools can detect if the alternative text is linked to an image but cannot judge its accuracy without interpreting the image's content. Consequently, manual evaluation is always needed to provide higher accuracy and coverage of accessibility issues [13, 27]. It is, moreover, the most accurate and reliable way of identifying accessibility issues on a website [26]. In this study, we used the Google Chrome Screen Reader to test each selected homepage individually. Afterward, we attempted to access each selected homepage from their respective websites.

3 Results

3.1 Manual Evaluation (with a Screen Reader)

We classified the various issues detected in the evaluation into different groups as per the categorization framework defined by WebAim [32]. These groups included focus indicators, navigation order, items that should not receive keyboard focus, inaccessible custom widgets, and lengthy navigation. The tests indicated that the provision of alternative text for non-textual content on the websites must be more consistent. Images that lack descriptive information, especially when text is already present within the image, should have alternative text to comply with regulations. Also, some web pages provided comprehensive descriptions of their images, while others did not include alternative text for non-textual content - or offered only perfunctory descriptions. There were tendencies for some websites to use animations; however, these elements were either not focusable or did not contain alternative text. Needless to say that providing accurate and comprehensive alternative text consistently for images, videos, and other non-textual content is crucial for users who rely on screen readers.

The websites also exhibited problems with keyboard access, making it difficult to follow the order of the content. On some pages, the keyboard focus shifted abruptly between different sections of the page, causing confusion and making it hard to determine the precise location. To ensure that website users can access all information on a page, regardless of their mode of access, websites must be designed to accommodate keyboard-based navigation. Additionally, some websites demonstrated illogical and unintuitive default keyboard navigation orders, particularly evident in the tabbing order - deviating from the standard visual flow from top to bottom and left to right. In some instances, some crucial areas were skipped, while insignificant portions were read aloud. Furthermore, some websites featured inaccessible custom widgets, such as buttons, hamburger menus, and chat bubbles.

A notable accessibility challenge in web design involves the limited functionality of screen readers, which may fail to accurately capture and convey certain text elements. Consequently, users who fully rely on screen readers may require assistance in interpreting the page content and may thus face incomplete or inaccurate information. The evaluation showed instances where screen readers selectively ignored the critical text and focused solely on links present on the page. Given the significance of these challenges, websites must be optimized to ensure that all content is accessible. Failure to do so can result in substantial barriers to accessing and comprehending important information, hence excluding and discriminating against screen readers.

The study also identified challenges in the navigation process on many of the websites. i.e., the abundance of interactive elements requires users to tab through numerous components, a process which exacerbates the challenge of accessing the desired information. Although the 'skip to the main content' feature enables easy keyboard navigation, it could have been more effective on some websites. In sum, this confuses the user's location on the page, disrupts their sense of orientation, forces them to spend additional time figuring out their position, and highlights the need for such features.

3.2 Tool-Based Evaluation

The tool-based evaluation generally complemented the manual review by addressing similar issues. The results showed that none of the university websites were error-free (see Table 1). As a matter of fact, all websites displayed a certain number of errors in web accessibility and were furthermore not consistent with accessibility guidelines. In total, the University of Stavanger had the highest number of checkpoint violations (n = 1661), followed by the Norwegian University of Life Sciences (n = 465), Nord University (n = 111), the University of Adger (n = 97), the University of South-Eastern Norway (n = 75), and the University of Bergen (n = 72). Conversely, the Norwegian University of Science and Technology (n = 13), the University of Oslo (n = 18), Oslo Metropolitan University (n = 24), and the University of Tromsø - The Arctic University of Norway (n = 25) contained the least number of violations.

The most frequent accessibility issue detected (n = 1464) was 'very low contrast', which relates to 1.4.3 Contrast (minimum) at the conformance Level AA. Insufficient contrast between image and text color negatively impacts user experience, particularly for individuals with limited vision or color deficiency. Therefore, background and foreground color combinations should be suitable for all users. The University of Stavanger (n = 796) and the Norwegian University of Life Sciences (n = 408) had the highest number of issues with very low contrast, while the Norwegian University of Science and Technology and Oslo Metropolitan University only had three contrast errors each.

Table 1. Frequently repeated errors across the universities

Error types	NTNU	NMBU	UiB	UiO	UiS	UiT	UiA	Nord	USN	OsloMet
Very low contrast	3	408	72	15	796	17	65	52	33	3
Linked image missing alternative text	–	3	–	1	780	–	4	12	2	–
Empty link	–	1	–	–	25	–	1	30	10	9
Missing alternative text	–	25	–	–	34	–	–	7	2	–
Empty button	10	27	–	–	–	–	14	–	–	10
Missing form label	–	–	–	2	2	8	11	2	9	2
Empty heading	–	1	–	–	9	–	1	8	12	–
Image map area missing alternative text	–	–	–	–	15	–	–	–	–	–
Language missing or invalid	–	–	–	–	–	–	–	–	7	–

The 'linked image missing alternative text' error was the second-highest error incidence, relevant to 1.1.1 Non-text Content (Level A) and 2.4.4 Link Purpose (Level A). This error occurs when images and links lack alternative text and images within a link - that do not contain alternative text, results in an empty link. Another common error was the absence of alternative text, indicating that the universities did not provide descriptive text for non-text content. Without this, non-text content will be unavailable to screen readers. Hence, it is necessary to add the 'alt' attribute to each non-text content along with an adequate and equivalent description describing the content, as well as presenting the function of the link.

Other errors with a high incidence were 'empty link' (n = 76), 'missing alternative text' (n = 68), 'empty button' (n = 61), 'missing form label' (n = 36), and 'empty heading' (n = 31). Relevant checkpoints include 1.1.1 Non-text Content (Level A), 1.3.1 Info and Relationships (Level A), and 2.4.4 Link Purpose (Level A). Only one university included the following errors; 'image map area missing alternative text' (n = 15), relevant to 1.1.1 Non-text Content and 2.4.4 Link Purpose, and 'language missing or invalid' (n

= 7), relevant to 3.1.1 Language of Page. These errors can negatively impact the ability of people to comprehend the content and navigate the website efficiently. Sufficient descriptions must accompany all design elements to prevent the loss of control and confusion for screen readers. Rectifying these issues can be achieved by incorporating a descriptive title for the form element and providing text within the link.

Table 2. Accessibility errors identified on evaluated homepages

Evaluated homepages	NTNU	NMBU	UiB	UiO	UiS	UiT	UiA	Nord	USN	OsloMet
Homepage	3	66	8	3	561	1	13	10	9	2
Library	1	55	9	2	445	11	9	12	10	3
Faculty	2	59	10	0	184	3	16	17	12	2
Department	1	62	4	0	254	3	13	3	6	2
Staff	1	52	4	0	2	1	5	4	5	2
Admission (bachelor)	1	50	4	3	27	1	11	11	7	2
Admission (master's)	1	36	4	3	29	1	8	8	7	2
Admission (PhD)	1	36	10	0	25	1	6	27	5	2
Exchange study	1	48	8	4	110	1	8	14	5	4
Student life	1	1	11	3	24	2	8	5	9	3

Moreover, the findings indicate that the university homepages exhibited the highest number of accessibility errors (n = 676), followed by the library (n = 557), department (n = 348), and faculty (n = 305) homepages (Table 2). Among the universities, the highest number was detected on the University of Stavanger homepage (n = 561), followed by the Norwegian University of Life Sciences (n = 66). Conversely, the homepages of the University of Tromsø - The Arctic University of Norway (n = 1) and Oslo Metropolitan University (n = 2) had the least number of errors. The student life (n = 67) and staff (n = 76) homepages were found to have the least accessibility issues. In terms of admission homepages, the bachelor's, master's, and Ph.D. program admission pages contained 117, 99, and 113 accessibility errors, respectively. These results suggest that university homepages are particularly prone to accessibility errors, and efforts should be made as soon as possible to enhance the accessibility of these pages - thus ensuring a more inclusive and user-friendly online experience for all users.

4 Discussion

This study explored the current state of accessibility of ten Norwegian university websites by performing both manual and tool-based evaluations to determine their level of compliance with WCAG 2.1 Level AA. The results showed that all websites failed to meet accessibility compliance, i.e., they lacked the required features to adhere to the recommended level of accessibility conformity and had a considerable number of accessibility errors. Consequently, this implies that the impact on user navigation, particularly for those with visual impairment and blindness, is adverse.

The most common errors were related to providing a text equivalent for non-text content, as outlined in WCAG 2.1 checkpoint 1.1.1 Non-text content. The main violations identified in the tool-based evaluation included missing alternative text, linked images missing alternative text, and image map areas missing alternative text - findings that are consistent with previous research [1, 2, 12, 17, 18]. Moreover, the manual evaluation revealed that the websites show inconsistency in offering alternative text for non-textual content to further enhance the use of screen readers. Some pages on the same website provided detailed descriptions for their images, while others did not - or provided only brief descriptions that may not accurately convey the image's essence and content. Previous research supports this finding and concludes that people with visual impairments cannot comprehend the content properly unless an adequate and equivalent description of non-text content is provided [10].

Concerning design elements, the tool-based evaluation identified empty links, empty buttons, empty headings, and missing form labels as the primary accessibility violations, which are all necessary to provide clear and relevant information on a website. Alhadreti [2] and Calvo et al. [4] reported that the lack of adequate description for design elements and inappropriate use of headings is the most commonly violated accessibility error, respectively. Both issues can leave screen readers feeling disoriented, severely impacting their engagement and performance. The tool-based evaluation also revealed that all websites had low contrast between the background color and foreground text color, which causes problems for users with low vision and color deficiency. This finding aligns with those of Laamanen et al. [17], who identified inadequate color contrast of the text and background on higher education institutions' web pages, with 58% of the total errors relating to low color contrast. Likewise, the research of Alim [3] reported that almost three-quarters of the university websites contained contrast errors - with an average of nine errors.

Regarding keyboard access, the manual evaluation identified numerous issues that negatively impact screen readers' comprehension of the website's structure. On some pages, the content order was extra challenging to follow; and, in some cases, the keyboard focus suddenly changed between different sections leading to confusion and difficulty pinpointing the exact location. Besides, some websites had unintuitive keyboard navigation orders, which should be structured from top to bottom and left to right. These findings are consistent with Parajuli and Eika's [19] study, where navigation was identified as the most frustrating issue screen readers encounter when accessing websites. Furthermore, some websites lacked functional focus indicators - notably with sufficient color contrast - enabling users to navigate through interactive elements such as links, buttons, images, and input fields on the page.

Last but not least, testing the websites using a screen reader showed that the navigation process often was excessively lengthy, which creates a significant obstacle for screen readers. Adding a 'skip to main content' feature is an effective way to improve the navigation of websites. However, some of the websites were found to have implemented this feature ineffectively. This improper usage may lead to additional user confusion and, moreover, users feeling a lack of control over their browsing experience.

Taken together, these findings clearly show that an absence of conformity with the accessibility guidelines results in web accessibility barriers that may impact an individual's daily life to various extents. The violations prevent users, particularly those with visual impairments, blindness, and difficulties in controlling mouse movements due to various physical and motor conditions, from easily accessing and navigating any text, image, audio, video, or program on a web page. Considering the fact that all people have the same rights when it comes to accessing online information and services provided by public institutions, e.g., universities and university colleges, the urgent need for equal access to information for all cannot be ignored to the same degree as today. Inal and Ismailova [9] suggest that web accessibility is an indication of human development, measuring various countries' levels of social and economic growth. Moreover, seeing that the EU's Action plan on human rights and democracy was implemented in 2020 [6], prioritizing human rights and democracy ought to be the primary goal for every European country by now.

Despite the fact that legal obligation has been implemented in many countries - Norway included - to ensure the accessibility of web content, and furthermore that country-specific regulations have been instrumental in promoting awareness among practitioners concerning implementing accessibility practices in the web development process [2, 8], a significant number of websites still remain inaccessible. Needless to say that this is a serious situation that hampers diversity, equity, and inclusion in digital society worldwide [e.g., 3, 10, 17]. Moreover, it indicates that enacting laws and regulations at the national level does not necessarily guarantee accessibility, and additionally, that changing practitioners' mindsets, etc., might take more time and effort than first expected. That said, previous studies show that raising awareness among practitioners regarding the importance of accessibility leads to the incorporation of accessibility attributes into digital systems [11, 17], and so we argue that a positive change is possible.

5   Conclusion and Recommendations for Further Work

This study aimed to assess the accessibility of ten university websites in Norway through a combination of manual and tool-based evaluations conducted in accordance with WCAG compliance. Overall, none of the university websites passed the test and the most common violations were lack of alternative text and very low contrast. As discussed above, the results from this study provide clear evidence that not adhering to accessibility guidelines creates obstacles to web accessibility - with a variety of negative consequences for the users. Thus, we recommend improvements in the following key areas:

- Provide text equivalents for non-text content
- Address design element issues

- Optimize keyboard access
- Streamline navigation process
- Raise awareness and provide education amongst all stakeholders
- Embrace inclusive education - therefore, accepting diversity amongst students

In line with the UN's focus on "leaving no one behind" [24] and the European higher education policies, that strongly promote inclusive education to provide equal opportunities for diverse students [5], the universities examined in this study should consider increasing both understanding *for* - and awareness *of* the accessibility requirements to further enhance the accessibility, usability, and inclusion of their websites. Seeing that most of the detected errors in this study were associated with a lack of awareness and a general understanding of the accessibility prerequisites of people regardless of skills or abilities, we find it imperative to keep educating and training all stakeholders - including content editors, designers, developers, and managers - in the ecosystem to ensure an even more accessible web, thus promoting access and improved outcomes for all students in higher education in Norway. Also, we call upon the research society to conduct more studies focusing on user evaluation, including potential users with various disabilities, as this would help to understand the bigger picture and why it is important.

References

1. Acosta-Vargas, P., Acosta, T., Lujan-Mora, S.: Challenges to assess accessibility in higher education websites: a comparative study of Latin America universities. IEEE Access **6**, 36500–36508 (2018). https://doi.org/10.1109/ACCESS.2018.2848978
2. Alhadreti, O.: Accessibility, performance and engagement evaluation of Saudi higher education websites: a comparative study of state and private institutions. Univ. Access Inf. Soc., 1–18 (2023). https://doi.org/10.1007/s10209-023-00971-6
3. Alim, S.: Web accessibility of the top research-intensive universities in the UK. SAGE Open **11**(4), 1–18 (2021). https://doi.org/10.1177/21582440211056614
4. Calvo, R., Iglesias, A., Moreno, L.: Accessibility barriers for users of screen readers in the Moodle learning content management system. Univ. Access Inf. Soc. **13**, 315–327 (2014). https://doi.org/10.1007/s10209-013-0314-3
5. ECEDS (European Commission: European Disability Strategy) 2010–2020: A renewed commitment to a barrier-free Europe. https://www.cedefop.europa.eu/en/news/european-disability-strategy-2010-2020-renewed-commitment-barrier-free-europe. Accessed 11 Mar 2023
6. EEAS - EU Action plan on human rights and democracy. High Representative of the European Union for Foreign Affairs and Security Policy and the European Commission. EEAS, Brussels (2020)
7. Espadinha, C., Pereira, L.M., Da Silva, F.M., Lopes, J.B.: Accessibility of Portuguese public universities' sites. Disabil. Rehabil. **33**(6), 475–485 (2011). https://doi.org/10.3109/09638288.2010.498554
8. Inal, Y., Guribye, F., Rajanen, D., Rajanen, M., Rost, M.: Perspectives and practices of digital accessibility: a survey of user experience professionals in Nordic countries. In: Proceedings of the 11th Nordic Conference on Human-Computer Interaction: Shaping Experiences, Shaping Society, pp. 1–11. ACM (2020). https://doi.org/10.1145/3419249.3420119
9. Inal, Y., Ismailova, R.: Effect of human development level of countries on the web accessibility and quality in use of their municipality websites. J. Ambient. Intell. Humaniz. Comput. **11**, 1657–1667 (2020). https://doi.org/10.1007/s12652-019-01284-4

10. Inal, Y., Mishra, D., Torkildsby, A.B.: An Analysis of web content accessibility of municipality websites for people with disabilities in Norway: web accessibility of Norwegian municipality websites. In: Proceedings of the 12th Nordic Human-Computer Interaction Conference, pp. 1–12. ACM (2022). https://doi.org/10.1145/3546155.3547272

11. Inal, Y., Rızvanoğlu, K., Yesilada, Y.: Web accessibility in Turkey: awareness, understanding and practices of user experience professionals. Univ. Access Inf. Soc. **18**, 387–398 (2019). https://doi.org/10.1007/s10209-017-0603-3

12. Ismailova, R., Inal, Y.: Accessibility evaluation of top university websites: a comparative study of Kyrgyzstan, Azerbaijan, Kazakhstan and Turkey. Univ. Access Inf. Soc. **17**, 437–445 (2018). https://doi.org/10.1007/s10209-017-0541-0

13. Ismailova, R., Inal, Y.: Comparison of online accessibility evaluation tools: an analysis of tool effectiveness. IEEE Access **10**, 58233–58239 (2022). https://doi.org/10.1109/ACCESS.2022.3179375

14. Korbel, D.M., Lucia, J.H., Wenzel, C.M., Anderson, B.G.: Collaboration strategies to facilitate successful transition of students with disabilities in a changing higher education environment. N. Dir. High. Educ. **154**(2), 17–25 (2011)

15. Król, K., Zdonek, D.: Local government website accessibility - evidence from Poland. Administrative Sciences **10**(2), 22 (2020). https://doi.org/10.3390/admsci10020022

16. Kuppusamy, K.S., Balaji, V.: Evaluating web accessibility of educational institutions websites using a variable magnitude approach. Univ. Access Inf. Soc. **22**, 241–250 (2023). https://doi.org/10.1007/s10209-021-00812-4

17. Laamanen, M., Ladonlahti, T., Puupponen, H., Kärkkäinen, T.: Does the law matter? An empirical study on the accessibility of Finnish higher education institutions' web pages. Univ. Access Inf. Soc., 1–17 (2022). https://doi.org/10.1007/s10209-022-00931-6

18. Laufer Nir, H., Rimmerman, A.: Evaluation of web content accessibility in an Israeli institution of higher education. Univ. Access Inf. Soc. **17**, 663–673 (2018). https://doi.org/10.1007/s10209-018-0615-7

19. Parajuli, P., Eika, E.: A comparative study of accessibility and usability of Norwegian university websites for screen reader users based on user experience and automated assessment. In Universal Access in Human-Computer Interaction. Design Approaches and Supporting Technologies: 14th International Conference, UAHCI 2020, Held as Part of the 22nd HCI International Conference, HCII 2020, Copenhagen, Denmark, vol. 12188, pp. 300–310. Springer, Cham (2020). https://doi.org/10.1007/978-3-030-49282-3_21

20. The Directorate for Higher Education and Skills (DHES). https://dbh.hkdir.no/

21. The Norwegian Digitalization Agency (Digdir). Digitale barrierar på norske nettstader 2018: Status for universell utforming. https://www.digdir.no/media/514/download. Accessed 12 Mar 2023

22. Thompson, T., Burgstahler, S., Moore, E.J.: Web accessibility: a longitudinal study of college and university home pages in the Northwestern United States. Disabil. Rehabil. Assist. Technol. **5**(2), 108–114 (2010). https://doi.org/10.3109/17483100903387424

23. UN Department of Economic and Social Affairs Disability: Convention on the Rights of Persons with Disabilities (CRPD), Article 2 - Definitions.https://www.un.org/development/desa/disabilities/convention-on-the-rights-of-persons-with-disabilities/article-2-definitions.html. Accessed 14 Apr 2023

24. UN Sustainable Development Group (UNSDG): Universal values principle two: leave no one behind. https://unsdg.un.org/2030-agenda/universal-values/leave-no-one-behind. Accessed 11 Apr 2023

25. Uutilsynet. https://www.uutilsynet.no/regelverk/gjeldende-regelverk-og-krav/746. Accessed 15 Mar 2023

26. Verkijika, S.F., De Wet, L.: Determining the accessibility of e-government websites in Sub-Saharan Africa against WCAG 2.0 standard. Int. J. Electr. Gov. Res. (IJEGR) **13**(1), 52–68 (2017). https://doi.org/10.4018/IJEGR.2017010104

27. Vigo, M., Brown, J., Conway, V.: Benchmarking web accessibility evaluation tools: measuring the harm of sole reliance on automated tests. In: Proceedings of the 10th International Cross-Disciplinary Conference Web Accessibility, pp. 1–10 (2013). https://doi.org/10.1145/2461121.2461124

28. W3C WAI Guidelines. WCAG 2 overview. https://www.w3.org/WAI/standards-guidelines/wcag/. Accessed 2 Feb 2023

29. W3C WAI Policy: Web Accessibility Laws & Policies. https://www.w3.org/WAI/policies/. Accessed 11 Mar 2023

30. W3C WCAG 2.1 Understanding Docs. https://www.w3.org/WAI/WCAG21/Understanding/. Accessed 11 Mar 2023

31. WAVE (Web accessibility evaluation tool). https://wave.webaim.org/. Accessed 5 Feb 2023

32. WebAim - Keyboard Accessibility. https://webaim.org/techniques/keyboard/#testing. Accessed 5 Feb 2023

33. Youngblood, N.E., Youngblood, S.A.: User experience and accessibility: an analysis of county web portals. J. Usability Stud. **9**(1), 25–41 (2013)

Wesee: Digital Cultural Heritage Interpretation for Blind and Low Vision People

Yalan Luo[1], Weiyue Lin[2], Yuhan Liu[1], Xiaomei Nie[1](✉),
Xiang Qian[1](✉), and Hanyu Guo[1]

[1] Tsinghua Shenzhen International Graduate School, Tsinghua University,
Guangdong, China
luoyl20@mails.tsinghua.edu.cn,
{nie.xiaomei,qian.xiang}@sz.tsinghua.edu.cn
[2] Peking University, Beijing, China
linweiyue@stu.pku.edu.cn

Abstract. When museums worldwide are introducing digital technology to help the heritage interpretation for visitors, blind and low vision (BLV) people are still excluded by various challenges. What BLV people need in museums is an in-depth learning and independent exploration process. However, the audio guide provided in museums is mostly simple descriptions, and cultural relics can not be touched, which cannot meet the cultural needs of BLV people. In this paper, we designed and implemented *Wesee*, an interactive platform that combined interactive narrative, voice interaction, and tactile interaction, to help BLV people experience cultural heritage more independently and interactively. The preliminary evaluation was conducted with 20 BLV participants. The results show that this platform is effective in helping BLV people experience cultural heritage.

Keywords: Multi-model interaction · Digital cultural interpretation · Blind and low vision

1   Introduction

The needs of blind and low vision (BLV) people are no different from those of sighted people when visiting museums. People won't lose interest in cultural heritage and historical knowledge because of blindness [8]. There have been growing efforts to make museums and cultural heritages accessible to BLV people. Museums often provide accessible services, including audio guides, tactile books, and accessible talks [5]. Some regular group tours offer special guides and explanation services [6]. However, there is still a gap between the current accessible design in

Y. Luo and W. Lin–Co-authors Supported by Shenzhen Key Laboratory of next-generation interactive media innovative technology (No: ZDSYS20210623092001004).

J. Abdelnour Nocera et al. (Eds.): INTERACT 2023, LNCS 14142, pp. 123–131, 2023.
https://doi.org/10.1007/978-3-031-42280-5_8

museums and the needs of BLV people. The audio introduction provided to BLV visitors is relatively plain and simple, which cannot meet their profound cultural learning needs [2]. Although museums offer information that can be heard and touched, they are still unable to visit independently. Research showed that only 5% of BLV people in Europe visited museums [4]. BLV people are a group from different backgrounds, what they need is diverse and interactive content rather than a unified introduction [8].

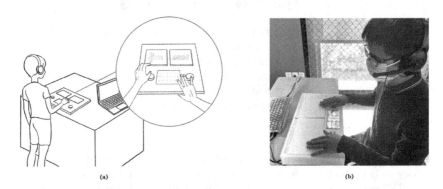

Fig. 1. (a): *Wesee* is an interactive platform designed and implemented for the BLV people to help them experience cultural heritage more independently and interactively; (b): A blind participant was interacting with *Wesee*.

Digital technology should be more widely used to improve the accessibility of museums and enable BLV people to visit more independently. Hafizur Rahaman et al. proposed an interpretive framework (PrEDiC) [10] to help users attain the desired perceptual sense of heritage culture. This framework has been applied to many digital heritage projects and proved effective in interpreting digital cultural heritage. Based on this framework, we designed and implemented *Wesee* (Fig. 1), an interactive platform that can be used in museums to help BLV people experience cultural heritage more independently and interactively. Through *Wesee*, BLV people can experience interactive narration and perform auditory-tactile interaction. In addition, a comparative experiment was conducted with 20 BLV participants to verify the effectiveness of *Wesee*. The results show that this platform is effective in helping BLV people experience cultural heritage.

2   Related Work

Over the years, the accessibility of museums has garnered increasing attention. Existing works have offered approaches to help BLV people visit museums and learn about cultural relics. Kyle Rector et al. realized a live installation [11] that can provide different audio descriptions according to the spatial distance between BLV visitors and artworks to help them feel more immersed during their appreciation. Using a 3D printing board combined with a fingertip sensor, Tooteko [3] provided a cultural heritage accessible design that provided audio descriptions based on where BLV visitors are touching. The Victoria & Albert Museum proposed several measures for BLV visitors to improve the museum's accessibility, including audio description, tactile books, accessible talks, and events [5]. Art Beyond Vision is Fine Arts Houston's monthly gallery tour for BLV visitors [6] to explore exhibits through verbal descriptions and combining observations. Furthermore, several works provided facilities for the wayfinding of BLV visitors. To help BLV visitors better access multidimensional information, Xiyue Wang et al. designed 3D maps for each floor of a museum [13], and BLV visitors can stack them or place them on a touch screen to learn about different levels of detail. Saki Asakawa et al. developed a solution that can continuously track the location of BLV people and link the navigation and the audio introduction of the different exhibits [1].

Previous works have improved the experience of BLV people in visiting museums in different ways. However, the BLVs prefer to explore the museum's cultural heritage independently and own a complete experience [2]. One study by Vaz et al. examined the trend in visiting museums from the perspective of BLV visitors [12]. They found that museums worldwide continue to provide innovative experiences for the sighted. However, to varying degrees, millions of BLV people still face difficulties in accessing the information they want and enjoying the exhibits independently. A study investigating BLV people in museums and galleries [2] reported that the accessible education of museums could not meet the needs of BLV people because the audio tours were often general and simple, and what they want was a more comprehensive and in-depth introduction. Moreover, museums' one-to-one tour guide service often lacks clear publicity and contact information. For various reasons, BLV people need to spend a lot of time and energy to get the resources and information they want in museums and exhibitions.

In recent years, human-computer interactions have been constantly applied in museums to improve cultural heritage interpretation as an effective learning and communication tool that increases sighted visitors' awareness and empathy to heritage [9]. Developments in digital technology and human-computer interaction have also opened up many new possibilities for museum experiences for BLV people. However, the process of digital heritage interpretation for BLV people has not been discussed. Based on a digital heritage interpretation framework (PrEDiC) [10] that has been proposed, we implemented an interactive platform called *Wesee*. This platform can be used in museums to help BLV people experience cultural heritage more independently and interactively.

3   Wesee

We designed and implemented a platform named *Wesee* (Fig. 2). The platform consists of a tactile integration board, a headset, and a control system that control the overall process. *Wesee* is designed according to the interpretive framework (PrEDiC) proposed by Hafizur Rahaman in 2018 [10], which puts forward a set of methods to help the users to attain the desired perceptual sense of heritage culture and artifacts. Presentation, culture learning, embodiment, and dialog interaction are considered four aspects of digital heritage interpretation.

Fig. 2. Based on the interpretive framework (PrEDiC), we designed and implemented a platform named *Wesee*.

Wesee combines interactive narrative, voice interaction, and tactile interaction to show BLV users the historical stories and cultural connotations of *Chinese rites of the Zhou Dynasty*. The interactive narration of this platform is based on non-linear storytelling rather than simple audio descriptions. Users can conduct voice questions answering in the interactive narration. And the tactile integration board displays 3D patterns and braille for users. Tactile interaction on the tactile integrated board is combined with voice interaction to achieve multi-modal interaction in the experience. Users can share messages with other participants through voice or braille dialog.

3.1   Presentation-Interactive Narration

The effective presentation helps users access new information in a simpler and freer way. We designed an interactive narration to present the content of *Chinese rites of the Zhou Dynasty*, which combines background music, sound effects, and picture descriptions. Users experience it from a first-person perspective under guidance. During the experience, BLV users can choose the introduction content through the physical buttons on the tactile integration board. They can also select ritual objects (bronze or jade) and patterns (phoenix pattern or moire pattern) to learn about further. This way can provide immersion in the context and help BLV users raise their interest and engagement in the experience.

3.2   Culture Learning-Voice Question Answering

Cultural learning enables users to construct cognition of cultural heritage and gain an in-depth understanding of symbolic meanings of heritages. So we design voice questions answering in the interactive narration. The questions are based on verified cultural knowledge and historical allusions. After the user says the answer, the system recognizes the keywords and gives a corresponding reply. In this process, the BLV user's concentration will be improved, and the understanding and memory of the content will be deepened.

3.3   Embodiment-Tactile Board Interaction

Embodiment provides effective feedback and helps users engage actively. Tactile interaction will promote embodied interaction of BLV users and encourage their active participation. We implemented a tactile integrated board(Fig. 3a) as the tactile interaction carrier of *Wesee*, including three interaction areas: pattern display area, braille display area, and physical buttons. The pattern display area emerges different three-dimensional patterns according to the narration. The braille display area displays the braille content. The entity button allows users to select interested content in interactive narration. The tactile integrated board can display patterns and braille, enhancing BLV visitors' concrete and abstract cognition.

Fig. 3. (a): There are three interaction areas on the tactile integrated board; (b): The pattern display area uses the pneumatic actuator to emerge different three-dimensional patterns; (c): Constant sinusoidal alternating current (AC) voltages applied to different electrets cause them to vibrate, thus forming braille.

Figure 3b shows the pattern display area, which uses the pneumatic actuator to emerge different three-dimensional patterns according to the user's choice. Similar to Ye Xing's work [14], the pattern display board is made of polylactic acid (PLA) and a flexible membrane of thermoplastic polyurethane (TPU) material. The 3D-printed plate is engraved with a concave pattern of external outline and internal texture. TPU film is used for sealing bonding with an inflatable interface and connected to the air pump. By controlling the air pump to drive different parts, the film changes under the action of air pressure, forming touchable patterns. Two pattern display boards are distributed respectively on the tactile integrated board's card slot, which makes it possible to present more patterns. Figure 3c shows the braille display area based on previously proposed flexible electret actuator arrays by Jiang Tao [7]. A braille unit is composed of six electrets arranged as a 3*2 matrix. The current braille, most widely used in China, consists of three braille units. Therefore, the braille display area adopts a 3*2*3 matrix design. Constant sinusoidal AC voltages applied to different electrets cause them to vibrate, thus forming palpable braille. Two push-type physical buttons are distributed on the left and right sides of the integrated board, through which users can issue interactive commands.

3.4 Dialog Interaction-Messages Sharing

Dialogue allows users to explore and contribute at the narrative level to enhance the interaction. Communication and dialogue of BLV users are mostly carried out through voice and braille. Therefore, through the process of message sharing, users can be encouraged to leave voice messages and share them with other participants. The voice messages left by users are recorded and translated into braille. Other users can listen to the voice messages or read the messages by touching the braille display area on the tactile integrated board.

4 Preliminary Evaluation

To verify the effectiveness of the *Wesee* platform in cultural heritage interpretation for BLV people, we tested its performance through controlled experiments.

4.1 Participants and Procedure

20 BLV participants were recruited to participate in our preliminary experiment. The experiment was agreed upon by the participants, and we obtained the informed consent of the experiment from participants to participate in this study. Participants are between 24 and 52 years old, including 7 females and 13 males.

The entire process of the experiment is presented in Fig. 4a. After filling out the background prior questionnaire, the experimental group (EG, n = 10) experienced our platform *Wesee*, and the control group (CG, n = 10) simulated the tour of the traditional museum and listened to the audio introduction by wearing headphones (Fig. 4b). The information provided by the two groups of participants was consistent. After the experience, both groups filled out a questionnaire designed based on a 5-point Likert scale to evaluate the interpretation effect. According to the framework, our evaluation points include presentation, embodiment, cultural learning, and dialog interaction. All the evaluation spots were designed in the questionnaire, with seven questions ranging from 1 (not at all) to 5(extremely). The questionnaire content is provided in the supplementary material. Finally, we conducted semi-structured interviews with the participants at the end of the study. The whole process was video and audio recorded for further analysis.

4.2 Results

We collect and analyze all the questionnaire data. Firstly, We analyze the reliability and validity of the questionnaire. The Cronbach's α of interpretation effect ($Cronbach\alpha = 0.893, KMO = 0.716$) is greater than 0.8, and KMO is

Fig. 4. (a): Overall process of the experiment; (b): The experimental group experienced our platform *Wesee* and the control group simulated the tour of the traditional museum and listened to the audio descriptions.

greater than 0.7, showing the questionnaire has good reliability and validity. Secondly, we study the difference between the *EG* and *CG* groups through variance analysis. The two groups show significant differences in presentation ($F = 20.307, p = 0.000$), embodiment ($F = 5.696, p = 0.028$), cultural learning ($F = 16.2, p = 0.001$), and dialog interaction ($F = 5.236, p = 0.034$). All the detailed analysis results are provided in the supplementary material. In addition, we show the average level and fluctuation degree of samples in different groups through the box chart. As shown in Fig. 5.

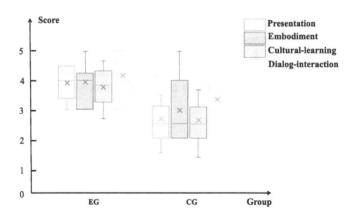

Fig. 5. Questionnaire data boxplot of interpretation effect

4.3   Discussion

According to the results, the questionnaire used in the experiment has good reliability and validity, and the difference between the *EG* and *CG* groups is significant. The box chart shows that the score of *EG* is higher than that of

CG in both dimensions. And the data of *EG* shows less fluctuation than *CG*, showing a higher consistency.

Results show that *Wesee* is significantly better than traditional visiting in the effect of interpretation. This phenomenon is also confirmed in the interview. P4 mentioned that *"It (Wesee) tells cultural stories in the form of stories. At the same time, some patterns can be touched, which is a feast for the senses of hearing and touch... It left a deep impression on me"*. For the traditional visiting, P16 said, *"Offline museum explanation is a simple introduction of some basic information. We can't see the appearance of the cultural relics, nor can we touch them. It is difficult to form their appearance just by listening to them."*

5 Conclusion and Future Work

In this paper, we implemented an interactive platform called *Wesee* based on the interpretive framework of PrEDiC. In addition, we designed and developed a tactile integrated board as the carrier of tactile interaction. A preliminary experiment was conducted with 20 BLV participants, and the results show the platform's effectiveness.

In the future, we will further enrich the interactive ways of *Wesee* in the dialogue and message sharing, and explore the possibility of allowing multiple BLV users to participate together. The display of different types of cultural heritage will be further explored to improve the flexibility of *Wesee* in the presentation content. We will optimize the structure and function of the tactile integrated board to achieve a more diverse content presentation in the pattern display area. The braille display area will be enlarged to enable the long presentation of braille content. Moreover, it is a potential tool for BLV children to learn braille, and we will carry out relevant applications and research. In addition, we will collaborate with local museum institutions to conduct more extensive applications in museums.

References

1. Asakawa, S., et al.: An independent and interactive museum experience for blind people. In: Proceedings of the 16th International Web for All Conference. W4A 2019, Association for Computing Machinery, New York, NY, USA (2019). https://doi.org/10.1145/3315002.3317557
2. Candlin, F.: Blindness, art and exclusion in museums and galleries. Int. J. Art Des. Educ. **22**(1), 100–110 (2003)
3. D'Agnano, F., Balletti, C., Guerra, F., Vernier, P.: Tooteko: A case study of augmented reality for an accessible cultural heritage. digitization, 3d printing and sensors for an audio-tactile experience. Int. Arch. Photogram. Remote Sens. Spatial Inf. Sci. **40**(5), 207 (2015)
4. Dash, K., Grohall, G.: Economic impact of creating and exhibiting 3d objects for blind and visually impaired people in museums. Economica Institut für Wirtschaftsforschung (2016)

5. Ginley, B.: Museums: a whole new world for visually impaired people. Disabil. Stud. Q. **33**(3) (2013)

6. Hoyt, B.O.: Emphasizing observation in a gallery program for blind and low-vision visitors: art beyond sight at the museum of fine arts, Houston. Disabil. Stud. Q. **33**(3) (2013)

7. Jiang, T., et al.: Programmable tactile feedback patterns for cognitive assistance by flexible electret actuators. Adv. Funct. Mater. **32**(4), 2107985 (2022). https://doi.org/10.1002/adfm.202107985, https://onlinelibrary.wiley.com/doi/abs/10.1002/adfm.202107985

8. Levent, N., Reich, C.: Museum accessibility: combining audience research and staff training. J. Museum Educ. **38**(2), 218–226 (2013). https://doi.org/10.1080/10598650.2013.11510772

9. Pirbazari, A.G., Tabrizi, S.K.: Recordim of iran's cultural heritage using an online virtual museum, considering the coronavirus pandemic. J. Comput. Cult. Herit. **15**(2) (2022). https://doi.org/10.1145/3500925

10. Rahaman, H.: Digital heritage interpretation: a conceptual framework. Digital Creativity **29**(2-3), 208–234 (2018). https://doi.org/10.1080/14626268.2018.1511602

11. Rector, K., Salmon, K., Thornton, D., Joshi, N., Morris, M.R.: Eyes-free art: exploring proxemic audio interfaces for blind and low vision art engagement. Proc. ACM Interact. Mob. Wearable Ubiquitous Technol. **1**(3) (2017). https://doi.org/10.1145/3130958

12. Vaz, R., Freitas, D., Coelho, A.: Visiting museums from the perspective of visually impaired visitors: experiences and accessibility resources in Portuguese museums. Int. J. Inclusive Museum **14**(1) (2021)

13. Wang, X., Kayukawa, S., Takagi, H., Asakawa, C.: Bentomuseum: 3d and layered interactive museum map for blind visitors. In: Proceedings of the 24th International ACM SIGACCESS Conference on Computers and Accessibility. ASSETS 2022, Association for Computing Machinery, New York, NY, USA (2022). https://doi.org/10.1145/3517428.3544811

14. Ye, X., Zhu, S., Qian, X., Zhang, M., Wang, X.: V-shape pneumatic torsional actuator: a building block for soft grasper and manipulator. Soft Robot. **9**(3), 562–576 (2022)

Accessibility and Aging

Accessibility Inspections of Mobile Applications by Professionals with Different Expertise Levels: An Empirical Study Comparing with User Evaluations

Delvani Antônio Mateus[1] , Simone Bacellar Leal Ferreira[2] , Maurício Ronny de Almeida Souza[1] , and André Pimenta Freire[1]([⊠])

[1] Universidade Federal de Lavras, Lavras, MG 37200-900, Brazil
{mauricio.ronny,apfreire}@ufla.br
[2] Universidade Federal do Estado do Rio de Janeiro,
Rio de Janeiro, RJ 22290-250, Brazil
simone@uniriotec.br

Abstract. Providing accessibility in mobile applications is essential for the appropriate use by people with disabilities. Different evaluation methods yield different results, and professionals and researchers must be aware of the types of results obtained by user evaluations and inspections performed by professionals with different expertise levels. This study aimed to compare the results from manual inspection of mobile apps performed by two groups of professionals with different expertise levels and to compare them with user evaluations conducted by users with visual disabilities. The Saraiva and Receita Federal applications usability evaluations carried out with nine visually impaired users encountered 189 problems divided into 39 violations of accessibility guidelines. Then, the applications were inspected by two groups of professionals: 17 specialists in different areas of software development (full-stack developers, testers, and front-end developers) and ten specialists in Human-Computer Interaction (HCI) with previous experience in accessibility. The results indicated a difference between accessibility assessment methods. In accessibility inspections, there was a difference between software development specialists (DEV group) and HCI specialists (HCI group). The results indicated a difference in the number of violations the DEV group encounters compared to the HCI group. Inspections by HCI experts and testing with users with disabilities encountered a greater diversity of problem types. HCI professionals also showed a broader repertoire of accessibility inspection approaches. The results allow for an initial understanding of the extent to which evaluations by developers without HCI background can cover compared to inspections by HCI specialists and users with disabilities.

Keywords: Mobile · Accessibility · User · Inspections

J. Abdelnour Nocera et al. (Eds.): INTERACT 2023, LNCS 14142, pp. 135–154, 2023.
https://doi.org/10.1007/978-3-031-42280-5_9

1   Introduction

Mobile applications have been used in countless everyday tasks, such as social networks, online banking services, shopping and access to messaging services. However, many mobile applications still have accessibility barriers that jeopardize their use by people with disabilities. Understanding which evaluation methods effectively detect violations in different contexts is crucial for developing such applications. These methods include approaches such as evaluations by users with disabilities and inspections by professionals. Each method provides distinct input for developers, testers, and designers to allocate. It is essential to know how to assign different methods appropriately to varying stages of the development cycle.

Several studies focused on the web platform compared different accessibility assessment methods. Mankoff [15] showed the importance of comparing professionals with experience in accessibility and professionals without expertise in accessibility and user. Their results showed that experienced developers tend to encounter more accessibility violations. Other studies [4,14,21] showed that different assessment methods find specific accessibility problems on websites.

In accessibility inspections, other studies have shown how evaluators with different expertise levels conduct their inspections [5–7]. Such studies showed that non-expert evaluators find fewer problems with low precision and validity. However, despite showing the objective differences in how expert and non-expert evaluators perform inspections on websites, such studies did not show qualitative aspects concerning the strategies used by evaluators with different levels of expertise on accessibility.

One important aspect that motivate the present study was the low number of studies on accessibility evaluation methods focused on mobile devices. Most studies comparing accessibility evaluation methods have focused on websites, and few have addressed the accessibility evaluation of mobile applications. Mobile applications have a number of particularities, such as different structures of interface components and different ways of employing assistive technologies than those used in websites, for example.

This study aimed to compare the results from manual inspection of mobile apps performed by two groups of professionals with different levels of expertise in accessibility and to compare with user evaluations conducted by users with visual disabilities. The study consisted of the inspections of two apps: Saraiva and Receita Federal by two groups of professionals. The apps were inspected by 17 specialists in different areas of software development (full-stack developers, testers, and front-end developers) and ten specialists in Human-Computer Interaction (HCI) with previous experience in accessibility. The results from the inspections were compared with a set of 189 instances of problems encountered by nine users with visual disabilities who had previously evaluated the same applications [9,10].

The following research questions were defined:

RQ1: *"Is there a difference between the violations encountered by users, software developers and HCI professionals?"*.

RQ2 *"What factors impact manual accessibility inspections of mobile apps performed by specialists?"*

This paper is organized as follows. Section 2 presents concepts related to mobile accessibility and related work. Section 3 presents the methods employed in the study. Section 4 presents the results and discussion and, finally, Sect. 5 presents conclusions and future work.

2   Theoretical Background

This section presents basic concepts and related studies that have approached accessibility inspections, tests with users, automated tests, and comparisons between evaluation methods in mobile applications.

2.1   Accessibility in Mobile Applications

Accessibility is defined by ISO 9241-11 as "Usability of a product, service, environment or installation by people with the widest range of resources" [13]. ISO 9241-11 defines usability as "The extent to which a system, product or service can be used by specific users to achieve specific objectives with effectiveness, efficiency and satisfaction in a specific context of use" [13].

Accessibility guidelines are commonly used to guide the development of applications intended to promote best practices. However, these guidelines alone cannot cover all accessibility requirements by users [11,16,21]. Accessibility guidelines were created to promote accessibility of digital technology, such as the Web Content Accessibility Guidelines (WCAG 2.1) [24], the British Broadcasting Corporation's (BBC) HTML Accessibility Standards v 2.0 [3] and BBC Mobile Accessibility Standards and Guidelines v1 .0 [8].

In October 2022, the Brazilian Standard NBR 17060 for the accessibility of mobile apps was released [2]. This standard is based on the WCAG Web Content Accessibility Guidelines), whose principles are; 1 Perception and understanding; 2 Control and interaction; 3 Media; and 4 Codification. Its main objective is to support article 63 of the Brazilian Inclusion Law (LBI 13.146/2015) [12].

The set of guidelines developed by the World Wide Web Consortium (W3C) as the Web Content Accessibility Guidelines (WCAG) has its version 3.0 under development [26]. Version 2.2 was published as a working draft in 2021 [25], which extends from version 2.1, published in 2018 [24]. Those are extensions to version 2.0, published in 2008 [23], originating from the first publication published in 1999 [22]. This set of guidelines is the most widely used worldwide.

The evaluation of mobile applications, like web applications, may be performed by different methods. The main types of evaluations are automated tests performed by tools [1], manual inspections by specialists and evaluations by users with disabilities [17]. As described in the following section, each method has advantages and disadvantages and can be used in different stages of development.

2.2 Related Work

The study by Power et al. [16] revealed problems with web accessibility in sixteen sites, with thirty-two users with visual impairment. Using the WCAG 2.0 guidelines, they observed that only 50.4% of the problems would be covered by the guidelines. This result demonstrated that methods based solely on guidelines cannot find all accessibility problems.

Rømen and Svanæs [18] conducted tests with thirteen users on two sites in Norway - three people with visual impairments, two with dyslexia, two with motor disabilities and six without disabilities. As a result, the study showed that WCAG 2.0 coverage corresponds to approximately 49% and WCAG 1.0 to 42% of the problems users encountered. Even if developers followed the guidelines, they could not cover all problems.

Vollenwyder et al. [21] also evaluated the impact that compliant and non-compliant websites have on 66 users with visual disabilities and 65 users without disabilities. The study showed that compliance with technical accessibility standards did not account for significant differences in usability measures but showed improvements in the perceptions expressed by users with disabilities. The study confirmed the value of using accessibility guidelines for addressing common issues but also confirmed they have limitations.

Another study conducted by some of the authors of this paper in Brazil [9,10] aimed to understand the types of problems encountered by visually impaired users in mobile applications. This study provided input from the user evaluations used in the present dissertation. The study involved user evaluations of four applications: Caixa Econômica Federal (government-owned bank), Receita Federal (National Treasury), Decolar (tourism agency), and Saraiva (bookseller) on Android and iOS platforms. The study recruited eleven users, six blind and five with low vision. The results yielded 39 types of problems and 415 problem instances. Table 1 and Table 2 present the problems with higher instances encountered by blind users and users with low vision, respectively. In addition to the accessibility problems identified, this study [9,10] showed that users with visual impairments had more significant difficulties completing tasks than users without disabilities and that the severity of the problems encountered is also greater.

The problems encountered in that study [9,10] were categorized using a categorization scheme adapted from Power et al. [16]. The most frequently encountered problems by blind users and their frequencies are shown in Table 1. Table 2 presents the list of partially-sighted users' most frequently encountered problems in the same study [9,10].

Other related studies have also investigated the interplay between different accessibility evaluation methods, including specialist inspections. Accessibility studies using different assessment methods can target whether websites follow accessibility guidelines. The study by Jaeger [14] sought to identify the accessibility of ten US government websites to determine if they followed the Sect. 508 accessibility guide. The following evaluation methods were used: tests by specialists, tests with users carried out by visually and motor impaired peo-

Table 1. Most frequently encountered problems by blind users and their frequencies [9, 10]

Problem category	Total (N)
3.4.1 Inappropriate feedback (Controls, forms and functionality)	34
3.4.5 Unclear or confusing functionality (Controls, forms and functionality)	25
3.5.1 Lack of identification (Buttons)	22
3.4.9 Users inferred that there was functionality where there wasn't (Controls, forms and functionality)	18
1.1.3 Users cannot make sense of content (Content - meaning)	15
3.4.8 Sequence of interaction is unclear or confusing (Controls, forms and functionality)	15
3.5.2 Button functionality is nuclear or confusing (Buttons)	15
2.2.1 No textual alternative (Image)	14
1.1.4 Inconsistent Content organization (Content - meaning)	12
3.4.10 Default presentation of control or form element is not adequate (Controls, forms and functionality)	11
3.4.4 Expected functionality not present (Controls, forms and functionality)	10
6.1.3 System problems with assistive technology (System characteristic)	8
1.1.7 Meaning in content is lost (Content - meaning)	6
2.3.1 No textual alternative (Audio, video and multimedia)	6
3.4.2 Functionality does not work (as expected) Controls, forms and functionality	6

Table 2. Most frequent problems encountered by partially-sighted users [9, 10]

Problem category	Total (N)
3.4.1 Inadequate feedback (Controls, forms and functionality)	15
3.4.10 Default presentation of control or form element is not adequate (Controls, forms and functionality)	12
2.1.5 Default presentation is not adequate (Text)	11
6.1.4 System too slow (System characteristic)	11
3.4.2 Functionality does not work (as expected) Controls, forms and functionality	10
3.4.9 Users inferred that there was functionality where there wasn't (Controls, forms and functionality)	9
3.5.1 Lack of identification (Buttons)	8
6.1.1 Server not working appropriately (System characteristic)	8
1.1.4 Inconsistent content organization (Content - meaning)	6
3.4.8 Sequence of interaction is unclear or confusing (Controls, forms and functionality)	6
1.1.3 Users cannot make sense of content (Content - meaning)	5
3.4.4 Expected functionality not present (Controls, forms and functionality)	5
4.1.1 Inadequate navigation elements (Navigation)	5
1.1.7 Meaning in content is lost (Content - meaning)	4
2.2.5 Default presentation not adequate (Image)	4

ple, automated tests and questionnaires for webmasters and professionals from the selected sites. This study showed that implementing Sect. 508 improved the accessibility of websites. However, it showed that testing with users offered greater detail about the problems encountered.

Brajnik *et al.* [6, 7] analyzed how two groups with 19 expert and 57 non-expert inspectors performed web accessibility evaluations using the barriers walkthrough method. The results showed significant differences between the number of problems encountered and the reports' quality concerning the inspectors' validity and precision. However, the study did not provide in-depth qualitative information about the strategies employed by the inspectors. In another study, Brajnik *et al.* [5] demonstrated that novice evaluators tend to encounter a broader range of problems when they conduct evaluations in groups.

Vollenwyder *et al.* [21] conducted a study analyzing the relationship between the conformance of websites to the Web Content Accessibility Guidelines (WCAG) [24] the evaluation by users with visual disabilities and sighted users. Their study showed no statistically significant difference in usability and user experience measures in conformant and non-conformant sites, in alignment with previous results from the literature [11,16,18]. However, comments from participants with visual disabilities showed that conformant websites provided more positive experiences than non-conformant sites. They highlight that conformance contributed to the improvement of the usability of websites but needs to be complemented by user-centred design and evaluation.

3   Methods

3.1   Study Design

The study involved the following methodological components:

1. Consolidation of results from evaluations of mobile apps by users with visual disabilities [9,10];
2. Inspection of the mobile apps by software development and Human-Computer Interaction professionals in different areas;
3. Follow-up interviews with professionals regarding their experiences in the inspections.

The study started with analysing the results of the user evaluations of the apps Saraiva and Receita Federal performed in previous studies [9,10]. We classified the issues identified by users according to related WCAG 2.1 success criteria. The consolidation of the results from that study allowed us to analyze how the results from manual inspections from specialists compared to user evaluations. The university's research ethics approved the previous study, with CAAE code 49781115.9.0000.5148.

The next step was a manual inspection task and recruiting software developers and HCI professionals for an empirical study. We compared the results of these inspections with the results of user tests. In the study design, we observed what types of problems were encountered by each group of participants (users and professionals).

Further to the analysis of the results from the evaluations, we also used observation and interview data to identify possible factors that impacted the inspections performed. The university's Research Ethics Committee approved the study with professionals under the code CAAE 41956121.7.0000.5148.

For the present study, we considered data from three groups of participants: users (USER), software developers (DEV), and HCI specialists (HCI). The USER group is composed of eleven participants, six blind and five with low vision.

3.2   Participants and Recruitment

The recruitment of participants for the DEV and HCI groups occurred through the researcher's social circle and social networks. Contact was made by e-mail, WhatsApp and telephone. Tasks were performed remotely through Google Meet. Participants received the Free and Informed Consent Form (ICF) and all the guidelines and clarifications about the process. Participants who agreed to complete the evaluation responded via e-mail, expressing their acceptance.

We recruited 27 professionals, 17 software developers and 10 HCI professionals. The DEV group comprised developers of three professional expertise: front-end and full-stack developers and testers. Following is the description of the members of the DEV group.

- Front-end developers: responsible for coding interfaces;
- Tester: responsible for carrying out tests on the system;
- Full-stack developers: people who can act as a back-end or front-end developers, and tester.

A summary of the academic and professional training profiles of the DEV group is presented as follows:

- Front-end developers: six professionals with work experience ranging from one year to six years, all with a BSc degree in Computing-related courses or PhD in Computing;
- Tester: two professionals with work experience ranging from one year to two years, all with a BSc degree in Computing;
- Full-stack developers: nine professionals with work experience ranging from one year to twelve years, all with a BSc degree in Computing, one with a post-graduate continuous-developement degree in Computing and three with research degrees (Master's and PhD degrees).

A summary of the academic and professional training profiles of the HCI group is presented as follows:

- HCI: ten professionals with experience in accessibility research, professors, professionals from private companies and public companies with a BSc degree in computing, and four with a continuous development postgraduate, master's or PhD in Computing.

The front-end group consisted of 7 participants, with four males with a median age of 36 and six months and an average age of 37 years and six months. They had undergraduate degrees in computer science and approximately one year of front-end development experience in private and public sector companies. The group also includes three female participants with a median age of 38 years and an average age of 35 and three months. They have undergraduate degrees in computing and around one year of experience in front-end development in the public sector.

The tester group comprised two participants, one male aged 30, with a degree in Computer Engineering and approximately one year of experience in software testing in a private company. The other participant is a 25-year-old female with a degree in Information Systems and around two years of experience in software testing in a private company.

The full-stack group consists of 9 participants, with eight males and a median age of 36 years, and an average age of 34 years. They have undergraduate degrees in computer science and an average of 5 years of experience in both the public and private sectors. The other participant is a 34-year-old female with a degree in Information Systems, a master's and a PhD in Computational Ontology, and approximately eight years as a full-stack developer in the public sector.

The HCI group comprised 10 participants, with six males with a median age of 33 and an average age of 37. They have undergraduate degrees in Computer Science, with two having master's degrees and one holding a PhD in Computer Science. Additionally, one participant is an HCI professor. The other 4 participants are females with a median age of 37 and six months and an average age of 34 and six months. They have undergraduate degrees in computer science, with one having a postgraduate degree, one holding a master's degree, and one holding a PhD, all in Computer Science. Moreover, all participants have experience in accessibility implementation and accessibility testing. 50% had published articles in the field of accessibility, and 40% conducted tests with disabled users.

Users Group: The six blind users included in the previous study from which the data were drawn [9,10] were five males and one female. Participants aged between 23 and 63 years old, with an average age of 42. The average experience with mobile devices, on a scale of 1 (none) and 7 (substantial experience), is 6. One participant had postgraduate study, two were undergraduate students, two completed higher education, and one completed high school.

Low-vision participants were three females and two males. The age varied between 20 and 42 years, averaging 31 years. Following the same experience scale as blind users, the average experience is 5. Regarding the level of education, two completed high school, two had an undergraduate degree, and one had a postgraduate degree.

3.3 Inspection Procedures

Based on the problems identified in user tests [9,10], we designed a WCAG checklist for success criteria, as shown in Table 3. Participants should manually inspect each application and fill out the checklist provided. We provided the participants with guidelines for filling out the checklist, and we also provided them with links to the BBC mobile guidelines and WCAG 2.1 guidelines. Evaluation techniques were not provided. Each participant was supposed to use whichever technique they knew.

Before starting the evaluations, the following guidelines were given to developers: (i) to use the Talkback screen reader on a mobile phone to perform the tests; and (2) participants were strongly encouraged to comment on their actions. For filling out the checklist, participants were instructed to assign an "X" in the columns "Yes" or "No" for each problem category they identified.

3.4   Applications Evaluated

We selected two applications that provided electronic, one of them from the Brazilian government (Receita Federal) and one from the commercial sector (Saraiva) [9,10]. The versions of the applications are the same ones used in the previous user study, obtained from ApkPure[1].

– Receita Federal: Federal Revenue app with consultation of the CPF (Individual Taxpayer Registry) and income-tax services.
– Saraiva: Brazilian e-commerce app that sells books and other products.

The applications evaluated were Android native apps. We acknowledge that Android and iOS apps may have different accessibility features. However, this study aimed at examining how different profiles of evaluators conduct their inspections, and not the specific differences in the accessibility of Android and iOS apps. Unlike countries in the Global North, the share of Android users in Brazil was nearly 85% in 2022 [19], whilst iOS had more than 50% of the market share in the US [20].

3.5   Scenarios for Evaluations

The test scenario performed in all assessments was obtained from the study with users [9,10].

– Saraiva Scenario 1: Look for the Harry Potter book in print in Portuguese for a gift. Find out how much this gift will cost you in total and the deadline.
– Saraiva Scenario 2: After choosing the book, you would like to know the ways to payment that Saraiva accepts.
– Federal Revenue Scenario 1: Make an appointment with your CPF and check if it is valid.
– Federal Revenue Scenario 2: You would like to estimate the Income Tax of 2015 to be paid, considering income and deductions (provided in the task).

3.6   Data Gathering and Analysis

We monitored the inspections performed by each participant individually using the Google Meet[2] platform and the Teamviewer[3] remote area sharing software. All professionals performed the inspections using the same device: a notebook with the Linux Mint operating system and the Android Studio program with Android 8.0. The professionals were encouraged to report the techniques and strategies used to verify violations during this process. We recorded all interactions for qualitative analysis. The professionals were also free to report violations they encountered and not present in the checklist.

---

[1] https://m.apkpure.com/br/.
[2] https://meet.google.com/.
[3] https://www.teamviewer.com/.

Table 3. Violation encountered by users in the Saraiva and Federal Revenue apps

WCAG 2.1 criteria	Federal Revenue	Saraiva
1.1.1 Non-text content	YES	YES
1.2.3 Audio desc. or media alternative (pre-recorded)	NO	YES
1.3.1 Information and relationships	YES	YES
1.3.2 Significant Sequence	NO	YES
1.4.1 Use of Color	NO	YES
1.4.10 Reflux	NO	YES
1.4.3 Contrast (minimum)	No	YES
1.4.4 Resize Text	YES	YES
2.1.1 Keyboard	NO	YES
2.1.2 No keyboard trap	NO	YES
2.2.2 Pause, Stop, Hide	NO	YES
2.4.3 Focus Order	YES	YES
2.4.4 Purpose of the link (in context)	NO	YES
2.4.6 Headers and Labels	NO	YES
2.4.8 Location	YES	YES
2.5.5 Target Size	YES	NO
3.1.1 Language of the page	YES	YES
3.1.4 Abbreviations	NO	YES
3.2.3 Consistent Navigation	NO	YES
3.3.1 Error Identification	YES	YES
3.3.2 Labels or instructions	YES	YES
3.3.5 Help	YES	YES
4.1.1 Parsing	YES	NO
4.1.2 Name, Function, Value	YES	YES

We compared the violations the HCI and DEV participants encountered to those identified in user tests (USER) for the same two apps. The analysis quantitatively compared the violations encountered by the HCI and DEV groups to those encountered by the USER group. The violations identified by the USER group consisted of 24 violations, mapped in Table 3. The DEV group comprised participants with different expertise levels, so we mapped specific violations encountered by specific roles.

We also considered the qualitative data obtained from observation, the comments from the participants in the execution of the inspections, and interviews. We conducted a content analysis and derived categories of factors that may have impacted the inspection process performed by the professionals.

We applied open coding to synthesize the qualitative data into factors and categories that may have impacted the inspection process performed by the

Table 4. Violations by WCAG principles encountered by all groups

Principles	Violated guidelines - Front	Violated guidelines - Tester	Violated guidelines - Fullstack	Violated guidelines - HCI	Violated guidelines - User
Perceivable	8	6	8	8	8
Operable	7	6	8	8	8
Understandable	5	7	7	8	6
Robust	0	2	2	2	2
Other	0	0	0	8	14

professionals. The lead researcher analyzed the responses and marked relevant segments with "codes" (keyword tagging). The codes represented features related to evaluations and experiences voiced by the participants or observed by the researchers. This stage generated 24 codes.

After generating the first selection of codes, two other researchers discussed the codes until a consensus was reached. We grouped these codes into relevant categories, with five categories at the end of the analysis.

4   Results and Discussion

This section presents the results obtained from the accessibility inspections carried out by DEV and HCI specialists. It also presents the qualitative analysis of the data obtained during the tests. Both groups completed the checklist stating whether each guideline was violated during the guideline review process.

4.1   Results DEVs Groups, HCI Group, and User Groups (RQ1)

Table 4 presents all violations encountered by all groups at the principles perceivable, operable, understandable and robust. Success criteria from principle "Perceivable" start with number 1, principle "Operable" number 2, principle "Understandable" number 3 and "Robust" number 4. Only the HCI and User groups identified violations not covered by WCAG, categorized as "Other".

The six front-end developers detected 20 types of WCAG-related problems. Table 4 concentrated on the principles perceivable (8), understandable (7) and operable (5). It was surprising that no problems were encountered related to guidelines concerning the robust principles. The problems listed according to the success criterion from principle "Perceivable" start with number 1, non-text content, audio description or media alternative (pre-recorded), information and relationships, significant sequence, use of colour, reflux, contrast (minimum), resize text. The principle "Operable" has criteria starting with number 2: keyboard, no keyboard trap, pause, stop, hide, focus order, focus order, headers and labels, location, and target size. The principle "Understandable" has criteria starting with number 3, the language of the page, the language of parts, error identification, and error prevention (legal, financial, data). The principle "Robust" has criteria starting with number 4. No participants from the DEV group encountered problems with this principle. The front-end developers did not encounter the following violations: the purpose of the link (in context), consistent navigation, labels or instructions, help, parsing, and name and function.

The two testers detected 21 types of violations related to WCAG. Table 4 focuses on the problems encountered by principles: perceptible (6), operable (7), understandable principles (6) and robust (2). The problems listed according to the success criteria from principle "Perceivable" principle had: non-text content, significant sequence, use of colour, reflux, contrast (minimum), and text resize. The "Operable" principle had: no keyboard trap, focus order, the purpose of the link (in context), headers and labels, location, and target size. The "Understandable" principle had problems with the language of the page, the language of parts, consistent navigation, error identification, labels or instructions, error prevention (legal, financial, data), and help. The "Robust" had: parsing and name, function, and value. The DEV tester did not encounter the following violations: abbreviations, no keyboard trap, text resize, information and relationships, audio description or media alternative (pre-recorded).

The nine full-stack developers detected 25 types of WCAG-related problems. Table 4 presents the WCAG principles that had violations: perceivable (8), operable (8), understandable (7), and robust (2). It was surprising that no problems were encountered at understandable and robust levels. The problems listed according to the success criteria from principle "Perceivable" principle start with number 1: non-text content, audio description or media alternative (pre-recorded), information and relationships, meaningful sequence, use of colour, reflux, contrast (minimum), and resize text. The "Operable" principle has criteria with the number 2, keyboard, no keyboard trap, pause, stop, hide, focus order, the purpose of the link (in context), headers and labels, location, and target size. The "Understandable" principle has criteria starting with number 3: the language of the page, the language of parts, consistent navigation, error identification, labels or instructions, error prevention (legal, financial, data), and help. The "Robust" principle has criteria starting with number 4: parsing, name, function, and value. The DEV full-stack encountered no problems with abbreviations.

The ten professional HCI could detect 26 WCAG-related problems. Table 4 shows the WCAG principles with violations: perceivable (8), operable (8), understandable (8), and robust (2). No violations were encountered at understandable and robust levels. Success criteria from principle "Perceivable" start with number 1, principle "Operable" with number 2, principle "Understandable" with number 3 and "Robust" with number 4. The violations listed in principle 1 were: non-text content, audio description or alternative media (pre-recorded), information and relationships, significant sequence, use of colour, reflux, contrast (minimum), and text resize. Violations listed in principle 2 were: keyboard, no keyboard trap, pause, stop, hide, focus order, purpose of the link (in context), headers and labels, location, and target size. Violations listed in principle 3 were:

the language of the page, the language of parts, abbreviations, consistent navigation, error identification, labels or instructions, error prevention (legal, financial, data), and help. Violations listed in principle 4 were: parsing and name, function, and value.

It is worth mentioning that HCI professionals encountered problems not listed in the checklist Table 6: layout problems, wrong form entries, lack of identification of items per page, lack of adequacy of calendars and lack of descriptive icons. They were the only group that defined the severity of each problem encountered.

All violations encountered by the DEV, HCI, and User groups are in Table 5. In aggregating the results by group, we observed that only the HCI group listed all expected violations, followed by the DEV full-stack. These two groups of professionals listed approximately the same number of violations as users. On the other hand, front-end DEVs encountered fewer violations.

Responding to **RQ1**, the front-end DEV professionals encountered violations in three principles, mostly in "Perceivable". These violations were directly linked to their area of expertise. They did not find any violations related to "Robust". Only two DEV testers listed one more violation than the front-end DEVs. They listed violations in all principles. Full-stack DEVs encountered the highest number of violations, totalling 25. Table 4 shows the number of violations.

The User group encountered 38 types of violations, and the HCI group encountered 34 of them. Some violations were not covered by WCAG 2.1. Table 4 presents the number of violations by WCAG principles, and others not covered by the guidelines. These results corroborate with other studies [9,16,18].

4.2   Factors that Influence the Inspection Process (RQ2)

This section presents a qualitative analysis involving DEV and HCI professionals on the factors influencing the accessibility inspection process. The factors were divided into five themes: Professional background; Guidelines used for inspection; Practical experience; Visual perception; and Techniques applied in the inspection. Figure 1 shows an overview of these factors with their categories. In the following subsections, the five factors are detailed. The categories used in the codes grouped under each theme are highlighted in the description.

4.3   Influence of Professional Background

Knowledge was linked to accessibility and software development. Elements related to the category **Accessibility knowledge** were mentioned five times by the DEV group and ten times by the HCI group. Elements related to **Knowledge in software development** were mentioned 17 times by the DEV group and three times by the HCI group.

Table 5. Violation encountered by WCAG, DEV group and IHC group

WCAG 2.1 criteria	Front	Full-stack	HCI	Tester	User
1.1.1 Non-text content	Yes	Yes	Yes	Yes	Yes
1.2.3 Audio desc. or media alternative (pre-recorded)	Yes	No	Yes	No	Yes
1.3.1 Information and relationships	Yes	Yes	Yes	Yes	Yes
1.3.2 Significant Sequence	Yes	Yes	Yes	Yes	Yes
1.4.1 Use of Color	Yes	Yes	Yes	Yes	Yes
1.4.10 Reflux	No	Yes	Yes	Yes	Yes
1.4.3 Contrast (minimum)	Yes	Yes	Yes	Yes	Yes
1.4.4 Resize Text	Yes	Yes	Yes	No	Yes
2.1.1 Keyboard	Yes	Yes	Yes	Yes	Yes
2.1.2 No keyboard trap	No	Yes	Yes	No	Yes
2.2.2 Pause, Stop, Hide	No	Yes	Yes	Yes	Yes
2.4.3 Focus Order	Yes	Yes	Yes	Yes	Yes
2.4.4 Purpose of the link (in context)	Yes	Yes	Yes	Yes	Yes
2.4.6 Headers and Labels	No	Yes	Yes	Yes	Yes
2.4.8 Location	No	Yes	Yes	Yes	Yes
2.5.5 Target Size	Yes	Yes	Yes	Yes	Yes
3.1.1 Language of the page	Yes	Yes	Yes	No	Yes
3.1.2 Language of Parts	No	Yes	Yes	No	No
3.1.4 Abbreviations	No	No	Yes	No	Yes
3.2.3 Consistent Navigation	No	Yes	Yes	Yes	Yes
3.3.1 Error Identification	No	Yes	Yes	Yes	Yes
3.3.2 Labels or instructions	No	Yes	Yes	Yes	Yes
3.3.4 Error prevention (legal, financial, data)	No	Yes	Yes	Yes	No
3.3.5 Help	No	Yes	Yes	Yes	Yes
4.1.1 Parsing	No	No	Yes	Yes	Yes
4.1.2 Name, Function, Value	No	Yes	Yes	Yes	Yes

DEV professionals reported having knowledge as **partial in accessibility**. Some understood that accessibility was in having buttons to increase and decrease the font or having a high-contrast button. HCI professionals reported having mastery in **accessibility** through academic research or professional experience. DEVs also demonstrated knowledge of software development. Following are excerpts from the responses of professionals DEV-15 and HCI-07.

"... I work for the state administration and until then we intended that accessibility on the site was to put the A+ (increase letter) and A- (decrease letter) in the letter, make a contrast and such putting a little thing (object) and another what we usually see." (DEV-15).
"... today I work with users with low literacy in my doctoral research, I am a professor of HCI." (HCI-07).

Table 6. Violations encountered not covered by WCAG, IHC group and USER group

Violations	HCI	User	Median Severity
Layout problems (broken)	Yes	No	2
Wrong form entries	Yes	No	1
Lack of identification of items per page	Yes	No	2
Lack of adequacy of calendars	Yes	No	1
Lack of descriptive icons	Yes	No	1
Inconsistent navigation	No	Yes	1
System issues with the assistive technolog	No	Yes	3
Irrelevant content	No	Yes	2
No alternative	No	Yes	1
Lack of alternative to data	No	Yes	1
Users can't make sense of content	No	Yes	1
Functionality not clear	No	Yes	1
No alternative to functionality	No	Yes	3
No way to return to home page	No	Yes	4
Web Server not working properly	No	Yes	4
System too slow	No	Yes	2
Inadequate feedback	No	Yes	1

Fig. 1. Factors related to the inspection process.

Another factor of professional background is knowledge of software development. DEVs and HCI reported having theoretical and practical knowledge in **software development**. This knowledge helped them in the inspection process.

4.4 Do the Guidelines Used for Inspection Influence the Results?

In the inspection process, the guidelines used in the inspection interfered with the results. The professionals reported the complexity of the guidelines. Elements related to the **usability of guidelines** (or lack thereof) were reported five times by the DEV group and twice by the HCI group.

Professional DEVs reported that the **guidelines are complex**, especially WCAG. The items seemed to have the same meaning. Participants also reported that the BBC had **practical examples**, and the understanding was very clear regarding the problem. Following is the response from participants on the usability of the DEV-15 guidelines: "... correctly identify the guideline items within the application, I didn't sometimes understand, because it was not a very clear understanding of that item, sometimes they clashed with other items.".

The HCI professionals also reported that the description of the guideline items is similar, bringing **confusion to the understanding of the item**. Following is the report of the professional HCI-05: "...the WCAG guideline I found a bit confusing, it has similar terms with others.". The study provided evaluators with guidelines derived from professional practice available from the BBC [8]. However, we noticed that using complex guidelines that need to adapt from the Web context to the mobile context poses extra challenges to evaluators. At the time of the evaluations, the Brazilian standard for the accessibility of mobile applications was not available [2].

4.5   Does Visual Perception Contribute to Problem Detection?

Some problems can be identified visually, and professionals reported problems regarding visual elements. The **ease of identifying problems in visual elements in the interface** was mentioned three times by the DEV group and twice by the HCI group. HCI professionals reported problems on visual elements, **layout breakage**, and **lack of pre-defined format mask** in the CPF field.

DEV professionals reported having trouble spotting visual interface elements (e.g., **large banner without alt text**), **lack of a number of items per page**, and lack of **masking in numeric fields**. DEV-08 reported: "... the non-text content was straightforward to identify as it had the banner passing through.".

4.6   Hands-On Experience with Inspection or Software Development

During the inspection, professionals reported having practical experience in software development in accessibility tests with blind users, older people and others. Different aspects were reported concerning the category **Practical experience**. Some elements were reported only by the DEV group: **lack of experience in accessibility testing** (6 times) and **software development negative habits** (twice). HCI specialists also had particular practices not reported by the DEV group, namely: **experience in software development for users with heading disabilities** (once), **experience in software testing for users without disabilities** (three times), **experience in software testing with blind users** (twice), **experience in testing software with people with low literacy** (once) and **experience in software testing with older adults** (once).

Only the HCI group reported having experience in software development for elderly and **deaf and hard of hearing** users. They also reported experience in testing with **blind users**, **elderly users**, and users with **low literacy**. These experiences came with academic research and professional experiences in public and private sector organizations. Some DEV professionals reported having **no experience** with accessibility before the inspection in the study. They had a macro view of usability problems, but it was **not aimed at users with disabilities**. Following is the report of the professional DEV-16: "... The tests were aimed at users as a whole. I didn't have this view of the limitation of some users with accessibility issues.".

Professionals also reported having experience in **software development**. With this experience, they reported having **greater power** in identifying problems related to **poorly developed coding**, bugs caused by **improper error handling**, and **lack of error handling**. Following is the report of the professional DEV-17: "... Some crashes and bugs caused by improper error handling and system boot errors, due to poorly developed coding.". Professionals also **reported frustration** in finding so many accessibility problems in applications. They also reported satisfaction in acquiring **practical experience**.

4.7   Techniques Applied in the Inspection

Professionals reported having several techniques to carry out inspections. Regarding the category **Techniques applied in inspections**, different aspects were reported by the DEV and HCI groups. **Security-level tests** were only reported once by a developer. **Creating personas with different characteristics** and **Strategy to check the description of the guideline items and interface icons** were only reported by HCI specialists. **Usability-level tests** were reported eight times by HCI specialists and only once by developers. **Ad hoc evaluation strategy** and **Functional-level tests** were reported once by participants from the DEV and once from the HCI group.

Several professionals use techniques in their domain to carry out inspections in this context. There was the **Ad hoc evaluation strategy**. Professionals reported that they **do not have a defined technique**, that they identify problems as they go. A report from HCI-07 states: "... I don't have a strategy to test, I'm doing the task and identifying the problems.".

Most professionals used usability techniques to check navigation. They reported turning **off the monitor** and navigating using the screen reader. Some tried to navigate using the right-swipe gesture (which generates a similar effect as the **TAB key** on computers) to jump between content items. This same technique was used to identify problems related to focus.

Professionals reported that some accessibility violations could be identified by performing functional tests. For example, the calculate shipping **button does not work**, and the **back button does not work**. HCI-05 reported: "... The calculate shipping button is not working. It does not return the calculation.".

That HCI professional reported the **creation of personas** to carry out the inspections, each persona has a different characteristic, and it brings the obligation to **inspect with a different look**, making them find **different problems** whenever **inspecting the usability**. HCI-05 reported: "... I create personas to test usability in ways that I can identify issues from different perspectives.".

Answering **RQ2**, the qualitative analysis provided preliminary indications that the difference between the DEV and HCI groups was mostly in the strategies used in inspections. The DEVs focused on the code and techniques that analyze the written code. The HCI professionals displayed a broader repertoire of usability techniques, especially those that interfere with the user experience. For example, they identified almost all navigation problems in the apps.

5   Conclusion and Future Work

This study compared the results from manual inspection of mobile apps performed by two groups of professionals with different levels of expertise in accessibility and compared with evaluations with users with visual disabilities. The results included comparing accessibility evaluations of the Saraiva and Receita Federal applications carried out by nine visually impaired users. That study found 189 instances of problems divided into 39 violations of accessibility guidelines in a previous study [10]. The results from user evaluations were compared with inspections by two groups of professionals: 17 specialists in different areas of software development (full-stack developers, testers, and front-end developers) and ten specialists in Human-Computer Interaction (HCI).

The study provided preliminary indications that professionals with more expertise in accessibility could find a higher proportion of the types of problems that users with visual disabilities encountered in user evaluations. However, the study's results indicated that many types of problems were only encountered by users. These results are in line with previous studies stating that user evaluation involving users with disabilities is essential for accessibility evaluations. Further to these results, the study provided initial insights into the factors that influence the accessibility inspection of mobile apps, including practice experience, professional background, the different techniques they employ, the guidelines they use for inspections and visual perception.

The results provided initial indications of issues that may help future studies to improve accessibility inspection practices for experts and non-experts. The study provided important information about the types of problems that evaluators commonly encountered with different levels of expertise compared to those encountered by users with visual disabilities.

The study was limited in different aspects considering its methodology and problems analyzed. The first limitation was the number of applications evaluated. The previous study on which this analysis was based had four apps [9,10]. However, the older versions that users evaluated were not operating. The sampling method for professionals was another limitation. Convenience sampling was used to invite participants. Due to this, the results cannot be generalized, as there might be biases in the selection. The participants are not representative of all developers or HCI specialists. We could not balance the sample to have the same number and variability of different groups.

Future studies should include a broader range of evaluators to perform a quantitative analysis. Other studies should also analyze the use of specific standards for mobile accessibility, such as the recently approved Brazilian ABNT NBR 17060 [2]. We also intend to compare the results encountered in accessibility inspections and those from evaluations with users with other disabilities.

Acknowledgements. We would like to thank all the participants who took part in this study for their valuable contribution. We also thank FAPEMIG, CNPq and FAPESP.

References

1. Abascal, J., Arrue, M., Valencia, X.: Tools for web accessibility evaluation. In: Web Accessibility: A Foundation for Research, pp. 479–503 (2019)
2. Associação Brasileira de Normas Técnicas (ABNT): ABNT NBR 17060 - Acessibilidade em aplicativos de dispositivos móveis - Requisitos (Accessibility in Mobile Apps - requirements) (2022). shorturl.at/lvwJ2
3. BBC: HTML accessibility standards v2.0 (2014). http://www.bbc.co.uk/guidelines/futuremedia/accessibility/html/. Accessed 15 Feb 2021
4. Brajnik, G.: A comparative test of web accessibility evaluation methods. In: Proceedings of the 10th International ACM SIGACCESS Conference on Computers and Accessibility, pp. 113–120 (2008)
5. Brajnik, G., Vigo, M., Yesilada, Y., Harper, S.: Group vs individual web accessibility evaluations: effects with novice evaluators. Interact. Comput. **28**(6), 843–861 (2016)
6. Brajnik, G., Yesilada, Y., Harper, S.: Testability and validity of WCAG 2.0: the expertise effect. In: Proceedings of the 12th International ACM SIGACCESS Conference on Computers and Accessibility, pp. 43–50 (2010)
7. Brajnik, G., Yesilada, Y., Harper, S.: The expertise effect on web accessibility evaluation methods. Hum.-Comput. Interact. **26**(3), 246–283 (2011)
8. British Broadcasting Corporation - BBC: Mobile accessibility standards and guidelines v1.0 (2014). http://shorturl.at/wCPX3. Accessed 15 Feb 2021
9. Carvalho, M.C.N., Dias, F.S., Reis, A.G.S., Freire, A.P.: Accessibility and usability problems encountered on websites and applications in mobile devices by blind and normal-vision users. In: Proceedings of the 33rd Annual ACM Symposium on Applied Computing, SAC 2018, pp. 2022–2029. Association for Computing Machinery, New York (2018)
10. Dias, F.S.: Análise de causas técnicasde problemas de acessibilidade encontrados em aplicativos nativos para dispositivos móveis. UFLA, Lavras (2018)
11. Freire, A.P.: Disabled people and the Web: User-based measurement of accessibility. Ph.D. thesis, University of York (2012)
12. Governo Brasileiro: Lei brasileira de inclusão da pessoa com deficiência (2015). https://www.planalto.gov.br/ccivil_03/_ato2015-2018/2015/lei/l13146.htm. Accessed 31 Jan 2023
13. ISO - International Organization for Standardization: ISO 9241-11. usability: Definitions and concepts (2018). https://www.iso.org/obp/ui/iso:std:iso:9241:-11:ed-2:v1:en. Accessed 31 Jan 2023
14. Jaeger, P.T.: Assessing section 508 compliance on federal e-government web sites: a multi-method, user-centered evaluation of accessibility for persons with disabilities. Gov. Inf. Q. **23**(2), 169–190 (2006)
15. Mankoff, J., Fait, H., Tran, T.: Is your web page accessible? A comparative study of methods for assessing web page accessibility for the blind. In: Proceedings of the SIGCHI Conference on Human Factors in Computing Systems, pp. 41–50 (2005)

16. Power, C., Freire, A., Petrie, H., Swallow, D.: Guidelines are only half of the story: accessibility problems encountered by blind users on the web. In: Proceedings of the SIGCHI Conference on Human Factors in Computing Systems, pp. 433–442 (2012)
17. Power, C., Petrie, H.: Working with participants. In: Web Accessibility: A Foundation for Research, pp. 153–168 (2019)
18. Rømen, D., Svanæs, D.: Validating WCAG versions 1.0 and 2.0 through usability testing with disabled users. Univers. Access Inf. Soc. **11**(4), 375–385 (2012)
19. Statista: Market share of mobile operating systems in Brazil from January 2019 to August 2022 (2022). https://www.statista.com/statistics/262167/market-share-held-by-mobile-operating-systems-in-brazil/. Accessed 20 May 2023
20. Statista: Mobile OS share in North America 2018–2023 (2022). https://www.statista.com/statistics/1045192/share-of-mobile-operating-systems-in-north-america-by-month/. Accessed 20 May 2023
21. Vollenwyder, B., Petralito, S., Iten, G.H., Brühlmann, F., Opwis, K., Mekler, E.D.: How compliance with web accessibility standards shapes the experiences of users with and without disabilities. Int. J. Hum.-Comput. Stud. **170**, 102956 (2023)
22. W3C: Web content accessibility guidelines 1.0, web accessibility initiative (1999). https://www.w3.org/TR/WCAG10/. Accessed 31 Jan 2023
23. W3C: W3c - world wide web consortium. web content accessibility guidelines (WCAG) 2.0 (2008). https://www.w3.org/TR/WCAG20/. Accessed 31 Jan 2023
24. W3C: W3c. web content accessibility guidelines (WCAG) 2.1 (2018). https://www.w3.org/TR/WCAG21/. Accessed 31 Jan 2023
25. W3C: W3c. web content accessibility guidelines (WCAG) 2.2 (2020). https://www.w3.org/TR/WCAG22/. Accessed 31 Jan 2023
26. W3C: W3c. web content accessibility guidelines (WCAG) 3.0 (2021). https://www.w3.org/TR/wcag-3.0/. Accessed 31 Jan 2023

Evaluating the Acceptance of a Software Application Designed to Assist Communication for People with Parkinson's Disease

Julia Greenfield[1] , Káthia Marçal de Oliveira[1(✉)] , Véronique Delcroix[1] , Sophie Lepreux[1] , Christophe Kolski[1] , and Anne Blanchard-Dauphin[2]

[1] Univ. Polytechnique Hauts-de-France, LAMIH CNRS UMR 8201, Le Mont-Houy cedex 9, 59313 Valenciennes, France
{julia.greenfield,kathia.oliveira,veronique.delcroix, sophie.lepreux,christophe.kolski}@uphf.fr
[2] Lille University Hospital Center - Physical Medicine and Rehabilitation Service,Rue André Verhaeghe, 59000 Lille, France
anne.blanchard@chu-lille.fr

Abstract. Parkinson's disease (PD) is a neurodegenerative disorder that affects a huge number of people. People with PD may have trouble speaking. Impeded speech affects 70% of people with PD and this can have particularly harmful consequences linked to social exclusion and isolation. Considering this context, we have been working for the last three years in the development of a software application to assist people with PD to communicate with others. To assure the use and adoption of this application an evaluation of its acceptance was carried out. To that end the Unified Theory of Acceptance of Use of Technology (UTAUT) was applied. The results showed acceptation of the application for people with PD that has serious problems of communication. This paper presents this evaluation from its design to the discussion of the results.

Keywords: UTAUT · Communication tool · Assisted technology · Acceptance · Parkinson

1 Introduction

Parkinson's disease (PD) is a neurodegenerative disorder that affects a huge number of people. It is the second most common neurodegenerative disorder in the world, following Alzheimer's disease [27]. The symptoms of PD are often associated with dysfunctional motor control; however people with PD may have speech disturbances, swallowing, depression and anxiety [7]. Impeded speech affects 70% of people with PD [27] and this can have particularly harmful consequences linked to social exclusion and isolation. Aware of this situation we have been worked for three years in the development of an specific software application [20], named ParkinsonCom to help people with PD to communicate.

J. Abdelnour Nocera et al. (Eds.): INTERACT 2023, LNCS 14142, pp. 155–164, 2023.
https://doi.org/10.1007/978-3-031-42280-5_10

A certain number of mobile applications already exist for people with speech difficulties (e.g. Proloquo2go [6] and Vocalyx [1]) that can also be used for people with PD but not developed considering their particularities and needs. ParkinsonCom was developed using a user-centred approach [3,15] where people with PD and their carers expressed their needs, participated in the co-design of the user interfaces and evaluated the developed application. The main functionality of the application is to support the person with PD to write a text and use a vocal synthesizer to communicate with people who are nearby, or send the texts by SMS or email to a contact previously saved in the application. For this, a specific virtual keyboard for people with PD was designed (e.g., keys more widely spaced, larger, in contrasting colors) in addition to allowing the choice of a classic AZERTY or ABCD keyboard. Complementary functionalities include an agenda to recall the medication schedule and a relaxation space to listen to music, see family photos, etc. To the best of our knowledge, this is the first app developed with and for people with PD that aims to increase and assist communication.

Once we had developed and tested the software application we carried out a study in which people with PD were asked to use the application and then evaluate it. To that end we have evaluated the usability of the application with CSUQ (Computer System Usability Questionnaire) [16] and then its acceptance for daily use. This article is focused on the acceptance evaluation of the proposed application through the use of the UTAUT (Unified Theory of Acceptance of Use of Technology) model [23] by target and non-target users (explained in the methods section). Ethical approval for this study was obtained from the ethical committees of Lille University (France) and Mons University (Belgium) under the respective references 2021-548-S100 and 10062022EB.

2   Background: Technology Acceptance

The integration of any new tool (physical or digital) into society undergoes a certain scrutiny by potential users. The notion of intending to use a new tool can be defined by acceptability (prior to first use) and acceptance (after first use). These constructs can be measured through questionnaires such as the Technology Acceptance Model [13], Theory of Planned Behaviour [4], and the Unified Theory of Acceptance of Use of Technology (UTAUT [22]), the latter providing the highest level of prediction of technology adoption [14].

The UTAUT model [22,23] is composed of seven constructs that influence behavioral intention to use a technology and as a result, technology use. Those constructs are defined as follows: (1) *Performance expectancy* is the degree to which using a technology will provide benefits to consumers in performing certain activities; (2) *Effort expectancy* is the degree of ease associated with consumers' use of technology; (3) *Social influence* is the extent to which consumers perceive that important others (e.g., family and friends) believe they should use a particular technology; (4) *Facilitating conditions* refer to consumers' perceptions of the resources and support available to perform a behavior effort expectancy; (5) *Hedonic motivation* refers to the fun or pleasure derived from using a technology;

(6) *Price value* is the consumers' cognitive trade off between the perceived benefits of the applications and the monetary cost for using them (7) *Experience and habit* in which Experience reflects an opportunity to use a target technology and is typically considered as the passage of time from the initial use of a technology by an individual, and Habit refers to the extent to which people tend to perform behaviors automatically because of learning. The questionnaire is composed of a total of 28 items evaluated in a 7-point Likert scale.

Several studies can be found regarding the acceptance of assistive technologies in health care using (e.g. [5,8,9,11,12,17,19,24,25]) or not (e.g. [10,21]) the UTAUT model. The users of the technology that evaluated its acceptance were therapists and health professionals [8,10–12,17,21], caregivers [9,25], and also the affected individuals [5,8,19,24]. The common aim of all these studies is the assessment of the acceptance identifying factors that would most influence future use behaviour of the given application or technology. The studies that applied the UTAUT confirmed its utility for the acceptance evaluation of applications in health care.

From these quoted articles, only two concern Parkinson's health care [8,19]. The first one [8] aims to evaluate the uses of an interactive digital tool (tablet and inertial sensor) for the self-rehabilitation of patients with PD. Patients use bracelets equipped with motion sensors and a tablet application guides them in the activity rehabilitation work. Physiotherapists and patients answered the UTAUT questionnaire for the acceptance evaluation. The second article [19] aims to evaluate a self-management application that records symptoms and medication information. To that end, the patients with PD performed a set of defined tasks in the application and then answer the UTAUT questionnaire. Both studies showed the feasibility of use of UTAUT by people with PD. However, to the best of our knowledge there is no study on acceptance evaluation of a tool for people with impeded speech (nor for Parkinson's or any other disease/disability). Experiments should be defined considering this element for the identification of the population and analysis of the results.

3   Methods

This section presents the research protocol approved by the French and Belgium national ethical committees.

Population and Recruitment. Participants were recruited through advertising and word of mouth, explaining the need to evaluate a system to support communication for people with PD. We decide to accept all volunteers for the experimentation. Participants were first contacted by email or telephone and the study procedure was explained to them. In total, 30 participants agreed to take part in this study, 15 from Belgium and 15 from France. Mean age was 68.7 ± 8.8 years, with a Parkinson's disease diagnosis history of 12.1 ± 7.1 years. In total, 18 men and 12 women were recruited for this study.

Procedure. The execution and evaluation procedure is composed of three steps:

1. Software presentation and collect of profile data - A first meeting was organized for demonstration of the software application, explanation of any unclear points, signing of the consent form and answer of some questions about age, gender and some questions of Parkinson's Well-being Map^{TM} [2] questionnaire related to speech difficulties. To protect identity and ensure anonymity, participants were assigned a colour as an identification code for the collected data.
2. Use of the application - The participants were left with a tablet for a minimum of one week and, during this time, they were asked to use the software application as an aid to their daily lives.
3. Feedback - Following the 7-day minimum period, a second meeting was carried out. Participants were able to express their views on the application, suggest modifications, and were also asked to answer questionnaires for usability (not explored in this paper) and acceptance (UTAUT) evaluation.

Data Collection, Measures and Processing. The questionnaire was printed and manually filled out by the participants (with help of careers if necessary) in the presence of the researchers, which allowed for questions to be asked should any item be unclear. Each item of the UTAUT was answered using a 7-point Likert scale from 1 ("strongly disagree") to 7 ("strongly agree"). Measures collected included the UTAUT model variables: performance expectancy (PE), effort expectancy (EE), social influence (SI), Facilitating Conditions (FC), Hedonic Motivation(HM), Habit (H) and Behavioural Intention (BI). The *Price value* item was not included since the application would be available online for free. In addition, age, gender and self-evaluation of difficulty of speech are also registered. This last information was collected by answering the item "I have slowness of speech and/or people often ask me to repeat myself" of Parkinson's Well-being map questionnaire [2] using a 5-point Likert scale ranging from 1 ("strongly disagree") to 5 ("strongly agree"). The completed questionnaires (Well-being map selected items and UTAUT) were transcribed to an Excel spreadsheet for further analysis.

Applied Techniques and Statistical Analysis. Data were divided into two subgroups: a target population and a non-target population. As the primary objective of the application is to provide assistance in communication, a target participant was considered as someone who had severe speech communication difficulties. A score relating to 4 (agree) or 5 (strongly agree) for the related item of the Well-being map questionnaire distinguish target participants from non-target participants. Using the spreadsheet previously completed, median scores for each participant and each subgroup were calculated for each category of the Well-being map and for each UTAUT construct. Demographics, including participant age and history of diagnosis were averaged for each subgroup.

The two data pools (target and non-target) were assessed for normality using the Shapiro-Wilk test. Next, based on the Shapiro-Wilk test result, an independent samples t-test or a Mann Whitney-U test was used to evaluate the differences between the two groups' scores for each UTAUT construct. Effect sizes were calculated using Cohen's d where 0.2 is considered small, 0.5 medium and 0.8 large, and confidence intervals were determined at the 95% level. Kendall's Tau B was used to quantify the relationship between the Behavioural intention UTAUT construct and the remaining six UTAUT constructs (PE, EE, SI, FC, HM, H) for each population group in order to evaluate the underlying factors influencing future use of the system. All statistical analyses were performed in JASP software (version 0.16, JASP Team 2021). The threshold for significance was set at 0.05.

4   Results

Of the 30 participants initially included in the study, data from three participants were removed as these participants chose to abandon the study. Of the data from the 27 participants included in the statistical analyses, the mean age was 68.3 ± 9.2 years, with a diagnosis history of 13.6 ± 7.3 years. A total of seven participants qualified for the target population group, leaving 20 participants in the non-target group.

4.1   Acceptance of the Software Application

Results from the UTAUT questionnaire are given in Table 1. Data are presented as medians and interquartile ranges (IQR). Performance expectancy, social influence, habit and behavioural intention are all significantly higher in the target group than in the non-target group. However, in the non-target group effort expectancy and hedonic motivation were higher; although these differences were not significant. The facilitating conditions construct displayed equal scores for both population groups, although the non-target group had a slightly lower interquartile range.

The greatest difference lies in the social influence construct, where the median score for the target group (6.0) is more than 2-fold that of the non-target group (2.0); this difference is significant ($p < 0.01$) and is also coupled with a high effect size. All other significant differences (PE, H, and BI) demonstrate medium effect sizes, despite differences in H and BI being highly significant between the two population groups.

4.2   Behavioural Intention Influences

The results from correlation analyses showed that behavioural intention was not influenced by the same factors depending on the target and on-target population groups. A summary of the six UTAUT constructs (PE, EE, SI, FC, H, and HM) and their correlation level with BI is given in Table 2.

For the target group, BI was influenced by EE and FC, with these constructs displaying a significantly positive correlation with BI (Tau-B = 0.51 and 0.48, respectively). Although not significant, the correlation with SI (Tau-B = 0.31, $p = 0.14$) was also relatively high. For the non-target group, all UTAUT

Table 1. Median [interquartile range] UTAUT construct scores for the target and non-target population with the p-value from Mann Whitney-U tests, and effect given as Cohen's d with upper and lower confidence intervals (CI). (* = significantly higher score; CI = confidence interval)

UTAUT construct	Target group score (n = 7)	Non-target group score (n = 20)	P-value	Effect [low CI - high CI]
Performance expectancy	6.0 [2.0]*	4.0 [4.0]	0.01	−0.38 [−0.60 - −0.11]
Effort expectancy	6.0 [1.5]	7.0 [2.0]	0.34	0.12 [−0.18 – 0.36]
Social influence	6.5 [1.0]*	2.0 [3.0]	< 0.01	−0.86 [−0.93 – −0.75]
Facilitating conditions	6.0 [2.0]	4.0 [4.0]	0.44	0.10 [−0.16 – 0.35]
Hedonic motivation	5.5 [2.5]	6.0 [1.3]	0.67	0.07 [−0.24 – 0.36]
Habit	4.5 [3.0]*	2.0 [4.0]	< 0.01	−0.46 [−0.64 – −0.22]
Behavioural intention	2.0 [5.0]*	4.0 [4.0]	< 0.01	−0.54 [−0.71 – −0.30]
Total (all constructs)	5.0 [5.0]	4.0 [4.0]	< 0.01	0.24 [0.13 – 0.34]

constructs significantly and positively influenced behavioural intention. The most influential construct was PE, with a correlation coefficient of 0.74, followed closely by SI (Tau-B = 0.67). All other constructs presented only moderate correlations; however, all were significant. Hedonic motivation correlated with a coefficient of 0.45 with BI. The remaining three constructs (EE, FC, and H) all produced moderate correlations of between 0.3 and 0.4.

Table 2. Correlations between UTAUT constructs and behavioural intention (BI) with p-value for the target and non-target population groups. (* = significant correlation)

UTAUT construct	Correlation with BI Target group (p-value)	Correlation with BI Non-target group (p-value)
Performance expectancy	0.11 (0.61)	0.74 (< 0.01)*
Effort expectancy	0.51 (< 0.01)*	0.30 (0.01)*
Social influence	0.31 (0.14)	0.67 (< 0.01)*
Facilitating conditions	0.48 (0.01)*	0.37 (< 0.01)*
Hedonic motivation	0.20 (0.31)	0.34 (< 0.01)*
Habit	0.21 (0.31)]*	0.45 (< 0.01)*

4.3   Discussion

Within the UTAUT constructs, the Mann Whitney-U tests found significantly higher PE, SI, H, and BI scores in the target group compared to the non-target group. These results indicate that, in comparison to those in the non-target group, the people in the target group find this application more useful than those in the non-target group (performance expectancy); this population also had a social entourage who were more encouraging in the use of the application (social influence). The target group also had a greater need to use this app (habit), and have a greater intention to continue using this system (behavioural intention). Regarding other results, the non-target group found the application easier to use (greater effort expectancy) than the target group. Although not significant, this difference may be due to other factors of Parkinson's disease affecting the patients. If people in the non-target group also had less motor symptoms, for example, or perhaps were younger or more used to using technology, then this will have influenced the ease of use of this system. The non-target population also gave the application a higher score for hedonic motivation (i.e. they found the system more fun to use). The latter phenomenon may also be linked to past and current experience with technology, the UTAUT model from Venkatesh and colleagues [22] have displayed that both HM and EE are influenced by experience and that greater past experience with similar technology (in this case, a tablet with apps installed) will lead to a higher EE (the new technology will be easier to use) and a higher HM (they will take more pleasure in using the technology).

The score given for facilitating conditions (6/7) was identical in both the target and non-target population groups, indicating that all participants had a similar access to the required technology for use of the application, and also all had the sufficient skills and knowledge to use an app on a mobile tablet. Facilitating conditions is the only construct, other than BI, to directly influence use behaviour.

The lower behavioural intention score given by the non-target group can be explained by the fact that the app is primarily aimed at those having partially or fully lost the ability to speak. Although the app provides other functions, such as easy access to off-period activities and an activity and medication planner, the use of such a system for communication will naturally be less attractive to those who are still able to communicate with their peers. The app offers the possibility for live communication by typing out a text and having the tablet read it out loud, but a user can also send the text a given contact via email or text messaging. This function is highly similar to that offered by a telephone but the app's keyboard is designed in such a way that the keys are bigger, more spaced out, and it is less sensitive to possible trembling - a typical symptom of Parkinson's disease. The use of the BI construct to evaluate the factors influencing future system use is based on the original UTAUT model by [22,23]. The former studies have shown that system usability is directly influenced by behavioural intention and, since our study did not assess long-term use of the application, the BI construct is considered as a strong predictor of future use.

Some limitations of the study are the relatively small sample size, in particular for the target group and also the absence of an acceptability study carried out before the development of the app. For future studies concerning this application, it would be of interest to conduct a longitudinal study on use behaviour, or plan a follow-up study at the end of a given trial period. Further development of the app may wish to build on the constructs with lower scores cited here, such as habit for the target group, and PE, SI, H and BI for the non-target group.

4.4   Threats to Validity

Following [26] we analysed four threats to validity as described below:

- *construct validity* regards the choice of the questionnaire used in the study. To mitigate this threat, we used UTAUT questionnaire that has high level of reliability as shown in [23];
- *internal validity* is associated with the potential bias of the participants involved in the study. To mitigate this threat we made an open call on the internet (emails, social network and project website), requesting volunteers for evaluation. All persons who answered the call participated in the study. No prior selection was carried out;
- *conclusion validity* regards the ability to draw the correct conclusion of the study. To mitigate this threat we performed a careful analysis with reliable static methods and we separated the participants for the analysis into target and non target groups;
- *external validity* regards the ability to generalize the results of our experiment outside the scope of our study. Although the call was open, the users are only of French nationality, so we cannot generalise the result to any people with Parkinson.

5   Conclusion

This article has presented the evaluation of the acceptance of a communication tool for people with Parkinson's disease using UTAUT model. Thirty users with PD were initially involved, and data from 27 of them could be exploited. To our knowledge, this is the first study that applies UTAUT for an evaluation of a tool by people with varying speech capacities. Considering that the aim of ParkinsonCom is to support communication, for a better analysis, we divide the answers to the questionnaire in two main groups based on the severity of speech communications difficulties of the person with PD. The UTAUT analysis of each of the factors proved adequate in this context.

The results showed that the application has a good acceptance for people with severe difficulties in communication. However, it shows that the application is not adequate for people that have small to moderate difficulties on communication. Therefore, it should be improved to answer the need of personalisation taking into account the evolving nature of Parkinson's disease [18]. The software application is currently available for download (https://www.parkinsoncom.eu). Further evaluations could aim to study how differences related to speech capacity influence the use of the tool, given that we are dealing with an evolving disease.

Acknowledgements. The authors warmly thank all participants who took time to assist in the development and evaluation of the ParkinsonCom application. This project is supported by the European regional development fund, FEDER (Interreg V France-Wallonie-Vlaanderen) and the Agency for quality life AVIQ (l'Agence pour une Vie de Qualité), Belgium, to which the are are deeply grateful.

References

1. Vocalyx. https://vocalyx.com/. Accessed 14 Apr 2023
2. Wellbeing map. https://www.parkinsonseurope.org/about-parkinsons/symptoms/wellbeing-map/. Accessed 08 Jun 2023
3. Iso 9241–210:2019 ergonomics of human-system interaction - part 210: Human-centred design for interactive systems. Standard, International Organization for Standardization (2019)
4. Ajzen, I.: The theory of planned behaviour: reactions and reflections. Psychol. Health **26**(9), 1113–1127 (2011). https://doi.org/10.1080/08870446.2011.613995, pMID: 21929476
5. Al Shehri, W., Almalki, J., Alshahrani, S., Alammari, A., Khan, F., Alangari, S.: Assistive technology acceptance for visually impaired individuals: a case study of students in Saudi Arabia. PeerJ. Comput. Sci. **8**, e886 (2022). https://doi.org/10.7717/peerj-cs.886
6. Assistive ware: S'exprimer avec la CAA basée sur des symboles. https://www.assistiveware.com/fr/produits/proloquo2go. Accessed 14 Apr 2023
7. Beitz, J.M.: Parkinson's disease: a review. Front Biosci (Schol Ed) **6**(1), 65–74 (2014). https://doi.org/10.2741/S415
8. Blanc, M., et al.: Evaluation of a digitally guided self-rehabilitation device coupled with telerehabilitation monitoring in patients with parkinson disease (telep@rk): Open, prospective observational study. In: JMIR serious games (2022). https://doi.org/10.2196/24946
9. Bsharat, B., Al-Duhoun, A., Ghanouni, P.: The acceptance and attitudes towards using assistive technology for people with stroke in jordan: caregivers' perspectives. Assistive Technol. Official J. RESNA 1–11 (2023). https://doi.org/10.1080/10400435.2023.2202723
10. Calisto, F.M., et al.: Assertiveness-based agent communication for a personalized medicine on medical imaging diagnosis. In: Proceedings of the 2023 CHI Conference on Human Factors in Computing Systems. CHI 2023, Association for Computing Machinery, New York, NY, USA (2023). https://doi.org/10.1145/3544548.3580682
11. Calisto, F.M., Nunes, N., Nascimento, J.C.: Modeling adoption of intelligent agents in medical imaging. Int. J. Hum.-Comput. Stud. **168**, 102922 (2022). https://doi.org/10.1016/j.ijhcs.2022.102922
12. Cruz, A., Perez, H., Daum, C., Rutledge, E., King, S., Liu, L.: Technology acceptance and usability of a mobile application to support the workflow of health care aides who provide services to older adults residing in a care facility: a pilot mixed methods study (preprint). JMIR Aging **5**, e37521 (2022). https://doi.org/10.2196/37521
13. Davis, F., Davis, F.: Perceived usefulness, perceived ease of use, and user acceptance of information technology. MIS Q. **13**, 319 (1989). https://doi.org/10.2307/249008
14. Legris, P., Ingham, J., Collerette, P.: Why do people use information technology? a critical review of the technology acceptance model. Inf. Manage. **40**(3), 191–204 (2003). https://doi.org/10.1016/S0378-7206(01)00143-4

15. Lepreux, S., Apedo, K., Oliveira, K.M.D.: Vers une conception centrée sur l'utilisateur ayant un profil évolutif: Une étude de cas avec des personnes atteintes de la maladie de parkinson: Towards a user-centered design with an evolving profile: A case study with people with parkinson's disease. In: 32e Conférence Francophone Sur l'Interaction Homme-Machine. IHM 2021, Association for Computing Machinery, New York, NY, USA (2021). https://doi.org/10.1145/3451148.3458646
16. Lewis, J.R.: IBM computer usability satisfaction questionnaires: psychometric evaluation and instructions for use. Int. J. Hum.-Comput. Interact. **7**(1), 57–78 (1995). https://doi.org/10.1080/10447319509526110
17. Liu, L., Cruz, A.M., Rincon, A.R., Buttar, V., Ranson, Q., Goertzen, D.: What factors determine therapists' acceptance of new technologies for rehabilitation - a study using the unified theory of acceptance and use of technology (utaut). Disabil. Rehabil. **37**(5), 447–455 (2015). https://doi.org/10.3109/09638288.2014.923529, pMID: 24901351
18. McNaney, R., Tsekleves, E., Synnott, J.: Future opportunities for IoT to support people with parkinson's. In: Proceedings of the 2020 CHI Conference on Human Factors in Computing Systems, CHI 2020, pp. 1–15. Association for Computing Machinery, New York, NY, USA (2020). https://doi.org/10.1145/3313831.3376871
19. Memedi, M., Lindqvist, J., Tunedal, T., Duvåker, A.: A study on pre-adoption of a self-management application by parkinson's disease patients. In: 39th International Conference on Information System (2019)
20. de Oliveira, K.M., et al.: ParkinsonCom project: towards a software communication tool for people with Parkinson's disease. In: Antona, M., Stephanidis, C. (eds.) HCII 2021. LNCS, vol. 12768, pp. 418–428. Springer, Cham (2021). https://doi.org/10.1007/978-3-030-78092-0_28
21. Sivaraman, V., Bukowski, L.A., Levin, J., Kahn, J.M., Perer, A.: Ignore, trust, or negotiate: understanding clinician acceptance of AI-based treatment recommendations in health care. In: Proceedings of the 2023 CHI Conference on Human Factors in Computing Systems. CHI 2023, Association for Computing Machinery, New York, NY, USA (2023). https://doi.org/10.1145/3544548.3581075
22. Venkatesh, V., Morris, M.G., Davis, G.B., Davis, F.D.: User acceptance of information technology: toward a unified view. MIS Q. **27**(3), 425–478 (2003)
23. Venkatesh, V., Thong, J.Y.L., Xu, X.: Consumer acceptance and use of information technology: extending the unified theory of acceptance and use of technology. MIS Q. **36**(1), 157–178 (2012)
24. Wang, H., Tao, D., Yu, N., Qu, X.: Understanding consumer acceptance of healthcare wearable devices: an integrated model of utaut and ttf. Int. J. Med. Inf. **139**, 104156 (2020). https://doi.org/10.1016/j.ijmedinf.2020.104156
25. Wasić, C., Bahrmann, F., Vogt, S., Böhme, H.J., Graessel, E.: Assessing professional caregivers' intention to use and relatives' support of use for a mobile service robot in group therapy for institutionalized people with dementia - a standardized assessment using an adapted version of utaut. In: Miesenberger, K., Kouroupetroglou, G., Mavrou, K., Manduchi, R., Covarrubias Rodriguez, M., Penáz, P. (eds.) Computers Helping People with Special Needs, pp. 247–256. Springer, Cham (2022). https://doi.org/10.1007/978-3-031-08645-8_29
26. Wohlin, C., Runeson, P., Höst, M., Ohlsson, M., Regnell, B., Wesslén, A.: Experimentation in Software Engineering. Springer-Berlin Heidelberg (2012). https://doi.org/10.1007/978-3-642-29044-2
27. World health organization: Parkinson disease. https://www.who.int/news-room/fact-sheets/detail/parkinson-disease. Accessed 13 Jan 2023

"The Relief is Amazing": An In-situ Short Field Evaluation of a Personal Voice Assistive Technology for a User Living with Dementia

Ana-Maria Salai[1]($\boxtimes$), Glenda Cook[2], and Lars Erik Holmquist[3]

[1] School of Design, Northumbria University, Newcastle upon Tyne, UK
salaianamaria@gmail.com
[2] Nursing, Midwifery and Health, Northumbria University, Newcastle upon Tyne, UK
glenda.cook@northumbria.ac.uk
[3] Nottingham Trent University, Nottingham, UK
lars.holmquist@ntu.ac.uk

Abstract. We present a first short field evaluation of *IntraVox*, a smart home assistive technology that has the potential to support older adults with dementia living independently at home. Based on sensor data, IntraVox uses a *personalized human voice* to send prompts and reminders to end-users to conduct daily life activities. During a short field study of seven days, IntraVox was installed in the home of an end-user with advanced dementia to prompt a lifestyle change. Additional feedback was collected from their family supporter and three carers. Results show that IntraVox has the potential to prompt end-users with complex needs into changing their actions. In particular, the family supporter found that IntraVox was *"100% successful"* in that it allowed the family more time together rather than focusing on caregiving, and the relief afforded by the system was considered *"amazing"*. Thus, we argue the system has the potential to improve the quality of life of both the end-users and their carers. These preliminary findings will inform future larger studies that will assess the usability and feasibility of such systems.

Keywords: Smart Home · Assistive Technology · Dementia

1 Introduction

Individuals across the globe are living longer. A consequence of this is that people develop complex comorbidities and social problems. Dementia is currently one of the major causes of disability and dependency amongst older adults and affects the ability to perform daily activities such as cooking, washing, and maintaining

Supplementary Information The online version contains supplementary material available at https://doi.org/10.1007/978-3-031-42280-5_11.

J. Abdelnour Nocera et al. (Eds.): INTERACT 2023, LNCS 14142, pp. 165–175, 2023.
https://doi.org/10.1007/978-3-031-42280-5_11

personal hygiene [12]. Technology is an important factor in supporting people with dementia to live independently in their homes. One response by carers is to provide reminders or cues [19] using various assistive technologies.

IntraVox [27] is a novel voice-based assistive technology, which has the potential to prompt older adults with dementia to change their actions. In collaboration with a city council, we conducted an initial field study of IntraVox in a home setting. The system is composed of a speaker and a Raspberry Pi 4B computer with various smart home sensors attached. Based on the sensor data collected and using a *personalized human voice*, IntraVox *verbally* sends prompts and reminders to end-users to conduct tasks according to their needs and aspirations (e.g., enhance continence). The system introduces a high level of personalization as the human voice can be that of e.g. a carer, a family member, or a friend. All prompts and reminders verbalized by IntraVox are tailored to the individual's needs and capacity to understand the instructions (e.g., tailored keywords and sentence structure). Whilst popular voice assistants (e.g., Amazon Alexa, Google Home) can provide prompts and reminders using standard voices [34], the IntraVox system is unique in that it uses a personalized human voice for delivering prompts, which could have benefits of security and comfort [27].

The work was conducted during the COVID-19 pandemic, at which time many research studies had stagnated [4,25]. Despite these challenges, we recruited one end-user, their family supporter, and three carers. We installed IntraVox in the end-user's home for seven days and asked participants to interact with it in an uncontrolled way. We wished to address the following research questions: *RQ1: Does IntraVox have the potential to prompt people with dementia to change their behaviour?* and *RQ2: Do the tailored prompts used by IntraVox have an emotional impact on people with dementia and their carers?*

This paper is structured as follows. We start by providing an overview of assistive technologies, highlighting also the importance of conducting short field evaluation studies. We then present the study conducted to evaluate IntraVox. Finally, we discuss the contributions we bring to the Human-Computer Interaction (HCI) field.

2   Background

In this section, we present the current research regarding assistive technologies and we highlight the importance of conducting short field evaluation studies.

Voice Assistive Systems. Most voice assistive systems are composed of off-the-shelf devices such as Amazon Alexa and Google Home. These have been introduced in the home as they have the potential to support independent living [4,11,15,22]. For example, Shalini et al. [29] developed a customized voice assistant system using the two devices for older adults to use in the home. The system was developed as a consumer interface for the end-users and their family members that can provide health information on-demand, based on spoken queries. Simpson et al. [30], on the other hand, used an open source framework to design a conversational agent and provide companionship to older adults. The device engages in a casual conversation with the user regarding a past memory in their life or by suggesting activities that might be of interest to them. Despite the benefits, most users face challenges in interacting with the assistants. Whilst most users start by interacting in a natural language, they are later forced to learn how to speak to the assistant in order to successfully enable and interact with it, i.e., limit themselves to specific keywords, remember the proper commands and verbalize them clearly, loudly and in a short amount of time in the case of Amazon Alexa and Google Home [10,18].

Prompting and Reminding. Cognitive assistive technologies supporting adults with dementia can provide them with an increased level of independence by considering their specific needs, emotions, and preferences [22,27]. For example, systems using sensors, smart bulbs, and pressure detectors can direct individuals to the bathroom at night [1], whereas other systems can guide individuals to prepare meals [5], wash hands and prepare a cup of tea [20]. König et al. [16] highlight that a one-size-fits-all style of prompting should be avoided as people with dementia have different emotional responses to prompts, thus the user's background and *"sense of self and identity"* should be considered when designing assistive technologies. Furthermore, Boyd et al. [6] concluded that prompts for people with dementia that are delivered in a familiar and explicit language can increase the success of a tailored intervention.

Short Field Evaluations. Technology evaluation is essential in HCI. Despite being complex and time-consuming, it is important to conduct short field evaluations as laboratory-based ones could leave mistakes unrevealed [14,17]. Rogers et al. [24] argue that laboratory studies are *"poor at capturing the context of use"* and highlight that in-situ evaluations can indicate how people interact with technology in their intended setting. Bacchetti et al. [2] highlight that studies of new technologies and ideas *"often must start small (sometimes even with n of 1) because of cost and feasibility concerns."*. Similarly, Caine [9] notes that *"small"* sample size studies can bring important findings to the HCI community by informing future studies and revealing the most obvious usability problems.

3   Short Field Evaluation Study

Together with a city council team, we identified an opportunity for IntraVox to be piloted with one of the city council's customers. The end-user was a woman with advanced dementia, who lived alone at home (referred to as *'the mother'*). A family supporter (her *son*) stayed with her during evenings and mornings and three carers (city council employees) attended daily to prepare meals (lunch and dinner) and provide medication.

The study had three phases: *Phase(1)* - a pre-study interview with the son to understand the requirements and how IntraVox could provide an intervention; *Phase(2)* – an uncontrolled field study of seven days when IntraVox was installed in the mother's home together with additional questionnaires the son and the three carers were asked to complete, and *Phase(3)* – a post-study interview to explore the son's views regarding the system and his views of the impact it had on his mother. Ethical approval was obtained from the University and the city council to install the system in the mother's house. Informed consent was attained by the son and carers, whereas the son acted as a consultee for the involvement of his mother who lacked the capacity to consent [31].

3.1   Phase 1 – Pre-study Interview

The interview was composed of open-ended questions to understand the son's experience with smart home devices and how IntraVox could support the mother (to answer RQ1). The son was also presented with videos depicting scenarios where IntraVox could support end-users with complex needs [27].

Findings. The son had previously installed technology in his mother's house. This included smart cameras to monitor the carers [23], USB-controlled gas, smart switches, and an Amazon Alexa for controlling lighting. His mother was unable to interact with the devices as a result of her advanced dementia.

With the deterioration of the mother's cognitive abilities, she was in need of more personal care. One aspect that also impacted the son was the mother urinating in the utility room rather than her bathroom. The son suggested that IntraVox could *"remind her that the utility room is not the bathroom and that she should go upstairs to use the toilet."*. Regarding the voice, the son stated: *"Her dementia is very advanced, but she is strong-willed, and she would listen to a familiar voice, especially a carer's voice. She doesn't always listen to me, but she follows the carer's instructions really well. Accents that she recognises make her feel more comfortable."*.

3.2   Phase 2 - Short Field Study

In collaboration with the son and three city council officers (an occupational therapist (OT), a dementia carer who has previously supported the mother, and an IT representative familiar with the mother's situation), we held a separate discussion to explore how we could install the system in the mother's home in compliance with COVID-19 pandemic restrictions, and to agree on the intervention. It was agreed to use IntraVox to provide prompts to use the bathroom rather than the utility room for voiding. It was decided that IntraVox would be installed in the utility room. Whenever motion would be detected (i.e., the mother entered the room), a prompt would be played: *"Mary, the toilet is upstairs."*. As advised by the son, the prompt would be repeated twice. As the mother cooperates when recognising a familiar accent, we used the OT's voice for the prompt. IntraVox was deployed for seven days to collect sufficient qualitative and quantitative data [13].

Development. IntraVox was comprised of a Raspberry Pi 4B computer, embedded in a case, with speakers attached to play the prompt (Fig. 1 left). As per the city council officers' recommendation, we used the Samsung SmartThings motion sensor [28] for detecting motion in the utility room. The city council officers suggested the use of a Message Queue Telemetry Transport (MQTT) protocol [21], a standard Internet of Things protocol designed for transferring messages. Python software was used to connect to the city council's server and to subscribe to the topic of interest (motion in a room). Whenever a message was received (motion detected), the prompt played.

Fig. 1. IntraVox installed inside a cabinet (left) and the motion sensor (right).

Procedure. The system was installed following COVID-19 safety measurements [25]. As per the son's advice, the system was installed in a hidden cabinet to avoid it being disturbed by the mother, and the motion sensor was placed on top of a light switch (Fig. 1 right). Data was collected in the background to log the time motion was detected and a prompt was played.

The son and the three carers were asked to complete two questionnaires, every day. The first questionnaire had two open-ended questions and a 5-Likert-scale question to capture their views regarding IntraVox. The questionnaire also included an emotion wheel to capture their emotion and emotional distress when interacting with the system [8]. We used Baillie et al.'s emotion wheel [3] to capture their emotions when entering the room and the prompt was played. For each emotion wheel, participants were asked to provide a primary and secondary emotion, with each emotion being grouped into its corresponding quadrant [3]. The second questionnaire, containing an open-ended question and an emotion wheel, aimed to capture the mother's reaction and emotions when hearing the prompt (to answer RQ2). Participants were asked to view and describe the mother's interaction with the system. The scope was to make sure the audio messages were not causing any emotional distress, e.g. being perceived as auditory hallucinations or making the mother think someone is in the house.

Findings. Due to their busy schedules, the son and the three carers managed to complete the two questionnaires only once. Positive emotions were provided when filling out the emotion wheels, with the majority being in the Very Passive – Very Positive quadrant (Table 1). This indicates that participants had a pleasant interaction with the system.

Inconsistencies were, however, noticed in the feedback. Despite indicating positive feelings when entering the utility room and hearing the prompt, participants provided mixed feedback on the 5-Likert-scale question if the prompt was annoying, i.e., the son disagreed, Carer 1 neither agreed nor disagreed, whilst Carer 2 and 3 agreed.

Table 1. Participants' emotions when hearing the prompt played by IntraVox.

Participant	Primary Emotion	Secondary Emotion	Annoyance
The Son	Pleased	Relaxed	No
Carer 1	Alarmed	Glad	Neutral
Carer 2	Happy	Relaxed	Yes
Carer 3	Glad	Satisfied	Yes

Positive emotions were described by the son and carers with regards to the mother's interaction with the system, with the majority being in the Very Passive – Very Positive quadrant (Table 2). She had a positive reaction to the system and no signs of distress when hearing the prompt. This contradicts previous findings indicating that IntraVox might only be suitable for people with mild and moderate dementia as the familiar voice might cause confusion [27].

Table 2. The mother's emotions when hearing the prompt played by IntraVox.

Participant	Primary Emotion	Secondary Emotion	Comment
The Son	Calm	Relaxed	*"She listened and left."*
Carer 1	Amused	Calm	*"She seemed interested in the prompt."*
Carer 2	Pleased	Relaxed	*"She listened and asked about it."*

3.3   Phase 3 – Post-study Interview

The second interview with the son was composed of open-ended questions and aimed to understand his views regarding IntraVox and whether it was beneficial to the mother (to answer RQ1).

Findings. IntraVox received positive feedback from the son who stated: *"The idea is massive. The study was 100% successful as we did not have any incident in the utility room since IntraVox was installed."*. Confirming previous findings [27], the son felt that the human voice contributed to a sense of security and comfort, and helped his mother adhere to a routine. The son also believed that IntraVox can improve the quality of life of both of them, stating that: *"It can definitely improve her quality of life as sometimes she feels embarrassed of her actions. It* *gives me more time to spend with my mother, rather than cleaning around the house. The relief is amazing.".* When asked about the mother's interaction with the system, the son declared that: *"She would open the door and stop when she would hear the voice. She acknowledged that somebody was talking, she listened and paid attention to the second prompt. It didn't scare her, she didn't seem upset. She didn't seem surprised either.".*

The son highlighted that the familiar voice *"was annoying to me and the other carers who were in and out for 4 - 5 times.".* The son believed that IntraVox might be *"better for people living alone",* or, as suggested by the carers, to trigger the prompts only for the mother. However, in other circumstances, the son declared he would like to hear the voice all the time: *"If the sensor was installed on the front door, then I would definitely like to hear it and have an alert on my phone.".* All in all, despite the annoyance the familiar voice can sometimes trigger to non-end-users, the son added that: *"The benefit of having it outweighs that, and the voice would not stop me from installing it.".*

The log data collected also indicates a need to distinguish between individuals. As advised by the son, *"only triggers between 1 pm - 6 pm would be accurate"* as the mother was visited by carers during the day. Focusing on this time interval, the prompt was triggered on average 8.75 times per day. Importantly, there were no incidences of voiding in inappropriate locations during the study. This suggests that IntraVox was an effective prompt.

4 Discussion

Here we discuss the outcomes of the study and how they address our RQs:

RQ1: Does IntraVox have the potential to prompt people with dementia to change their behaviour? Results show that IntraVox has the potential to prompt a lifestyle change by prompting end-users with dementia to change their routines and behaviours. Whilst embodied conversational agents also have great potential in supporting older adults [32], IntraVox is unique in that it uses a *personalized human voice* for delivering prompts and reminders to users with dementia with the purpose of supporting them in their daily activities. Moreover, IntraVox does not require any interaction as the system is not composed of any voice assistive device available on the market (Amazon Alexa, Google Home). We argue that overcoming the need to verbalize commands and remembering syntaxes results in an increased usability. IntraVox can always be adjusted and its purpose can be changed over time following an evaluation of the end-user's needs. For example, IntraVox can also be used as a guiding system by using a motion sensor and a smart bulb and/or bar. Similar to previous findings [6,16,27], the results indicate that assistive technologies using tailored prompts to the end-user's needs and the use of a human voice can be beneficial to people with dementia. Researchers designing voice assisting interfaces for people with cognitive impairments should consider using a familiar voice (e.g., a carer, a family member, or a friend) as this could create a sense of security and comfort.

RQ2: Do the tailored prompts used by IntraVox have an emotional impact on people with dementia and their carers? Prompts and reminders are important in dementia care [19]. The positive feedback and the emotions provided demonstrate that IntraVox was not received as a negative experience by the mother, it did not cause any emotional distress and has the potential to improve the quality of life of both the end-user and their carers. The son and carers were pleased that previous voiding in inappropriate places ceased, without intervention from them. This enabled their interaction to refocus on being together and enjoying positive interaction rather than focusing on cleaning the utility room. We believe that IntraVox's main outcome demonstrated here was the improvement in the quality of life of the cared-for and carers, together with a reduced carer burden. People with dementia live with a range of symptoms and their response to the use of IntraVox will differ. Hence, careful assessment is required to ensure that technology is useful, appropriate, and, importantly, does not enhance anxiety.

We conducted the study as an experience-centred project [33] focusing on the mother's interaction with IntraVox and her reactions and emotions when hearing the prompt. Having no incident during the study represented a huge achievement for her. This field study highlights the importance of designing assistive technologies based on the end-users' needs and aspirations. Similar to [7], we believe that the findings could inform future larger studies focusing on evaluating assistive technologies for prompting and supporting end-users with dementia. Below we present additional key points arising from the study's findings:

Multiple evaluation forms might need to be applied when evaluating assistive technologies and their emotional impact on users. Inconsistencies were noticed in the feedback provided, i.e., despite providing positive feelings when entering the utility room and hearing the prompt, participants found the prompt to be annoying. Similar to [26], this inconsistency can indicate that researchers may want to consider using more than one technique when assessing the success of an assistive technology and its emotional impact on users.

Understanding the end-user and the environment can improve the user experience when interacting with assistive technologies. When technology migrates to real-life settings, more usability problems are discovered than during laboratory evaluations [14,17,24]. The findings from this study indicate a need to distinguish between individuals and play the prompts accordingly. This is due to the fact that IntraVox does not recognize the person entering the room and plays the prompt whenever motion is detected. This led to the carers and the son sometimes being irritated by the voice repetition, whilst the mother was not. This indicates that researchers can design an assistive technology that may seem annoying to a regular user but not to the intended end-user.

5   Limitations and Future Work

The main limitation is the small number of participants taking part in the study. We would like to conduct more field studies with a higher number of participants to determine whether IntraVox would be suitable for people experiencing various cognitive disabilities. To develop the system further, we would introduce sensors that could differentiate between different users, as suggested in the discussion. In the future, thanks to recent developments in generative Artificial Intelligence, a synthetic voice might also be created to mimic a known human voice.

6   Conclusion

In this paper, we present the short field evaluation we conducted to evaluate *IntraVox*, a novel voice-based interaction system that uses a highly personalized human voice to send prompts to older adults with dementia. Results show the system has the potential to prompt a lifestyle change and increase the quality of life of the end-user and their carers. Despite the small sample, we believe that the findings can be generalized to individuals experiencing a wide range of cognitive disabilities. Moreover, the lessons learned can inform larger studies focusing on evaluating assistive technologies for prompting and reminding end-users with complex needs to conduct various daily activities.

References

1. Ault, L., Goubran, R., Wallace, B., Lowden, H., Knoefel, F.: Smart home technology solution for night-time wandering in persons with dementia. J. Rehabil. Assist. Technol. Eng. **7**, 2055668320938591 (2020)
2. Bacchetti, P., Deeks, S. G., McCune, J. M.: Breaking free of sample size dogma to perform innovative translational research. Sci. Transl. Med. **3**(87), 87ps24-87ps24 (2011)
3. Baillie, L., Morton, L., Moffat, D.C., Uzor, S.: Capturing the response of players to a location-based game. Pers. Ubiquit. Comput. **15**(1), 13–24 (2011)
4. Bakhai, A., Constantin, A., Alexandru, C.A.: Motivate me!: an Alexa skill to support higher education students with Autism. In: International Conferences Interfaces, Human Computer Interaction, Game and Entertainment Technologies (2020)
5. Bouchard, B., Bouchard, K., Bouzouane, A.: A smart cooking device for assisting cognitively impaired users. J. Reliab. Intell. Environ. **6**(2), 107–125 (2020). https://doi.org/10.1007/s40860-020-00104-3
6. Boyd, H.C., Evans, N.M., Orpwood, R.D., Harris, N.D.: Using simple technology to prompt multistep tasks in the home for people with dementia: an exploratory study comparing prompting formats. Dementia **16**(4), 424–442 (2017)
7. Bradford, D., Zhang, Q.: How to save a life: could real-time sensor data have saved Mrs Elle?. In: Proceedings of the 2016 CHI Conference Extended Abstracts on Human Factors in Computing Systems, p. 910–920 (2016)
8. Brave, S., Nass, C.: Emotion in Human-Computer Interaction, pp. 53–68 (2009)
9. Caine, K.: Local standards for sample size at CHI. In: Proceedings of the 2016 CHI Conference on Human Factors in Computing Systems, pp. 981–992 (2016)
10. Carroll, C., Chiodo, C., Lin, A.-X., Nidever, M., Prathipati, J.: Robin: enabling independence for individuals with cognitive disabilities using voice assistive technology. In Proceedings of the 2017 CHI Conference (2017)

11. Cheng, A., Raghavaraju, V., Kanugo, J., Handrianto, Y. P., Shang, Y.: Development and evaluation of a healthy coping voice interface application using the Google home for elderly patients with type 2 diabetes. In 2018 15th IEEE Annual Consumer Communications and Networking Conference (CCNC), pp. 1–5. IEEE (2018)

12. Dementia. https://www.who.int/news-room/fact-sheets/detail/dementia. Accessed 10 Apr 2023

13. Hakobyan, L., Lumsden, J., Shaw, R., O'Sullivan, D.: A longitudinal evaluation of the acceptability and impact of a diet diary app for older adults with age-related macular degeneration. In Proceedings of the 18th International Conference on Human-Computer Interaction with Mobile Devices and Services - MobileHCI 2016 (2016)

14. Klasnja, P., Consolvo, S., Pratt, W.: How to evaluate technologies for health behavior change in HCI research. In: Proceedings of the SIGCHI conference on Human Factors in Computing Systems, pp. 3063–3072 (2011)

15. Kowalski, J., et al.: Older adults and voice interaction: a pilot study with google home. In Extended Abstracts of the 2019 CHI Conference on Human Factors in Computing Systems (2019)

16. König, A., Francis, L. E., Joshi, J., Robillard, J. M., Hoey, J.: Qualitative study of affective identities in dementia patients for the design of cognitive assistive technologies. J. Rehabil. Assist. Technol. Eng. 4, 2055668316685038 (2017)

17. Kjeldskov, J., Skov, M.B.: Was it worth the hassle? Ten years of mobile HCI research discussions on lab and field evaluations. In: Proceedings of the 16th International Conference on Human-Computer Interaction with Mobile Devices and Services, pp. 43–52 (2014)

18. Luger, E., Sellen, A.: Like having a really bad PA the gulf between user expectation and experience of conversational agents. In: Proceedings of the 2016 CHI Conference on Human Factors in Computing Systems (2016)

19. Mihailidis, A., Boger, J., Canido, M., Hoey, J.: The use of an intelligent prompting system for people with dementia. Interactions 14(4), 34–37 (2007)

20. Mihailidis, A., Boger, J.N., Craig, T., Hoey, J.: The COACH prompting system to assist older adults with dementia through handwashing: an efficacy study. BMC Geriatr. 8(1), 1–18 (2008)

21. MQTT: the standard for IoT messaging. https://mqtt.org/. Accessed 10 Apr 2023

22. Pradhan, A., Mehta, K., Findlater, L.: Accessibility came by accident use of voice-controlled intelligent personal assistants by people with disabilities. In Proceedings of the 2018 CHI Conference on Human Factors in Computing Systems (2018)

23. Ring. https://eu.ring.com/pages/security-cameras. Accessed 10 Apr 2023

24. Rogers, Y., Connelly, K., Tedesco, L., et al.: Why it's worth the hassle: the value of in-situ studies when designing ubicomp. In: UbiComp 2007: Ubiquitous Computing, pp. 336–353 (2007)

25. Saberi, P.: Research in the time of coronavirus: continuing ongoing studies in the midst of the COVID-19 pandemic. AIDS Behav. 24(8), 2232–2235 (2020)

26. Salai, A.M., Baillie, L. : A wee bit more interaction: designing and evaluating an overactive bladder app. In: Proceedings of the 2019 CHI Conference on Human Factors in Computing Systems, pp. 1–14 (2019)

27. Salai, A.-M., Cook, G., Holmquist, L.E.: IntraVox: a personalized human voice to support users with complex needs in smart homes. In: Ardito, C., et al. (eds.) INTERACT 2021. LNCS, vol. 12932, pp. 223–244. Springer, Cham (2021). https://doi.org/10.1007/978-3-030-85623-6_15

28. Samsung smartthings motion sensor. https://bit.ly/3vTxva5. Accessed 10 Apr 2023
29. Shalini, S., Levins, T., Robinson, E.L., Lane, K., Park, G., Skubic, M.: Development and comparison of customized voice-assistant systems for independent living older adults. In: Zhou, J., Salvendy, G. (eds.) HCII 2019. LNCS, vol. 11593, pp. 464–479. Springer, Cham (2019). https://doi.org/10.1007/978-3-030-22015-0_36
30. Simpson, J., Gaiser, F., Macik, M., Bressgott, T.: Daisy: a friendly conversational agent for older adults. In: Proceedings of the 2nd Conference on Conversational User Interfaces, pp. 1–3 (2020)
31. Slaughter, S., Cole, D., Jennings, E., Reimer, M.A.: Consent and assent to participate in research from people with dementia. Nursing Ethics **14**(1), 27–40 (2007)
32. Ter Stal, S., Broekhuis, M., van Velsen, L., Hermens, H., Tabak, M.: Embodied conversational agent appearance for health assessment of older adults: explorative study. JMIR Hum. Factors **7**(3), e19987 (2020)
33. Wallace, J., Wright, P. C., McCarthy, J., Green, D. P., Thomas, J., Olivier, P.: A design-led inquiry into personhood in dementia. In: Proceedings of the SIGCHI Conference on Human Factors in Computing Systems, pp. 2617–2626 (2013)
34. Zubatiy, T., Vickers, K.L., Mathur, N., Mynatt, E.D.: Empowering dyads of older adults with mild cognitive impairment and their care partners using conversational agents. In: Proceedings of the 2021 CHI Conference on Human Factors in Computing Systems, pp. 1–15 (2021)

Towards an Automatic Easy-to-Read Adaptation of Morphological Features in Spanish Texts

Mari Carmen Suárez-Figueroa[1]([⊠])(iD), Isam Diab[1](iD), Álvaro González[1],
and Jesica Rivero-Espinosa[2]

[1] Ontology Engineering Group (OEG), Universidad Politécnica de Madrid (UPM),
Madrid, Spain
mcsuarez@fi.upm.es, isam.diab@upm.es, a.gsanz@alumnos.upm.es
[2] Inserta Innovación, Madrid, Spain
jrivero@fundaciononce.es

Abstract. The Easy-to-Read (E2R) Methodology was created to improve the daily life of people with cognitive disabilities. This methodology aims to present clear and easily understood documents. The E2R Methodology includes, among others, a set of guidelines related to the writing of texts. Some of these guidelines focus on morphological features that may cause difficulties in reading comprehension. Examples of those guidelines are: (a) to avoid the use of adverbs ending in -mente (-ly in English), and (b) to avoid the use of superlative forms. Both linguistic structures are quite long, which is also related to another E2R guideline ("The use of long words should be avoided"). Currently, E2R guidelines are applied manually to create easy-to-read text materials. To help in such a manual process, our research line is focused on applying the E2R Methodology in Spanish texts in a (semi)-automatic fashion. Specifically, in this paper we present (a) the inclusive design approach for the development of E2R adaptation methods for avoiding adverbs ending in -mente and superlative forms, (b) the initial methods for adapting those morphological features to an E2R version, and (c) a preliminary user-based evaluation of the implementation of those methods.

Keywords: Easy-to-Read Methodology · Cognitive Accessibility · Artificial Intelligence

1 Introduction

People with cognitive disabilities present some difficulties related to reading comprehension processes. Hence, a methodology called Easy-to-Read (E2R) [1,13,17] was created with the goal of presenting clear and easily understood content. This methodology provides a collection of guidelines concerning both the content of texts and their design and layout, such as to use short and simple sentences, to avoid the use of long words, to divide ideas into paragraphs, or to use images that complement the content of the text.

© The Author(s), under exclusive license to Springer Nature Switzerland AG 2023
J. Abdelnour Nocera et al. (Eds.): INTERACT 2023, LNCS 14142, pp. 176–198, 2023.
https://doi.org/10.1007/978-3-031-42280-5_12

Currently, the E2R methodology is applied in a manual fashion. This adaptation process is iterative and involves three key activities: analysis, adaptation, and validation [1]. This manual process is labour-intensive and costly, and it would benefit from having a technological support. In this context, our research line is focused on applying different Artificial Intelligence (AI) methods and techniques[1] to (semi)-automatically perform the analysis and the adaptation of documents to obtain easy-to-read versions of original documents written in Spanish. Specifically, this paper is focused on two of the E2R guidelines that affect the writing of texts [1]: (a) to avoid the use of adverbs ending in -mente (-ly in English) and (b) to avoid the use of the superlative form of adjectives and adverbs. These two guidelines are considered useful for the daily work of E2R experts by one in every four experts as reported in [27].

In linguistic terms, these two structures are the result of the so-called process of word formation. Among other word classes, this process results on derived words, those formed from another word by the addition of morphological features called morphemes (e.g. *walk: walker*). Both the adverbs ending in -mente and the superlatives are examples of morphologically-derived words, as they are made up of a base attached to a morpheme (i.e. a suffix). With these notions in mind, it is important to note that morphological awareness, defined as the ability to recognise and manipulate morphemes [10], is related to the reading comprehension ability for different target groups including persons with cognitive impairments such as dyslexia (e.g. [25,26]). Research on this topic (see [26] for review), indeed, supports that poor comprehenders' difficulties have to do with derivational morphology, since the process of derivation can change the word class of the base (for instance, from an adjective to an adverb, e.g. *dulce* ('gentle'): *dulcemente* ('gently')). Therefore, these types of words are normally long and can clutter the text if used too often, since the more stimuli (in letter or syllable form) a text contains, the more cognitive processing the reader requires in the comprehension task [12]. Besides, one of the morphology-based linguistic accessibility criteria set by Jenge and colleagues [14] warns that morphologically complex words can impose a considerable burden to the human language processing system. Moreover, the reduction of morphological complexity of these features is related to another E2R guideline that recommends to avoid the use of long words, as they negatively affect language comprehension [4,6].

To improve the E2R adaptation process, technological aids could be developed. In this regard, to the best of our knowledge, research work on an automatic E2R analysis for Spanish is quite scarce. We can only mention an E2R conformance checker called Easy-to-Read Advisor [28]. Regarding E2R transformations for Spanish texts in an automatic way, it is worth mentioning Simplext [22], LexSIS [8], DysWebxia [20], and easier [16], which are based on simplification techniques. In such works, both lexical and syntactic simplification tasks are performed. However, none of the aforementioned works specifically addresses the E2R adaptation of either adverbs ending in -mente nor superlative forms.

To cover the identified gap, we pose the following research question: "Is it possible to develop an automatic method for adapting sentences written in

---

[1] We are investigating both the symbolic and subsymbolic approaches in AI.

Spanish that include both adverbs ending in -mente (-ly in English) and superlative forms into a simpler version, that is, an E2R version?" To answer our research question, we decided to follow an inclusive design approach [30], with the goal of involving a diverse set of stakeholders in our research. This approach implies that we conducted a user study to include people with cognitive disabilities in the activity of selecting the best proposal for adapting sentences with such morphological features (adverbs ending in -mente and superlatives). Based on these results, we have created declarative[2] methods for identifying and adapting these types of morphologically-derived words to the E2R Methodology and implement a pair of proofs of concept based on such methods. Since most of E2R experts prefer an application providing suggestions of E2R adaptations [27], when possible we create our methods based on different possible E2R adaptations. Finally, we performed a preliminary user-based evaluation of those proofs of concept.

The rest of the paper is organised as follows: Sect. 2 is devoted to the state of the art on (a) the most relevant linguistic features of adverbs in -mente and superlatives in Spanish, and (b) the automatic approaches for identifying and adapting these types of morphologically-derived words. In Sect. 3 we explain the user study we conducted with the aim of selecting the best proposal for adapting sentences with adverbs ending in -mente and/or superlatives. Section 4 presents our first attempts of methods for adapting both types of words to the E2R Methodology, the first versions of proofs of concept for those methods, and the summary of the preliminary user-based evaluation. In addition, the most essential drawbacks of the research presented in this paper are shown in Sect. 5. Finally, we present some conclusions and future work on this research.

2   State of the Art

As mentioned in Sect. 1, in this work we concentrate our efforts on developing initial methods to automatically detect derived words by morphological features such as adverbs ending in -mente and superlative forms in Spanish, and adapt them into easy-to-read versions, in the light of the guidelines provided by the E2R Methodology [1]. Thus, this section is devoted to (a) highlight some notes on both linguistic structures to better understand the problematic they raise (Sects. 2.1 and 2.3), and (b) summarise the automatic approaches for identifying and adapting such morphological features (Sects. 2.2 and 2.4).

2.1   Linguistic Features of Adverbs Ending in -mente

Adverbs ending in -mente belong to the so-called adverbs of manner. Formally, they are composed of feminine and singular adjectives (*lenta: lentamente*, 'slow: slowly'), or of single-ending adjectives (*feliz: felizmente*, 'happy: happily').

These adverbs conform a paradox, not always noticed in classical grammatical studies, but recognised directly or indirectly in modern ones [19]. Such a paradox

---

[2] Human knowledge is explicitly represented in a declarative form (e.g. facts and rules). This way to proceed is part of the so-called symbolic AI.

is a consequence of the fact that the noun *manera* ('manner') acquires a very abstract meaning in the paraphrase "de manera + adjective". Hence, when we say *Los votantes acudieron masivamente a las urnas*[3], we literally express a certain 'manera de acudir' ('manner of attendance'), but, at the same time, it is not evident that the property of 'ser masivo' ('to be massive') can express any manner itself [19].

In accordance with the Spanish Royal Academy [19], we distinguish among the following types of adverbs in -mente: (a) **Subject-oriented adverbs**, which refer to a certain property of an action, but also of the person or thing designated in the situation being described. Some examples of these adverbs are[4]: *deliberadamente, descuidadamente, or (in)conscientemente*. Moreover, (b) **Object-oriented adverbs** indicate the way in which the action affects the complement of some predicate. For instance, in *Cortó el pastel profundamente*[5], the adverb *profundamente* ('deeply') conveys indeed a way of slicing, but it mainly reports a certain change of state in the object which receives the cut, and not a situation of the subject who caused the deep cut. Following, (c) **Action-oriented adverbs** refer to certain obstacles that the action has to overcome, or to other circumstances that intrinsically characterise the action (e.g. *arduamente, dificultosamente, dolorosamente, or fácilmente*[6]). Finally, (d) **Adverbs of point of view or relational adverbs** are derived from relational adjectives. Since such adjectives establish a connection with a certain field or domain represented by the modified noun instead of denoting a property or quality, relational adverbs are hardly commutable by the paraphrase "de manera/forma + adjective".

2.2 Automatic Approaches for Identifying and Adapting Adverbs Ending in -mente

In Spanish the attempts on identifying and/or transforming this type of adverbs are way scarce. The automatic identification has been covered in some studies dealing with adverbs in general [21]; however, in the case of transformation, the way forward is still open. On the contrary, in other languages, such as French [29] or Portuguese [5], progress has been made along this way. On the one hand, the goal of Tolone and Voyatzi [29] is to extend the adverbial entries of LGLex, a Natural Language Processing (NLP) oriented syntactic resource for French. To do that, they first identify the adverbs ending in -mente, and then, for each type of adverb, they include the different paraphrasing alternatives in the lexical tables of LGLex. On the other hand, Baptista [5] aimed to provide a comprehensive set of paraphrasing strategies, which can be used in several natural language applications, such as text simplification or even machine translation. In this case, an annotated corpus was used to propose different paraphrases for each type of adverb, considering the lexical-semantic information. Then, they formalised such paraphrases through a finite-state automata to transform the equivalent adverb.

---

[3] Translation: *Voters went massively to the polls.*
[4] Translation: *deliberately, negligently, (un)consciously.*
[5] Translation: *He sliced the cake deeply.*
[6] Translation: *arduously, difficultly, painfully, easily.*

2.3   Linguistic Notions of Superlative Forms

Superlative is understood as the ponderation in a maximum or minimum degree of quantity or quality [18]. The superlative degree can be denoted by grammatical categories such as adjectives and adverbs. The expression of the superlative can be performed by means of numerous formulas [9]: (a) **Morphemic expression**, also called synthetic form, which is expressed through the process of affixation on adjective and adverbial bases, i.e. the use of prefixes such as "super- + base" (e.g. *supergrande* ('superlarge')) and suffixes such as "base + -ísimo/a or -érrimo/a[7]" (e.g. *grandísimo* ('mighty')) or *libérrimo* ('very free')). Another formula is the so-called (b) **Lexical expression**. In that case, the expression of the superlative occurs when a word carries itself the feature 'superlative', such as some quantifier adverbs (e.g. *demasiado* ('too much')), absolute adjectives (e.g. *excelente* ('excellent')), or adverbs ending in -mente, e.g. *completamente* ('completely')). For its part, the (c) **Syntagmatic expression**, also called analytic form, it is denoted by the adverb mark *muy* ('very') preceding an adjective or adverb (e.g. *muy triste* ('very sad')). Such a formula is the most common in Spanish [18]. Finally, superlative structures can be made up by some expressions as *un montón* or *miles de* (both mean 'a lot' and belong to a colloquial register of language), called (d) **Locutions or superlative expressions.**

Since the superlative structure affects the degree of the word it quantifies, it can only occur with words that are susceptible to gradation, which means that it must be possible to place them on a scale of comparison, at a position higher or lower than the one indicated by the adjective or adverb alone. In the case of adjectives, most of the so-called qualifying adjectives accept gradation, with some exceptions such as the adjectives of extreme degree (also called *elatives*) which correspond to the aforementioned lexical expression of superlative, since they express themselves the maximum degree of gradation, so they do not admit any type of affixation (e.g. *fabuloso: *fabulosísimo; enorme: *enormísimo[8]*). Due to their affective connotations, adjectives derived through this suffix (in this case, we refer only to the form -ísimo/a) are very rare in scientific and technical language, but very frequent in the colloquial language [19].

At last but not least, following Olmos [18] the morphemic expression using the suffixes -ísimo/a and -érrimo/a represent an exceptional paradigm in the word derivation process, due to the excessive length of the result (the suffixes

---

[7] Both suffixes express the same superlative feature. However, superlatives ending in -ísimo/a are widespread used in comparison to those in -érrimo/a. The suffixes -ísimo and -érrimo refer to the masculine gender, while -ísima and -érrima to the feminine gender. (Henceforth, we will use the slash symbol (/) to include both genders).

[8] In the colloquial register it is common to use the suffix -ísimo/a in elative adjectives to focus on the meaning of the adjective, so we can find this type of structures in spoken language, even though they are non-normative. (Henceforth, the asterisk symbol (*) will be used to indicate ungrammatical or non-normative structures).

add three syllables to the base) and the resulting proparoxytone[9] schema of the superlative, which can be a hard-to-pronounce word.

2.4   Automatic Approaches for Identifying and Adapting Superlatives

Although superlative forms have received considerable attention in formal linguistics [7], this interest is not mirrored in computational linguistics and NLP.

For such a reason, the study carried out in [7] is seen as the first automated approach to the interpretation of superlatives for open-domain texts in English. In such a research work, they present a corpus annotated for superlatives and propose an interpretation algorithm that uses a wide-coverage parser. The system they implemented is able to recognise a superlative expression and its comparison set. In addition, Jindal and Liu [15] studied the identification of superlatives in the framework of identifying comparative sentences in evaluative texts, and extracting comparative relations from them. To achieve such aims, they proposed two techniques to perform the tasks, based on class sequential rules and label sequential rules. Furthermore, it is worth mentioning the work led by Scheible [23], who proposed a computational treatment of superlatives aimed to automatically extract useful information from superlatives occurring in free text. Further on, the author extended this work in her doctoral thesis [24]. In the case of Spanish language, there are no automatic approaches for identifying superlatives and transforming them into simpler paraphrases.

3   E2R Adaptation Design via a User Study

As mentioned in Sect. 1, our intention is to involve a diverse set of stakeholders[10] in our research work. In this regard, we decided to apply an inclusive design approach [30] including people with cognitive disabilities in the team in charge of designing the most appropriate E2R adaptations for both adverbs ending in -mente and the so-called morphemic superlatives. Out of the scope of this paper, and thus one limitation of this research work, is the involvement of E2R experts in such an inclusive design approach.

To materialise the approach, we created an inclusive co-design process for selecting the most appropriate E2R adaptations. Thus, we developed a pair of questionnaires written in Spanish and implemented as a Google Form[11]. The goal of these questionnaires is to gather opinions of people with cognitive impairments on the use of adverbs in -mente and superlatives. Such questionnaires were

---

[9] Linguistic term for a word with stress on the antepenultimate (third last) syllable such as the words in English *cinema* and *operational*.

[10] The main actors who affect and/or are affected by our research line on cognitive accessibility are people with cognitive disabilities and E2R experts.

[11] Questionnaires are available at https://doi.org/10.5281/zenodo.8018593.

launched in February 2022 through mailing lists of autonomous federations and associations of people with cognitive disabilities in Spain[12].

3.1 User Study Design

Both questionnaires are divided into two main parts: (1) a section that includes single-answer multiple choice questions to capture data about which linguistic structures (adverb paraphrasing formulas in the case of adverbs ending in -mente and superlative forms in the other case) are easier or better understood; and (2) a part with questions on participants' demographics, knowledge, background, and experience. In the first part of the questionnaires, questions are of two different types. Such types of questions used in the questionnaire were validated by an E2R expert in a pilot survey before the user study began. On the one hand, the questionnaire poses questions where the participant has to choose an answer. In this case, participants are asked about their preferences or about the simplest answer. Possible answers to these questions consist of (a) sentences including original linguistic structures (i.e. adverbs in -mente or a superlative form that used a suffix (e.g. -ísimo/a)) and (b) one or more sentences that are the result of adapting the original linguistic structures with an E2R approach in mind, that is, trying to find a synonym formula which is easier to understand. On the other hand, there are questions where participants have to complete a sentence by selecting one of the possible answers. The set of answers includes the original linguistic structure and one or more synonym formulas. As an illustration, Table 1 shows two examples of these types of questions.

The collection of original sentences used in the questionnaire was built using two oral corpus: COSER[13] and C-Or-DiAL[14]. Synonym formulas were manually built by consulting several dictionaries such as WordReference[15] and Reverso[16]. A linguistic expert validated the collection of synonym formulas.

In the case of the questionnaire involving adverbs ending in -mente, the first part is composed of 16 questions of which four include sentences with subject-oriented adverbs, six include sentences with action-oriented adverbs, and six include sentences with adverbs of point of view or relational adverbs, based on the classification presented in Sect. 2.1.

While in the case of the questionnaire about superlatives, the first part is composed of 11 questions including morphemic superlative expressions (see Sect. 2.3). Out of these questions, nine contain sentences with superlative adjectives and two with superlative adverbs.

---

[12] Plena Inclusion España, an associative movement who fights in Spain for the rights of people with intellectual or development disabilities and their families, played the key role of (a) finding federations willing to participate in the user study and (b) distributing the information about this research work through those federations.

[13] https://hispanismo.cervantes.es/recursos/coser-corpus-oral-sonoro-del-espanol-rural.

[14] http://lablita.it/app/cordial/corpus.php.

[15] https://www.wordreference.com/.

[16] https://synonyms.reverso.net/sinonimo/.

Table 1. Sample questions from the questionnaires of both cases.

CASE 1: Adverbs ending in -mente
Question
Por favor, completa el principio de esta frase con una de las opciones: "......... Ana necesita más vocabulario técnico."   (Translation (Tr.): *Please complete the beginning of this sentence with one of the options:*   "*......... Ana needs more technical vocabulary*".*)*
Options
1. Definitivamente (Tr.: *Definitely*)   2. Sin lugar a dudas (Tr.: *Without doubt*)   3. Está claro que (Tr.: *It is clear that*)   4. En definitiva (Tr.: *In the end*)   5. No lo sé. (Tr.: *I do not know*)   6. Otro: (texto libre) (Tr.: *Other* (Participants can freely write their own proposals)).
CASE 2: Superlatives
Question
Por favor, lee las siguientes 2 frases. Qué frase te parece más sencilla?   (Tr.: *Please read the next 2 sentences. Which sentence do you think is easier?*)
Options
1. David vive lejísimos de su prima Anabel. (Tr.: *David lives far away from his cousin Anabel*).   2. David vive muy lejos de su prima Anabel. (Tr.: *David lives very far away from his cousin Anabel*).   3. Niguna de las frases es sencilla. (Tr.: *None of the sentences is simple*).   4. Todas las frases son sencillas. (Tr.: *All sentences are simple*).   5. No lo sé. (Tr.: *I do not know*).   6. Otro: (texto libre) (Tr.: *Other* (Participants can freely write their own proposals)).

3.2 Participants in User Studies

On the one hand, for the survey on adverbs in -mente, 139 people responded the questionnaire (72 male, 60 female, and 7 participants who preferred not to provide gender information). Participants include representatives from five different autonomous communities in Spain[17]: Andalucía (73), Madrid (32), Comunidad Valenciana (31), one participant from Galicia and another one from Cataluña. Most of the participants (73.5%) answered the questionnaire alone, while the rest needed the support of another person. On the reading comprehension level[18], 51.1% of the participants had a medium level of reading comprehension, whereas 35.3% had a high level, 0.7% a medium-high level, and 5.8% a low level.[19]

Regarding the age range, half of the participants ranged from 31 to 45 years old, 25.9% from 18 to 30, 18.7% were from 46 to 60, two participants was over 60 years old, and 3.6% of the participants declined to provide their age. With

---

[17] Autonomic Federations from Andalucía, Comunidad Valenciana and Madrid played the crucial role of distributing the goal of this user study as well as the link to the questionnaire through different organisations of people with cognitive disabilities.

[18] The level of comprehension is based on a self-assessment question.

[19] 4.3% of the participants declined to provide their level, while 2.9% did not know it.

respect to their impairments, most of the participants (80.3%) had an intellectual disability, followed by those (8%) who had intellectual and physical disabilities. On the most frequent occupation of the participants, from the 139 participants, 68 were users of occupational centres, 10 were public examination candidates, 7 were unemployed, while 7 were E2R validators.

On the other hand, 121 participants (62 male, 54 female, and 5 participants who preferred not to provide gender information) took part in the survey on superlative forms. In this case, these participants came from seven different autonomous communities in Spain: Andalucía (68), Comunidad Valenciana (29), Madrid (20), one participant from Galicia, one from Cataluña, one from Castilla y León, and another one from Extremadura. Most of the participants (80.2%) answered the questionnaire alone, while the rest needed the support of another person. Regarding their occupation, 58.7% were occupational center users. With respect to participant's level of reading comprehension, 48.8% had a medium level of reading comprehension, while 0.8% had a very high level, 34.7% had a high level, 0.8% a medium-high level, and 9.9% a low level[20]. On the age range, around half of the participants (52.1%) ranged from 31 to 45 years old, 21.5% from 18 to 30, 20.7% were from 46 to 60, 2.5% were over 60 years old, 2.5% of the participants declined to provide their age and 0.8% provides a non-valid age. On their impairments, most of the participants (86%) had an intellectual disability, followed by those (6.6%) who had intellectual and physical disabilities.

3.3 User Study Outcomes: E2R Adaptation Proposals

Findings indicate that, overall, participants consider simpler those sentences that have been manually simplified by means of substituting the original linguistic structure (adverbs ending in -mente and superlatives) by other synonym formulas. In the questionnaire on adverbs ending in -mente, only in 3 out of 16 questions the preferred option was the one with the adverb ending in -mente. While in the case of questionnaire involving superlatives, in the 11 questions the preferred option was the one with a synonym paraphrasing of the original superlative form. The detail analysis of the data gathered is organised in Case 1 (Adverbs ending in -mente) and Case 2 (Superlatives).

Case 1: Adverbs ending in -mente. The situation in which the preferred option was the original sentence with an adverb ending in -mente includes, in particular, the following adverbs *directamente* ('directly'), *normalmente* ('normally') and *seriamente* ('seriously'). Our first hypothesis for explaining this outcome was that these three words would be very frequent in Spanish. In order to confirm such an hypothesis we analysed the frequencies of these three adverbs in the list of most frequent words in CORPES XXI (Corpus del Español del Siglo XXI)[21]. However, these adverbs were not in the top of frequencies; indeed, other

---

[20] 1.7% of the participants declined to provide their level, while 0.8% did not know about their level and 2.5% did not know how to read.

[21] https://www.rae.es/banco-de-datos/corpes-xxi.

adverbs in our questionnaire have highest frequencies (e.g. *actualmente* ('currently') and *solamente* ('only')). Nevertheless, in very broad terms, we could interpret this situation from a morphological point of view, since these three preferred adverbs (*directamente* ('directly'), *normalmente* ('normally') and *seriamente* ('seriously')) belong to the group of relational adverbs, and thus they are made up by relational adjectives, as we mentioned in Sect. 2.1. This type of adjectives do not express a single property or quality of the noun they accompany, but denote a set of properties and link them to those of the modified noun, thus they establish different types of more complex semantic relations [11]. In addition, the constituent -mente neither alters the semantics of the adjective nor changes its category, hence the adjective still exhibits all the formal properties that it exhibited as an independent adjective [2]. This means that, for example, in the paraphrase "de manera + adjective" the adjectives *seria*, *normal* and *directa* do not qualify the property of the noun *manera*, but express a set of properties that affect the whole sentence. For such a reason, the replacement of those three adverbs (*directamente, normalmente* and *seriamente*) by the paraphrase "de manera + relational adjective" may seem unusual for persons with reading comprehension difficulties.

A more in depth analysis[22] of the survey data reveals that participants' preferred selections can be classified into the following scenarios:

- **Scenario A.** Sentences that are adapted by using the following pattern "de forma + adjective", e.g. original sentence: *Antonio escribe correctamente, sin faltas de ortografía*[23]; adapted sentence: *Antonio escribe de forma correcta, sin faltas de ortografía*[24]. Two survey responses fall into this category.

- **Scenario B.** Sentences that are adapted by replacing the adverb ending in -mente by synonym paraphrasing structure, e.g. original sentence: *Probablemente los pintores necesiten más botes de pintura*[25]; adapted sentence: *Puede que los pintores necesiten más botes de pintura*[26]. Six responses fall into this grouping.

- **Scenario C.** Sentences that are adapted by eliminating the adverb ending in -mente, e.g. original sentence: *María asiste a clase de español solamente un día por semana*[27]; adapted sentence: *María asiste a clase de español Ø un día por semana*[28]. Two survey responses fall into this category.

- **Scenario D.** Sentences that are adapted by replacing the adverb ending in -mente by a synonym word, e.g. original sentence: *Antiguamente, los niños entraban en la escuela con 6 años*[29]; adapted sentence: *Antes, los niños entraban en*

---

[22] The analysis and aggregation of ratings was performed manually grouping the different percentages of response types (no statistical analysis tool was used). Data gathered from the questionnaires are available at https://doi.org/10.5281/zenodo.8018593.

[23] Translation: *Antonio writes correctly, without spelling mistakes.*

[24] Translation: *Antonio writes in a correct way, without spelling mistakes.*

[25] Translation: *The painters will probably need more paint cans.*

[26] Translation: *Painters may need more cans of paint.*

[27] Translation: *María attends Spanish classes only one day a week.*

[28] Translation: *María attends Spanish classes one day a week.*

[29] Translation: *Formerly, children entered school at the age of 6.*

la escuela con 6 años[30]. Three survey responses fall into this group. In this case, it is worth mentioning that the sentence with the adverb ending in -mente was the third preferred option in all the questions.

In addition, we analysed the data gathered for each scenario with respect to the following variables: age, level of comprehension and origin. Table 2 shows the corresponding percentages[31].

Table 2. Summary of percentages for each scenario in Case 1.

Case 1: Adverbs ending in -mente					
Variable		Scenario A	Scenario B	Scenario C	Scenario D
Age	**18–30**	9%	47%	4%	12%
	31–45	12%	45%	6%	12%
	45–60	9%	49%	10%	18%
Reading Comprehension	**High**	22%	44%	3%	16%
	Medium	18%	49%	11%	13%
	Low	9%	42%	10%	13%
Geographical Origin	**Madrid**	11%	39%	6%	14%
	Andalucía	12%	41%	7%	10%
	Comunidad Valenciana	9%	45%	8%	12%

Figure 1 shows which percentage of participants selected the most preferred option and what percentage the sentence with adverb ending in -mente in the four identified scenarios. For each scenario, it is shown the percentage of answers of the participants who have chosen the sentence with the adverb in -mente, or the sentence with the adapted paraphrase. As we can see in the figure, in all the scenarios there is a clear difference between the percentage of participants who selected the most preferred option and those who selected the sentence with the adverb in -mente. In fact, the percentages for the most preferred options are in almost all cases more than double the percentages for the sentences with adverbs in -mente. As a summary, the situation represented by Scenario B has been the one that has appeared the most, followed by the situation described in Scenario D. Finally, the situations represented by Scenarios A and C have been the ones that have occurred the least.

Case 2: Superlatives. A deeper analysis of the survey data reveals that participants' preferred selections (that is, those options with the highest percentage) can be classified into the following scenarios:
- **Scenario A.** Sentences that are adapted by directly using the original adjective or adverb, without including any mark for its gradation, e.g. original sentence: *El suegro de Alba está contentísimo*[32] and the preferred adapted sentence: *El suegro*

---

[30] Translation: *Earlier, children entered school at the age of 6.*

[31] The regions of Galicia and Cataluña have not been considered as there is only one participant for each.

[32] Translation: *Alba's father-in-law is very happy.*

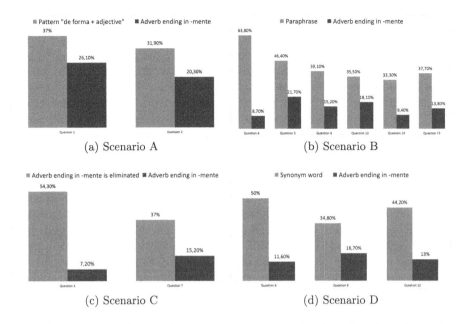

Fig. 1. Percentage of selections for the most preferred option from the adapted formulas and for the sentence with adverb in -mente in the four scenarios.

de Alba está contento[33]. Five survey responses fall into this category. In this scenario, it is worth noting that we have identified two sub-scenarios regarding the participants' second preferred option: (1) **Sub-scenario A.1.** Synonym of the original adjective or adverb is used as an E2R paraphrasing. For instance, *feliz* ('happy') is a common synonym for *contento* ('pleased'). Three survey responses fit this category; and (2) **Sub-scenario A.2.** The original adjective or adverb including the gradation mark *muy* ('very') is used as E2R paraphrasing. For example, *rarísimo* ('strange') is substituted by *muy raro* ('very strange'). Two survey responses fall into this category. Given that, this Scenario A indicates the participants' preference in selecting the lexical expression of superlative when (a) an extreme-degree adjective is proposed as synonym of the morphemic expression ending in -ísimo/a (e.g. most participants prefer the extreme-degree synonym adjective *feliz* ('happy') instead of the morphemic form *contentísimo* ('very pleased')); and (b) the morphemic expression with the suffix -ísimo/a is added to a extreme-degree adjective or adverbial base (e.g. most participants prefer the original adjective *enojada* ('angry') instead of its morphemic version of superlative *enojadísima* ('very angry'), since *enojada* carries itself the maximum degree of superlative). Hence, we can find that participants consider easier or better understood the lexical expression of the superlative rather than its morphemic version with the suffix -ísimo/a.

---

[33] Translation: *Alba's father-in-law is happy.*

- **Scenario B.** Sentences that are adapted by replacing the original superlative by the original adjective or adverb, including the gradation mark *muy* ('very'), e.g. the original sentence: *Ana es guapísima*[34]; and the preferred adapted sentence: *Ana es muy guapa*[35]. Six questions fall into this grouping. In such a scenario, we observed that those six cases correspond to the so-called restrictive qualifying adjectives, which point out characteristics that distinguish nouns among their peers, i.e. for instance, in the previous example *Ana es muy guapa*, the adjective *guapa* is "differentiating" Ana from the rest.

Although both the morphemic expression (suffix -ísimo/a and -érrimo/a) and the syntagmatic expression (formula "*muy* + adjective or adverb") are considered synonymous structures for expressing superlative, there are semantic differences in their use. According to [18], the synthetic form with -ísimo/a expresses a higher gradation than the analytic formula "*muy* + adjective or adverbial base". However, thanks to the findings extracted in this first approach, people with reading comprehension difficulties lean towards the latter form using *muy*, either due to the phonetic and morphological difficulties posed by the suffix -ísimo mentioned in Sect. 2.3, or due to the common use of this formula in Spanish.

In addition, we analysed the data gathered for each scenario with respect to the following variables: age, level of comprehension and origin. Table 3 shows the corresponding percentages[36].

Table 3. Summary of percentages for each scenario in Case 2.

Case 2: Superlatives			
Variable		Scenario A	Scenario B
Age	**18–30**	31%	49%
	31–45	29%	51%
	46–60	35%	47%
	Over 60	30%	50%
Reading Comprehension	**High**	30%	48%
	Medium	35%	49%
	Low	31%	48%
Geographical Origin	**Madrid**	35%	50%
	Andalucía	30%	48%
	Comunidad Valenciana	32%	50%

Figure 2 presents which percentage of participants selected the most preferred option for those responses that fall into Scenario A (five responses) and Scenario

---

[34] Translation: *Ana is gorgeous.*

[35] Translation: *Ana is very pretty.*

[36] The regions of Galicia, Cataluña, Castilla y León, and Extremadura have not been considered as there is only one participant for each.

B (six responses), respectively. For each scenario, it is shown the percentage of answers of the participants who have chosen the sentence with the suffix form in -ísimo/a, or the sentence with the adapted paraphrase. As can be seen in the figure, there is a clear difference between the percentage of participants who selected as the most preferred option the superlative paraphrasing (original adjective or adverb, with or without the gradation mark *muy* ('very')) and those who selected the sentence with the superlative form using a suffix. In fact, the percentages for the most preferred options are in almost all the cases more than double the percentages for the sentences with superlative features.

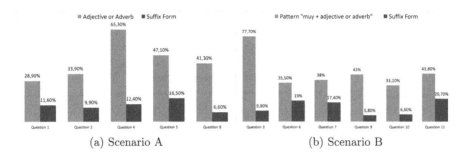

(a) Scenario A   (b) Scenario B

Fig. 2. Percentage of selections for the most preferred adapted paraphrase and for the sentence with the superlative (using the suffix form) in the two scenarios.

Finally, it is worth mentioning that considering the data shown in Tables 2 and 3, there is no evidence that participants' responses are influenced (or mediated) by any of the categorical variables used to describe the sample (age, level of reading comprehension and region of origin), as the percentages are similar for each scenario in the three variables.

4   Initial Methods for an E2R Adaptation of Morphological Features

The general aims of the proposed methods are (a) to detect a couple of derived words by morphological features in texts written in Spanish, and (b) to provide the most appropriate E2R paraphrasing formulas for such linguistic structures. The selected paraphrasing formulas are based on the data gathered from people with cognitive disabilities during the inclusive design action explained in Sect. 3. Our initial methods are composed of the following activities: (1) NLP, which includes a cleanup of the text using regular expressions and a tokenization step, (2) Morphological Feature Identification, and (3) Morphological Feature Adaptation. The following sections explain the E2R adaptation method for adverbs ending in -mente (Sect. 4.1) and the method for adapting morphemic superlatives ending in -ísimo/a or -érrimo/a (Sect. 4.2) as well as the services[37] that implement such methods. Finally, Sect. 4.3 shows our initial efforts for evaluating the implemented methods.

4.1 Method for Adapting Adverbs Ending in -mente

Adverbs identification activity relies first on a pre-filter of the words in the text in order to obtain only those words ending in -mente and second on a selection of the words that are adverbs from this pre-filtered set. The activity of adapting adverbs was conceived as an activity to provide first the most appropriate substitution and, second, an ordered list with other possible substitutions. This design decision was based on the E2R experts preferences about having adaptation suggestions in a support application [27]. All possible adaptations are based on the data gathered from people with cognitive disabilities described in Sect. 3.3. As outcomes of those data we obtained the following ranking of preferences for adapting adverbs in -mente: (1) using a synonym paraphrasing structure, (2) using a synonym word, (3) using the pattern "de forma + adjective", and (4) eliminating the adverb in -mente. Based on these outcomes, our initial method proposes as first adaptation the option described in Scenario B, i.e. a synonym paraphrasing structure. This was the first option because it is the most recurrent situation as shown in Sect. 3. The ordered list of possible substitutions is created with (1) the option presented in Scenario D (synonym word), (2) the option described in Scenario A (pattern "de forma + adjective", and (3) the option in Scenario C (deleting the adverb). The first two adaptation formulas imply the automatic identification of synonyms (a non trivial task).

We have developed a proof of concept, as a RESTful web service, to detect adverbs ending in -mente in Spanish texts and providing the most appropriate E2R adaptation formulas, based on the aforementioned method. Such a service requires as input a text written in Spanish and provides as output a set of possible E2R adaptations for adverbs ending in -mente in the input text.

The developed service has been implemented in Python 3.9, using the development framework Flask. This services uses LibrAIry[38] [3] for detecting adverbs ending in -mente. In particular, our service uses the following LibrAIry functionalities: Part-of-Speech (PoS) tagging and stemming. As a first attempt the method was implemented using a declarative mapping catalogue with adverbs in -mente and possible synonym paraphrasing structures or synonym words. This catalogue was used to obtain the first two adaptation formulas described in our method. We realised that this solution is not scalable, thus we decided to plan as a future activity the research of a more flexible solution. For this reason, currently, the service implements as possible E2R adaptation formulas those represented by Scenarios A (pattern "de forma + adjective", and C (deletion of the adverb). In addition, after discussing with a linguistic expert, we decided to include an additional pattern for Scenario A, that is, "de manera + adjective".

---

[37] Services are not currently available due to privacy constrains in the context of the project in which they has been developed.

[38] http://librairy.linkeddata.es/nlp/api.html.

We tested the identification functionality of our service with a collection of 2502 texts written in Spanish extracting from minutes of sessions held in municipalities[39]. We manually created a set of 2502 unit tests for testing the identification of adverbs ending in -mente. Each test is composed of the text written in Spanish and the annotation. This annotation contains the adverbs ending in -mente that appears in the text and was created in a manual fashion. Then, we developed an ad hoc testing code, written in Python, for (a) using our service for identifying adverbs ending in -mente in the text that is included in each unit test and (b) comparing the output of the service with the annotation included in the unit tests. After the testing activity, our service passed 2433 unit tests. Based on this, we can mention that our service identify adverbs ending in -mente with a 97% of success. An ongoing work is the design of evaluating activity for the adaptation functionality of our service.

4.2   Method for Adapting Superlatives

As in the case of adverbs ending in -mente, the activity of adapting superlatives was conceived as an activity for providing first the most appropriate substitution and, second, an ordered list with other possible substitutions. The idea is to have adaptation suggestions as preferred by E2R experts [27]. All possible substitutions are based on the data gathered from people with cognitive disabilities described in Sect. 3.3. As outcomes of those data we obtained the following ranking of preferences for adapting superlatives: (1) using the pattern "muy + adjective/adverb" and (2) using the adjective or adverb without gradation mark. Based on these outcomes, our initial method proposes as main adaptation the most recurrent situation shown in Sect. 3.3; that is, the option described in Scenario B (to use "muy + adjective/adverb" as a synonym paraphrasing structure). The ordered list of possible substitutions is created with (1) the option presented in Scenario A, that is, using the original adjective or adverb, without including any mark for its gradation; and (2) a synonym of the original adjective or adverb (Sub-scenario A.1). We considered interesting and useful to include an additional adaptation to have a more rich list of suggested adaptations. After selecting the most appropriate substitution, a post-processing should be performed in order to maintain the syntactic coherence in the sentence.

We have developed a proof of concept, as a RESTful web service, based on the aforementioned method. Such a service requires as input a sentence written in Spanish and provides as output a set of possible E2R adaptations for superlatives appearing in the input text.

The developed service has been implemented in Python 3.9, using the development framework Flask. This service uses spaCy[40] for sentence tokenization and TextServer[41] for tagging the obtained tokens with EAGLE PoS tags[42] The

---

[39] https://ayuntamientoboadilladelmonte.org/tu-ayuntamiento/gobierno-municipal/los-plenos/actas-municipales.

[40] https://spacy.io/.

[41] http://textserver.cs.upc.edu/textserver/login?hl=es.

[42] https://www.cs.upc.edu/~nlp/tools/parole-sp.html.

superlatives detection is based on a filtered process using the following PoS tags: category A (adjective) and degree S (superlative). When the superlatives have been identified, TextServer is used again in order to get the gender and number of such superlatives. This information is needed to maintain the syntactic coherence in the adapted sentence. Regarding the adaptation formulas, the service only implements as possible E2R adaptation formulas the ones represented by Scenarios B (pattern "muy + adjective/adverb") and A (adjective or adverb without gradation mark). Since the situation represented by sub-scenario A.1 implies the automatic identification of synonyms, which is not a trivial task, we decided not to implement in our service the option of adapting the superlatives by means of using a synonym of the original adjective or adverb.

We tested the identification functionality of our service with a collection of 566 sentences written in Spanish and extracted randomly from CREA Corpus[43]. We manually created a set of 566 unit tests for testing the identification of superlatives. Each test is composed of the text written in Spanish and the testing annotation. This annotation contains the superlatives that appears in the text and was created in a manual fashion. For performing the testing activity, we developed an ad hoc testing code, written in Python, for (a) using our service for identifying superlatives in the text that is included in each unit test and (b) comparing the output of the service with the testing annotation included in the unit tests. After the testing activity, our service passed 540 unit tests. Based on this, we can mention that our service identifies superlatives with a 95% of success. At present, we are designing the approach for evaluating the adaptation functionality of our service.

4.3 Preliminary Evaluation of E2R Adaptation Services

To evaluate the E2R adaptation services described in Sects. 4.1 and 4.2, we decided to perform an initial user-based validation via online questionnaires. Two validation settings have been considered: one devoted to the case of adverbs ending in -mente (Case 1) and the other to the use of superlatives (Case 2). For each setting, the questionnaire[44] was divided into two main parts: (1) one part with questions related to participants' demographics, knowledge, background and experience; and (2) the other part that includes 10 single-answer multiple choice questions to capture participants' opinions about how easy is the adaptation provided by our service. The format of these 10 questions is always the same. Each question has 2 sentences (one is an original sentence and the other one is the sentence adapted by our service). After reading each question calmly, participants should choose one option among the following ones: (a) Sentence 1 is the one you understand best; (b) Sentence 2 is the one you understand best; (c) I understand both sentences well; and (d) I do not understand either of the two sentences. The two questionnaires were validated by an E2R expert before

---

[43] https://www.rae.es/banco-de-datos/crea/crea-version-anotada.

[44] Questionnaires are written in Spanish, implemented as a Google Form, and available at https://doi.org/10.5281/zenodo.8018593.

starting the evaluation activity. 17 participants responded each questionnaire, 7 males and 10 females, all from Madrid. 13 of them had a medium level of reading comprehension and 4 a low level. Their distribution by age is 5, 3 and 9 participants in the ranges 18–30, 31–45 and 46–60 respectively. Regarding the impairments, 14 had an intellectual disability, one person had intellectual plus physical disability, one other had intellectual plus mental disability and the last one declared to have neurological issues. As for their occupation, 10 were users of occupational centres, 2 were E2R validators and the remaining were a cognitive accessibility professional, an unemployed person, a retired person, a receptionist, and a kit man.

Table 4. Summary of percentages in the user-based evaluation.

		Q1	Q2	Q3	Q4	Q5	Q6	Q7	Q8	Q9	Q10
Original	Case 1	6	6	12	12	6	18	6	0	6	35
	Case 2	12	18	6	6	6	24	6	12	6	6
Adapted	Case 1	76	70	70	64	82	64	82	94	88	41
	Case 2	59	59	88	76	82	76	76	53	59	65
Both	Case 1	18	18	12	12	12	12	12	6	6	0
	Case 2	29	23	6	12	12	0	6	35	35	29
None	Case 1	0	6	6	12	0	6	0	0	0	24
	Case 2	0	0	0	6	0	0	12	0	0	0

Table 4 shows the percentages of participants who choose each of the available options for both settings (Case 1 and Case 2), i.e. choosing whether their preferences in terms of understanding were the original sentence (Original), the E2R adaptation (Adapted), both sentences (Both) or none of them (None). Analysing the first setting (Case 1), percentages clearly show their preference for the adapted text; they manifest it is the easiest to understand in almost the whole set of questions. Sentences in questions 1, 5, 7, 8 and 9 were understood by every participant. The percentage of them who prefer the adapted version is over 75%. Specifically, for question 8, all participants chose the adapted form except one who chose both forms. Question number 10 is the one furthest from this pattern, as it seems the hardest to understand. Despite this fact, the E2R adaptation is still the preferred one. When analysing the second setting (Case 2), again, the E2R adaptation is the preferred one. In this case, the comprehension of questions 1, 8, 9 and 10 is less impacted by the adaptation as the percentages of people who chose they understand both sentences are the highest. Yet, these percentages are always lower than the ones for the E2R option. Compared to Case 1, it seems the impact of the adapted forms in helping to understand superlatives is higher than the impact in adverbs in -mente. This is supported by the fact that 8 out of 10 questions in Case 2 have no observations in category

None, meaning everyone ended up understanding the sentence and preferring the E2R form.

Overall, these figures in Table 4[45] show the usefulness in terms of understanding of the E2R adaptation carried out by the developed E2R adaptation services.

5 Discussion

Regarding the user study described in Sect. 3, what is currently missing is to include people without cognitive disabilities, in particular, E2R experts in the design of the most appropriate E2R adaptations for adverbs ending in -mente and for superlatives. The opinion of E2R experts would be a very useful complement to the results obtained from people with cognitive disabilities. In this sense, the E2R adaptation design would include the visions of the two main actors who are interested in our research work.

Concerning the proposed methods for adapting adverbs in -mente and superlatives, we considered as E2R adaptation results the ranking of preferences obtained in the user study described in Sect. 3. These results were based on two surveys with 139 participants for the case of adverbs in -mente and 121 participants for the case of superlatives. However, those methods have been implemented as proofs of concept with slight adjustments in order to have more scalable services. Thus, this difference between the methods and the services is the main limitation of this part of our contribution. More intensive research is needed to find the best solution to have methods and services describing the same situations and providing the same results. In addition, we need to evaluate in a more exhaustive way both the identification and adaptation in our services.

Finally, with respect to the evaluation of the automatic methods described in Sect. 4, we performed an initial user-based validation of the services for adapting to an easy-to-read version adverbs ending in -mente and superlatives. The validation involved 17 participants. Results of this validation provides us with brief insights about the benefits of having adaptation services for these linguistic structures. The data analysis of this validation activity suggests that the service outcomes, in general, are easy to understand by people with cognitive disabilities, thus, such outcomes improve the understanding of people with cognitive disabilities. However, we should confirm these conclusions by means of performing a larger user-based validation that involves a higher quantity of people with cognitive disabilities.

6 Conclusions and Future Work

With the general aim of improving the cognitive accessibility of texts written in Spanish, in this paper, we present a pair of straightforward declarative methods

---

[45] Data gathered from the questionnaires as well as reports generated by Google Forms are available at https://doi.org/10.5281/zenodo.8018593.

for adapting sentences written in Spanish which include morphological features of derived words, such as adverbs ending in -mente and superlative forms, following an E2R approach. Although the initial methods we propose for the E2R identification and adaptation of adverbs ending in -mente and superlative forms are simple and direct, we consider them as a useful contribution in the context of cognitive accessibility and assistive technologies. Based on our service development, we can respond in a positive manner to the research question presented in Sect. 1 ("Is it possible to develop automatic methods for adapting sentences written in Spanish that include both adverbs ending in -mente (-ly in English) and superlative forms into a simpler version, that is, an E2R version?"). A crucial task in the development of those methods has been the selection of the most appropriate E2R paraphrasing formulas for such morphologically-derived words. To perform this task we applied an inclusive design approach involving people with cognitive disabilities. Their involvement was materialize by participating in two surveys. In those surveys participants were asked about their preferences with respect to the simplicity of a collection of short sentences written in Spanish. Thanks to the data collected in such questionnaires, we discovered the patterns to be used in the E2R adaptation of adverbs ending in -mente and superlatives in Spanish. After analysing those patterns, we realised that involving E2R experts in this inclusive design approach would have provided us with a more exhaustive vision of the E2R adaptation options.

The proposed methods have been implemented, with slight changes, as proof of concepts in the form of services. Such services has been initially evaluated by means of involving people of cognitive disabilities. This user-based evaluation has been performed by means of two questionnaires. This is a first approximation to a deeper evaluation of the services since the sample size was not large, but prospects are optimistic. Thus, currently, we could say that adaptations obtained from our services seem to be easier than original texts.

As further research, we have planned three specific directions: one pragmatical, one more analytical and another one more technical. First of all, we are going to organise a working session with E2R experts with the goal of complementing the data gathered from people with cognitive disabilities about the most convenient ways to adapt adverbs ending in -mente and superlatives to an easy-to-read form. Second, we are going to analyse in more depth the data gathered in our inclusive co-design process for selecting the most appropriate E2R adaptations for adverbs ending in -mente and superlatives. We would like to find linguistic patterns to explain the selection made by participants with respect to the types of such morphological features and the identified scenarios. And third, several technical actions are planned: (a) we are going to design the evaluation activity for the adaptation functionality of our services; (b) we are going to investigate different ways to obtain, in an automatic fashion, the equivalences between original morphological features and possible synonym paraphrasing structures; and (c) we have plan to integrate our services in a web user interface. After these technical improvements, we plan to perform a set of user-based studies to evaluate both the web user interface and the services. The plan is to involve both E2R experts and people with cognitive disabilities in these studies.

Acknowledgments. This research has been financed by Asociación Inserta Innovación (part of Grupo Social Once) through Prosvasi Ciencia y Tecnología Para La Inclusión, A.I.E., within the project ACCESSJOBS. We would like to thank Plena Inclusión España for its help in organising the study with users, as well as the Federations of Organisations of People with Intellectual or Developmental Disabilities in Madrid, Comunidad Valenciana, and Andalucía for their participation in the study. We would like to thank Isa Cano and María José Sánchez for their help in organising the user-based validation of our services. In addition, we really appreciate the collaboration provided by (a) ACCEDES (Entornos y Servicios Accesibles SL.) and its cognitive accessibility validation team, made up of people with intellectual disabilities, from the "Así Mejor" Program of workshops and activities of the Tres Cantos City Council (Madrid) and (b) the users of the COFOIL "cuarentainueve" of the Association Somos Diferencia (AMP) for their participation in the initial service validation. Finally, we would like to express thanks to Arminda Moreno for her help in the analysis of the data gathered in the user-based evaluation of our services.

References

1. AENOR: Lectura Fácil. Pautas y recomendaciones para la elaboración de documentos (UNE 153101:2018 EX). Inclusion Europe (2018)
2. Alfaro, A.F.: Adverbios en -mente y la estructura del adjetivo en español. Revista de Lengua Española y Lingüística en General 21 (2007)
3. Badenes-Olmedo, C., García, J.L.R., Corcho, Ó.: Distributing text mining tasks with librAIry. In: Camilleri, K.P., Bonnici, A. (eds.) Proceedings of the 2017 ACM Symposium on Document Engineering, DocEng 2017, Valletta, Malta, 4–7 September 2017, pp. 63–66. ACM (2017). https://doi.org/10.1145/3103010.3121040
4. Balthazar, C.: The word length effect in children with language impairment. J. Commun. Disord. **36**, 487–505 (2003). https://doi.org/10.1016/S0021-9924(03)00033-9
5. Baptista, J.: Paráfrase de advérbios terminados em -mente em Português. Linguamática **10**(2), 21–30 (2018)
6. Barton, J., Hanif, H., Björnström, L., Hills, C.: The word-length effect in reading: a review. Cogn. Neuropsychol. **31** (2014). https://doi.org/10.1080/02643294.2014.895314
7. Bos, J., Nissim, M.: An empirical approach to the interpretation of superlatives. In: Proceedings of the 2006 Conference on Empirical Methods in Natural Language Processing (EMNLP 2006), pp. 9–17. Association for Computational Linguistics, Sydney (2006)
8. Bott, S., Rello, L., Drndarevic, B., Saggion, H.: Can Spanish be simpler? LexSiS: lexical simplification for Spanish. In: Proceedings of COLING 2012. The COLING 2012 Organizing Committee (2012)
9. Calvo, J.M.G.: Sobre la expresión de lo "superlativo" en español (I). Anuario de estudios filológicos **7**, 173–205 (1984)
10. Carlisle, J.F.: Morphological awareness and early reading achievement. In: Morphological Aspects of Language Processing, pp. 189–209 (1995)

11. Demonte, V.: El adjetivo: clases y usos. La posición del adjetivo en el sintagma nominal. In: Ignacio Bosque and Violeta Demonte (ed.) Gramática descriptiva de la lengua española, vol. 1, pp. 129–216 (1999)
12. Difalcis, M., Ferreres, A., Abusamra, V.: Syllabic length effect in Spanish - evidence from adult readers. Ocnos Revista de Estudios sobre Lectura **19**, 19–28 (2020). https://doi.org/10.18239/ocnos_2020.19.3.2295
13. Inclusion Europe: Information for All. European standards for making information easy to read and understand. Inclusion Europe (2009)
14. Jenge, C., Hartrumpf, S., Helbig, H., Osswald, R.: Automatic control of simple language in web pages. In: Miesenberger, K., Klaus, J., Zagler, W.L., Karshmer, A.I. (eds.) ICCHP 2006. LNCS, vol. 4061, pp. 207–214. Springer, Heidelberg (2006). https://doi.org/10.1007/11788713_31
15. Jindal, N., Liu, B.: Mining comparative sentences and relations. In: Proceedings of the 21st National Conference on Artificial Intelligence, AAAI 2006, vol. 2, pp. 1331–1336. AAAI Press, Boston (2006)
16. Moreno, L., Alarcon, R., Martínez, R.: EASIER system. Language resources for cognitive accessibility. In: The 22nd International ACM SIGACCESS Conference on Computers and Accessibility, ASSETS 2020. Association for Computing Machinery (2020). https://doi.org/10.1145/3373625.3418006
17. Nomura, M., Nielsen, G.S.: International Federation of Library Associations and Institutions, Library Services to People with Special Needs Section: Guidelines for easy-to-read materials. IFLA Headquarters, The Hague (2010)
18. Olmos, B.P.: El afijo -ísimo en el español actual. Verba: Anuario galego de filoloxia **28**, 159–185 (2001)
19. Real Academia Española and Asociación de Academias de la Lengua Española: Nueva gramática de la lengua española. Espasa Calpe (2009)
20. Rello, L., Baeza-Yates, R., Saggion, H.: DysWebxia: Textos más Accesibles para Personas con Dislexia. Procesamiento del Lenguaje Natural **51**, 205–208 (2013)
21. Rodrigo, A.: Tratamiento automático de textos: el sintagma adverbial núcleo. Ph.D. thesis, Universidad Nacional de Rosario (2011)
22. Saggion, H., Stajner, S., Bott, S., Mille, S., Rello, L., Drndarevic, B.: Making it simplext: implementation and evaluation of a text simplification system for Spanish. ACM Trans. Access. Comput. **6**(4) (2015). https://doi.org/10.1145/2738046
23. Scheible, S.: Towards a computational treatment of superlatives. In: Proceedings of the ACL 2007 Student Research Workshop, pp. 67–72. Association for Computational Linguistics, Prague (2007)
24. Scheible, S.: A computational treatment of superlatives. Ph.D. thesis, University of Edinburgh, Edinburgh, UK (2009)
25. Siegel, L.: Morphological awareness skills of English language learners and children with dyslexia. Top. Lang. Disord. **28**, 15–27 (2008). https://doi.org/10.1097/01.adt.0000311413.75804.60
26. Spencer, M., et al.: Examining the underlying dimensions of morphological awareness and vocabulary knowledge. Read. Writ. **28** (2015). https://doi.org/10.1007/s11145-015-9557-0
27. Suárez-Figueroa, M.C., Diab, I., Ruckhaus, E., Cano, I.: First steps in the development of a support application for easy-to-read adaptation. Univ. Access Inf. Soc. (2022). https://doi.org/10.1007/s10209-022-00946-z
28. Suárez-Figueroa, M.C., Ruckhaus, E., López-Guerrero, J., Cano, I., Cervera, Á.: Towards the assessment of easy-to-read guidelines using artificial intelligence techniques. In: Miesenberger, K., Manduchi, R., Covarrubias Rodriguez, M., Peňáz, P.

(eds.) ICCHP 2020. LNCS, vol. 12376, pp. 74–82. Springer, Cham (2020). https://doi.org/10.1007/978-3-030-58796-3_10

29. Tolone, E., Voyatzi, S.: Extending the adverbial coverage of a NLP oriented resource for French. In: Proceedings of 5th International Joint Conference on Natural Language Processing, pp. 1225–1233. Asian Federation of Natural Language Processing (2011)

30. Trewin, S., et al.: Considerations for AI fairness for people with disabilities. AI Matters 5(3), 40–63 (2019). https://doi.org/10.1145/3362077.3362086

Accessibility for Auditory/Hearing Disabilities

Challenges Faced by the Employed Indian DHH Community

Advaith Sridhar[1,2]($\boxtimes$), Roshni Poddar[2,3]($\boxtimes$), Mohit Jain[3]($\boxtimes$),
and Pratyush Kumar[1,2,3]($\boxtimes$)

[1] Indian Institute of Technology Madras, Chennai, India
[2] AI4Bharat, Chennai, India
advaithsridhar08@gmail.com,roshni.poddar28@gmail.com
[3] Microsoft Research, Bangalore, Karnataka, India
{mohja,pratykumar}@microsoft.com

Abstract. One-sixth of the global Deaf or Hard-of-Hearing (DHH) population resides in India. However, most of the research on the DHH population is situated in the Global North. In this work, we study the accessibility issues faced by the DHH community in India by conducting 15 interviews and surveying 131 people. We focus on the employed DHH community for two reasons: (a) to gauge the effectiveness of the widespread intent to increase diversity, equity, and inclusion in workplaces, and (b) to establish the state of early adoption of (accessible) technology. Our work reveals that our participants face acute communication challenges at the workplace primarily due to non-availability of certified interpreters critically impacting their outcomes at work. We report the consequent workarounds used, including the human infrastructure available to our participants and how at times it impacts their agency and privacy. We identify socio-cultural and linguistic contexts that contribute to our participants' reduced language proficiency both in sign language and English. We also identify that our participants use a variety of technologies, from video conferencing tools to ride hailing apps, and identify their current usability failings. Based on our findings, we recommend several assistive technologies, such as providing access to on-demand interpreters and accessibility improvements for current video conferencing and smartphone telephony apps.

Keywords: Accessibility · Disability · Assistive Technologies · Workplace · Empirical study · Deaf · Hard-of-Hearing

1 Introduction

The Deaf or Hard-of-Hearing (DHH) community constitutes over 5% of the global population [58]. Due to the inaccessible nature of their environments, this community faces a variety of challenges in their everyday lives. Most of the accessibility research works that study these challenges are situated in the Global North. These studies explore the socioeconomic context of the lives of the DHH community, such as the role of family [23], communication challenges

© The Author(s), under exclusive license to Springer Nature Switzerland AG 2023
J. Abdelnour Nocera et al. (Eds.): INTERACT 2023, LNCS 14142, pp. 201–223, 2023.
https://doi.org/10.1007/978-3-031-42280-5_13

in educational institutions [44], and access to healthcare [35]. Other work has explored accessibility issues faced by the employed DHH community especially in the workplace setting—examining communication patterns, career barriers and difficulties faced by DHH in Australia [60], communication preferences of DHH professionals in supervisory roles in the USA [25], and a literature survey about experiences of stress and fatigue among the members of the DHH community at work in USA, Europe, and Australia [61]. Such studies assume well-resourced settings and explore technological interventions to aid communication between DHH and hearing people, like custom camera setups to recognize sign language [3], use of video relay services to make calls [15], and teletypewriter technology for emergency calls [73].

Many of these solutions and insights do not generalize to a country like India due to the large differences in cultural and economic context, and access to technology. One example of this cultural difference is the nature of Indian Sign Language (ISL). Unlike American or British Sign Language, ISL is not a *single* language. It has a variety of dialects, such as Delhi Sign Language and Bombay Sign Language [26]. This diversity has impeded standardization and makes communication within the Indian DHH community hard. Other factors specific to India include accessibility-related cultural taboos (reported in work on the Indian blind population [36,38]), limited opportunities for education in mainstream schools [36], and the lack of trained interpreters [40]. Moreover, the Indian DHH population warrants its own study due to its large size—India is home to 63 million DHH people or one-sixth of the global DHH population [28]. Additionally, hearing loss is the second most common disability in India, representing 18.9% of the disabled population [55]. Despite the above, formal studies on the challenges faced and potential technological solutions for the DHH community in India has not received much research attention.

In this work, we seek to address and focus on a part of this gap by asking the research question: *"What are the key communication challenges faced by the working Indian DHH population today?"* We focus on communication as it is a fundamental challenge faced by the DHH community [25,60]. Additionally, we focus on the employed DHH demography for two reasons. First, it provides an opportunity to gauge the effectiveness of the widespread intent of employers and the government to increase the diversity, equity, and inclusion in workplaces [8]. Second, it establishes the state of early adoption of (accessible) technology given that employed members of the community have more access to such technology given their financial independence. Moreover, employed members have experiences spanning the workplace, home, and commute settings, thus providing richer context for our study. Hence, we focus on the demography of employed DHH and study challenges faced by them at and related to their work.

Towards the above end, we conducted a mixed-methods study of the employed Indian DHH community. Our qualitative study consisted of 15 virtual interviews; our quantitative study consisted of 131 responses to an online form circulated amongst employed members of the DHH community. Our work reveals that our participants face acute communication challenges at the workplace primarily due to non-availability of certified interpreters critically impacting their outcomes at work. We report the consequent workarounds used, including the human infrastructure available to our participants and how at times it impacts their agency and privacy. For instance, our participants report taking help of colleagues as intermediaries in communicating with their managers, at the risk to their privacy. We identify socio-cultural and linguistic contexts that contribute to our participants' reduced language proficiency both in sign language and English. Specially, we show that cultural taboos around signing and the lack of a national standardized signing system, delays our participants' development of high proficiency in sign language. We also identify that our participants use a variety of technologies, from video conferencing tools to ride hailing apps, and identify their current usability failings. Based on our findings, we recommend several assistive technologies, such as providing access to on-demand interpreters and accessibility improvements for current video conferencing and smartphone telephony apps. We hope that this work invites attention from both the global DHH research community and the accessibility research community in India.

2 Related Work

In this section, we examine existing work in two related areas—research on DHH community globally and on accessibility in India.

2.1 Research on Challenges Faced by the DHH Community

The DHH community relies mainly on assistive technology to understand speech. The methods used by the DHH community to communicate with hearing people have been well studied [25,31], and several workarounds have been identified, such as avoidance, lip reading, optimizing volume of speech, confirming the message, and using simpler words and signs. Simple aids such as exchanging written/text messages can work, but are much slower and thus not effective for sustained conversation [29]. Several technological solutions have been proposed such as video relay services [15], Internet Captioned Telephone Services [14], and Assistive Listening Devices [18].

Specific contexts such as home, workplace and educational settings have been studied. Several studies are specific to the context of education: the experiences of DHH students in educational institutions [44,56], hearing students' perspectives on the inclusion of DHH students [13,33], methods to teach and assess DHH students [11,53], and reading experiences with assistive tools like text simplification [39,50]. These studies have found that DHH students may not always disclose their needs and often settle for sub-par accommodations [12,44]. They also dismantle misconceptions that technology can remove all access barriers generalizing across an entire population [44].

Another context that has been well studied is the home. The home sensitively shapes the experiences of DHH children, since more than 90% of deaf children are born to hearing parents [19], who have to make several decisions regarding communication and language choices on behalf of their children. Research on this decision-making [20,34] reveal that parents view hearing loss in one of two ways: the *sociocultural* view of deafness aligning with the use of sign language, or the *audiological* view aligning with the use of the family's spoken language. While the efficacy of these choices vary, it is observed that parents often make decisions based on inadequate information [72].

Lastly, several studies chronicle the experiences of the DHH community in the workplace context [25,54,60,61]. Quantitative findings indicate that meetings are the most difficult workplace situations, followed by training activities and work-related social functions [60]. There exist multiple accommodations to address these challenges, such as better lighting and furniture rearrangement to facilitate seeing other people better, access to sign language interpreters, and automatic live captioning during meetings [54]. Apart from these accommodations, certain personal attributes like persistence and self-advocacy skills, as well as the presence of supportive and helpful co-workers are important to facilitate job satisfaction and success for DHH employees [21]. Awareness of the Americans with Disabilities Act (ADA)[1] [69] among employers, and the perspective of hearing managers of Deaf workers [70] have also been studied.

2.2 Accessibility Research in India

There is limited work on the DHH community in India. Existing work has primarily focused on educating DHH children [55,74], methodologies to teach English to DHH students [24,59], and teachers' perspectives on the education of DHH children [57]. We did not find any existing research that studies the broader set of challenges faced by the employed DHH community in India. In the wider space of accessibility research, significant work has been done over the past decade on the visually impaired community in India. This body of research has studied various aspects of the life of people with vision impairment, such as navigation [42,43], education [37,38], technology adoption [45], and has proposed accessible solutions [62,71]. Beyond the visually impaired community, there has also been research on developmental disabilities such as autism [1,64], cerebral palsy [66], and speech and motor impairment [17].

More recently, researchers have studied the Indian Sign Language (ISL) [67, 68]. These studies focus on the diversity of ISL and its unique characteristics that differ from other sign languages as well as the many spoken languages of India. They examine the several regional dialects of ISL used across India [26], and its high iconicity and use of compound signs [22]. Another crucial feature of ISL that has been examined is its variation across class [22]. Members of the educated middle-class DHH community use a unified and relatively standardized sign language, while the rural DHH have no exposure to this urban form. Instead, the rural DHH community use organically evolved *home-sign systems* [63], specialized to the socio-linguistic context of their communities. To further research

---

[1] ADA is a comprehensive civil rights law in USA prohibiting discrimination based on disability in employment, state and local government programs, public accommodations, commercial facilities, transportation and telecommunications.

on ISL and promote its standardisation and usage, the Government of India established the ISL Research and Training Centre in 2015. Moreover, as part of a new National Education Policy announced in July 2021, the Indian government launched an ISL dictionary of 10,000 words and suggested introducing ISL in the school curriculum to improve accessibility and create awareness [46].

In summary, most of the work on challenges faced and solutions adopted by the DHH community in the contexts of education, home, and workplace are situated in the Global North. These do not directly generalize to a country like in India with vast differences in both the socio-economic context and the nature and diversity of the adopted sign language. Accessibility research in India is also limited, with a primary focus on visually impaired, and more recent work on datasets for Indian Sign Language. Given this background, our work focuses on the challenges faced, workarounds employed, and their effectiveness for DHH community in India for the specific context of workplace.

3   Method

To understand the communication challenges faced by the employed DHH community in India, we circulated an online survey amongst employed DHH, followed by semi-structured video interviews. Both the survey and the interviews contained questions about accessibility issues faced in a workplace setting by this demography. The study was approved by the Institutional Review Board at Indian Institute of Technology, Madras. In this section, we present our survey and interview methodologies, along with our data collection and analysis techniques.

3.1   Survey

Our survey consisted of 18 questions—12 multiple-choice questions and 6 open-ended questions—and was administered via Google Forms. The survey was organised in two sections. The first section consisted of demography questions (such as gender, age, occupation, and level of hearing disability). The second section focused on the workplace context (such as *"Does your workplace have a sign language interpreter?"*, *"How often do you have meetings at work?"*, and *"How do you communicate with your coworkers?"*). The final, optional question asked survey participants to provide their email and phone number if they wanted to participate in a follow-up interview. No Personally Identifiable Information was collected unless the participants volunteered to participate in the interviews.

The survey was administered in English. All the survey questions were short, simple, and unambiguous to make them accessible to participants with low English proficiency. The survey was piloted with two researchers and a certified ISL interpreter who provided feedback on question framing. At the start of the survey, its purpose was explained in English and ISL. The survey form was distributed by a certified ISL interpreter, an NGO working for the DHH community, and a philanthropic organization supporting work on the Deaf, within their networks using WhatsApp and email. Furthermore, we asked the survey participants to share the survey within their WhatsApp groups. In order to be included in the survey, participants needed to be Deaf or Hard-of-Hearing, currently living in India, and employed (either currently or in the recent past).

In total, we received 131 valid responses (107 male, 24 female, age=27.9±5.9 years) over 30 days spanning Jan–Feb 2022. All the survey respondents self-attested as DHH, out of which 42.2% of respondents have profound hearing loss (*i.e.*, complete deafness), 25.9% have moderate hearing loss, and 31.9% have mild hearing loss. Our participants were educated, with 24.4% having Master's degrees, 49.6% having Bachelor's degrees, and the rest having a high school diploma. At the time of answering the survey, due to the COVID-19 pandemic, 65.8% of survey participants worked from home, 22.2% worked solely from the office, and 12.0% worked in a hybrid model.

3.2   Interview

We conducted semi-structured interviews after the survey during Feb–Aug 2022 period. Interview participants were recruited from two sources—survey participants who volunteered to participate in the interview, and recruitment messages shared by a certified ISL interpreter within her network using WhatsApp and email. In the interviews, we asked participants about their sign language education, how they communicate with hearing people (coworkers, managers, and other work related personnel), and accessibility challenges, workarounds and the role of technology in various work settings (like workplace and commute). We also asked them to recall a recent accessibility-related incident and their approach to handle that situation. At the end of the interview, participants were invited to share open comments and express any concerns.

All interviews were conducted remotely by the first two authors using the Google Meet video conferencing tool in the presence of a certified ISL interpreter (female, 27 years old). All the calls were video-recorded with the consent of the participants. Participants were informed that the data would only be used for research purposes. The interviews lasted 30–75 min. The authors and the ISL interpreter interacted in English, while the ISL interpreter and the participant communicated in ISL. The interviews were transcribed soon after they were conducted, and we use the exact translation provided by the interpreter when quoting participants. Participants were paid 500 INR for participation.

In total, we interviewed 15 participants (8 male, 7 female, age = 21–34 years). Only one participant was currently unemployed, but was employed in the last 6 months. The interview participant demographics are available in Table 1.

3.3   Data Analysis

We conducted a mixed-methods analysis to systematically analyze the collected data: quantitative analysis of surveys and grounded theory analysis of interviews.

We subjected our interview data to open coding and rigorously categorized our codes to examine communication challenges, workarounds and the role of technology by the employed DHHs in India. All authors regularly participated in the coding process and iterated upon the codes until consensus was reached. Over the course of analysis, they interacted over multiple days to: (1) discuss coding plans, (2) develop preliminary codebook, (3) review the codebook and refine/edit codes, and (4) finalize categories and themes. The first-level codes were specific, such as "communication with coworkers", "lip-reading", and "sign language proficiency". After several rounds of iteration, the codes were condensed into high-level themes, such as "ISL education" and "workplace-related challenges". Please note that we refer to survey respondents as 'respondents' and interview participants as 'participants' in the rest of the paper.

Table 1. Demographic details of the interview participants

ID	Age	Sex	Hearing Loss	Location	Education	Sector	Occupation
P1	26	M	Mild	Hyderabad	Bachelor's	IT/BPO	Movie editor
P2	26	F	Moderate	Coimbatore	Bachelor's	IT/BPO	Security Guard
P3	37	M	Moderate	Bombay	High School	Education	Teacher
P4	34	M	Moderate	Hyderabad	Bachelor's	IT/BPO	Expenditure Auditor
P5	25	M	Profound	Theni	Master's	Retail	Data Entry Operator
P6	25	M	Profound	Coimbatore	Bachelor's	E-commerce	Warehouse Assistant
P7	29	M	Profound	Coimbatore	Master's	IT/BPO	Process Executive
P8	21	F	Profound	Hyderabad	Bachelor's	NGO	Video Creator
P9	25	F	Profound	Hyderabad	Master's	IT/BPO	Customer Support
P10	24	F	Profound	Hyderabad	Bachelor's	IT/BPO	Expenditure Auditor
P11	32	F	Profound	Delhi	Bachelor's	Education	Teacher
P12	33	F	Profound	Hyderabad	Bachelor's	IT/BPO	Expenditure Auditor
P13	26	M	Moderate	Trivandrum	Bachelor's	Education	Teacher
P14	25	M	Moderate	Trivandrum	Bachelor's	IT/BPO	Software Developer
P15	21	F	Profound	Hyderabad	Bachelor's	NA	Unemployed

4   Findings

In this section, we discuss findings from our survey and interviews. We first describe various accessibility challenges faced by the employed DHH community in the workplace. Along with challenges, we also present workarounds and the role of technology. Moreover, we provide insights from our study that might explain the core reasons behind the identified challenges.

4.1   Work-Related Challenges and Workarounds

We asked survey respondents—"*Where do you find it difficult to communicate with hearing people? (Select all that apply)*" The results show that most respondents (53.4%) experience communication challenges at work, followed by home (38.9%), hospital (36.6%), and commute (29.0%).

Job Descriptions. Our survey respondents were working at 53 different organizations, which we mapped to 12 sectors. We found that the IT-BPO (Information Technology-Business Process Outsourcing) and Finance sectors are the most common sectors employing 38.6% and 15.9% of our survey respondents, respectively. Our interview participants worked in 6 of these sectors, with a majority of them (8) working in the IT-BPO sector. Respondents of the IT-BPO sector mainly worked in roles such as software engineers (13.7%), expense auditors (13.0%), and data entry operators (6.1%). P4 described his job as an expense auditor in an IT-BPO organization:

> "There is an app called Concur. We approve bills there. Bills come from third party, and we see if the amount being claimed matches the amount on the bill. If the amount is not matching, we have to manually delete it and enter the amount printed on the bill. Then we get to the next bill... We have to check each bill within 10 seconds, otherwise our reports per hour goes down. We have to reach [at least] 97% of the weekly target... We have to login for 8 hours per day with an hour of break." – *P4*

We found such job descriptions to be typical. They were designed to minimise communication with other colleagues and/or customers, and required minimal English literacy. In spite of being a white-collar technical job, it was menial requiring minimal (technology) expertise. Moreover, we found 99.2% of survey respondents and all our interview participants worked in individual contributor roles, mainly because such roles require "*no communication with colleagues*". P6 stated that he was "*unable to grow*" in leadership roles in his organization due to communication challenges. As an exception, P8 did not face communication challenges in her workplace, as she worked for a DHH-focused NGO.

Lastly, despite already having a Bachelor's degree, 10 interview participants had to complete additional training courses—like English writing, typing on keyboard, using Microsoft Excel, and video editing—to get employed. Our participants found these courses to be valuable, as "*it taught* [them] *the in-demand skills*" and connected them with prospective employers, thus significantly increasing their likelihood of getting employed.

Access to Interpreters. 49.6% of survey respondents had access to interpreters at work, while another 8.5% had interpreters present only during major events. The rest of them (41.9%) did not have access to any interpreter at their respective workplaces. In contrast, 76.3% of survey respondents used sign language at work, indicating that sign language is used even without interpreters at the workplace. Six of our interview participants stated that their office lacked an interpreter, but four of them still used ISL at their workplace. This was made possible using interesting workarounds, such as:

> "We don't have any interpreter. Initially we faced difficulty in talking to the supervisor but later we started teaching them sign language. We started with alphabets and a few words. Now they can sign!" – *P2*

We also found our participants attending meetings over teleconferencing platforms (like Teams, Zoom) even when they were physically present in their workplace, in order to use the live caption feature offered by these platforms. However, that limited their participation to passive consumer of the ongoing discussion rather than actively participating in it. Still our participants found that to be *"better than being uninformed"*.

Meetings. Meetings are a crucial component of office life, with employees across organizations attending meetings for an average 6 h/week [52]. 30.2% of our survey respondents reported having meetings everyday, with another 34.1% having meetings at least once a week, 16.7% having 1–2 meetings per month, and 19.0% having no meetings. Among our interview participants, these meetings mainly comprised of daily/biweekly work assignments, weekly performance discussions, and monthly training for future assignments. When asked the question *"Are you able to actively participate in meetings?"*, 53.7% of survey respondents responded with 'yes', 24.8% responded 'sometimes', and the rest 21.5% stated 'no'. To understand these challenges better, we asked our interview participants about their meetings-related communication experiences.

We found participants with access to interpreters at workplace successfully participated in meetings. In the organizations of P4, P10 and P12, the interpreter jointly leads the team with another manager. That way the interpreter has both work context and is comfortable with ISL. In case of P9's organization, the interpreter does not have a management role; the interpreter conducts a separate follow-up meeting with the DHH employees after a meeting concludes, to *"reiterate everything that was discussed"*. Among participants who did not have access to interpreters, P5 reported that he *"mostly skips meetings"* and relies on meeting minutes prepared by the team leader. While such workarounds allowed DHH participants to be updated, it precluded them from meaningfully contributing to such discussions.

A few participants use lip reading to follow meeting discussions. For instance, P7, who learned lip reading and received speech therapy during his childhood, can 'listen' and respond to others, as conversations happen during a meeting. However, this approach could get frustrating, as P7 described:

> "I cannot lipread when others are speaking fast... I can't tell them to slow down. If someone is talking to me fast and I am unable to understand then I ask someone else to explain what that person is saying. The person usually summarizes it instead of telling me the whole story and treats me

like a baby... I don't like that... I sometimes turn off my video and sit because I don't understand what people are saying." – *P7*

Five participants mentioned using the auto-generated captions feature offered by video conferencing platforms. While they found the feature useful, they stated two reasons that obstructed their usage of live captions. First, participants struggled to read and understand captions when someone spoke fast: "*If a person is speaking too fast... only 50% of the caption I can read, rest of it I miss.*" (P1). Second, the caption generator often make errors in understanding Indian accents and pronunciations, especially for Indian names.

Conversations with Managers. Communication with one's manager is vital to success at work. Participants preferred organizations with interpreters acting as the team lead for DHH employees. Although a few such participants had another hearing reporting manager, their single point of contact was still the (team lead) interpreter, who resolved their doubts and raised concerns with the reporting manager, acting as the intermediary between the DHH employee and his/her reporting manager. In workplaces without interpreters, communication between DHH employees and hearing managers is challenging. The default mode of communication in such cases is written messages, on a piece of paper or over email/WhatsApp. While written messages enable limited communication, it has two drawbacks. First, it is slow and becomes impractical for long, two-way conversations. Second, participants were concerned that writing about an issue "*appears excessively formal*" and may be taken out of context as a complaint. For example, P6 described his hesitation with writing an email requesting promotion:

> "Initially, my [DHH] seniors helped me understand and do my current work. Now I want to go to the next level... I don't like doing the same work for a long time. But [my] manager is not able to understand what I'm trying to say. If I have to write and ask about the promotion, they [the management team] will be asking questions... I am afraid that they will give me lecture on it, so its better to not talk about it." – *P6*

Two participants stated that they took the help of their hearing colleagues often to communicate with their manager. They were more comfortable in having a long written exchange with their colleagues, as the colleagues were not as busy as their managers. E.g., P14, who is the sole deaf engineer in his organization:

> "When I need to have some conversation with my manager, I will first talk to a coworker. Then he/she will come with me to explain to the manager. I used to write [on paper] and explain to coworker for long conversations. Now I use WhatsApp to communicate [with the coworker]... Conversations are usually about work-related issues... I have never discussed my salary with my manager." – *P14*

This apprehension of discussing salary and other private matters may be because the co-worker will become privy to the DHH employee private information.

Other participants (like P6) reported having very limited conversations with their managers. P6 works at an e-commerce warehouse that does not employ an interpreter. His job is to pack products into boxes before they get shipped to customers. Due to his blue-collar work profile, he finds it difficult to communicate even over WhatsApp/email.

"Before I joined, there were Deaf people working already. They taught the manager some sign language, but not much. I cannot talk about my job role to my manager. I can only say hi/bye to him. He [my manager] only understands conversations like 'did you have your tea?'." – P6

Conversations with Colleagues. All participants reported that the frequency and quality of interactions with their hearing colleagues were poor. For instance, *"I have only hearing colleagues at work. Conversations with them won't go beyond simple greetings like 'Hi', 'Bye', etc."* (P14). Such interactions happen using simple, intuitive signs that hearing colleagues can understand without any sign language training/knowledge. Even offices with interpreters, access to interpreters was limited to meetings. Interpreters were not available for informal, unscheduled water-cooler conversations. This resulted in minimal social interaction for the DHH employees.

Results to the survey question, *"How do you communicate with your colleagues at work?"*, show that WhatsApp (81.7%) is the most common app used to communicate with colleagues, followed by email (66.4%) and various video conferencing tools, such as Zoom (48.1%), Microsoft Teams (25.2%) and Google Meet (23.7%). While Zoom is the most commonly used video conferencing tool among our survey respondents, this may only reflect their organization's adoption of specific tools and not necessarily the accessibility of these tools. Coincidentally however, our interview participants preferred Zoom (even in offices using Teams/Meet), as Zoom allows a user to quickly shift between participant video tiles on a call (even on a mobile device), thus enabling DHH users to focus on the person speaking or signing. Google Meet on the other hand, automatically identifies the speaker and prominently displays the speaker's video on the user's screen by default, which our participants found *"unusable, as an interpreter was also on the call"*. This was also reported as a challenge when viewing shared content such as slide decks which also occupy majority of the screen real-estate by default. Finally, this accessibility challenge also manifests in recordings of meetings where the content recorded depends on automatic choices made by the tool which are not necessarily informed by DHH accessibility.

Transportation. Our participants use three modes of transportation for their daily commute—cabs, auto-rickshaws, and public buses. Ride-hailing cab drivers call their passengers for (a) *confirmatory calls*: informing the service requester that they have arrived at their doorstep, and (b) *query calls*: asking for guidance to reach the exact address of the service requester. Addresses in India are not well-defined, hence such query calls are not uncommon [5]. Our participants never make audio calls. However, they frequently receive confirmatory and query audio calls from ride-hailing drivers (e.g., Uber, Ola) and food delivery personnel (e.g., Swiggy, Zomato). Such calls cause distress to our participants as they can neither understand nor reply to the callers.

> "When I book a cab, it is difficult to guide the person to my place... If I go to the doctor for fever or any problem, I can at least write and show them. But with drivers, there is no way to make them understand. Sometimes I text, but they don't reply and keep calling." – *P9*

All our participants have experienced their rides being cancelled by the driver when they did not pick up the driver's phone calls. Attempts by our participants to interact with them over text messages were mostly unsuccessful, as drivers were usually driving when our participants messaged, and hence were unable to check and reply to messages. This inability to communicate with cab drivers emerged as a major challenge, with 9 participants complaining about it. The most common workaround (reported by five participants) was to take the help of a family member, nearby hearing neighbour or work colleague to interact with the driver. P4 stated another workaround, wherein his organization provides a free cab pick-up and drop service at a fixed time for its DHH employees. If the employee does not show up on time for his/her pickup, the driver calls the office interpreter and the interpreter checks with the DHH employee.

Despite the phone call related challenges, our participants preferred app-based ride-hailing services over hailing auto-rickshaws on the road: *"It is still much easier to book a cab on the app than to catch an auto [-rickshaw] on the road as it is difficult to explain the destination to auto drivers. In ride-hailing apps, it is easy to put the office address in text."* (P1). Moreover, due to language differences between auto-rickshaw drivers and our participants, written message-based communication may not be feasible.

Lastly, our participants face unique challenges while using public buses. Public buses are the most affordable means of transportation in India and hence tend to be overcrowded. Moreover, the rider needs to know the correct bus stop to get down at, and the name of the next stop is usually announced by the bus conductor. Thus, a bus ride requires communication with the bus conductor or co-passengers, which is difficult using written messages, both due to the crowd and language differences between co-passengers and our participants. E.g.:

> "While travelling in the bus when I ask 'Which place is this?', they [co-passengers] cannot understand and sometimes ignore me. When I write and ask them, people don't understand English because they are from village. At times, writing in Tamil works." – *P7*

However for office commute, as the source and destination are fixed, public buses provide the most frictionless travel experience for the DHH community.

4.2 Insights into Indian Sign Language

In this subsection, we present findings about ISL that we learnt over the course of our study. Specifically, we examine the state of sign language education in

India, the influence of ISL on the way the DHH community perceives English, and the difficulties in communication due to the diversity of ISL.

Sign Language Education. A majority of our participants (11) attended schools for DHH children; the remaining 4 participants attended mainstream schools and struggled throughout. Participants attended mainstream schools mainly because their parents did not want them to be seen as *"different"*. They recalled that they were given a hearing aid at school and asked to sit in the front, in an attempt to ensure that they could hear and lipread the teachers.

> "I studied with other hearing students near my house. I went to NISH [National Institute of Speech and Hearing] for college where I learnt sign language. It was difficult for me while studying in school. I sat in the first row. I used hearing aids and could understand slightly. Sometimes I could not understand some words and kept asking the teacher... If it gets cold like in the winter season, then my hearing reduces and I could not hear anything at all, and relied completely on lip reading." – *P14*

This approach resulted in negative experiences—P2 and P12 also mentioned not able to understand their teachers and relied solely on notes written by their friends, while P14 complained of social isolation in school due to his disability.

Interestingly, even participants who attended schools for DHH children were forbidden to use sign language at school, and students were encouraged to lipread and speak instead. P10 mentioned:

> "I can read lips a little now, but I mostly use ISL. I don't speak at all now... When I was a child, the teacher used to teach me and force me to speak. I went to a deaf school where there was a speech therapist, but I could not understand him." – *P10*

A key finding from our survey results is that this encouragement to speak is widely prevalent in India, as 49.6% of our survey respondents responded 'yes' to the question *"Have you had speech therapy?"*. P4 shared that he was encouraged to *"practice speaking slowly and clearly"* by his parents and teachers, as they feared that he would be socially isolated if he relied only on sign language. Despite this, there was an overwhelming consensus amongst our interview participants that they preferred and were comfortable using ISL over speech.

Five of our participants did not learn ISL at home or school, but picked it up informally from peers, by watching YouTube videos, or through apps like the DEF-ISL app[2]. Interview participants stated that they found peer learning to be the most effective way to learn ISL. Three participants mentioned clearing doubts by asking their friends, and stated, *"practising with friends gave the confidence needed to use sign language in public"*. All our participants later learnt ISL formally, either in college as part of their undergraduate studies or by completing a sign language diploma course.

---

[2] https://play.google.com/store/apps/details?id=in.eightfolds.deafenabled.

English Literacy. As mentioned earlier, using ISL to communicate with the hearing community is often not feasible due to the lack of interpreters. Moreover, these interpreters are very expensive (costing 13–20 USD/hour). Thus, written English becomes the dominant method to communicate with the hearing people. However, we found our participants to face various challenges in reading and writing English, due to a variety of reasons—learning deficit in schools due to late diagnosis of deafness and social stigma, and linguistic differences between ISL and English. Below are a few examples of the unique sentence structure used by our participants, provided by our interpreter from her WhatsApp conversations with them:

> "I go start my exercise walking now it" instead of "I shall now start my walking exercise".
> "Hard exercise some same gym" instead of "I do some hard exercise in the same gym".
> "Before I wash shirt and jeans" instead of "I washed my shirt and jeans before this".

The most apparent difference between ISL and English is the underlying sentence structure. While English follows the SVO (subject - verb - object) order for arranging words in a sentence, ISL follows the SOV (subject - object - verb) order [67]. Due to this, the DHH community tends to follow the SOV order even while communicating in English, resulting in sentences that are confusing to read for non-ISL users. The other major difference between ISL and English is the absence of articles (like 'a' or 'the') and connectives (like 'and' or 'or') in ISL [4]. This results in missing articles/connectives when DHH people write in English too. Finally, P13 (a teacher) noted that DHH students often have difficulty in understanding idioms such as *"time flies"*.

Diversity of ISL. ISL is not a single, standardised sign language. Variations in ISL became a frequent topic of conversation during our interviews as our interpreter (who is from Hyderabad) would sometimes fail to understand signs used by our participants who were from different parts of India. For instance:

> "The sign for 'marriage' is shown by a mangalsutra (an auspicious necklace used in Hindu weddings) *[performs a sign that draws out a necklace]* in Chennai, while in Hyderabad it is shown by the holding of hands *[performs a sign by touching right hand with left]*, just like how the bride and groom hold hands during weddings..." – *Interpreter*

We observed that these variations in sign language are reflective of India's cultural and linguistic diversity. India comprises of 29 culturally-diverse states and is home to 184 languages (spoken by more than 10,000 speakers). ISL, just like spoken languages, is strongly influenced by the culture of its signers. Three participants mentioned knowing multiple signs for a given word, as they had grown up in multiple cities. P9 stated that even signs for basic words like the days of the week varied across different regions she grew up in.

Participants reported instances where these variations in ISL caused problems during lectures, training workshops, and workplace meetings.

"Sometimes she [my manager at work who knows sign language] will stop and say 'I can't understand what you are signing.' She'll ask me twice or thrice again. She won't understand as she is from North [India]. Sometimes I get fed up and just text her to explain." – *P1*

Apart from the ISL diversity, four participants (from tier-1 cities like Delhi and Mumbai) reported mixing of American Sign Language (ASL) with ISL. This phenomenon is similar to code-switching, wherein a speaker alternates between two or more languages in the same conversation or utterance [2]. In particular, we found the ISL-ASL switch similar to the Hindi-English switch (called *Hinglish*), which is commonly observed among Hindi-speaking Indians [49]. Our participants specified that the reason for code-switching is the unique advantage offered by ASL. Unlike the two-handed ISL, all ASL alphabets can be signed using one hand [16], thus enabling them to sign while holding objects with their other hand. All the four participants mentioned using ASL mainly for WhatsApp video calls as they could hold their phone with one hand and use the other hand for signing. However, all of them reported that they were not fluent in ASL, and could only fingerspell the alphabets in ASL and know of a few basic ASL signs. Other participants who did not use ASL would sign by using their body or face as a substitute for one hand while holding objects.

5 Discussion

Here, we examine key findings in the broader context of existing work and provide design recommendations.

Comparison to Global North. Most of our participants were employed in the technology sector as (semi) skilled workers with the interpreters often as their reporting managers. Conversely, the DHH community in the Global North were predominantly employed in the manufacturing sector as unskilled workers [27]. A significant distinction in the workplace communication is the varying availability and role of interpreters. In India, we found an acute shortage of interpreters and notably interpreters often doubled up as managers and supported DHH employees with other activities such as cab booking. This provided crucial human infrastructure for the DHH employees. In more rewarding roles (such as software development), managerial roles may require specialized skills perhaps precluding their combination with interpreter roles. In contrast, interpreters are more accessible in Global North [25,61] and their roles were specialized and did not intersect with managerial responsibilities, leading to distinctly different power structures. There were also major concerns raised around privacy with an interpreter in the Global North [48] or of agency with intermediary hearing colleagues. Consistent with our findings, studies conducted in the Global North indicate that DHH employees face challenges in actively participating in meetings and have limited social interaction with coworkers [25,60,61], with a few hearing supervisors learning sign language [32].

In contexts outside work, a notable finding in India was the need for DHH to rely on hearing friends and family to use services for food delivery and commute, as service providers often call to confirm availability and for directions. In contrast, such services are usually contact-less in the Global North reducing dependence of DHH individuals on people around them. In terms of the sign language, a particular challenge in India is the relatively nascent stage of standardization with many local and even home signs in active usage impeding learning and interoperability, in contrast to relatively standardized languages such as ASL. Interestingly, our participants engaged in code-mixing, incorporating ASL signs within their ISL communication.

Human Infrastructure and Agency. Our participants relied on support from their family, friends, co-passengers, colleagues, interpreters, and even strangers, for their communication needs. Human infrastructuring played a crucial role. In the workplace setting, interpreters played several roles such as being a reporting manager, signing during meetings and important discussions, and also communicating with service providers such as cab drivers for office pick-up. However, our participants reported a challenge in discussing complex matters due to limited knowledge of sign language amongst colleagues. Another challenge was privacy in critical conversations such as discussing salary hike with a manager at work. Such privacy concerns have been raised in prior works as well [25,48].

Agency and social stigma often conflicted in the choices exercised by guardians of DHH individuals. For instance, our participants were encouraged by their parents and teachers from early childhood to speak, lipread, use hearing aids, and undertake speech therapy to avoid signing in public given the stigma associated with it. These methods were prevalent in both mainstream schools and schools for DHH children. While such approaches worked with moderate success for hard-of-hearing children, the deaf children struggled to communicate throughout. Thus, well-meaning efforts by members of the hearing community to increase the agency of DHH individuals actually have the opposite effect. The role of such stigma has previously reported for the Indian blind population [36]: Parents did not provide white canes to their children with vision impairments to make their children 'look less blind' [36], which curtailed their children's physical and mental growth. This suggests that social stigma supersedes agency in India and serves as an additional hurdle for people with disabilities.

Role of Technology. Technology plays a crucial and multi-dimensional role in the lives of our DHH participants. Many of our participants are employed in the technology sector and work on computers (as data entry operators, expense auditors, and software engineers). The IT sector has a major footprint in India: It contributes ∼8% to the Indian economy and employs ∼4.5 million people [30,41]. Also, multinational corporations are increasingly becoming more inclusive [47], resulting in active policies to hire from the disabled community. Our participants also mentioned the suitability of their technology job roles as they required limited communication.

Our participants relied on technology as their primary mode of communication, utilizing emails, WhatsApp video calls, and teleconference calls to connect with colleagues and friends. They were also active users of online food delivery and cab booking services. However, they often faced accessibility issues with existing technologies and provided suggestions for improvement. For example, they proposed features like pinning interpreters in teleconferencing platforms and receiving feedback in video calls if their hands are getting cropped from the live video feed. With the rise of hybrid workplaces, technology will continue to play a significant role in the lives of DHH individuals. It is important to note that while technology facilitates communication, connection, and employment for our participants, it also has the potential to contribute to social isolation [9]. The existing barriers of sign language further amplify these challenges for the DHH community [7]. Interestingly, technology served as both an enabler for communication, connection, and employment, as well as a facilitator of isolated work with minimal communication requirements in the workplace.

5.1 Designing Inclusive Technology

Given the diverse needs and constraints in India, it is crucial to collaborate with NGOs and end users to iteratively develop tailored technological solutions.

Interpreters on Demand: Access to an interpreter emerged as the most reliable solution for the DHH community. All of our participants mentioned the ease of interacting with hearing individuals in the presence of an interpreter and the reduction in anxiety during such conversations. However, constant accessing interpreters is infeasible due to the high cost of hiring an interpreter and the dearth of certified interpreters in India [40]. Technologies like on-demand online interpreter[3] have potential to address this. It is expected that such on-demand hiring would reduce costs as interpreters are able to serve more people more efficiently. Privacy concerns on such a platform can be alleviated by anonymizing both the DHH user and the interpreter with generative avatars. While an early prototype solution is available in India[4] none of our participants were aware of it. We believe that a platform for on-demand interpreters that pays the interpreters fairly while efficiently interfacing them with DHH users will be very effective in meeting several challenges that our work identifies.

Ambient Conversation: There are other situations like informal social conversations with colleagues at workplace (such as at the water cool) which do not warrant an interpreter, but enable building of relationships and mental well-being at work. Smartphone apps (like Talk to Deaf[5]) enable DHH users to listen to ambient conversations, by using STT technology to display captions for conversations happening around the user's smartphone. However, we found that

---

[3] Jeenie: https://jeenie.com/.

[4] SignAble: https://play.google.com/store/apps/details?id=org.signable.apprtc.

[5] https://play.google.com/store/apps/details?id=unique2040.com.text2speech.

these apps to be limited in their utility as they work only when spoken directly into the smartphone's microphone. Improved microphone technology for indoor settings is available on consumer-grade smart speaker devices, which can be adapted to enable the DHH to listen in to ambient conversations.

Accessible Video Conferencing Platforms: Our participants utilized speech-to-text (STT) technology in video conferencing platforms to auto-generate live captions during office meetings. However, participants with limited English proficiency found it challenging to read the captions at the required pace. A possible solution is to provide a history of the generated captions for later reference, however that still limits active participation. A more technically challenging solution would be to integrate automatic tools for real-time text simplification [65] such as Lexi [6]. Prior research on the accessibility of videoconferencing platforms has identified barriers to inclusive meetings such as insufficient frame rates required to understand sign language, identifying active speakers based on audio, and sub-optimal presentation of visual sources [51]. Proposed design considerations include customizable layouts to consolidate visual information [10].

Accessible Phone Calls: While efforts to build novel applications to improve accessibility continues, several problems can be solved by designing existing applications more inclusively. In particular, a majority of our DHH participants faced challenges in interacting with cab drivers and food delivery personnel over phone calls, and have to seek help from family members, work colleagues, or strangers. These service apps should add a "Do not disturb/DHH mode" informing the driver/delivery personnel that the service requester is a DHH individual. In such cases, communication should be automatically restricted to text messages, instead of phone calls. More generally, our participants pointed challenges in attending audio phone calls. Recent smartphone apps (such as Rogervoice[6] attempt to make audio phone calls accessible for the DHH community. Rogervoice auto-generates captions for incoming audio calls, and the DHH person can either talk to the caller or type out a message that is read to the caller using TTS technology. Unfortunately, no similar app is available in India. The technological barriers to build such an app are higher in India, given the diversity in spoken languages and accents, and presence of code-mixing.

6   Conclusion

In this work, we study the challenges faced, workarounds, and role of technology in the life of employed DHH Indians, by interviewing 15 DHH participants and surveying 131 DHH respondents. We emphasize the specificity of our study here as a reminder to readers that this study is at best a first step towards characterizing accessibility challenges for the DHH community outside of the developed regions context. Our study reveals various challenges faced by the Indian DHH community on a day-to-day basis, in a variety of work-related settings.

---

[6] Rogervoice: https://play.google.com/store/apps/details?id=com.rogervoice.app).

Specifically, we highlight technology-related challenges with video conferencing applications, automated captioning services, audio phone calls, and app-based service delivery, along with workarounds. We also discuss foundational challenges due to the stigma associated with signing in India and problems arising due to linguistic variations in ISL and English. We conclude by proposing technology and design recommendations to tackle the identified challenges.

References

1. Ahuja, K., et al.: Gaze-based screening of autistic traits for adolescents and young adults using prosaic videos. In: COMPASS (2020)
2. Bali, K., Sharma, J., Choudhury, M., Vyas, Y.: "I am borrowing ya mixing?" an analysis of English-Hindi code mixing in Facebook. In: Proceedings of the First Workshop on Computational Approaches to Code Switching. ACL (2014). https://doi.org/10.3115/v1/W14-3914
3. Berke, L., Thies, W., Bragg, D.: Chat in the hat: a portable interpreter for sign language users. In: ASSETS. ACM, New York (2020). https://doi.org/10.1145/3373625.3417026
4. Bhatia, P., Verma, S., Kaur, S.: Sign language generation system based on Indian sign language grammar. ACM Trans. Asian Low-Resour. Lang. Inf. Process. (TALLIP) 19(4), 1–26 (2020)
5. Bhattacharya, D.S., Sai Sri Sathya, Rustogi, D.K., Raskar, D.R.: Economic Impact of Discoverability of Localities and Addresses in India (2018). https://arxiv.org/pdf/1802.04625.pdf
6. Bingel, J., Paetzold, G., Søgaard, A.: Lexi: a tool for adaptive, personalized text simplification. In: Proceedings of the 27th International Conference on Computational Linguistics (2018)
7. Bott, A., Saunders, G.: A scoping review of studies investigating hearing loss, social isolation and/or loneliness in adults. Int. J. Audiol. (2021). https://doi.org/10.1080/14992027.2021.1915506
8. Brimhall, K.C., Barak, M.E.M.: The critical role of workplace inclusion in fostering innovation, job satisfaction, and quality of care in a diverse human service organization. Hum. Serv. Organ. Manag. Leadersh. Gov. 42(5), 474–492 (2018). https://doi.org/10.1080/23303131.2018.1526151
9. Carwile, R.: Technology makes us more alone (2021). https://whsgrassburr.com/opinion/2021/02/01/technology-makes-us-more-alone/
10. Cavender, A.C., Bigham, J.P., Ladner, R.E.: Classinfocus: enabling improved visual attention strategies for deaf and hard of hearing students. In: ASSETS. ACM (2009). https://doi.org/10.1145/1639642.1639656
11. Cawthon, S.W.: Science and evidence of success: two emerging issues in assessment accommodations for students who are deaf or hard of hearing. J. Deaf Stud. Deaf Educ. (2010). https://doi.org/10.1093/deafed/enq002
12. Cawthon, S., Leppo, R.: Assessment accommodations on tests of academic achievement for students who are deaf or hard of hearing: a qualitative meta-analysis of the research literature. Am. Ann. Deaf 158(3), 363–376 (2013). https://doi.org/10.1353/aad.2013.0023
13. Cawthon, S.W., Leppo, R.: Accommodations quality for students who are d/deaf or hard of hearing. Am. Ann. Deaf (2013). https://doi.org/10.1353/aad.2013.0031

14. Federal Communications Commission: Internet Protocol (IP) captioned telephone service (2011). https://www.fcc.gov/consumers/guides/internet-protocol-ip-captioned-telephone-service
15. Federal Communications Commission: Video Relay Services (2011). https://www.fcc.gov/consumers/guides/video-relay-services
16. Cormier, K., Schembri, A.C., Tyrone, M.E.: One hand or two? Sign Lang. Linguist. **11** (2008). https://doi.org/10.1075/sll.11.1.03cor
17. Dasgupta, T., Sinha, M., Basu, A.: Web browsing interface for people with severe speech and motor impairment in India. In: ASSETS (2014). https://doi.org/10.1145/2661334.2661396
18. The National Institute on Deafness and Other Communication Disorders: Assistive devices for People with Hearing, Voice, Speech, or Language Disorders. https://www.nidcd.nih.gov/health/assistive-devices-people-hearing-voice-speech-or-language-disorders
19. The National Institute on Deafness and Other Communication Disorders: Quick statistics about hearing. https://www.nidcd.nih.gov/health/statistics/quick-statistics-hearing
20. Decker, K.B., Vallotton, C.D., Johnson, H.A.: Parents' communication decision for children with hearing loss: sources of information and influence. Am. Ann. Deaf (2012). https://doi.org/10.1353/aad.2012.1631
21. Dong, S., Guerette, A.R.: Workplace accommodations, job performance and job satisfaction among individuals with sensory disabilities. Aust. J. Rehabil. Couns. **19**(1), 1–20 (2013)
22. Doval, A.: The people's linguistic survey of India sign language. https://www.academia.edu/34740076/
23. Eleweke, C.J., Rodda, M.: Factors contributing to parents' selection of a communication mode to use with their deaf children. Am. Ann. Deaf (2000). http://www.jstor.org/stable/44393224
24. Fan, H.: An E-learning ecosystem for deaf young adult learners' English literacy attainment in India. Ph.D. thesis, University of Central Lancashire (2019)
25. Foster, S., Macleod, J.: Deaf people at work: assessment of communication among deaf and hearing persons in work settings. Int. J. Audiol. (2003). https://doi.org/10.3109/14992020309074634
26. Frawley, W.J.: International encyclopedia of linguistics: 4-volume set. In: International Encyclopedia of Linguistics. Oxford University Press (2003)
27. Garberoglio, C.L., Palmer, J.L., Cawthon, S., Sales, A.: Deaf people and employment in the United States: 2019. Technical report, National Deaf Center on Post-secondary Outcomes (2019)
28. Garg, S., Chadha, S., Malhotra, S., Agarwal, A.K.: Deafness: burden, prevention and control in India. Natl. Med. J. India **22**, 79–81 (2009)
29. Glasser, A., Kushalnagar, K., Kushalnagar, R.: Deaf, hard of hearing, and hearing perspectives on using automatic speech recognition in conversation. In: ASSETS. ACM (2017). https://doi.org/10.1145/3132525.3134781
30. GoI: Employment generation (2021). https://www.meity.gov.in/content/employment
31. Hallam, R.S., Corney, R.: Conversation tactics in persons with normal hearing and hearing-impairment. Int. J. Audiol. (2013). https://doi.org/10.3109/14992027.2013.852256
32. Heyko, D., Flatla, D.R.: Identifying the factors that influence dhh employee success under hearing supervisors. In: DIS (2021)

33. Hung, H.L., Paul, P.V.: Inclusion of students who are deaf or hard of hearing: secondary school hearing students perspectives. Deaf. Educ. Int. (2006). https://doi.org/10.1179/146431506790560229

34. Hyde, M., Punch, R., Komesaroff, L.: Coming to a decision about cochlear implantation: parents making choices for their deaf children. J. Deaf Stud. Deaf Educ. (2010). https://doi.org/10.1093/deafed/enq004

35. Iezzoni, L.I., O'Day, B.L., Killeen, M., Harker, H.: Communicating about health care: observations from persons who are deaf or hard of hearing. Ann. Intern. Med. (2004). https://doi.org/10.7326/0003-4819-140-5-200403020-00011

36. India, G., Jain, M., Swaminathan, M.: Understanding motivations and barriers to exercise among people with blindness in India. In: Ardito, C., et al. (eds.) INTERACT 2021. LNCS, vol. 12932, pp. 444–454. Springer, Cham (2021). https://doi.org/10.1007/978-3-030-85623-6_27

37. India, G., Ramakrishna, G., Bisht, J., Swaminathan, M.: Computational thinking as play. In: ASSETS (2019). https://doi.org/10.1145/3308561.3354608

38. India, G., et al.: Teachers' perceptions around digital games for children in low-resource schools for the blind. In: CHI (2021). https://doi.org/10.1145/3411764.3445194

39. Inui, K., Fujita, A., Takahashi, T., Iida, R., Iwakura, T.: Text simplification for reading assistance: a project note. In: Proceedings of the 2nd IWP: Paraphrase Acquisition and Applications (2003)

40. ISLRTC: Indian Sign Language Interpreters Directory. http://islrtc.nic.in/sites/default/files/Interpreter%20Directory.pdf

41. IT and BPM Industry Report: IT & BPM Industry in India (2022). https://www.ibef.org/industry/information-technology-india

42. Jain, D.: Path-guided indoor navigation for the visually impaired using minimal building retrofitting. In: ASSETS (2014). https://doi.org/10.1145/2661334.2661359

43. Jain, D.: Pilot evaluation of a path-guided indoor navigation system for visually impaired in a public museum. In: ASSETS (2014). https://doi.org/10.1145/2661334.2661405

44. Jain, D., Potluri, V., Sharif, A.: Navigating graduate school with a disability. In: The 22nd International ACM SIGACCESS Conference on Computers and Accessibility (2020). https://doi.org/10.1145/3373625.3416986

45. Jain, M., Diwakar, N., Swaminathan, M.: Smartphone usage by expert blind users. In: CHI (2021). https://doi.org/10.1145/3411764.3445074

46. Jain, P.: Indian sign language dictionary for hearing impaired students is inclusive in nature (2021). https://www.news9live.com/education-career/isl-dictionary-for-hearing-impaired-students-is-inclusive-120346

47. Jonsen, K., Point, S., Kelan, E.K., Grieble, A.: Diversity and inclusion branding: a five-country comparison of corporate websites. Int. J. Hum. Resour. Manag. (2021). https://doi.org/10.1080/09585192.2018.1496125

48. Kim, E.J., Byrne, B., Parish, S.L.: Deaf people and economic well-being: findings from the life opportunities survey. Disabil. Soc. (2018). https://doi.org/10.1080/09687599.2017.1420631

49. Kumar, A.: Certain aspects of the form and functions of Hindi-English code-switching. Anthropol. Linguist. (1986). https://www.jstor.org/stable/30028409

50. Kushalnagar, P., Smith, S., Hopper, M., Ryan, C., Rinkevich, M., Kushalnagar, R.: Making cancer health text on the internet easier to read for deaf people who use American sign language. J. Cancer Educ. (2018)

51. Kushalnagar, R.S., Vogler, C.: Teleconference accessibility and guidelines for deaf and hard of hearing users. In: ASSETS (2020)
52. Lehmann-Willenbrock, N., Rogelberg, S.G., Allen, J.A., Kello, J.E.: The critical importance of meetings to leader and organizational success. Organ. Dyn. (2018). https://doi.org/10.1016/j.orgdyn.2017.07.005
53. Leigh, G., Crowe, K.: Evidence-based practices for teaching learners who are deaf or hard of hearing in regular classrooms. In: Oxford Research Encyclopedia of Education (2020). https://doi.org/10.1093/acrefore/9780190264093.013.1258
54. Lempka, C.: Employees who are deaf or hard of hearing: perceptions of workplace accommodations. Ursidae: The Undergraduate Research Journal at the University of Northern Colorado (2019)
55. Mandke, K., Chandekar, P.: Deaf education in India. In: Deaf Education Beyond the Western World (2019). https://doi.org/10.1093/oso/9780190880514.003.0014
56. Marschark, M., et al.: Do you see what i see? School perspectives of deaf children, hearing children and their parents. Eur. J. Spec. Needs Educ. **27**(4), 483–497 (2012)
57. Mohanty, E., Mishra, A.J.: Teachers' perspectives on the education of deaf and hard of hearing students in India: a study of Anushruti. Alter **14**(2), 85–98 (2020). https://doi.org/10.1016/j.alter.2020.02.002
58. World Health Organization: Deafness and hearing loss. https://www.who.int/news-room/fact-sheets/detail/deafness-and-hearing-loss
59. Papen, U., Tusting, K.: Using ethnography and 'real literacies' to develop a curriculum for English literacy teaching for young deaf adults in India. Compare (2020). https://doi.org/10.1080/03057925.2019.1585756
60. Punch, R., Hyde, M., Power, D.: Career and workplace experiences of Australian university graduates who are deaf or hard of hearing. J. Deaf Stud. Deaf Educ. (2007). https://doi.org/10.1093/deafed/enm011
61. Punch, R.: Employment and adults who are deaf or hard of hearing: current status and experiences of barriers, accommodations, and stress in the workplace. Am. Ann. Deaf (2016). http://www.jstor.org/stable/26235284
62. Rajput, N., Agarwal, S., Kumar, A., Nanavati, A.A.: An alternative information web for visually impaired users in developing countries. In: ASSETS (2008). https://doi.org/10.1145/1414471.1414542
63. Richie, R., Yang, C., Coppola, M.: Modeling the emergence of lexicons in homesign systems. Top. Cogn. Sci. (2014). https://doi.org/10.1111/tops.12076
64. Sharma, S., et al.: Gesture-based interaction for individuals with developmental disabilities in India. In: ASSETS (2016). https://doi.org/10.1145/2982142.2982166
65. Siddharthan, A.: A survey of research on text simplification. ITL-Int. J. Appl. Linguist. (2014)
66. Sinha, M., Dasgupta, T., Basu, A.: Development of accessible toolset to enhance social interaction opportunities for people with cerebral palsy in India. In: ASSETS (2014). https://doi.org/10.1145/2661334.2661408
67. Sinha, S.: Indian Sign Language: A Linguistic Analysis of Its Grammar. Gallaudet University Press, Washington DC (2018). https://books.google.co.in/books?id=cy6_tAEACAAJ
68. Sridhar, A., Ganesan, R.G., Kumar, P., Khapra, M.: Include: a large scale dataset for Indian sign language recognition. In: Proceedings of the 28th ACM International Conference on Multimedia. ACM (2020). https://doi.org/10.1145/3394171.3413528
69. Stokar, H.: Reasonable accommodation for workers who are deaf: differences in ADA knowledge between supervisors and advocates. JADARA (2020). https://nsuworks.nova.edu/jadara/vol53/iss2/2

70. Stokar, H., Orwat, J.: Hearing managers of deaf workers: a phenomenological investigation in the restaurant industry. Am. Ann. Deaf (2018). https://doi.org/10.1353/aad.2018.0009

71. Vashistha, A., Cutrell, E., Dell, N., Anderson, R.: Social media platforms for low-income blind people in India. In: ASSETS (2015). https://doi.org/10.1145/2700648.2809858

72. Young, A.: Factors affecting communication choice in the first year of life - assessing and understanding an on-going experience. Deaf. Educ. Int. (2002). https://doi.org/10.1179/146431502790560935

73. Zafrulla, Z., Etherton, J., Starner, T.: TTY phone: direct, equal emergency access for the deaf. In: ASSETS. ACM, New York (2008). https://doi.org/10.1145/1414471.1414536

74. Zeshan, U., Vasishta, M., Sethna, M.: Implementation of Indian sign language in educational settings. Asia Pac. Disabil. Rehabil. J. **16**(1), 16–40 (2005)

Haptic Auditory Feedback for Enhanced Image Description: A Study of User Preferences and Performance

Mallak Alkhathlan[1]([✉])(iD), M. L. Tlachac[2]([✉])(iD),
and Elke A. Rundensteiner[1]([✉])(iD)

[1] Computer Science Department, Worcester Polytechnic Institute,
Worcester, MA, USA
{malkhathlan,rundenst}@wpi.edu

[2] Information Systems and Analytics and Center for Health and Behavioral Sciences,
Bryant University, Smithfield, RI, USA
mltlachac@bryant.edu

Abstract. Our research has focused on improving the accessibility of mobile applications for blind or low vision (BLV) users, particularly with regard to images. Previous studies have shown that using spatial interaction can help BLV users create a mental model of the positions of objects within an image. In order to address the issue of limited image accessibility, we have developed three prototypes that utilize haptic feedback to reveal the positions of objects within an image. These prototypes use audio-haptic binding to make the images more accessible to BLV users. We also conducted the first user study to evaluate the memorability, efficiency, preferences, and comfort level with haptic feedback of our prototypes for BLV individuals trying to locate multiple objects within an image. The results of the study indicate that the prototype combining haptic feedback with both audio and caption components offered a more accessible and preferred among other prototypes. Our work contributes to the advancement of digital image technologies that utilize haptic feedback to enhance the experience of BLV users.

Keywords: Haptics · Touchscreens · Smartphones · Accessibility

1 Introduction

The use of images on the World Wide Web, including social media, email, mobile applications, and online games, is widespread. Social media, in particular, has seen a rapid increase in the number of available images [36], with over 4.5 billion digital images being uploaded to WhatsApp in 2017 alone [41]. As the number of online images grows, it becomes increasingly important for people with vision impairments, including blindness and low vision, to be able to understand and access these images and their properties. However, currently, most image content is largely inaccessible to the more than 1.3 billion people [56] worldwide who have

© The Author(s), under exclusive license to Springer Nature Switzerland AG 2023
J. Abdelnour Nocera et al. (Eds.): INTERACT 2023, LNCS 14142, pp. 224–246, 2023.
https://doi.org/10.1007/978-3-031-42280-5_14

a vision disability [1]. Even when alternative text is available for screen readers, it often lacks the image details recommended by the Web Content Accessibility Guidelines. While research on image descriptions has informed the development of reliable technologies, recent studies have also begun exploring strategies to capture more detailed information about images [49]. For instance, a study [38] that used image tags to record the spatial positions of objects within an image found that 71.4% of participants with vision impairments expressed enjoyment at being able to understand the relative locations of objects. Recent advances in smartphone technology have led to the creation of more immersive and informative experiences for users. [40] With over 3 billion worldwide users in 2021, smartphones have become ubiquitous devices. One of the key features that contribute to the user experience on smartphones is haptic feedback, or "haptics". Haptics is the physical response created by a touchscreen interface through the use of actuators that can operate at low voltages and provide high-speed touch sensations. There are two main components of haptic technology: force feedback, which relates to the muscles and tendons and can produce physical characteristics such as force and mechanical compliance, and tactile feedback, which is based on the human senses and is triggered by manual input.

Touchscreen technologies have significantly improved in the past two decades through various means, including higher touch resolution, multitouch capabilities, improved screen brightness and resolution, and the incorporation of resistive and capacitive technologies that allow for new forms of interaction and gesture recognition [52]. Smartphones of the current generation offer haptic feedback for virtual keyboard apps and long presses on both Android and iOS devices [26]. While the Taptic Engine is designed to help users locate objects through haptic feedback [52], to the best of our knowledge, there has been no research on how combining haptic feedback with audio might enhance image understanding for blind and low vision (BLV) users.

The purpose of this study is to examine the use of haptic feedback as a means of improving the understanding of images by blind or low vision (BLV) individuals on touchscreen mobile phones. Previous research has suggested that haptic feedback has the potential to address certain accessibility issues faced by BLV users. Our focus is on the use of two types of haptic notifications to convey a sense of touch and to determine whether or not users are successful in locating objects within an image. We have designed and tested various prototypes in order to determine the feasibility of using haptic feedback to help BLV users form a mental model of the images and to improve their overall understanding of the images.

Recognizing that all prototypes include haptic feedback, we have sometimes combined haptic notifications with auditory components, and in other cases, we have paired them with image captions, which we will discuss further in the study design section. Our goal is to verify and update the findings of previous studies in the context of current touchscreen mobile technology. Our research has made the following contributions:

– Development of three prototypes that use haptic feedback to interact with images: Prototype *(F1)* utilizes haptic feedback only, prototype *(F2)* combines haptic feedback with auditory facial recognition, and prototype *(F3)* combines haptic feedback with both auditory facial recognition and auditory captions.

- Evaluation of the memorability, efficiency, preferences, and comfort level with haptic feedback in our prototypes for BLV individuals when locating multiple objects within an image, accompanied by an analysis of the user experience, emphasizing the influence of varying audio and caption components.
- Exploring the design implications of incorporating haptic technology into smartphone applications to improve visual accessibility for BLV users.

2   Related Work

Our research is similar to that of Morris et al. [38] in that we both investigate the spatial exploration of images by blind or low vision (BLV) users. Morris et al. [38] developed a prototype for Android phones that allows users to interact directly with an image by touching a specific region, which is an improvement on the outdated image description standards that have been in place since 1995. These standards, while still used, are no longer considered best practice as they can lead to suboptimal outcomes for both content creators and users. We believe that even more engaging and immersive experiences can be achieved using newer technologies such as haptic feedback.

Our study builds upon the work of Morris et al. [38] and Seeing AI by incorporating haptic feedback to enhance image navigation for BLV users. We have designed prototypes that use two different types of haptic notifications to distinguish between successful and unsuccessful interactions with image regions. These prototypes differ from Seeing AI[1], which uses only one type of haptic notification, potentially resulting in less feedback and longer image search times for users. Our research is unique in that we also conducted a study to evaluate how users interact with the haptic notifications alone and in combination with auditory image descriptions, and how this combination can improve spatial awareness and image accessibility for BLV individuals.

2.1   Haptic Technologies

Haptic functionality, which allows users to experience tactile sensations through technology, has only recently become widely available on smartphones. However, the first commercial desktop haptic display, called Phantom (Sensable Technologies), was released as early as 1996. [35] MacLean highlighted the potential for incorporating haptic functions into contemporary design trends, such as enhancing a graphical user interface. It is worth noting that while many applications now utilize haptic technology, few were designed specifically for blind or low vision (BLV) users and none focus on providing image descriptions.

Mobile apps that use tactile feedback can enhance touch interactions through stimulation when touching a haptic device [28]. Previous research has focused

---

[1] https://www.microsoft.com/en-us/ai/seeing-ai.

on haptic feedback techniques, such as tapping, path following, and dragging and dropping, using current smartphone-based haptic technologies [26]. This research included experimental conditions involving walking and sitting, as well as three different types of feedback: physical haptics, virtual haptics, and visual only. The participants in this study reported a positive experience, in addition to improvements in task speed and accuracy [26]. Other studies have also examined the use of haptic feedback to improve user performance, such as finger dragging tasks on a touchscreen augmented by electrostatic haptic feedback [61] and the rapid prototyping of haptic interfaces for touch devices, including buttons, sliders, switches, and dials [59].

In this study [54], researchers focused on combining visual, auditory, and haptic elements in multisensory interactions to create a richer sensory context. This approach has been shown to enhance memory encoding and retrieval. Consequently, the implementation of mid-air haptic technology in museums can result in more vivid and enduring memories for visitors. Studies [19] have shown that multisensory information enhances semantic and autobiographical memory. Therefore, incorporating multisensory elements in museum experiences should be a central focus to ensure that all visitors have engaging, memorable, and accessible experiences.

Haptics technology has also been incorporated into other devices. Campbell et al. [10] demonstrated that tactile feedback can improve user performance in an isometric joystick, either by reducing the error rate or increasing steering speed. These findings are similar to previous research indicating that using a force feedback mouse improves speed and accuracy [16]. Studies on touch interaction have also found that the introduction of haptic feedback improves both speed and accuracy [12,34]. Kruijff et al. present another interesting method involving a haptic layer above the screen that allows users to distinguish between firmness and contour characteristics to enhance onscreen feedback.

Engel et al. [22] created an initial prototype that automatically generates maps based on OpenStreetMap data, using a digital pen and smartphone application for detailed information and navigation assistance. Researchers [60] have developed a multimodal user interface with a large-scale Braille display, introduced innovative techniques like blinking pins for fast map element location, and incorporated gesture recognition for intuitive navigation. Other studies have also focused on investigating the potential of different tactile chart designs to improve accessibility for BLV [20,21].

There is also a growing body of literature on the use of preemptive force-feedback systems in human-computer interaction (HCI). For example, Kasahara et al. [33] studied the optimal time to deliver a haptic actuation using electrical muscle stimulation (EMS) to tune preemptive force feedback systems and provide users with more control over automated haptic interfaces. This allows synchronization of muscle contraction timing without relying on visual or audio feedback.

2.2 Exploring Digital Graphics

There has been a recent emphasis on non-visual interactions for exploring digital graphics in a tactile manner, allowing for the full utilization of the benefits of digital information, such as easy modification [18] and interactivity [4]. Bardot et al. [4] introduced virtual spatial map exploration techniques as an alternative to traditional raised-line maps, using a smartwatch for input and feedback along with hand tracking. Zhao et al. [62] utilized Delayed-Matching-to-Samples (DMTS) to assess accuracy by having participants trace two lines and determine if they were the same. Their study focused on raised-line graphics, such as contours, paths, or shapes, and aimed to reduce tracing errors through the use of vibrations applied to the hand as a tactile cue.

The researchers in this study [53] concentrate on investigating the perception and processing of vibrations on touchscreens, specifically examining two-dimensional geometric shapes. They recognize the limitations of commercially available touchscreens in replicating the physical cues from 3D objects and raised line graphics. By exploring different vibration patterns for shape vertices and basic shape lines, the researchers aim to enhance shape recognition and facilitate the creation of mental representations of essential shape features.

In previous research, audio has also been utilized to replace visual information and describe semantically visual graphics Melfi et al. [37], and Poppinga et al. [43]. While audio descriptions can assist people with visual impairments in understanding graphics, it is still challenging to convey the spatial layout of graphics solely through audio.

Multimodal interactions are also commonly employed in this field. For instance, Giudice et al. [23] proposed a multimodal system allowing blind or low vision (BLV) individuals to interact with graphics through vibrations and audio feedback. Similarly, Goncu et al. [24] suggested the use of simple vibrations coupled with audio for learning about 2D graphics.

In other areas of research, such as materials engineering, haptic gloves and cameras have been developed to assist BLV individuals in interpreting their surroundings [48]. A wearable VR controller that simulates standard cane techniques and provides tactile and audio feedback has also been created to help BLV users navigate immersive environments research [63]. These developments demonstrate the potential for haptic technology to enhance non-visual interactions and improve accessibility for individuals with visual impairments.

2.3 Accessible Images

Smartphones equipped with screen readers have made it convenient for blind users to access information and services. These screen readers, built into the mobile operating system, allow users with low vision to read the contents of each screen within an app and navigate using gestures. A number of practical accessibility testing tools have been developed for developers, such as Android Lint [17], Accessibility Scanner [47], and other accessibility testing frameworks [3]. While these tools can identify problems, they cannot fix issues with missing labels, which can be addressed through education [11], guidelines [9], and functional testing tools [7]. Despite these efforts, progress in making apps accessible has been slow [27].

Alt text is important for image accessibility, and there is a significant amount of literature on the generation of alt text for images. These approaches can be classified as machine-generated, human-generated, or hybrid. Automated approaches use machine learning models to provide alt text, but these models can have challenges and constraints such as a limited number of training images, image size, and caption format. The greatest challenge is creating a description that captures not only the objects contained in an image but also expresses how these objects are related [50].

Research has identified the preferred structure and content for prioritizing image descriptions for BLV individuals [46]. Human-powered approaches involve crowd sourcing, friend sourcing, and social micro-volunteering, but they can be limited by participant payment, social caution, and changing needs of the vision impaired community [6]. Hybrid approaches, also known as "Human-in-the-Loop," involve a combination of automated and manual processing, but can be time-consuming to implement [46].

2.4   Addressing Insufficient Metadata

Accessibility features such as screen readers depend on apps offering complete and accurate metadata for their user interface (UI) elements. In applications, metadata refers to information about app components, like UI elements, that enables better understanding and interaction; for instance, metadata for a button could indicate its function (e.g., "play") and provide an accessible description (e.g., "Play button"). Addressing the longstanding challenge of insufficient metadata is essential for improving accessibility features. Apps may not be fully accessible due to various factors, including developers being unaware of accessibility needs, lacking the expertise to design accessible apps, or assigning low priority to accessibility issues [45].

Various methods have been developed to extract information about user interface (UI) elements from screen pixels to generate metadata for accessibility services. Initial efforts concentrated on non-pixel sources like accessibility and instrumentation APIs or software tutorial videos metadata [13]. However, these approaches faced limitations stemming from their restricted access to comprehensive UI.

Two primary categories exist for pixel-based interpretation of interfaces: traditional image processing methods and deep learning models. Traditional methods encompass edge/contour detection, which is effective for simple GUIs, and template matching, which demands feature engineering and templates [39]. In contrast, deep learning models employ neural networks such as CNN-RNN models and object detection models to locate and classify UI elements [5]. Some hybrid techniques merge traditional image processing with deep learning-based classification [14].

3   Study Design

Our research employs a mixed-methods approach, combining both qualitative and quantitative data collection and analysis. The study consists of two phases: the first phase involves conducting semi-structured interviews, while the second phase focuses on prototype trials.

In the first phase, we conducted semi-structured interviews with seven participants who later participated in the prototype trials. The interview process aimed to explore the participants' experiences, preferences, and challenges with technology, emphasizing their personal opinions on digital image trust and experiences with haptic technology (additional information regarding the interview process can be found in the interview section of the study). The insights gained from these interviews were crucial in informing our selection of appropriate prototype tasks, tailored to the participants' backgrounds and abilities for the prototyping phase.

The interview questions were designed to address various topics relevant to the research objectives. These questions have been provided in the supplementary materials for reference. The purpose of each question was to gain a deeper understanding of the participants' experiences with the technology being studied, as well as to identify potential areas for improvement. By asking these questions, we were able to gather valuable information that contributed to the development and evaluation of the prototypes in the second phase of our study.

3.1   Interview

We conducted a qualitative analysis of semi-structured interviews with participants using Braun and Clarke's method of thematic analysis [8]. We then applied axial coding [51] to identify codes and relate them to one another. Two researchers cleaned the transcripts and coded randomly selected portions of the transcripts. Through iterative review, they developed and refined the coding schemes. While many child codes were identified, we focused on the two codes that most closely aligned with our research questions. These codes received complete agreement between raters.[2]

The first code, *Personal experiences with haptic technology*, concerned participants' previous use of haptic feedback technology, such as on smartphones, games, or watches. Out of the seven participants, only one had no prior experience with haptic technology, the remaining six participants had used it in the past. While some participants found haptic feedback to be distracting or unhelpful, others appreciated its ability to communicate notifications or the time without making a sound. For example, participant **P1** shared, *"I really enjoyed using*

---

[2] We have chosen not to conduct a thematic analysis of the responses to the interview questions regarding 'Experiences using entertainment system' and 'Using technology to read e-books and digital magazines' in the present study, as a majority of the responses are not relevant to the scope of the present study. We plan to publish these responses in a separate study at a later date.

haptic technology for telling time, It gives me the feeling of subtlety and I can check the time without any disturbance to anyone else". "It was a great feature for me". P1 enjoyed being able to check the time using haptic technology (such as a haptic watch or phone) without having to hear the time announced audibly. This may be useful in situations where the speaker does not want to make noise or disturb others around them. **P4** noted, *"It's pretty common for me to have my phone on silent, so being able to get notifications through haptic feedback is a real lifesaver... It lets me know something's up without having to hear it and bother anyone around me"*. This suggests that the participant values being able to receive notifications discreetly, without the phone making a sound. Haptic technology allows them to do this by providing a tactile notification rather than an auditory one. Participant **P3** mentioned using haptic feedback in gaming, saying, *"The first time I ever felt haptic feedback was on my Playstation 5 controller, it was so cool. I felt like I was really in the game, like when I'd get hit or move around different areas, my controller would vibrate in different ways and it was an awesome experience."*. Participant P3 experienced haptic feedback while moving around and interacting with the game. It seems that the haptic feedback was triggered by certain actions or events in the game, such as "various hits," and provided participant P3 with a tactile sensation.

The second code, *Personal opinion on digital image trust*, pertained to participants' views on trustworthiness when it comes to digital images with no descriptions. Participants expressed frustration at the lack of reliable image descriptions and often had to rely on trusted family and friends. For instance, participant **P1** said, *"For me, not being able to see images is a major barrier as a blind person. It's difficult to fully grasp the world around us, when visual information is so prevalent .... However, I have found that having someone to describe images to me, like my parents, can provide me with a better understanding of those images and at least give me a sense of what they look like...."*. Participant P1 seems to be expressing frustration with the lack of accessibility of images and the need to rely on others for information about them. **P2** added, *"I rely on my sighted friends to describe images that don't have captions in articles. I wish I could enjoy them the same way others do, but it seems like people don't take the time to add descriptions."*. P2 Participant is unable to fully experience and understand images in the same way as sighted people. This can be a source of disappointment for individuals who are blind or visually impaired. **P5** shared, *"Sometimes, when people ask me to describe something or give more details, it can be really tiring. It's tough to know who I can really trust to help me."*. **P5** expresses dissatisfaction with the inaccessibility of images for individuals who are BLV, and the challenges they face in obtaining reliable information about them. **P9** said, *"it's just trying to find someone you trusted who is willing to describe, you know; it's sad that's a lot."*. P9 feels a sense of isolation or exclusion due to their inability to fully experience and understand images on their own.

3.2 Prototypes

Based on the results of our interviews, we conducted an experiment to explore the use of haptic feedback in novel interactions. To do this, we designed and prototyped three different interactions that incorporated haptic feedback. Our prototypes use a feedback generator called (UIFeedbackGenerator) to play predefined haptic patterns [2, 30] as a way to help users navigate images. The haptic notifications, or tactile responses, allow users to distinguish between different regions of the image (UINotificationFeedbackGenerator), and provide feedback when tasks are completed successfully or not. A medium haptic notification indicates success while a heavy haptic notification indicates failure, and only a single finger interacting with the image is required to trigger these notifications. This tactile response helps to enhance the user's attention and understanding of the objects depicted in the image.

While our prototypes can be used with any type of image, we chose to focus on images of people for our prototypes, as a previous study [46] found that people were the most frequently mentioned objects in image-based questions. Therefore, we included a facial recognition feature in prototypes *F2* and *F3*, and synchronized the audio with the haptic feedback in prototype *F3*. Moreover, a screen reader reads the image caption aloud in prototype *F3*. It is important that the objects that are labeled as actionable through haptic feedback are distinct from non-actionable objects, such as the background. To prevent unintentional actions during touch, we use the touchend event and the (UINotificationFeedbackGenerator) to trigger actions and communicate whether an action has succeeded or failed.

We conducted a user study with seven diverse BLV participants in order to address four research questions related to our prototypes. The study was designed to gather information on the following topics:

1. Which prototype would improve the memory of BLV users?
2. How does the number of people in each scenario affect the time it takes to complete the task?
3. Is the level of haptic feedback enough to notify BLV users?
4. Which prototype do BLV users prefer?

Participant Recruitment: We sent our IRB-approved recruitment request to several organizations that support individuals with visual impairments via direct messages on Twitter. Due to the COVID-19 pandemic, we informed potential participants that the user study would be conducted over video conference. To be eligible, participants had to meet the following criteria: 18 years of age or older, proficient in English, blind or visually impaired (BLV), using a magnifier, owning an Apple mobile device and screen reader (for interacting with VoiceOver), and possessing a computer with a webcam and Zoom app for the purposes of testing the prototypes. Participants received a $100 Amazon gift card as a token of appreciation for their time upon completion of the study.

In Table 1 we summarize the participants' demographic information. The three women and four men had an age range of 21 to 51 with occupations ranging from student to retiree. The participants also shared their level of visual impairment and Snellel Visual Acuity category [55]. The participants were either blind or had partial blindness levels of visual impairment. The Snellen Visual Acuity categories of the participants ranged from category 1 to category 3. While all participants reported some experience with haptic in response to the statement *"I have used haptic on my phone previously"*, the amount of experience varied from rarely to always.

Table 1. Participant user study demographics. Demographics include the Snellen Visual Acuity (SVA) category. Category 1: No light perception. Category 2: 20/1200 to light perception. Category 3: 20/200 to 20/400. Category 4: 20/70 to 20/200. Mobile haptic experience ranges from never (1), rarely (2), occasionally (3), often (4), and always (5).

PID	Age	Gender	Occupation	Level of Visual Impairment	SVA	Haptic Experience
P1	21	W	Student	Blindness	Category 1	4
P2	43	W	Teacher	Blindness	Category 2	4
P3	22	M	Student	Blindness	Category 2	5
P4	24	M	Student	Blindness	Category 2	5
P5	37	W	Unemployed	Partial Blindness	Category 3	2
P6	51	M	Social workers	Partial Blindness	Category 3	3
P7	31	M	Student	Blindness	Category 2	3

Procedure: In this study, we asked participants to download and install the app from TestFlight onto their iPhones. They were instructed to enable haptic feedback for supported models [29] by navigating to the Sounds and Haptics settings and activating System Haptics. A 15-minute tutorial was provided to familiarize the participants with the app, including demonstrations of mobile touch, audio playback for the face recognizer, and screen reader audio for captions. Participants were given the opportunity to practice with sample images.

Four distinct scenarios *a, b, c,* and *d* were presented to participants using three prototypes *F1, F2, and F3*. These scenarios contained between two and five objects to evaluate the participants' ability to locate multiple objects. Our study utilized image and caption pairs sourced from Google's Conceptual Captions Dataset [25], which contains web-sourced images with captions of varying lengths. It is important to note that not all image captions in our work are short sentences. We aimed to provide a realistic representation of the types of image captions that individuals with visual impairments may encounter in their daily lives. By including captions of different lengths and complexities, we sought to understand the challenges that individuals with visual impairments may face in accessing information conveyed in image captions. This insight could inform the development of more accessible image captioning techniques that can effectively communicate information to individuals with visual impairments.

To minimize the influence of order effects, the prototypes and scenarios were presented using a counterbalanced Latin square design. The assignment of prototypes to participants for testing was conducted randomly to control for potential biases. The following are comprehensive descriptions of the prototypes:

1. **Prototype *F1*:** has only haptic feedback; prototype. (a) shows scenario a: image with two objects, (b) shows scenario b: image with three objects, (c) shows scenario c: image with four objects, and (d) shows scenario d: image with five objects. This prototype, illustrated in Fig. 1.
2. **Prototype *F2*:** has haptic feedback with auditory facial recognition. We use audio feedback for each object to indicate the face recognizer. (a) shows scenario a: image with two objects; first object audio is *"Here is Denzel Washington"*, and second object audio is *"Here is Viola Davis"*. (b) shows scenario b: image with three objects; first object audio is *"Here is Edward Carstens"*, second object audio is *"Here is Virginia Madsen"*, and third object audio: *"Here is Elaine Madsen"*. (c) shows scenario c: image with four objects; first object audio is *"Here is Laura Harris"*, second object audio is *"Here is Aubrey dollar"*, third object audio is *"Here is Angie Harmon"*, and fourth object audio is *"Here is Paula Newsome"*. (d) shows scenario d: image of five objects; first object audio is *"Here is Benjamin"*, second object audio is *"Here is Olivi"*, third object audio is *"Here is Isabella"*, fourth object audio is *"Here is Emma"*, and fifth object audio is *"Here is Sophia"*. This prototype, illustrated in Fig. 2. (Note: Fig. 2 display audio feedback as text for illustration purposes; however, the actual images don't contain text on them).
3. **Prototype *F3*:** has haptic feedback with auditory facial recognition and auditory caption. We use audio feedback for each object to indicate the face recognizer. (a) shows scenario a: image with two objects; first object audio is *"Here is Denzel Washington"*, and second object audio is *"Here is Viola Davis"*; the caption is *"Actors attend the opening night"*. (b) shows scenario b: image with three objects; first object audio is *"Here is Edward Carstens"*, second object audio is *"Here is Virginia Madsen"*, and third object audio: *"Here is Elaine Madsen"*; caption is *"Actor, dramatist and person arrive at the premiere"*. (c) shows scenario c: image with four objects; first object audio is *"Here is Laura Harris"*, second object audio is *"Here is Aubrey dollar"*, third object audio is *"Here is Angie Harmon"*, and fourth object audio is *"Here is Paula Newsome"*; caption is *"Actors attend the upfront presentation"*. (d) shows scenario d: image of five objects; first object audio is *"Here is Benjamin"*, second object audio is *"Here is Olivi"*, third object audio is *"Here is Isabella"*, fourth object audio is *"Here is Emma"*, and fifth object is *"Here is Sophia"*; caption is *"Happy children and adults with a shopping cart inside retail"*. This prototype, illustrated in Fig. 3. (Note: Fig. 3 display audio feedback as text for illustration purposes; however, the actual images don't contain text on them).

The evaluation instrument for the haptic feedback system comprises four components: memory recall, time measurement, sensitivity level, and user preference. Failure regions, which do not contain people, trigger a failure notification when touched with one finger. These failure notifications utilize impact haptics to create the sensation of a collision between the finger and the failure region, generating a strong physical metaphor. On the other hand, success regions, which contain people, trigger a success notification when touched with one finger. Success notifications are accompanied by medium impact haptics, providing the sensation of a collision between the finger and the success region, and conveying a moderate level of physical feedback. These haptic notifications serve to indicate the presence of a person in the image for the success region. Heavy and medium impact haptics are employed for failure and success notifications, respectively. It is important to note that the success and failure notifications, as illustrated in the prototype legend (Table 2), can be viewed in the accompanying supplemental videos.

(a) Image with 2 objects. (b) Image with 3 objects. (c) Image with 4 objects. (d) Image with 5 objects.

Fig. 1. Prototype *(F1)*

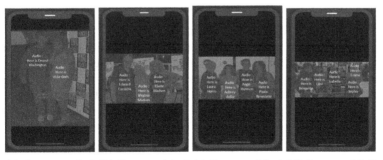

(a) Image with 2 objects. (b) Image with 3 objects. (c) Image with 4 objects. (d) Image with 5 objects.

Fig. 2. Prototype *(F2)*

(a) Image with 2 objects.   (b) Image with 3 objects.   (c) Image with 4 objects.   (d) Image with 5 objects.

Fig. 3. Prototype *(F3)*

Table 2. Haptic feedback legend for prototypes *F1, F2,* and *F3*.

Failure region ■ Notification of failure ⅲ Success region ■ Notification of success ‖

4   Analysis

Memory Recall: Participants were asked to complete four trials, each of which involved being presented with a different number of objects. After each trial, they were asked to recall the sequence of objects presented to them by stating the number of objects in the correct order, e.g. "There were 5, 3, 4, and 2 objects." Their ability to correctly recall the sequence of objects was recorded as a binary outcome: a score of 1 was given if they accurately remembered the sequence, and a score of 0 was given if they were unable to do so. The results of these memory recall tests were used to assess the participants' memory abilities.

Time Measurement: Usability is commonly assessed using time as a metric [38]. In order to maintain consistency and accuracy in timestamping, we utilized Unix Time as the benchmark for our study. To gauge usability, we monitored the time it took for participants to navigate through images with varying numbers of objects, recording the time taken for each object to be located. In order to address our second research question, we displayed the time in seconds on the screen at the end of each scenario.

Sensitivity Level: After completing the session, participants were asked to evaluate the appropriateness of the haptic feedback strength they experienced while exploring the images. Haptic notifications were used to assess participants' comfort levels. A three-point Likert scale was employed for responses, ranging from $-1 = too\ weak$ to $0 = just\ right$ to $1 = too\ strong$. Participants were explicitly instructed on the meaning of -1, 0, and 1 in relation to haptic feedback strength and informed that these values corresponded to their individual sensitivity levels. For example, a participant with thick skin who cannot feel anything would rate -1, indicating the haptic feedback was too weak for them; someone with normal skin may rate 0 if they feel just right, while someone with sensitive skin may give a 1. These self-reported scores were used to address the third research question.

Preference: Upon reviewing all three prototypes, participants were asked to rate their preferences for each prototype on a five-point Likert scale, with *1* representing the least preferred and *5* the most preferred. This scale enabled us to compare the relative preferences between the prototypes. These self-reported preferences were used to address the fourth research question.

5 Findings

Memory Recall: The objective of this study was to investigate the influence of different feedback channels (haptics and audio) on memory recall accuracy. To analyze the data, a mixed logistic regression model was employed, considering the fact that each participant underwent multiple memory recall tests with binary outcomes.

The analysis of the data, using models with categorical predictors for prototype and scenario, revealed that the type of feedback channel (haptics and audio) used in the prototype was a statistically significant predictor of memory recall accuracy ($\chi^2(2, N = 7) = 16.88, P = .0003$). In contrast, the number of objects (ranging from two to five) present in the image did not have a statistically significant impact on memory recall.

When evaluating the results of the chi-square statistic for the prototypes, it was found that the odds of correctly recalling the sequence were 12.8 times higher for prototype *F2* compared to prototype *F1*, although this result was not statistically significant at $p = 0.06$ due to Bonferroni adjustment for three comparisons. In contrast, the odds of correctly recalling the sequence were 4.5 times higher for prototype *F3* compared to prototype *F2*, which was statistically significant at $p < 0.05$. The odds of correctly recalling the sequence for prototype *F3* were also found to be substantially higher than for prototype *F1*, with an odds ratio of 57, which was statistically significant at $p < 0.01$.

In conclusion, the results of this study demonstrate that the integration of haptic and auditory feedback in the prototype significantly improves memory recall accuracy. The number of objects present in the image, however, does not appear to have a significant impact on memory recall. Further research on the integration of different scenarios may be beneficial in understanding their impact on image recall.

Time Measurement: We recorded the time taken by participants to locate each object in images with varying numbers of objects. The time required to locate each object was the dependent variable, while the predictors were categorical variables for the scenario, prototype, and number of objects. A linear mixed model was used to analyze the data, considering the continuous nature of the outcome variable and the presence of multiple observations for each participant in the repeated measures design.

The analysis did not reveal any statistically significant results for the model that included an interaction between prototype and scenario. However, the completion time for finding object 2 and object 3 (using data from scenarios *b, c* and *d*) was found to be different between prototype *F1* and prototype *F2*. The model that included an interaction between prototype and object also did not show a significant difference ($\chi^2(8, N = 7) = 14.48, P = .07$). These results suggest that the completion time was similar for two, three, and four objects, but appeared to increase when a fifth object was added to the image. Future studies could explore the completion time for images with more than five objects to determine if there are ceiling effects for the number of effective objects.

Sensitivity Level: At the end of the session, participants were asked to evaluate the appropriateness of the strength of the haptic feedback they experienced while exploring the images. The haptic notifications were used to assess the level of comfort experienced by the participants. Our prototypes contained two different haptic notifications: a heavy strength notification indicated failure at finding an object, while a medium strength notification indicated success. It is worth noting that, with the exception of one participant, all participants reported that the haptic feedback notification level was appropriate. The majority of participants therefore approved of the strength of both types of notifications.

Preference: The objective of the statistical analysis conducted on the preference data for three different prototypes *(F1, F2, and F3)* was to determine if there were significant differences in preferences among the prototypes. To achieve this, a repeated measures ANOVA was carried out, followed by a Tukey's HSD test for multiple comparisons. The dependent variable in this analysis was the preference score, and the within-subjects factor was the prototype. Participants were treated as subject identifiers.

The analysis revealed significant differences in preferences among the prototypes $p < 0.05$, with a grand mean preference score of 2.86 across all prototypes. The Tukey's HSD test identified significant differences between the following pairs of prototypes: *F1* and *F2* p-value: 0.0126, *F1* and *F3* p-value: 0.0001, and *F2* and *F3* p-value: 0.0343. Based on the estimated mean differences obtained from the Tukey's HSD test, the order of preference for the prototypes, from most preferred to least preferred, is as follows: Prototype *F3*, Prototype *F2*, and Prototype *F1*.

These results suggest that participants preferred prototype *F3*, which conveyed information using haptic feedback with both auditory notifications to identify people and auditory caption. These findings provide valuable insights into the preferences of the participants, which can be utilized to guide decision-making processes related to the development and improvement of the prototypes

Reflections on the Prototypes: We sought feedback from participants on the prototypes through their reflections, in order to gauge the prototypes' effectiveness in enhancing the participants' experience. At the end of the prototyping session, we asked participants to share any additional insights or noteworthy observations they may have. BLV participants enjoyed the experience of navigating images with haptic. In the words of **P2**, *"This type of app and the idea behind it are laudable."* **P4** expressed, *"This is a great way to get instant feedback."*. Although user P5 has less experience with haptic, the experience exploring images in our prototypes was positive. In fact, **P5** shared, *"So far, I have been highly impressed and grateful for the exceptional precision and feedback I have received."*. From the experience of this participant, we expect haptic accessibility features will prove to have a low barrier to entry and thus anticipate a quick rate of adoption among BLV users.

The participants also confirmed that finding the location of objects with haptic feedback improved the image interaction experience. **P3** shared, *"By taking the time to understand where the people in the image were located, I felt more confident and comfortable in my decisions on how to navigate it. This made me feel more positive."* As **P4** noted, *"I got a better idea of what was happening in the picture by comparing it to other stuff and knowing where everyone was. It helped me understand more."*. **P6** expressed, *"When you can examine pictures along with the descriptions, you get more information, which makes you feel more intense emotions."*. Haptic technology could therefore make BLV users more independent by making them comfortable with navigating images by themselves and less reliant on family and friends to describe the images. This is especially important as prior research has found that BLV users tend to mistrust public image descriptions due to the potentials for errors or insufficient details [58]. Haptic feedback could then serve to verify the details provided by the alt text as well as depart additional image details. For example, the participants were able to discern the spatial relations between image elements in our prototypes, which was not conveyed through the captions alone and proved challenging to communicate solely through auditory feedback.

Notably, one of the participants recommended an alternative application where haptic feedback would be useful. Specifically, **P7** suggested, *"I believe that by adding haptic audio to educational books through a smartphone app specifically for blind students, it will greatly improve their learning experience and be highly valued and appreciated by those students."*. This comment encapsulates how essential it is to add a new accessibility features such as haptic feedback to audio applications to improve interactions with images.

Some participants offered critiques of the haptic feedback that could be used to improve the image interaction experience. For example, **P7** observed, *"The haptic feedback on the device is not strong enough for me to be able to feel the vibration."*. Similarly, **P3** noted, *"Having more options for the level of haptic feedback would be useful."*. Overall, no participants expressed that they disliked receiving haptic feedback when interacting with the images. This suggests that haptic features would be welcome in future applications.

6   Discussion

In light of the growing scale, meaning, and significance of digital imagery, it is important to consider how haptic technology can be used to enhance the visual content available to screen reader users. In this study, we developed prototypes with haptic feedback in order to make digital images more accessible to individuals who are blind or have low vision (BLV).

Our research questions (RQ1-RQ4) support the information access theory of blind spatial cognition [42,57], which posits that the spatial differences observed between BLV and sighted individuals in their understanding of images are not due to a lack of visual experience or the necessary result of visual loss, but rather due to inadequate environmental information from non-visual sensing and insufficient spatial education.

Addressing the difficulties that blind and low vision users face when using touch screens requires a solution that helps them memorize the location of on-screen objects [31,32,44]. Memorizing these locations is critical for promoting independence and minimizing the need for sighted assistance. As a result, there is a growing demand for effective accessibility solutions, such as tactile haptic feedback, to better support blind and low vision users in their interactions with touch screen devices.

Previous research has shown that haptic feedback can be used to make objects visible through vibrations on a smartphone or the rumbling of a game controller [15]. However, there has been a shift towards creating more natural haptic experiences that mimic the feel of natural materials and facilitate more intuitive interactions. Therefore, it is important to design haptic feedback in mobile applications in a touch-like and perceptible manner to enhance image understanding for the BLV.

In summary, recent advancements in haptic technology by companies such as Apple and Android have spurred developers to create more engaging and empowering experiences for BLV users by utilizing the synchronizing touch and sound. However, our experiment uncovered several design considerations that will be elaborated on in the upcoming part of our discussion.

Design Implications: In our analysis and evaluation of touchscreen actions enhanced with active haptic feedback, we used the latest smartphone releases and three prototypes to assess the benefits and limitations of such feedback. Based on our findings, we have identified four design considerations for near-term product decisions and future advancements in input and haptic system design:

1. The participants in our user study preferred haptic feedback paired with auditory feedback. However, the appropriate prototype to use depends on the purpose of the application:
   - There is a tradeoff between speed and detail, and BLV users may prefer a more detailed image, even if the results are slower. In this case, prototype *F3* may be preferred over *F1* or *F2*.

– There is a tradeoff between speed and the number of objects in each image. Images with fewer objects may be easier for BLV users to navigate using haptic feedback. In this case, scenarios (a) or (b) with fewer objects may be preferred.

2. Tablets and laptops have different shapes and uses than smartphones, so they need special haptic designs for the best user experience

3. Introducing more objects to images may require new haptic designs to accommodate the increased complexity. Future work could assess the number of objects that can be remembered when touching an image and the amount of time it takes to navigate images with many objects.

4. It is important to provide settings that allow users to customize the interface to their preferences and the characteristics of their specific device. Our study participants suggested that these settings should include options for layout (portrait or landscape orientation).

5. Designers and developers must consider individual skin sensitivity differences when testing haptic feedback. Users with thickened skin may not perceive sensations, while sensitive-skinned users could experience discomfort. Designers should explore alternative approaches or measures, like objective skin sensitivity assessments, rather than solely relying on a 3-point Likert scale to validate self-reported sensitivity levels.

To effectively use a given interface, it is important to provide clear instructions such as overlays, tooltips, and tutorials. These instructions should be easily accessible and discoverable, and should be available to the user at any time, not just on the first use of the interface. It may be particularly useful to highlight the instructions on the first use to ensure that they are noticed by the user.

7 Future Work and Conclusion

In future research, we plan to explore various haptic notifications for individuals with visual impairments. We aim to identify optimal configurations and investigate built-in image understanding for iOS apps, including interactive image highlighting and custom haptic patterns. Further experiments with larger participant groups and AI-powered services for efficient image description pipelines on smartphones will be conducted to validate and expand upon our findings.

In conclusion, our study used a multi-method approach to investigate haptic feedback's role in digital image understanding for BLV individuals. By combining haptic feedback with facial recognition and captions, we demonstrated enhanced image comprehension. Our research, based on three prototypes and feedback from seven participants, highlights haptic feedback's potential to improve user experience and accessibility. Our findings pave the way for integrating touchscreen and haptic interfaces, creating a more inclusive user experience and driving innovation in AI-based digital image processing and human-computer interaction.

Acknowledgments. We thank Imam Abdulrahman Bin Faisal University (IAU) and The Saudi Arabian Cultural Mission (SACM) for financially supporting Mallak Alkhathlan.

References

1. Alkhathlan, M., Tlachac, M.L., Harrison, L., Rundensteiner, E.: "Honestly i never really thought about adding a description": why highly engaged tweets are inaccessible. In: Ardito, C., et al. (eds.) INTERACT 2021. LNCS, vol. 12932, pp. 373–395. Springer, Cham (2021). https://doi.org/10.1007/978-3-030-85623-6_23
2. Alvina, J., Zhao, S., Perrault, S.T., Azh, M., Roumen, T., Fjeld, M.: OmniVib: towards cross-body spatiotemporal vibrotactile notifications for mobile phones. In: Proceedings of the 33rd Annual ACM Conference on Human Factors in Computing Systems, pp. 2487–2496 (2015)
3. Apple: Testing for accessibility on OS X (2022). https://developer.apple.com/library/archive/documentation/Accessibility/Conceptual/AccessibilityMacOSX/OSXAXTestingApps.html
4. Bardot, S., Serrano, M., Jouffrais, C.: From tactile to virtual: using a smartwatch to improve spatial map exploration for visually impaired users. In: Proceedings of the 18th International Conference on Human-Computer Interaction with Mobile Devices and Services, pp. 100–111 (2016)
5. Beltramelli, T.: pix2code: generating code from a graphical user interface screenshot. In: Proceedings of the ACM SIGCHI Symposium on Engineering Interactive Computing Systems, pp. 1–6 (2018)
6. Brady, E., Morris, M.R., Bigham, J.P.: Gauging receptiveness to social microvolunteering. In: Proceedings of the 33rd Annual ACM Conference on Human Factors in Computing Systems, pp. 1055–1064 (2015)
7. Brajnik, G.: A comparative test of web accessibility evaluation methods. In: Proceedings of the 10th International ACM SIGACCESS Conference on Computers and Accessibility, pp. 113–120 (2008)
8. Braun, V., Clarke, V.: Using thematic analysis in psychology. Qual. Res. Psychol. **3**(2), 77–101 (2006)
9. Caldwell, B., et al.: Web content accessibility guidelines (WCAG) 2.0. WWW Consortium (W3C) **290**, 1–34 (2008)
10. Campbell, C.S., Zhai, S., May, K.W., Maglio, P.P.: What you feel must be what you see: adding tactile feedback to the trackpoint. In: Proceedings of INTERACT 1999: 7th IFIP Conference on Human Computer Interaction. Citeseer (1999)
11. Carter, J.A., Fourney, D.W.: Techniques to assist in developing accessibility engineers. In: Proceedings of the 9th International ACM SIGACCESS Conference on Computers and Accessibility, pp. 123–130 (2007)
12. Casiez, G., Roussel, N., Vanbelleghem, R., Giraud, F.: Surfpad: riding towards targets on a squeeze film effect. In: Proceedings of the SIGCHI Conference on Human Factors in Computing Systems, pp. 2491–2500 (2011)
13. Chen, J., et al.: Wireframe-based UI design search through image autoencoder. ACM Trans. Softw. Eng. Methodol. (TOSEM) **29**(3), 1–31 (2020)
14. Chen, J., et al.: Object detection for graphical user interface: old fashioned or deep learning or a combination? In: Proceedings of the 28th ACM Joint Meeting on European Software Engineering Conference and Symposium on the Foundations of Software Engineering, pp. 1202–1214 (2020)

15. Culbertson, H., Schorr, S.B., Okamura, A.M.: Haptics: the present and future of artificial touch sensation. Ann. Rev. Contr. Robot. Auton. Syst. **1**, 385–409 (2018)
16. Dennerlein, J.T., Martin, D.B., Hasser, C.: Force-feedback improves performance for steering and combined steering-targeting tasks. In: Proceedings of the SIGCHI Conference on Human Factors in Computing Systems, pp. 423–429 (2000)
17. Android Developers: Improve your code with lint checks (2022). https://developer. android.com/studio/write/lint
18. Ducasse, J., Brock, A.M., Jouffrais, C.: Accessible interactive maps for visually impaired users. In: Pissaloux, E., Velázquez, R. (eds.) Mobility of Visually Impaired People, pp. 537–584. Springer, Cham (2018). https://doi.org/10.1007/978-3-319-54446-5_17
19. Eardley, A.F., Mineiro, C., Neves, J., Ride, P.: Redefining access: embracing multimodality, memorability and shared experience in museums. Curator Museum J. **59**(3), 263–286 (2016)
20. Engel, C., Konrad, N., Weber, G.: TouchPen: rich interaction technique for audio-tactile charts by means of digital pens. In: Miesenberger, K., Manduchi, R., Covarrubias Rodriguez, M., Peňáz, P. (eds.) ICCHP 2020, Part I. LNCS, vol. 12376, pp. 446–455. Springer, Cham (2020). https://doi.org/10.1007/978-3-030-58796-3_52
21. Engel, C., Müller, E.F., Weber, G.: SVGPlott: an accessible tool to generate highly adaptable, accessible audio-tactile charts for and from blind and visually impaired people. In: Proceedings of the 12th ACM International Conference on PErvasive Technologies Related to Assistive Environments, pp. 186–195 (2019)
22. Engel, C., Weber, G.: ATIM: automated generation of interactive, audio-tactile indoor maps by means of a digital pen. In: Miesenberger, K., Kouroupetroglou, G., Mavrou, K., Manduchi, R., Covarrubias Rodriguez, M., Penáz, P. (eds.) Computers Helping People with Special Needs ICCHP-AAATE 2022, Part I. LNCS, vol. 13341, pp. 123–133. Springer, Cham (2022). https://doi.org/10.1007/978-3-031-08648-9_15
23. Giudice, N.A., Palani, H.P., Brenner, E., Kramer, K.M.: Learning non-visual graphical information using a touch-based vibro-audio interface. In: Proceedings of the 14th International ACM SIGACCESS Conference on Computers and Accessibility, ASSETS 2012, pp. 103–110. Association for Computing Machinery, New York (2012). https://doi.org/10.1145/2384916.2384935
24. Goncu, C., Marriott, K.: GraVVITAS: generic multi-touch presentation of accessible graphics. In: Campos, P., Graham, N., Jorge, J., Nunes, N., Palanque, P., Winckler, M. (eds.) INTERACT 2011. LNCS, vol. 6946, pp. 30–48. Springer, Heidelberg (2011). https://doi.org/10.1007/978-3-642-23774-4_5
25. Google: Conceptual captions dataset. Envision empower (2021). https://ai.google. com/research/ConceptualCaptions/
26. Gordon, M.L., Zhai, S.: Touchscreen haptic augmentation effects on tapping, drag and drop, and path following. In: Proceedings of the 2019 CHI Conference on Human Factors in Computing Systems, CHI 2019, pp. 1–12. Association for Computing Machinery, New York (2019). https://doi.org/10.1145/3290605.3300603
27. Hanson, V.L., Richards, J.T.: Progress on website accessibility? ACM Trans. Web (TWEB) **7**(1), 1–30 (2013)
28. Hightower, B., Lovato, S., Davison, J., Wartella, E., Piper, A.M.: Haptic explorers: supporting science journaling through mobile haptic feedback displays. Int. J. Hum. Comput. Stud. **122**, 103–112 (2019)
29. Apple Inc.: Models with haptic feedback (2021). https://devstreaming-cdn.apple. com/videos/wwdc/2019/810fdftstga66w4hfadq/810/810_designing_audiohaptic_ experiences.pdf?dl=1

30. Apple Inc.: Haptic feedback provides a tactile response (2021). https://developer. apple.com/documentation/uikit/uifeedbackgenerator
31. Kane, S.K., Bigham, J.P., Wobbrock, J.O.: Slide rule: making mobile touch screens accessible to blind people using multi-touch interaction techniques. In: Proceedings of the 10th International ACM SIGACCESS Conference on Computers and Accessibility, Assets 2008, pp. 73–80. Association for Computing Machinery, New York (2008). https://doi.org/10.1145/1414471.1414487
32. Kane, S.K., Morris, M.R., Perkins, A.Z., Wigdor, D., Ladner, R.E., Wobbrock, J.O.: Access overlays: improving non-visual access to large touch screens for blind users. In: Proceedings of the 24th Annual ACM Symposium on User Interface Software and Technology, pp. 273–282 (2011)
33. Kasahara, S., Nishida, J., Lopes, P.: Preemptive action: accelerating human reaction using electrical muscle stimulation without compromising agency, CHI 2019, pp. 1–15. Association for Computing Machinery, New York (2019). https://doi. org/10.1145/3290605.3300873
34. Levesque, V., et al.: Enhancing physicality in touch interaction with programmable friction. In: Proceedings of the SIGCHI Conference on Human Factors in Computing Systems, pp. 2481–2490 (2011)
35. MacLean, K.E.: Haptic interaction design for everyday interfaces. Rev. Hum. Factors Ergon. 4(1), 149–194 (2008)
36. Meeker, M.: Internet trends 2014 (2014). https://cryptome.org/2014/05/internet-trends-2014.pdf
37. Melfi, G., Müller, K., Schwarz, T., Jaworek, G., Stiefelhagen, R.: Understanding what you feel: a mobile audio-tactile system for graphics used at schools with students with visual impairment. In: Proceedings of the 2020 CHI Conference on Human Factors in Computing Systems, pp. 1–12 (2020)
38. Morris, M.R., Johnson, J., Bennett, C.L., Cutrell, E.: Rich representations of visual content for screen reader users. In: Proceedings of the 2018 CHI Conference on Human Factors in Computing Systems, pp. 1–11 (2018)
39. Nguyen, T.A., Csallner, C.: Reverse engineering mobile application user interfaces with REMAUI (T). In: 2015 30th IEEE/ACM International Conference on Automated Software Engineering (ASE), pp. 248–259. IEEE (2015)
40. O'Dea, S.: Number of smartphone users worldwide from 2016 to 2021, 10 December 2020. https://www.statista.com/statistics/330695/number-of-smartphone-users-worldwide/
41. BT Online: Whatsapp users share 55 billion texts, 4.5 billion photos, 1 billion videos daily (2017). https://www.businesstoday.in/technology/news/whatsapp-users-share-texts-photos-videos-daily/story/257230.html
42. Pascual-Leone, A., Hamilton, R.: The metamodal organization of the brain. Prog. Brain Res. 134, 427–445 (2001)
43. Poppinga, B., Magnusson, C., Pielot, M., Rassmus-Gröhn, K.: Touchover map: audio-tactile exploration of interactive maps. In: Proceedings of the 13th International Conference on Human Computer Interaction with Mobile Devices and Services, pp. 545–550 (2011)
44. Postma, A., Zuidhoek, S., Noordzij, M.L., Kappers, A.M.: Differences between early-blind, late-blind, and blindfolded-sighted people in haptic spatial-configuration learning and resulting memory traces. Perception 36(8), 1253–1265 (2007)

45. Ross, A.S., Zhang, X., Fogarty, J., Wobbrock, J.O.: Epidemiology as a framework for large-scale mobile application accessibility assessment. In: Proceedings of the 19th International ACM SIGACCESS Conference on Computers and Accessibility, pp. 2–11 (2017)
46. Salisbury, E., Kamar, E., Morris, M.: Toward scalable social alt text: conversational crowdsourcing as a tool for refining vision-to-language technology for the blind. In: Proceedings of the AAAI Conference on Human Computation and Crowdsourcing, vol. 5 (2017)
47. Accessibility Scanner: Improve your code with lint checks (2022). https://play.google.com/store/apps/details?id=com.google.android.apps.accessibility.auditor
48. Shrewsbury, B.T.: Providing haptic feedback using the kinect. In: The Proceedings of the 13th International ACM SIGACCESS Conference on Computers and Accessibility, pp. 321–322 (2011)
49. Stangl, A., Morris, M.R., Gurari, D.: "Person, shoes, tree. Is the person naked?" What people with vision impairments want in image descriptions. In: Proceedings of the 2020 CHI Conference on Human Factors in Computing Systems, pp. 1–13 (2020)
50. Stangl, A.J., Kothari, E., Jain, S.D., Yeh, T., Grauman, K., Gurari, D.: Browse-WithMe: an online clothes shopping assistant for people with visual impairments. In: Proceedings of the 20th International ACM SIGACCESS Conference on Computers and Accessibility, pp. 107–118 (2018)
51. Strauss, A., Corbin, J.: Basics of qualitative research techniques. Citeseer (1998)
52. Tactile Technologies: The five different touch screen technologies, February 2021. https://tactiletechnologies.com/Tactile/The-Five-Different-Touch-Screen-Technologies-Choosing-The-Best-One
53. Tennison, J.L., Gorlewicz, J.L.: Toward non-visual graphics representations on vibratory touchscreens: shape exploration and identification. In: Bello, F., Kajimoto, H., Visell, Y. (eds.) EuroHaptics 2016, Part II. LNCS, vol. 9775, pp. 384–395. Springer, Cham (2016). https://doi.org/10.1007/978-3-319-42324-1_38
54. Vi, C.T., Ablart, D., Gatti, E., Velasco, C., Obrist, M.: Not just seeing, but also feeling art: mid-air haptic experiences integrated in a multisensory art exhibition. Int. J. Hum. Comput. Stud. **108**, 1–14 (2017)
55. WHO: Definitions of blindness (2021). https://www.who.int/news-room/fact-sheets/detail/blindness-and-visual-impairment
56. World Health Organisation (WHO): Blindness and vision impairment (2020). https://www.who.int/news-room/fact-sheets/detail/blindness-and-visual-impairment
57. Wolbers, T., Klatzky, R.L., Loomis, J.M., Wutte, M.G., Giudice, N.A.: Modality-independent coding of spatial layout in the human brain. Curr. Biol. **21**(11), 984–989 (2011)
58. Wu, S., Wieland, J., Farivar, O., Schiller, J.: Automatic alt-text: computer-generated image descriptions for blind users on a social network service. In: Proceedings of the 2017 ACM Conference on Computer Supported Cooperative Work and Social Computing, pp. 1180–1192 (2017)
59. Yasu, K.: MagnetAct: magnetic-sheet-based haptic interfaces for touch devices. In: Proceedings of the 2019 CHI Conference on Human Factors in Computing Systems, pp. 1–8 (2019)
60. Zeng, L., Weber, G.: Audio-haptic browser for a geographical information system. In: Miesenberger, K., Klaus, J., Zagler, W., Karshmer, A. (eds.) ICCHP 2010, Part II. LNCS, vol. 6180, pp. 466–473. Springer, Heidelberg (2010). https://doi.org/10.1007/978-3-642-14100-3_70

61. Zhang, Y., Harrison, C.: Quantifying the targeting performance benefit of electrostatic haptic feedback on touchscreens. In: Proceedings of the 2015 International Conference on Interactive Tabletops & Surfaces, pp. 43–46 (2015)
62. Zhao, K., Serrano, M., Oriola, B., Jouffrais, C.: VibHand: on-hand vibrotactile interface enhancing non-visual exploration of digital graphics. Proc. ACM Hum.-Comput. Interact. 4(ISS), 1–19 (2020)
63. Zhao, Y., et al.: Enabling people with visual impairments to navigate virtual reality with a haptic and auditory cane simulation. In: Proceedings of the 2018 CHI Conference on Human Factors in Computing Systems, pp. 1–14 (2018)

Using Colour and Brightness for Sound Zone Feedback

Stine S. Johansen[1]([⊠]) , Peter Axel Nielsen[2] , Kashmiri Stec[3] ,
and Jesper Kjeldskov[2]

[1] Queensland University of Technology, Brisbane, Australia
stine.johansen@qut.edu.au
[2] Aalborg University, Aalborg, Denmark
{pan,jesper}@cs.aau.dk
[3] Bang & Olufsen, Struer, Denmark
ksh@bang-olufsen.dk

Abstract. We investigate the use of colour and brightness for feedback from sound zone systems. User interaction with sound zones suffer from them being invisible. Hence, spatial properties such as volume, size, and overlaps need to be represented through, *e.g.*, light. Two studies were conducted. In the first study (N = 27), participants experienced different colour and brightness values shown on an LED strip attached to a volume controller and related those to sound zone volume, size, and overlaps. In the second study (N = 36), participants created an overlap between two sound zones by turning up the volume, triggering 12 animated light patterns. Our findings show that brightness reflects well the size of a sound zone, and that instant patterns are better indicators of overlaps compared to gradual patterns. These contributions are useful for designing sound zone visualisations.

Keywords: Sound zone · Light · Colour · Brightness

1 Introduction

In this paper, we argue that brightness and colour animations are useful to novice users as feedback for sound zone systems. A sound zone system is a speaker-based solution to create delimited areas of sound in a room. There is a clear boundary for sound, and users' proximity to a sound zone inversely impacts the amplitude of the sound. This allows for multiple persons to share a room while listening to different music tracks or other sounds without using headphones, thereby enabling social interactions and higher awareness of the surroundings. Sound zone systems have reached a state where they are considered useful for various settings, including car cabins [7], hospital wards [33], and homes [22]. Even though limitations still exist for constructing sound zone systems, they are on their way to becoming commercially available. Given the imminent availability to consumers, ensuring suitable feedback mechanisms to the sound zone users poses important challenges for human-computer interaction.

J. Abdelnour Nocera et al. (Eds.): INTERACT 2023, LNCS 14142, pp. 247–272, 2023.
https://doi.org/10.1007/978-3-031-42280-5_15

Our work is anchored in ethnographic research on social and subjective experiences of sound in homes [22]. One challenge relating to feedback and control of sound zones is that the sound inhabits a physical space in a way that is significantly different when compared to other sound systems, *e.g.*, headphones or current standard home speaker systems. Offering more background into this, Lundgaard et al. [23] position sound zones as one type of technological intervention into soundscapes, unique for their spatial properties that headphones and standard speaker systems do not have. Since sound zones are inherently intangible and invisible, their spatial properties are not obvious. This necessitates the development of interfaces and displays to provide relevant feedback about the new properties that sound zones introduce, including size and overlaps. For novice users, forming an understanding of overlaps is important. Overlaps can happen when adjusting the volume, and thereby size, of a sound zone. Previously [17], we investigated direct and indirect representations of the size and location of sound zones, comparing a "spot-light" projection on the ceiling to an LED strip on the wall. This study showed potentials for exploring indirect mappings further, leading us to investigate the use of colour and brightness as part of small objects on a table (see Fig. 1). Early research has shown that subjective estimations of brightness and loudness stimuli were analogous [26]. We extend this by investigating how light and sound are experienced together.

Sound properties can be visualised in different ways, both for artistic purposes [28] and for sound design [27]. Lima et al. conducted a survey on visualisation techniques of musical features, showing that colour is used extensively for tone, frequency, and harmonic structure [16]. Here, we are interested in using light for visualising information in the novel context of sound zone systems. We consider light as an opportunity for feedback about the spatial properties of sound zones. Previous research shows that light affects people's perception of physical properties of objects and spaces, such as dimensions and weight [21]. While light and sound waves are different, they also share common traits (*e.g.*, high intensity at the source and a gradual drop-off out into a physical space) that we suggest are useful for visualising complex spatial behaviour of sound.

In this paper, we present two consecutive studies, investigating the use of colour and brightness as feedback for sound zone volume, size, and overlaps. We ask the research question: *How can feedback about sound zone volume, size, and overlaps be provided using light?* In Study 1, we investigated colour and brightness as feedback about volume and size of one sound zone. In Study 2, we focused on sound zone overlaps. Novice users experienced animated light patterns and were asked how well each pattern provided information about overlaps,

Fig. 1. Controllers with LED strips.

size increase and decrease, and how well it notified them of these issues. We also gathered qualitative insights into how novice users experienced sound zone behaviour in relation to particular light feedback. With this research, we provide insights that are useful in feedback design for sound zone systems in particular. This can also be extended to other sound systems with similar spatial properties.

2   Related Work

2.1   Personal Sound Zones

As part of a broader paradigm shift from channel-based to object-based audio reproduction [12], there is a potential for users to control new aspects of their soundscape. Spatial sound has become a subject of investigations in HCI, *e.g.*, for connecting auditory and biomechanical cues [30] and for designing auditory displays where visual displays are inappropriate [34]. One type of system in the object-based paradigm is sound zones. The vision behind sound zone systems is to provide different users in the same shared physical space with personal listening experiences without wearing headphones [3]. This can be useful in many situations, such as shared office spaces, car cabins [6], and homes [22], the latter of which is expanded below. Sound zones can be implemented in different ways. Examples of commercial products are the directional speakers Audio Spotlight by Holosonics, Sennheiser AudioBeam or Soundlazer that use ultrasound. In this case, the ultrasonic waves can only be heard when they collide. Limitations to these systems exist such as their inability to reproduce low-frequency sound. Another method for creating sound zones is by using a combination of microphones and loudspeakers. Microphones capture the sound pressure of audio signals directed at predefined areas, and those measurements can then be used to create filters that enhance the acoustic contrast between the zones [7], *i.e.*, the decibel difference of an audio signal between the area where a user wants to hear it and the areas in which users do not want to hear it. To help achieve this, Rämö et al. present a model which shows that if the acoustic contrast between two or more sound zones is too low, users become distracted by the chaotic mixing of sounds [29].

Previous research provides an overview of the interaction design challenges for domestic sound zones and approaches to addressing them [23]. Sound zone systems are intangible and invisible, making it difficult, especially for novice users, to understand their behaviour in comparison to experiences they have with other sound systems. This behaviour is further complicated by different implementation methods for sound zone systems typically resulting in different behaviours. Current methods result in low acoustic contrast when sound zones are close to each other or when the volume of one sound zone is much higher than another sound zone in the same room. We refer to this as overlaps.

A study on domestic situations for sound zones points to different social aspects of using sound zone systems [22]. For example, one use situation includes persons who engage in their own sound-producing activities but stay within the same room. Here, they are not actively engaged in social activities which also means that they may not be aware of how their own sound is affecting the others. In another situation, persons may want to listen to the same sound from a television but have different preferences for sound properties such as the volume. This means that the persons might be actively engaged with each other, changing their awareness of how their own sound adjustments affect the other. The research by Lundgaard et al. [23] includes descriptions of design concepts to visualise sound zones. These visualisations particularly focus on projections on floors or ceilings. Jacobsen et al. [17] recently presented an experiment evaluating the precision with which users can position themselves and sound zones from either ceiling projections, a relative wall display, or no visualisation, respectively. They show that visualisations aid users significantly in positioning tasks. Similarly, Johansen et al. [18] conducted an elicitation study of shape-changing visualisations that showed the effect different visualisations have on user experiences of and expectations for sound zone behaviour. These prior studies suggest that visualisations play an important role in sound zone interaction. All of them, however, rely on users having to map a 2-dimensional visualisation with a relative position to the 3-dimensional space within which the sound zones exist.

2.2 Light as Feedback

Using light for visualising information is not novel outside the context of sound zone systems to, *e.g.*, show states such as on or off. A common way to do this is through point lights where one small LED lights up. This can be varied at different brightness levels and in different colours. Previous research investigates how the vocabulary for light can be expanded with more expressions that still make sense to users [14]. This includes categories for notification, active state, low energy state, and turning on. In relation to using expressive lights in robots, research shows that participants' interpretation is dependent on the situation [1].

Many conventions and culturally inherent meanings are attached to colours. Early research shows that colour affects the perceived size of an object [35]. Similarly, dark coloured objects tend to be perceived as heavier than light coloured objects when the objects are only observed and not touched [32]. Löffler et al. investigate how these psychological traits can be combined with metaphors to convey meaning through colour in tangible user interfaces [21]. Their study shows that there can be other uses for colour that not only come from culturally derived symbolic meaning, but are instead based on sensorimotor experiences independent from language and culture. In terms of brightness, previous research within architecture shows an effect of light on perceived size and dimensions of physical spaces [20,24]. The research shows that increased brightness is related to increased perceived size of a room. Furthermore, different light patterns affect perception of dimensions. For example, vertical lights projected onto a church resulted in perceptions of a taller church compared to no projections. Impressions of these spatial properties is shown by a study by Lindh et al. to relate to the gaze of participants [20]. They found that participants tended to direct their gaze towards areas with high brightness.

In previous research and art, sound has been visualised in many ways. This includes 2D visualisations of sound in 3D space, *e.g.*, for the design of GUIs [4, 13]. Another example includes using opacity to represent sound volume [28] with a broad focus on generation of spatial forms from music. McGregor et al. developed visualisations of soundscape elements to assist interaction designers in capturing data about and identifying problems within a soundscape [27]. Different aspects of a sound were represented with particular visual features. Dynamics was represented with different sizes where small is soft, and big is loud. To represent this spectrally, they used hues where blue is low, and red is high. Spatiality was represented as a 2D position of depth and panning. In some cases, sound is visualised in a more direct way. For example, an art installation for the 2013 GLOW festival featured a large, dark room with projectors on the ceiling [31]. When a member of the audience produced a sound such as a whistle, the sound waves would be projected onto the floor. Given these possibilities of communicating with light, we set out to investigate how light is experienced together with sound zones, and what information can be communicated to users about specific properties of sound zones.

3   Experimental Setup

We conducted two studies of the use of colour and brightness for sound zone feedback. The second study was planned in response to the findings from the first to further investigate light pattern feedback when two sound zones overlap. The two studies use a highly similar experimental setup, illustrated in Fig. 2. The soundbar was constructed from a 20-channel speaker array positioned in two rows, with a displacement of half a speaker. This was to ensure the shortest distance from centre to centre as that impacts the maximum frequency possible to use. The speaker is a 3″ full-range unit from Tymphany, covering a range from 100 Hz to 8 kHz. The sound zones centres were positioned at a distance of 4.8 m from each other and 2.47 m from the soundbar. This enabled us to create a total separation between the sound zones greater than 15 dB. The setup mimics a situation where the participant shares a room, *e.g.*, a living room or an office, with another person, and want to listen to different music tracks without disturbing each other, the type of situation termed "social-connected" by Lundgaard and Nielsen [22]. In this situation, users are engaged in different activities but still desire to be physically close to each other. Since listening to sound is a secondary activity for both users, we wanted to make the interaction with the sound zone familiar through the use of a physical volume controller.

Colour can be described according to the HSB (Hue, Saturation, Brightness) model where hue is the "attribute of a visual sensation according to which an area appears to be similar to one of the perceived colors", brightness is when that area "appears to emit more or less light", and saturation is the assessment of the area's colourfulness "in proportion to its brightness" [10], which all impact the perception of physical properties differently. As a first step, we focused on hue, henceforth referred to as colour, and brightness, independently, where a larger amount of prior research can be relied upon. This includes the animated patterns defined by [14] and the findings on brightness for object perceptions by [20,24]. In contrast to previous research that proposes light projections, wall displays, and shape-changing displays as potential approaches [17,18,23], we investigate if integrating the feedback directly as light onto the control device enable users to understand the spatial properties of sound zones. For this purpose, we designed two sound zone volume controllers with an LED strip that can display light in various brightness and colour settings. The motivation behind the specific design choices for our experiments was to enable the study of different patterns of colour and brightness in order to learn about their individual strengths and limitations. We chose to augment physical volume controllers as opposed to constructing a smartphone application because users' smartphones are not always visually accessible, especially when engaged in activities such as reading or watching television. While volume controllers can also be occluded by, *e.g.*, furniture and people, this will more rarely be the case in comparison to smartphones. We invite readers to watch the supplementary video, linked in Appendix 4, for further description of the envisioned setup. Each controller is constructed of two 3D printed cylinders that are connected through a 10K rotary potentiometer. Outside the bottom cylinder, we attached a NeoPixel strip that can display light through 11 LEDs. Since the study included light transitions, which can affect how specific colours are perceived, we used a gamma correction function as specified in the NeoPixel library. The potentiometer and LED-strip were connected to an Adafruit Feather HUZZAH ESP8266 board. To ensure a non-painful and safe experience for participants, the maximum loudness in the room was 75 dB.

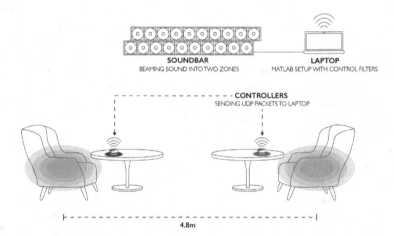

Fig. 2. The setup for the studies consisted of one or two volume controllers, a laptop and a soundbar. The volume controllers communicated with the laptop through UDP packets which were processed and resulting in a final output from the soundbar.

4   Study 1: Volume and Size of One Sound Zone

The purpose of Study 1 was to investigate the research question: *How can colour and brightness be used as feedback about volume and size of one sound zone?* We conducted a mixed methods evaluation, including a quantitative investigation into the perceptions of users on colour and brightness as a mechanism for feedback in sound zones, and interviews about participants' understanding of what they saw and heard. The study was approved by the ethics board of the institution. Even though the size of a sound zone can be set independently of its volume, these properties can be experienced as related, because the sound from a louder zone can be heard in a wider area. With a focus on users' experiences in this research, we view sound zone size and volume as dependent characteristics. We hypothesised that high brightness would be related to loud sounds and low brightness to quiet sounds. Furthermore, we expected that colours could be used for volume in a systematic way, meaning that participants would organise them according to wavelength (e.g. in the order of blue, green, yellow, and red).

4.1   Method

Participants. Due to the novelty of sound zone systems, we recruited novice users with no prior experience with nor knowledge of sound zone systems. Recruitment was done through social media. We recruited 27 participants (12 female and 15 male) within an age range of 23 to 48 (M = 33.2). We screened participants for hearing impairments, colour blindness (including Tritanopia), and synesthesia related to sound and vision. All participants signed an informed consent form and were paid $24.

Setup. The study took place in a lab with two active sound zones (see Fig. 2). Participants were asked to stand inside the left sound zone. Two different pop-rock music tracks (by The Killers and Muse) were played, one in each zone.

4.2   Procedure

Participants were introduced to the sound zone system by walking around the room for 1 to 2 min. We did not provide a verbal explanation of the system in order for participants to only rely on their auditory and visual impressions. The facilitator instructed them to walk into each sound zone and listen to the sound within both of them as well as the sound around the zones. Participants were then informed that the aim of the prototype was to display feedback about their own sound zone and the room surrounding it. They were then asked to adjust the volume of their own sound zone from minimum to maximum and, again, walk into both sound zones and listen to the sounds. This also served as a manipulation check to ensure that they noticed a difference in volume of their own sound zone. Each trial then consisted of two phases as shown in Fig. 3), with feedback displayed on the participant's controller.

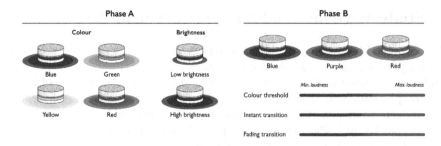

Fig. 3. Left: Colour and brightness settings for phase A. Right: Colour transitions for phase B. Each line shows which colour is displayed from minimum to maximum volume.

Phase A: Colour and Brightness. First, four colour settings were displayed in a randomized order. Then, two brightness settings were displayed. We chose the blue colour for displaying brightness settings, because it is the brightest, perceptually [9]. For each colour and brightness setting, participants were asked to rate how loud they would expect their sound zone to be on a scale from 0 to 100 (0 being silence, and 100 being maximum volume). They were then given a map of the room in which the centers of the two sound zones were marked. The facilitator asked each participant to draw a circular area within which they would expect to hear their music track without being disturbed by the other track. After all variations had been displayed, participants were given the opportunity to correct responses and drawings. Phase A was conducted with no sound in order to remove the possibility that participants would provide answers based on what they heard rather than the light.

Phase B: Colour Transitions. We designed three colour transitions that were displayed when participants adjusted the volume of their sound zone. Based on the hypothesis that colours would be systematically organized according to wavelength, we assigned blue to low volume and red to high volume. Participants were instructed to adjust the volume of their sound zone from minimum to maximum and focus on the colour and sound. The colour transition was initiated when the volume of one sound zone was predicted to disturb another sound zone. This was based on the distraction model developed in previous research [29]. The facilitator then asked each participant to describe what each colour threshold signified to them. Additionally, the facilitator asked participants to describe how they believed the adjustment had affected the other sound zone. Participants were exposed to all three versions in randomised order.

4.3   Analysis

Participants' assessments of sound zone size and volume in relation to colour were analyzed using a repeated measures ANOVA to compare responses across all colour settings (blue, green, yellow, and red). This method is appropriate for continuous numerical response data with one variable when the distribution of responses is approximately normally distributed. If the null-hypothesis (no statistical significance exists between the independent variable, $i.e.$, colours) could be rejected with an alpha value below .05, we conducted a pairwise post hoc analysis with Bonferroni correction (to correct for multiple t-tests) to determine which pairs were significantly different. For responses regarding brightness for sound zone size and volume (low brightness and high brightness), we conducted t-tests to determine significantly different pairs ($p < .05$). For significantly different pairs, we report effect sizes calculated using the Cohen's d formula. We annotated the interviews and conducted a thematic analysis [8] in order to investigate experiences of the light. We used an open-coding process, identifying and developing themes in two iterations. In the first iteration, 13 themes were identified. Through the second iteration, these themes were consolidated to five regarding (1) types of transitions, (2) illusions of sound behaviour, (3) conventions, (4) experiences of how the sound distributes in the space, and (5) synchronisation of sound zones.

4.4 Findings

Colour and Brightness for Volume and Size. We found that participants related low brightness to low volume and small size, and high brightness to high volume and large size. The mean volume responses were 12.7 for low brightness and 79.5 for high brightness. The difference between these responses was statistically significant ($F_{1,52} = 207.81$, $p < .01$), effect size 4.329 (indicating a large effect). 24 participants (89%) drew differently sized zones in relation to different brightness values. The difference between low and high brightness in relation to size was also statistically significant ($F_{1,52} = 63.18$, $p < .01$), effect size 2.175 (indicating a large effect). The mean sound zone size responses were 3.5 cm for low brightness and 8.6 cm for high brightness on a map that measured 16×14.5 cm. For colour, we found a significant difference in participants' volume responses ($F_{1,104} = 6.20$, $p < .01$) which was due solely to the difference between blue (mean = 37) and red (mean = 67), effect size 0.973 (indicating a large effect), as well as green (mean = 42) and red, effect size 0.876 (indicating a large effect), both $p < .05$. However, we found that 24 participants (89%) ranked colours in similar ways. 15 participants (56%) placed red at the high end of their volume responses, followed by yellow, green, and blue. 7 participants (26%) placed the colours in the reverse order.

Instant Versus Fading Transitions. 15 participants described that a colour fade better represented the behaviour of the sound as compared to instant transitions. Some expanded that instant transitions were experienced as volume levels whereas a fading transition supported what they heard and felt on the volume controller. In other words, the fading transition matched the visual sense to the auditory and haptic senses. This was also supported by some participants being surprised when the colour changed instantly. Furthermore, even though we used the same colours for all transitions, participants experienced a bigger volume change for the instant transition as compared to the fade. Some participants were confused that the brightness did not increase with the volume since they believe that would have enhanced the representation of the sound behaviour.

Sound Zone Illusions. In several cases, participants described non-existing sound behaviour. One participant described that the volume did not change noticeably within each colour range, but it changed noticeably when the colour changed. Some participants experienced that the sound responded differently between the instant colour transition and the fading colour transition. For example, one described that the volume level increased abruptly when the colour changed instantly, but it increased gradually when the colour faded. One participant explained that the fading colour transition was less noticeable and therefore, he was aware of the sound in a different way compared to the instant colour transition. Six participants believed that the zones switched places when the colour changed on the controller. For most of these cases, participants believed that the volume of the zones was constant, and they instead controlled the position of the sound zones with the controller. Some participants mentioned this in relation to the instant colour transition but not the fading transition.

Colour Conventions. As expected, participants relied on experiences with colours as feedback about sound properties, but not all relied on the same conventions. 12 participants mentioned that they perceived red as a warning, and some specifically experienced it as a signal about potential hearing damage. Relating the colour transitions to conventions in sound displays only applied to the instant colour transitions and not the fading transition. We found that even though some participants rated blue and green as high volume colours, several of these participants changed this view quickly to match our settings where red is related to high volume. In some cases, participants mentioned that they wanted to modify their responses according to this newly established system. The purple colour in the 'colour threshold' transition was only displayed within a small volume range. Some described that this allowed them to more easily adjust their own sound zone to a volume level equal to that of the other sound zone.

A Bubble Effect. Seven participants believed that adjusting the volume of one sound zone would not affect the other zone, as if the sound was contained inside a closed bubble. We did not anticipate this response, because of the initial introduction to the sound zones. During the introduction, only one participant reported that he could not hear both music tracks in one zone with the other on maximum volume. Some participants explained that they forgot about the other sound zone when they could not hear it. In one case, a participant described that the fading colour transition made it easier to forget the other zone. Seven participants believed that the sound zones were acoustically isolated from each other regardless of volume levels. Furthermore, our findings show that some participants relied on the displayed light for knowing whether or not sound zones could overlap. For example, one participant believed that 'colour threshold' transitions signified disturbing another sound zone or not, while the fading colour transition would lead to increased volume but no disturbance.

Synchronisation and Movement of Sound Zones. Eight participants believed that the volume levels of the two sound zones were synchronised. We found that participants described this synchronisation in different ways. Three participants believed that increasing volume in one zone would lead to decreased volume in the other zone. Another participant believed she was adjusting the volume of both zones simultaneously. Finally, four believed that the purple colour signified an equilibrium between zones where they were at equal volume levels.

5   Study 2: Overlaps Between Two Sound Zones

For the second study, we investigated the research question: *How can animated light patterns be used as feedback for showing that sound zones overlap?* To address this, we investigated how patterns compare with each other in terms of supporting users' understanding of sound zone overlaps and for notification. This study was also approved by the ethics board of the institution.

5.1   Method

Participants. We followed the same procedure for recruiting participants as in Study 1. Since overlapping sound zones can only occur when multiple sound zones are active, and social aspects of the experience could affect the experience of certain patterns, we asked participants to bring a friend. No participants from the first study participated in the second. None reported hearing impairments, colour blindness (including Tritanopia), or synesthesia related to sound and vision, and none had prior experience with sound zone systems. We recruited 36 participants (22 female and 14 male) aged 19 to 28 (M = 22.8). Similar to Study 1, all signed an informed consent form and were paid US$24.

Setup. Study 2 used the same setup as Study 1 with two active sound zones (see Fig. 2). For each trial, we asked the participant and their friend to sit in their own sound zones. Both participant and friend had a controller to adjust the volume of their own sound zone. Participants were asked to respond to questions about the light patterns on a tablet placed in front of them. They took turns being an active and passive user. The active user turns up the volume of their sound zone, and the passive user just listens to the music.

Feedback Settings. We used either white on both controllers or red or blue for each controller. When increasing the volume of one sound zone to the point where the sound zones overlapped, an animated light pattern was displayed on the affected sound zone. See Fig. 4 for the patterns. In study 1, we learned that displaying feedback on participants' own controllers made them less aware of, or completely forget, the other sound zone. It could even emphasise the focus on that person's own sound zone. Based on that, we displayed the patterns on the passive participant's controller. We hypothesised that this would serve our goal of showing how a volume increase by the active participant would affect the passive participant's sound zone, *i.e.*, the fact that the active participant's sound zone overlaps with the passive participant's sound zone.

We used six patterns in two categories, 'Instant' and 'Gradual'. We included instant patterns, 'beacon', 'bright flash', and 'blink increasing', as Harrison et al. showed that their participants related these patterns to particular notification states [14] and effectively grabbed their attention. This would be especially useful for overlapping sound zones, since a user adjusting their volume cannot otherwise hear or see overlaps with other sound zones. Instant patterns might be useful for bringing users' attention to these other sound zones and prompt them to adjust the sound again to avoid disturbing other users. To complement the study of these instant patterns, we included Harrison et al.'s gradual patterns [14], 'staircase blink', 'gradual build', and 'lighthouse', which we believed could give a different understanding of how sound zones overlap, based on the research by Löffler et al. [21]. Where instant patterns might notify users well, we aimed to investigate whether the gradual patterns give users a more realistic imitation of how the sound from one sound zone interferes with another sound zone. Our investigation relied on animations shown on the entire LED strips as opposed to parts of the LED strips. As such, this is a first step to identify whether or not light animations can be utilised for sound zone feedback. Utilising the spatial features of the LED strips is a next relevant step.

5.2 Procedure

Participants were first allowed to explore the room to create an initial experience of the sound zones. They then received a short introduction to the prototype. This included a description of the use situation for the prototype (*i.e.*, "You are in a shared living room with a friend, and you are listening to different music tracks without wanting to disturb each other"). For half of the trial, participants took an active role by increasing the volume of their sound zone and focusing on the light on the other volume controller. For the other half, they took a passive role and watched their own controller while the friend increased the volume of their own sound zone. We counterbalanced whether they started the trial as active or passive. After up to 1 min of watching a pattern, participants were asked to rate it in a Likert-item format from 'Strongly disagree' to 'Strongly agree' according to how well it provided information in the form of six statements about the sound zones. We incorporated recommendations from previous research, including a mid-point option ('Neither agree nor disagree') [5], using a 7-point scale [11], and labelling all options on the scale [5]. Participants could provide additional comments. The six statements were phrased to investigate sound zone overlaps, volume, and size: "The sound zones are overlapping", "My

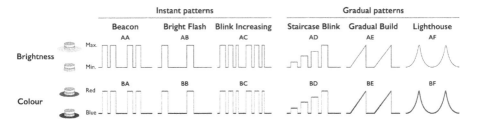

Fig. 4. Brightness and colour patterns for study 2 categorized as 'Instant' and 'Gradual'. For brightness patterns, the height of the line signifies the intensity of the brightness (from minimum to maximum). For colour patterns, the height is related to the colour, and the default state of the volume controllers were blue (bottom) and red (top). Here, the passive user's controller is blue, and the active user's controller is red. (Color figure online)

sound zone is increasing in size", "The other sound zone is decreasing in size", "The person in the other sound zone can hear my music", "I am being warned", and "I should adjust the volume of my sound zone". The order of the patterns and statements were randomized for each pattern. At the end of the trial, we conducted a small follow-up interview asking participants to elaborate on their answers and describe how the light was experienced with the sound.

5.3 Analysis

Similar to Study 1, we performed a statistical analysis on the quantitative data followed by a reflective thematic analysis with open coding of the follow-up interviews. Methods for analysing Likert items are widely debated [5]. The debate is mainly centered on interpreting the responses as either ordinal or interval data. For this study, we followed an ordinal interpretation and therefore conducted a non-parametric analysis. We conducted a related-samples Friedman's two-way analysis of variance by ranks (using an alpha level of 0.05 as cutoff for significance) because of its suitability for analyzing non-parametric ordinal data with repeated measures. To determine which pairs were significantly different, we conducted a pairwise Dunn test. Finally, we conducted a Kendall's W test which indicates the effect size as a value between 0 and 1, representing the agreement between participants. We used Cohen's effect size interpretation guidelines of $0.1 - < 0.3$ (small effect), $0.3 - < 0.5$ (moderate effect), and $> = 0.5$ (strong effect). The thematic analysis was conducted in two iterations by coding of transcriptions of the interviews. In the first iteration, six themes emerged concerning (1) colours mixing, (2) gradual transitions as overlaps, (3) associations for the colours and patterns, (4) ability to perceive light patterns according to the participant's role, (5) ability to act on overlaps based on the participant's role, and (6) feeling powerless when passive. In the second iteration, these themes were consolidated within the five themes presented together with the quantitative findings below.

5.4 Findings

An overview of the results of the analysis for each statement described above can be seen in Fig. 7 in Appendix 2. Boxplots showing the differences in ratings can be seen in Appendix 3. Our analysis indicates that the patterns perform statistically differently for five of the information statements but not the statement "The other sound zone is decreasing in size". We found that the Beacon (BA) and Blink Increasing patterns (BC) perform best for all three categories. The follow-up interviews conducted at the end of each trial offer qualitative insights into why certain patterns performed better than others. These insights sometimes contradicted the quantitative findings. In the following, we group our findings according to categories of the information statements for which two fit into each category.

Overlapping Sound Zones. The two information statements related to over-laps were "The sound zones are overlapping" and "The person in the other sound zone can hear my music". For information about overlapping sound zones, $W = .124$, indicating a small effect, we found that patterns with two colours performed better than patterns in white for all except when comparing the Bright Flash in white (AB) to the Gradual Build in two colours (BE) where the Bright Flash performed significantly better. For example, the Bright Flash pattern performed better in two colours (BB) than in white (AB) for the statement that the other person can hear the participant's music, $W = .140$, indicating a small effect. We also found that instant patterns perform better than gradual patterns for both white and two colours.

Some participants experienced the patterns and colours as a metaphor for the sound zones. For some, this was the case for gradual patterns which were described as more realistic than instant patterns. One participant explained that the transition towards an overlap was fluid. Related to that, others mentioned the colours mixing as a supportive metaphor for the music tracks mixing for both instant and gradual light patterns. For one participant who put the instant patterns highest, the colours signified what caused the blinking pattern to occur: *"I think the fact that I was red and that was blue added something. Then I could see that my colour was blinking on the blue one which indicated that mine was disturbing the blue one. It was also visible without colour, but I think it made more sense that my colour was blinking on it."* (P11). Similarly, another participant described that the instant patterns better supported her in seeing the overlap between zones. She explained that the high-frequency shifting between two colours indicated that both sounds were present in the same area of the room. A third described a similar experience: *"I think that with the [gradual patterns], they were too slow which made you think: Is it happening now? Oh, I guess it is. I could better understand it with shifts of a higher pace"* (P23). One participant expanded on his experience of assessing how much each music track could be heard in the other sound zone: *"It was hard that thing about, is this loud enough that they can hear? Because I can't hear their music. It was tricky to figure out how much my sound affected them"* (P19).

Sound Zone Size. The two information statements related to sound zone size were "My sound zone is increasing in size" and "The other sound zone is decreasing in size". For the first statement, $W = .059$, indicating a small effect, we found that the Blink Increasing pattern in colour (BC) performed significantly better than the Lighthouse pattern in white (AF) and colour (BF) as well as the Bright Flash in white (AB) and Gradual Build in colour (CE). This was the most significant difference. The findings for these patterns followed a similar direction as above where instant patterns perform better than gradual patterns. When asked to clarify their preference for Blink Increasing, participants underlined the fact that it featured blinks at an increasing frequency. No patterns performed significantly better than others for informing about the impacted sound zone decreasing in size. Participants related the feedback to the sound zone they were modifying instead of the affected sound zone. One participant noted: *"I thought it was difficult regarding whether or not they got bigger or smaller. I don't really think the light indicated that to me in any way"* (P36).

Notification Level. For the statements "I am being warned" and "I should adjust the volume of my sound zone", we expected that results would align with previous research [14], from which we defined the instant patterns. As expected, the notification level was rated significantly higher for patterns with colours compared to patterns only using brightness in white colour, $W = .364$, indicating a moderate effect. This was especially true for the Beacon (AA, BA) and Blink Increasing (AC, BC) patterns that blinked at a higher frequency. For a call to action on adjusting their volume, participants put the Beacon pattern in colour (BA) statistically higher than other patterns (except for the Bright Flash (BB) and Blink Increasing (BC)), $W = .190$, indicating small effect. The Beacon pattern in white (AA) performed statistically better than the Lighthouse patterns in white (AF) and colours (BF). This indicates a tendency that, even though colours are good for alerting participants, short blinks generally signal a call to action for participants more than fading patterns, regardless of colour. Participants commented that the gradual patterns, particularly the Gradual Build (AE, BE) and Lighthouse (AF, BF) patterns did not attract their attention or make a call to action as much as other patterns. One participant described that the patterns were easier to separate from the colours when passive. In contrast, when she was in the active role, she noticed the colours more. Several participants described the patterns as more intrusive when passive. While instant patterns in colour performed best, these were also described as most intrusive.

Passive or Active Role. We did not find any statistically significant differences in how participants responded to the light patterns when comparing responses from when they were passive to when they were active. However, the thematic analysis showed that some participants experienced the feedback differently because, in the passive role, they could hear the overlap, and in the active role, they could only see it. One participant expanded on this, saying that in the active role, he could see there was an overlap but he did not know the extent to which he was affecting the other sound zone. Sitting far away from the light pattern in the active role, some participants noted that it was more difficult to see the pattern. Some elaborated, explaining that the colours can help make the pattern more clear. In the passive role, however, the patterns were more easily distinguished from each other. Some related the meaning of a pattern to whether or not they were acting, and others related to what they heard (their own volume getting louder or hearing the other music track overtaking their sound zone).

Light Patterns and Music. Some participants mentioned that they looked for whether or not the light patterns matched the tempo or beat of the music. For some, the gradual patterns reportedly seemed like a music feature, *e.g.*, following the beat, whereas the instant patterns more clearly did not align with the music. Because the instant patterns did not appear to align with the music, participants mentioned that they seemed less like a visualisation of the music and therefore related to sound zone properties. One participant experienced that the blinking patterns began at different volume levels. This aligns with other participants commenting that the instant patterns better indicated the precise volume level at which the overlap occurred. There was no clear indication of preference when asked to choose between patterns in colour and in white. However, when asked in the follow-up interviews, participants preferring white patterns explained that these were more aesthetically pleasing and less intrusive for a home situation.

6   Discussion

6.1   Brightness Mimics Sound Zone Size

The goal of the first study was to investigate light as feedback about the volume and size of one sound zone. We specifically focused on colour, brightness, and animated light patterns. Our findings extend previous research in the effect of light on spatial experience to show that those spatial experiences can also be used for supporting control of sound zones. Where previous research investigated the effect of light on perception of room and object sizes [20, 21, 24], we have used light as a visual overlay on an otherwise invisible experience. Our results show that brightness can be used as an indicator for sound zone volume and size. From the interviews, we deduce that this is due to participants' experience of the light behaviour as something that mimics sound behaviour. Interpreting these results, we note that while the controllers have a fixed maximum brightness, this is not initially known by novice users. While our findings suggest that brightness is useful, this has two main implications for further investigations. First, we expect that there is a learning curve in becoming familiar with the feedback design which would be relevant to explore in further research. Second, the experience of brightness will change according to the physical environment. This will become especially relevant to investigate as sound zone systems move outside the lab setting and into homes, hospitals, and other domains. Customisation of the feedback to fit personal preferences and the characteristics of the physical environment is part of the next steps in this research.

6.2   Instant Light Patterns Mimic Overlapping Sound Zones

Study 2 investigated animated light patterns for feedback on overlapping sound zones. The findings revealed participants' understanding of what constitutes an overlap between sound zones. The fact that the instant patterns rank highest for all three information categories can have several reasons. First, we confirm previous work on the effectiveness of instant patterns for notifications [14]. Second, we expand on this work by showing that these patterns can also be used in the specific context of sound zone systems for showing that sound zones overlap—especially for patterns in colour that, according to some participants, provide a metaphor for the two music tracks mixing. This interpretation could be dependent on the situation as pointed out in previous research [1]. We acknowledge that the statements on increasing and decreasing sound zones might have skewed participants into a particular understanding of the sound zone behaviour. The fact that no significant differences were found for the statement "The other sound zone is decreasing in size" but were found for all other statements indicates that no animations visualised a decrease in the size of the other sound zone. Future research could include a broader range of statements to support or contend this.

The findings for notification levels are more general and not only applicable to sound zone systems. This means that they do not necessarily carry particular information about sound zones, such as whether or not the zones are overlapping. Further research could investigate whether or not novice users expect one sound zone to decrease in size when affected by another sound zone. Since participants felt affected by a pattern when in a passive role, further research could also investigate the case where feedback is only displayed on the side of the controller that is visible to the active user as feedback can otherwise be confusing and intrusive. This would also be relevant to explore outside lab setups to allow for further insights into how the light is experienced in situations in homes where it should not intrude on users' primary activities, as stated by Hazlewood et al. [15]. Our findings point to two distinct interaction paradigms for sound zone interaction, either emphasising the behaviour of sound through gradual patterns or the more abstract notion of sound zone bubbles through instant patterns. Based on the follow-up interviews, our findings indicate that choosing either interaction paradigm leads to different subjective conceptualisations of how the sound zone affects the rest of the physical space. This will also affect the utilisation of the spatial features of the LED strips. To emphasise sound behaviour, a design could include sound direction. On the other hand, notification patterns could be useful to provide differential information to active and passive users.

6.3   Metaphors Confused with Symbolism

We included colours (blue, green, yellow, and red) in Study 1 to explore whether these colours could represent characteristics of sound zone volume and size through a similar affordance as brightness. However, while brightness and animated light patterns have shown to be useful, our findings confirm that colours in relation to sound have different symbolic meanings to users. This suggests that colour cannot be used in the same way as brightness, where users rely on tacit knowledge about object properties [21]. This does not necessarily mean that colour cannot be used in displays for sound zone feedback, but they do not reliably carry information about spatial properties themselves. Instead, colour can be used in animated light patterns that mimic sound behaviour, such as transitions between colours. A possible future avenue is to provide a colour "identity" for each sound zone which can be, *e.g.*, chosen by the user. This will be especially useful in situations with more than two users. For Study 1, we found that while participants typically ordered the four colours in a sequential way (red, yellow, green, and blue – or mirrored), it also led to confusion among some participants. Because the aim is to show volume intervals, a future research avenue could be to explore other colour mappings such as sequential color mappings with single colours [25] or with inspiration from the use of nodes by Bastian and Heymann where colours reflect proximity to other nodes [2]. This could also extend Löffler et al.'s prior research [21] by investigating the effect of the saturation parameter on perception of sound zone properties. Drawing inspiration from previous research on the effect of light on perception of spatial properties of space and objects [20, 21] for Study 2, we expected that gradual light animation patterns would provide participants with realistic information about sound zones overlapping. However, while many participants understood and appreciated the metaphor offered by these patterns, our analysis indicates that they do not allow participants to easily adjust the volume of their sound zone with reassurance that they are not disturbing someone in a different sound zone. A key takeaway, therefore, is that light patterns for sound zones should have distinguishable contrasts to support understanding of overlaps.

7   Conclusion

Sound zones are invisible and thereby challenging to understand. We tackle this design challenge by using brightness and colour for feedback about sound zone volume, size, and overlaps based on prior research showing a relation between variations of light and experience of object properties. We confirm that brightness can be used to inform users about both sound zone size and volume. We also show that instant patterns in colour are useful for overlaps. Future research could investigate other light settings and designs, *e.g.*, by including saturation as a parameter for adjusting the light. Another opportunity is to utilise the spatial features of the volume controller to, *e.g.*, show the direction from which the sound is coming. Other avenues include using light on other interfaces and varying what light is visible to each user in a multi-user setup. Second, future research could investigate different situations where light is used as feedback for sound zones to clarify the effect the situation has on the user experience.

A Appendix 1

See Figs. 5 and 6.

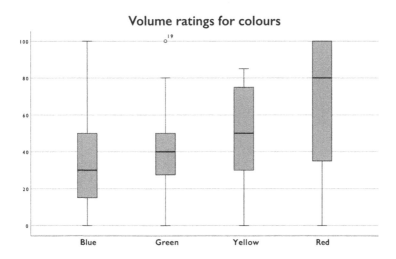

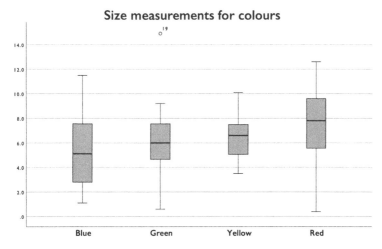

Fig. 5. Top: Participant ratings on colour settings for sound zone volume. Bottom: Participant ratings on colour settings for sound zone size.

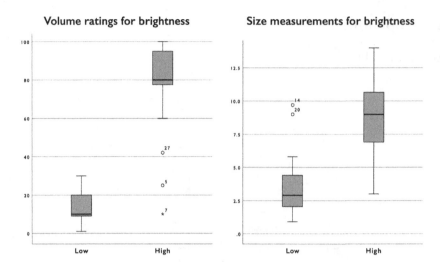

Fig. 6. Left: Participant ratings on brightness settings for sound zone volume. Right: Participant ratings on brightness settings for sound zone size.

Appendix 2

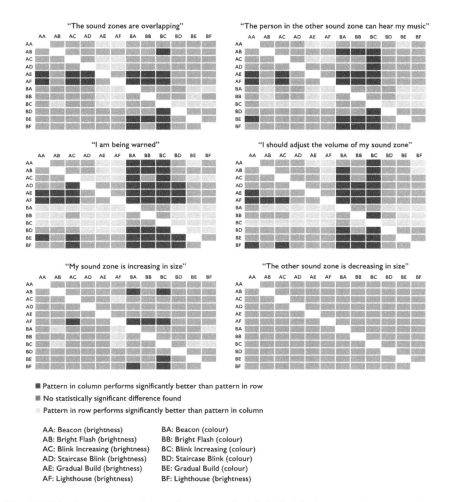

Fig. 7. This figure shows the performance of each individual pattern in comparison to the other patterns according to each of the six statements investigated. Dark blue: The pattern in the column performed significantly better than the pattern in the row ($p < 0.05$). Yellow: The pattern in the row performed significantly better than the pattern in the column ($p < 0.05$). Green: No statistically significant difference found. (Color figure online)

Appendix 3

See Figs. 8, 9 and 10.

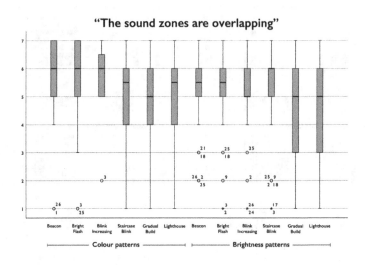

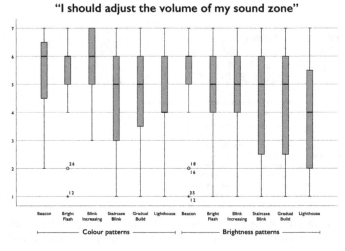

Fig. 8. Top: Participants' responses to the statement "The sound zones are overlapping". Bottom: Participants' responses to the statement "I should adjust the volume of my sound zone".

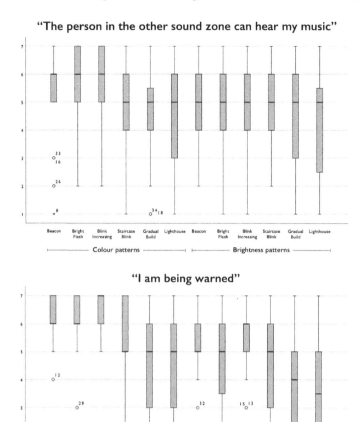

Fig. 9. Top: Participants' responses to the statement "The person in the other sound zone can hear my music". Bottom: Participants' responses to the statement "I am being warned".

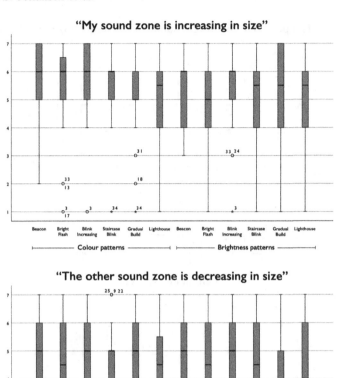

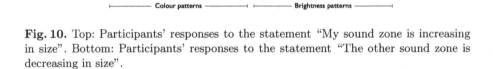

Fig. 10. Top: Participants' responses to the statement "My sound zone is increasing in size". Bottom: Participants' responses to the statement "The other sound zone is decreasing in size".

Appendix 4

The following supplementary materials can be located here:
https://www.dropbox.com/sh/poc15eypbnvl0af/AAAhO5jnWsMJLIEw0kt6DI
X8a?dl=0

- Data from Likert-item responses in Study 2
- Video figure that shows the experimental setup and the light patterns used in Study 2
- Questionnaires used in Study 1, including (1) for brightness settings and (2) for colour settings

– Likert-item questionnaire used in Study 2
– Information sheets handed out to participants in both studies

References

1. Baraka, K., Rosenthal, S., Veloso, M.: Enhancing human understanding of a mobile robot's state and actions using expressive lights. In: 2016 25th IEEE International Symposium on Robot and Human Interactive Communication (RO-MAN), pp. 652–657. IEEE (2016)
2. Bastian, M., Heymann, S.: Diseasome: the human disease network. In: Börner, K. (ed.) Atlas of Knowledge: Anyone Can Map, pp. 128–129. The MIT Press (2015)
3. Betlehem, T., Zhang, W., Poletti, M.A., Abhayapala, T.D.: Personal sound zones: delivering interface-free audio to multiple listeners. IEEE Signal Process. Mag. **32**(2), 81–91 (2015)
4. Bullock, J., Michailidis, T., Poyade, M.: Towards a live interface for direct manipulation of spatial audio. In: Proceedings of the International Conference on Live Interfaces. REFRAME Books Sussex (2016)
5. Cairns, P.: Doing Better Statistics in Human-Computer Interaction. Cambridge University Press, Cambridge (2019)
6. Cheer, J., Elliott, S.J., Gálvez, M.F.S.: Design and implementation of a car cabin personal audio system. J. Audio Eng. Soc. **61**(6), 412–424 (2013)
7. Choi, J.-W., Kim, Y.-H.: Generation of an acoustically bright zone with an illuminated region using multiple sources. J. Acoust. Soc. Am. **111**(4), 1695–1700 (2002)
8. Clarke, V., Braun, V., Hayfield, N.: Thematic analysis. In: Qualitative Psychology: A Practical Guide to Research Methods, pp. 222–248 (2015)
9. Corney, D., Haynes, J.-D., Rees, G., Lotto, R.B.: The brightness of colour. PloS one **4**(3), e5091 (2009)
10. Fairchild, M.D.: Color Appearance Models. Wiley, Milton (2013)
11. Finstad, K.: Response interpolation and scale sensitivity: evidence against 5-point scales. J. Usability Stud. **5**(3), 104–110 (2010)
12. Geier, M., Spors, S., Weinzierl, S.: The future of audio reproduction. In: Detyniecki, M., Leiner, U., Nürnberger, A. (eds.) AMR 2008. LNCS, vol. 5811, pp. 1–17. Springer, Heidelberg (2010). https://doi.org/10.1007/978-3-642-14758-6_1
13. Graves, A., Hand, C., Hugill, A.: MidiVisualiser: interactive music visualisation using VRML. Organised Sound **4**(1), 15–23 (1999)
14. Harrison, C., Horstman, J., Hsieh, G., Hudson, S.: Unlocking the expressivity of point lights. In: Proceedings of the 2012 CHI Conference on Human Factors in Computing Systems, pp. 1683–1692. ACM (2012)
15. Hazlewood, W.R., Stolterman, E., Connelly, K.: Issues in evaluating ambient displays in the wild: two case studies. In: Proceedings of the 2011 CHI Conference on Human Factors in Computing Systems. ACM (2011)
16. Lima, H.B., Dos Santos, C.G.R., Meiguins, B.S.: A survey of music visualization techniques. ACM Comput. Surv. **54**(7), 1–29 (2021)
17. Jacobsen, R.M., van Berkel, N., Skov, M.B., Johansen, S.S., Kjeldskov, J.: Do you see what i hear? - Peripheral absolute and relational visualisation techniques for sound zones. In: Proceedings of the 2022 CHI Conference on Human Factors in Computing Systems, New Orleans, LA, USA. ACM (2022). https://doi.org/10.1145/3491102.3501938

18. Johansen, S.S., Merritt, T., Jacobsen, R.M., Nielsen, P.A., Kjeldskov, J.: Investigating potentials of shape-changing displays for sound zones. In: Proceedings of the 2022 CHI Conference on Human Factors in Computing Systems, New Orleans, LA, USA. ACM (2022). https://doi.org/10.1145/3491102.3517632
19. Kunchay, S., Wang, S., Abdullah, S.: Investigating users' perceptions of light behaviors in smart-speakers. In: Conference Companion Publication of the 2019 on Computer Supported Cooperative Work and Social Computing, pp. 262–266. ACM (2019)
20. Wänström Lindh, U., Billger, M., Aries, M.: Experience of spaciousness and enclosure: Distribution of light in spatial complexity. J. Sustain. Des. Appl. Res. **8**(1), 5 (2020)
21. Löffler, D., Arlt, L., Toriizuka, T., Tscharn, R., Hurtienne, J.: Substituting color for haptic attributes in conceptual metaphors for tangible interaction design. In: Proceedings of the TEI 2016: Tenth International Conference on Tangible, Embedded, and Embodied Interaction, pp. 118–125. ACM (2016)
22. Lundgaard, S.S., Nielsen, P.A.: Personalised soundscapes in homes. In: Proceedings of the 2019 on Designing Interactive Systems Conference, pp. 813–822. ACM (2019)
23. Lundgaard, S.S., Nielsen, P.A., Kjeldskov, J.: Designing for domestic sound zone interaction. Pers. Ubiquitous Comput., 1–2 (2020)
24. Matusiak, B.: The impact of lighting/daylighting and reflectances on the size impression of the room. Full-scale studies. Archit. Sci. Rev. **47**(2), 115–119 (2004)
25. Munzner, T.: Visualization Analysis and Design. CRC Press, Boca Raton (2014)
26. Stévens, J.C., Hall, J.W.: Brightness and loudness as functions of stimulus duration. Percept. Psychophys. **1**, 319–327 (1966)
27. McGregor, I., Turner, P., Benyon, D.: Using participatory visualisation of soundscapes to compare designers' and listeners' experiences of sound designs. J. Sonic Stud. **6**(1) (2014)
28. Radojevic, M.D., Turner, R.: Spatial forms generated by music-the case study. In: International Conference on Generative Art, pp. 1–11. CumInCAD (2002)
29. Rämö, J., Christensen, L., Bech, S., Jensen, S.: Validating a perceptual distraction model using a personal two-zone sound system. Proc. Meetings Acoust. **30**(1), 050003 (2017)
30. Riecke, B.E., Feuereissen, D., Rieser, J.J., McNamara, T.P.: Spatialized sound enhances biomechanically-induced self-motion illusion (Vection). In: Proceedings of the 2011 CHI Conference on Human Factors in Computing Systems. ACM (2011). https://doi.org/10.1145/1978942.1979356
31. Waves: See Your Own Sound Waves. http://rombout.design/openlight/. www.openlight.nl/waves.html. Accessed 14 Jan 2023
32. Walker, P., Francis, B.J., Walker, L.: The brightness-weight illusion. Experimental Psychology (2010)
33. Walker, L., Karl, C.A.: The hospital (Not So) quiet zone: creating an environment for patient satisfaction through noise reduction strategies. HERD Health Environ. Res. Des. J. **12**(4), 197–202 (2019)
34. Wang, M., Lyckvi, S.L., Chen, C., Dahlstedt, P., Chen, F.: Using advisory 3D sound cues to improve drivers' performance and situation awareness. In: Proceedings of the 2017 CHI Conference on Human Factors in Computing Systems. ACM (2017)
35. Warden, C.J., Flynn, E.L.: The effect of color on apparent size and weight. Am. J. Psychol. **37**(3), 398–401 (1926)
36. Waves - See your own sound waves. http://rombout.design/openlight/. www.openlight.nl/waves.html. Accessed 14 Jan 2023

Co-design

Common Objects for Programming Workshops in Non-Formal Learning Contexts

Nathalie Bressa[1,2](✉) ⓘ, Susanne Bødker[2] ⓘ, Clemens N. Klokmose[2] ⓘ,
and Eva Eriksson[2] ⓘ

[1] i3 (UMR 9217), CNRS, Télécom Paris, Institut Polytechnique de Paris, Palaiseau,
France
nathalie.bressa@telecom-paris.fr
[2] Aarhus University, Aarhus, Denmark
{bodker,clemens}@cs.au.dk, evae@cc.au.dk

Abstract. We investigate common objects as material support for programming workshops for children and adolescents in non-formal learning contexts. To this end, we engaged in a one-year participatory design process with a facilitator of programming workshops. Based on observations of workshops and interviews with the facilitator, we mapped out their artifact ecologies to investigate how the multiple artifacts and common objects were orchestrated by the facilitator and then adopted by the participants of the workshops. Building on these findings, we explored the development of a collaborative teaching tool, MicroTinker, through a participatory design process with the facilitator. This paper presents the results of our analyses and shows their constructive use to design technology in a non-formal learning setting.

Keywords: Artifact ecology · non-formal learning · participatory design · programming education

1 Introduction

Research on learning programming has a long tradition [31]. This research has shifted over the years from a predominantly individualistic and tool-oriented focus to one that is sociologically and culturally grounded [29]. In line with this, we investigate the social and material structures that constitute a set of programming workshops for children and adolescents in non-formal learning environments, outside of formal education [39]. Such non-formal settings are key for the development of technology skills, such as programming [32]. Early exposure to programming can bring many benefits, increasing children's interest in computing and promoting their social, emotional, and cognitive development [8,21].

However, current software tools for educational settings are often designed around a laptop programming paradigm that tends to restrict collaboration rather than encourage shifting of roles and sharing of experiences when learning

J. Abdelnour Nocera et al. (Eds.): INTERACT 2023, LNCS 14142, pp. 275–296, 2023.
https://doi.org/10.1007/978-3-031-42280-5_16

Fig. 1. Two programming workshops for children and adolescents that we ob served: *Workshop 1 Technology Play and Workshop 2 Robot Art.*

technology skills [47]. Because the availability of tools and the purposes of the learning activity, as set by the facilitator or the participant, affect the intended outcomes, it is important for facilitation to match tools with purpose, space, and characteristics of the participants [20,36]. HCI studies of technology education in non-formal learning contexts typically have a specific single focus, such as factors that impact learning [41], a specific technology like Scratch [35], or a specific context such as a makerspace [49]. The real-world integration between a heterogeneous set of technologies and broader social and cultural concerns within educational technologies is missing [48], except for a few culturally grounded studies of technology use in non-formal learning environments [4].

We present findings from an artifact ecology analysis of non-formal programming workshops for children and adolescents and a participatory design process where we designed a collaborative teaching tool together with a facilitator with life-long experience in technology education. Focusing on multiplicities of artifacts, objects and, purposes [34], we first conducted an artifact ecology analysis based on observations of six programming workshops (see Fig. 1) and interviews with the facilitator. An artifact ecology analysis foregrounds the relationships of artifacts to practices in the context of individuals or groups [34] and has been applied to different contexts such as collaborative writing [33] and volunteer communities [17]. We used these theoretical concepts generatively [7] i.e., analytically, critically, and constructively to make them actionable in a participatory design process over six months with the facilitator whose workshops we had observed. We built a collaborative teaching tool, MicroTinker, focusing on sharing and common objects to support the facilitation of workshops. As a starting point, we used a locally developed software platform, CoTinker, for orchestrating learning activities around programming. We implemented an activity for micro:bit with MicroTinker and explored it in two workshops with teachers and children.

Our findings highlight how an artifact ecology analysis focused on the facilitator's orchestration and participants' adoption can help identify both explicit and implicit knowledge about these types of learning environments. Using the insights in the PD process allowed us to formulate situated implications for design and point towards possibilities for remediation of the material support.

2   Background

Non-formal learning takes place outside of formal learning environments, such as schools but within an organizational framing, for instance, in museums, libraries, computer clubs, or maker spaces [24,39]. It is supportive and guided or teacher-led. The workshops we observed and designed for were all set in non-formal learning contexts with some structure in their organization to emphasize learning about programming and technology. In the following, we provide more background specifically on computing and technology support in informal and non-formal learning contexts and work on artifact ecologies and common objects.

2.1   Material Support and Non-Formal Learning Contexts

In non-formal technology education environments, activities are typically constituted of diverse programming and making activities, integrating playfulness and creativity [52]. However, research is still scattered across disciplines, for instance, in education, library science, and computer science [36]. Some studies investigate factors of learning [24] like the role of age and gender [52], while other research focuses on specific learning technology like Scratch [35], a specific context such as makerspaces [49], or specific formats like hackathons and game jams [25]. Studies of the Scratch online programming community [19,30,43,45] expand the focus on tangible construction kits and programming tools to also include more intangible aspects, such as social and cultural dimensions [45].

In non-formal learning contexts factors such as the use of design materials, spaces, and collaborative aspects are important to consider [27,45]. Previous work has covered after-school programs to foster computing and technological literacy [4] investigating the affordances for social interaction with technology [3,22], the development of situated learning practices [4], and socially embodied performance as an important element in children's programming activities to complement more cognitive foci, such as memory, perception and conceptual understanding [26]. Whereas education around technology and micro-controllers is often set in collaborative group contexts, most software tools available are still designed around a laptop programming paradigm that tends to restrict collaboration rather than encourage shifting of roles and sharing of experiences [47].

Upon this background, we see learning to program in non-formal learning environments as mediated by a variety of artifacts from robots to programming environments, and tools where participants are collaborating and focusing on the objects of their activity [11]. To provide the means to further analyze these material and collaborative aspects, we move on to presenting artifact ecologies and common objects [2,15–17,33,34].

2.2   Artifact Ecologies and Common Objects

Human activity is mediated, social, and happening through common objects and artifacts according to the basic principles of activity theoretical HCI [11, 14]. Technological objects exist in ecologies with other objects, used by people, not in singular activities, but together across webs of activities. Human use of particular artifacts and objects happens across activities, configurations of people, applications, and devices, and it is analytically important to embrace such transitions and substitutions [14,15].

Objects are held in *common* through the simple exchange of objects, sharing of objects, and common views of the same object [33]. Such objects are in the making as the object moves from (shared) material to product and they contain and represent for the user an idea of the end product (or intermediate products along the way). It is important to be able to analyze the multiplicity of objects and artifacts [16] and artifact ecology as a concept foregrounds the relationships of artifacts to practices, in the context of individuals or groups of people [34]. Hence, the notion of artifact ecologies allows for examining the multiple interactive artifacts in use and highlights the multiplicity and dynamics of computer-mediated collaborative activity including the interplay between the personal and the shared [33]. It puts emphasis both on the multiplicity of devices through which common objects are accessed and activated, on changing configurations of tools (software and hardware), the settings and contexts in which use happens, and the connected activities; for instance, whether there is a particular, possibly enforced order of things [2].

Artifact ecologies help understand common objects and mediators in the context of other objects and mediators that are used in an activity. As such, the dynamic relationships between artifacts in an ecology may be used to analytically frame developments in how activities are carried out and what meaning each artifact holds in relation to the activity [2]. In the following, we are primarily concerned with how joint learning activity is supported through common objects, mediators, and their dynamics.

3   Process and Method

This paper investigates how artifacts in programming workshops mediate the activities with a focus on shared and common objects using these concepts both analytically and constructively [2,6] to design material support.

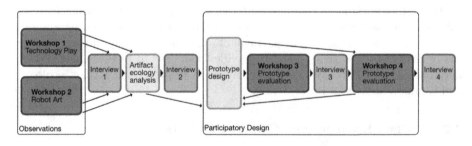

Fig. 2. Overview of the research process from observations to participatory design.

We employed a participatory design approach [12,13] (see Fig. 2). First, we collected empirical data from participant observations [51] of two programming workshops in six instances (*Workshop 1 Technology Play* and *Workshop 2 Robot Art*), followed by *Interview1* with the facilitator of the workshops (henceforth referred to as *Facilitator*). Based on this, we conducted an artifact ecology analysis [28], mapping the different workshop activities to investigate the ecologies, technologies, layouts, and the collaboration and sharing between participants.

Based on the findings from the artifact ecology analysis, we interviewed the Facilitator again (*Interview2*), and carried out a participatory design process where we iteratively co-designed, developed, and explored a web-based teaching tool with the Facilitator. We analyzed the design interactively with the finding from the artifact ecology analysis and used and evaluated it in two different workshops (*Workshop 3 Prototype evaluation* and *Workshop 4 Prototype evaluation*). Interwoven with this, we also conducted two additional interviews (*Interview3* and *Interview4*) with the Facilitator.

Our methodological approach is to study the very particular [9] where we engaged with a Facilitator throughout a one-year process. The Facilitator works at the computer science department of a university, has a long career teaching university students, and is the leading educator of high school teachers in the municipality. The Facilitator has developed teaching materials on programmable robots and is organizing various formal, informal, and non-formal learning events for children, such as local maker fairs, programming clubs, and international programming competitions such as the World Programming Olympiad.

3.1 Observations and Workshops

We conducted observations [51] of two different workshops (*Workshop 1 Technology Play* and *Workshop 2 Robot Art*) in six different instances over four months. This included one workshop series (*Workshop 1 Technology Play*) with the same participants consisting of five consecutive events. The workshops were organized by the Facilitator. All workshops were set in a non-formal learning context for children and adolescents (aged 9–21) within the general theme of programming for beginners. The participants were recruited by the Facilitator. All activities were free of charge and provided food and drinks for participants. The participants and their parents were informed of the researchers' presence and the purpose and type of data that we collected. We conducted the observations by attending each of the workshops and collecting field notes without interacting with the participants. We used an observation grid consisting of the dimensions: space and tools, children, facilitators, and procedure. The observation grid served as a reminder to reflect on each of the dimensions as different points of focus. The two workshops studied were:

Workshop 1 Technology Play. This workshop series took place for five consecutive weeks for two hours with nine participants in the evenings in a robotics workshop at a university. The activity targeted girls aged 9–11 and was co-organized by an organization and the university. The participants built a concert stage with light, music, and moving singers and dancers using LEGO Spike Prime which is a learning tool that enables building with LEGO and programming of motors and sensors with a block-based programming language[1]. In the first two gatherings, the participants got familiar with LEGO Spike Prime by building walking grasshopper robots in groups of two. In the next three instances, they built stages in wooden cubes. In the last instance, each group presented their stage through a performance.

Workshop 2 Robot Art. This workshop was organized within an IT Camp for girls at a university. Participants, between the ages of 16–21, participated in a range of activities and lectures over a week. The workshop took place in a lecture room with 28 participants for two hours. The theme of the activity was to build a drawing robot with LEGO Spike Prime in groups of three to create an art piece. The drawing robot held a pen and could be programmed to draw different shapes with a block-based programming language. Each group created one art piece that was then presented at the end in an art exhibition.

3.2   Interviews 1–4

We recruited the Facilitator for four semi-structured interviews, conducted by one of the researchers. These interviews were carried out in person, lasted around 45–100 min, and were audio recorded and transcribed. The interviews were conducted at different points in the process (see Fig. 2). With the interviews, we aimed to better understand the reasoning and motivations of the Facilitator with regard to how workshops were organized, to supplement the observations, and to get insights into the experience with the participatory design process.

3.3   Artifact Ecology Analysis

We conducted an artifact ecology analysis and visual mapping of the observed workshops and coded the interviews and notes from the observations. Visual mappings [28] were done by visually grouping artifacts based on empirical data (see Fig. 3). We did a spatial mapping of the room layout for the start and end of the activity, focusing on space, people, tools, and spatial positions. This led to a detailed map of the technologies, materials, and processes.

For the coding of the empirical material, we used notes from observations and transcribed interviews. We developed the codes over multiple iterations and discussed them in meetings among researchers. We then structured the emerging themes into categories, condensed descriptions, and illustrative quotes.

---

[1] An   example   of   such   a   workshop: https://www.youtube.com/watch?v=0YGq7cjs9Xw.

3.4   Prototype Design

We conducted a participatory design (PD) [13] process with the Facilitator that tied into the findings from the artifact ecology analysis. The focus of the design explorations was to scaffold collaboration and knowledge sharing of programming through software. We used our CoTinker platform [38] as a foundation for prototyping which is an experimental platform for exploring collaboration and facilitation in computational thinking-related learning activities. As a starting point, we used our first CoTinker-based prototype [38] designed for a learning activity in high-school biology as a *provotype* [37] because the pedagogical and didactical approach it embodied differed drastically from the one practiced by the Facilitator. Together with the Facilitator, we designed and developed a collaborative teaching tool, *MicroTinker* that integrates micro:bit [1] Microcontrollers such as the micro:bit are increasingly used in classroom settings to teach skills, attitudes, and knowledge around technology [1], and are commonly used in schools in Denmark. The iterative PD process ran as a series of bi-weekly design sessions between the Facilitator, researchers, and developers of CoTinker, as well as ad-hoc meetings between the Facilitator and the two developers. As part of the process, we explored MicroTinker in teaching activities in two different prototype trials (see Fig. 7).

Workshop 3 Prototype Evaluation. This was a one-hour workshop with a group of five high school teachers in informatics, set up to get didactic feedback for further iterations. It took place in a meeting room at the university, with two researchers present for observations. The Facilitator presented the tool, the teachers tried it out in several exercises and provided feedback and ideas for further development.

Workshop 4 Prototype Evaluation. We iterated on the exercises and the tool that were then tried out in a two-hour workshop targeting children aged 10–15. It took place in the robotics lab at the university with eight child participants, one parent, three researchers, and the Facilitator.

4   Artifact Ecology Analysis of Programming Workshops

We start by presenting the artifact ecologies of the programming workshops by describing the orchestration of activities by the facilitator based on the facilitator's intentions with regard to technology and layout of activities. Then, we highlight observations from the adoption of the orchestrated ecologies by participants during the different activities.

4.1   Orchestration

For *Workshop 1 Technology Play* and *Workshop 2 Robot Art*, the Facilitator prepared orchestrated ecologies of different artifacts for the participants. Orchestration in the context of artifact ecologies [46] describes the process of aligning

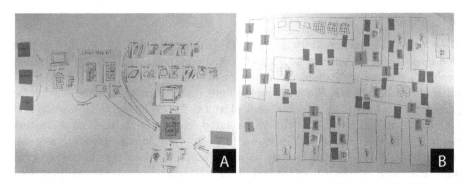

Fig. 3. Examples from the visual mapping in the artifact ecology analysis. (A) Overview of *Workshop 1 Technology Play* (B) Layout of *Workshop 2 Robot Art*.

constellations of technologies between the involved actors in a group. *Workshop 1 Technology Play* and *Workshop 2 Robot Art* were mainly pre-orchestrated by the Facilitator based on the assumptions of how the ecologies would be adopted by participants in the activity. During the activity, the participants adopted from the pre-orchestrated potential ecology [33] which are all artifacts available to the participants. The orchestration included devices, software, other building materials (LEGO bricks, cardboard, paper), and tools (scissors, glue, knife). This process of orchestration was planned by the Facilitator based on the intention of the specific activities and happened on different levels: both for the individual ecologies of participants working on the same project (either individually or in groups) as well as the overall ecology of all the materials in the room. These were set up in the same way for all groups and formed the overall ecology of all the actors taking part. For instance, in *Workshop 2 Robot Art* the ecology of one group of three was a laptop with one robot to create an art piece and together with all the groups in the room and the Facilitator formed the overall ecology.

Technology. In both observed workshops, participants used LEGO Spike Prime to control sensors and movement with a block-based programming language. The activities included various other building materials such as LEGO bricks and pen and paper in *Workshop 2 Robot Art* and string, stuffed animals, cardboard, feathers, foam, and stickers in *Workshop 1 Technology Play*. The Facilitator intended for participants to *"express [themselves] by means of programming"* where physical computing provided opportunities to learn programming: *"It's not very easy to make the correspondence to what's happening on the screen and then the program, as it is with robots or light or movement"*. Both *Workshop 1 Technology Play* and *Workshop 2 Robot Art* revolved around a shared object that the group built together (a drawing robot and a music stage) that was used in an exhibition or performance at the end as a shared activity. The participants approached the task independently in groups with the goal of enabling self-expression: *"I think you can make them program, if it has a purpose and [...]*

they end up with something that expresses themselves, within that purpose". The Facilitator took on the role of assisting the groups with achieving the goals they had set for themselves.

The selection of technology happened by negotiating a tension between *why* the technology was used, *what* it was used for, and *how* it was used [14]). For instance, in *Workshop 1 Technology Play*, the participants were not intended to learn how professionals code, instead, they were supposed to experience being creative with computation (*why*) by controlling sensors and actuators (*what*) through programming with whatever means were available (*how*).

Fig. 4. Layout: (A) *Workshop 1 Technology Play* , (B) *Workshop 2 Robot Art*.

Layout of Activities. *Workshop 2 Robot Art* was set in a bigger classroom with desks for each group on the sides of the room (see Fig. 4). On one side of the room, there were desks with materials such as paper, LEGO bricks, and writing utensils for participants to pick up if needed. Additionally, a large strip of paper was taped to the floor in the middle of the room between the desks where participants could test out their drawing robots.

Workshop 1 Technology Play, was a series set in the robotics lab of the university, a medium-sized room with a big table in the middle (see Fig. 4). The robotics workshop lab had multiple different materials such as LEGO, fabric, stuffed toys, and cardboard that participants could use.

Workshop 1 Technology Play and *Workshop 2 Robot Art* focused on work in groups. This was reflected in the spatial organization of the workshops and how the Facilitator orchestrated the ecologies. Both *Workshop 1 Technology Play* and *Workshop 2 Robot Art* provided a shared desk and shared paper for interactions between groups, enabling participants to see what the other groups were doing. For the Facilitator, this spatial organization was intentional: *"I do not tell them they can take a piece of paper from the table and sit at their own table to do drawings. In the beginning, I say: "Do it without the pen in the beginning, on the floor, so it doesn't fall down. Then do it with a pen on the common paper [...] to make some initial drawings... and finally, do it on your own paper.' "* with the goal to *"get some building activity that we have in common in the middle"* and create *"something like a fire camp, where we can sit around and do something"*. For the Facilitator, the goal was to create a shared place where participants could meet and communicate: *"To make the room inviting, to stand up and draw in the middle, because then they see each other and see each other's activities and maybe talk to each other"*. The Facilitator wanted to create a layout where the ecologies of the individual groups were visible to the other groups to create awareness of the joint activity.

4.2   Adoption

In the adoption of the orchestrated ecologies, participants used the different artifacts provided to them both in ways that were intended by the Facilitator and in unanticipated ways. In the following, we highlight findings regarding shared and common objects, copying, and collaboration.

Common Objects. The focus of the common object in *Workshop 1 Technology Play* changed throughout the activity. At first, the groups made sketches of their stages, then they built the stage with the different singers, dancers, and decorations, and finally, they integrated the motors of LEGO Spike Prime to make the elements move. Instead of working mainly with LEGO Spike Prime, participants spent a lot of time decorating their stages and had to be pushed by the Facilitator to integrate the technology into their stages. The Facilitator remarked that *"a lot of you will do what you are good at with the materials that I have around the table, which is not programming and building with Lego [...] and that's what happened with the girls [...] they put up this Christmas stuff instead of making it turn"* suggesting that the participants focused on what they already knew and were good at. The Facilitator had to encourage the participants to bring the technology back into the activity since they *"didn't see the LEGO as material in the design process"*. As a result, the Facilitator was considering changing the activity for future workshops by starting with the technology for the stages. While the activity was structured by the Facilitator using different materials, the participants adopted these in ways that were different and unintended.

Figure 5 illustrates how the common objects changed as the activity in *Workshop 1 Technology Play* unfolded. In Fig. 5A, the common object was the laptop and robot shared by pairs of children, the large screen shared by all in the room, and the table that all pairs were gathered around. In Fig. 5B, the common object was mainly the robot and the laptop with which the groups could make the robot move. In Fig. 5C, the common object was no longer the digital technology but pen and paper, used for dreaming up a vision and idea for their final product as a sketch. When the sketch was done, the physical materials were allocated and assembled for construction. When the physical materials started to take over, the Facilitator reminded the participants of incorporating movement and light into the stage, so that the physical and digital materials would merge (Fig. 5D). The product, the stage, the motors, and the laptop were the shared object within groups, while the groups were also aware of and inspired by each other's objects.

By the end of the activity, (Fig. 5E), the products were presented and exhibited to parents and families, and the object shared was now also a part of a larger ecology of objects being on show. The workshop participants were simultaneously working, collaborating, and focusing on the objects of their activity [11], where these objects were held in common [44]. However, they changed through the process and were always intermediary [33].

Fig. 5. Examples of common objects from the early, middle, and final stages of the workshop series *Workshop 1 Technology Play*. (A) Initial setup, (B) Robot, (C) Sketch, (D) Stage, (E) Performance and exhibition.

Copying and Collaborating. For *Workshop 1 Technology Play* and *Workshop 2 Robot Art*, participants worked in groups on a shared task. In addition, the Facilitator wanted to enable cross-group interaction and communication among groups so that they could *"see each other and see each other's activities and maybe talk to each other"* to *" make sure that they knew, what each there were doing"*. The visibility of the ecologies of the groups was also meant to enable copying of what other participants were doing. This was rooted in the Facilitator's belief that *"normally in their play culture, they [...] go out into the playground and then they copy and remix what the other kids are doing"*. By arranging the room to enable visibility between groups, the participants started picking up elements of the others' stages and when one group would discover a new feature, like playing sound, the other groups would follow. In *Workshop 1 Technology Play* and *Workshop 2 Robot Art*, the spatial organization and group constellations changed over time. Especially in *Workshop 2 Robot Art*, participants were seated only in the beginning and then spread out over the whole space, some sitting on the floor in groups or on the desks. First, the focus was on assembling the robot, then on programming and making it move, and finally on testing out different robot movements to create an art piece. The activity centered on the shared piece of paper on the floor that the robots would draw on, and participants walked around to grab materials or look at the work of other groups. In *Workshop 1 Technology Play*, participants similarly started seated and would then move around the table to other groups or to shelves for materials. In this case, the groups transitioned to different configurations of the spatial arrangement of their tools depending on the stage of their projects.

4.3 Summary of the Artifact Ecology Analysis

The findings of the artifact ecology analysis demonstrate the link between the Facilitator's intention, orchestration of the room and the artifact ecology, and the participants' adoption as the activity unfolds. This follows findings from Barkhuus and Lecusay [4] pointing to the importance of acknowledging already established infrastructures in the learning environment, and that those infrastructures are flexible enough for adjustment. Flexibility was needed as the Facilitator's intention and orchestration were supported by the room and physical materials, but less so by the technology: The software environment for motors and sensors was not designed for sharing between different groups and the participants would need to physically gather around one computer to collaborate or to view code from different groups. This is a reason for exploring possibilities of how to remediate the material support and these findings served as a starting point for the PD process.

5   Prototyping MicroTinker

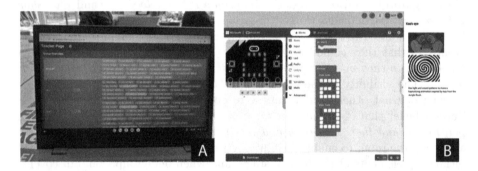

Fig. 6. MicroTinker. (A) The teacher page with groups and exercise repository, green marks in which exercise each group is. (B) The participant page with an embedded MakeCode editor and instructions for the current step of the learning activity. (Color figure online)

Building on the findings from the artifact ecology analysis, we employed an iterative PD process in order to develop and try out a new digital teaching tool for facilitating programming workshops in non-formal learning contexts. Particularly, to explore how the digital aspects of a learning activity could become a common object. The goal of exploratively developing the tool was to facilitate collaboration and sharing of code between participants and enable the Facilitator to share and discuss the code of individual groups with the whole group. Based on previous experience in building collaborative systems and software to facilitate learning activities, we used CoTinker which is an in-house developed platform for creating web-based collaborative and flexible learning environments for programming and computational thinking. The teaching activity imagined together with the Facilitator revolved around the different sensors of the micro:bit. The tool and the content were intended to be used in a teaching activity where small groups would work together in a room with a facilitator. The central idea was a stepwise tutorial where each step can include both the instructions and the interactive means to solve the given part of the tutorial. Through the PD process, we came to imagine two main parts: *the teacher page* where the Facilitator can administrate groups and steps, and the *participant page* where the participants program and solve the steps of the learning activity.

Participant Page. The participant page is what the participants load on their laptops and where they program in groups (Fig. 6). The page integrates a version of the MakeCode interface and an additional panel with instructions from the Facilitator. An activity is divided into steps that participants can go through. A step includes instructions and/or inspiration for the given assignment and a pre-loaded starting point for a micro:bit program. Additionally, the participant page enables participants to share their code in a code library to access and reuse their programs. The participant page is collaborative, and anyone with the link can modify and access the project in real-time.

Teacher Page. The teacher page functions as a space for the Facilitator to manage the groups and the learning activity. The Facilitator can access the participant page of all groups to, for instance, share their work with the whole class on a project or large display. The Facilitator sees exactly the same as the groups and can collaboratively edit the micro:bit code. The teacher page shows an overview of the progress of each group, which enables the Facilitator to move all the groups to the same step in the learning activity.

Fig. 7. Prototype evaluation. (A) With high school teachers, (B), with children.

5.1   Learning Activity

The Facilitator authored an activity for MicroTinker consisting of several exercises for the micro:bit which all revolved around the sensors of the micro:bit such as sound, light, and the accelerometer. The exercises involved creating patterns on the light panel of the micro:bit to create hypnotizing eyes (of a snake or Odin) by holding the micro:bit behind a cardboard cut-out, and the creation of a step-counter where the micro:bit can be attached to a shoe.

6   Exploring MicroTinker

In the following, we report on the findings from the PD process of developing MicroTinker with regard to sharing and common objects in the workshops and how the tool shaped and integrated into the teaching and orchestration process.

6.1   Sharing and Common Objects

During the observed workshops (*Workshop 1 Technology Play*, *Workshop 2 Robot Art*), sharing of the physical products (the stages, art pieces, and robots) was done through the spatial layout of the activity: *"you can go around between the groups and you can see what they have been building"*. However, this was not the case in the same way for the code: *"but you can't see what they've been programming because you [seldom] look at the computer"*. Therefore, one of the main goals for the development of MicroTinker was to make the digital material, i.e., the code, accessible and shareable like the physical material: *"each have their own app and you can't share it [...] There's a lot of places where the programming is hidden somehow. This tool can make it as visible as the physical stuff"*. For the Facilitator, being able to share the digital material could make participants aware of the shared activity and show the value of seeing other participants' solutions: *"the possibility of sharing screens made it more explicit that we also have this to share [...] Instead of sitting each with their own screen we are aware that we all have a screen, and we're doing the same thing, and we're doing it different ways, and maybe it's a good idea to see what the others are doing."* In this case, the option of sharing code had the potential of creating awareness of the code as a common object between participants within the wider context of the joint workshop activity.

During *Workshop 4 Prototype evaluation*, sharing of the products was enabled in the same way as in the observed workshops through the room layout, with cardboard cut-outs at the front where the participants could try out their programs making these visible to the other participants (see Fig. 7). Sharing with all participants was mediated through the large screen at the front where the Facilitator could open participants' programs. In this case, sharing code and sensor values on the large screen facilitated communication between participants by transitioning between individual work and shared group activities.

The code became common between the participants, as did the teaching material which had previously been PowerPoint slides that were now integrated with the code editor. However, after reflecting on the prototype evaluations, the Facilitator found it better if the slides would not show on the participants' screens in the tool as *"there's no reason for them to see the whole screen as a PowerPoint"*. It suited the Facilitator better if participants would look at the slides on the projector to help attract their full attention. In this case, having the shared focus of the group during instructions was more useful to the Facilitator than having the teaching material shared on all laptops.

6.2 Between Improvisation and Structure

At first, the Facilitator was skeptical of CoTinker as it would be *"getting rid of the teacher"* and thus did not fit with the Facilitator's way of teaching: *"my first reaction was [...]: 'come one, that's not how you teach'"*. For the Facilitator, it was important to maintain an active role during the teaching whereas the initial CoTinker prototype was focused on supporting autonomous work of students. Therefore, in the PD process, one goal became to develop a tool that would give the Facilitator control and an active role during the workshops.

There was a tension between how the Facilitator was involved in the progression of the prototype evaluation workshop with children and how this role was externalized through the tool: The Facilitator wanted to be able to orchestrate the activity while having room for improvisation during the workshop. On the one hand, the tool provided fine-grained steps: *"what the tool gives me is to have extremely simple programming exercises in a series where every step is very minor"*, on the other hand, a balance was needed with the different progress of participants and the freedom to adapt the teaching to that: *"somehow you need to plan using CoTinker so that you can have some [...] do whatever they like, and some of the other students do what I say they should do"*. Whereas previously these activities were spontaneous and improvised during the workshop, the tool made the Facilitator plan and externalize parts of it: *"but normally that's part of the planning of the activity on the fly [...], it is not something you do beforehand sitting with a tool. But that [CoTinker] tool, as every other tool, makes you aware of how you should plan the teaching activity"*.

The tool made the Facilitator reflect on the process and the individual steps during the workshop: *"then I would realize where I should make sure that everybody was at the same slide as I, or where should I let them do something else?"*. The Facilitator thought that there could be benefits to this, such as making teachers reflect on the different aspects and steps of the activity serving as an educational tool for planning teaching: *"maybe for an inexperienced teacher it might be good to have [...] the activities and the planning of the activities within embedded in such a tool, so they can learn how to teach programming by means of the tool"*. The tension between structure and improvisation highlighted that externalization of the facilitation through the tool was an important design concern and balance to maintain.

6.3 Integration of Functionality

MicroTinker integrated functionality that the Facilitator had previously used with other tools and it thus became a substitute. Before, the Facilitator made slides in PowerPoint to plan workshops. As these functions became integrated, the Facilitator needed to figure out how to orchestrate the workshop: *"it was a learning process to figure out how to prepare some learning activity by means of a tool that, it's not PowerPoint but it's like PowerPoint. It's not sharing a common screen, [...] I show something up there with the tool on my screen and then they are supposed to do it with their tool on their screen. These things I really had to think about it and adjust to [...] the media of the new tool"*. When reflecting on this, the Facilitator remarked that the tool could take a role that was not only specific to the context that we had designed it for: *"now it's like any other tool. It's PowerPoint with a programming tool integrated or the other way around, and then you can share screens in a more elegant way. That's it. That's a tool you can use for anything. It's not built into the tool how to use it"*.

Similarly, when adopting the tool in *Workshop 4 Prototype evaluation*, the Facilitator remarked that using it required a conscious adaption throughout the workshop facilitation: *"there [was] one occasion where I forgot that I can actually see what they're doing [...] and I should have said 'let me look at your page' so I can correct or see what's wrong [...] that's because I'm not used to using it like that."* Other functionalities integrated into the tool, like the ability to move all participants to the same step, were not used by the Facilitator: *" I actually didn't use the tool to make them go to a specific page because normally you would just shout out 'are you all on this page?' "*

Using MicroTinker changed the dynamics of the artifacts previously used by the Facilitator and required a rethinking of the orchestration and adoption for the tool to be integrated into the new artifact ecology in the wider context of the activity and teaching practice.

7 Future Work and Iterations

In the current version of MicroTinker, the focus was not specifically on the preparation of teaching material. Instead, these steps involved the software developer.

The Facilitator wanted to be able to author the teaching material in future versions: *"I need to be able to write my own material [...], with PowerPoint you sit and then you mingle until the very last moment before you present it to people. And here I barely remembered what I had put on the slide I sent [name] a week ago"*. The workflow of producing teaching material did not fit with the practice of the Facilitator when preparing workshops. Designing and developing authoring tools that would allow teachers to create, edit and adapt learning activities through a graphical direct manipulation interface is a next step beyond the scope of this prototype.

The Facilitator reflected on the prototype evaluations and how using a more stable version of MicroTinker to prevent technical difficulties in longer, consecutive workshops would provide more insights into the sharing functionality. For instance, during the *Workshop 4 Prototype evaluation*, participants did not use the shared code library: *"they actually do not use that they can save code. That might be because it's not a long enough sequence of activity"*. Similarly, the Facilitator was interested in organizing workshops with a higher level of complexity and thought that this would make differences more pronounced: *"I would be curious about what will happen if they see each other's programs when the programming is a little more complex than we had in the workshop. Because then you can see that they express themselves by means of these blocks differently"*.

8 Summary and Discussion

This study contributes to the understanding of programming in non-formal learning contexts that are still under-explored [36,52]. In related work, the components and intentions of each study vary significantly [36], not only in the variability of countries, and disciplines but also in their scope [4,23,25,35,36,41,42,52]. Related work shows that it is relevant to consider the characteristics and aim of facilitators, the tools and materials available, the spaces, and the social and cultural structures [4,36,52]. We have done so by investigating the artifact ecologies and common objects in a non-formal learning environment of six programming workshops. We have used the findings of these analyses for a PD process of a new teaching tool together with a Facilitator of programming workshops.

The findings from the artifact ecology analysis demonstrate the link between the Facilitator's intention, orchestration of the room and the artifacts, and the participants' adoption as the activity unfolds. The tool developed served as an exemplification of how these insights can be turned into design constructively [2,6]. This is only one such possible design and its usefulness lies in the PD process. The digital tools did not support the collaborative setup to the same extent as physical artifacts, as also noted by Roumen and Fernaeus [47]. The artifact ecology analysis and visual mapping enabled us to identify and analyze common objects and their roles as mediators of sharing for the participants. These findings provided opportunities to design a tool to address code sharing, creating awareness among participants of the joint activity, seeing the digital material as common, and enabling the Facilitator to share and discuss the code of individual groups with the whole group. As such, the tool complements and extends the traditional laptop programming paradigm, which tends to restrict collaboration rather than encourage shifting of roles and sharing of experiences [47], and addresses the identified lack of a social context for learning programming [31].

Through introducing CoTinker as a provotype, we ended up with additional design implications with regard to facilitation. It helped externalize the Facilitator's needs and practices for how to structure the activity, and the role of the tool and the Facilitator became clearer. These findings extend previous knowledge on the role of facilitation style and the facilitator in technology education [10,20,36,50], and shed light on the importance of the facilitator's practices and ability to identify the types of instructional support necessary for individual needs [5, 18, 40]. In contrast to formal learning contexts, the purpose of a learning activity in a non-formal programming context can be set either by the facilitator or the participants [20, 36].

The artifact analysis helped gain insights into how the Facilitator orchestrated the activities with regard to the material support, but less so on the process and practice of the orchestration itself. By introducing a new tool into the Facilitator's teaching, the process of orchestration and authoring of teaching material changed as tools previously used got integrated into MicroTinker. An authoring tool to support the process of orchestrating the workshops is needed to support the Facilitator's planning and preparation. This requires a thorough understanding of how these activities unfold which is a topic of future work.

9 Conclusion

We have presented results from a PD process with a facilitator of programming workshops in a non-formal learning context. We conducted an artifact ecology analysis based on observations and interviews. The results have been used in an iterative PD process in which we developed a new tool to support collaboration and sharing of code.

The empirical setting is rich with multiplicities of artifacts and objects, some of which are everyday and mundane, while others are rather specialized for the teaching situation. The Facilitator sets up and orchestrates combinations that are then shared and adopted and held in common by the groups in entire workshops as they are both able to monitor the activities of other groups and explicitly share them with the help of the Facilitator. The common objects represent the workshop participants' ideas of the end product, their intermediate designs along the way, and the steps in the design process. In this study, we have seen how both slides and code serve as common objects as they move from being part of the orchestration of the Facilitator to becoming parts of the joint end product of the groups. It is important to notice that they are not only shared material, and they help students and the Facilitator share a vision of a future outcome of the groups' building process.

The type of study presented here can be useful for others who intend to better understand both the explicit and implicit social and material structure of non-formal learning environments. Analyzing the Facilitator's orchestration and intention with the artifact ecology and setup, and the participants' adoption, enabled not only identifying what dynamics impact the artifact ecology, but also more specific needs and new technological possibilities.

Acknowledgements. We would first like to thank Ole Caprani at Aarhus University for his dedication and time. The research is co-funded by the European Union's Horizon 2020 Research & Innovation programme under Grant Agreement no. 870612 for the ySkills project. This work also was supported by the European Research Council (ERC) under the European Union Horizon 2020 research and innovation programme (grant agreement No 740548), by IT-Vest networking universities (grant agreement No AU-

2020-49), and the Carlsberg Foundation (grant agreement No CF17-0643). The authors would like to thank the Co-Coders organization, and finally CAVI.

References

1. Austin, J., et al.: The BBC micro:bit: from the U.K. to the world. Commun. ACM **63**(3), 62–69 (2020). https://doi.org/10.1145/3368856
2. Avdic, M., Bødker, S., Larsen-Ledet, I.: Two cases for traces: a theoretical framing of mediated joint activity. Proc. ACM Hum.-Comput. Interact. **5**(CSCW1) (2021). https://doi.org/10.1145/3449289
3. Barab, S.A., Evans, M.A., Baek, E.O.: Activity theory as a lens for characterizing the participatory unit. In: Handbook of Research on Educational Communications and Technology, vol. 2, pp. 199–213 (2004)
4. Barkhuus, L., Lecusay, R.: Social infrastructures as barriers and foundation for informal learning: technology integration in an urban after-school center. Comput. Support. Coop. Work (CSCW) **21**(1), 81–103 (2012). https://doi.org/10.1007/s10606-012-9157-3
5. Barton, A.C., Tan, E., Greenberg, D.: The makerspace movement: sites of possibilities for equitable opportunities to engage underrepresented youth in STEM. Teach. Coll. Rec. Voice Scholarsh. Educ. **119**(6), 1–44 (2017). https://doi.org/10.1177/016146811711900608
6. Beaudouin-Lafon, M.: Instrumental interaction: an interaction model for designing post-wimp user interfaces. In: Proceedings of the SIGCHI Conference on Human Factors in Computing Systems, CHI 2000, pp. 446–453. ACM, New York (2000). https://doi.org/10.1145/332040.332473
7. Beaudouin-Lafon, M., Bødker, S., Mackay, W.E.: Generative theories of interaction. ACM Trans. Comput.-Hum. Interact. **28**(6) (2021). https://doi.org/10.1145/3468505
8. Bers, M.: Coding as a Playground. Routledge, London (2017)
9. Bertelsen, O., Bødker, S., Eriksson, E., Hoggan, E., Vermeulen, J.: Beyond generalization: research for the very particular. Interactions **26**(1), 34–38 (2018). https://doi.org/10.1145/3289425
10. Blikstein, P., Gomes, J.S., Akiba, H.T., Schneider, B.: The effect of highly scaffolded versus general instruction on students' exploratory behavior and arousal. Technol. Knowl. Learn. **22**(1), 105–128 (2016). https://doi.org/10.1007/s10758-016-9291-y
11. Bødker, S.: Through the Interface: A Human Activity Approach to User Interface Design. L. Erlbaum Associates Inc., Hillsdale (1990)
12. Bødker, S., Dindler, C., Iversen, O.S., Smith, R.C.: Participatory Design. Springer, Cham (2022). https://doi.org/10.1007/978-3-031-02235-7
13. Bødker, S., Grønbæk, K., Kyng, M.: Cooperative design: techniques and experiences from the scandinavian scene. In: Schuler, D., Namioka, A. (eds.) Participatory design. Principles and practices, pp. 157–176. Lawrence Erlbaum Associates (1993)
14. Bødker, S., Klokmose, C.N.: The human–artifact model: an activity theoretical approach to artifact ecologies. Hum.-Comput. Interact. **26**(4), 315–371 (2011). https://doi.org/10.1080/07370024.2011.626709
15. Bødker, S., Klokmose, C.N.: Dynamics in artifact ecologies. In: Proceedings of the 7th Nordic Conference on Human-Computer Interaction: Making Sense Through Design, NordiCHI 2012, pp. 448–457. Association for Computing Machinery, New York (2012). https://doi.org/10.1145/2399016.2399085

16. Bødker, S., Klokmose, C.N.: Dynamics, multiplicity and conceptual blends in HCI. In: Proceedings of the 2016 CHI Conference on Human Factors in Computing Systems, CHI 2016, pp. 2538–2548. ACM, New York (2016). https://doi.org/10.1145/2858036.2858530

17. Bødker, S., Lyle, P., Saad-Sulonen, J.: Untangling the mess of technological artifacts: investigating community artifact ecologies. In: Proceedings of the 8th International Conference on Communities and Technologies, C&T 2017, pp. 246–255. ACM, New York (2017). https://doi.org/10.1145/3083671.3083675

18. Bransford, J., Brophy, S., Williams, S.: When computer technologies meet the learning sciences. J. Appl. Dev. Psychol. **21**(1), 59–84 (2000). https://doi.org/10.1016/s0193-3973(99)00051-9

19. Ching, C.C., Kafai, Y.B.: Peer pedagogy: student collaboration and reflection in a learning-through-design project. Teach. Coll. Rec. **110**(12), 2601–2632 (2008)

20. Christensen, K.S., Iversen, O.S.: Articulations on form properties and action-function couplings of maker technologies in children's education. Entertain. Comput. **18**, 41–54 (2017). https://doi.org/10.1016/j.entcom.2016.09.001

21. Clements, D.H., Gullo, D.F.: Effects of computer programming on young children's cognition. J. Educ. Psychol. **76**(6), 1051–1058 (1984). https://doi.org/10.1037/0022-0663.76.6.1051

22. Cole, M., Consortium, D.L., et al.: The Fifth Dimension: An After-school Program Built on Diversity. Russell Sage Foundation, New York (2006)

23. Einarsson, Á.M.: Sustaining library makerspaces: perspectives on participation, expertise, and embeddedness. Libr. Q. **91**(2), 172–189 (2021). https://doi.org/10.1086/713050

24. Eshach, H.: Bridging in-school and out-of-school learning: formal, non-formal, and informal education. J. Sci. Educ. Technol. **16**(2), 171–190 (2007)

25. Falk Olesen, J., Halskov, K.: 10 years of research with and on hackathons, pp. 1073–1088. ACM, New York (2020). https://doi.org/10.1145/3357236.3395543

26. Fernaeus, Y., Tholander, J.: Designing for programming as joint performances among groups of children. Interact. Comput. **18**(5), 1012–1031 (2006)

27. Griffith, A.L.: Persistence of women and minorities in stem field majors: is it the school that matters? Econ. Educ. Rev. **29**(6), 911–922 (2010)

28. Jung, H., Stolterman, E., Ryan, W., Thompson, T., Siegel, M.: Toward a framework for ecologies of artifacts: how are digital artifacts interconnected within a personal life? In: Proceedings of the 5th Nordic Conference on Human-Computer Interaction: Building Bridges, NordiCHI 2008, pp. 201–210. ACM, New York (2008). https://doi.org/10.1145/1463160.1463182

29. Kafai, Y.B., Burke, Q.: The social turn in k-12 programming: moving from computational thinking to computational participation. In: Proceeding of the 44th ACM Technical Symposium on Computer Science Education, SIGCSE 2013, pp. 603–608. ACM, New York (2013). https://doi.org/10.1145/2445196.2445373

30. Kafai, Y.B., Fields, D.A., Burke, W.Q.: Entering the clubhouse: case studies of young programmers joining the online scratch communities. J. Organ. End User Comput. **22**(2), 21–35 (2010). https://doi.org/10.4018/joeuc.2010101906

31. Kelleher, C., Pausch, R.: Lowering the barriers to programming: a taxonomy of programming environments and languages for novice programmers. ACM Comput. Surv. **37**(2), 83–137 (2005). https://doi.org/10.1145/1089733.1089734

32. Koschmann, T.: Introduction to special issue on learning and work. Comput. Support. Coop. Work (CSCW) **17**(1), 1–3 (2007). https://doi.org/10.1007/s10606-007-9069-9

33. Larsen-Ledet, I., Korsgaard, H., Bødker, S.: Collaborative writing across multiple artifact ecologies, pp. 1–14. ACM, New York (2020). https://doi.org/10.1145/3313831.3376422
34. Lyle, P., Korsgaard, H., Bødker, S.: What's in an ecology? A review of artifact, communicative, device and information ecologies. In: Proceedings of the 11th Nordic Conference on Human-Computer Interaction: Shaping Experiences, Shaping Society. ACM (2020). https://doi.org/10.1145/3419249.3420185
35. Maloney, J.H., Peppler, K., Kafai, Y., Resnick, M., Rusk, N.: Programming by choice: urban youth learning programming with scratch. In: Proceedings of the 39th SIGCSE Technical Symposium on Computer Science Education, SIGCSE 2008, pp. 367–371. Association for Computing Machinery, New York (2008). https://doi.org/10.1145/1352135.1352260
36. Mersand, S.: The state of makerspace research: a review of the literature. TechTrends 65(2), 174–186 (2021)
37. Mogensen, P.: Towards a provotyping approach in systems development. Scand. J. Inf. Syst. 4(1), 5 (1992)
38. Musaeus, L.H., Sørensen, M.L.S.K., Palfi, B.S., Iversen, O.S., Klokmose, C.N., Petersen, M.G.: CoTinker: designing a cross-device collaboration tool to support computational thinking in remote group work in high school biology. In: Nordic Human-Computer Interaction Conference, pp. 1–12 (2022)
39. OECD: Recognition of non-formal and informal learning - home (2022). https://www.oecd.org/fr/education/apprendre-au-dela-de-l-ecole/recognitionofnon-formalandinformallearning-home.htm
40. Pellegrino, J.W.: A learning sciences perspective on the design and use of assessment in education. In: The Cambridge Handbook of the Learning Sciences, pp. 233–252. Cambridge University Press (2014). https://doi.org/10.1017/cbo9781139519526.015
41. Pienimäki, M., Kinnula, M., Iivari, N.: Finding fun in non-formal technology education. Int. J. Child-Comput. Interact. 29, 100283 (2021). https://doi.org/10.1016/j.ijcci.2021.100283
42. Pitkänen, K., Iwata, M., Laru, J.: Exploring technology-oriented fab lab facilitators' role as educators in K-12 education: focus on scaffolding novice students' learning in digital fabrication activities. Int. J. Child-Comput. Interact. 26, 100207 (2020). https://doi.org/10.1016/j.ijcci.2020.100207
43. Resnick, M., et al.: Scratch: programming for all. Commun. ACM 52(11), 60–67 (2009). https://doi.org/10.1145/1592761.1592779
44. Robinson, M.: Design for unanticipated use... In: Proceedings of the Third Conference on European Conference on Computer-Supported Cooperative Work, ECSCW 1993, pp. 187–202. Kluwer Academic Publishers, USA (1993)
45. Roque, R., Kafai, Y., Fields, D.: From tools to communities: designs to support online creative collaboration in scratch. In: Proceedings of the 11th International Conference on Interaction Design and Children! IDC 2012, pp. 220–223. ACM, New York (2012). https://doi.org/10.1145/2307096.2307130
46. Rossitto, C., Bogdan, C., Severinson-Eklundh, K.: Understanding constellations of technologies in use in a collaborative nomadic setting. Comput. Support. Coop. Work 23(2), 137–161 (2013). https://doi.org/10.1007/s10606-013-9196-4
47. Roumen, G.J., Fernaeus, Y.: Envisioning arduino action. Int. J. Child Comput. Interact. 29(100277), 100277 (2021)
48. Selwyn, N.: Looking beyond learning: notes towards the critical study of educational technology. J. Comput. Assist. Learn. 26(1), 65–73 (2010). https://doi.org/10.1111/j.1365-2729.2009.00338.x

49. Sheridan, K., Halverson, E.R., Litts, B., Brahms, L., Jacobs-Priebe, L., Owens, T.: Learning in the making: a comparative case study of three makerspaces. Harvard Educ. Rev. **84**(4), 505–531 (2014). https://doi.org/10.17763/haer.84.4. brr34733723j648u
50. Smith, R.C., Iversen, O.S., Hjorth, M.: Design thinking for digital fabrication in education. Int. J. Child-Comput. Interact. **5**, 20–28 (2015). https://doi.org/10. 1016/j.ijcci.2015.10.002
51. Spradley, J.P.: Participant Observation. Waveland Press, Long Grove (2016)
52. Tisza, G., et al.: The role of age and gender on implementing informal and non-formal science learning activities for children. In: Proceedings of the FabLearn Europe 2019 Conference, FabLearn Europe 2019. ACM, New York (2019). https:// doi.org/10.1145/3335055.3335065

Engaging a Project Consortium in Ethics-Aware Design and Research

Päivi Heikkilä[(✉)] [iD], Hanna Lammi [iD], and Susanna Aromaa [iD]

VTT Technical Research Centre of Finland, Espoo, Finland
{paivi.heikkila,hanna.lammi,susanna.aromaa}@vtt.fi

Abstract. Ethics is an important perspective in project work. For a research and development project, ethics plays a key role when creating a shared understanding of societal goals and the intended long-term impacts of the project. It is an essential part of designing novel solutions and an integral part of conducting research. However, ethics is typically an area dedicated to ethics experts only, even though it would be important to embed it in the work of all project participants. In a European project on smart manufacturing, we have pursued to involve the whole project consortium to discuss and consider ethics in design and research throughout the project. This paper describes our ethical approach and the results of the engagement activities. Finally, we discuss the practical means we applied to create awareness and commitment towards ethics.

Keywords: Ethics · Design Ethics · Research Ethics · Co-creation · Industrial Work

1 Introduction

The role of ethics is drawing more attention in research and design projects due to the application of emerging technologies, as well as emphasis on societal impacts and sustainability in the project goals and outcomes. The development and application of novel technologies, such as artificial intelligence, increases the efficiency of completing tasks, but also creates social concerns, for example, on the privacy of technology users, competences in using new tools and the true benefits of the tools.

While ethics is acknowledged as an important perspective of research and design work, it may be challenging to embed it into project work and make a project group or a consortium aware of and committed to ethical aspects related to research and design. Although technology ethics is widely discussed in literature, a lack of practical examples of design processes including ethics and engaging a project group or a consortium in considering ethics may hinder the adoption of ethics in project work.

This paper explores a process to engage members of a project consortium in ethical thinking across the project lifecycle. The goal of our work was to engage our project consortium to proactively discuss and consider ethics in the project work and to foster maintaining an ethics-aware mindset throughout the project. In this paper, we share

J. Abdelnour Nocera et al. (Eds.): INTERACT 2023, LNCS 14142, pp. 297–306, 2023.
https://doi.org/10.1007/978-3-031-42280-5_17

the results of our engagement activities and thus, aim at informing researchers, designers, developers and other practitioners to foster ethical thinking in research and design projects.

Our ethics-related work was conducted in a four-year, EU-funded research and development project, in which 20 partners develop novel software solutions to support smart manufacturing work. The partners of the project represent research organisations, technology developers and manufacturing companies. The engagement activities were targeted at all participants of the project, encouraging everyone to consider ethics in their own work. The emphasis of our ethics-related work was on design ethics, which is also the main focus in this paper.

The paper is structured as follows. First, we introduce the background on the role of ethics in design. We then describe the process and methods used in the engagement activities during the research project and present the results of the activities. Finally, we discuss the practical means we applied to create awareness and commitment towards ethics.

2   Related Work

Although ethics is a relatively new perspective in design and research work, there are several design approaches that emphasise the role of ethics in design. Ethics can be considered in design, for example, by identifying and responding to the values of the target users [1], assessing the impacts of new solutions [2], or by creating and following ethical guidelines (e.g., [3]). The Ethics by Design approach [4] refers to forward-looking ethical thinking to address ethical aspects proactively in the design process. Ethics can also be addressed as one perspective of several aspects to be considered during the design and evaluation of novel solutions [5]. In addition, on a more general level, attention to ethics has been paid through associations and institutions that promote responsible behaviour [6, 7].

While existing approaches and frameworks provide an understanding on ethical design, there is less knowledge on how to engage a project consortium in considering ethics in their own project tasks. Based on Value-sensitive Design [1], Shilton and Anderson [8] explore the roles and responsibilities related to ethics in design teams, highlighting the question of whether responsibility of ethics work should be borne by ethics experts or designers of a design team. To support a design team, ethics experts can work as *values advocates* [8, 9], bringing knowledge of ethics literature and making bridges between abstract values and concrete technological affordances [8]. They can broaden the values considered in design [9] and spot ethical challenges during design [8]. However, this approach has been criticised for bringing a prescriptive list of values to a project [8, 10] and, due to time commitment, required to integrate into design teams.

The challenges of ethics interventions by experts have led to fostering the *ethical reflection embedded in design* [8]: the aim of incorporating ethics directly into the work of designers or developers. The approach has helped developers to experience ethical concerns as personal and relevant [8] and highlighted the connection between social concerns and design decisions [11]. However, this approach lacks deeper expertise that an ethics expert could bring to the process. A solution for this is yet a different role of bringing ethics to the project work: training ethics expertise to technical developers that Shilton and Anderson call *moral exemplars* [12, 13].

To encourage a whole project consortium to consider ethics in their work, the ethical approach can be based on the ideology of *co-creation*, a widely and successfully used approach of involving different stakeholders in the design process [14, 15]. Co-creation is defined as creativity that is shared by two or more people and can be applied throughout the whole design process [14]. Accordingly, co-creation refers to a practice of developing systems, products, or services through collaboration with the stakeholders [16].

One of the main building blocks of co-creation is *dialogue*, referring to interactivity, engagement, and propensity to act [17]. Through dialogue, the different perspectives, and a productive combination of them [18], may lead to successful outcomes. Concerning ethics, co-creation may also prevent challenges of ethical guidelines or checklists feeling extraneous or irrelevant that has been observed in previous studies when practitioners have not been involved in the design of them [19, 20].

3   Process and Methods

The process of engaging the project consortium in considering ethics in their design and research work consisted of engagement activities and support provided when needed (Fig. 1). The engagement activities included a workshop to identify potential ethical challenges in the beginning of the project, a workshop for introducing a set of ethical guidelines for the project and collecting feedback to it, and a questionnaire to review whether and how ethics had been considered during the project work. The participants of the workshops were researchers, developers, and project managers of the project consortium, consisting of twenty partners from nine European countries. The consortium included twelve research organisations, four manufacturing companies and four other companies, focusing, for example, on technology or business development.

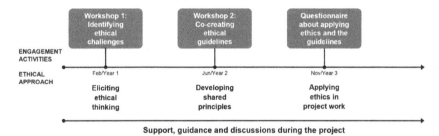

Fig. 1. Process of engaging the project consortium in considering ethics in their project work.

The first ethics workshop was organised as a part of the first project consortium meeting, organised as a face-to-face event. The aim of the workshop was to raise the project members' awareness of ethics and to identify potential ethical challenges related to the project. The area of ethics was first introduced to the participants by giving them a short presentation on research ethics and ethical principles in design. The presentation on research ethics focused on the need to protect the privacy of the volunteer test users in accordance with the GDPR (General Data Protection Regulation) and on the need to use informed consent forms in user studies. Ethical principles in design were introduced with the examples of an earlier research project on human-centric smart manufacturing [5] and principles for trustworthy AI [21]. The participants were asked to form pairs or small groups, discuss ethical aspects related to research or development of ethically sound solutions, and as a result, write down one ethical challenge or question to be considered during the project and addressed in the ethical guidelines for the project. Twenty-four members of the project consortium participated in the workshop.

Before the second workshop, three researchers categorised the challenges identified in the first workshop under six ethical themes applied in earlier research [3] and, based on the categorisation, created twelve initial ethical guidelines. The second ethics workshop was organised as an online meeting, and all project members were encouraged to participate. The aim of the workshop was to obtain feedback on the initial ethical guidelines. After a brief introduction of the initial guidelines, the participants were divided into three subgroups with moderators to give feedback on the clarity and relevance of the guidelines and discuss topical ethical issues. At the end of the workshop, the participants conducted an exercise of writing down the personally relevant key take-aways of the workshop to foster considering ethics from the perspective of their own project work. After the workshop, the guidelines were modified based on the feedback and shared with the consortium to be iterated. Eighteen members of the project consortium participated in the workshop.

At the end of the third project year, as a third engagement activity, an online questionnaire was sent to the project consortium to review whether and how the ethical guidelines or other ethics-related methods had been utilised in the project activities. The questionnaire also included a question to describe ethical challenges faced during the project and a possibility to request support for ethics-related activities. Twenty-one members of the project consortium responded to the questionnaire.

Parallel to the three main engagement activities, ethics was supported through documentation, short presentations, and discussions with project members. To support design, ethics was included as one perspective in a design and evaluation framework, developed to guide the design activities and pilot experiments of the project [22]. Ethical research practices were supported by providing guidance and material for the use of the consortium, for example a template for an informed consent form. Furthermore, ethics was discussed in case of specific challenges when designing and piloting software components and tools developed in the project.

4   Results

This section describes the results of the ethics-related engagement activities conducted during the project. Each sub-section ends with a short summary of the role of the activity as part of the ethical approach from the perspective of the project consortium.

4.1   Engagement Activity 1: Identifying Ethical Challenges

The first ethics workshop was organised to identify ethical challenges to be addressed later in the ethical guidelines for the project. The workshop resulted in eight potential challenges or questions related to developing and deploying new solutions or conducting research in an ethically sustainable way.

The potential challenges related to developing and deploying new solutions included issues such as monitoring employee performance and collecting data of employees. As a more general notion, the issue that machines should assist people, and not take over their work, was raised. The potential challenges and questions related to research ethics included specific questions on ethical procedures, such as the criteria when an ethical committee needs to be contacted before conducting a user study or procedures on processing personal data. As a more project-related issue, the issue of publishing results of other partners was raised.

From the perspective of the ethical approach, the first workshop served as a starting point for considering ethics during the project. It engaged all the participants of the consortium meeting to discuss ethics and provided common ground for co-creation of the ethical guidelines for the project.

4.2   Engagement Activity 2: Co-creation of Ethical Guidelines for the Project

The second ethics workshop was organised to co-create ethical guidelines for the project. The workshop resulted in feedback to the initial ethical guidelines that were introduced to the workshop participants and refined after the workshop.

The resulting twelve ethical guidelines were connected to six ethical themes identified as important in previous research [3]: privacy, autonomy, dignity, reliability, inclusion and benefit to society, two guidelines for each theme. The guidelines addressed the aspects of designing ethically sound solutions and piloting or deploying the solutions at work in an ethically sustainable way [23]. For example, the guidelines related to privacy emphasised respecting of workers' privacy when collecting data at the workplace and making workers aware if data is collected. In the guidelines on reliability, workers' safety and informing them of the reliability of new solutions were highlighted. Related to benefit to society, the guidelines stated that technological solutions should assist workers, supporting focus on value-adding work, and they should not cause harm to anyone, to their users or stakeholders. The complete list of guidelines is presented in [23].

From the perspective of the ethical approach, the second workshop and the co-creation process of the ethical guidelines served as the main activity for engaging project members in ethics. It provided understanding of ethical values relevant to the project, a possibility to have an impact on the guidelines and a forum for discussing topical ethical questions. After the workshop, the ethical guidelines were refined, and the project consortium had the possibility to comment on them. Based on the comments, suggestions of practices to apply the guidelines in project work were added to give the project consortium concrete examples of the guidelines.

4.3   Engagement Activity 3: Questionnaire on Application of Ethics

As the third ethics engagement activity, the members of the project consortium were asked to respond to an online questionnaire on applying ethics and the ethical guidelines during the project. The ethical guidelines of the project were included in the questionnaire.

According to the questionnaire, almost all respondents (20/21) had considered ethics in their project work. Thirteen respondents had either followed or applied the ethical guidelines of the project, and eight respondents had considered ethics with other means (Fig. 2). Only one respondent considered ethics irrelevant in his/her project work.

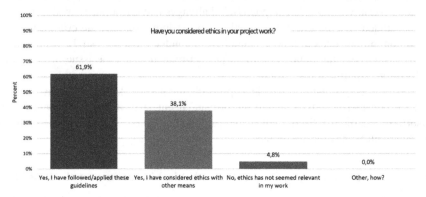

Fig. 2. Responses (N = 21) to the question, "Have you considered ethics in your project work?"

Concerning the ethical themes of the ethical guidelines, the respondents identified privacy, reliability and benefit to society as the most relevant themes for the project, followed by autonomy and inclusion (Fig. 3). The free-form descriptions of considering ethics were in line with this, particularly emphasising privacy that was addressed in most of the free-form responses (9/17 responses).

Considerations on privacy were related to procedures on collection of personal data, such as minimising it or deploying ways to collect anonymous data, for example in the case of tracking workers. Related to reliability, a need to inform stakeholders on the reliability and limitations of the developed solutions was emphasised, including identification and documentation of liability and responsibility issues. Benefit to society was highlighted in responses describing work for fostering safety and well-being of workers. Autonomy had been considered especially in tasks where humans and robots interact, in giving freedom to workers to organise their task flow, and when involving workers in design and development activities. Inclusion was mentioned to be considered in design and trials not excluding workers with different capabilities, skills and disabilities.

In addition to describing how ethics had been applied, the respondents also described the ethical challenges that they had faced during the project. The challenges included, for example, the risk of excessive data collection with sensors or wearables and facing worker concerns on losing their job. The latter had been addressed by informing workers on the potential benefits of the new solutions and involving them in the development work.

From the perspective of an ethical approach, the questionnaire served as a reminder of the ethical guidelines and a trigger to reflect on ethics related to one's project work. In addition, it worked as a channel for support in ethics-related issues, as the need for it was inquired.

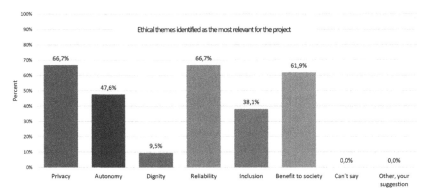

Fig. 3. Responses (N = 21) to the question, "Which ethical themes do you find the most relevant for our project?" The respondents were instructed to select maximum three ethical themes from the six themes of the ethical guidelines.

5 Discussion

Our aim was to engage the project consortium to consider ethics in their project work, and thus promote ethical thinking and design throughout the project. In line with the Ethics by Design approach [4], we aimed at encouraging positive and proactive ethical thinking, starting from the beginning of the project. Even though it is impossible to predict all issues related to the adoption of emerging technologies in advance [24], ethical design choices can be encouraged by paying attention to ethical values or principles considered as important by the project consortium. In the context of industrial work, for example colleting sensitive information on workers (e.g. [25]) or more generally, aiming at enhancing well-being of workers (e.g. [26]) are topics that require addressing ethical aspects when designing and piloting new solutions. While the goal of our work was to facilitate the development of ethically sustainable solutions, raising awareness of ethics in the project consortium also supports the wider aim to foster responsible and ethics-aware working in the technology industry [6, 7].

Our work on engaging the project consortium in considering ethics has elements of the roles of working as design advocates [8, 9] and fostering the ethical reflection embedded in design [8]. The engagement activities can be perceived as ethics interventions, but they also aimed at including ethical reflection to the design processes and guiding project members in considering ethics. Instead of training a few developers to work as moral exemplars [12, 13], our approach was based on the idea of co-creation [14, 15], to create shared understanding on ethics and encourage project partners to consider ethics in their work.

During the engagement process, we aimed at involving the whole project consortium to ethics work and creating awareness and commitment to ethics through practical means and methods: explicitly welcoming everyone to attend to ethics-related activities and using several methods, such as pair work, group work and discussions, to elicit ethical thinking. Attention was paid to using positive expressions when introducing the area of ethics and the engagement activities. Instead of identifying problems, we aimed at creating ethically sound solutions. To make the area of ethics easier to comprehend during the project, research ethics and ethics-aware design were separated in the workshops and ethics-related material. In addition, clarity was pursued by summarizing the results of the co-creation process into short guidelines with descriptions and examples.

In our research and development project, we have aimed at supporting industrial work with novel technological solutions. The results of our ethics work provide an understanding on ethical aspects relevant to this context. While the ethical guidelines co-created in the project focus on industrial work, and thus can best be applied in industrial contexts, our ethical approach and the process of engagement activities are also applicable in other research and design contexts. The engagement activities presented in this paper focused on the project consortium. In the future, also involving shop floor workers in a similar process could bring new perspectives to considering ethics or highlight different ethical values. In addition, it would be interesting to focus closer on design practices and the impact of ethics on the actual design decisions.

6 Conclusions

This paper presented the ethical approach and the results of the engagement activities to involve the project consortium to considering ethics in a European research and development project. The project consortium was engaged in ethics through workshops to identify ethical challenges and to co-create ethical guidelines for the project, as well as by providing guidance and support. The results provide understanding on ethical aspects related to designing novel tools to support industrial work. However, the main contribution is on increasing understanding on the ways to encourage project partners' ethics awareness and commitment to ethics.

Acknowledgements. We would like to thank all the project partners who have participated in the engagement activities presented in this paper. The project has received funding from the European Union's Horizon 2020 research and innovation programme under grant agreement No. 873087 (project SHOP4CF).

References

1. Friedman, B., Kahn, P.H., Borning, A., Huldtgren, A.: Value sensitive design and information systems. In: Doorn, N., Schuurbiers, D., van de Poel, I., Gorman, M.E. (eds.) Early engagement and new technologies: Opening up the laboratory. PET, vol. 16, pp. 55–95. Springer, Dordrecht (2013). https://doi.org/10.1007/978-94-007-7844-3_4
2. Wright, D.: A framework for the ethical impact assessment of information technology. Ethics Inf. Technol. **13**(3), 199–226 (2011)
3. Ikonen, V., Kaasinen, E., Niemelä, M.: Defining ethical guidelines for ambient intelligence applications on a mobile phone. In: Intelligent Environments (Workshops), pp. 261–268 (2009)
4. Niemelä, M., Kaasinen, E., Ikonen, V.: Ethics by design - an experience-based proposal for introducing ethics to R&D of emerging ICTs. In: ETHICOMP 2014 - Liberty and Security in an Age of ICTs (2014)

5. Kaasinen, E., et al.: A worker-centric design and evaluation framework for operator 4.0 solutions that support work well-being. In: Barricelli, Barbara Rita, Roto, Virpi, Clemmensen, Torkil, Campos, Pedro, Lopes, Arminda, Gonçalves, Frederica, Abdelnour-Nocera, José (eds.) Human Work Interaction Design. Designing Engaging Automation. IAICT, vol. 544, pp. 263–282. Springer, Cham (2019). https://doi.org/10.1007/978-3-030-05297-3_18
6. ACM. ACM code of ethics and professional conduct (2018). https://www.acm.org/code-of-ethics. Accessed 26 Apr 2023
7. IEEE. IEEE Code of ethics (2020). https://www.ieee.org/about/corporate/governance/p7-8.html. Accessed 26 Apr 2023
8. Shilton, K., Anderson, S.: Blended, not bossy: Ethics roles, responsibilities and expertise in design. Interact. Comput. 29(1), 71–79 (2017)
9. Van Wynsberghe, A., Robbins, S.: Ethicist as designer: a pragmatic approach to ethics in the lab. Sci. Eng. Ethics 20, 947–961 (2014)
10. Le Dantec, C.A., Poole, E.S., Wyche, S.P.: Values as lived experience: evolving value sensitive design in support of value discovery. In: Proceedings of the SIGCHI Conference on Human Factors in Computing Systems, pp. 1141–1150 (2009)
11. Shilton, K.: Values levers: building ethics into design. Sci. Technol. Hum. Values 38(3), 374–397 (2013)
12. Huff, C., Barnard, L., Frey, W.: Good computing: a pedagogically focused model of virtue in the practice of computing (part 1). J. Inf. Commun. Ethics Soc. 6, 246–278 (2008)
13. Huff, C., Barnard, L., Frey, W.: Good computing: a pedagogically focused model of virtue in the practice of computing (part 2). J. Inf. Commun. Ethics Soc. 6, 284–316 (2008)
14. Sanders, E.B.N., Stappers, P.J.: Co-creation and the new landscapes of design. Co-design 4(1), 5–18 (2008)
15. Robertson, T., Simonsen, J.: Participatory design: an introduction. In: Routledge International Handbook of Participatory Design, pp. 1–17. Routledge (2012)
16. Ramaswamy, V., Gouillart, F.J.: The Power of Co-creation: Build It With Them to Boost Growth, Productivity, and Profits. Simon and Schuster, New York (2010)
17. Prahalad, C.K., Ramaswamy, V.: Co-creation experiences: The next practice in value creation. J. Interact. Mark. 18(3), 5–14 (2004)
18. Steen, M., Manschot, M., De Koning, N.: Benefits of co-design in service design projects. Int. J. Des. 5(2) (2011)
19. Hagendorff, T.: The ethics of AI ethics: an evaluation of guidelines. Mind. Mach. 30(1), 99–120 (2020)
20. Madaio, M.A., Stark, L., Wortman Vaughan, J., Wallach, H.: Co-designing checklists to understand organizational challenges and opportunities around fairness in AI. In: Proceedings of the 2020 CHI Conference on Human Factors in Computing Systems, pp. 1–14 (2020)
21. AI, H.: High-level expert group on artificial intelligence set up by the European commission. In: Ethics guidelines for trustworthy AI. European Commission (2019)
22. Aromaa, S., Heikkilä, P.: Design of a human factors questionnaire to evaluate digital solutions developed for industrial work. Ergon. Des. 47, 635–641 (2022)
23. Heikkilä, P., Lammi, H., Aromaa, S.: Co-creation of ethical guidelines for designing digital solutions to support industrial work. In: Proceedings of the 18th International Joint Conference on Computer Vision, Imaging and Computer Graphics Theory and Applications - Volume 2: HUCAPP, ISBN 978–989–758–634–7, ISSN 2184–4321, pp. 185–192 (2023)
24. Brey, P.A.: Anticipatory ethics for emerging technologies. NanoEthics 6(1), 1–13 (2012)

25. Heikkilä, P., Honka, A., Mach, S., Schmalfuß, F., Kaasinen, E., Väänänen, K.: Quantified factory worker - expert evaluation and ethical considerations of wearable self-tracking devices. In: Proceedings of the 22nd International Academic Mindtrek Conference, pp. 202–211 (2018)
26. Heikkilä, P., Honka, A., Kaasinen, E., Väänänen, K.: Quantified factory worker: field study of a web application supporting work well-being and productivity. Cogn. Technol. Work **23**(4), 831–846 (2021). https://doi.org/10.1007/s10111-021-00671-2

Exploring Emotions: Study of Five Design Workshops for Generating Ideas for Emotional Self-report Interfaces

Carla Nave[1]([⊠]) ⓘ, Francisco Nunes[2] ⓘ, Teresa Romão[3] ⓘ, and Nuno Correia[3] ⓘ

[1] iNOVA Media Lab, ICNOVA, Faculdade de Ciências Sociais E Humanas, Universidade Nova de Lisboa, Lisbon, Portugal
carlanave@fcsh.unl.pt
[2] Fraunhofer Portugal AICOS, Porto, Portugal
[3] NOVA LINCS, NOVA School of Science and Technology, Costa da Caparica, Portugal

Abstract. Accurately reporting our emotions is essential for various purposes, such as men-tal health monitoring and annotating artificial intelligence datasets. However, emotions are complex and challenging to convey, and commonly used concepts such as valence and arousal can be difficult for users to understand correctly. Our main goal was to explore new ways to inform the design of affective self-report instruments that can bridge the gap between people's understanding of emotions and machine-interpretable data. In this paper, we present the findings of five de-sign workshops to generate ideas and solutions to represent emotion-related con-cepts and improve the design of affective self-report interfaces. The workshops originated seven themes that informed the derivation of design implications. These implications include representing arousal using concepts such as shape, movement, and body-related elements, representing valence using facial emojis and color properties, prioritizing arousal in questioning, and facilitating user con-firmation while preserving introspection.

Keywords: Design Workshops · Emotion · Self-Report

1 Introduction

The significance of emotions in our lives has spurred researchers to develop systems that can detect and respond to users' emotional states. These systems have the potential to significantly improve our well-being by enabling mental health symptom recognition and care interventions [17], adapting home functionalities for improved well-being [29], or adjusting car characteristics to reduce stress impact during driving [16]. Emotion Recognition, a key topic in Affective Computing, is fundamental for building such intelligent technologies.

Emotion Recognition involves detecting emotional states from visual, audio, and physiological data, which requires training algorithms with ground-truth data. Ground-truth data is collected and annotated through affective self-report, essential for obtaining valid and accurate datasets for emotion recognition systems [3]. The instruments used

© The Author(s), under exclusive license to Springer Nature Switzerland AG 2023
J. Abdelnour Nocera et al. (Eds.): INTERACT 2023, LNCS 14142, pp. 307–316, 2023.
https://doi.org/10.1007/978-3-031-42280-5_18

can influence the accuracy of collected data and its labels in assessing emotional states. Various tools are available to measure affect, ranging from pen-and-paper long questionnaires. However, there is a growing need in the research community for a valid, generic, quick-to-use, and intuitive instrument for self-reporting affect [5, 11, 15].

2   Background and Related Work

Although there is no universally accepted definition of emotion, researchers concur that emotional states involve coordinated changes across multiple components, including a physiological component, a behavioral or expressive component, and a subjective feeling component [13, 19]. Although sensors can implicitly measure the physiological component and facial expression recognition can assess the expressive component to some extent, accessing the subjective feeling component requires explicit subjective self-report. Russel refers to this subjective emotional component as "core affect" - a consciously available neurophysiological state described as a point in a valence (pleasure-displeasure) and arousal (sleepy-activated) space [26]. Valence and arousal are also fundamental to a prominent dimensional model used to classify emotions, known as the circumplex model of affect [24], which is widely utilized in fields such as psychology [8] and HCI [11]. Furthermore, these dimensions are commonly employed to rate emotional stimuli sets [7, 9, 10] and annotate ground-truth datasets [3, 31].

Arousal, also known as energy, activation, or intensity, is widely recognized as the intensity of the experienced emotion. On the other hand, valence, also known as pleasantness, refers to the hedonic quality that reflects an emotion's degree of positivity or negativity. Researchers in the affective sciences and related disciplines commonly use the terms arousal and valence. However, these terms do not typically carry the same meaning in everyday English, which can cause confusion. For instance, valence is often associated with the ability of atoms to combine with others, while arousal is often associated with sexual excitement. This disparity in usage may result in users misunderstanding the intended meaning of these terms when encountered in interfaces for self-assessing emotional states. Therefore, it is crucial to investigate how users perceive and interpret these concepts concerning emotional states.

Various instruments enable individuals to self-report their affect using the dimensions of arousal and valence, ranging from traditional pen-and-paper psychology instruments like the PANAS scales [30] to modern digital interfaces. For example, the-Assessment Manikin (SAM) (Fig. 1 -A) [4] is a widely recognized pictorial scale that portrays the dimensions of the Pleasure-Arousal-Dominance (PAD) model [27] using manikin figures arranged in three rows. Users can select the level that best represents their perception of each dimension using a nine-point Likert scale accompanying each row. SAM has been extensively validated and employed. However, researchers have identified some limitations, including the need for clear instructions and compliance with the SAM usage protocol [2, 5]. Another drawback is the potential misinterpretation of arousal, represented by an "explosion" in the stomach area, which may result in incorrect responses [28]. The Affect Grid (Fig. 1 -B) [27] is a paper-based, single-item scale developed in 1989 for quick and easy assessment of affect through valence and arousal, based on Russell's Circumplex Model [24]. It uses a 9x9 table as its interface, where the center cell represents a neutral feeling, the vertical dimension means arousal and the horizontal dimension represents valence. Participants mark the grid to indicate their emotions. The Affective Slider (AS) (Fig. 1 -C) [2] is a digital scale composed of two slider controls that measure valence and arousal. Emoticons are placed at the edges of the sliders to represent bipolar affective states, and two opposed triangles underneath each slider serve as visual cues for intensity. The Photographic Affect Meter (PAM) (Fig. 1 -D) [23] is designed for mobile, with a user interface based on a 4x4 grid containing 16 randomly selected photographs that represent a diversity of emotions. Users choose the image that best captures their feelings at the moment, and each photo maps to a score in Russell's Circumplex. The Circumplex Affect Assessment Tool (CAAT) (Fig. 1 -E) [6] is a widget for assessments of emotional experiences. It displays 25 selectable emotion nodes, each with its feeling word and color, arranged in a layout based on Plutchik's model [22]. The AffectButton (Fig. 1 -F) [5] is a button displaying a changing face as the user's mouse pointer moves inside. Users select the facial expression that represents their feelings. The x and y coordinates within the button define values on the PAD model [21].

3   Method

We conducted five design workshops where participants were asked to brainstorm designs of a graphical interface for reporting emotions using the arousal and valence dimensions. The main objective of these sessions was to generate ideas and solutions for effectively representing emotion-related concepts and enhancing the design of affective self-report interfaces. A total of 29 participants partook in the workshops, with Workshop 1 (WS1) having 6 participants, WS2 having 4 participants, WS3 having 7 participants, WS4 having 6 participants, and WS5 having 6 participants. The participants (22 males and seven females, averaging 33 years old) were recruited via social media and word-of-mouth, mainly targeting designers and software engineers. The study took place in Portugal.

The workshops, each lasting approximately 2.5 h, commenced with introductions, consent forms, and a brief demographic questionnaire. Subsequently, we provided instruction on valence and arousal and the Circumplex Model [24]. Participants were then prompted to brainstorm and sketch potential design options for a digital interface intended for self-reporting emotional states, drawing upon the concepts they had just learned. We told participants that the interfaces should ideally be generic and cross-platform, but they were free to consider specific platforms if they preferred, as our primary objective was to generate many ideas and observe how valence and arousal would be depicted.

We utilized thematic analysis as our qualitative data analysis approach to identify and organize recurring themes in the data. Due to space limitations, we summarize the coding process, highlighting the key codes and categories. Our research team followed a systematic coding process that involved conducting open coding to generate an initial list of codes, which were then refined and organized into categories. Consistency and validity were ensured through team-based reviews and discussions of the codes and categories. Based on our analysis, we identified several key codes and categories that emerged from the data. Through the investigation, several patterns and themes emerged, and this paper presents the study of the seven most relevant themes and their design implications.

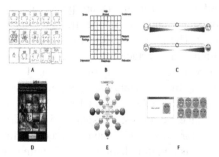

Fig. 1. Images of the interfaces of A- The Self-Assessment Manikin; B- Affect Grid; C- The Affective Slider; D- Photographic Affect Metter; E- Circumplex Affect Assessment Tool; F- AffectButton.

4   Results

4.1   Arousal and Shape

Participants generally associated high arousal levels with irregular and shaky lines, while they connected low arousal levels with smooth lines. For example, P5.2 (participant 2 from Workshop 5) correlated arousal with the lines in electrocardiogram charts. This association between shape and emotions, where high-arousal emotions like anger are often depicted with spikes, and low-arousal emotions like sadness are often represented by round shapes, is also commonly seen in everyday design.

4.2   Arousal and Movement

During the workshops, participants frequently discussed how to depict arousal, often starting with high arousal levels, and linking them to energetic movements. For example, participant P3.5 designed a wristwatch (Fig. 2) that required users to shake their wrists to indicate their level of arousal, with more vigorous movements indicating higher arousal levels.

4.3   Arousal and Body-Related Concepts

For instance, P2.1 suggested a slider for arousal that changes the body's position as it moves, while P3.1 mentioned relating arousal to a fast or slow heartbeat. The connection between arousal (also referred to as body activation) and the body is well-established, as arousal has been linked to activity in the sympathetic nervous system [24] and is relevant to the perception and identification of emotions [20]. In addition, Interoception, which refers to the perception of sensations from within the body and how they relate to emotional states, has positively contributed to health and well-being [25] positively. Users need to be aware that investigating their bodily signals can help gauge their arousal levels during self-reporting of affect. Therefore, the interface should convey that arousal is experienced intrinsically in the body and encourage users to pay attention to their bodily sensations when measuring arousal.

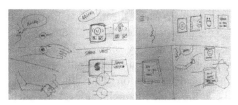

Fig. 2. The two images depict sketches of one of the proposed solutions. In this design, the user initiates the process by verbally expressing their emotion, which is interpreted as valence. Next, the user adds the level of arousal by shaking their arm.

4.4 Valence and Facial Emojis

Participants in the debate consistently considered facial features and emojis as potential representations of valence, which may be due to the widespread use of emojis in messaging apps to convey emotions. For example, P2.1 stated, "We can use smileys, which are very popular and commonly used in WhatsApp." P3.7 also emphasized the significance of eyebrows in conveying emotional expressions in Comics. These considerations are supported by research indicating valence measures correlate with facial muscles involved in emotional expression [24].

4.5 Valence, Arousal, and Color Properties

In the workshops, participants discussed using colors to represent arousal or valence. Consensus was challenging due to cultural differences, but some groups agreed on specific color properties. Saturation was chosen to represent valence, while brightness was selected for arousal. Participants associated negative valence with "dark" and "lifeless" colors, and positive valence with bright, vivid colors, aligning with artistic and design practices [1]. For instance, P5.5 remarked "If it is colorless, normally a person associates it with negative state" referring to dark colors and shades of grey. On the other hand, P2.1 mentioned "I also like the idea of going from the darkest color to the lighter color" referring to the transition from negative to positive valence.

4.6 The Relationship Between Arousal and Valence

Most participants seemed to believe valence was the emotion per se and that arousal was its intensity (i.e., arousal was a property of valence). For instance, Fig. 3 shows an interface where the buttons "+" and "−" control the intensity of each face (meant to denote valence).

Fig. 3. One of the proposed solutions: the user begins by selecting a face that represents their desired valence, then adjusting arousal levels using the "+" and "−" buttons below.

Similarly, Fig. 2 shows a design where the interface first asks the user to evaluate the valence by responding to the question "How happy?" and then rate the intensity of that response (i.e., the intensity of valence) by shaking the wrist. Despite some opposition [18], scientific literature mainly states that valence and arousal are separate dimensions equally important when related to emotion. Thus, the elements in the interface that represent them should be at the same hierarchical level. As such, the two parts should be visually similar in shape, size, color, proximity, and direction (Gestalt principle of similarity [12]). However, we believe that if users think first about arousal, they will think about it independently and not dependent upon valence. We can achieve this by placing arousal first in the interface, either horizontally or vertically.

4.7 Feedback and Introspection

Participants consistently emphasized the importance of feedback to confirm the accuracy of their input in terms of arousal and valence values aligning with their intended emotion label. P4.1 explicitly stated this need: *"as you navigated through different zones, there would be pop-ups with keywords associated with feelings to help you understand what that feeling was like, to see if it corresponded to what you were feeling."* Building on this concept, participants in WS4 devised solutions where users could view the emotion label simultaneously while using the self-assessment interface element.

An integral aspect of interface design is providing timely feedback to keep users informed [14]. However, some participants expressed concerns about immediate feedback, such as displaying the emotion label, as it could impede introspection and adversely impact the process of emotional self-assessment. For instance, P1.6 remarked, *"I liked the slider better. At the end, you could even submit, and it would give you a final face, that would be OK. But not at the moment you are still trying to figure it out"* and *"I think that if we want to make an assessment, it is better not to see the final result."* In addition, this participant highlighted how seeing an emotion label while selecting arousal and valence values could influence the final answer, potentially leading users to search for a label rather than focusing on separate variables. P2.1 also shared similar views, stating, *"I think it is cool that you give people control of the two dimensions separately, but you can see the joining of the two to what it corresponds to. But she has to work on both separately, contributing to that awareness. It seems to me that this is more important."* This participant emphasized the significance of users reflecting on arousal and valence separately before receiving feedback (i.e., an emotion label corresponding to the chosen values). Affective self-reports need introspection, and this psychological process should be considered during the design phase. Displaying a label immediately as users select arousal and valence values might hinder introspection, resulting in less focused and truthful choices based on the two dimensions. Furthermore, it is worth noting that there is no scientifically proven mapping of arousal and valence to specific emotion labels. Therefore, assessing arousal and valence values directly is imperative, as inferring values from a label may not be accurate. Additionally, separating an emotion into two variables, arousal, and valence, could enhance the final assessment, as users need to contemplate various aspects of emotion.

5   Design Implications

5.1   Representing Arousal Through Shape

Based on our findings, it is recommended that when representing arousal in an interface through shapes, they should transition from soft to shaky as the intensity increases. For instance, smooth and delicate shapes should indicate low arousal levels, while wobbly and thick shapes should be used to depict higher levels of this dimension.

5.2   Representing Arousal Through Movement

According to our research, vigorous movements could indicate the expression of higher arousal levels. Expressing arousal by shaking a watch or other objects could accommodate a broader range of users, including those with visual impairments.

5.3   Representing Arousal Through Body-Related Concepts

Users need to recognize that assessing arousal involves interpreting the body's signals. Therefore, the interface should emphasize that arousal is an intrinsic sensation that originates from the viscera. As a result, incorporating body-related images and metaphors can be beneficial for conveying arousal in the interface. Alternatively, audible instructions, such as those used in guided meditations, may also be helpful.

5.4   Representing Valence Through Facial Emojis

Our research suggests that using facial emojis and facial features to represent valence is a good choice. However, it is important to consider that different emojis can carry different meanings in different cultures.

5.5   Representing Valence and Arousal Through Color Properties

Cultural barriers can make establishing relationships between colors and emotional properties challenging. However, our findings suggest that saturation and brightness may be worth exploring as a way to indicate varying levels of valence or arousal. Dark and lifeless colors could represent negative values at one end of the spectrum, while bright and vivid colors could be set at the opposite end, representing positive values.

5.6 Ask for Arousal First

During our study, we discovered a common misconception: many people mistakenly perceive valence as the emotion itself, and arousal as its intensity, i.e., a property of valence. To address this issue, the interface layout must communicate to users that valence and arousal are independent dimensions. We propose two steps to achieve this. Firstly, both dimensions should be visually represented similarly, with equal size and parallel positioning, following the Gestalt Principle of Similarity, to convey equal importance. Secondly, we suggest presenting arousal information to users first, followed by valence, either horizontally or vertically, such as on top or the left. This sequence aims to prompt users to consider arousal as a separate dimension, independent of valence, and prevent them from conflating arousal as a property of valence.

5.7 Help Users Confirm Their Choices but Preserve Introspection

Assessing emotional states is a deeply personal and introspective experience. However, providing users immediate and explicit feedback can hinder introspection and bias responses. To address this dilemma, there are several solutions. One approach is offering abstract or subjective feedback, such as adjusting the screen's brightness or incorporating abstract designs. Another option is to implement a "submit" button that only displays objective feedback, such as an emotion label after the user completes the assessment by clicking on it. Additionally, strategically placing prototypical emotion labels on the interface can help guide users during the assessment process, providing further assistance without compromising their introspective experience.

6 Conclusion and Future Work

To correctly understand emotional states, gathering data from several components, including the conscious subjective feeling, which is only graspable through self-report, is necessary. Our findings, derived from five design workshops focused on investigating how individuals comprehend emotion-related concepts, provide insight into the representation of arousal and valence dimensions, the interface layout, and feedback. Furthermore, by converting our results into design implications, we offer potential considerations for developing graphical interfaces that facilitate emotion reporting. Our future endeavors entail conducting a replicated study with a sample that is gender-balanced and encompasses multiple countries. This approach aims to yield more robust and reliable results. Subsequently, we will proceed to develop prototypes to assess the effectiveness of the design implications.

Acknowledgements. This work is supported by NOVA LINCS (UIDB/04516/2020) with the financial support of FCT.IP, as well as by FCT grand PD/BD/114141/2015.

References

1. Barbiere, J.M., Vidal, A., Zellner, D.A.: The color of music: correspondence through emotion. Empirical Stud. Arts **25**, 193–208 (2007)
2. Betella, A., Verschure, P.F.M.J.: The affective slider: a digital self-assessment scale for the measurement of human emotions. PLoS ONE **11**(2), e0148037 (2016)
3. Bota, P.J., et al.: A review, current challenges, and future possibilities on emotion recognition using machine learning and physiological signals. IEEE Access **7**, 140990–141020 (2019)
4. Bradley, M.M., Lang, P.J.: Measuring emotion: the self-assessment manikin and the semantic differential. J. Behav. Ther. Exp. Psychiatry **25**(1), 49–59 (1994)
5. Broekens, J., Brinkman, W.-P.: AffectButton: a method for reliable and valid affective self-report. Int. J. Hum. Comput. Stud. **71**(6), 641–667 (2013)
6. Cardoso, B., Romão, T., Correia, N.: CAAT - a discrete approach to emotion assessment. In: CHI '13 Extended Abstracts on Human Factors in Computing Systems on - CHI EA '13. ACM Press (2013)
7. Carvalho, S., et al.: The Emotional Movie Database (EMDB): a self-report and psychophysiological study. Appl. Psychophysiol. Biofeedback **37**(4), 279–294 (2012)
8. Ciuk, D., Troy, A., Jones, M.: Measuring emotion: self-reports vs. physiological indicators (2015)
9. Dan-Glauser, E.S., Scherer, K.R.: The Geneva affective picture database (GAPED): a new 730-picture database focusing on valence and normative significance. Behav. Res. Methods **43**(2), 468–477 (2011)
10. Douglas-Cowie, E., et al.: The HUMAINE database: addressing the collection and annotation of naturalistic and induced emotional data. In: Paiva, A.C.R., Prada, R., Picard, R.W. (eds.) Affective Computing and Intelligent Interaction. Lecture Notes in Computer Science, vol. 4738, pp. 488–500. Springer, Heidelberg (2007). https://doi.org/10.1007/978-3-540-74889-2_43
11. Fuentes, C., Herskovic, V., Rodríguez, I., Gerea, C., Marques, M., Rossel, P.O.: A systematic literature review about technologies for self-reporting emotional information. J. Ambient. Intell. Humaniz. Comput. **8**(4), 593–606 (2016). https://doi.org/10.1007/s12652-016-0430-z
12. Graham, L.: Gestalt theory in interactive media design. J. Human. Soc. Sci. (2008)
13. Gross, J.J., Thompson, R.A.: Emotion regulation: conceptual foundations. In: Handbook of Emotion Regulation, pp. 3–25. Guilford Press, New York (2007)
14. Harley, A. Visibility of System Status (Usability Heuristic #1) (2018). https://www.nngroup.com/articles/visibility-system-status/. Accessed 28 Dec 2022
15. Healey, J., et al.: Circles vs. scales. In: Proceedings of the 20th International Conference on Human-Computer Interaction with Mobile Devices and Services, pp. 1–11 (2018)
16. Healey, J.A., Picard, R.W.: Detecting stress during real-world driving tasks using physiological sensors. IEEE Trans. Intell. Transp. Syst. **6**(2), 156–166 (2005)
17. Ji, S., et al.: Suicidal ideation and mental disorder detection with attentive relation networks. Neural Comput. Appl. **34**(13), 10309–10319 (2022)
18. Kron, A., et al.: How are you feeling? Revisiting the quantification of emotional qualia. Psychol. Sci. **24**(8), 1503–1511 (2013)
19. Mauss, I.B., Robinson, M.D.: Measures of emotion: a review. Cogn. Emot. **23**(2), 209–237 (2009)
20. Mayer, J.D., Salovey, P.: What is emotional intelligence? In: Emotional Intelligence: Key Readings on the Mayer and Salovey Model. Dude Publishing (2004)
21. Mehrabian, A.: Pleasure-arousal-dominance: A general framework for describing and measuring individual differences in Temperament. Curr. Psychol. **14**(4), 261–292 (1996)

22. Plutchik, R.: The nature of emotions - human emotions have deep evolutionary roots, a fact that may explain their complexity and provide tools for clinical practice. Am. Sci. **89**(4), 344–350 (2001)
23. Pollak, J.P., Adams, P., Gay, G.: PAM. In: Proceedings of the SIGCHI Conference on Human Factors in Computing Systems. ACM (2011)
24. Posner, J., Russell, J.A., Peterson, B.S.: The circumplex model of affect: an integrative approach to affective neuroscience, cognitive development, and psychopathology. Dev. Psychopathol. **17**(03), 715–734 (2005)
25. Price, C.J., Hooven, C.: Interoceptive awareness skills for emotion regulation: theory and approach of mindful awareness in body-oriented therapy (MABT). Front. Psychol. **9**, 798 (2018)
26. Russell, J.A.: Core affect and the psychological construction of emotion. Psychol. Rev. **110**(1), 145–172 (2003)
27. Russell, J.A., Weiss, A., Mendelsohn, G.A.: Affect grid - a single-item scale of pleasure and arousal. J. Pers. Soc. Psychol. **57**(3), 493–502 (1989)
28. Toet, A., Heijn, F., Brouwer, A., Mioch, T., van Erp, J.B.: An immersive self-report tool for the affective appraisal of 360° VR Videos. Front. Virtual Reality **1** (2020)
29. Tsoukalas, A., et al.: IoT enhancements for an in-house calm computing environment. In: 2022 8th International Conference on Automation, Robotics and Applications (ICARA). IEEE (2022)
30. Watson, D., Clark, L.A., Tellegen, A.: Development and validation of brief measures of positive and negative affect: the PANAS scales. J. Pers. Soc. Psychol. **54**(6), 1063–1070 (1988)
31. Zhao, S., et al.: Affective computing for large-scale heterogeneous multimedia data. ACM Trans. Multimed. Comput. Commun. Appl. **15**(3s), 1–32 (2019)

Moving Away from the Blocks: Evaluating the Usability of EduBlocks for Supporting Children to Transition from Block-Based Programming

Gavin Sim[1]([⊠]) [iD], Mark Lochrie[1] [iD], Misbahu S. Zubair[2] [iD], Oliver Kerr[1] [iD], and Matthew Bates[1] [iD]

[1] University of Central Lancashire, Preston, UK
grsim@uclan.ac.uk
[2] Manchester Metropolitan University, Manchester, UK

Abstract. When learning to code, children and novice programmers often transition from block-based to traditional text-based programming environments. This paper explores the usability problems within a block-based authoring environment, EduBlocks, that may hinder children's learning. Using domain-specific heuristics, a usability evaluation was performed by expert evaluators, which was later combined with data from an analysis of problems reported in Forums, to produce a corpus of usability problems. The corpus was subsequently analysed using thematic analysis, and seven design guidelines were synthesized. Using the guidelines, a model of interaction was created to inform the design of block-based authoring environments that support the transition to text-based authoring. The model examines the interplay between learning within a school environment to independently using the authoring environment and how the interface can support these differing scenarios. This paper contributes to the design of effective user interfaces to support children learning to code and provides guidelines for developers of hybrid authoring environments to support the transition away from blocks.

Keywords: Heuristic Evaluation · Programming Interfaces · Usability · Design Guidelines

1 Introduction

Since the creation of Logo in the 1960s, which was the first computer programming language designed for children, there has been considerable research into how children learn to program, and the programming environments have evolved. Over the last twenty years, the Child Computer Interaction (CCI) community has explored how children program, the use of programming environments to support STEM subjects, the development of computational skills and exploring new interaction paradigms such as augmented reality. Currently, the predominant programming environment that is used with children in elementary schools appears to be Scratch.

© The Author(s), under exclusive license to Springer Nature Switzerland AG 2023
J. Abdelnour Nocera et al. (Eds.): INTERACT 2023, LNCS 14142, pp. 317–336, 2023.
https://doi.org/10.1007/978-3-031-42280-5_19

Scratch was publicly launched in 2007 as a visual programming environment designed for children. The key design goal is to support children's self-directed learning through tinkering and collaboration with peers [1]. Based on the concept by Papert [2] Scratch facilitates a "low floor", meaning it is easy to learn and has a "high ceiling", thus allowing more complex projects to be developed. Researchers have demonstrated the effectiveness of Scratch as a programming environment [3]. Other programming environments have emerged such as App Inventor and EduBlocks. In a comparison study of Scratch and App Inventor, researchers developed a rubric for evaluating the effectiveness of these environments based on seven criteria [4]. The results showed that Scratch was more effective against three criteria and App Inventor two. It would suggest that overall children can effectively learn from visual programming, however, whether the interfaces are effective at ensuring the "low flow" is debatable, as there are several studies that highlight usability problems with visual programming environments.

Usability problems have been reported in earlier versions of the Scratch interface for experienced programmers [5], whilst in a more recent study of novice programmers aged 18 to 24 [6] three notable usability problems were identified, and it is conjectured that these would also be applicable to children. These problems impacted the learner's ability to navigate and create programs.

Once children are familiar with visual programming applications there are very few tools that support the transition to text-based authoring environments. This presents new challenges to children or novice programmers as they start needing to comprehend and understand the syntax and semantics of the language. Usability evaluations have been performed on traditional authoring environments [7] revealing usability anomalies in languages and the interfaces. Within these environments users can make syntax errors and the error messages cannot always be comprehend which impacts on the learning [8]. It is apparent that the design of these environments can influence the ability to successfully acquire the confidence and ability to create programs. Despite this there appears to be little research on how to design effective interfaces to help support the transition from visual to text-based authoring environments, as reflected in Dijkstra's comment, "The tools we use have a profound (and devious!) influence on our thinking habits, and, therefore, on our thinking abilities" [9]. Given the view that learning to program solely using a visual environment does not teach students to program, rather it teaches them to think logically [10], there is, therefore, a clear need for research into designing effective interfaces to help support the transition from visual to text-based authoring environments.

This paper aims to investigate the usability of EduBlocks a hybrid authoring software that uses block-based programming whilst also revealing the generated source code for each block to the user. From the identified usability problems guidelines will be synthesised to not only improve the usability but help foster an environment for children to learn whilst using the software.

2 Related Work

The related work section will examine theory related to learning to code, the usability of novice programming environments and the Blocky API. The API is used in a range of block-based authoring environments and can have a direct impact on usability.

2.1 Learning to Code

There is a general view held by students and teachers alike, that programming is a difficult topic to learn [11]. Learning to program can often be a daunting process, as it requires students to not only learn to apply and understand the syntax and semantics of the language they are trying to learn, but also develop appropriate mental models of core programming concepts which often have no real-world counterpart, in addition to developing their problem-solving abilities to produce working solutions [12]. As such, Du Boulay [13] proposed an outline of the key areas of difficulty a student will encounter when learning to program:

1. General Orientation – students must develop an understanding of what programming can be used for and how it can be used to solve problems.
2. Notional Machine – students can have difficulty understanding how the instructions within a program are executed by the computer through a lack of understanding of the *notional machine*; a general representation of the computer being used to execute the program [14].
3. Notation – students may struggle to learn the syntax and semantics of a particular language.
4. Structures – students may encounter issues in applying the notation of a language when attempting to apply or adapt known approaches (schemas) to fit the requirements of the program they are trying to develop, such as adapting a loop to compute a numerical sum.
5. Pragmatics – students must be able to apply their knowledge of programming to specify, develop, test, and debug a program. This not only requires an understanding of how to write a program, but also how to identify and solve problems effectively.

The five areas of difficulty, as highlighted by Du Boulay [13], cannot be fully separated from each other, which can consequently lead to students becoming overwhelmed when they attempt to try and comprehend all of the different issues at once, particularly if they are using an Integrated Development Environment (IDE) which has been designed for professional use, rather than for use within a classroom environment, where students will regularly be encountering cryptic error messages which makes the task of debugging their programs all the more difficult [15].

A typical introductory programming course which uses a text-based language would not engage with the interests of children [16, 17]. Subsequently, block-based languages such as Scratch, have attempted to create an environment which is more engaging for children, whilst also abstracting away from the complex syntax and semantics of traditional text-based languages, by allowing students to construct programs by 'snapping' blocks of code together, as if they were solving a puzzle [18]. This, therefore, allows students to focus on developing an appropriate understanding of the underlying concepts being learnt, and applying them in order to produce an appropriate solution.

Although Lin and Weintrop [18] review of the literature surrounding students' transition from block-based programming to a traditional text-based language revealed that Block-based programming has been shown to be an effective way of introducing children to programming, mixed views were reported as to whether having prior experience of a block-based language benefits students. To that end, Kolling et al. [19] compiled a list of 13 distinct issues which students face when transitioning from a block-based language to a text-based one, including, amongst others, students' lack of memorisation of commands and syntax, struggling with the readability of the text-based language, how to layout code effectively and how to comprehend error messages. There is, therefore, a clear need to support students with the transition from block-based languages to text-based ones in order to overcome the issues highlighted by Kolling et al. [19].

2.2 Usability of Visual Programming

There has been considerable work over the years looking at the usability of various programming IDEs. Storey et al. [20] performed a usability evaluation with three participants, with the main issue being confusion between the edit and debug modes. IDEs have continued to evolve of the years in an attempt improve the programming experience for users, reduce usability problems and make environments more accessible. For example, a frame-based IDE was developed, by combining elements of blocks and text programming [21] with the rational for this being the poor usability of older editors. In general, the common issues with VPE include:

- Limited expressiveness: difficult for users to go beyond the confines of the environment [22, 23].
- Difficulty with debugging: the visual representation doesn't map to the underlaying logic (text-based) [24].
- Limited scalability: used for purposes of learning rather than building complex software projects [25].
- Limited extensibility: Many VPE's lack the ability to customise Blocks in terms of their presentation or functionality [26].
- Limited domains: designed for one programming language [25].

One of the key features of visual programming environments is the reliance on using colour to distinguish different code elements. It has been reported that most of these block-based environments have either been reported to be inaccessible or present significant barriers to novices with visual impairments learning how to program [27]. Researchers have tried to overcome accessibility issues through modifications to the interface via plugins or development of environments such as TabGo which is a tangible programming environment based around Scratch.

It is difficult to decouple usability problems and programming experiences as they are intertwined. Shepperd at el. [28] within the context of programming a robot suggests that a block-based environment can simplify the industrial robot programming experience, the choice of available commands and their semantics has a large effect on the usability. Thus, navigating the possible programming commands without, or with limited, prior experience could impact on the usability. A usability study was performed with five proficient programmers of the Scratch interface looking at learnability, errors, memorability and efficiency [5]. In this study very few usability problems were reported, notably problems in using sprites to organize projects, issues with variables and scrolling issues. It is worth noting that all evaluators were adults with prior experience of programming and often block-based environments target children.

The System Usability Scale (SUS) was used to evaluate the usability of Scratch with 96 teenagers after completing four practical activities [29]. The results showed the overall rating was under satisfactory with the construct learnability scoring the lowest. These types of evaluation do not identify the issues faced by the users or provide data that can help iterate the design of the system to alleviate any problems.

A great deal of the research into block-based environments with children has focused on making block-based programming more accessible through novel interaction techniques including gestures [30], tangible interaction [31] and speech [32]. There have been hybrid systems developed to help children transition from Scratch [33]. In this study they identified formula manipulation within Scratch to be problematic and developed a hybrid system that displays the logic in text format for editing. The usability testing with 17 children demonstrated the effectiveness of this approach and children perceived it to be easy to use. Despite these promising results the design and use of hybrid programming environments for children is still rather limited with the majority of studies focusing on the design of Scratch to mitigate problems faced by the user.

2.3 Issues with Block Based APIs

Although numerous Visual Programming Environments (VPEs) exist in the wild, Holwerda and Hermans' analysis of VPEs found most to belong to either the "Scratch family" or the "Blockly family" [34]. Tools in the Scratch family include Scratch 2.0 and below [1], and VPEs created as their extensions such as Snap!/BYOB [35] and GP [36]. The Blockly family on the other hand includes both VPEs created by extending Blockly and by using the Blockly API for developing block-based visual programming languages and editors, they include several popular children's visual programming environments such as Scratch 3.0 [37] and App Inventor [38].

Pasternak et al. [37] state the importance of noting that APIs like Blockly serve only as tools for developers to utilize when creating their vocabulary of programming blocks, and it is up to the developers to determine the output produced by building the blocks and to provide a way of communicating or visualising said output. Therefore users of a VPE and its context of use must be considered by developers during the development process to produce a VPE that is fit for purpose. However, Pasternak et al. [37] also highlight that varying levels of differences that may arise across VPEs of the same API as a result of these considerations; these differences, which can range from differences in levels of abstraction and functions of blocks to the visual layout of the VPE could confuse users.

Issues and inconsistencies across VPEs of the same API can be caused by other factors other than user-based design decisions, for example, Holwerda and Hermans [34] reported complaints from users of a Blockly-based VPE about the use of only buttons for zooming despite Blockly's additional support of the use of the mouse scroll wheel or the zoom gesture on a trackpad.

Despite the design differences that may exist between VPEs of the same API, some features will stay the same and provide consistency in both positive and negative forms. For example, one of the "things" learnt by the Blockly Team as reported by Fraser [39] is that the lack of a connector inside c-shaped blocks (e.g. if-block) makes it difficult for some users to see how other blocks can fit inside the 'c', this issue was also found and reported by Weintrop et al. [40] when testing their Blockly based VPE for programming robots. Additionally, although both the Scratch and Blockly families of VPEs are provided with the ability to customize block colours, accessibility and usability issues as a result of similarities between colours of different block categories have been faced by users [32, 41]. Similarly, both VPE families have been found to have no search support to ease the difficulty of finding blocks, and as such, this issue is inherited by VPEs belonging to both families [34].

3   Method

A study was devised to investigate whether there are usability problems within the interface of EduBlocks that may hinder the children's ability to transition away from block-based programming to a traditional line-based environment using the heuristic set the usability of EduBlocks for Python programming. To establish the usability of the software two approaches were taken, a heuristic evaluation and an analysis of discussion forums and feedback sites to find reported problems from end users.

3.1   EduBlocks

EduBlocks is a cross-platform web-based, opensource, drag-and-drop programming environment designed to teach children (8–13 years old) and novice programmers how to programme in various languages [42]. The platform was developed by Joshua Lowe in 2017 at the age of 12 as a solution to a problem he was facing learning to code in Python. He found that the transient from blocks (Scratch) to Python wasn't as easy as it could be and as he was familiar with other block-based environments (Scratch, Mi-crosoft Make-Code). His main issue with the transition was the lack of visual interface and the speed of being able to prototype something quickly due to the drag and drop interface and the error safety net that platforms such as Scratch 3 conceals. Being a child at secondary school, Joshua was able to observe the same issues from his fellow pupils when they were beginning their transition into text-based programming. He states, "going from the cat in Scratch to hello world in Python, can quickly put you off and not want to do coding or Computer Science (CS)" [43]. Noting that, typing skills vary across pupil abilities with the rise in touch-screen interfaces and the removal of the traditional desktop computer from classrooms [42]. This raises another problem when using your first text-based programming environment where there is no visual interface or drag-and-drop snippets of code, you are presented with a white background no different to a basic text editor. You are expected to type code with little to no support, and if you incorrectly type something you won't have the same fail-safe catch as seen in Scratch, Python will complain, and the user is expected to understand what is wrong from the error message. Furthermore, teachers will have varying levels of experience in CS and the lack of knowledge teaching the subject, leaves the learner in distress from not understanding what is happening or how to solve the problem and consequently loose interest in the subject [43].

The platform is designed like many VLE's, to allow users to learn the syntax of a programming language using a visual interface to explore and discover how code is structured and assembled. The aim of EduBlocks is to provide a route to transition from blocks to text-based programs easier for users and teachers. The design of EduBlocks was inspired by the block-based environments (colourful blocks, ease and use of drag-and-drop: size of blocks and functionality) combines with text-based code. As you drag blocks, code is added to the text editor. Which makes EduBlocks unique from other alternatives. Over the years EduBlocks has expanded to accommodate other programming languages and platforms – making it a versatile VLE to learn programming.

Inspired by Scratch, EduBlocks (Fig. 1) uses the exact same style of blocks to Scratch and MakeCode to support learners transitioning from these to EduBlocks. The plat-forms afford a split-view User Interface (UI) between the visual elements and the code. On the left is the 'EduBlocks Editor'. Blocks can be dragged in the same manner as Scratch and MakeCode with the main difference of the code appearing in the 'Code Editor' (right side of the UI) as blocks are added to the stage. Where one block is one line of Python. The idea behind this is to help learners understand how the block relates to the line of code. EduBlocks provides a fun and engaging experience using visual libraries taken from Python such as Turtle and Processing which enablers learners to create visual experiences that were similarly observed in Scratch [42].

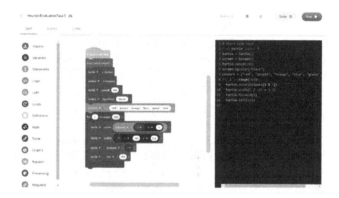

Fig. 1. EduBlocks *programming environment demonstrating task 4*

Lowe insists EduBlocks like Scratch provides 'low floors' easy for anyone to get going, 'wide walls' range of platforms/languages and libraries and 'high ceiling' for advanced and extensible use [43]. Additionally, as the platform focusses on learning to sup-port learners and teachers, work can be distributed to Google Classroom and Microsoft Teams, enabling teachers to push templates to learners and submit work for making. EduBlocks doesn't just support learners in coding software but also hardware from platforms like the Raspberry Pi, BBC MicroBit and Circuit Python to access platform specific hardware such as GPIO pins and on-board sensors.

Aside from the core programming environment, Lowe has supported teachers in building a EduBlocks curriculum[1] with slides, scheme of work, lesson plans and assessment and mark scheme to get started with teaching EduBlocks. Recognising the similarities and differences between Scratch and EduBlocks, '123 Coding Cards' were

---

[1] EduBlocks Curriculum https://curriculum.edublocks.org/.

designed to support learners' transitions from Scratch to EduBlocks to Python as an onboarding activity.

The curriculum and coding cards 'activities' are grounded by AQA specification for programming concepts to support learners become familiar and confident with the en-vironment. Furthermore, understanding how learning should take place, Lowe has extended the learning materials to support users at home with more scaffolding to support learners outside the classroom environment. These home learning resources include getting started with EduBlocks and worksheet activities consist of providing starter code, documenting observations and extension tasks for advanced users. Furthermore, the community backing EduBlocks is heavily supported by teachers creating guides and video lessons to teach within the classroom and at home [42].

3.2 Evaluators

A total of 4 lecturers in Computer Science with experience of usability research and teaching programming were recruited. This included two senior academics and two Early Career Researchers. The evaluators had between 5- and 11-years' experience of teaching programming and only one had no experience of performing usability studies including heuristic evaluations. Where one of the evaluators had conducted a heuristic evaluation before whilst one had been involved in a usability evaluation. Therefore, the evaluators were judged to be double experts in usability when it came to performing the evaluation of the EduBlocks interface.

3.3 Heuristic Set

The heuristics that had been specifically developed for evaluating visual programming environments were selected for use in this study [44]. This heuristic set has been shown to be effective for evaluating the usability of the Scratch platform and thus it was deemed more appropriate than generic heuristic sets such as Nielsen's [45]. The heuristics are:

Engagement: The system should engage and motivate the intended audience of learners. It should stimulate learners' interest or sense of fun.

Non-threatening: The system should not appear threatening in its appearance or behaviour. Users should feel safe in the knowledge that they can experiment without breaking the system or losing data.

Minimal language redundancy: The programming language should minimise redundancy in its language constructs and libraries.

Learner-appropriate abstractions: The system should use abstractions that are at the appropriate level for the learner and task. Abstractions should be driven by pedagogy, not by the underlying machine.

Consistency: The model, language, and interface presentation should be consistent, internally and with each other. Concepts used in the programming model should be represented in the system interface consistently.

Visibility: The user should always be aware of system status and progress. It should be simple to navigate to parts of the system displaying other relevant data, such as other parts of a program under development.

Secondary notations: The system should automatically provide secondary notations where this is helpful, and users should be allowed to add their own secondary notations where practical.

Clarity: The presentation should maintain simplicity and clarity, avoiding visual distractions. This applies to the programming language and to other interface elements of the environment.

Human-centric syntax: The program notation should use human-centric syntax. Syntactic elements should be easily readable, avoiding terminology obscure to the target audience.

Edit-order freedom: The interface should allow the user freedom in the order they choose to work. Users should be able to leave tasks partially finished and come back to them later.

Minimal viscosity: The system should minimise viscosity in program entry and manipulation. Making common changes to program text should be as easy as possible.

Error-avoidance: Error-avoidance: Preference should be given to preventing errors over reporting them. If the system can prevent, or work around an error, then it should.

Feedback: The system should provide timely and constructive feedback. The feedback should indicate the source of a problem and offer solutions.

As no bespoke severity rating scales have been developed within the context of visual programming environments the decision was made to use the 4 point scale proposed by Nielsen [46].

3.4 Task Design

To provide reasonable tasks that the evaluators could perform whilst conducting the heuristic evaluation of EduBlocks, it was necessary to review the UK national curriculum and sample code tutorials. Four tasks were created by the researcher, two in visual form showing the blocks and two showing just the code. The tasks covered a range of programming concepts in Python including arrays, loops, logic and visual output to the screen. These are all activities that would be expected to teach to children learning to code in Python. The four tasks are:

- Task 1 was creating a dance narrative (showing the blocks)
- Task 2 was creating a word guessing game (showing the code)
- Task 3 was to draw a star (showing the blocks)
- Task 4 was to draw a triangle (showing the code)

3.5 Procedure

All the evaluators performed the heuristic evaluation in the same laboratory and the evaluators were required to bring their own laptops. Three of the evaluators used Microsoft Surfaces that were the same specifications, and one evaluator used a Microsoft Surface 2. There may been some technical variability, such as monitor resolution, but this would be expected within a school environment. The whole evaluation was scheduled to last 3 h and the evaluators were asked to:

- Locate EduBlocks website and set up a new Python 3 project.

- Individually go through the four tasks and record any usability problems on the form provided.
- In groups merge the individual problem sets into an aggregated list of usability problems.

Whilst completing the individual tasks the evaluators were required to record any usability problems encountered on a form provided (see Fig. 2), this was based on the evaluation forms provided in the DR-AR model [47]. The evaluators were allowed to categorise a usability problem as a violation of multiple heuristics, this method is seen in other studies [48].

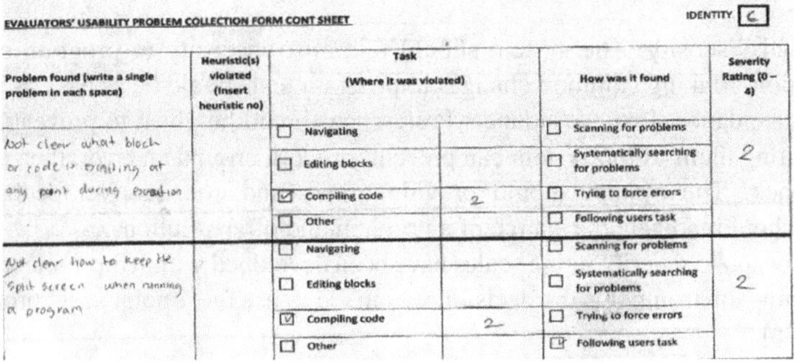
EVALUATORS' USABILITY PROBLEM COLLECTION FORM CONT SHEET

IDENTITY C

Problem found (write a single problem in each space)	Heuristic(s) violated (Insert heuristic no)	Task (Where it was violated)		How was it found	Severity Rating (0 – 4)
Not clear what block or code is executing at any point during execution		☐ Navigating		☐ Scanning for problems	2
		☐ Editing blocks		☐ Systematically searching for problems	
		☑ Compiling code	2	☐ Trying to force errors	
		☐ Other		☐ Following users task	
Not clear how to keep the split screen when running a program		☐ Navigating		☐ Scanning for problems	2
		☐ Editing blocks		☐ Systematically searching for problems	
		☑ Compiling code	2	☐ Trying to force errors	
		☐ Other		☑ Following users task	

Fig. 2. Individual Evaluators Data Capture Form

Once the evaluators had completed the fours tasks and documented problems, they were then asked to form a group to merge their individual problem sets, into a single list using Excel which was projected onto a screen.

The evaluators were informed that problems could be merged if they were judged to be the same based on the description. For each problem the evaluators had to provide a description of the problem, record the frequency of discovery within the group and assign an agreed severity rating. This merging stage lasted approximately 1.5 h as there were considerable discussion relating to the interface and at times EduBlocks was opened to explain the problem.

After the heuristic evaluation was completed, so not to bias the results of the study, two of the authors then analysed the data from the EduBlocks support site, along with other sites including Reddit, Fandom and CodeGuru to identify any reported usability problems. This consisted of identifying websites that are used for help and support in programming and determining whether there are specific queries relating to EduBlocks by using the search feature within the forum. It became apparent that there is very little online support other than the EduBlocks main website. Other platforms such as Scratch appear to be much more widely used and have an active support community on platforms such as Google Groups and Fandom in comparison to EduBlocks.

3.6 Analysis

Heuristic Data
The aggregated forms were analysed by the 1st author of this paper and an CCI specialist to verify that the problems predicted were not 'false positives'. The heuristic evaluation method is an inspection method where evaluators are required to predict problems that they think users will encounter, this means that on occasions, usability problems can be included in the aggregated list that are not real problems, in that a user, in this case a child, would not have a problem hence the phrase 'false positives'. If the reported problem was judged by the CCI experts and the 1st authors to potentially be a 'false positive', it was further analysed by re-examining the software to determine whether it is a viable problem or whether it was indeed a false positive. No problems were removed from the dataset following this analysis.

Forum Data
The 5 forums that were identified yielded very little data with respect to the EduBlocks IDE. Usability problems were only reported on the official EduBlocks website and there were 60 feedback posts in total. Each one of these posts were read to determine whether it was a usability issue or a recommendation for new features. There were some instances were multiple posts related to the same topic, for example code not compiling although the syntax was correct, these were just merged to a single problem. This resulted in 9 usability problems being identified from the Forum data.

Thematic Analysis
The aggregated data from the heuristic evaluation and the forums was then examined using thematic analysis to produce themes [49]. For thematic analysis, a 6-step approach was used where step 1 was to familiarize with the usability problems from the forums and heuristic evaluation, each problem was read. Step 2 involved the manual creation of initial codes from the 32 problems set. In total 19 codes were created, and these were examined to find themes in step 3. Codes such customization and colour mismatch were found to be most repeated code. These codes were then merged to form 9 themes generated from these codes. In step 4 the researchers evaluated and finalized these themes which were further clustered to 7 themes. Step 5 involved defining the 7 themes with final refinement and concluded with step 6 which synthesized the descriptions relating to how they might address the usability problems identified.

4   Results

The results are presented in 3 sections, the first is the individual evaluators' results, followed by the aggregated results and finally the data from the analysis of the for-rums.

4.1   Individual Evaluators Performance

The individual evaluators collectively identified 54 problems before their individual sheets were aggregated. As expected, there was variance in the numbers of problems found with evaluator B identifying the fewest problems with 10 whilst evaluator C reported the highest with 17 problems being identified. All except evaluator C mapped the problems to the heuristic set and the spread can be seen in Table 1 below.

Table 1. Frequency of problems matched to a heuristic

	Heuristic Number													
	1	2	3	4	5	6	7	8	9	10	11	12	13	NA
Number of problems	1	1	2	0	8	7	3	7	2	3	7	0	6	6

When examining the problems that were not categorized it may have been feasible to map these to one of the heuristics. For example, evaluator C reported cannot resize execution window, but this could have been mapped to consistency as it is feasible to resize windows in most programming IDEs.

There were two heuristics that appeared to be redundant with no reported problems associated with them, these were Learner-appropriate abstractions and Error avoid-ance.

The severity of the problems was also examined, and the number of problems mapped to each severity scale is shown in Table 2 below.

Table 2. Frequency of Severity Rating

	Severity Scale			
	1	2	3	4
Number of problems	7	21	17	9

There were 9 problems that were initially judged to be a usability catastrophe by an evaluator with most problems, 21, judged to be a minor usability problem.

When examining the programming task, where the errors were associated as shown in Fig. 2 column 3, 23 out of 54 problems were linked to editing blocks, however only 3 of these were judged to have a severity rating of 4 and these were:

- The block colour doesn't match the code colour making it difficult to see changes to code
- Coloured blocks are too similar when printed (sheet) and on screen
- You can follow the code exactly with the correct logic, but the code won't run. This is because you need to use the correct blocks for example while userGuess! = randomWord need the logic + variable blocks to work correctly.

For children or novice programmers, these problems may hinder the user's ability to successfully complete programming tasks and make it difficult to learn the fundamentals of programming.

In addition, 15 problems related to navigating within the software, 7 problems occurred whilst compiling the code and 9 problems were classified as others. The problems classified as others mainly related to understanding code generated and writing code.

4.2 Aggregated Problems

The individual problems were aggregated into a single list of 23 usability problems. When analysing the frequency of discovery, there was only 1 problem that was identified by all four evaluators, and this received a severity rating of 4. The problem was:

- Language and terminology are difficult to follow without prior knowledge and understanding or with prior knowledge of programming – either no hover help or non-readable.

Of the other 26 problems, 8 were identified by a single evaluator, 11 by two evaluators and the remaining 3 problems were identified by 3 evaluators. The three problems reported by the three evaluators and the severity ratings are shown below:

- Block operation is difficult when used on a small screen for moving and decoupling from the main thread (severity 3)
- Block colours are difficult to distinguish when printed/on screen (severity 3)
- The console hides the code and refers to the line of code, but you can't reference this to see all panels to debug the problem (severity 4)

It is evident that many of the problems reported with the interface could impact on the teaching and learning of programming, especially impacting on the transition away from blocks-based programming.

4.3 Usability Problems from Forums

The EduBlocks website has a feedback forum[2] where issues and suggested improvements can be made by users. There were 60 posts in total on the site, recommending new features and reporting problems. The problems that were documented within the forum are:

- I have a student who has created a simple Python Turtle program (just a simple for loop) and although it is correctly formatted, there is no output on the screen. Tried it on Chrome and Edge, same result. Anyone had similar issues? 20 other students have the same code, and it works fine.
- No ability to rename project.
- How do students get a password reset please? No link for those that cannot remember.
- Need to be able to add comments on projects.
- I wrote a 300+ long code and it was completely deleted to 27 lines when I went back on. I did not open my block tab at all, I have no way of going back and it was for a school project.
- Can't add assignments to my class.

---

[2] EduBlocks Feedback Forum https://app.edublocks.org/feedback.

- When using it in class you need to be able to increase the font size
- Need to be able to change the background colour to make it more accessible.
- It would be useful to have greater language support for non-English speaker.

Many of these problems were not identified in the heuristic evaluation, as the tasks were not designed from a teacher's perspective.

4.4 Hybrid Block-Based Programming Guidelines

The data from the forums and heuristic evaluations were then coded to produce the following 7 themes. These themes encompass all the usability problems and recommend interactions and behaviours within the user interface to mitigate the problems identified. The guidelines are:

User Interface Customisation: Children and teachers need to be able to modify the interface characteristics including, colour, fonts, window size and language to make sure it is suitable for the classroom environment and accessible. In addition to support novice programmers the number of operations could be reduced.

Support New Users: The system should provide initial onboarding through prompts to support new users understand the features. This could include prompts to support assisting users resume where they left off and ensuring autosave.

Language and Syntax Support: It should be assumed that the users have limited programming knowledge thus terminology relating to programming terms and syntax should be in the user's language. For example, it was difficult without prior knowledge selecting colour based on RGB values.

Visualising Blocks and Code: The colour of the blocks should reflect the colour of the code. The colour of blocks should be distinguishable from one another to enable children to easily follow tutorials online or in print. During compiling it should highlight what block is being executed to provide visual feedback.

Flexibility in Code Editing and Manipulation: There should be flexibility in the manipulation of code with edits to the textual code reflected in changes to the blocks and vise versa. If blocks are not attached to other blocks and are floating on the canvas this should still appear in the code view and be editable. Correct code in the text panel should still compile if this has been modified.

Appropriate Error Feedback and Intervention: Error message should be visible and meaningful to the user. When error messages occur, the fix should be accessible from within the user interface.

Simplify Interaction: It should be possible to duplicate blocks to reduce the need to locate previous code. If there are subblocks it should be distinguishable the number of operators that are available.

5 Discussion

It is evident from the usability evaluation of EduBlocks that the requirements to understand computer science concepts and terminology may impact the novice programmer's ability to easily transition from block to text-based authoring environments. For example, the drawing tools within EduBlocks required that participants access the 'Turtle' drawing tools of Python to both create a canvas and map a path for a pen tool to draw a basic shape. The EduBlocks commands to set colour values are presented as an RGB system by default, with no immediate access to a simplified colour description (e.g., 'red' vs. 'blue') or an 8-bit 'colour palette' as part of the interface. By offering the user a more varied set of default blocks, which prioritise colour descriptions over their RGB values may offer users a more convenient method translating their intentions into the Blockly space. Conversely, it could be argued that use of an RGB system demands greater specificity from the end user in colour designation, instilling good practice in acutely selecting and differentiating between colours as part of the activity. Promotion of experimentation with new technologies has been shown to be an important part of colour recognition and description as part of early school learning for children, as part of 'play' [50].

Such considerations are evident in wider introductory programming programmes such as the 'Code Playground' resources by Barclays in the UK, whose resources introduce the drawing features of EduBlocks using both colour descriptions and RGB notations to actively encourage experimentation. The innovation agency 'Nesta' [51] cite Barclays contribution to the learning space in their 2015 review of opportunities for digital creativity in the UK, illustrating the importance of 'creativity' alongside technical understanding when discussing 'digital making' as a process. It is therefore important that visual programming tools such as EduBlocks offer alternate methods for defining colour, which satisfy user expectations and experiences from alternate environments (e.g., Scratch).

The primary users of block-based authoring tools including EduBlocks are novices, predominately children. The PLU-Model [52, 53] has been used to characterize software designed for use with children under three dimensions, play, learning and use. Based on the assumption that most children will be introduced to programming within schools, Fig. 3 below models' children's programming journey and how these three dimensions influence their ability to progress. Children's introduction into programming is usually within a school context facilitated by a teacher who will have designed or appropriated learning activities. Children will then use the software within this environment to complete the activities before using the platform independently either through the need to complete homework or through motivation to learn outside of school.

Within the classroom context usability problems reported in the forums, including needing to resize fonts and language support may impact the willingness of teachers to use the software and the children's learning experience. The learning activities presented to the children may impact their fun and enjoyment of the software. Fun is an important design requirement to motivate children to use software [54, 55] and is a construct that is often examined when evaluating educational software for children [56, 57]. The heuristic evaluation identified problems in the material describing the tasks and in particular difficulty to distinguish colour in the block examples provided. Thus, the design of the UI can impact the creation of learning resources which may make it difficult to learn. The activities that are being designed by teachers also need to be fun and engaging to help motivate the children to learn. Research has shown that the activities can promote children having fun whilst learning to code [3]. An alternative view is that to develop learning environments that foster intrinsic motivation and engagement by triggering

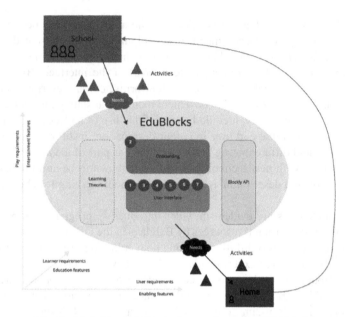

Fig. 3. Modelling EduBlocks Interaction to the PLU Model

the learners' curiosity [58]. It is evident that Fun whether designed into the system or activities can have a positive influence on children's motivation to learn to code and their perceived learning [58].

Within the EduBlocks platform onboarding for new users is rather limited and thus the guideline Support for New Users address this challenge. The concept of adaptive user interfaces has been around for decades, and these have not transcended into programming environments [59]. Having an adaptive block-based environment may help new users to navigate and find the code blocks easier. When designing tasks for class teachers could specify the functionality that needs to be visible and as their learning progresses then additional functionality can be revealed. This would help children learn to program by improving their general orientation [13].

Most of the problems and proposed guidelines (6 out of 7) relate to the user interface. The UI interaction is influenced by the constraints within the Blocky API and the design should also be informed by learning theory relating to programming. The reliance on the use of colour to differentiate blocks was highlighted as a server problem in the heuristic evaluation and contributes to accessibility issues [32]. When blocks are generating the programming syntax it is important to be able to form a mental model of the block and the corresponding syntax to help with comprehension. It has been suggested that novices struggle with notation having difficulty in learning the syntax and semantics of a particular language [13]. Creating a playful environment were the relationship between the blocks and the code is evident and either can be manipulated may promote exploratory learning [60]. This interaction may not only cause syntax errors but logic errors within the code and therefore appropriate feedback messages and assistance with debugging is essential. In the analysis of the Forum results, it was reported that the teacher struggled to understand why the code would not compile and there were no obvious errors. It could be conjectured that children would disengage from the activity if this occurred and failure with the activities could impact motivation to learn [61].

These problems within the interface may be compounded if the child is using the software outside of the school context. They may be reliant on teacher support to overcome syntax errors, difficulty in saving and loading projects, resetting passwords and navigating the interface. Based on the PLU-Model [52] enabling features may be more important for children when they are working independently so that the interface can scaffold their learning.

6   Conclusions

This paper aimed to investigate the usability problems that may impact on children's ability to transition away from block-based programming environments to traditional text-based authoring environment. The heuristic evaluation and analysis of problems reported in forums, relating to the EduBlocks software, revealed severe usability problems that could impact on children's ability to learn and a willingness to use the software by teachers. In line with other studies looking at usability, it was important to complement the heuristic evaluation with other data. Although the heuristic set was designed for novice programming environments, they do not consider children's characteristics or behaviours.

From the data, guidelines were synthesized using thematic analysis and this paper contributes a set of 7 guidelines to improve the usability of hybrid programming environments for children. The child's learning journey with respect to programming was modelled considering learning theory and the Blocky API. Building on from CCI literature it is recommended that the software is flexible in the way children interact, this could promote accessibility and foster playful learning.

Further work will examine how modification to the EduBlocks environment can improve the usability of the software and children's learning of programming. Through manipulation of the program source code, it will be possible to manipulate the colours of the blocks and minimize the number of blocks visible to the child. This modified interface will be tested with children to establish perceived learning, actual learning and the overall usability of the system. Although no falsification testing of the usability problems from the heuristic evaluation was performed, expert evaluators were used, and data was gathered from the forums. This corpus of usability problems will be used to compare the usability of the modified interface.

References

1. Maloney, J., Resnick, M., Rusk, N., Silverman, B., Eastmond, E.: The scratch programming language and environment. ACM Trans. Comput. Educ. (TOCE) **10**, 1–15 (2010)
2. Papert, S.A.: Mindstorms: Children, Computers, and Powerful Ideas. Basic Books, New York (2020)
3. Papavlasopoulou, S., Sharma, K., Giannakos, M.N.: How do you feel about learning to code? Investigating the effect of children's attitudes towards coding using eye-tracking. Int. J. Child-Comput. Interact. **17**, 50–60 (2018)

4. Park, Y., Shin, Y.: Comparing the effectiveness of scratch and app inventor with regard to learning computational thinking concepts. Electronics **8**, 1269 (2019)
5. Tanrikulu, E., Schaefer, B.C.: The users who touched the ceiling of scratch. Procedia Soc. Behav. Sci. **28**, 764–769 (2011)
6. Jimenez, Y., Kapoor, A., Gardner-McCune, C.: Usability challenges that novice programmers experience when using scratch for the first time. In: 2018 IEEE Symposium on Visual Languages and Human-Centric Computing (VL/HCC), pp. 327–328. IEEE (2018)
7. Leßenich, O., Sobernig, S.: Usefulness and usability of heuristic walkthroughs for evaluating domain-specific developer tools in industry: evidence from four field simulations. Inf. Softw. Technol. 107220 (2023)
8. Denny, P., et al.: On designing programming error messages for novices: readability and its constituent factors. In: Proceedings of the 2021 CHI Conference on Human Factors in Computing Systems, pp. Article 55, Yokohama, Japan. Association for Computing Machinery (2021)
9. Dijkstra, E.W.: How do we tell truths that might hurt? ACM Sigplan Notices **17**, 13–15 (1982)
10. Robinson, W.: From scratch to patch: easing the blocks-text transition. In: Proceedings of the 11th Workshop in Primary and Secondary Computing Education, Münster, Germany, pp. 96–99. Association for Computing Machinery (2016)
11. Konecki, M., Petrlic, M.: Main problems of programming novices and the right course of action. In: Central European Conference on Information and Intelligent Systems, p. 116. Faculty of Organization and Informatics Varazdin (2014)
12. Khalife, J.T.: Threshold for the introduction of programming: providing learners with a simple computer model. In: 28th International Conference on Information Technology Interfaces, pp. 71–76. IEEE (2006)
13. Du Boulay, B.: Some difficulties of learning to program. J. Educ. Comput. Res. **2**, 57–73 (1986)
14. Sorva, J.: Notional machines and introductory programming education. Trans. Comput. Educ **13**, 1–31 (2007)
15. Becker, B.A., et al.: Compiler error messages considered unhelpful: the landscape of text-based programming error message research. In: Proceedings of the Working Group Reports on Innovation and Technology in Computer Science Education, pp. 177–210 (2019)
16. Moors, L., Luxton-Reilly, A., Denny, P.: Transitioning from block-based to text-based programming languages. In: 2018 International Conference on Learning and Teaching in Computing and Engineering (LaTICE), pp. 57–64. IEEE (2018)
17. Resnick, M., et al.: Scratch: programming for all. Commun. ACM **52**, 60–67 (2009)
18. Lin, Y., Weintrop, D.: The landscape of Block-based programming: characteristics of block-based environments and how they support the transition to text-based programming. J. Comput. Lang. **67**, 101075 (2021)
19. Kölling, M., Brown, N.C., Altadmri, A.: Frame-based editing: easing the transition from blocks to text-based programming. In: Proceedings of the Workshop in Primary and Secondary Computing Education, pp. 29–38 (2015)
20. Storey, M.-A., et al.: Improving the usability of Eclipse for novice programmers. In: Proceedings of the 2003 OOPSLA Workshop on Eclipse Technology eXchange, pp. 35–39 (2003)
21. Kölling, M., Brown, N.C., Hamza, H., McCall, D.: Stride in BlueJ--computing for all in an educational IDE. In: Proceedings of the 50th ACM Technical Symposium on Computer Science Education, pp. 63–69 (2019)
22. Weintrop, D., Wilensky, U.: To block or not to block, that is the question: students' perceptions of blocks-based programming. In: Proceedings of the 14th International Conference on Interaction Design and Children, pp. 199–208 (2015)

23. Bak, N., Chang, B.-M., Choi, K.: Smart Block: A visual block language and its programming environment for IoT. J. Comput. Lang. **60**, 100999 (2020)
24. Kim, C., Yuan, J., Vasconcelos, L., Shin, M., Hill, R.B.: Debugging during block-based programming. Instr. Sci. **46**, 767–787 (2018)
25. Strong, G., North, B.: Pytch—an environment for bridging block and text programming styles (Work in progress). In: The 16th Workshop in Primary and Secondary Computing Education, pp. 1–4 (2021)
26. Burnett, M.M., McIntyre, D.W.: Visual programming. In: COMPUTER-LOS ALAMITOS, vol. 28, p. 14 (1995)
27. Mountapmbeme, A., Okafor, O., Ludi, S.: Accessible Blockly: an accessible block-based programming library for people with visual impairments. In: Proceedings of the 24th International ACM SIGACCESS Conference on Computers and Accessibility, pp. 1–15 (2022)
28. Shepherd, D., Francis, P., Weintrop, D., Franklin, D., Li, B., Afzal, A.: [Engineering Paper] An IDE for easy programming of simple robotics tasks. In: 2018 IEEE 18th International Working Conference on Source Code Analysis and Manipulation (SCAM), pp. 209–214. IEEE (2018)
29. Morales, J., Rusu, C.: Usability perception of visual programming language: a case study. In: CEUR Workshop Proceedings, pp. 83–88 (2020)
30. Toro-Guajardo, S., Lizama, E., Gutierrez, F.J.: Gesture coding: easing the introduction to block-based programming languages with motion controls. In: Bravo, J., Ochoa, S., Favela, J. (eds.) Ubiquitous Computing and Ambient Intelligence, pp. 840–851. Springer, Cham (2023). https://doi.org/10.1007/978-3-031-21333-5_84
31. De Siqueira, A.G., Feijóo-García, P.G., Stanley, S.P.: BlockXR: a novel tangible block-based programming platform. In: 2021 IEEE Symposium on Visual Languages and Human-Centric Computing (VL/HCC), pp. 1–4. IEEE (2021)
32. Okafor, O., Ludi, S.: Voice-enabled blockly: usability impressions of a speech-driven block-based programming system. In: Proceedings of the 24th International ACM SIGACCESS Conference on Computers and Accessibility, pp. 1–5 (2022)
33. Koitz, R., Slany, W.: Empirical comparison of visual to hybrid formula manipulation in educational programming languages for teenagers. In: Proceedings of the 5th Workshop on Evaluation and Usability of Programming Languages and Tools, pp. 21–30 (2014)
34. Holwerda, R., Hermans, F.: A usability analysis of blocks-based programming editors using cognitive dimensions. In: 2018 IEEE Symposium on Visual Languages and Human-Centric Computing (VL/HCC), pp. 217–225. IEEE (2018)
35. Harvey, B., Mönig, J.: Bringing "no ceiling" to scratch: can one language serve kids and computer scientists. Proc. Constructionism 1–10 (2010)
36. Monig, J., Ohshima, Y., Maloney, J.: Blocks at your fingertips: blurring the line between blocks and text in GP. In: 2015 IEEE Blocks and Beyond Workshop (Blocks and Beyond), pp. 51–53. IEEE (2015)
37. Pasternak, E., Fenichel, R., Marshall, A.N.: Tips for creating a block language with blockly. In: 2017 IEEE blocks and beyond workshop (B&B), pp. 21–24. IEEE (2017)
38. Patton, E.W., Tissenbaum, M., Harunani, F.: MIT app inventor: objectives, design, and development. In: Kong, S.-C., Abelson, H. (eds.) Computational thinking education, pp. 31–49. Springer, Singapore (2019). https://doi.org/10.1007/978-981-13-6528-7_3
39. Fraser, N.: Ten things we've learned from Blockly. In: 2015 IEEE Blocks and Beyond Workshop (Blocks and Beyond), pp. 49–50. IEEE (2015)
40. Weintrop, D., Shepherd, D.C., Francis, P., Franklin, D.: Blockly goes to work: block-based programming for industrial robots. In: 2017 IEEE Blocks and Beyond Workshop (B&B), pp. 29–36. IEEE (2017)

41. Zubair, M.S., Brown, D., Hughes-Roberts, T., Bates, M.: Evaluating the accessibility of scratch for children with cognitive impairments. In: Antona, M., Stephanidis, C. (eds.) UAHCI 2018. LNCS, vol. 10907, pp. 660–676. Springer, Cham (2018). https://doi.org/10.1007/978-3-319-92049-8_49
42. Lowe, J.: Hello World. The Magazine for Computing and Digital Making Educators. Raspberry Pi Foundation (2020)
43. Youtube. https://www.youtube.com/watch?v=Sp6o6S15sPM&ab_channel=CASTV
44. Kölling, M., McKay, F.: Heuristic evaluation for novice programming systems. ACM Trans. Comput. Educ. (TOCE) **16**, 1–30 (2016)
45. Nielsen, J.: Finding usability problems through heuristic evaluation. In: Proceedings of the SIGCHI Conference on Human Factors in Computing Systems, pp. 373–380. ACM (1992)
46. Nielsen, J., Molich, R.: Heuristic evaluation of the user interface. In: SIGCHI Conference on Human Factors in Computing Systems: Empowering People, Seattle, pp. 249–256. ACM (1990)
47. Woolrych, A., Cockton, G.: Testing a conjecture based on the DR-AR model of usability inspection method effectiveness. In: 16th British HCI Group Annual Conference, pp. 1–4. British HCI Group (2002)
48. Zhang, J., Johnson, T.R., Patel, V.L., Paige, D.L., Kubose, T.: Using usability heuristics to evaluate patient safety of medical devices. J. Biomed. Inform. **36**, 23–30 (2003)
49. Kiger, M.E., Varpio, L.: Thematic analysis of qualitative data: AMEE Guide No. 131. Med. Teach. **42**, 846–854 (2020)
50. Shen, Y., Qiu, Y., Li, K., Liu, Y.: Beelight: helping children discover colors. In: Proceedings of the 12th International Conference on Interaction Design and Children, pp. 301–304 (2013)
51. Quinlan, O.: Young Digital Makers: Surveying Attitudes and Opportunities for Digital Creativity Across the UK [online]. London (2015). Accessed 7 Feb 2018
52. McKnight, L., Read, J.C.: PLU-E: a proposed framework for planning and conducting evaluation studies with children. In: Proceedings of the 25th BCS Conference on Human-Computer Interaction, Newcastle-upon-Tyne, United Kingdom, pp. 126–131. British Computer Society (2011)
53. Read, J.C., Bekker, M.M.: The nature of child computer interaction. In: Proceedings of HCI 2011 the 25th BCS Conference on Human Computer Interaction, vol. 25, pp. 1–9 (2011)
54. Blythe, M.A., Monk, A.F., Overbeeke, K., Wright, P.C.: Funology: From Usability to Enjoyment. Human Computer Interaction Series. Kluwer Academic Publishers, Dordecht (2003)
55. Malone, T.W., Lepper, M.R.: Making learning fun: a taxonomy of intrinsic motivations for learning. In: Snow, R.E., Farr, M.J. (eds.) Aptitude, Learning and Instruction. Volume 3: Cognitive and Affective Process Analysis. Erlbaum, Hillsdale (1987)
56. Sim, G., MacFarlane, S., Read, J.C.: All work and no play: measuring fun, usability and learning in software for children. Comput. Educ. **46**, 235–248 (2006)
57. Sim, G., Nouwen, M., Vissers, J., Horton, M., Slegers, K., Zaman, B.: Using the Memoline to capture changes in user experience over time with children. Int. J. Child-Comput. Interact. (2016)
58. Tisza, G., Markopoulos, P.: Understanding the role of fun in learning to code. Int. J. Child-Comput. Interact. **28**, 100270 (2021)
59. Liu, J., Wong, C.K., Hui, K.K.: An adaptive user interface based on personalized learning. IEEE Intell. Syst. **18**, 52–57 (2003)
60. Rieman, J.: A field study of exploratory learning strategies. ACM Trans. Comput.-Hum. Interact. (TOCHI) **3**, 189–218 (1996)
61. Henrie, C.R., Halverson, L.R., Graham, C.R.: Measuring student engagement in technology-mediated learning: a review. Comput. Educ. **90**, 36–53 (2015)

Cybersecurity and Trust

Dark Finance: Exploring Deceptive Design in Investment Apps

Ivana Rakovic and Yavuz Inal[(✉)] [iD]

Department of Design, Norwegian University of Science and Technology, Gjøvik, Norway
yavuz.inal@ntnu.no

Abstract. This study aimed to explore how financial technology companies employed dark patterns to influence investors' financial decision-making and behavior. We examined 26 mobile apps that are available in Norway and allow users to purchase stocks, funds, and cryptocurrencies. Our goal was to identify any design strategies that may be deemed unethical. We detected several methods or deceptive tactics deliberately devise to evade the purpose of GDPR. Nearly all the studied apps incorporate dark patterns to varying degrees, and the manipulation level using these practices differs between bank and non-bank apps. Banks have more transparent apps with fewer dark patterns. They give more importance to safeguarding users' personal information than non-bank fintech companies and are less likely to exploit the data shared by users. Non-bank apps display more intrusive data policies and subpar default settings than banks. They utilize deceptive practices to conceal pricing, encourage user interaction, and dissuade users from exiting the platform.

Keywords: Dark Pattern · Deceptive Design · Financial Technology · Fintech · Investment Apps · Dark Finance

1 Introduction

Advancements in financial technology (fintech) have transformed the way ordinary individuals manage their assets by enabling investment through mobile applications. Fintech has made investing enjoyable and exciting; however, it can lead to impulsive and reckless investment behavior. While certain interaction design features contribute to a more enjoyable user experience, they may also introduce bias in users' decision-making when investing. Researchers have been studying design practices that manipulate user behavior to benefit businesses. These practices are collectively known as dark patterns [2, 6]. Gray et al. [6] define them as methods used to deceive and exploit users by tricking them, for example, into signing up for things they did not intend to or buying things they did not want to.

The term 'dark pattern' was initially coined and popularized by Brignull [2] in 2010, but he has since redefined it as 'deceptive design'. Patterns have been employed in various fields to capture solutions to recurring issues [2]. Since the research area on dark patterns is still developing, there are variations in how researchers define and categorize

J. Abdelnour Nocera et al. (Eds.): INTERACT 2023, LNCS 14142, pp. 339–348, 2023.
https://doi.org/10.1007/978-3-031-42280-5_20

them within the existing literature [2–4, 6, 7]. Although researchers often use Brignull's categories as a starting point, they frequently modify and redefine the definitions of the various types to improve understanding of dark patterns. Unfortunately, the categories can be ambiguous and often overlap between studies, making it challenging to measure dark patterns objectively. Researchers continue to build upon and refine the existing knowledge of dark patterns [e.g., 6, 8].

After the adoption of the General Data Protection Regulation (GDPR) in 2016, the research community began paying more attention to privacy-related dark patterns. Initially, researchers focused on identifying and categorizing deceptive designs, but recent work has become more specialized. For example, Bösch et al. [1] studied privacy-specific dark patterns to extract as much user data as possible and discovered new patterns in this area. Soe et al. [11] analyzed dark patterns in cookie consent forms on online newspaper outlets in Scandinavia. They built on the taxonomy of Gray et al. [6], aiming to define dark patterns so that they are easily identifiable and detectable by a computer, thus making dark patterns automatically quantifiable. In another study, Mathur et al. [8] used an automated tool to search for dark patterns in 11,000 shopping websites, identifying 1,818 instances, and developed a taxonomy that connects similarly Gray et al.'s [6] dark patterns with five strategies for online manipulation and six types of cognitive biases they exploit. In our study, we adopted taxonomies developed based on the most cited papers in the literature, including [1, 2, 6], and [8]. The taxonomy we developed based on these papers is given in the Appendix.

Dark patterns can cause significant harm to users, such as financial losses and compromised personal data. They generally involve leading users away from their intended actions and influencing their decision-making in ways not in their best interests. Although there are many examples of how app design influences decision-making, there needs to be more research on how design features in finance management apps affect users' investments. To this end, we conducted a descriptive analysis of 26 investment applications that allow users to purchase stocks, funds, and cryptocurrencies in Norway. Our goal was to identify deceptive designs and explore their effects. The research was limited to the Norwegian fintech market, as not all investment apps available worldwide can be used in Norway. Consequently, we scrutinized only relevant bank and non-bank apps legally accessible in Norway.

2   Implementation of the Dark Pattern Taxonomy

The study's primary goal was to identify dark patterns present in a group of 26 capital market mobile apps available in Norway. The study aimed to determine the proportion of apps using dark patterns, the number of dark patterns utilized by each app, the purpose and location of these patterns, and the most common types [10]. These apps included Bitcoin Wallet, Binance, Coinbase, CoinGecko, Crypto.com Exchange, DNB, eToro, Firi, FTX crypto trading, Gjensidige, Handelsbanken, IBKR Mobile, Koinal, Kraken, Kron, KuCoin, Nordea Bank, Nordnett, OKX, Plus500 Trading, Sbanken, Sparebank 1, Sparebanken Møre, Storebrand Mine penger, StormGain, and Trading 212. The selection of apps for analysis was based on their capacity for users to invest in funds, stocks, and cryptocurrencies, regardless of whether they utilized various fintech business models.

First, we focused on analyzing banking apps that provide online brokerage services. To identify these apps, we used lists of Norwegian banks, such as Finansportalen [5] and Neste Bank [9], and carefully examined all Norwegian banks to see which ones offered investment products. We then filtered out banks that did not have apps allowing users to open brokerage accounts and invest in financial instruments. Finally, the banking apps that met these criteria were downloaded and tested for the study.

Although banks are the primary destination for investment services in Norway, there are trading platforms that operate differently from traditional banks. These platforms, also known as shadow banks (i.e., non-banks), do not offer standard customer services like bank accounts, loans, or credit cards but provide platforms for trading securities. Even though these platforms appear similar to investment banks' services and platforms, it is crucial to examine how they differ from each other and how they utilize mobile app features. Therefore, trading platforms that enable users to purchase stocks, funds, and cryptocurrencies, but are not provided by banks, were also considered in the study. To be eligible for inclusion, platforms had to allow users to create an account using Norwegian credentials. Apps that were excessively basic (with only one or two features), received poor ratings (with a rating of 3.5 stars or less in the App Store), or were clearly in the early stages of development were excluded.

We followed a process that involved setting up brokerage accounts, exploring and buying financial products, and carefully scrutinizing each screen. We analyzed each screen encountered during this process to identify any designs that could be considered unethical, and any instances of dark patterns were highlighted, referenced, explained, and categorized.

3 Found Dark Patterns

Forced Registration. Many investment apps employ a deceptive design practice called forced registration. Out of the apps that were examined, 10 allow access to basic content without any registration, four require an email address for demo mode access, and 11 require complete account registration, which involves providing personal identification through a national ID or passport, disclosing address and phone number, and completing questionnaires about intended activities on the platform. Norwegian banks use BankID, a national solution for multi-factor online identification, to authenticate their users. International apps usually ask users to provide identification information manually and sometimes submit selfies or images of their ID documents. Nordea's app falls somewhere in the middle, initially appearing to lock out users until they become a customer. The app's welcome page only displays two options: 'Log in' or 'Become a customer'. However, a demo function is concealed behind the login button in a menu.

Hidden Information. All of the apps have some degree of hiding information in their privacy policy and terms and conditions documents, but the type and severity of information hidden vary. Common characteristics of these legal documents are that they are lengthy, difficult to read and navigate, and often written in legal terminology. The documents are typically in the form of PDFs that have to be downloaded or accessed through a web browser. Information is deemed hidden in this context if it is relevant to the user during app usage but only accessible through these documents, not on the app's actual interface. Furthermore, users can access these documents through links on the landing screen or the menu, which nine cases are positioned at the bottom of the page in small, light-colored type.

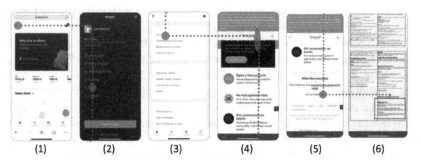

| (1) | (2) | (3) | (4) | (5) | (6) |

Fig. 1. Locating fees on the eToro application.

It is typical for apps to acknowledge the existence of inactivity fees in their documents, but the specific amount of these fees often needs to be disclosed. For instance, eToro only mentions their inactivity fee at the end of a lengthy PDF document that users need to navigate through six steps to find (Fig. 1). The app's fees page only listed the products for which fees are not charged, with only one line dedicated to locating the actual products that incur fees. Another app's terms and conditions document stated that 'Client Money' would be terminated if the account remained inactive for six years.

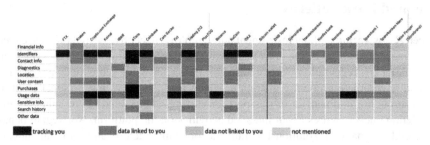

Fig. 2. Platforms and personal data policies.

The policies related to cookies and data are often concealed within lengthy documents that are difficult for users to read and have to be downloaded. Commonly, these documents disclose poor default settings and how user data is shared with third-party entities. In nine apps, the data policies are hidden from view, either by removing the content entirely from the app or making links to external pages challenging to locate (Fig. 2). Nine apps demonstrate transparency and clarity in their use of personal data, providing users with clear information on the reasons for collecting and sharing data and offering simple opt-out options.

None of the commission-free platforms openly discuss or provide clear details about their execution policies regarding payment for order flow (PFOF). They tend to present this information in a vague manner, often hidden within complex legal language (as shown in Fig. 3a). However, when we closely analyzed these policies, we discovered discrepancies between the statements made in the policies and the information advertised on the platforms.

False Hierarchy. Besides the common practice of hiding fees, the false hierarchy pattern is utilized to deceive regarding the fees. For example, eToro prioritizes the promotion of its free products by allocating significant space, utilizing large fonts, and employing vivid colors (Fig. 1). Conversely, the statement 'other fees may apply' is presented in a basic fashion, isolated from the free products section, and is not hyperlinked. This strategy downplays the significance of the fees and could result in users ignoring them.

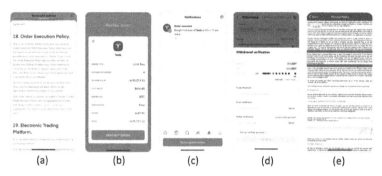

Fig. 3. Dark patterns detected in various apps.

Hidden Cost. Apps typically present an estimated price to users during the order placement process, but the actual charge may vary from what is shown (Fig. 3b). This lack of transparency about the actual cost of the trade is compounded by the absence of feedback on the execution quality of orders, which together comprise a dark pattern. This practice was identified on all PFOF platforms, all of which are apps, except for Norwegian banks. Norwegian banks usually charge a brokerage or platform fee, which is clearly indicated in the pricing of each product.

Additional Costs. Another strategy used by platforms to charge fees while appearing to offer free services is by imposing additional costs. They claim that they do not charge a brokerage fee but instead charge a currency exchange fee. However, this practice could have been acceptable if most platforms were upfront about disclosing these fees to users early in the process (Fig. 3b). Platforms that do not resort to this dark pattern explicitly state their fees during account registration and furnish a link for users to examine pricing.

Intermediate Currency. Using intermediate currency is a common practice in investment because international money exchange is an essential aspect of the process. Different platforms utilize various currencies in different places, complicating the user's ability to determine the total cost of their investments (Fig. 3c). Another way that apps can take advantage of currency is by stating their fees in cryptocurrency, such as Ethereum or their proprietary digital currency, making it challenging for users to predict the cost of essential services (Fig. 3d). eToro, for instance, presents conversion fees in PIPs, which is a function of USD and is commonly used in professional settings to describe forex currency pairs.

Bad Defaults. Nine applications have poor default settings, which include automatic sign-ups for marketing content, excessive disclosure of personal information, and acceptance of invasive cookie policies (Fig. 3e). These settings are typically located in the settings menu, but in some cases, they are only mentioned in the terms and conditions documents without any option to modify the default.

Forced Continuity. Three platforms implement the forced continuity or roach model using inactivity fees, which charge users who do not trade actively, with fees ranging from 1 to 10$ per month, to keep them engaged (Fig. 4a). It's important to note that if users sell their investments all at once, they could incur losses. The dark pattern of forced continuity also manifests in immortal accounts, which are difficult or impossible to delete. Eight apps have such accounts and deleting them often requires users to contact customer service or follow a complex multi-step process that needs to be clearly outlined on the platform. It is also unclear whether deleting the account would erase all user data and the implications of deleting it.

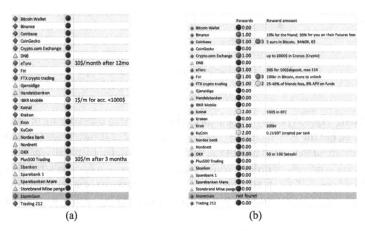

Fig. 4. Inactivity fees (a) and earn cryptocurrency features (b) in various apps.

Gamification. Many cryptocurrency apps incentivize users to complete tasks within the app, such as taking a course about cryptocurrencies in exchange for earning, winning, or obtaining coins (Fig. 4b). These apps use gamification techniques such as daily check-ins, completing 'learn-to-earn' courses, and practicing depositing or trading to make the experience more engaging. However, this type of gamification may be considered a dark pattern because users may only feel comfortable with cryptocurrencies after investing significant time and effort in earning them. Figure 5 shows instances of reward features in cryptocurrency apps, with ten apps offering rewards, including referral rewards, rewards for investing specific amounts, and rewards for completing tasks. Three of these apps provide multiple ways to earn rewards.

Among 10 apps that offer rewards, four disclose the monetary value of the reward in local currency or USD, even though the reward is paid in the app's preferred cryptocurrency. One app offers either 50 or 100 Satoshi, based on the task, while another uses Chronos as its reward unit. One app states all rewards in USDT, which is a cryptocurrency linked to the US dollar, and two apps provide rewards in the form of a percentage of the fees that their referred friends paid without disclosing the actual fee amounts.

Fig. 5. Inactivity fees and earn cryptocurrency features in various apps.

Social Proof. The presence of social proof is evident through testimonials displayed on Kron and eToro. These testimonials are selected from unidentified sources and showcased to increase credibility. eToro further employs social proof by indicating the number of people who copied the portfolios of its influencers to enhance their trustworthiness.

Disguised Ads. Several apps use deceptive tactics in their 'earning' section, enticing users to invite their friends to invest in exchange for a monetary reward ranging from just over 8 USD to 30 USD for each new user recruited. However, all seven applications have a condition that the recruited friend must invest a certain amount in unlocking the reward, which ranges from 879 to 1000 NOK. In most apps, both the referrer and the friend receive the reward if the conditions are met, with the exception of one Norwegian bank that offers only a referral bonus. Additionally, disguised ads in the form of inbox messages are found in three apps. These apps also include disguised advertisements in the inbox section, where clients typically receive important messages such as order notifications and purchase summaries. Some of these ads are nagging pop-ups that could be deactivated in the notification settings, while others could not be deactivated at all.

Aesthetic Manipulation. The practice of aesthetic manipulation involves highlighting certain positive words or phrases taken out of context and using them to hide negative information in the rest of the text. This is frequently seen in the pricing sections of the apps, where words like 'zero commission', 'no extra fees', 'free', and 'no hidden costs' are emphasized, while the costs that users need to pay are presented in the small, light grey text that is difficult to read. This tactic is often used in combination with the use of complex language to bury information that the platform does not want users to pay attention to. eToro's FAQ section is a good example of this, where they answer the question 'Is eToro free?' by first highlighting the free services they offer before vaguely mentioning that they charge 'fees for some trades and withdrawals', without specifying which ones, and that they also have an inactivity fee.

4 Summary

This study aimed to determine how fintech firms utilized dark patterns to influence investors' financial decision-making and behavior. In general, the findings suggest a divergence between bank apps and fintech apps operating as shadow banks (i.e., non-banks). Although dark patterns are present in most of the apps examined in the study, the findings suggest that banks are less inclined to use dark patterns to manipulate their users than shadow bank fintech. The dark patterns employed by banks are also less likely to directly aim at enticing users to spend more on brokerage services. While banks often require users to register for services before allowing access to app features, non-bank platforms employ dark patterns to hide pricing, retain user engagement, and discourage users from leaving the platform. Several apps utilize deceptive design techniques and marketing strategies to entice users to start spending on their platforms, in addition to simplifying the process of getting started with the app.

Non-banks exhibit more invasive data policies and poor default settings than banks. Users are more likely to engage in risky financial behavior, such as trading CFDs, with shadow bank fintech, as banks are more regulated and transparent about their services. They are also more likely to suffer from poor order execution, incur unexpected fees, or be unable to withdraw their profits since pricing information is not revealed to them. The results show that banks prioritize the protection of users' personal information more than non-bank fintech does and are less prone to exploiting the data shared by users.

Platforms utilizing the PFOF model employ deceptive design to make users believe that trading is commission-free. They achieve this by hiding pricing information from users. The platforms also offer rewards to incentivize users to deposit money, trade frequently, and recruit their friends to join. However, users need to be provided with full information about potential fees for leaving the platform or for inactivity. These platforms have poor default settings that lead users to unknowingly share too much personal data and receive excessive marketing communications. While some banks are transparent and helpful in guiding customers on how to delete their accounts and personal data, one bank follows a roach model where such information is not easily accessible. This practice is more prevalent among non-bank platforms.

This study provides a descriptive analysis of the extent to which investment apps involve deceptive design practices. Especially non-bank applications should be more sensitive and careful about the design practices that might affect investors' financial decision-making and behavior. It is important to note that deceptive design practices may cause financial losses to users. In the study, several apps were not included in the sample due to their support of only CFD trading, which is considered an extremely risky financial instrument and not a form of investment. These apps were deemed out of scope. Considerably more work needs to be done by including all investment-related apps to obtain a more comprehensive understanding of financial dark patterns.

Acknowledgments. This paper was based on the master's thesis of the first author conducted under the direction of the second author.

Appendix

A dark pattern taxonomy developed based on the most cited papers of literature.

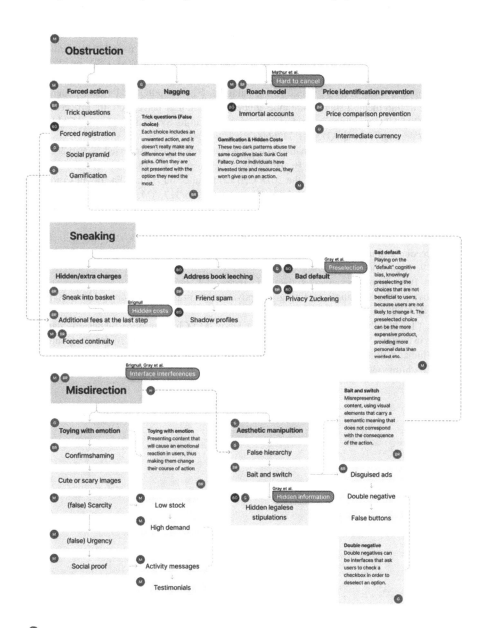

- ⬤ BR — Brignull's original dark patterns (Brignull, 2018)
- ⬤ M — Dark patterns contributed by Mathur et al. (2019)
- ⬤ G — Dark patterns contributed by Gray et al. (2018)
- ⬤ BÖ — Dark patterns contributed by Bösch et al. (2016)

References

1. Bösch, C., Erb, B., Kargl, F., Kopp, H., Pfattheicher, S.: Tales from the dark side: privacy dark strategies and privacy dark patterns. Proc. Priv. Enhancing Technol. **2016**(4), 237–254 (2016)
2. Brignull, H.: Deceptive design. https://www.deceptive.design/. Accessed 20 Mar 2023
3. Conti, G., Sobiesk, E.: Malicious interface design: exploiting the user. In: Proceedings of the 19th International Conference on World Wide Web, North Carolina, USA, pp. 271–280. ACM (2010). https://doi.org/10.1145/1772690.1772719
4. Di Geronimo, L., Braz, L., Fregnan, E., Palomba, F., Bacchelli, A.: UI dark patterns and where to find them: a study on mobile applications and user perception. In: Proceedings of the 2020 CHI Conference on Human Factors in Computing Systems, pp. 1–14. ACM (2020). https://doi.org/10.1145/3313831.3376600
5. Finansportalen. https://www.finansportalen.no/plassere-penger/. Accessed 22 Feb 2022
6. Gray, C.M., Kou, Y., Battles, B., Hoggatt, J., Toombs, A.L.: The dark (patterns) side of UX design. In: Proceedings of the 2018 CHI Conference on Human Factors in Computing Systems, pp. 1–14. ACM (2018). https://doi.org/10.1145/3173574.3174108
7. Lewis, C.: Monetary dark patterns. In: Irresistible Apps, pp. 111–117. Apress, Berkeley, CA (2014). https://doi.org/10.1007/978-1-4302-6422-4_10
8. Mathur, A., et al.: Dark patterns at scale: findings from a crawl of 11K shopping websites. In: Proceedings of the ACM on Human-Computer Interaction (CSCW), vol. 3, pp. 1–32. ACM (2019). https://doi.org/10.1145/3359183
9. Neste Bank. https://nestebank.no/banker/. Accessed 22 Feb 2022
10. Rakovic, I: Dark finance: exploring deceptive design in investment apps. Master's Thesis, NTNU (2022)
11. Soe, T.H., Nordberg, O.E., Guribye, F., Slavkovik, M.: Circumvention by design - dark patterns in cookie consent for online news outlets. In: Proceedings of the 11th Nordic Conference on Human-Computer Interaction: Shaping Experiences, Shaping Society, pp. 1–12. ACM (2020). https://doi.org/10.1145/3419249.3420132

Elements that Influence Transparency in Artificial Intelligent Systems - A Survey

Deepa Muralidhar[1]([✉]) [iD], Rafik Belloum[2] [iD], Kathia Marçal de Oliveira[2] [iD], and Ashwin Ashok[1] [iD]

[1] Georgia State University, Atlanta, Ga 30302, USA
deepa.muralidhar@gmail.com
[2] Univ. Polytechnique Hauts-de-France, LAMIH, CNRS, UMR 8201, 59313 Valenciennes, France

Abstract. Artificial Intelligence (AI) models operate as black boxes where most parts of the system are opaque to users. This reduces the user's trust in the system. Although the Human-Computer Interaction (HCI) community has proposed design practices to improve transparency, work that provides a mapping of these practices and interactive elements that influence AI transparency is still lacking. In this paper, we conduct an in-depth literature survey to identify elements that influence transparency in the field of HCI. Research has shown that transparency allows users to have a better sense of the accuracy, fairness, and privacy of a system. In this context, much research has been conducted on providing explanations for the decisions made by AI systems. Researchers have also studied the development of interactive interfaces that allow user interaction to improve the explanatory capability of systems. This literature review provides key insights about transparency and what the research community thinks about it. Based on the insights gained we gather that a simplified explanation of the AI system is key. We conclude the paper with our proposed idea of representing an AI system, which is an amalgamation of the AI Model (algorithms), data (input and output, including outcomes), and the user interface, as visual interpretations (e.g. Venn diagrams) can aid in understanding AI systems better and potentially making them more transparent.

Keywords: Transparency · Explainablity · Usability · HCI · AI models · Data · Interpretability

1 Introduction

Machine-learning based systems that make predictions or recommendations to its users and explain why a decision was made increases the user's understanding of the system and improves the overall user-experience of the system. Transparency is an explanation given by a system on how it works or why an algorithm made a decision [7,32]. Automated systems using AI are helping humans make important decisions in areas such as recidivism risk assessment to identifying qualified

© The Author(s), under exclusive license to Springer Nature Switzerland AG 2023
J. Abdelnour Nocera et al. (Eds.): INTERACT 2023, LNCS 14142, pp. 349–358, 2023.
https://doi.org/10.1007/978-3-031-42280-5_21

applicants using applicant tracking systems. For a system to be transparent, users need a clear follow-up explanation why a decision was taken and if the system worked correctly [4]. These systems make decision or recommendations based on data input, implicit rules and decisions made by machine learning models [36]. When the user of the AI system receives the algorithm's output, they are unable to understand how or why the inputs resulted in the outcome. As a result the end-users when they do not understand the decision, feel discriminated against and demand explanations for the decisions taken [3].

When we think of an AI system being transparent, we expect that the system is interpretable and explainable. Interpretability is being able to explain what the AI model and the algorithms does [6]. Explanations help understand the data used by the model and they expose how the data used by the algorithms logically arrived at a decision and provide additional information to the user about the expected output. Explanations improve user trust and increase the transparency of the system [11,33]. With regards to transparent systems, user interfaces are a less discussed aspect, but are critical to this discussion since they display the outcomes of the model [9,14]. While using interactive user friendly interfaces users feel they have a better insight into the outcomes of the AI system.

- We conducted a survey of 223 research papers around HCI and AI around explainability, interpretability and transparency. We then conducted an in depth review and identified 48 papers that addressed our research questions.
- We identified three elements that impact transparency of a system. The AI model, the algorithms that work with the model and the data (the input and the output) that influence the outcome the model and interactive user interfaces.

2 Survey Approach and Methodology

AI systems that exhibit human-like intelligence are being used to do general tasks that humans were doing. The problem is it is difficult to understand or predict the decision or recommendations of these systems. In such cases not only do user's lose trust in the system, but as a society our overall trust in these AI systems goes down [11]. We conducted a review of papers to understand better the state of the art on transparency in AI systems. Our perspective is that making systems transparent may help us understand and control these AI systems. Our research work started by trying to find an answer to the question RQ1: *"what the elements that influence transparency in machine learning systems"*. We examined and downloaded 223 papers that were relevant and placed them in content relevant folders. Then we conducted an in-depth research and identified 48 papers. We used search terms such as: **HCI** AND **AI** AND *Transparency*,OR *explainability* OR *mental models* OR *user interfaces*.

We followed an iterative process in two phases(see Fig. 1). In phase I we addressed RQ1. As we read through these papers and found answers to this question, we identified two other related research questions analysed in phases II and III: RQ2: *"how is transparency different from explainability?"* and RQ3:

"what kinds of explanations will authentically improve transparency?". As the next step, we examined each of the 48 research papers and classified them based on each of the three research questions. We found different definitions for transparency depending on the context it operates. We define transparency as **"the ability of the AI system to be able to convey clearly what it can and cannot do"** [36].

Our research was done using Google scholar and selecting papers after 2000. For understanding on work around artificial intelligence and software engineering usability principles, we examined papers around 1990. Topics related to HCI and the concept of Mental Models included papers that were published in the 1980 s.s. The following HCI areas were identified in the papers: IUI (Intelligent User Interfaces), HCAI (Human Centered AI) and HAII (Human-AI Intelligence). For every paper that we reviewed we looked at the abstract,introduction and discussion sections. If we found the paper to be relevant we saved it to folders and revisited them again for a detailed study according to the research question it addressed. By following this process we found a research gap. Within AI systems the design of user-interfaces that follow usability principles so that they have effective interaction with users is an open research area. Further research in the area of Intelligent User Interfaces helped us outline our research agenda.

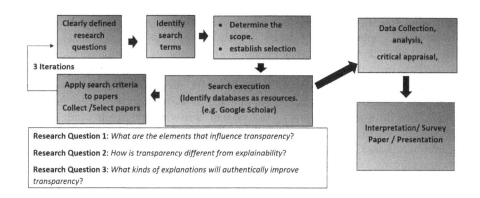

Fig. 1. Methodology used to conduct the review.

3   RQ1: "What Are the Elements that Influence Transparency?"

When considering a system that is "AI-enabled" through machine learning, independent of the domain it functions, there are three elements that impact the transparency of a system [13,34,36], as follows:

- **AI Model and Algorithms** - Transparency is an understanding of the mechanism by which the model works [6]. Such a model is an interpretable model [37]. For a model to be trustworthy we are interested not only about accuracy and accuracy rates, but also the examples for which the model makes accurate decisions.(e.g. are outcomes biased towards a gender, race, etc.?) Also, there is mismatch between a human's need for reasoning and explanation and the algorithm's ability to provide this information in an understandable fashion [3].

- **Data** - The data is the input and the output of an AI system [27]. The output data includes the outcome such as a decision or a recommendation produced by an AI model. Building operational data is part of the process used to prepare training data that impact the performance of the machine learning systems [11].
- **Interactive User Interfaces** - The third element in AI systems that impact transparency is are user-interfaces that facilitate interaction between AI systems and humans. By developing methodologies and building tools that improve the intelligent interactive pieces of the AI system, user interfaces should be such that users intuitively understand the AI system's reasoning related to its outcome [18]. For example, when the user sees a direct relationship between their action that conveyed a desired goal and the AI system responding to that action and satisfying the goal, the system does not have to explain its reasoning on *how* it understood the user's goal [17].

Discussion A fundamental machine learning problem is that when a computer learns from the training data, it produces an outcome, and is presented to the user as a recommendation or decision without any regard for human comprehension. This lack of transparency is not just because of the poor user interface design that could mislead the user, but it is as a result of the actual design of the automated tasks [16]. The more accurate an AI model and its algorithms are in their prediction, the greater its opacity. Transparency is lost in this process [8]. The data that is input to the system is used to train the model on its outcome. Biases that are introduced during this training process can be seen in the system's behaviour, and as a result, it is quite likely that the decision or recommendation by the system is unfair [1,11]. Solutions to such problems lie in data transparency which discloses the data and the metadata used, as well as the purpose of the data within the AI system [1]. Similarly, feature transparency reveals the data points used by the AI systems and their origin [2,35]. Users regardless of their expertise want data-centric explanations as it improves their trust in the system. The users are less wary and trust the system more when there are text and visual explanations presented using virtual agents [3]. In particular, users benefit by having explanations that use user interface elements and design patterns [18]. Transparency can be increased by designing intelligent interfaces that adapt usability principles for machine-learning based AI systems increasing its interactivity [28]. The problem is user needs change depending on the AI system. Recommender systems studies found that designing systems that are efficient, that deliver effective outcomes help users make faster and good decisions, and makes the user experience more enjoyable. Users rate such systems to be easier to use [30]. User studies have found that using virtual agents that had a speech recognition system along with a visual, interactive interface increased the transparency and trust of the AI system [4]. The interaction between the users and the AI system should be rich using natural language, providing human-understandable explanations and use any other forms of communication that are effective [17,23].

4   RQ2: "How Is Transparency Different from Explainability?"

When a system is transparent it is explainable [11]. However, a system that provides an explanation for a decision may not be transparent. Not all questions seek honest explanations and explanations that do not reveal the true reason for a decision made by an AI system do not aid in the design of a honest transparent system. "Dark patterns" in the explanations make assumptions about an AI model [12]. Assumptions impact the transparency of the system negatively [11]. Additionally, explanations that have dark patterns embedded within the user interface do not improve transparency for user [5]. The phrasing of explanations and the methods in which they are embedded within the interface makes a pattern *dark*. Often explanations that are not valid or accurate or just not useful, increase user trust and convey a sense of transparency just because they exist. Transparency of this kind is known as placebo transparency [10]. Systems that display such explanations provide a false sense of certainty in the system. In other situations, users do not pay close attention to the explanations and view the system as transparent because they are not highly motivated about the context in which the AI system functions. Explanations given to such users called heuristic cueing do not increase the transparency of the system [21]. Without a standard for transparency in AI systems, it can be easy to deceive users about system accuracy or quality of the AI system [32].

Discussion. AI experts and domain experts who have the know-how about the actual mechanics regarding the AI models provide explanations for the layman about the AI model making assumptions about the behaviour of the model. For an AI model to be transparent it could be interpretable. Often a model that is interpretable is considered to be transparent or "glass-box". Explanations about the outcomes such as *why* and *how* the system arrived at a decision can increase trust in the system [10]. Since transparency is a positive feature for AI to have, users may rate an AI system more positively if they see it provides explanations for its decisions, even without carefully examining the explanations' quality. When individuals are "mindless," not the content of an explanation but its explanatory form becomes persuasive [21]. In these cases, transparency just functions as a heuristic cue [21]. AI system designers, while designing explanations should keep in mind how users perceive explanations, the value the explanations can provide to the user and ensure that they are easy to process.

5   RQ3: "What Kinds of Explanations Will Authentically Improve Transparency?"

If the user who watches the system's behavior and understands the explanations provided by the system, is able to explain the working of the system with no errors, then the system output is transparent [15]. Explanations that model how human's explain decisions to each other are likely to be effective [24]. Explanations can be classified into four categories, one that explains the terminology, that which explains the control or strategy, which justifies or supports the outcome and that which can trace a line of reasoning for the outcome [7]. To build a transparent system, and increase trust users, developers and domain experts should be able to provide explanations that answer questions such as *what* was the reasoning behind the outcome of the AI system [9]. *Where* did the data for the AI model come from [33]. *How* was the data collected, and *how* did the AI model arrive at the decision. Experiments conducted on context-aware system and found explanations to"why the system" and "why not" explanations were useful in increasing user trust when compared to "how" and "what if" explanations [20]. Further the *why* explanations helped users understand how the system performed when compared to *why not* explanations [19].

A Well-Designed Explanation Should Be Complete and Sound. A complete and sound explanation that explains how the data is processed, addresses the *why* questions, and those that explain the internal data structures in a program address the *what* questions [13]. Soundness is defined as, *"nothing but the truth"* while Completeness is *"the whole truth"* [19]. The **what if** and **how** questions address the *gulf of execution*, which is the difference in what can be done with the system and what the user perceives can be done with the system [29]. The **what,why,why not** questions address the *gulf of evaluation*, which is difference between what the user perceives to be the functionality of the system and the user's expectation of the system. Users create mental models of the systems they use which aid in observing the effectiveness of the explanations [22]. Often there is a difference in the user's perception of the system and the actual conceptual model of the system. This could be because of "persistence of mental model", that is users apply their prior knowledge while using the system and do not pay careful attention to the explanations [29]. To make sure that users gain from these explanations, we have to ask the right questions. Explanations that bring the user's mental model closer to the actual working model minimizing these gulfs are explanations that improve transparency.

Explanations that Clarify What Is at Stake. This ensure higher levels of transparency of the system and increase authenticity and trust in systems [38]. Algorithms that have a high impact are considered high stakes. In such cases transparency standards should be sensitive to considering explanations that state what is at stake more valuable than other kinds of explanations.

Interactive Visualizations. Such as concentric circles, saliency maps, Venn diagrams and others aim to convey the outcome and the impact of the outcome to the user [37]. This idea supports the well-known adage, *"a picture is worth 1000 words".* Interactive AI systems benefit from explanations related to questions such as *how* and *what if* [20]. A problem with textual explanations is that they can overwhelm the user with too much information and often the language is English and hence not universally accessible. Hybrid explanations that include visualizations supplemented with text increase the user's understanding being an effective way of presenting explanations while reducing the cognitive load [30]. They improve the usability of the system and users perceive these systems to be transparent.

Discussion. Post hoc interpretable explanations responses discuss how and why a system arrived at a decision [25]. The trust a user places on a system is closely related to the usability of the system and the explanations provided by it [14]. Richard Feyman's popular quote, *if you can't explain it to a six year old, you don't really understand it"* is a good test for explanations [36]. The problem with such explanations is that they may not accurately describe the AI model's decisions. User studies have shown that to be complete is more important than being accurate(sound) [19]. Explanations should therefore try to provide a complete picture related to the output within established expectations of the system [31].

6   Findings on Open Questions for Future Work

Transparency in machine learning systems is about theoretically examining what powerful machines can reveal about their decision making [16]. A system is said to be opaque if it is easier to experiment with it than understand it [26]. The user interface helps the user interact with the system and can help understand the reasoning of the AI model on how it arrived at the decision. The idea of making available different levels of transparency is an important design decision [9,30]. We use Fig. 2 to define concepts and their role in transparency considering the three element identified in RQ1. Transparency can be achieved by implementing interpretability and explainability, explainability and usability or interpretability and usability within the AI systems. The issue is that interpretability cannot generate trust by itself [13]. In order to gain the trust of the user, interpretability should be accompanied by complete explanations. Interpretability is defined as when the user with the aid of the explanations provided by the AI system understands the decision made by the system [34]. This aids the system's transparency. We present that *Explainable models are interpretable by default, but the reverse is not always true.* is only part of the story [13]. For a system to be fully transparent the user interface for these AI system should follow usability guidelines. In human-human interactions, some of a human's actions are intuitive enough that they do not need explanations [18]. Using usability principles can help improve human-machine interactions [24]. A developer often wonders, *Is the system working as designed?* [25,27]. Systems that have an ability to interact with people using explanations can use the knowledge provided to improve the decision making process. When explanations are communicated to the user following usability principles, the user understands the reasoning of the decision made easily and system's transparency increases. An approach to address the limitations of explanations is to design systems where the architecture simplifies the interpretation of the model's behaviour and presents its outcomes to the user [13]. This sort of *interactive machine learning* and ease of use of the system lends itself to being transparent, since the user can verify *what* the system is doing [14].

Putting all the above ideas together we propose that transparency is the intersection between AI models, its algorithms, the data and its interactive user interfaces. In such a scenario, the machine provides enough information so that the user is not only satisfied, but they are willing to take responsibility for the decision [13]. We acknowledge that is still an open area of research since it current XAI research does not properly address how users interact and visualize the explanations provided by the AI systems [22].

7   Conclusion

In this paper we presented our insights gained from a literature review based on the notion of answering three research questions that we set for ourselves to understand the impact of transparency on AI systems. Due to space constraints, all the papers we reviewed are not listed. They can be provided under request. We conclude that the AI model and its associated algorithms, the data, and the user interface of the AI system together enable complete transparency of the system. Our future work (see Fig. 2) is to find a way to quantify transparency for two classes of AI systems such as music, book, recommender systems, conversational AI agents, or grammar checkers, and have visualizations that inform users about the level of transparency of an AI system.

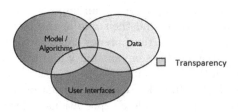

Fig. 2. The three elements that impact transparency, where intersection of all represents highest level of transparency.

References

1. Anik, A.I., Bunt, A.: Data-centric explanations: explaining training data of machine learning systems to promote transparency. In: Proceedings of the 2021 CHI Conference on Human Factors in Computing Systems (2021)

2. Bertino, E., Merrill, S., Nesen, A.: A multidimensional approach. Computer, Redefining data transparency (2019)
3. Burrell, J.: How the machine 'thinks': Understanding opacity in machine learning algorithms. Big Data Soc. **3**(1), 2053951715622512 (2016)
4. Cheng, H.F., et al.: Strategies to help non-expert stakeholders, Explaining decision-making algorithms through UI (2019)
5. Chromik, M., Eiband, M., Völkel, S.T., Buschek, D.: Dark patterns of explainability, transparency, and user control for intelligent systems. In: IUI Workshops (2019)
6. Clinciu, M., Hastie, H.: A survey of explainable AI terminology. In: Proceedings of the 1st Workshop on Interactive Natural Language Technology for Explainable Artificial Intelligence, pp. 8–13. Association for Computational Linguistics (2019)
7. Cramer, H., et al.: The effects of transparency on trust and acceptance in interaction with a content-based art recommender. User Model. User-Adapt. Interact. **18**, 455–496 (2008)
8. Diakopoulos, N.A.: Accountability in algorithmic decision making. Commun. ACM **59**(2), 56–62 (2016)
9. Fallon, C.K., Blaha, L.M.: Improving automation transparency: addressing some of machine learning's unique challenges (2018)
10. Ferrario, A., Loi, M., Viganò, E.: In AI we trust incrementally: a multi-layer model of trust to analyze human-artificial intelligence interactions. Philos. Technol. **33**(3), 523–539 (2019). https://doi.org/10.1007/s13347-019-00378-3
11. Ozmen Garibay, O., et al.: Six human-centered artificial intelligence grand challenges. Int. J. Hum.-Comput. Interact. **39**(3), 391–437 (2023)
12. Gilpin, L., Paley, A., Alam, M., Spurlock, S., Hammond, K.: Explanation is not a technical term: the problem of ambiguity in xai (2022)
13. Gilpin, L.H., Bau, D., Yuan, B.Z., Bajwa, A., Specter, M., Kagal, L.: Explaining explanations: an overview of interpretability of machine learning. In: 2018 IEEE 5th International Conference on Data Science and Advanced Analytics (DSAA) (2018)
14. Glass, A., McGuinness, D.L., Wolverton, M.: Toward establishing trust in adaptive agents. In: Proceedings of the 13th International Conference on Intelligent User Interfaces (2008)
15. Gregor, S., Benbasat, I.: Explanations from intelligent systems: theoretical foundations and implications for practice. MIS Q. **23**(4), 497–530 (1999)
16. Hollanek, T.: Ai transparency: a matter of reconciling design with critique. AI & Soc. (2020). https://doi.org/10.1007/s00146-020-01110-y
17. Höök, K.: Steps to take before intelligent user interfaces become real. Interact. Comput. **12**(4), 409–426 (2000)
18. Kirsch, A.: Explain to whom? putting the user in the center of explainable AI. In: Proceedings of the First International Workshop on Comprehensibility and Explanation in AI and ML (2017)
19. Kulesza, T., Stumpf, S., Burnett, M., Yang, S., Kwan, I., Wong, W.K.: Too much, too little, or just right? ways explanations impact end users' mental models. In: 2013 IEEE Symposium on Visual Languages and Human Centric Computing (2013)
20. Lim, B.Y., Dey, A.K., Avrahami, D.: Why and why not explanations improve the intelligibility of context-aware intelligent systems. In: Proceedings of the SIGCHI Conference on Human Factors in Computing Systems (2009)

21. Liu, B.: In AiIwe trust? effects of agency locus and transparency on uncertainty reduction in human-AI interaction. J. Comput.-Med. Commun. **26**(6), 384–402 (2021)
22. Lopes, P., Silva, E., Braga, C., Oliveira, T., Rosado, L.: A review of human and computer-centred methods. Appl. Sci. Xai Syst. Eval. **12**(19), 9423 (2022)
23. Miller, C.: Delegation and transparency: Coordinating interactions so information exchange is no surprise, June 2014
24. Miller, T.: Explanation in artificial intelligence: Insights from the social sciences. Artif. Intell. **267**, 1–38 (2019)
25. Mittelstadt, B., Russell, C., Wachter, S.: Explaining explanations in AI. In: Proceedings of the Conference on Fairness, Accountability, and Transparency (2019)
26. Montavon, G., Lapuschkin, S., Binder, A., Samek, W., Müller, K.-R.: Explaining nonlinear classification decisions with deep taylor decomposition. Pattern Recogn. **65**, 211–222 (2017)
27. Montavon, G., Samek, W., Müller, K.R.: Methods for interpreting and understanding deep neural networks. Digit. Sig. Process. **73**, 1–15 (2018)
28. Nielsen, J.: Enhancing the explanatory power of usability heuristics. In: Proceedings of the SIGCHI conference on Human Factors in Computing Systems, pp. 152–158 (1994)
29. Donald, A.: Norman. Basic Books Inc, The Design of Everyday Things (2002)
30. Ribeiro, M.T., Singh, S. and Guestrin, C.: Why should i trust you?: explaining the predictions of any classifier (2016)
31. Rubin, V.: Ai opaqueness: what makes AI systems more transparent? In: Proceedings of the Annual Conference of CAIS/Actes du congrès annuel de l'ACSI, November 2020
32. Springer, A., Whittaker, S.: Progressive disclosure: when, why, and how do users want algorithmic transparency information? ACM Trans. Interact. Intell. Syst. **10**(4), 1–32 (2020)
33. Tintarev, N., Masthoff, J.: Designing and evaluating explanations for recommender systems (2011)
34. Tomsett, R., Braines, D., Harborne, D., Preece, A., Chakraborty, S.: Supriyo: interpretable to whom? A role-based model for analyzing interpretable machine learning systems, CoRR (2018)
35. van Nuenen, T., Ferrer, X., Such, J.M., Cote, M.: Transparency for whom? assessing discriminatory artificial intelligence. Computer **53**(11), 36–44 (2020)
36. Weller, A.: Transparency: motivations and challenges (2019)
37. Lipton Zachary, C.: The mythos of model interpretability. Queue **16**(3), 31–57 (2018)
38. Zerilli, J., Knott, A., Maclaurin, J., Gavaghan, C.: Transparency in algorithmic and human decision-making: is there a double standard? Philos. Technol. **32**(4), 661–683 (2018). https://doi.org/10.1007/s13347-018-0330-6

Empowering Users: Leveraging Interface Cues to Enhance Password Security

Yasmeen Abdrabou[1,2]([✉]), Marco Asbeck[3], Ken Pfeuffer[4],
Yomna Abdelrahman[2,5], Mariam Hassib[2,6], and Florian Alt[2]

[1] Lancaster University, England, UK
y.abdrabou@lancaster.ac.uk
[2] University of the Bundeswehr Munich, Munich, Germany
[3] LMU Munich, Munich, Germany
[4] Aarhus University, Aarhus, Denmark
[5] European Universities in Egypt, Cairo Governorate, Egypt
[6] Fortiss GmbH, Research Institute of the Free State of Bavaria, Munich, Germany

Abstract. Passwords are a popular means of authentication for online accounts, but users struggle to compose and remember numerous passwords, resorting to insecure coping strategies. Prior research on graphical authentication schemes showed that modifying the interface can encourage more secure passwords. In this study ($N = 59$), we explored the use of implicit (website background and advertisements) and explicit (word suggestions) cues to influence password composition. We found that 60.59% of passwords were influenced by the interface cues. Our work discusses how designers can use these findings to improve authentication interfaces for better password security.

Keywords: Passwords · Authentication · User Interface · Usability

1 Introduction

Up to date, passwords remain the most popular means for authentication [10]. Although different authentication techniques such as behavioral biometrics or facial recognition, it is unlikely that password usage will be eliminated anytime soon [3]. This is due to the advantage of passwords over other techniques such as ease of use, and security [4]. As a result, people have on average 80 accounts they are protecting with an average of 3.5 passwords. This makes password memorability challenging [7].

Numerous methods have been developed to help users obtain stronger passwords. Besides explicit approaches, such as password policies which may force users to create secure passwords, there are also promising implicit attempts to steer the user in a certain direction. Von Zezschwitz et al. [18] presented an interesting approach, where they showed that by carefully choosing a background image to the Android lock pattern, they were able to significantly reduce the use of popular start positions.

In this work, we adopt this approach for text-based passwords. In a remote study, we explore the concept of integrating explicit (i.e. word suggestions to be added to the password) and implicit (i.e. UI elements, advertisements, background images) UI cues on password composition. We found that 60.59% of composed passwords were influenced by the interface cues. To our knowledge, this is the first study exploring the effect of UI cues on password composition.

2   Related Work

The trade-off between usability and security has been the subject of continuous research in both academia and industry. Security experts consider users to be the weaker link in the security of systems because they lack the motivation to create secure passwords. The enormous number of accounts per user (80 on average) [7] makes password memorability challenging. Hence, users create mitigation techniques, such as reusing passwords [13].

To address these problems, researchers have proposed different approaches. Yan et al. [17] suggested using mnemonic phrase-based passwords, integrated into the generated passwords. The results showed that this approach is as secure as random passwords and more secure than regularly chosen passwords. Furthermore, Jermyn et al. [8] suggested altering the order of the chosen password after creating it. Other schemes explored include fictional news headlines [9], word associations [11] or use passphrases [12]. Seitz et al. [14] suggested using the *Decoy Effect* to influence password composition. The authors developed concepts to improve persuasive approaches to nudge users towards stronger password creation. Recent works suggest adding gaze as a behavioral aspect to increase password strength and reduce reuse [1,2].

Another body of research investigates influencing users' password composition. For example, research showed that adding a background image to the authentication screen guided participants to create stronger and lock patterns. For example, Dunphy et al. [5] showed that adding a background picture to the "Draw A Secret" graphical password approach significantly increased the complexity of the drawn passwords. A similar study by Von Zezschwit et al. [18] showed that users choose patterns based on their interest in the geometric properties of the resulting shapes. Hence, the authors implemented an approach to nudge users to create more diverse passwords by adding or animating a background image. Furthermore, Ur et al. [15] implemented a password meter that provides accurate strength measurement and actionable, detailed feedback to users to help them modify their created passwords.

Finally, one work that explored altering text-passwords generation is the research by Forget et al. [6]. They introduced *Persuasive Text Passwords (PTP)*, a text password system that leverages Persuasive Technology principles to influence users to create more secure passwords. After users choose a password during creation, the PTP system improves the password's security by placing randomly-chosen characters at random positions into the password. Users can shuffle the order and position of the randomly-chosen characters until they find a memorable combination. Results showed that the PTP variations significantly improved the security of users' passwords.

Motivated by prior research, in this paper, we will investigate using implicit (i.e., background images) and explicit (i.e., word suggestion) UI cues to influence users' text-password choice on different websites with different protected information sensitivity.

3 User Interface Cues and Password Composition

In this section, we will reflect on the study design and the design choices. This research covers one research question **RQ**, *What are the implications of adding implicit/explicit UI cues on text-password composition?*

3.1 Study Design

To address our research question, we conducted a within-subjects study with remote participants who completed all conditions. Our study had two independent variables: 1) implicit and 2) explicit UI cues, and 1) high and 2) low sensitivity of website information. The dependent variable was the generated passwords. Our study was GDPR compliant, with participants able to opt-out at any time, and their data being deleted. We obtained consent from participants to analyze and share their collected passwords. Eye-tracking data was collected to gain insights into the participants' password choices. Moreover, we collected participants' eye gaze data on the website to map where did they look during the study. Finally, we collected post-study questionnaire that asked participants to reflect on their collected passwords and provide Likert scale responses on how frequently they use PayPal and 9GAG (ranging from 1 "rarely" to 5 "daily").

3.2 User Interface Design and Cues

To investigate the impact of interface cues on password creation, we utilized two different types of cues: 1) implicit and 2) explicit cues. Implicit cues were added to the interface to inspire participants to incorporate them into their passwords, including a background image, advertiser logo, dynamic content, ticking counter for PayPal, and GIFs for 9GAG. Explicit cues suggested a phrase or password that users could use partially or fully to create their passwords. The plain registration webpage included only the website logo, and after 2 s, a fading sentence suggesting a word to make the password more personalized appeared. Users could select two categories of interest from 15 presented at the beginning of the study, such as education, literature, gaming, and others. We used two different websites to assess the influence of data sensitivity levels: PayPal, with high-sensitivity information such as users' full name, address, gender, and bank details, and 9GAG, with almost no personal user information saved. Both websites included three fields to enter: email, password, and password re-entry. Our design was based on the original website designs to collect ecologically valid data, with a password strength meter included to encourage participants to create stronger passwords. Figure 1 shows the different interface designs.

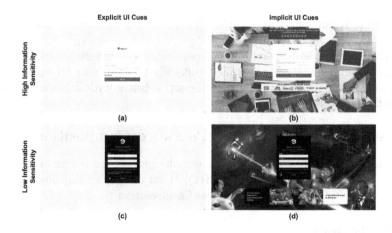

Fig. 1. A screenshot of our implemented two websites with their two variations. (a) and (b) represent high information sensitivity webpages, and (c) and (d) represent low information sensitivity webpages.

3.3 Apparatus and Participants

As our study was remote, we implemented a JavaScript and Node.js website for the study. We used MongoDB Atlas for the database, we hosted it on Heruku and we use GazeRecorder for eye tracking[1]. We also disabled auto-completion for passwords to make sure that participants created the passwords and did not use password meter suggestions.

We recruited 59 participants (30 Females and 29 Males), aged 18 to 54 ($M = 24.67; SD = 5.83$). Participants had diverse nationalities and backgrounds, including, Engineering, law, secretaries, and workers. Participants had different nationalities from USA, Germany, Italy, UK, Turkey, India, and Russia. 12 participants had glasses on, and 7 had corrected vision using lenses. Participants did not have IT security background or experience ($M = 1.5$ on a scale from 1 (novice) to 5 (expert))), and finally, most of our participants use PayPal frequently (71.19%); however, they do not use 9GAG frequently (89.83%).

3.4 Procedure

We recruited participants via university mailing lists and directed them to a study URL. After reading the study's aim and consenting to data collection and analysis, they were directed to an eye-tracking calibration page. Participants were asked to register and sign in on two different websites with two variations, shown in counterbalanced order. Participants were informed that the interfaces are only replicas of the original websites. Afterwards, they filled a demographics form. The study lasted 15 min and participants received 5 Euros as compensation.

---

[1] https://gazerecorder.com/gazecloudapi/.

As this was a deception study, we debriefed participants with the main aim of the study in the end, and they were allowed to opt-out.

3.5   Limitations

Our study was able to overcome some of the limitations of remote studies by collecting ecologically valid data, while also being able to maintain a high level of participant engagement, as evidenced by the lack of reported interruptions. Furthermore, our study showed promising results in terms of short-term password memorability. To build on these findings, future research could explore the long-term effects of using cues to enhance password memorability.

4   Evaluation Methodology

To decide if the interface inspires the passwords, we defined key aspects that would indicate that the password is inspired by the implicit cues such as:

1. Website name or adapted website name (replacing letters with numbers or special characters) (i.e. PayPal30EusikR)
2. Background item names (i.e. Zalando5432)
3. Items description (Name, Color, Size, Position, etc) (i.e. bigEyesCat9)

For the explicit cues, we indicate that the explicit cue inspires the password if the password contained the cue itself (i.e. Sports5432), or a subtopic of the cue (i.e. p!zZa123 when primed with the category. If a password, for example, contained the website name (implicit cue) and the explicit cue, then we consider the longest (in terms of the number of characters) of them, and we use its respective category for counting.

We used a two-step approach for both categories: First, we used an automated process to compare collected passwords to a predefined set of words (e.g., PayPal, pizza, blue). Second, we manually checked the remaining passwords for letter replacements with numbers or special characters (e.g., p!zza, P@yPal).

5   Results

5.1   Passwords Overview

In total, we gathered 236 passwords from participants who agreed to share them, with an average length of 11.5 characters. Table 1 presents a selection of passwords collected for each cue type (implicit and explicit) and website content sensitivity level (high and low). Before analyzing the passwords, we needed to verify that participants had not simply entered random characters. To achieve this, we employed the zxcvbn password meter [16] to evaluate password strength. Our analysis revealed that the average password strength score was 2.43 out of 4 (on a scale from 0 (easily guessable) to 4 (hard to guess)), indicating that participants created passwords that were not easily guessable.

To assess the memorability of the passwords, we asked participants to log in to the websites at the end of the study. Our results showed that 86% of the logins were successful, which suggests that the passwords were reasonably memorable.

Table 1. Sample of the passwords collected per cue type (Implicit and Explicit) and per website content sensitivity (High and Low)

	Implicit Cues (Background)	Explicit Cues (Word Suggestion)
High Information Sensitivity (PayPal)	dbToLate247	TravelSriLanka94
	Paypa!123	MoviesCollection1999!
	Zalando5432	1234Petsarecute
	Netto123123	Fashion@Style.1998
	banking4518	spo3rtsisFun
Low Information Sensitivty (9GAG)	ExploringMemes	CocaColaisGreat
	alienCakememe	Footballer94!
	pokemonfstgen	Studytechnology1
	bigEyesCat9	9GAG4FUNtechnology
	9gagsonde3851	Timis1niceActor

5.2   Password Characteristics per Webpage Content Sensitivity

Looking at the password strength relative to the content sensitivity, we found that high-sensitivity information (PayPal) is slightly stronger (average strength score of 2.59 (on a scale from 0 (very week) to 4 (very strong))) than low-sensitivity webpage (9GAG) 2.34. A repeated-measures ANOVA with Bonferroni correction showed that the content sensitivity significantly affects the created password strength ($F_{2,118} = 4.44$, $P = .037$). We also found that the length of the passwords created for PayPal and 9GAG 11.89 and 11.10 characters, respectively, is another indication of our participants' website sensitivity perception, which confirms the literature [1]. However, stronger passwords can also mean less memorability. Evidence of this is provided by the login success rate, which is 82% for PayPal compared to 89% for 9gag.

5.3   Password Characteristics per UI Cue Type

Implicit cues resulted in slightly stronger passwords (avg. strength score of 2.52) compared to explicit cues (2.41), but this difference was not statistically significant according to a repeated measures ANOVA. Passwords affected by explicit cues were slightly longer than passwords inspired by implicit cues (11.63 vs. 11.36 characters), but the cue type did not have a statistically significant effect on password length. Passwords affected by implicit cues had a higher successful login rate (92%) compared to ones affected by explicit cues (80%).

5.4   Cues Impact on Passwords Generation

Of the 236 passwords collected in our study, 60.59% (143 passwords) were influenced by the interface cues. Of these, 44.76% (64 passwords) were influenced by implicit cues (i.e. background) and 55.24% (79 passwords) by explicit cues (i.e. word suggestion). Our statistical analysis, using repeated measures ANOVA with Bonferroni correction, showed that the type of cue significantly influenced the generated password ($F_{1,118} = 83.904$, $P < .001$). Users' gaze heatmaps on the different interfaces also reflected this finding, as seen in Fig. 2.

Participants created stronger passwords when using interface cues (score of 2.86 on a scale from 0 to 4) compared to not using any cues (score of 2.18), as shown in Fig. 3. Interface cues significantly influenced the strength of passwords (ANOVA $F_{1,59} = 19.98$, $P < .001$). Successful login attempts were associated with passwords inspired by interface cues in 60.89% (123 out of 202) of cases, compared to 39.11% (79 out of 202) of attempts with passwords not influenced by interface cues.

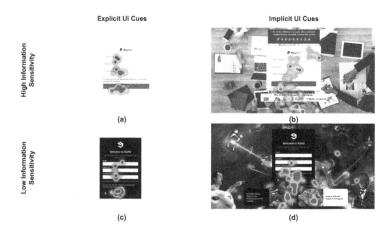

Fig. 2. Eye gaze heatmaps for the four interfaces highlighting P2 gaze data. The heatmaps show that for implicit cues, users looked at background objects that they later used in their passwords. Similarly, for the explicit cues, users who looked at the word suggestion were inspired by it.

For the *High Sensitivity Webpage (PayPal)*, we found that 59.32% (35 out of 59 passwords) of the passwords generated were influenced by the implicit cues, and 79.66% (47 out of 59 passwords) were influenced by the explicit cues. This is slightly higher than the percentages for the *Low Sensitivity Webpage (9GAG)* where we found that 49.15% (29 out of 59 passwords) of the passwords were inspired by the implicit cues and 61.10% (36 out of 59 passwords) were inspired by the explicit cue, comparison can be seen in Fig. 4. However, for both implicit and explicit cues, we could not find a statistically significant effect of the interface cues on the passwords generated according to each information sensitivity level ANOVA test, $P > .05$.

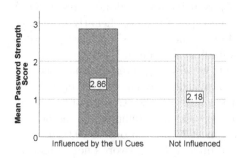

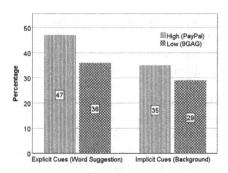

Fig. 3. Mean password strength score for passwords influenced and not influenced by the UI cues.

Fig. 4. Percentage of passwords influenced by a) Implicit & b) Explicit cues added to registration webpages with information sensitivity levels a) High and b)Low.

6   Discussion

The results of this study have several implications for the design of website registration pages and the use of UI cues to impact users' password composition. Our findings suggest that incorporating UI cues into the registration process can have a positive impact on the strength and memorability of passwords. This is an important contribution to the field, as it demonstrates how UI cues can influence password composition and highlights the potential benefits of incorporating such cues into the design of registration pages.

In particular, our study found that UI cues increased the strength of passwords created by users compared to passwords not influenced by the cues. This is a significant finding, as it suggests that UI cues can be an effective tool for improving the security of user-generated passwords. Additionally, we observed that having UI cues enhanced the memorability of passwords, as reflected in the proportion of successful login attempts. While our preliminary findings are promising, a longer-term study is needed to test the lasting effect of UI cues on password memorability.

Another interesting finding from our study is that passwords influenced by implicit cues were stronger than those influenced by explicit cues, although the difference was not statistically significant. One possible explanation for this result is that explicit cues limit users to the word suggestion, whereas implicit cues provide a broader range of suggestions. This highlights the potential benefits of providing implicit cues throughout the registration process to encourage users to generate stronger and more memorable passwords.

However, it is important to note that there may be potential security risks associated with the use of UI cues in password composition. Specifically, if users become too reliant on UI cues to generate passwords, they may be more vulnerable to various types of attacks. Moreover, UI designers could potentially manipulate users to choose a certain type of password, which raises ethical concerns.

Further research is needed to investigate these potential threats and to ensure that cue-based text passwords are sufficiently secure.

Despite these concerns, our findings suggest that incorporating personalized UI cues into website registration pages can be an effective tool for improving the security and memorability of passwords. These cues can be learned from users' behavior or entered by the user in advance into the system. Our approach can also leverage personality traits and adaptive user interfaces to create UI cues accordingly. We envision that our approach can be integrated into internet browsers to add personalized content to websites or can be used by designers to create adaptive, personalized registration pages. Overall, our study offers valuable insights into the potential benefits and limitations of UI cues for improving password composition and highlights avenues for future research in this area.

7 Conclusion and Future Work

In this study, we aimed to investigate the impact of using implicit (e.g. website background and advertisements) and explicit (e.g. word suggestions) cues on password composition. To achieve this, we conducted a remote user study and collected passwords from 59 participants. Our analysis revealed that 60.59% of the generated passwords were influenced by the UI cues. Additionally, we found that the use of UI cues led to stronger passwords compared to those not influenced by the cues. However, it would be valuable to conduct a follow-up study to investigate password memorability over longer periods and explore alternative representations of UI cues that can implicitly impact password choice.

References

1. Abdrabou, Y., et al.: Your eyes tell you have used this password before: identifying password reuse from gaze and keystroke dynamics (2022)
2. Abdrabou, Y., et al.: GazeMeter: exploring the usage of gaze behaviour to enhance password assessments. Association for Computing Machinery, New York, NY, USA (2021). https://doi.org/10.1145/3448017.3457384
3. Alt, F., Schneegass, S.: Beyond passwords-challenges and opportunities of future authentication. IEEE Secur. Priv. **20**(1), 82–86 (2021). http://www.florian-alt.org/unibw/wp-content/publications/alt2021ieeesp.pdf, alt2021ieeesp
4. Bonneau, J., Herley, C., van Oorschot, P.C., Stajano, F.: Passwords and the evolution of imperfect authentication. Commun. ACM **58**(7), 78–87 (2015). https://doi.org/10.1145/2699390
5. Dunphy, P., Yan, J.: Do background images improve draw a secret graphical passwords? In: Proceedings of the 14th ACM Conference on Computer and Communications Security, pp. 36–47. ACM (2007)
6. Forget, A., Chiasson, S., Van Oorschot, P.C., Biddle, R.: Improving text passwords through persuasion. In: Proceedings of the 4th Symposium on Usable Privacy and Security, pp. 1–12. ACM (2008)
7. Hanamsagar, A., Woo, S.S., Kanich, C., Mirkovic, J.: Leveraging semantic transformation to investigate password habits and their causes, pp. 1–12. Association for Computing Machinery, New York, NY, USA (2018). https://doi.org/10.1145/3173574.3174144

8. Jermyn, I., Mayer, A., Monrose, F., Reiter, M.K., Rubin, A.: The design and analysis of graphical passwords. In: 8th USENIX Security Symposium (USENIX Security 99). USENIX Association, Washington, D.C., August 1999. https://www.usenix.org/conference/8th-usenix-security-symposium/design-and-analysis-graphical-passwords

9. Jeyaraman, S., Topkara, U.: Have the cake and eat it too - infusing usability into text-password based authentication systems. In: 21st Annual Computer Security Applications Conference (ACSAC 2005), pp. 10 pp.-482 (2005)

10. Komanduri, S., et al.: Of passwords and people: measuring the effect of password-composition policies. Association for Computing Machinery, New York, NY, USA (2011). https://doi.org/10.1145/1978942.1979321

11. Pond, R., Podd, J., Bunnell, J., Henderson, R.: Word association computer passwords: the effect of formulation techniques on recall and guessing rates. Comput. Secur. 19(7), 645–656 (2000). https://doi.org/10.1016/S0167-4048(00)07023-1

12. Porter, S.N.: A password extension for improved human factors. Comput. Secur. 1(1), 54–56 (1982)

13. Seitz, T., Hartmann, M., Pfab, J., Souque, S.: Do differences in password policies prevent password reuse? In: Proceedings of the 2017 CHI Conference Extended Abstracts on Human Factors in Computing Systems, CHI EA 2017, pp. 2056–2063. Association for Computing Machinery, New York, NY, USA (2017). https://doi.org/10.1145/3027063.3053100

14. Seitz, T., von Zezschwitz, E., Meitner, S., Hussmann, H.: Influencing self-selected passwords through suggestions and the decoy effect. In: Proceedings of the 1st European Workshop on Usable Security, Internet Society, Darmstadt. vol. 2, pp. 1–2 (2016)

15. Ur, B., et al.: Design and evaluation of a data-driven password meter. In: Proceedings of the 2017 Chi Conference on Human Factors in Computing Systems, pp. 3775–3786 (2017)

16. Wheeler, D.L.: zxcvbn: low-budget password strength estimation. In: 25th USENIX Security Symposium (USENIX Security 16), pp. 157–173. USENIX Association, Austin, TX, August 2016. https://www.usenix.org/conference/usenixsecurity16/technical-sessions/presentation/wheeler

17. Yan, J., Blackwell, A., Anderson, R., Grant, A.: Password memorability and security: empirical results. IEEE Secur. Priv. 2(5), 25–31 (2004). https://doi.org/10.1109/MSP.2004.81

18. von Zezschwitz, E., et al.: On quantifying the effective password space of grid-based unlock gestures. In: Proceedings of the 15th International Conference on Mobile and Ubiquitous Multimedia, pp. 201–212. ACM (2016)

Friendly Folk Advice: Exploring Cybersecurity Information Sharing in Nigeria

James Nicholson[1]([⊠]), Opeyemi Dele Ajayi[2], Kemi Fasae[3],
and Boniface Kayode Alese[4]

[1] Northumbria University, Newcastle Upon Tyne, UK
`james.nicholson@northumbria.ac.uk`
[2] Meta, London, UK
`ajayiopeyemi@meta.com`
[3] Stemres Learning Initiative, Lagos, Nigeria
[4] Federal University of Technology, Akure, Nigeria
`bkalese@futa.edu.ng`

Abstract. The risk of cyber crimes continues to increase as more Nigerians continue to adopt digital and online tools and services. However, we do not know enough about citizens' understanding of cybersecurity behaviours and habits. In this paper, we explored the cybersecurity behaviours of Nigerians using a mixed-methods approach to understand how citizens stay safe online. Using a survey, we collected data (n = 208) on how citizens protect themselves online and where they get cybersecurity advice from. We then further explored the reported behaviours using semi-structured interviews (n = 22). We found that Nigerian citizens discussed cybersecurity incidents openly and shared tips and advice with peers through social media and through broadcasts on messaging platforms. We discovered that this has resulted in relatively high adoption rates for protective technologies like 2FA, particularly on WhatsApp. However, we also report how the adoption of 2FA on one account did not necessarily lead to enabling it on other accounts and how some citizens were being socially engineered to bypass those 2FA protections. Finally, we discuss some recommendations for how tools could provide more information to improve users' understanding of both security threats and the countermeasures the tools offer.

Keywords: Cybersecurity · two-factor authentication · cyberhygiene

1 Introduction and Related Work

Citizens in Nigeria have been adopting internet-enabled technologies at an accelerated rate due to the continued transition to the digital economy [1]. As such, the rate of cybercrime in Nigeria has skyrocketed in recent years [2]. In fact, cybercrime costs the Nigerian economy $500 million every year [3], and these losses will only increase with time as more people get online.

Over the past decade, attackers have been turning to targeting users rather than systems, e.g., via SMS fraud [4]. This trend also rings true for developing countries,

J. Abdelnour Nocera et al. (Eds.): INTERACT 2023, LNCS 14142, pp. 369–378, 2023.
https://doi.org/10.1007/978-3-031-42280-5_23

with reports of social engineering being amongst the most likely attack vectors year-on-year [5, 6]. These social engineering attacks are effective because security is rarely a citizen's main priority when using digital devices, yet simple mistakes can be very costly.

An essential defense against cyberthreats is to maintain good cybersecurity habits, such as correctly managing passwords and enabling two-factor authentication (2FA). Research has shown that good cybersecurity habits significantly reduce the chances of account hijacking by eliminating opportunistic, low-effort attacks [7]. This results in attackers having to target specific users at greater economic and time cost.

Of course, information seeking and sharing plays a significant role in users' adoption of secure behaviours and tools. From research in developed nations we know that facts-and-advice from security experts generally work better than sharing simple stories, the stories work much better when told by a peer which suggests that sharing of experiences may be beneficial for understanding cybersecurity and ultimately taking preventive measures [8]. As such, social triggers have been shown to play a significant role in motivating users to both adopt and promote cybersecurity prevention tools [9].

Despite the potential of this peer-to-peer information sharing and the opportunities for individuals to learn from their social groups and network, research has shown that people tend not to openly talk about issues around cybersecurity, privacy and preventive measures [10], and instead rely on online news [11] to keep updated on these topics. Some user groups, e.g. older adults, however, may need to rely on physical social networks [12] or coordination with co-habiting family members [13] to make sense of security and privacy information. Recent work has attempted to address this problem by embedding knowledgeable peers into older communities to improve reliable information sharing and improve the basic cyberhygiene behaviours of citizens [14].

However, prior work has highlighted how citizens in developing nations face different contextual challenges in order to maintain the security of their online accounts and devices [4, 15, 16]. While previous work has touched on the types of cyber crime that affect the Nigerian banking sector, and the security practices that the industry employs to protect itself [17], we do not know how citizens protect themselves from these threats. Although we know that Nigerians seek information from multiple online sources [18], we know very little specifically about their understanding of cybersecurity or how they seek information and advice on how to stay safe online.

This paper reports on the findings from a mixed-method study exploring the cybersecurity behaviours of Nigerian citizens and their motivations for adopting security tools, in particular two-factor authentication (2FA). We find that our sample had a higher adoption rate of 2FA compared with previous work in developed countries [19] and this was largely driven by online social interactions, namely broadcasts through messaging groups and the sharing of incidents on social media. This paper makes two contributions: (i) we uncover information-sharing techniques that could be used in developed countries to improve the adoption of security tools such as 2FA, while also (ii) highlighting possible design considerations for increasing the understanding of these tools amongst citizens.

2 Method

The overall goal of this study was to explore the cybersecurity behaviours of Nigerians so as to better understand the barriers and opportunities for sustainable good cybersecurity advice. We adopted a mixed-methods approach to this study consisting of an initial large-scale online survey to collect baseline information on how Nigerian citizens are protecting themselves online followed by semi-structured interviews to better understand these behaviours. The interview data was analysed using thematic analysis [20] and consisted of the lead author conducting the first pass at the analysis, and then the research team engaged in the process of 'researcher triangulation' whereby themes and subthemes were vetted by team members [21].

2.1 Participants

Respondents were recruited using emails and text communications broadcasted by our Stemres in Nigeria. Following the initial recruitment, other participants were recruited via word of mouth and snowball sampling. The recruitment criteria included participants aged at least 18 years and who have been living in Nigeria for the past 12 months. Participants were entered into a draw to stand a chance of winning £10 each.

Survey
A total of 208 respondents completed the online survey. The sample consisted of 56% male and 44% female. The age distribution was similar between 18–25 (30%), 26–30 (24%) and 31–40 years old (29%), with a few aged 41–50 years old (10%) and 51 + (4%). The majority of respondents were students (26%), with those in teaching service (17%), self-employed (12%) and public service (10%) also contributing. We also had respondents from I.T. employees (6%), lawyers (5%), engineers (3%), and other or undisclosed job roles (21%). The majority of the respondents had access to the internet through their mobile phone (97.1%) followed by a laptop (65.4%), The respondents are predominantly Android users (82.9%).

Interviews
Participants who completed the survey were given the option to sign up for a follow-up interview to discuss their answers in more detail for compensation of £10. Of the 208 people who completed the survey, 132 indicated further interest in being interviewed. We selected 20 out of the 132 and prioritised the recruitment of individuals who had reported enabling two-factor authentication on their accounts (see Sect. 4.2) to better understand their motivations and experiences. We then further selected participants based on gender, age, and occupation to match the demographics of our survey. The sample consisted of 50% male and 50% female. The age distribution was 18–25 years old (20%), 26–30 years old (25%), 31–40 years old (20%), 41–50 years old (15%), 51–60 years old (15%) and 61 + years (5%). The occupation distribution was public service (30%), self-employed (15%), teaching service (15%), students (15%), I.T employee (10%), retired (10%), and nursing (5%).

2.2 Materials

We developed a survey instrument with 16 questions that asked respondents about their habits online, cybersecurity practices including if and how often they update their digital devices, how they stay safe online, and password management practices. The questions were based on the security behaviours identified in the SeBIS questionnaire [22] but also featured open-ended questions where participants were encouraged to expand on their answers. We also asked a few demographic questions to better understand the responses. We piloted the survey with a small group of Nigerian citizens (n = 30) and reworded some of the questions to achieve better clarification.

2.3 Procedure

The survey was deployed online between April and July 2020. The semi-structured interviews were carried out approximately one month later remotely via Zoom. The interviews were conducted in English and were led by a researcher with expertise in cybersecurity. However, two other researchers who were familiar with the Nigerian context and local languages joined the interviews as well to help with any translation needs. A local researcher in Nigeria briefed each participant before they joined the interview and encouraged them to ask any clarification questions before, during and after the interviews. Participants were also told that their continued involvement in the research activities remained voluntary and they could refuse to answer any question or choose to withdraw from the interview at any time. The interviews were recorded and transcribed by a member of the research team.

The interviews focused predominantly on their usage of two-factor authentication on their online accounts, but did allow for discussions around other security habits and cybersecurity information seeking. We also explored participants' experiences of cybersecurity breaches or compromises, from details on how it originated to how it was fixed. Finally, we asked participants how and where they get information about staying safe online and what steps they take to keep their devices safe online. The order of the topics we explored varied from participant to participant depending on their individual experiences. Both studies were approved by our institution's Ethics Committee.

3 Findings

This section introduces the key findings from our work. We initially present descriptive findings on how citizens in Nigeria protect their accounts online and where they obtain cybersecurity protective information (n = 202). We then present the findings from the semi-structured interviews (n = 20) to better understand the motivations of citizens for enabling 2FA on their online accounts.

Most survey respondents (42%) reported visiting 'safe websites' as being their number one prevention of online attacks, although it was not clear how the safety of the website was evaluated. Using strong passwords (19%) was another method for keeping accounts safe from bad actors, while being careful with what information was disclosed (11%) and using an antivirus (11%) were also common amongst respondents.

Interestingly, we found that 30% of our respondents had enabled two-step verification (often referred to as 2FA) on their WhatsApp accounts, which is considerably higher than previously reported figures for 2FA adoption in developed countries [19]. 2FA was enabled on email accounts by 18% of respondents, and 5% explicitly mentioned their Google account, while social media accounts were also protected by 2FA (Facebook - 13%, Instagram & Twitter - 5% each).

The majority of respondents obtained information on how to stay safe online on the internet itself (total: 53%), in particular through social media (30%). The most popular social media platform reported was WhatsApp (23%) and closely followed by Twitter (20%). 8% relied on friends and relatives for cybersecurity information, while 5% had access to cybersecurity students and experts. We should note that 14% of respondents admitted not having a source of cybersecurity information.

3.1 Understanding the Adoption of Two-Factor Authentication (2FA)

The percentage of citizens enabling 2FA on accounts reported in the survey (30% for WhatsApp) was considerably higher than previously published numbers on 2FA adoption in developed countries – i.e. less than 10% of Google users who enable 2FA [19]. Hence, we decided to investigate the reasons behind this high adoption in our interviews with selected respondents and report on four themes: Visibility of Advice, Visibility of Attacks, Flawed Mental Models, and Visibility of Protection.

Visibility of the Advice
In order to enable two-factor authentication on accounts, participants first had to become aware of the feature and the process to enable it. It became apparent that a key source for discovering information on two-factor authentication was group broadcasts on WhatsApp, with the majority of participants interviewed explaining the importance of protecting the overall security of the group by promoting the security feature: *"I encourage my participants in my group to enable this two-way verification because it's not just for my own safety as a group admin of which they are a participant. But for the fact that it's also for their safety and for their privacy. To ensure their chats and their conversations are private, I encourage them to enable that two-way verification. From time to time, I remind... When I have new participants to my groups, I encourage them to do that."* (P5).

The motivation of group administrators (e.g., participant 5 above) to protect their groups from security incidents was crucial for increasing the visibility of security advice to lay users, and supports previous work [9] showing that some individuals feel a sense of obligation to protect others and this leads to sharing security information. However, individuals' own experiences of cyber attacks also played a role in keeping their contacts informed about methods for protecting themselves online and possible threats to look out for: *"I could remember the day I got my [Facebook] account back I posted it on my account, I hardly post on my Facebook account but I did that day, trying to preach the message of people activating their two-factor authentication, I did the same on my WhatsApp status telling people to activate and then, of course, I got a lot of messages from people asking me how can I go about it and... I told them all how to go about it.*

Like, okay go here, go here, then some that couldn't do it themselves, I helped those people." (P11).

Our participant above described a common security information sharing process: how hacked users take up a sense of duty to inform others on how they can prevent these attacks. Our participants explained how one of the first things that many of them did after restoring accounts was to share their experience of the hack, including tools and methods for preventing similar attacks. This is important as previous work has demonstrated that citizens in developing nations do not always know how to manage the privacy and security settings of messaging platforms [23]. Our insights also extend previous work looking at triggers for the uptake of security tools and motivations for sharing advice [9, 11] by showing how a personal adverse experience can motivate citizens to improve their own behaviours, but also share protective information with others. This also highlights the importance of having open conversations about cybersecurity threats and countermeasures, which is less common in developed countries [10]. Of course, the challenge here is understanding how to encourage citizens to adopt these protective technologies prior to experiencing security breaches.

Visibility of the Attacks

While it is important to be aware of how to protect online accounts (see above), the perceived vulnerability of the account is equally as important to help action further protection of these accounts. Across our participants, we see how visual confirmation of account takeovers drives the awareness of account vulnerability, while those that result in obscure hackings are perceived as being more secure: *"You know, as I told you, I'm mostly active on WhatsApp and Messenger. So, I've done that, I've done [2FA]. Other applications that I use like Twitter and...I think I use Zoom too. But you know, I don't think the problem of hacking is all that pronounced."* (P19).

Participants predominantly enabled 2FA for messaging and social media accounts, and while these roughly correlate with the most popular usage of smartphones in developing nations [23], it also demonstrates the importance of the visibility of account takeovers: a WhatsApp account or Facebook account that is taken over is typically used to try and compromise contacts, resulting in very clear visual instances of attempted attacks. However, when other accounts, e.g., Google, are compromised, their effect is not always visible to other users, thus many citizens do not feel the need to protect this account with further security tools. This observation is in line with Protection Motivation Theory and ensuring that the threat is salient [24] before any protective behaviour changes. Here, we see that word of mouth and sharing personal experiences of hacks is effective in this context, supporting previous work suggesting that previous experience of compromises drives the adoption of protective tools [9], but we extend this by showing that peer experiences of compromises also drives the adoption of protective tools. We also see the power of peer stories in action (e.g. [8]) once again highlighting the need for open communications around cybersecurity in communities.

Flawed Mental Models

While the adoption of 2FA was high compared to other published work (e.g. [19]), we found that many participants who had enabled 2FA due to announcements and posts from contacts as detailed above showed a lack of understanding of how the tool helped protect the accounts. In particular, we observed how some participants perceived their accounts to be completely safe after enabling 2FA, which then led to social engineering compromises: *"So when she called me to inform me that she has been hacked, I asked her all the details. Then when she told me that she gave out the number, I was like, the main purpose of two-factor authentication was that they would send you a code and that code, you just gave it to them."* (P10).

The adoption of security tools like 2FA are critical for ensuring that citizens are protected against opportunistic attacks [7]. However, what was clear from our participants was that bypassing these tools once enabled, either on purpose (e.g., sharing with a friend) or by mistake (as detailed by P10 above), was relatively common. Additionally, participants reported enabling 2FA for accounts that they perceived as being at high risk of compromise (see Visibility of Attacks) or that they had encountered advice for (see Visibility of Advice), yet had usually failed to protect other accounts that supported 2FA. Poor user mental models around security tools is well known [25], but it is important here to highlight that simply pushing for the adoption of tools may not be as effective as desired. Thus, it is of great importance to ensure that citizens understand *why* 2FA can protect online accounts, not just how to enable the security feature.

Visibility of Protection
A large number of participants enabled 2FA on their accounts due to observing large volumes of account compromises and being exposed to group announcements on how to protect their accounts. However, the realisation of the importance of the tools was typically only visible once they had first-hand experience with failed attacks: *"But there was a time when I was always receiving a WhatsApp OTP to confirm the code so that they can register your number. But then, I think that's one. Yeah. I think that's the only other time I think I feel my account is trying...it's being... it's almost being compromised."* (P21).

Having concrete confirmation that security attacks had been prevented was reassuring to citizens, and helped them to better understand the value of the tool. This was the case even when the tools were activated by mistake rather than by actual attacks: *"I have a friend... he actually wanted access to my WhatsApp and when he tried opening it, unlike before, if he opened my WhatsApp with a different phone, he will just completely have the access to it. So since I enabled that two-way verification, when he tried to open it, he...it demanded for a PIN from him which he didn't have. So he came back to me and told me it demanded for a PIN. So I think if it demanded for PIN from him and if he couldn't get the pin, that means I was safe. Cause that means someone else too wouldn't be able to get the PIN."* (P6).

We have seen in previous work that users appreciate the perception of security when it comes to security tools [26], yet here we extend this by suggesting that users may need to see the tool in action early on in the process to support their mental models of threats and protective measures.

4 Discussion

In this paper we report on how Nigerian citizens openly communicate about cybersecurity incidents and protective measures with peers, predominantly through social media posts and broadcasting on messaging platforms. This openness around cyber incidents has led to the relatively high uptake of 2FA which has also been facilitated by the visibility of account compromises, predominantly messaging and social media services that then lead to further attacks of contacts. Ensuring that group administrators are up to date with appropriate protective advice, and that they only share appropriate security information will be an important consideration for future investigation.

4.1 Recommendations for Improving 2FA Mental Models

While sharing personal experiences and broadcasting reminders on WhatsApp and social media did drive the adoption of 2FA on those accounts, they did not necessarily translate to enabling 2FA on other accounts or the full prevention of cyber attacks (e.g., social engineering). Here we discuss two recommendations for improving citizens' understanding of 2FA tools for better account protection.

First, we must make sure that such **advice includes details on *how* the tools protect the accounts** in order to prevent social engineering attacks and promote adoption across other services. Our participants commented on how they followed guidance from peers or group administrators due to social pressures or in an attempt to make their accounts impossible to hack, but it was clear that such advice typically did not include details on *how* 2FA practically protected accounts. As reported above, this then led to some citizens exhibiting behaviours that undermined 2FA – e.g., sharing the code.

Second, **services should include embedded tutorials or demonstrations of the process** to help users understand the mechanics of how 2FA can prevent attacks. Participants reported that experiencing the tool in action was reassuring and that it helped them understand both the security threat and the countermeasure more concretely. If tools can run through a demonstration which features how attacks are prevented during setup, then users may truly understand the importance of the tool. Additionally, increasing the visibility of prevented attacks may serve as regular reminders to enable 2FA and reinforce the value of the tool, but we must think very carefully about how to implement these warnings and messages in order to avoid habituation [27].

4.2 Conclusion

In this paper, we have reported how Nigerian citizens openly share details about account compromises and how this drives the adoption of the appropriate security tools. Of course, there is plenty of room for improvement (e.g., ensuring that users understand how these tools are protecting them so they cannot be circumvented or socially engineered) but it is a good first step towards driving the adoption of tools like 2FA.

References

1. Chakravorti, B., Chaturvedi, R.S.: Research: how technology could promote growth in 6 African Countries (2019). https://hbr.org/2019/12/research-how-technology-could-promote-growth-in-6-african-countries
2. Doyon-Martin, J.: Cybercrime in West Africa as a result of transboundary e-waste. J. Appl. Secur. Res. **10**, 207–220 (2015). https://doi.org/10.1080/19361610.2015.1004511
3. Fassassi, A., Akoussan, C.F.: Cybercrime in Africa: facts and figures (2016)
4. Pervaiz, F., et al.: An assessment of SMS fraud in Pakistan. In: Proceedings of the 2nd ACM SIGCAS Conference on Computing and Sustainable Societies, pp. 195–205. Association for Computing Machinery, New York (2019)
5. Kshetri, N.: Cybercrime and cybersecurity in Africa. J. Glob. Inf. Technol. Manag. **22**, 77–81 (2019). https://doi.org/10.1080/1097198X.2019.1603527
6. Kaimba, B.: Demystifying Africa's cyber security poverty line. SERIANU (2017)
7. Thomas, K., Moscicki, A.: New research: how effective is basic account hygiene at preventing hijacking (2019). https://security.googleblog.com/2019/05/new-research-how-effective-is-basic.html
8. Wash, R., Cooper, M.M.: Who provides phishing training? Facts, Stories, and People Like Me. In: Presented at the Proceedings of the 2018 CHI Conference on Human Factors in Computing Systems, 21 April 2018
9. Das, S., Dabbish, L.A., Hong, J.I.: A typology of perceived triggers for end-user security and privacy behaviors. In: Presented at the Fifteenth Symposium on Usable Privacy and Security ({SOUPS} 2019) (2019)
10. Watson, H., Moju-Igbene, E., Kumari, A., Das, S.: 'We Hold Each Other Accountable': unpacking how social groups approach cybersecurity and privacy together. In: Proceedings of the 2020 CHI Conference on Human Factors in Computing Systems, pp. 1–12. Association for Computing Machinery, Honolulu (2020)
11. Das, S., Lo, J., Dabbish, L., Hong, J.I.: Breaking! A typology of security and privacy news and how it's shared. In: Proceedings of the 2018 CHI Conference on Human Factors in Computing Systems, pp. 1:1–1:12. ACM, New York (2018)
12. Nicholson, J., Coventry, L., Briggs, P.: "If It's Important It Will Be A Headline": cybersecurity information seeking in older adults. In: Proceedings of the 2019 CHI Conference on Human Factors in Computing Systems, pp. 1–11. Association for Computing Machinery, Glasgow (2019)
13. Murthy, S., Bhat, K.S., Das, S., Kumar, N.: Individually vulnerable, collectively safe: the security and privacy practices of households with older adults. Proc. ACM on Hum.-Comput. Interact. **5**, 24 (2021)
14. Nicholson, J., Morrison, B., Dixon, M., Holt, J., Coventry, L., McGlasson, J.: Training and embedding cybersecurity guardians in older communities. In: SIGCHI Conference on Human Factors in Computing Systems (2021)
15. Vashistha, A., Anderson, R., Mare, S.: Examining security and privacy research in developing regions. In: Proceedings of the 1st ACM SIGCAS Conference on Computing and Sustainable Societies, pp. 1–14. Association for Computing Machinery, Menlo Park and San Jose (2018)
16. Chen, J., Paik, M., McCabe, K.: Exploring internet security perceptions and practices in Urban Ghana. In: Presented at the 10th Symposium On Usable Privacy and Security ({SOUPS} 2014) (2014)
17. Wang, V., Nnaji, H., Jung, J.: Internet banking in Nigeria: cyber security breaches, practices and capability. Int. J. Law, Crime Justice **62**, 100415 (2020). https://doi.org/10.1016/j.ijlcj.2020.100415

18. Obasola, O.I., Agunbiade, O.M.: Online health information seeking pattern among under-graduates in a Nigerian university. SAGE Open **6**, 2158244016635255 (2016). https://doi.org/10.1177/2158244016635255
19. Petsas, T., Tsirantonakis, G., Athanasopoulos, E., Ioannidis, S.: Two-factor authentication: is the world ready? Quantifying 2FA adoption. In: Proceedings of the Eighth European Workshop on System Security, pp. 4:1–4:7. ACM, New York (2015)
20. Braun, V., Clarke, V.: Using thematic analysis in psychology. Qual. Res. Psychol. **3**, 77–101 (2006). https://doi.org/10.1191/1478088706qp063oa
21. Nowell, L.S., Norris, J.M., White, D.E., Moules, N.J.: Thematic analysis: striving to meet the trustworthiness criteria. Int. J. Qual. Methods **16**, 1609406917733847 (2017). https://doi.org/10.1177/1609406917733847
22. Egelman, S., Peer, E.: Scaling the security wall: developing a security behavior intentions scale (SeBIS). In: Proceedings of the 33rd Annual ACM Conference on Human Factors in Computing Systems, pp. 2873–2882. Association for Computing Machinery, Seoul (2015)
23. Reichel, J., Peck, F., Inaba, M., Moges, B., Chawla, B.S., Chetty, M.: 'I have too much respect for my elders': Understanding South African mobile users' perceptions of privacy and current behaviors on Facebook and WhatsApp. In: Presented at the 29th {USENIX} Security Symposium ({USENIX} Security 20) (2020)
24. van Bavel, R., Rodríguez-Priego, N., Vila, J., Briggs, P.: Using protection motivation theory in the design of nudges to improve online security behavior. Int. J. Hum. Comput. Stud. **123**, 29–39 (2019). https://doi.org/10.1016/j.ijhcs.2018.11.003
25. Wash, R.: Folk models of home computer security. In: Proceedings of the Sixth Symposium on Usable Privacy and Security, pp. 1–16. Association for Computing Machinery, New York (2010)
26. Wiefling, S., Dürmuth, M., Lo Iacono, L.: More than just good passwords? A study on usability and security perceptions of risk-based authentication. In: Annual Computer Security Applications Conference, pp. 203–218. Association for Computing Machinery, New York (2020)
27. Amran, A., Zaaba, Z.F., Singh, M.K.M.: Habituation effects in computer security warning. Inf. Secur. J.: Global Perspect. **27**, 192–204 (2018). https://doi.org/10.1080/19393555.2018.1505008

Trust in Facial Recognition Systems: A Perspective from the Users

Gabriela Beltrão[(✉)] [iD], Sonia Sousa[iD], and David Lamas[iD]

Tallinn University, Tallinn, Estonia
{gbeltrao,scs,drl}@tlu.ee

Abstract. High-risk artificial intelligence (AI) are systems that can endanger the fundamental rights of individuals. Due to their complex characteristics, users often wrongly perceive their risks, trusting too little or too much. To further understand trust from the users' perspective, we investigate what factors affect their propensity to trust Facial Recognition Systems (FRS), a high-risk AI, in Mozambique. The study uses mixed methods, with a survey (N = 120) and semi-structured interviews (N = 13). The results indicate that users' perceptions of the FRS' robustness and principles of use affect their propensity to trust it. This relationship is moderated by external issues and how the system attributes are communicated. The findings from this study shed light on aspects that should be addressed when developing AI systems to ensure adequate levels of trust.

Keywords: Trust in Technology · Human-Centered Artificial Intelligence · User Studies

1 Introduction

Trust in technology has been increasingly discussed in Human-Computer Interaction (HCI) literature. Its importance is by now unquestionable, but there are obstacles to its measurement due to the multidimensionality of the concept [27] and the particularities of the interaction contexts. When moving to AI-enabled systems, trust is similarly essential but more complex. The autonomous nature of these technologies affects how individuals perceive and relate to them, and misconceptions become more common because AI capabilities are difficult for users to grasp. So, while it is essential that users have adequate levels of trust, it is still unclear how to assess it and what levels of trust are actually adequate [3,13].

This study primarily looks into challenges emerging from complex and riskier AI systems. Using mixed methods, we investigate the factors affecting the propensity to trust in Facial Recognition Systems (FRS) in Mozambique, aiming to include a region underrepresented in HCI literature. We rely on Mayer's [19] definition of trust and incorporate aspects concerning "calibration" [11], that is, aiming that trust is not too low (undertrust) nor too high (overtrust). We first

J. Abdelnour Nocera et al. (Eds.): INTERACT 2023, LNCS 14142, pp. 379–388, 2023.
https://doi.org/10.1007/978-3-031-42280-5_24

introduce related work about high-risk AI from a socio-technical [6] perspective; Next, we detail our study methodology and present the findings. The discussion synthesizes our insights and implications to current research on trust in high-risk AI.

2   Related Work

2.1   High-Risk AI

Recently, the European Union (EU) proposed the AI Act [8], a legal framework for regulating AI technologies. According to the document, AI systems are classified based on the risks they create, which can be (1) unacceptable, (2) high, (3) low, or (4) minimal. High risk refers to AI that creates risks for individuals' safety of fundamental rights, such as biometric identification and categorization or systems used for the selection of persons [7]. These systems are allowed in the EU but face legal requirements. This study relies solely on the AI Act classification due to its higher maturity and influence in other countries emerging legislation. However, we acknowledge that there are efforts toward AI regulation in other parts of the world.

It is noteworthy that the AI Act's principles are rooted in compliance with existing laws and regulations, which bleed into AI's technical agendas [28]. According to the document, trustworthiness is mostly about risk management and is controlled by legal clauses, which enable practical application but, at the same time, constrains it to it a shallow view of trust, which disregards broader social effects.

Users of High-Risk AI? One issue emerges from the loose definitions of the users and stakeholders of high-risk AI. In systems used for classification or categorization, thousands of individuals are scanned and affected by the AI. However, only a few specialized professionals actually interact with the tool and its outputs. In the AI Act, there are references to "affected persons", which are not considered users and thus only marginally contemplated in the document.

It is unclear how the citizens are contemplated from the design and HCI perspective, as even human-centered views fail to account for them. For clarity, in this paper, the term "user" is adopted broadly, referring to the citizens who (would) use the system regardless of actively interacting with an interface.

Facial Recognition Systems (FRS). Involve a set of technologies for face detection, imaging pre-processing, and identity recognition. These systems are based on algorithms designed to find and extract the faces in an image and classify them based on an existing database or, more recently, using deep learning methods [18]. This way, when referring to FRS, we mean a series of automated systems for pattern recognition. We explore the use of these systems for law enforcement, which would fall under the high-risk category within the EU.

Investment in these technologies is growing due to their potential as a convenient alternative for identity verification. However, many issues also arise from its uses. First, as with most AI systems, the classification's quality is bound to the data used to develop the algorithms, which can be biased. Another pressing issue regards the ethics of the usage of these systems: as regulations are still unclear, companies can deploy them with little accountability for possible consequences [9]. Although regulations have started to appear, they still lag behind, and problems are emerging across the globe [15–17].

2.2 Technology Adoption in Mozambique

It is estimated that only around 17% of the population can access the internet in Mozambique. Sub-Saharan Africa has the lowest access rates, at around 30%, while the average global access is 60% [25]. The slight penetration of technology in Mozambique is related to issues with infrastructure, lack of economic resources from individuals to pay for the services, and lack of knowledge to use technology. Nevertheless, there was an increase in access to the internet between 2015 and 2021, and the tendency is that it continues to grow, fostered by national and foreign funds [1]. Fast growth within limited regulation and unequal access can create an ambiguous context where benefits are tied to risks to the population.

3 Methodology

This study employs a mixed methods approach, following a triangulation design [10] to enable meta-inferences. Both methods were employed during the same time frame and held equal weight; they are described separately in this section to ensure clarity but are presented combined, prioritizing the insights [4].

We explore FRS using a scenario, that is, by presenting a concrete situation so the participants engage with the topic and have a common understanding of the otherwise abstract interactions. The same scenario was used as stimuli in both phases of the data collection. It consists of a short video about FRS for law enforcement created by the authors using excerpts from two existing videos.

3.1 Quantitative Phase

The quantitative phase consisted of a survey using the Human-Computer Trust Scale (HCTS) [14], a psychometric instrument to assess trust in technology from the user perspective, which has been applied in various contexts [5,12,14,26]. The validated questionnaire includes nine items measuring Competence, Benevolence, and Risk Perception. To account for the particularities of AI, three additional items were included in the scale, with predictive ability yet to be assessed, referring to the construct of Social Capital [23]. The questionnaire was used in Portuguese, following a validated translation of the HCTS [22]. The data was collected online and in person through LimeSurvey (www.limesurvey.org). We followed convenience sampling, with respondents recruited with the support of the local partners and their communication channels.

3.2   Qualitative Phase

We used semi-structured interviews to explore what affects individuals' trust in facial recognition systems and the reasons behind their perceptions. The interview guide was developed considering principles of contextual laddering [24], using free elicitation methods [21] to understand how attributes and values from FRS relate to trust.

The participants were recruited based on stratified criteria established by the authors, aiming to represent different socio-demographic groups of the population. All the interviews were conducted in Portuguese, the official but not the only language in the country. The data analysis happened through thematic analysis [20] in two iterations of inductive coding.

4   Results and Findings

The survey had 120 valid responses. Females accounted for 35.8% (N = 43), males for 63.3% (N = 76), and non-binaries for 0.8% (N = 1) - thus not considered in gender analyses. There are responses from "-17" to "65+" age ranges, but respondents are centered in the range of 18–34, with 83.3%(N = 100) of the participants.

Simultaneously, 13 interviews were conducted with six females and seven males between 17 and 45 years old. Six are university students from different fields, and seven are individuals working in different segments. Amongst them, three identify as part of minority groups: two as LGBTQ+ and one as a person with a disability.

Trust scores were calculated according to the HCTS procedures [14], ranging from 1 to 5. Cronbach's alpha coefficient was 0.737, indicating good internal consistency. The Trust score for the sample was 3.31 (SD = 0.708). Competence (COM) had the highest scores (M = 3.78, SD = 0.95), indicating that individuals perceive the technology to have the features and ability to perform its intended tasks. The lowest was from Risk Perception (RP) (M = 2.82, SD = 1.05), indicating that users are concerned about the technology's possible consequences. The scores for RP are reversed - so low scores indicate that high perception of risk. Table 1 presents the results of all constructs. Still, most interviewees (N = 8) believe an FRS system would be mostly beneficial in Mozambique.

Table 1. Human-Computer Trust Scale (HCTS). Results for N = 120

Construct	Mean	Std. Deviation	Variance
Trust	3.31	0.71	0.51
Risk Perception (rev)	2.82	1.05	1.12
Benevolence	3.39	1.12	1.27
Competence	3.78	0.95	0.92
Social Capital	3.24	1.08	1.17

Factors Affecting Trust. Despite a positive view of FRS, the participants had some concerns. From the interviews, we identified the main factors expressed to affect their propensity to trust the system. They refer to users' *perceptions*:

Potential Improvement According to the interviewees, the potential improvement brought by the system is crucial to their perception and trust in it. In this case, FRS was seen as a tool to improve safety. Placing cameras in the city would, first, be an effective measure to reduce crimes, an urgent problem in the country. As explained, *"there are many cases of kidnapping, so imagine if we had these systems already in place. I believe it would make it much easier to find the kidnapped people and find the kidnappers"* (P11). Some respondents also highlight that surveillance can positively change behaviors in a broader sense because *"the fact that people know they are being watched would bring up other ways to behave"* (P13), helping also prevent other minor acts of harassment or disrespect of the public space.

Usage The respondents were also concerned with how and by whom the system would be used, recognizing that there will always be a human in the process who can have their own intentions: *"If it was going to be used for the sake of protecting people, for the benefit of people, I think it would be a good system"* (P3). Additionally, the respondents express worry about a potential loss of privacy resulting from misuse, which emerged as sensitive points of implementing FRS.

Reliability The reliability of the information provided by the camera is one key attribute that shaped the respondents' perceptions, as the information is perceived to be more objective and unbiased; as explained, *"because with the cameras you can see everything that goes on"*(P5) and *"images worth more than words"* (P2). FRS can thus be considered more reliable than people's second-hand information.

Capability Most respondents talked about the system's capability, which is unclear to them: *"imagine, I'm leaving my house, and something hurts my face. And I go back, and it says it is not me"* (P2). They also worry about the system's accuracy over time, highlighting that if a criminal changed their appearance, they *"do not know if the camera would still be able to identify the person"* (P9). So the system's capabilities and respective limitations affect their trust in it.

When looking at the technology itself, these factors can be grouped under two major groups referring to *socio-technical characteristics*:

Principles of Use Broadly defined as the goals and intentions that underlie the use of the system, which can be expressed in norms, regulations, and informal practices. They affect the users' perceptions of why and how the system will be used. This way, it comprises perceptions of the "Potential Improvement" and "Usage".

Technical Robustness Refers to how well the system can perform its designated tasks. Technical robustness underlies their perceptions of the system's "Reliability" and "Capability".

Moderators. In addition, we identified factors that are external to the interaction but can shape participants' perceptions. They were classified as moderators of the interaction:

Communication The interviewees mentioned the importance of the system's characteristics being communicated to them adequately because *"people already run away if they see the television [channel] filming"* (P4). Another participant also explained: *"I first need to convince myself that it is working fine to trust it"*(P1). This way, we assume that how the system is communicated affects how the users perceive its characteristics.

External Issues Existing external issues also moderated the respondents' propensity to trust FRS. In Mozambique, there is a pervasive preoccupation with local structural problems that steered the participants' opinions. First, they affirmed that FRS would be limited to the capital, Maputo, as the country has an unequal infrastructure. As explained, *"You need to send money to someone, for example, who is at home [in a different region]. The person will tell you: 'no, it is not possible because here we do not even have a bank'*(P1). According to them, Mozambique is not yet prepared to implement FRS, and the governmental structures do not have sufficient ability to manage such a system adequately.

Differences in Propensity to Trust. The role of External Issues was corroborated by the differences identified between specific groups. When comparing the HCTS scores, females had higher Trust (M = 3.43, SD = .73) than males (M = 3.24, SD = .69), but the difference was not significant. In the interviews, females did not explicitly manifest that their opinions were related to being a woman but admitted that there are gender differences in Mozambique.

P10 explained that there are unequal opportunities because families usually see boys' education as a more significant contribution to the family's economic growth. Additionally, they highlight that the differences are not inherent but result from the context, *"there are some things that put women more at risk"*(P13, female). One inference is that despite the risks FRS brings, it can potentially mitigate other, more critical issues that females are susceptible to.

The survey also considered individuals who considered themselves as ethnic minorities, LGBTQ+, immigrants, and individuals with disabilities. To enable statistical analyses, these responses were regrouped, considering individuals who are part of at least one minority, thus not accounting for intersections. This group includes 32.5% (N = 39) of total responses.

Individuals belonging to at least one minority also had higher trust in FRS (M = 3.39, SD = 0.71) than the ones who are not (M = 3.26, SD = 0.71). The difference is not statistically significant, but the tendency prevailed among the four minority groups.

Among the interviewees, three are part of a minority group. They especially highlighted how adaptations of FRS and other AI systems could benefit society and their lives in a broader sense. For example, P12, LGBTQ+, explained that besides reducing crimes, FRS could assist in cases of vulnerability, and *"certain homophobic, pedophile behaviors would be reduced"*. For P2, who has a disability, FRS is majorly positive and could be used by decision-makers to see the situation in the public space and lead to more *"equity"*. Similar to what was observed for females, existing inequalities shape individuals' perceptions of the system's benefits. Figure 1 summarizes the relationships identified in our study.

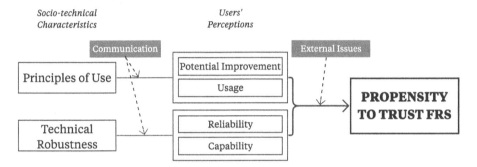

Fig. 1. Summary of the relationships identified

5 Discussion

The findings from both study phases help us identify some patterns in how Mozambicans trust FRS. It has implications for the (so far, hypothetical) use of these systems in the country and brings insights into an integrative view of the design and implementation of high-risk AI.

First, a general analysis of the HCTS reveals that FRS are perceived as competent but also risky. Still, most respondents admit they would still want it implemented due to the potential improvements it can bring, especially regarding citizens' safety. Therefore, in this case, the levels of Competence and Benevolence can mitigate the drawbacks of the Perceive Risk. Our results reinforce the validity of HCTS constructs [14] but show that other factors also shape users' propensity to trust.

The model presented in Fig. 1 helps us observe the interplay between different aspects within and outside the system. It demonstrates that technical characteristics, represented on the node "Technical Robustness, are only partially responsible for users' trust. Even so, users' perceptions of these characteristics can be steered by moderators. This finding adds depth to current views of trustworthy AI [2] and proposed legislation [8], which often focus on technical aspects.

Furthermore, both socio-technical characteristics (Principles of Use and Technical Robustness) pertain to the interaction, thus, falling under the scope of the HCI. So although high-risk AI does not necessarily have an interface for the general citizens, it is possible to work on aspects of the interaction that can affect users' propensity to trust it. Interaction aspects also bleed into the moderator "Communication" because communication can be tied to the system's design and implementation.

The study also identified indications of factors that affect users' propensity to trust. Both women and minorities had higher Trust scores, meaning they are more prone to trust FRS. However, the interviews demonstrated that their higher trust is not due to an inherent more accepting inclination but a result of existing obstacles related to their position in society, and they see in FRS the potential of counterbalancing these problems. In Fig. 1, these characteristics are represented within "External Issues". They are usually outside the scope of HCI but should be considered for an inclusive perspective.

It is then crucial that HCI practitioners working with high-risk technologies consider the existing sociodemographic differences and the local context to ensure that systems are used to empower and not aggravate existing problems. High-risk AI design should consider technical and usage aspects and include mechanisms to prevent amplifying existing inequalities.

6   Conclusions

This study explored the factors that affect the propensity to trust FRS in Mozambique. The findings help understand users' relationships with high-risk AI systems there and elsewhere. Using mixed methods was a valuable strategy that allowed us to identify patterns and add meaning to them. Although still preliminary, the findings contribute to a more holistic understanding of trust in high-risk AI. Adopting the users' perspective was useful for understanding the role of HCI in this interaction and providing insights for human-centered AI systems, even when the characteristics of the interaction are fuzzy.

7   Limitations

This study aimed to have an inclusive perspective of trust in technology by looking at different social groups in an underexplored country in HCI. Although this was achieved to some extent, our sample centered around young, educated groups, thus limited in size and representation, even among Mozambicans. This way, our perspective is not exhaustive. More efforts are necessary to include a broader population, provide a more accurate snapshot of Mozambican society, and validate our inferences to other populations.

Acknowledgements. This study was partly funded by the Trust and Influence Programme (FA8655-22-1-7051), European Office of Aerospace Research and Development, and US Air Force Office of Scientific Research.

References

1. Mozambique's Digital Transformation. https://www.trade.gov/market-intelligence/mozambiques-digital-transformation
2. on Artificial Intelligence, H.L.E.G.: Assessment list for trustworthy artificial intelligence (Altai) for self-assessment, July 2020. https://digital-strategy.ec.europa.eu/en/library/assessment-list-trustworthy-artificial-intelligence-altai-self-assessment
3. Bach, T.A., Khan, A., Hallock, H., Beltrão, G., Sousa, S.: A systematic literature review of user trust in AI-enabled systems: an HCI perspective. International Journal of Human-Computer Interaction, pp. 1–16 (2022). https://doi.org/10.1080/10447318.2022.2138826
4. Bazeley, P.: Issues in mixing qualitative and quantitative approaches to research. Appl. Qual. Methods Market. Manage. Res. **141**, 156 (2004)
5. Beltrão, G., Sousa, S.: Factors influencing trust in WhatsApp: a cross-cultural study. In: Stephanidis, C., et al. (eds.) HCII 2021. LNCS, vol. 13094, pp. 495–508. Springer, Cham (2021). https://doi.org/10.1007/978-3-030-90238-4_35
6. Bostrom, R.P., Heinen, J.S.: MIS problems and failures: a socio-technical perspective. part i: The causes. MIS Q. 17–32 (1977). https://doi.org/10.2307/248710
7. Commission, E.: Annexes to the proposal for a regulation of the european parliament and of the council laying down harmonised rules on artificial intelligence (artificial intelligence act) and amending certain union legislative acts (2021). https://ec.europa.eu/newsroom/dae/redirection/document/75789
8. Commission, E.: Proposal for a regulation of the European parliament and of the council laying down harmonised rules on artificial intelligence(artificial intelligence act) and amending certain union legislative acts (2021). https://eur-lex.europa.eu/legal-content/EN/TXT/?qid=1623335154975&uri=CELEX%3A52021PC0206
9. Crawford, K.: Halt the use of facial-recognition technology until it is regulated. Nature **572**(7771), 565–566 (2019)
10. Creswell, J.W., Clark, V.L.P.: Designing and Conducting Mixed Methods Research. Sage Publications (2017)
11. De Visser, E., et al.: Towards a theory of longitudinal trust calibration in human-robot teams. Int. J. Soc. Robot. **12**(2), 459–478 (2020). https://doi.org/10.1007/s12369-019-00596-x
12. Fimberg, K., Sousa, S.: The impact of website design on users' trust perceptions. In: Markopoulos, E., Goonetilleke, R., Ho, A., Luximon, Y. (eds.) Advances in Creativity, Innovation, Entrepreneurship and Communication of Design. AHFE 2020. AISC, vol. 1218, pp. 267–274. Springer, Cham (2020). https://doi.org/10.1007/978-3-030-51626-0_34
13. Gebru, B., Zeleke, L., Blankson, D., Nabil, M., Nateghi, S., Homaifar, A., Tunstel, E.: A review on human-machine trust evaluation: human-centric and machine-centric perspectives. IEEE Trans. Human Mach. Syst. (2022). https://doi.org/10.1080/0144929X.2019.1656779
14. Gulati, S., Sousa, S., Lamas, D.: Design, development and evaluation of a human-computer trust scale. Behav. Inf. Technol. **38**(10), 1004–1015 (2019). https://doi.org/10.1080/0144929X.2019.1656779
15. Hao, K.: South Africa's private surveillance machine is fueling a digital apartheid (2022). https://www.technologyreview.com/2022/04/19/1049996/south-africa-ai-surveillance-digital-apartheid/
16. Johnson, K.: How Wrongful Arrests Based on AI Derailed 3 Men's Lives (2022). https://www.wired.com/story/wrongful-arrests-ai-derailed-3-mens-lives/?mc_cid=187337992f

17. Johnson, K.: Iran Says Face Recognition Will ID Women Breaking Hijab Laws (2023). https://www.wired.com/story/iran-says-face-recognition-will-id-women-breaking-hijab-laws/
18. Li, L., Mu, X., Li, S., Peng, H.: A review of face recognition technology. IEEE Access **8**, 139110–139120 (2020). https://doi.org/10.1109/ACCESS.2020.3011028
19. Mayer, R.C., Davis, J.H., Schoorman, F.D.: An integrative model of organizational trust. Acad. Manag. Rev. **20**(3), 709–734 (1995). https://doi.org/10.5465/amr.1995.9508080335
20. Miles, M.B., Huberman, A.M., Saldaña, J.: Qualitative Data Analysis: A Methods Sourcebook. Sage publications (2018)
21. Miles, S., Rowe, G.: The laddering technique. Doing social psychology research, pp. 305–343 (2004)
22. Pinto, A., Sousa, S., Silva, C., Coelho, P.: Adaptation and validation of the HCTM scale into human-robot interaction portuguese context: a study of measuring trust in human-robot interactions. In: Proceedings of the 11th Nordic Conference on Human-Computer Interaction: Shaping Experiences, Shaping Society, pp. 1–4 (2020). https://doi.org/10.1145/3419249.3420087
23. Putnam, R.D.: Bowling alone: America's declining social capital. In: The City Reader, pp. 188–196. Routledge (2015)
24. Reynolds, T.J., Gutman, J.: Laddering theory, method, analysis, and interpretation. In: Understanding consumer decision making, pp. 40–79. Psychology Press (2001). https://doi.org/10.4324/9781410600844-9
25. Roser, M., Ritchie, H., Ortiz-Ospina, E.: Internet. Our World in Data (2015). https://ourworldindata.org/internet
26. Sousa, S., Kalju, T., et al.: Modeling trust in COVID-19 contact-tracing apps using the human-computer trust scale: online survey study. JMIR Hum. Factors **9**(2), e33951 (2022). https://doi.org/10.2196/33951
27. Sousa, S., Lamas, D., Dias, P.: A model for human-computer trust. In: Zaphiris, P., Ioannou, A. (eds.) LCT 2014. LNCS, vol. 8523, pp. 128–137. Springer, Cham (2014). https://doi.org/10.1007/978-3-319-07482-5_13
28. Urquhart, L.D., McGarry, G., Crabtree, A.: Legal provocations for HCI in the design and development of trustworthy autonomous systems. In: Nordic Human-Computer Interaction Conference, pp. 1–12 (2022). https://doi.org/10.1145/3546155.3546690

Data Physicalisation and Cross-Device

Comparing Screen-Based Version Control to Augmented Artifact Version Control for Physical Objects

Maximilian Letter$^{(\boxtimes)}$, Marco Kurzweg, and Katrin Wolf

Berlin University of Applied Sciences and Technologies (BHT), Berlin, Germany
{maximilian.letter,marco.kurzweg,katrin.wolf}@bht-berlin.de

Abstract. Besides referring to digital twins, the iterative development of physical objects cannot be easily managed in version control systems. However, physical content also could benefit from versioning for structured work and collaborative uses, thereby increasing equality between digital and physical design. Hence, it needs to be investigated what kind of system is most suitable for supporting a physical object version control. Focusing on the visualization of differences between states of a physical artifact, two systems were compared against each other in a lab study: a screen-based solution optimized for 3D models as baseline and an approach that augments a physical artifact with digital information as hypothesis. Our results indicate that the Augmented Artifact system is superior in task completion time but scores a lower usability rating than the baseline. Based on the results, we further provide design considerations for building a physical object version control system.

Keywords: Version Control · Augmented Reality · Physical Object

1 Introduction

Creating and altering physical objects is a fundamental ability of humans, which is supported by a natural understanding of tangible materials [26]. Therefore, working on physical artifacts is an intuitive way of bringing ideas to life. With the rise of computers, Computer Aided Design (CAD) software, and fabrication capabilities, however, creation of artifacts has seen a shift towards digital design workflows [22]. In digital design, work is done in front of a two-dimensional screen, iterating on fully digital representations. Physical results are then produced by dedicated fabrication machines, e.g. 3D printers or laser cutters. Working with CAD allows for precise manufacturing and offers the flexibility of virtual content, at the cost of being disconnected from the physical result during design as well as fabrication process. In addition, constant re-fabrication produces expenses in time and material, while amateur creatives often do not have

---

Supplementary Information The online version contains supplementary material available at https://doi.org/10.1007/978-3-031-42280-5_25.

J. Abdelnour Nocera et al. (Eds.): INTERACT 2023, LNCS 14142, pp. 391–415, 2023.
https://doi.org/10.1007/978-3-031-42280-5_25

equal access to such machines. Besides, there are application areas, e.g. architecture [1,18], fashion design [39], and crafting [16], where physical objects remain highly relevant. Physical creation, however, is restricted by its physicality. One constraint is that physical objects cannot be easily duplicated, and therefore it is difficult to save interim versions of an object during development. If different states of the object were captured, the current state could be compared to alternative versions, which is common practice with digital content. This appears to be a desirable feature for physical design, providing more equality in asynchronous and remote collaboration.

The structured use of saving, retrieving, and comparing interim states during design and development can be described as version control, which is provided by Version Control Systems (VCSs) [38]. This technology is especially well established in software development to the point that it has become an indispensable collaboration tool. It enables remote collaboration between software developers, while also supporting single users to comprehend and trace their progress of building software. The extensive use of VCSs brought forth numerous commercial applications, for example in the case of source code (SourceTree [2], GitKraken [3], and GitHub Desktop [19]) as well as 3D modeling (3D Repo [12], GrabCAD [25], and Onshape [34]). However, all these solutions are tailored toward digital design and do not include physical objects, besides working with virtual twins on two-dimensional displays. Research into VCSs for physical content has seen little exploration so far [28,36,44], leaving many remaining aspects to be studied. Such an approach represents an alternative route to digital design, focusing on working with and on physical objects. Therefore, it does not target professionals that usually work with CAD tools. We rather assume domains that could equally be carried out by novices (creative building, prototyping, craftsmanship). Therefore, general concepts of working with versioned physical objects are investigated, translating to people regardless of professional background.

To utilize the human's haptic interaction skills and natural understanding of the physical world [26], it is of importance to study if concepts and metaphors used in VCSs translate into physical space. We anticipate that this will preserve the artifact's tangibility and enables seamless interaction with virtual alternative versions in the real world. However, to this date, VCSs for physical objects are basically non-existent and metaphors of traditional VCSs have not been evaluated in the context of physical artifacts. Therefore, the question arises: "When building a physical-based VCS, which technology should be used, and how should the information be represented?". Accordingly, we performed a comparative study between two exemplary systems. One system builds and extends a concept that centers around the physical artifact using Augmented Reality (AR) [28], while the other one shows virtual twins on a screen. The evaluation focuses on displaying differences between versions of a physical artifact, where participants build from a given physical version to an alternative. Other aspects of VCSs, like the exploration of a version history, are not part of the evaluation.

2   Related Work

2.1   Digital and Physical Design

There exist many works that attempted to narrow the gap between physical and digital design by building on top of a digital design process, but also taking the physical artifact into account [21,37,41,45]. One area to do so is the intersection between digital and physical space by allowing users to interact with physical artifacts in-between or during fabrication [35,44,46]. As an example, a user can monitor and intervene a fabrication process in order to make manual changes to the produced object. In the work of Peng et al., the user wore a see-through Virtual Reality (VR) Head-mounted Display (HMD), in which upcoming changes were visualized on top of the fabricated physical object [35]. Yamaoka and Kakehi proposed an approach of including such a support in the fabrication machine, developing printer hardware which could show floating images on a 3D printer stage [46]. A similar approach was taken by Weichel et al. in their work from 2015 [44], displaying upcoming changes on a transparent projection screen, overlaid onto the physical outcome. Weichel et al. further supported versioning in their prototype, digitizing physical objects with 3D scanning inside the fabrication machine. Alternative versions could be viewed and selected on the mounted projection screen. As a workable material was chosen, the machine was able to alter the physical object to correspond to a selected alternative version. A drawback of these approaches is that they require a machining system, which is costly, highly specialized, and mostly stationary. In addition, many iterative physical design tasks do not require the fabrication of parts and live from the freedom of building and shaping with the own hands.

There have also been approaches of persisting information about its history in a physical object, like the machining of artifacts that are representative of the iterative development steps [43], or enhancing 3D-printed objects with markers that lead to a web-application for documentation purposes [14]. However, as this information was physically manifested, their appearance is static once fabricated. An additional drawback is the redundant production of material.

2.2   Version Control Systems

Version Control Systems (VCSs) are a widespread form of preserving the history of documents for later revision or comparison [38]. While being traditionally targeted at text-based content, there has been research on transferring the idea of VCS to other domains, such as images [48] and 3D modeling [8–11,13]. Doboš and Steed proposed an approach to mesh differencing and conflict resolution for 3D models [10], which was part of a revision control framework [11]. Doboš et al. further studied VCS-specific solutions in the context of 3D models in multiple publications, mainly targeted at computing and visualizing differences while also solving merge conflicts [9,13]. The proposed methods of Doboš were used in a comprehensive tool for collaboration on 3D models named 3D Repo [12,13]. A similar work by Denning and Pellacini determines the modified parts of a model and highlights them in a color-code [8]. The techniques used for displaying differing parts are used as inspirations for highlighting differences on the physical object itself.

The work by Perteneder et al. from 2015 attempted to build a VCS for physical objects [36]. In their prototype system, they used a motorized turntable and a monocular camera to digitize physical objects as a 360-degree collection of images. From the physical objects, that were identified via an RFID chip, a digital history of versions was created, which could be explored by co-located as well as by remote collaborators in a web interface. Versions, both the virtual and the physical ones, were presented in a 360°C view and could be annotated with notes. However, in the prototype by Perteneder et al., the physical object and version history were still separated between physical space and web interface.

Another approach in dealing with asynchronous work, including the work on physical artifacts, was taken by Fender and Holz, in their publication from 2022 [15]. They studied how changes and actions happening in the real world while a user spends time in VR could be preserved and replayed using 3D capture. Although the authors' approach also targets asynchronous work and collaboration as we do, the focus lies more on the correct causalities of (partly physical) actions than on the objects themselves.

Letter and Wolf proposed the concept of Tangible Version Control in 2022, utilizing AR and marker tracking to explore and compare alternative versions of a physical object [28]. In their prototype implementation, the concept was divided into two, timeline and comparisons. The timeline serves as a chronological representation of alternative versions that could be explored. Comparisons between a virtual version and the current physical state then took place directly on top of the physical artifact. The authors proposed three comparison modes, including a part-based detection of differences between the two objects. While their prototype conveyed a first glimpse at how AR could serve for a VCS, it was limited to part-based structures with all parts being pre-known. Further, the proposed metaphors and interaction designs were not evaluated.

3   User Study

In order to determine what type of system might be suitable for a physical object version control, we conducted a controlled lab study. For this purpose, an existing state-of-the-art VCS solution that can be used for managing 3D models in the web-browser was compared to a prototype implementation utilizing AR in combination with the physical artifact. We aim to evaluate the main difference between the two systems, which is the type of display – using a traditional 2D screen versus an AR experience – which results in having the physical object as a separate piece next to the screen versus merging virtual and physical information directly on top of the object. The two systems are referred to as Screen-Based 2D Version Control (2D) and Augmented Artifact Version Control (AA) accordingly. We used models built out of multiple LEGO®-like bricks for both, the virtual versions and the physical artifacts. This allowed the result of tasks to be controllable, while simultaneously being a familiar material to most participants. In both systems, participants worked with a physical object for which the differences to another version were shown through a computer monitor or a HMD respectively.

3.1 Experiment Design

The study focused on the inclusion of the physical object in the comparison process, which is the main novelty of AA. The evaluation followed a 1×2 within-subject design having the independent variable system, namely 2D and AA. Within-subject was the favored design as the participants had quite diverse backgrounds (see Sect. 3.5) and bias by individuals could be eliminated. The system was further studied as system per task, to gain more insight into how the systems are used. Therefore, each system was investigated three times (2D_add, AA_add, 2D_sub, AA_sub, 2D_exc, AA_exc). In the experiment, participants were asked to build a given physical version to a compared version.

3.2 Measurements

We selected our measurements on the basis of studies that were conducted in related work [9,13] as well as from publications where two or more systems were evaluated with a physical task [7,17,23]. The time participants required to fulfill a task was measured as Task Completion Time (TCT). In order to measure the effectiveness of a system, the Error Rate (ERROR) for each trial was calculated by recording how many of the parts were wrongly added or removed. System Usability (SU) was measured using the System Usability (SU) questionnaire [6]. In addition, we did measure Subjective Mental Load (SML) of participants using the Subjective Mental Effort Questionnaire (SMEQ) [47], as it was shown that it can be a suitable addition to usability questionnaires [40]. Besides the quantitative measures, we asked the participants for aspects they liked and disliked about the system in a semi-structured interview after a task was concluded.

3.3 Apparatus

Systems and Technologies. For the baseline system 2D, the 3D Repo [12] web app was used, as it is optimized for collaboration and version control of 3D models. It ran on a dedicated desktop computer in the Chrome [20] browser. The prototype for the AA system was built on the example of the work of Letter and Wolf [28]. It was implemented with Unity version LTS 2020.3 running on a HoloLens 2 [33] headset. Marker tracking was implemented using the Vuforia SDK in version 9.8. For managing information related to headset tracking and spatial understanding, the Mixed Reality Toolkit [32] was used.

The actual physical object was mounted on top of a three-dimensional marker. The marker was tracked by the HMD, therefore the position of the physical object in relation to it is known. Letter and Wolf proposed different comparison modes, which include the automated detection and highlighting of differences [28]. This is also the default visualization of differences for the 2D system.

Detection of Differences. To highlight differences in the paper from Letter and Wolf, they used an algorithm that detects differences using a part-based matching. This has the drawback of every part needing to be known beforehand, which makes it impractical and especially not usable for objects that are not made out of predefined parts. For this implementation, an alternative method is used that builds on surface-shaders, render queue, and stencil buffer. Therefore, three models are rendered on top of the physical object. First, the current version is drawn in a red highlight color, writing a stencil value for the rendered area. Afterward, the compared version is rendered, leaving only the removed areas in red and drawing everything else in green. At last, the current version is rendered a second time, testing for equal stencil values in the areas where the first two materials were rendered before. In this area, the object is displayed invisible as a phantom object [27], allowing it to see the real physical object. The phantom material has set a slight z-index offset to avoid flickering in the areas where all materials are rendered at the same depth. With the simple models used in this work, no noticeable overhead is produced, and the application runs stable at 60 frames per second. For the final visualizations, the physical object is not augmented in areas where no changes have to be made. Only areas that are subject to change are highlighted in either red or green highlights. This mimics the 2D implementation of displaying the model in neutral gray where no difference between versions was detected. A visualization of the augmentation effect can be found in the Figs. 1 and 2.

System-Specific Implementations. The two systems, 2D and AA, share the primary feature of displaying differences to another version as green and red highlights. Besides technological differences, like turning the model on 2D using mouse input versus the AA variant being physically transformed, there exist slight implementation differences. 3D Repo displays the red highlights as highly transparent colored areas, while green highlights are rendered as shaded opaque objects. In comparison, in the AA system, both red and green parts are rendered shaded. However, by technological differences, highlights cannot be displayed with full opacity due to the HoloLens display.

Another difference is the use of animated highlights for AA. Highlights pulse in a periodic pattern using a quartic easing function. At one end, highlights are turned off completely to allow the user to have a clear view of the physical object, while on the other end, highlights are fully visible. The animation takes 0.35 s to transition and then holds the state for one second before transitioning back to the other state. The use of animated highlights was implemented after the example of Letter and Wolf [28], as it enables users to check if they already placed or removed a part otherwise covered by highlights. To better convey the benefit, an example could be a pottery scenario, where an artifact is approximated step by step

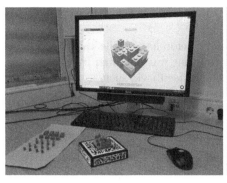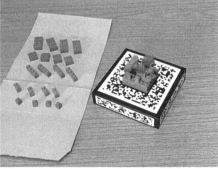

Fig. 1. Systems used in the user study. *Left:* workplace for 2D with a desktop monitor showing 3D Repo [12], on the bottom the physical object is located; *Right:* setup for AA, image taken from the HoloLens 2 HMD viewpoint focusing on the physical object.

towards the target form. The animation supports the reoccurring comparison of states when the object is modeled a tiny bit in each step.

Study Apparatus. The setups for the two systems were prepared in one room. For the 2D system, a computer with a mouse was set up. The same desk was used in the AA system, participants were seated in front of it. The computer mouse was moved away during the HMD use. The desk provided space for the user to maneuver the physical object. A visualization of the apparatus is shown in Fig. 1.

As the two systems were evaluated with three types of tasks each, 6 physical objects were prepared to work with. For each run, a prebuilt brick structure was placed right in front of the user, serving as the physical object to be altered in the task. The corresponding virtual twin as well as the alternative versions of the physical object were created in the Mecabricks workshop [31], a digital LEGO® builder software. A small selection of bricks was provided to build from one version to another. One additional physical artifact prepared to be used during the onboarding of a system.

The onboarding scenario was prepared as training before the actual study. In the case of 2D, the user was presented with a placeholder 3D Repo workspace, where they could manipulate a digital object with the mouse and get accustomed to the interface. In the case of AA, a physical placeholder-object was tracked and its outlines were highlighted. That way, the participant could inspect and move the object to see how the tracking worked. With both systems, the training object was not showing actual highlights on the object, since the onboarding rather focused on the interaction paradigms than on the task. The fact that participants were first confronted with highlights visualizations in their first actual run might affect the results of that system's task. However, since the system per task combinations were counter-balanced, see Sect. 3.6, this is unlikely to influence the overall results.

All versioned 3D models were prepared beforehand. The task completion time was measured using a secondary laptop that was operated by a researcher. Measurements that relied on active participant feedback, such as the used questionnaires, were filled out in between tasks using Google Forms [24]. The SMEQ was provided as a paper printout.

3.4   Tasks

Three types of tasks were designed to evaluate the systems. In each case, participants were required to alter the provided object. This process was varied in three tasks: (a) add parts to match the compared version; (b) remove parts to match the compared version; (c) exchange parts, which includes adding and removing parts to match the compared version. These kinds of tasks were chosen because they imply the users' understanding of differences between versions, which is otherwise difficult to assess, and provide more insights into how the systems can be used. For the *add*-tasks 2D_add and AA_add, 4 parts needed to be added, with one part being on top of another one that needs to be added. For the *subtract*-tasks 2D_sub and AA_sub, 4 parts needed to be removed, with one part being below another one that needs to be removed. The *exchange*-tasks 2D_exc and AA_exc required 3 parts to be removed and 3 parts to be added. The 6 system per task combinations, using 3 out of 6 objects, are shown in Fig. 2 in both the 2D and AA variant.

Fig. 2. The 6 system-per-task combinations, showing 3 out of 6 objects; same task-types are displayed on top of each other, from left to right (in tuples): 2D_add and AA_add, 2D_sub and AA_sub, 2D_exc and AA_exc.

Since the actions required to perform a task differ from each other by nature – e.g. adding a new part needs more steps than removing a part – the tasks are not of the same difficulty and therefore not directly comparable as individual variables but instead serve as different views onto one system. Also, the exchange-tasks, 2D_exc and AA_exc, are not a sum of the adding and subtraction tasks because they allowed for removing a part in one place and directly placing it on another spot. While the first two tasks represent single necessary actions of building from one version to another, the third one attempts to investigate the scalability of the concepts to more realistic and therefore more complex tasks. In order to have the tasks not drifting too far from each other in time to complete, the amount of steps needed for 2D_exc and AA_exc was increased, but not doubled.

3.5 Participants

We recruited 24 participants (of which 7 reported as male, 16 as female, and 1 as other gender) between the ages of 20 and 51 (mean 26.79, standard deviation 5.78). Participants were recruited from a university course and the personal network of a researcher, resulting in a diverse group of people with different backgrounds (e.g., computer science, social work, medicine, business management). The participants had no professional expertise in physical building, construction, or CAD design. They further had no prior experience with AR hardware like the one used in our study. Each participant received a short introduction to the concept of version control. None of the participants reported color-blindness.

3.6 Procedure

The procedure began with the signing of a consent form and data acquisition of demographic information. Afterward, participants were introduced to the apparatus (one system at a time) and could get accustomed to the interface and interaction design during onboarding. The onboarding lasted until participants stated that they were comfortable controlling the system.

Before the actual tasks began, the available building bricks were presented. The tasks were set up by a researcher so that a participant only had to click or lower the HMD visor to start. The order of system-per-task combinations was counter-balanced between all participants using a Latin square.

To further eliminate the potential of different task models affecting results, each task type could be carried out in one of two variants, which were also randomized in a balanced way for the used systems. At the end of each task, the participants were asked to complete the used questionnaires as well as to optionally give feedback about their experience. For the latter, they were asked what they liked about the system and what they did not like. The next task was prepared while the participant was filling out the post-task-questionnaire. This procedure was repeated for all 6 system-task-combinations. With the amount of 24 participants, the dataset contained 144 entries. In the finalization of the study, general ideas and thoughts towards the two used systems and the concept of version control for physical objects were collected from participants. The study took about 40 min in total per participant.

4 Results

We first analyze the quantitative results gathered for significant differences. Subsequently, qualitative answers taken from participants are investigated to explain the quantitative data obtained.

4.1 Quantitative Data

The quantitative data consisted of Task Completion Time (TCT), Error Rate (ERROR), Subjective Mental Load (SML), and System Usability (SU). We analyzed the findings comparing the systems 2D and AA, as well as a closer comparison of the systems using three tasks each, referred to as system-per-task. None of the data was normally distributed, as Shapiro-Wilk tests revealed (all data p < 0.0001). Therefore, we treated our data as non-parametric, utilizing Wilcoxon Signed-Rank tests for post-hoc analysis. When comparing systems, a p-value of 0.05 was used as a threshold for detecting significant differences. As the study design was 1×2 with multiple characteristics of the two systems, p-values were not corrected for multiple conditions. Tasks were not directly analyzed in comparison against each other, as this is neither the focus of the evaluation nor are the tasks directly comparable, as discussed in Sect. 3.4. Extensive quantitative results are also listed in the appendix.

Task Completion Time. The descriptive statistics for TCT led to the following results (in seconds): 2D (mean = 67.87, sd = 29.44) and AA (mean = 48.71, sd = 27.98), as well as for systems-per-task 2D_add (mean = 70.43, sd = 34.10), 2D_sub (mean = 59.42, sd = 23.86), 2D_exc (mean = 73.77, sd = 28.74), AA_add (mean = 54.94, sd = 30.84), AA_sub (mean = 36.64, sd = 24.21), and AA_exc (mean = 54.54, sd = 25.51). A Wilcoxon Signed-Rank test revealed a significant difference when comparing systems (p < 0.0001, z = −5.18). Subsequent comparison of systems per task with Wilcoxon Signed-Rank tests indicated significant differences between 2D_add and AA_add (p = 0.047, z = −1.99), 2D_sub and AA_sub (p = 0.0006, z = −3.41), as well as 2D_exc and AA_exc (p = 0.0003, z = −3.58). In each case, the AA variant resulted in faster completion times compared to their 2D counterpart, as shown in Fig. 3.

Error Rate. On average, participants produced 0.33 errors per task. Some executed all tasks flawlessly (n = 9), while some had one or more errors (n = 15), like misplaced bricks or missed differences. A Wilcoxon Signed-Rank test comparing 2D (mean = 0.24, sd = 0.59) and AA (mean = 0.42, sd = 0.82) showed no significance (p = 0.1188, z = −1.5597) and neither did the systems per task.

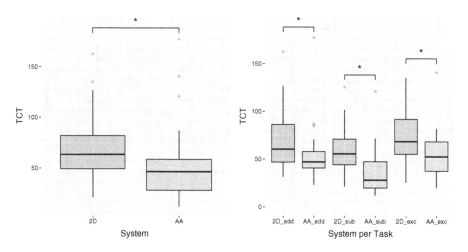

Fig. 3. Boxplots visualizing TCT data. *Left:* comparing the two systems 2D and AA against each other, resulting in a significant difference in favor of AA. *Right:* comparison of systems-per-task.

Mental Load. The descriptive statistics for SML led to the following results: 2D (mean = 49.78, sd = 41.72), AA (mean = 55.03, sd = 39.44). Wilcoxon Signed-Rank test comparing systems showed no significance (p = 0.1654, z = −1.3871). Also, no significant differences in SML for systems per task were found.

Usability. SU was measured through the SUS-questionnaire. When comparing system-wise with a Wilcoxon Signed Rank-test, the descriptive statistics of 2D (mean = 77.05, sd = 17.44) and AA (mean = 67.53, sd = 17.35) showed significant differences (p = 0.0021, z = −3.06). The descriptive statistics for systems-per-task were: 2D_add (mean = 81.04, sd = 16.01), 2D_sub (mean = 75.21, sd = 18.40), 2D_exc (mean = 74.90, sd = 17.87), AA_add (mean = 64.90, sd = 17.72), AA_sub (mean = 71.04, sd = 17.77), AA_exc (mean = 66.67, sd = 16.69). Post-Hoc analysis with Wilcoxon Signed-Rank tests comparing systems per task showed a significance between 2D_add and AA_add (p = 0.0025, z = −3.0283). A boxplot visualization of SU is shown in Fig. 4.

4.2 Qualitative Data

After each task, participants had the opportunity to give subjective feedback about the system they just worked with. Both, aspects that were liked and aspects that were disliked were explicitly asked for. At the end of the study, additional closing questions about the systems and their use were asked. Not every participant stated something, as it was optional. Further, some participants answered multiple times, adding up to a total number of 140 comments.

The qualitative data was coded using Grounded Theory [42]. In particular, we used axial and selective coding, starting with categories structured according

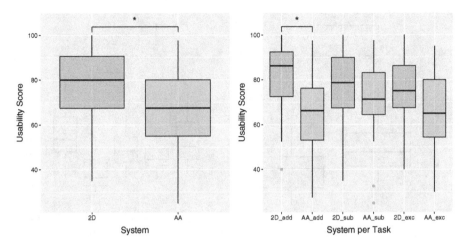

Fig. 4. Boxplots visualizing SU data. *Left:* comparing the significant difference between the two systems 2D and AA in favor of 2D. *Right:* task-wise comparison of systems, showing significant differences in the task type add.

to the questions that asked for positive or negative perceived aspects of a system [42]. To present results in a more understandable way, we grouped feedback by their main statements. In the following, stats are reported as n for the amount of participants and k as the amount of answers per statement.

Augmented Artifact has Clear Benefits: Multiple participants (n = 6, k = 8) mentioned the disconnect of physical and digital content when using the 2D system ("Control with the mouse and matching with the physical object [is] annoying", P7; "Had to change my hand very often from the Lego block to the computer mouse and thus had to reorient myself again and again", P1). Besides the challenge of working with the physical object and mouse, participants (n = 7, k = 9) stated the problem of aligning perspective ("Difficulty to find the starting point", P9) and keeping the orientation of digital and physical content in sync ("it was a bit difficult to put the digital object and the physical object in the same position to figure out where to place which stones").

Towards the Augmented Artifact system, participants (n = 10, k = 12) stated the benefit of having the highlight shown directly on top of the physical object ("Differences are immediately visible on the real object", P3; "Easily comprehensible three-dimensional AR representation", P8). Assumptions were made about the AR system's benefits ("In general I found it easier to perform the tasks with the glasses because using the computer screen made myself lose track of where I was with the real object", P4).

The majority of participants (n = 15, k = 15) stated a favored system in the closing question on the system feedback. Despite the benefits of the Augmented Artifact system, the distribution was almost equal, with 7 participants (47%)

stating a preference for the 2D system, while 8 (53%) participants favored the Augmented Artifact system.

Participants Anticipate Use for Physical VCSs: Asked about the concept, most participants (9 out of 11) mentioned that they like the idea and see potential in Augmented Artifact ("strong concept, never heard of it before, certainly useful in some industries, [...]", P15). One person added that the evaluation task was not a good fit for the Augmented Artifact system ("I think it's a cool idea, but it didn't feel very good in this case. Maybe it would be better for large scale models or machines", P3), which is in line with tracking issues, see Sect. 4.2. Some participants (n = 5, k = 5) named possible application areas, namely architecture, prototyping, arts with different materials, design and interior, and manufacturing (everything named once). As participants were not experts in one of the named domains, these suggestions should be taken with care.

HMD Issues Affect Augmented Artifact Usability: The most often made critique point on Augmented Artifact (n = 15, k = 23) was the imperfect tracking ("The real bricks have been slightly offset, slight confusion", P13; "did not fit exactly on the model", P16). This included fiddling with the headset ("The tracking didn't work that well. That's why I had to adjust the headset in the beginning from time to time", P2). Participants further criticized (n = 11, k = 15) the visuals through the HMD ("Sharpness of the objects varies in parts", P6; "Red looked more like an orange", P1). Another point of critique (n = 9, k = 12) was on the discomfort of wearing a HMD ("Unpleasant for eyes and head", P11; "Feeling of wearing the glasses", P9). Related to its novelty, participants (n = 6, k = 7) named their feeling of getting accustomed to the system ("I have noticed progress compared to the first task with the glasses", P11).

Physical and Virtual State Synchronicity Wanted: In the case of 2D, one participant suggested a new functionality for the controls ("It is easy to get confused if you have already removed/added the parts. If you could mark them as 'done' it would be easier", P14). Similarly, participants (n = 3, k = 4) proposed the removal of highlights after a brick has been added/removed for Augmented Artifact ("Perhaps it would also be possible to recognize the stones and thus indicate whether the respective stone has already been added/removed", P1). Multiple participants (n = 10, k = 12) further suggested that highlights should automatically disappear corresponding to an action ("might be even easier if the already removed parts could 'disappear' or change color", P14; "Remove highlighting after a part has been added. Show errors if necessary", P3). Some expected such behavior and were surprised that it did not work as they expected ("The highlights did not disappear after the stones were removed or added", P22; "that the remaining stones are not marked somehow", P18).

Visualizations are Understandable: With the Augmented Artifact system, positive comments were made on the overall design of the system (n = 12, k = 16), naming the highlight colors ("Clearly recognizable highlights", P13; "very clear representation", P11) and general visualization ("I feel I could see the parts that had to be placed under other ones and I find that okay", P4). Fewer participants (n = 6, k = 8) reported issues with the visuals ("the bricks in the back row are harder to see than the front bricks", P15). This is in line with 2D feedback being mostly positive about the visualizations (n = 13, k = 22), accompanied by some (n = 6, k = 6) geometry-related issues ("bricks were partially occluded", P0).

Animation Design has Room for Improvement: Some participants (n = 3, k = 6) liked the feature of using animated highlights on Augmented Artifact ("I like the fact that the stones to be added appear only briefly and then disappear again, so I can see more clearly where the stones should go"). One participant mentioned that the benefit was only apparent to him after some time ("[...] the flashing was helpful when removing after all", P5). Multiple participants (n = 5, k = 5) were surprised by the animation ("the flashing of the red stones was irritating at first", P15; "It was exhausting that the projection kept going on and off, I had to get used to it a bit", P17). As this was not part of the tutorial before the actual tasks, see Sect. 3.3, participants did not expect this behavior. One participant further recommended the ability to manually toggle the visibility of highlights on and off ("[...] instead of flashing the stones maybe manually fade them in and out, [...]", P5).

Transparent Parts in 2D are Disliked: The red display of bricks that have to be removed was criticized (n = 8, k = 9), as it was semi-transparent ("the red stones are too transparent", P16; "The red marked stones, which were on top of each other, were somewhat difficult to distinguish from each other", P13).

Not All Participants Like 2D Controls: Multiple comments (n = 8, k = 11) mentioned that the controls of 2D were easy to use as well as easy to learn ("easy and intuitive", P7; "Operation was very simple, known from other systems/programs", P11). Contrary to these statements, nearly half of the participants (n = 10, k = 13) disliked the mouse as interaction device ("I disliked the handling with the mouse a little", P2).

5 Discussion

Based on the results presented in Sect. 4, it can be stated that Augmented Artifact appears to be a promising system for comparing and converting between different versions of a physical object. While it has drawbacks in usability compared to the baseline Screen-Based 2D Version Control (2D) system, it also provides significant advantages in task efficiency. The qualitative feedback is closely aligned with the quantitative results, supporting our findings and providing additional insights in using a physical Version Control System (VCS).

5.1 Interpretation of Results

Using Augmented Artifact leads to significantly faster task completion time compared to the 2D system. As qualitative feedback underlines, the main factor lies probably in the AR technology, showing information directly on top of the physical object and removing the need to translate from one space to another. However, participants also experienced technical drawbacks, leading to poor usability. As a reason for this, participants named the HMD as rather inconvenient, pointing towards uncomfortable fit and imperfect display, see Sect. 4.2. Further, Augmented Artifact is strongly dependent on robust tracking, as highlights are directly connected to the real world and therefore prone to deviations. In accordance, imperfect tracking turned out to be a major influence. Fiducial markers were used to make the tracking as robust as possible, but computational capabilities remain limited on standalone HMDs, leading to offsets and delays.

Besides technical influences, the systems slightly varied in features and visuals, which was reflected in qualitative results. Feedback indicates that the semi-transparent visuals of 2D were disliked and may have influenced its usability. On the other hand, the non-static visuals of AA could have been a negative impact on usability or mental load of participants that felt stressed by them. Many participants commented on the missing detection of their physical changes in the AA system, even though both systems worked the same way - by not detecting if a manipulation of bricks took place. This points towards different anticipations of technologies, as that expectation was not made for the 2D variant.

Looking at usability results at last, James Lewis and Jeff Sauro [29] rate the 67.53 usability score of Augmented Artifact with grade C, just below 68, which marks the average value of being a usable product. Bangor et al. rate the 67.53 score in the area of 'marginally acceptable' [4]. It should be kept in mind that both systems have rather poor usability, indicating plenty of potential for improvement. We anticipate that in the case of Augmented Artifact, higher fidelity and less error-prone hardware would automatically result in higher usability.

5.2 Comparison to Related Work

As there is a limited amount of research in the area of version control for physical design, it is difficult to directly compare our contribution to other publications, as these are mostly parallel themes. The research on 3D model comparisons and differencing algorithms such as the ones presented by Doboš et al. [9,13] focus on fully digital 3D modeling. The research on hybrid fabrication, such as the work of Weichel et al. [44], represents the production of physical goods but with fabrication as medium. Our research on the other hand anticipates physical design first forming a third research branch. With one system providing higher usability (2D) and the other one faster task completion (Augmented Artifact), it is difficult to assess which system is more suitable as a physical VCS. Since Augmented Artifact is foremost limited by existing technology, we anticipate that it provides major potential for improvement.

5.3   Generalizability of Results

The study conducted in this work used an abstract physical design task. It can be assumed that the main benefit of Augmented Artifact - directly having information on the physical object - is maintained on other tasks regardless of complexity. Differences could even increase with bigger and more complex objects, where translation and zooming would become relevant on 2D.

LEGO®-like bricks were chosen as task-material in this work as a substitute for other materials, allowing for replication and comparability of results. It represents atomic tasks in a coherent system, similar to domains where standardized parts are used. However, LEGO®'s generalizability is probably reached for smaller content without placement regulations, as tracking offsets would be especially harmful. Continuous materials (i.e. clay) or the dynamic breaking down of one entity (i.e. carving) are also not supported and require further research.

Lastly, a tradeoff of greater efficiency for a more tedious user experience does not necessarily align with expectations for general-use technologies, hinting at professional application areas, see Sect. 5.5.

5.4   Limitations

Both systems do not regard the texture of objects, the versions and the physical objects in the user study were of uniform gray color. This differs from real world use cases where objects are of one or more colors. In that case, it needs to be studied to what degree such a color variance influences the understanding of the chosen highlighting metaphors if they interfere with the object's color.

The focus of the conducted study was on how the two systems support the understanding of differences between versions. While this is a crucial aspect of VCSs, it is not the sole factor that makes a system usable or efficient. Usually, a VCS also handles other repository related information, like the representation of multiple commits in tree structures. Therefore, it has to be stated that the findings of this work are not comprehensive for the topic of physical object VCSs but provide insights into a facet of these rather complex systems, namely the comparison of versions, one physical and one virtual.

Lastly, our conducted study had the following limitations. First, it only compared two systems and a limited amount of participants. Second, it is difficult to assess user understanding of the differences between objects Therefore building from one version to another was chosen as a task, implying understanding by the user. However, the act of building can be influenced by other factors. Lastly, since physical based VCSs are quite novel, the 2D system served as ground truth as it was not possible to provide another ground truth as manipulation test.

5.5   Future Work

As this field of research is relatively novel, there are many areas for improvement. Some future work packages result from qualitative participant feedback. For instance, the automated detection of physically added and removed parts can be named. Such a feature would require some form of live 3D scanning or shape recognition that runs alongside, thereby not interrupting the workflow. As non-disruptive digitization of intermediate versions is another facet still missing in an Augmented Artifact implementation, this issue lines up with it.

Besides, it must be considered what the best use of such a VCS might be. Creative physical modeling, prototyping, or craftsmanship appear suitable. However, participants rated Augmented Artifact's usability significantly lower than the 2D system despite higher efficiency and proposed its use in professional domains. This potentially suggests that participants saw it as a specialized technique.

In addition, more evaluation regarding different scopes and materials is required. Augmented Artifact could also be applied in relation to a lot bigger objects, thereby reducing tracking inaccuracies. An interesting case is the versioning of immobile objects that are so big that a user fits inside them, for example, a building site, which was suggested by a participant. Such an approach would result in the case in which the actually constructed and 3D-scanned walls could be compared to the original building plan or alternative layouts while being inside the object. Future studies on Augmented Artifact could look into realistic and more complex artifacts to version. Also, it is of interest how to support the use of real world materials, including glue and non-reversible work steps.

Lastly, following limitations discussed in Sect. 5.4, Augmented Artifact needs to be evaluated in more aspects of what a VCS is made of. For example, the exploration of alternative versions needs to be revisited. While metaphors from existing VCS might be transferable, as Letter and Wolf suggest [28], alternative metaphors and paradigms might be more applicable.

6   Design Considerations

To the best of our knowledge, there does not exist a fully built physical-based VCS. While this work does not provide a thorough implementation, we attempt at gaining a deeper understanding of the topic and how such a system could be designed. Based on our results, we provide recommendations for building and using an Augmented Artifact VCS. Naturally, these considerations are close to current benefits and challenges of AR. However, some aspects are especially relevant for the case of version control with AR and therefore pointed out.

Suitable Augmented Artifact application: Augmented Artifact is reasonable when good spatial understanding of the object and its changes is required. It helps to connect the information manifested in virtual versions straight to a real object. Artifacts like the ones used in the user study appear to be already of high enough complexity to justify the use of Augmented Artifact, as study results show faster task times compared to the 2D variant. For objects of lower complexity, a traditional desktop based approach might be sufficient. Another reason to use Augmented Artifact is when the user's hand should be free for physical tasks, as the 2D variant usually occupies at least one hand.

When using Augmented Artifact, fiducial markers should be applied for best tracking results. If the artifact is bigger, object tracking could be feasible as long as its appearance is suitable to be tracked [5,30].

Synchronous physical and virtual states: Qualitative answers clearly show that, when using a system that is closely connected to the physical world, users expect their physical actions to be reflected in the system state. This differs from AR applications in which the physical environment serves as a scene to place virtual objects on. Further investigation into how to best register physical changes is required, since this prototype does not offer any handling of this. As a possible predecessor to automated detection of physical changes by the system, users should be able to manually confirm their physical actions in the system.

Consistent and Adaptive Representations: Based on slight divergences in the representation of visuals between 2D and Augmented Artifact and the corresponding feedback of users, we conclude on how to best visualize version differences. Regardless of if content needs to be removed or added to the physical artifact, both variants should be differentiable but consistent in style, signaling equal importance. The overall visibility and transparency of highlights could be open for adjustments to user preference. The automated alteration of highlights with the use of animations can help users to perform physical actions by making the physical content briefly visible. However, this behavior might not be required in every state of a task. Further, it can confuse or stress users if they have no control over it. We therefore recommend allowing users to toggle animated differences based on what they require to fulfill the version transition.

7   Conclusion

Just as digital content creation is supported by version control systems, physical design could be enriched by information about alternative versions. Our proposal for designing such a system is Augmented Artifact, which utilizes augmented reality to enhance the physical artifact itself, while changes from one version to another are manually performed by users. In order to evaluate the concept of Augmented Artifact, a controlled user study was conducted, comparing a prototype implementation against a screen-based state-of-the-art system. Results indicate significantly faster completion times for the Augmented Artifact approach while scoring significantly lower usability. However, qualitative data indicates that this is majorly related to the limitations of the used hardware. Feedback further gave insights on how a physical version control system should look like and what features might be of importance. We derived design considerations that can help researchers how to build and use such a system:

(a) Augmented Artifact is suitable when objects are not of trivial complexity, free hands are beneficial, and tracking can be assured.

(b) Physical changes made by the user should be reflected in the system's state, as the physical artifact is perceived as an integral part of the system.

(c) Representation of changes should be consistent across task types and animations should be adaptive.

As version control for physical content is a novel approach, a thorough system remains to be built. The work presented here merely demonstrates the feasibility and benefits of Augmented Artifact and is an early approach to evaluating the comparison between physical and virtual versions. Thus, further research on physical version control systems and how to use them is worth to be conducted.

A   Appendix

Full results for the dependent variables Usability, Error Rate, Task Completion Time, and Mental Load. Only comparable tasks were tested against each other, variables were not compared cross-task. As no individual conditions were compared, but systems per task, a threshold of p < 0.05 is used for significance. Significant results are displayed in bold (Tables 1, 2, 3, 4 and Figs. 5, 6, 7 and 8).

Table 1. Results for the System Usability of Wilcoxon Signed Rank tests.

Usability	$Mean, SD$ **(2D)**	$Mean, SD$ **(AA)**	z-value	p-value
Across all tasks	**77.05, 17.44**	**67.53, 17.35**	**−3.065**	**0.0022**
Add parts	**81.04, 16.01**	**64.90, 17.72**	**−3.0284**	**0.0025**
Subtract parts	75.21, 18.40	71.04, 17.77	−0.9006	0.368
Exchange parts	74.90, 17.87	66.67, 16.69	−1.49	0.136

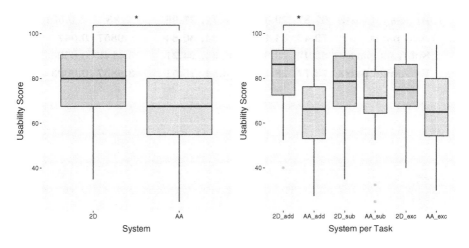

Fig. 5. Boxplots visualizing System Usability data. *Left:* comparing the two systems 2D and AA. *Right:* task-wise comparison of systems.

Table 2. Results for the Error Rate of Wilcoxon Signed Rank tests.

Error Rate	$Mean, SD$ (2D)	$Mean, SD$ (AA)	z-value	p-value
Across all tasks	0.24, 0.59	0.42, 0.82	−1.559	0.1188
Add parts	0.29, 0.69	0.58, 0.97	−1.3463	0.1782
Subtract parts	0.00, 0.00	0.21, 0.51	−1.7008	0.0889
Exchange parts	0.42, 0.72	0.46, 0.88	−0.2123	0.8318

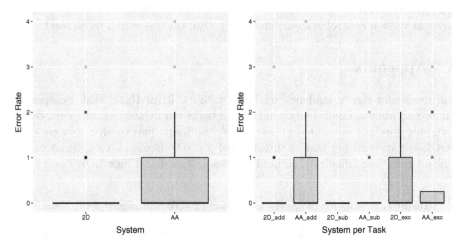

Fig. 6. Boxplots visualizing Error Rate data. *Left:* comparing the two systems 2D and AA. *Right:* task-wise comparison of systems.

Table 3. Results for the Task Completion Time of Wilcoxon Signed Rank tests.

Task Comp. Time	$Mean, SD$ (2D)	$Mean, SD$ (AA)	z-value	p-value
Across all tasks	**67.87, 29.44**	**48.71, 27.98**	**-5.188**	**< 0.001**
Add parts	**70.43, 34.10**	**54.94, 30.84**	**−1.9857**	**0.047**
Subtract parts	**59.42, 23.86**	**36.64, 24.21**	**−3.4142**	**0.0006**
Exchange parts	**73.77, 28.74**	**54.54, 25.51**	**−3.5857**	**0.0003**

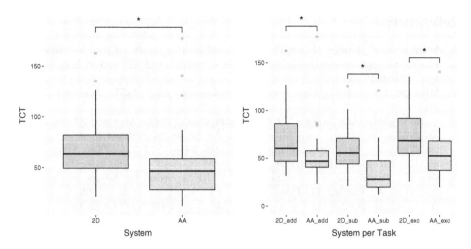

Fig. 7. Boxplots visualizing Task Completion Time data. *Left:* comparing the two systems 2D and AA. *Right:* task-wise comparison of systems.

Table 4. Results for the Mental Load of Wilcoxon Signed Rank tests.

Mental Load	$Mean, SD$ (2D)	$Mean, SD$ (AA)	z-value	p-value
Across all tasks	49.78, 41.72	55.03, 39.44	−1.387	0.1654
Add parts	46.79, 45.16	58.46, 42.94	−1.9002	0.0574
Subtract parts	49.08, 40.58	48.92, 43.18	−0.0857	0.9316
Exchange parts	53.46, 40.77	57.71, 32.18	−0.828	0.4076

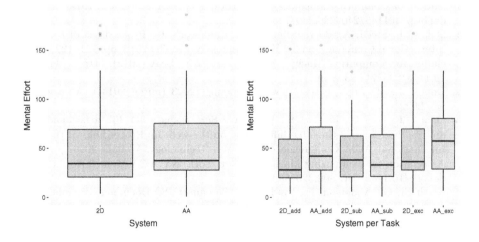

Fig. 8. Boxplots visualizing Mental Load data. *Left:* comparing the two systems 2D and AA. *Right:* task-wise comparison of systems.

References

1. Anshuman, S., Kumar, B.: Architecture and HCI: a review of trends towards an integrative approach to designing responsive space. Int. J. IT Archit. Eng. Constr. **2**(4), 273–284 (2004)
2. Atlassian: Sourcetree. https://www.sourcetreeapp.com/ (2023). Accessed 23 Jan 2023
3. Axosoft: GitKraken. https://www.gitkraken.com/ (2023). Accessed 23 Jan 2023
4. Bangor, A., Kortum, P.T., Miller, J.T.: An empirical evaluation of the system usability scale. Int. J. Hum.-Comput. Interact. **24**(6), 574–594 (2008). https://doi.org/10.1080/10447310802205776
5. Bay, H., Tuytelaars, T., Van Gool, L.: SURF: speeded up robust features. In: Leonardis, A., Bischof, H., Pinz, A. (eds.) ECCV 2006. LNCS, vol. 3951, pp. 404–417. Springer, Heidelberg (2006). https://doi.org/10.1007/11744023_32
6. Brooke, J., et al.: Sus-a quick and dirty usability scale. Usability Eval. Ind. **189**(194), 4–7 (1996)
7. Büttner, S., Prilla, M., Röcker, C.: Augmented reality training for industrial assembly work - are projection-based AR assistive systems an appropriate tool for assembly training? In: Proceedings of the 2020 CHI Conference on Human Factors in Computing Systems, CHI 2020, pp. 1–12. Association for Computing Machinery, New York, NY, USA (2020). https://doi.org/10.1145/3313831.3376720
8. Denning, J.D., Pellacini, F.: MeshGit: diffing and merging meshes for polygonal modeling. ACM Trans. Graph. **32**(4), 35:1–35:10 (2013). https://doi.org/10.1145/2461912.2461942
9. Doboš, J., Mitra, N.J., Steed, A.: 3d timeline: reverse engineering of a part-based provenance from consecutive 3d models. In: Computer Graphics Forum. vol. 33, pp. 135–144. Wiley Online Library, Computer Graphics Forum (2014)
10. Doboš, J., Steed, A.: 3D Diff: an interactive approach to mesh differencing and conflict resolution. In: SIGGRAPH Asia 2012 Technical Briefs, pp. 1–4. SA 2012, Association for Computing Machinery, New York, NY, USA, November 2012. https://doi.org/10.1145/2407746.2407766
11. Doboš, J., Steed, A.: 3d revision control framework. In: Proceedings of the 17th International Conference on 3D Web Technology, Web3D 2012, pp. 121–129. Association for Computing Machinery, New York, NY, USA (2012). https://doi.org/10.1145/2338714.2338736
12. Doboš, J.: 3D Repo. https://www.3drepo.io/ (2023 (initial 2014)). Accessed 01 Sep 2022
13. Doboš, J., Fan, C., Friston, S., Wong, C.: Screen space 3D diff: a fast and reliable method for real-time 3D differencing on the web. In: Proceedings of the 23rd International ACM Conference on 3D Web Technology, Web3D 2018, pp. 1–9. Association for Computing Machinery, New York, NY, USA, June 2018. https://doi.org/10.1145/3208806.3208809
14. Ettehadi, O., Anderson, F., Tindale, A., Somanath, S.: Documented: embedding information onto and retrieving information from 3D printed objects. In: Proceedings of the 2021 CHI Conference on Human Factors in Computing Systems, CHI 2021, pp. 1–11. Association for Computing Machinery, New York, NY, USA, May 2021. https://doi.org/10.1145/3411764.3445551
15. Fender, A.R., Holz, C.: Causality-preserving asynchronous reality. In: CHI Conference on Human Factors in Computing Systems, CHI 2022, Association for Computing Machinery, New York, NY, USA (2022). https://doi.org/10.1145/3491102.3501836

16. Frankjær, R., Dalsgaard, P.: Understanding craft-based inquiry in HCI. In: Proceedings of the 2018 Designing Interactive Systems Conference, pp. 473–484 (2018)
17. Funk, M., Kosch, T., Schmidt, A.: Interactive worker assistance: comparing the effects of in-situ projection, head-mounted displays, tablet, and paper instructions. In: Proceedings of the 2016 ACM International Joint Conference on Pervasive and Ubiquitous Computing, UbiComp 2016, pp. 934–939. Association for Computing Machinery, New York, NY, USA, September 2016. https://doi.org/10.1145/2971648.2971706
18. Gibson, I., Kvan, T., Wai Ming, L.: Rapid prototyping for architectural models. Rapid Prototyping J. **8**(2), 91–95 (2002)
19. GitHub, I.: GitHub Desktop. https://desktop.github.com/ (2023). Accessed 23 Jan 2023
20. Google: Chrome. https://www.google.com/intl/en_us/chrome/ (2023). Accessed 23 Jan 2023
21. Gulay, E., Kotnik, T., Lucero, A.: Exploring a feedback-oriented design process through curved folding. In: Proceedings of the 2021 CHI Conference on Human Factors in Computing Systems, CHI 2021, pp. 1–8. Association for Computing Machinery, New York, NY, USA, May 2021. https://doi.org/10.1145/3411764.3445639
22. Gulay, E., Lucero, A.: Integrated workflows: generating feedback between digital and physical realms. In: Proceedings of the 2019 CHI Conference on Human Factors in Computing Systems, CHI 2019, pp. 1–15. Association for Computing Machinery, New York, NY, USA, May 2019. https://doi.org/10.1145/3290605.3300290
23. Henderson, S.J., Feiner, S.K.: Augmented reality in the psychomotor phase of a procedural task. In: 2011 10th IEEE International Symposium on Mixed and Augmented Reality, pp. 191–200, October 2011. https://doi.org/10.1109/ISMAR.2011.6092386
24. Inc., G.: GoogleForms. https://docs.google.com/forms (2023). Accessed 23 Jan 2023
25. Inc., S.: GrabCAD. https://grabcad.com/workbench (2023). Accessed 23 Jan 2023
26. Ishii, H.: Tangible bits: beyond pixels. In: Proceedings of the 2nd International Conference on Tangible and Embedded Interaction, TEI 2008, pp. xv–xxv. Association for Computing Machinery, New York, NY, USA (2008). https://doi.org/10.1145/1347390.1347392
27. Kalkofen, D., Sandor, C., White, S., Schmalstieg, D.: Visualization techniques for augmented reality. In: Furht, B. (ed.) Handbook of Augmented Reality, pp. 65–98. Springer, New York, New York, NY (2011). https://doi.org/10.1007/978-1-4614-0064-6_3, http://link.springer.com/10.1007/978-1-4614-0064-6_3
28. Letter, M., Wolf, K.: Tangible version control: exploring a physical object's alternative versions. In: CHI Conference on Human Factors in Computing Systems Extended Abstracts, CHI EA 2022, Association for Computing Machinery, New York, NY, USA (2022). https://doi.org/10.1145/3491101.3519686
29. Lewis, J.R., Sauro, J.: Item benchmarks for the system usability scale. J. Usability Stud. **13**(3), 158–167 (2018)
30. Lowe, D.G.: Distinctive image features from scale-invariant keypoints. Int. J. Comput. Vis. **60**(2), 91–110 (2004)
31. Mecabricks: Mecabricks. https://mecabricks.com/en/workshop (2023). Accessed 23 Jan 2023
32. Microsoft: mixed reality ToolKit. https://docs.microsoft.com/en-us/windows/mixed-reality/mrtk-unity/packages/mrtk-packages (2023). Accessed 23 Jan 2023
33. Microsoft: HoloLens. https://www.microsoft.com/en-us/hololens (2023 (initial 2015)), Accessed 01 Sep 2022

34. Onshape: Onshape. https://www.onshape.com/en/features/data-management (2023). Accessed 23 Jan 2023
35. Peng, H., et al.: RoMA: interactive fabrication with augmented reality and a robotic 3D printer. In: Proceedings of the 2018 CHI Conference on Human Factors in Computing Systems, CHI 2018, pp. 1–12. Association for Computing Machinery, New York, NY, USA, April 2018. https://doi.org/10.1145/3173574.3174153
36. Perteneder, F., Grossauer, E.M., Xu, Y., Haller, M.: Catch-up 360: digital benefits for physical artifacts. In: Proceedings of the Ninth International Conference on Tangible, Embedded, and Embodied Interaction, TEI 2015, pp. 105–108. Association for Computing Machinery, New York, NY, USA (2015). https://doi.org/10.1145/2677199.2680564
37. Reipschläger, P., Dachselt, R.: DesignAR: immersive 3D-modeling combining augmented reality with interactive displays. In: Proceedings of the 2019 ACM International Conference on Interactive Surfaces and Spaces, ISS 2019, pp. 29–41. Association for Computing Machinery, New York, NY, USA, November 2019. https://doi.org/10.1145/3343055.3359718
38. Ruparelia, N.B.: The history of version control. SIGSOFT Softw. Eng. Notes **35**(1), 5–9 (2010). https://doi.org/10.1145/1668862.1668876
39. Särmäkari, N.: Digital 3d fashion designers: cases of atacac and the fabricant. Fashion Theor. **27**(1), 85–114 (2023)
40. Sauro, J., Dumas, J.S.: Comparison of three one-question, post-task usability questionnaires. In: Proceedings of the SIGCHI Conference on Human Factors in Computing Systems, CHI 2009, pp. 1599–1608. Association for Computing Machinery, New York, NY, USA (2009). https://doi.org/10.1145/1518701.1518946
41. Song, H., Guimbretière, F., Hu, C., Lipson, H.: ModelCraft: capturing freehand annotations and edits on physical 3D models. In: Proceedings of the 19th annual ACM symposium on User interface software and technology, UIST 2006, pp. 13–22. Association for Computing Machinery, New York, NY, USA, October 2006. https://doi.org/10.1145/1166253.1166258
42. Strauss, A., Corbin, J.M.: Grounded Theory in Practice. Sage, Newcastle upon Tyne (1997)
43. Tseng, T., Tsai, G.: Process products: capturing design iteration with digital fabrication. In: Proceedings of the Ninth International Conference on Tangible, Embedded, and Embodied Interaction, TEI 2015, pp. 631–636. Association for Computing Machinery, New York, NY, USA, January 2015. https://doi.org/10.1145/2677199.2687891
44. Weichel, C., Hardy, J., Alexander, J., Gellersen, H.: ReForm: integrating physical and digital design through bidirectional fabrication. In: Proceedings of the 28th Annual ACM Symposium on User Interface Software & Technology, UIST 2015, pp. 93–102. Association for Computing Machinery, New York, NY, USA, November 2015. https://doi.org/10.1145/2807442.2807451
45. Weichel, C., Lau, M., Kim, D., Villar, N., Gellersen, H.W.: MixFab: a mixed-reality environment for personal fabrication. In: Proceedings of the SIGCHI Conference on Human Factors in Computing Systems, CHI 2014, pp. 3855–3864. Association for Computing Machinery, New York, NY, USA, April 2014. https://doi.org/10.1145/2556288.2557090
46. Yamaoka, J., Kakehi, Y.: MiragePrinter: interactive fabrication on a 3D printer with a mid-air display. In: ACM SIGGRAPH 2016 Studio, SIGGRAPH 2016, pp. 1–2. Association for Computing Machinery, New York, NY, USA, July 2016. https://doi.org/10.1145/2929484.2929489

47. Zijlstra, F.: Efficiency in Work Behavior: A Design Approach for Modern Tools. Delft University Press, Delft, 01, 1993
48. Zünd, F., Poulakos, S., Kapadia, M., Sumner, R.W.: Story version control and graphical visualization for collaborative story authoring. In: Proceedings of the 14th European Conference on Visual Media Production (CVMP 2017), CVMP 2017, Association for Computing Machinery, New York, NY, USA (2017). https:// doi.org/10.1145/3150165.3150175

EmoClock: Communicating Real-Time Emotional States Through Data Physicalizations

Dennis Peeters[1], Champika Ranasinghe[3](✉) (iD), Auriol Degbelo[2](iD),
and Faizan Ahmed[4](iD)

[1] Creative Technology, University of Twente, Enschede, The Netherlands
d.w.m.peeters@utwente.nl
[2] Chair of Geoinformatics, TU Dresden, Dresden, Germany
auriol.degbelo@tu-dresden.de
[3] Data Management & Biometrics, University of Twente, Enschede, The Netherlands
c.m.eparanasinghe@utwente.nl
[4] Formal Methods & Tools, University of Twente, Enschede, The Netherlands
faizan.ahmed@utwente.nl

Abstract. Expressive interfaces that communicate human emotional state (e.g., level of arousal) are beneficial to many applications. In this work, we use a research-through-design approach to learn about the challenges and opportunities involved in physicalizing emotional data derived from biosignals in real-time. We present EmoClock, a physicalization that uses a clock as a metaphor to communicate arousal and valence derived from biosignal data and lessons learned from its evaluation.

Keywords: Data Physicalization · Biosignals and Biosensing ·
Soma-based design · Soma data · Emotion

1 Introduction

Data physicalization or physical visualizations of data [10,14] use material properties often in combination with sensing and actuation to create multisensory, expressive, embodied and engaging interactions with data. While data visualizations primarily focus on the sense of vision, data physicalizations focus on creating data representations that can not only be seen but also can be touched, smelled, heard or tasted thus enabling multisensory data experiences and perception [20]. The materiality of physicalizations offers new possibilities for engaging with data. In this work, we focus on the physicalization of users' emotional states.

Various fields (e.g., psychology, psychiatry, behavioural sciences, social sciences, human-computer interaction, affective computing, neurophysiology) require the measurement of the human emotional state during user studies [3]. Due to convenience and ease of interpretation, many researchers (e.g., in behavioural sciences, marketing and psychology) use subjective measurement

J. Abdelnour Nocera et al. (Eds.): INTERACT 2023, LNCS 14142, pp. 416–425, 2023.
https://doi.org/10.1007/978-3-031-42280-5_26

Fig. 1. Emotion physicalization: from sensing to physical actuation: (left) - the wearable sensing kit that senses heart rate (HR) and galvanic skin response (GSR) data and communicates them to a central server for further processing; (middle) - the data physicalization that represents the emotional state derived from HR and GSR data; (right) - a closer look at the representation of emotional state using LED light as a simple physical actuation.

tools such as the Self-Assessment Manikin (SAM) scale [2]. Nonetheless, human biosignal data (e.g., heart rate, heart rate variation, skin conductance, breathing rate) provide useful insights into human emotional and cognitive states and can be used to complement the measurements from subjective tools [12,16]. The current work intends to use the opportunities offered by biosignals to infer the real-time emotional states of users, and then use physicalizations to communicate these emotional states. There are at least five reasons to communicate the real-time emotional states of users through data physicalizations.

First, physicalizations of emotional states can be used for self-reflection - to reflect upon various stimuli and events that cause emotional arousal and valence. Second, they could be particularly relevant to showcase the emotions of specific user groups (e.g., caretakers of autistic people or cognitively impaired people can use them to learn about the emotions of their caretakees - as they are not good at describing/showcasing their emotions themselves). Third, physicalizations of emotional states derived from biosignals can be used to demonstrate the connection between vital signs (biosignals) and emotions to non-experts (general public). Fourth, they can be used as a tool during user studies to quantitatively measure the emotions of subjects. Fifth, these physicalizations can be used to evaluate the emotional journey of a user during virtual reality games.

Using an example of translating biodata to a physicalization, this work has explored the opportunities and challenges involved in communicating real-time emotional states through data physicalization. We designed a data physicalization that represents the human emotional state (arousal and valence) derived from heart rate and galvanic skin response sensing. The contributions of this article are (i) a physicalization that communicates a person's emotional state (arousal and valence) based on their physiological data and (ii) lessons learned from a preliminary evaluation of the prototype with 10 participants.

2 Related Work

Current research has shown that expressive interfaces that represent biosignals/emotion data that enable the exploration and engagement with biodata help mindful self-awareness, self-reflection and regulation of affect states, empathy, compassion and caregiving, relationship skills for authentic social connection, motivation, performance, and coordinative effort [18,24]. Expressive biodata interfaces are increasingly used also for the design of and research on somaesthetic experiences (e.g., the Breathing Light in [7,8], Breeze around your neck in [1], BrightHearts in [7,11], Balance Beam in [6]). Current research in soma-based design shows that such interactive material representations of soma (the felt-self) [5] enable not only the deepening of the awareness of one's soma but also the discovery of novel interactions with soma and help to understand the bodily engagement in somatic experiences [1]. Working on communicating biosignal data is arguably valuable and presents its own challenges. Nonetheless, a distinctive focus of this work is the use of biosignal data to derive other types of information (e.g., emotional states), which are then physicalized. Hence, the work is about the physicalization of information derived from biosignal data (as opposed to raw biosignal data).

Current research also shows that knowing about and communicating a person's emotional state helps well-being, emotion regulation and control, and social connection [13,25]. Thus, interfaces that represent and communicate emotions have been studied as a means of supporting this. Early research in this area focused mainly on screen-based representations such as visualizations, graphs and animated avatars (e.g., AffectAura [17], Significant Oter [13], Affective Diary [23], Affective Health [21]). Currently, there is an increasing interest in exploring non-traditional and non screen-based interfaces for representing and communicating emotion leveraging the material and interactive properties of material combined with actuation technologies (e.g., thermochromic materials and haptic actuators [25], smart textiles [9], light [7]). In order to enable such interactive and material representations of emotions, data acquired through biosensors should be translated into the properties of physical phenomena (e.g., material and actuation). While existing research in this area mostly focuses on expression and representation, in this research, we focus on studying this translation, the systematic physicalization process, from sensing to sensification.

3 Prototype

The objective of this work was to learn about the process of physicalizing emotional states (arousal, valence) derived from real-time biosignal data. We followed a method similar to the research through design process (RtD) [27] with the aim of learning about challenges through the design and evaluation of EmoClock. The process is shown in Fig. 2. The system consists of (a) a wearable sensing unit to sense biosignals required for inferring emotional states, (b) a server that stores and processes biosignal data and (c) an artefact that physically expresses and externalizes the emotional state (arousal, valence) of the wearer.

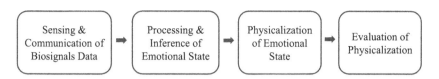

Fig. 2. Realtime physicalization of emotional state from biosignal data: from the sources to the sensification.

The Sensing Unit consists of a heart rate (HR) and Galvanic Skin Response (GSR) sensing units to acquire the biosignal data required to infer the emotional state (arousal and valence), and a microcontroller unit (ESP 32) to handle the processing and transmission (Fig. 1, left). The electronics circuitry is housed in a 3D-printed casing that can be wrist-worn. Attached to this wrist-worn unit is a glove that the user can wear on his or her two fingers, which houses two GSR electrodes (Fig. 1, left). The data read from the sensing unit is sent (via WiFi) to a web server that stores them together with the timestamp in its database server. The physicalization has the look and feel of a clock (Fig. 1, middle) and there are two LED rings on the inner round of the clock (Fig. 1, right). Therefore, the physicalization also looks like a table lamp. These design choices were made so that the physicalization can be integrated naturally into a user's environment without causing much distraction and privacy concerns. One of the LED stripes is used to display the level of arousal/valence by changing their colour according to the colour scheme shown in Fig. 1 (right). The other LED stripe is used to activate the physicalization as a normal lamp. The base contains two switches (c.f. Figure 1, middle): one of them is used to switch between the two modes (arousal, valence). The other one is used to switch off the data representation and activate it as a normal lamp (activate the second LED stripe). A user can relate to their arousal and valence level to the time using the clock engraved in the outer ring of the physicalization. The base of the clock contains a Raspberry Pi that pulls heart rate and GSR data from the web server, derives the components of the emotional state using a rule-based algorithm, and lights up the LED stripes accordingly.

4   Preliminary Evaluation

We conducted a pilot study to evaluate how effective and useful EmoClock is as a tool to convey a person's emotional state. The use case addressed in this pilot study was that of remote awareness of user states, that is, the use of a physicalization as a means for remote monitoring as done for example in [19].

4.1   Study Design and Procedure

We used standard emotion induction methods to stimulate known emotions in a user. Afterwards, these emotions were sensed using the EmoClock wearable.

We then evaluated the extent to which a second user can understand and inter-pret the emotions represented by EmoClock. The experiment was carried out in participant pairs (Participant A and Participant B). Participants A and B were separated into two separate rooms. Participant A was asked to wear the wearable on their wrist and Participant B interacted with EmoClock to understand the emotions Participant A was going through. During the experiment, participant A was asked to watch four short video clips. These video clips are standard video clips that are used in scientific experiments to induce specific emotions (arousal or valence) and are well accepted in affective computing research. Sources of the videos used in this experiment are Chieti Affective Action Videos (CAAV) [4] and FilmStim [22]. The length of a video clip was 2–3 min on average. These videos were expected to stimulate arousal and valence in A as follows: video 1: low arousal, positive valence; video 2: high arousal, positive valence; video 3: low arousal, positive valence; video 4: high arousal, negative valence. While Partic-ipant A was watching the videos, participant B was looking at and interacting with EmoClock and was asked to make a summary of valence and arousal levels together with the corresponding time slots. In the end, participant B answered the standard Usefulness, Satisfaction, and Ease of Use (USE) questionnaire [15] regarding the EmoClock. Afterwards, the two participants were involved in a discussion about what emotions Participant B observed from the physicaliza-tion and what emotions that A actually went through during the corresponding moment. The experimenter observed this discussion and took notes (behaviour, expressions, agreements, disagreements, comments, etc.). The experimenter also took notes of the informal feedback given by the participants. Ten participants (N=10, 5 pairs, 5 males and 5 females), aged between 20–30 years, recruited via word of mouth took part in the study. Each participant pair (A,B) knew each other and were comfortable with sharing their emotional state with each other.

4.2   Results

Usefulness, Ease of use, Satisfaction and Ease of learning: The perceived usefulness, ease of use, satisfaction and ease of learning of EmoClock measured by the USE questionnaire were overall very positive with many aspects rated above 5.0 on a 7-point Likert scale (Fig. 3).

Accuracy: In all five instances, we experienced different types of misclassifica-tions. One type of misclassification is a mismatch between the emotion (arousal, valence) shown in EmoClock and the type of emotion expected to be induced by the corresponding video. One reason for this could be that the actually induced emotion was different from the type of emotion that was defined to be induced by the video (according to the classification of the videos by their original authors). For example, a video that is defined as a high-arousal video may not provoke "high" arousal in users as the CAAV videos anticipated. Another reason could be the subjectivity of emotions and the algorithm's inability to cater for that sub-jectivity, i.e., the level of arousal or valence induced is very subjective thus the algorithm is not general for everyone. We also noticed that there were instances where the data were not classified at all thus the LED at that timestamp stayed off. A potential reason for this could be that the algorithm did not run in those instances because of resource limitations (the algorithm was running on a Raspberry Pi). When the lights did not turn on, the participants got confused and they thought that the system was not working, which affected their trust in the system. In one instance (participant pair 1), the heart rate readings were unavailable due to a misplacement of the sensor.

Informal User Feedback: The participants mentioned that it was difficult to distinguish the neutral state and the states immediately next to it (either before or after) due to the slight difference in the colours (LED) used. A user suggested using a different colour for different emotional states so that the interpretation is made easier. Also, participants found it difficult to observe the emotional state properly from a distance. Finally, three out of five participants mentioned that the videos are very outdated and that it might have affected their response.

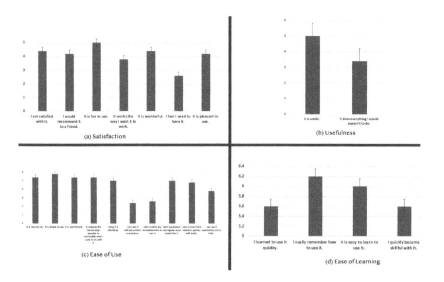

Fig. 3. Satisfaction, Usefulness, Ease of use, and Ease of learning of the EmoClock.

5   Opportunities and Challenges

Through the design and first evaluation of EmoClock, we identified some research directions worth further exploration. We classify the opportunities and challenges identified into five categories: (a) sensing biosignal data, (b) processing and calculating biosignal data, (c) deriving emotional states, (d) communicating uncertainty through physicalizations, and (e) evaluation challenges.

Sensing Biosignal Data: The availability of a wide range of sensors and wearable devices makes it possible to choose a range of biosignals that can capture several human body states and experiences. Furthermore, their increasing accuracy, smaller size, and the availability of Application Programming Interfaces (APIs) make them increasingly usable compared to early versions. In addition, advancements in microcontroller technology, their programmability, and their ability to communicate data via various means, especially, via WiFi (e.g., ESP 32) make it possible to sense and integrate data from multiple sensors. Despite these advancements, the collected signals can be noisy due to many factors such as interference, motion artefacts and placement of the sensors resulting in missing, erroneous data or outliers. Also, due to the battery concerns of ESP 32, the practical sampling frequency we could go for was one reading per second whereas a frequency of 20 or 30 readings per second could produce more accurate estimates. The development of technologies that improve the quality of the sensed data and their wearability is an important area for further research. Many wearables and sensing platforms use proprietary software and restrict access to raw biosignals. This hinders the use of smart wearables for physicalizing biosignal data. Enabling access to these raw biosignals will make it possible for physicalization researchers to use them in a customized way and to research on making everyday data artefacts that can be coupled with smart wearables.

Processing and Calculating Biosignal Data: The processing of biosignal data can be done at different logical places. For example, some processing can be done at the microcontroller level of the sensing unit (e.g., wearable unit of the EmoClock system) and some processing can be done by transmitting data to a central web/database server (e.g., webserver of the EmoClock system) while some processing can be done at the final physicalization level (e.g., the Raspberry Pi of the Physicalization of EmoClock system). Depending on the requirements of the system at hand, the choice of where the processing happens has pros and cons. For example, if the data is to be used for multiple physicalizations, and for physicalizing historical data (time-series physicalization), storing and processing them at the server level may be desirable over processing them locally at the sensing unit or at the physicalization. Handling real-time data is also challenging for example, with respect to missing values and outliers. Developing algorithms that do well with limited resources presents nice opportunities for future work.

Deriving Emotional States: Another challenge is the subjectivity of felt experiences and human affect. For example, for the same stimuli, the corresponding change in biosignal data can be different for different people. Classification algorithms learn and classify using models based on existing/learned data. Thus, subjectivity makes it harder to establish robust and stable affect classification algorithms. Also, machine learning models developed for standard computers might not be directly applicable to microcontroller-based systems as they have limited resources such as memory, computational power and power supply. There exists a range of algorithms that can be used to infer top-level affect states (e.g., stress, arousal) from body-sensing data. Although challenging, with the advancements in machine learning algorithms (e.g., Tiny Machine Learning (tinyML)), we can also be hopeful about the inference of different affect granularity (e.g., affect states in greater resolution [e.g., stress, nervousness, upsetness, excitement, happiness]). While this work focused on inferring emotional states through biosignals, we anticipate that the process of Fig. 2 will be relevant to the inference of other emotional states.

Communicating Uncertainty through Physicalization: During the implementation of EmoClock, we experienced missing, erroneous or low-quality data. This can have a direct impact on interpretation thus ways to deal with such low-quality or missing data at the physicalization level is essential. Such uncertainties should be treated as a characteristic of real-time affect sensing data rather than an exception. How the physicalization should represent missing or erroneous data or how it should adapt its behaviour in a way that it does not negatively affect the user experience is thus a crucial design decision. There is ample opportunity for future work in this area, especially when the data gaps are not present in historical, but real-time data.

Evaluation Challenges: As mentioned in Sect. 4, the evaluation of the physicalization requires emotion-inducing stimuli. The videos used in the experiment did not induce the emotional states to the extent anticipated, and this raises the question of designing better stimuli to provoke desired emotions in participants in the future. Individual differences with respect to age, gender, cultural background and previous experiences related to the context of the stimulus (e.g., image/video) might affect its effectiveness. Hence, there is a need for new techniques that reliably stimulate given emotions in users while remaining robust against the influence of their personal characteristics.

Limitations and Future Work: The current version of EmoClock used a rule-based algorithm on heart rate data coming directly from a heart rate sensor. In the future, we plan to use the raw ECG signal and use standard machine learning methods (e.g., [26]) to derive the arousal and valence. This could improve the accuracy of inferred emotional states. Also, this study involved a relatively small sample size of 10 participants, which limits the generalizability of results related to the user experience and usability. Our future plans include a more detailed and quantitative assessment of the performance of the system and its ability to accurately convey emotions as well as the impact of sensor placement or the reliability of the biosignal measurements on the overall performance of EmoClock. Our future plans also include a longitudinal study to evaluate the user experience and the potential challenges that might arise in real-world scenarios, especially with the prolonged usage of EmoClock.

6   Conclusion

Through the design and first evaluation of EmoClock, a physicalization that represents human emotional states, this work explored the opportunities and challenges of real-time physicalization of emotional states using the data obtained and derived from human biosignals. We identified some research directions worth further exploration and classified them into five categories: (a) sensing biosignal data, (b) processing and calculating biosignal data, (c) deriving emotional states, (d) communicating uncertainty through physicalizations, and (e) evaluation challenges. These research directions are applicable not only to physicalizing emotional data but also to physicalizing the derivatives of biosignal data more broadly. Thus we encourage the relevant research communities (e.g., data science, sensing and actuation, physicalization) to further research in these areas.

References

1. Alfaras, M., et al.: From biodata to Somadata. In: Proceedings of the 2020 CHI Conference on Human Factors in Computing Systems, pp. 1–14 (2020)
2. Bradley, M.M., Lang, P.J.: Measuring emotion: the self-assessment manikin and the semantic differential. J. Behav. Ther. Exp. Psychiatry 25(1), 49–59 (1994)
3. Choi, K.H., Kim, J., Kwon, O.S., Kim, M.J., Ryu, Y.H., Park, J.E.: Is heart rate variability (HRV) an adequate tool for evaluating human emotions?-a focus on the use of the international affective picture system (IAPS). Psychiatry Res. 251, 192–196 (2017)
4. Di Crosta, A., et al.: The Chieti affective action videos database, a resource for the study of emotions in psychology. Sci. Data 7(1), 32 (2020)
5. Hanna, T.: What is Somatics. Somat. Mag. J. Bodily Arts Sci. 5(4), 4–8 (1986)
6. Höök, K., et al.: Unpacking non-dualistic design The soma design case. ACM Trans. Comput. Human Interact. (TOCHI) 28(6), 1–36 (2021)
7. Höök, K., et al.: Embracing first-person perspectives in soma-based design. Informatics. 5, 8 (2018)
8. Höök, K., Jonsson, M.P., Ståhl, A., Mercurio, J.: Somaesthetic appreciation design. In: Proceedings of the 2016 CHI Conference on Human Factors in Computing Systems, pp. 3131–3142 (2016)
9. Howell, N., et al.: BioSignals as social cues: ambiguity and emotional interpretation in social displays of skin conductance. In: Proceedings of the 2016 ACM Conference on Designing Interactive Systems, pp. 865–870 (2016)
10. Jansen, Y., et al.: Opportunities and challenges for data physicalization. In: Begole, B., Kim, J., Inkpen, K., Woo, W. (eds.) Proceedings of the 33rd Annual ACM Conference on Human Factors in Computing Systems - CHI 2015, pp. 3227–3236. ACM Press, Seoul, Korea (2015)
11. Khut, G.: Designing biofeedback artworks for relaxation. In: Proceedings of the 2016 CHI Conference Extended Abstracts on Human Factors in Computing Systems, pp. 3859–3862 (2016)
12. Lee, S., El Ali, A., Wijntjes, M., Cesar, P.: Understanding and designing avatar biosignal visualizations for social virtual reality entertainment. In: Proceedings of the 2022 CHI Conference on Human Factors in Computing Systems, pp. 1–15 (2022)
13. Liu, F., et al.: Significant otter: understanding the role of biosignals in communication. In: Proceedings of the 2021 CHI Conference on Human Factors in Computing Systems, pp. 1–15 (2021)
14. van Loenhout, R., Ranasinghe, C., Degbelo, A., Bouali, N.: Physicalizing sustainable development goals data: An example with SDG 7 (affordable and clean energy). In: CHI Conference on Human Factors in Computing Systems Extended Abstracts, pp. 1–7 (2022)

15. Lund, A.M.: Measuring usability with the use questionnaire12. Usabil. Interface **8**(2), 3–6 (2001)
16. Mahlke, S., Minge, M.: Consideration of multiple components of emotions in human-technology interaction. In: Peter, C., Beale, R. (eds.) Affect and Emotion in Human-Computer Interaction. LNCS, vol. 4868, pp. 51–62. Springer, Heidelberg (2008). https://doi.org/10.1007/978-3-540-85099-1_5
17. McDuff, D., Karlson, A., Kapoor, A., Roseway, A., Czerwinski, M.: Affectaura: an intelligent system for emotional memory. In: Proceedings of the SIGCHI Conference on Human Factors in Computing Systems, pp. 849–858 (2012)
18. Moge, C., Wang, K., Cho, Y.: Shared user interfaces of physiological data: systematic review of social biofeedback systems and contexts in HCI. In: Proceedings of the 2022 CHI Conference on Human Factors in Computing Systems, pp. 1–16 (2022)
19. Pepping, J., Scholte, S., van Wijland, M., de Meij, M., Wallner, G., Bernhaupt, R.: Motiis: fostering parents' awareness of their adolescents emotional experiences during gaming. In: Lamas, D., Sarapuu, H., Lárusdóttir, M., Stage, J., Ardito, C. (eds.) NordiCHI 2020: Shaping Experiences, Shaping Society, Proceedings of the 11th Nordic Conference on Human-Computer Interaction, pp. 58:1–58:11. ACM, Tallinn, Estonia (2020)
20. Ranasinghe, C., Degbelo, A.: Encoding variables, evaluation criteria and evaluation methods for data physicalizations: a review. Multimodal Technol. Interact. **7**(73) (2023)
21. Sanches, P., et al.: Mind the body! designing a mobile stress management application encouraging personal reflection. In: Proceedings of the 8th ACM Conference on Designing Interactive Systems, pp. 47–56 (2010)
22. Schaefer, A., Nils, F., Sanchez, X., Philippot, P.: Assessing the effectiveness of a large database of emotion-eliciting films: a new tool for emotion researchers. Cogn. Emot. **24**(7), 1153–1172 (2010)
23. Ståhl, A., Höök, K., Svensson, M., Taylor, A.S., Combetto, M.: Experiencing the affective diary. Pers. Ubiquit. Comput. **13**, 365–378 (2009)
24. Umair, M., Sas, C., Alfaras, M.: Thermopixels: toolkit for personalizing arousal-based interfaces through hybrid crafting. In: Proceedings of the 2020 ACM Designing Interactive Systems conference. pp. 1017–1032 (2020)
25. Umair, M., Sas, C., Latif, M.H.: Towards affective chronometry: exploring smart materials and actuators for real-time representations of changes in arousal. In: Proceedings of the 2019 on Designing Interactive Systems Conference, pp. 1479–1494 (2019)
26. Wen, W., Liu, G., Cheng, N., Wei, J., Shangguan, P., Huang, W.: Emotion recognition based on multi-variant correlation of physiological signals. IEEE Trans. Affect. Comput. **5**(2), 126–140 (2014)
27. Zimmerman, J., Forlizzi, J., Evenson, S.: Research through design as a method for interaction design research in HCI. In: Proceedings of the SIGCHI Conference on Human Factors in Computing Systems, pp. 493–502 (2007)

Extending User Interaction with Mixed Reality Through a Smartphone-Based Controller

Georgios Papadoulis(✉) ⓘ, Christos Sintoris ⓘ, Christos Fidas ⓘ,
and Nikolaos Avouris ⓘ

Interactive Technologies Laboratory, University of Patras, 26500 Patras, Greece
g.papadoulis@upnet.gr, {sintoris,fidas,avouris}@upatras.gr
https://hci.ece.upatras.gr

Abstract. A major concern in mixed-reality (MR) environments is to
support intuitive and precise user interaction. Various modalities have
been proposed and used, including gesture, gaze, voice, hand-recognition
or even special devices, i.e. external controllers. However, these modalities may often feel unfamiliar and physically demanding to the end-user,
leading to difficulties and fatigue. One possible solution worth investigating further is to use an everyday object, like a smartphone, as an external
device for interacting with MR. In this paper, we present the design of
a framework for developing an external smartphone controller to extend
user input in MR applications, which we further utilize to implement a
new interaction modality, a tap on the phone. We also report on findings of a user study (n=24) in which we examine performance and user
experience of the suggested input modality through a comparative user
evaluation task. The findings suggest that incorporating a smartphone
as an external controller shows potential for enhancing user interaction
in MR tasks requiring high precision, as well as pinpointing the value of
providing alternative means of user input in MR applications depending
on a given task and personalization aspects of an end-user.

Keywords: Mixed-Reality · Head-Mounted-Displays · Usability · User
Study · Cross-Device Interaction

1 Introduction

Mixed Reality (MR) allows users to experience a synthesis of virtual and real
worlds [18], in which they are allowed to interact with digital content. An established way to access an MR environment is through the use of wearable Head-
Mounted Displays (HMDs). MR-HMDs support various interaction modalities to
enable user input and control [16]. These modalities may typically be divided into

Supplementary Information The online version contains supplementary material
available at https://doi.org/10.1007/978-3-031-42280-5_27.

J. Abdelnour Nocera et al. (Eds.): INTERACT 2023, LNCS 14142, pp. 426–435, 2023.
https://doi.org/10.1007/978-3-031-42280-5_27

two main categories; built-in and external. Built-in input modalities are characterized by the device's ability to detect the input without external hardware, only utilizing integrated sensors and software. These include gestures, gaze, voice, and hand-tracking. While intuitive, this category may lack precision, speed and can prove tiring for extended periods [5,22]. External inputs, in contrast, require additional hardware to provide input data. These include hand-held controllers, keyboards, joysticks, and other similar devices. External inputs often provide higher performance and precision but come at the cost of additional hardware and learning costs for users. Research on using hand-held devices has become a complex endeavor, as it entails a variety of technological and user-related factors that affect human behavior, performance and user experience in such tasks. Hand-held devices are the subject of cross-device interactions and environments in numerous works [7,11,17].

The ubiquity of the smartphone [15] makes it a perfect candidate for investigating cross-device interaction. Payy et al. [17] explore the use of four cross-device techniques (pinching, swiping, swinging, flicking) for interacting with a large display using a smartphone. MobiSweep [21] re-purposes a smartphone as a reference plane for spatial design ideation. Bergé et al. [6] present a technique for manipulating 3D elements on a distant display via hand gestures around the smartphone compared to typical touch and swipe techniques. Hartmann et al. [10] propose a system that allows for intuitive mode switching between typical smartphone use and using a smartphone for 3D manipulation in Spatial Augmented Reality (SAR). In [8], Büschel et. al. investigate an extension for 3D panning and zooming in head-mounted AR utilizing a smartphone's touch input and spatial movement and rotation as opposed to a typical AR gesture (air-tap) [12]. BISHARE [23] explores various bidirectional interactions between smartphones and headsets.

A rather interesting modality extension is making the smartphone an external 6DoF controller for interacting with MR environments to overcome issues such as the narrow field of view of most HMDs. TrackCap [13] tracks the smartphone in physical space by searching for a particular fiducial grid attached to the headset. Pocket6 [4] and Pair [20] utilize visual-inertial odometry (VIO) - typically implemented for smartphone AR applications [3,9] - to track the smartphone without additional equipment.

Motivation and Contribution. Reviewing the aforementioned works, we can conclude that beyond sporadic attempts [8], a rather limited body of research compares built-in and external interaction modalities using a smartphone in MR. Furthermore, while most of the works reference the technology used to pass input data from the smartphone to the controlled device, there is not an attempt to generalize the communication between them through a more generic framework. Our contribution is two-fold. Firstly, we propose and implement a communication framework between a smartphone and an MR-HMD to facilitate the development of applications that require the phone as an external controller. We believe that designing such frameworks is crucial from an HCI perspective to provide adaptive and personalised solutions to MR-applications, since it is well known that no interaction modality suits every user. Secondly, we utilize the proposed framework to replace the "select" gesture of the HMD (*air-tap*) by a tap on the smartphone (*phone-tap*). We then conduct a user study with 24 subjects to compare the two input modalities within a specific MR-application.

2   Framework

The main objective in designing the framework is to provide a modular, coherent and simple way to access a smartphone's input data in the headset. To accommodate that, we define a set of high-level terms: (a) **Smartphone Controller**: The application running in the smartphone, providing data to the HMD, (b) **MR-Gateway**: The application running in the HMD, receiving the data from the smartphone.

These are connected through the framework. The framework contains (c) **Shared Virtual Inputs**: a software description of an input, i.e., a touchscreen or an accelerometer that is shared between the two applications. These descriptions contain **events** that are triggered through user interaction within the application environment. The *virtual inputs* are shared between the *Smartphone Controller* and the *MR-Gateway* by means of an (d) **Input Mapper**. The *Input Mapper* is responsible for the communication between the two applications. Over the life-cycle of the framework, the *Input Mapper* accumulates events triggered by the user in the smartphone and periodically sends them to the HMD. The *MR-Gateway* subsequently triggers the events for the corresponding *Shared Virtual Input*.

As an example, a touchscreen now exists in the *MR-Gateway* without the HMD having a built-in touchscreen modality. The developer of the MR application may now access the touchscreen's *events*, i.e. a *tap* event, and implement new interactions quickly and efficiently, bypassing the communication between the two devices. Essentially, the necessary action to access a tap event from the smartphone to the HMD is to subscribe to the *Shared Touchscreen's tap event* in the *MR-Gateway*. The framework has inherently removed the barrier between built-in and external modalities in the HMD by providing a gateway to connect them. Lastly, we'd like to note that communication can be bi-directional; The HMD may equivalently provide input data to the smartphone. All the above are presented in Fig. 1.

For prototyping the framework, we utilized Unity Game Engine and specifically Unity's Input System [19] for best compatibility, and Mirror [1] for networking. The framework is available through a GPL-licensed open-source code under https://github.com/HeftyCoder/UnityInputTransfer.

3   Method of Study

3.1   Research Instruments

Utilizing the framework, we implemented, on an Android device, a smartphone-based input modality that we coined *phone-tap*, a simple tap to the smartphone's

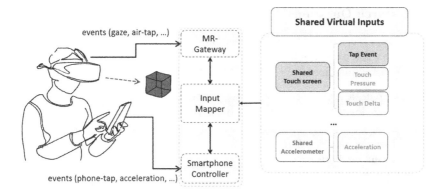

Fig. 1. An overview of the proposed communication framework between the smartphone and the HMD.

screen. This modality aims to be an alternative to *air-tap*, the provided barehanded select gesture in Microsoft HoloLens 2.

To compare the two input modalities, we conducted an in-lab study using a within-subjects design. Participants were asked to select preplaced digital content with both modalities for a multi-target selection task. They were presented with a fixed number of targets in close proximity, with one target colored blue and designated as the valid target for selection.

If the valid target was out of sight, an arrow pointer guided the participant towards it, as shown in Fig. 2a. When the participant placed the cursor over the target, a highlight was overlaid on top of it to signal that it was ready for selection. They subsequently confirmed their selection using either an *air-tap* or a *phone-tap*, as demonstrated in Fig. 2b and Fig. 2c respectively. For the *phone-tap* modality, participants tapped on the red section of the screen without requiring the smartphone be visible within the HMD's viewframe. After selecting the valid target, the next target was assigned randomly.

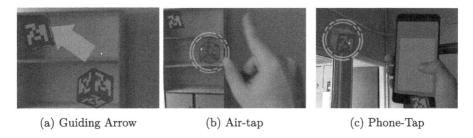

(a) Guiding Arrow   (b) Air-tap   (c) Phone-Tap

Fig. 2. (a) Arrow guiding to the next valid target. (b) Built-in air-tap modality used in HoloLens. (c) Experimental phone-tap modality. The smartphone is not required to be inside the HMD's viewframe.

3.2   Research Questions

In this study, we define the *air-tap* as the controlled input modality and the *phone-tap* as the experimental one. Based on this, we have formulated the following research questions:

RQ1: There is a significant difference in the **look-up time** needed for the participant to locate the next target between the controlled and experimental conditions; *essentially, we examine whether ease of navigation through head-movement or eye-gaze in MR-environments is significantly different between the two user input modalities.*

RQ2: There is a significant difference in the **selection time** needed for the participant to select the next target between the controlled and experimental conditions; *essentially, we examine whether the performance of user selection tasks in MR-environments (measured as time needed to select an item just after the item was looked-up) is significantly different between the two user input modalities.*

RQ3: There is a significant difference in the **number of targets selected** by the participants for **a given time** between the controlled and experimental conditions; *essentially, we further examine whether user selection performance is significantly different between the two user input modalities.*

RQ4: There is a significant difference between the controlled and the experimental conditions toward users' **perceived task completion, and mental and physical workloads.**

3.3   Data Metrics

We designed a *Time Measure* task to measure the *look-up* and *selection* times in seconds. In this task, the participant is presented with a fixed pool of targets and tasked with selecting twenty targets in succession, with no time constraint. We chose twenty targets based on trial and error to reduce participant fatigue and ensure sufficient data collection. For each valid target, we record the time taken to look-up the target relative to the previous target and the time taken to select the target after looking it up.

Moreover, we created a *Target Measure task* to measure the *number of selected targets*. In this task, the participant is given 45 s to select as many targets as possible. We selected this time frame after trial and error to ensure that it was sufficient for participants to complete the task but also challenging enough to measure their performance accurately.

3.4   Participants

A total of 24 participants were recruited (6 females), in the age range of 18–45 (28.5 ± 7.3). All individuals participated voluntarily and could opt out from the study at any time. Participants were informed that no personal data was collected aside from age. They all had no prior experience with mixed reality devices. As such, we allowed some time to experiment with the device as well as the two input modalities, specifically for selecting 3D digital targets. All data collected during this study was used anonymously.

3.5   Study Procedure

Phase a - Study Implementation: The participant was randomly assigned the controlled or experimental input modalities. Subsequently, they performed the *Time and Target Measure tasks* and repeated the test for the other user input modality.

Phase B - Post Study, User Questionnaire and Discussion: The participant was then instructed to fill out an adjusted version of NASA-TLX [14] in order to measure subjective physical and mental workload. Our version aims to compare the physical and mental workload between the two modalities, while the original provides an absolute metric for whether the participant was physically or mentally fatigued. After completing the user questionnaire, we conducted a series of semi-structured interviews to receive qualitative feedback to elicit the users' likeability and comments with regard to their experience with the controlled and experimental conditions.

4   Analysis of Results and Main Findings

4.1   RQ1: Look-Up Time Differences

We conducted a statistical analysis utilizing the paired-samples t-test to examine whether *look-up* time is significantly different between the two modalities. There were no outliers in the data based on boxplot inspection and residuals were normally distributed. *Look-up* time showed no statistically significant difference -0.065 ± 0.062 [*mean $\pm$ std*] seconds between air-tap and phone-tap $(95\%CI), t(24) = -1.045, p = 0.306$.

Main Finding Related to RQ1. As depicted in Fig. 3a, the analysis results indicate that using phone-tap instead of air-tap does not affect the amount of time it takes for the participant to locate the next target. As the phone tap requires moving the arm along with the HMD's frame, we can summarize that the additional arm movement is not correlated with the participant's ability to navigate in the MR environment.

4.2   RQ2: Selection Time Differences

The paired-samples t-test was further applied to examine whether *selection* time is significantly different between the two modalities. One significant outlier was presented during boxplot inspection. This particular participant had a significantly higher air-tap *selection* time than others. This was caused by the participant's inability to adapt to the unfamiliar air-tap modality. Following outlier identification and handling guidelines [2], we identified the outlier as an error outlier and, as suggested in the literature, proceeded to manually alter the air-tap *selection* time for this participant to the next highest value in the data-set. Data residuals were normally distributed. *Selection* time showed a statistically significant difference -0.46 ± 0.063 seconds [*mean* ± *std*] between air-tap and phone-tap $(95\%CI), t(24) = -7.258, p < 0.001$.

Main Finding Related to RQ2. As depicted in Fig. 3b, the analysis results indicate that using phone-tap instead of air-tap allows the participants to select a valid target faster when using the phone-tap, a result we may have expected given the ubiquity and ease of use of a smartphone. It further underscores the fact that natural gestures such as air-tap are slower and less precise compared to an input handled internally by another device, such as the phone-tap.

4.3   RQ3: Number of Targets Selected Differences

A third paired-samples t-test was employed to examine whether the *number of targets* is statistically different between the two modalities. Based on boxplot inspection, there were no outliers and residuals were normally distributed. *Number of targets* showed a statistically significant difference 6.28 ± 1.03 [*mean* ± *std*] between air-tap and phone-tap. $(95\%CI), t(24) = 6.124, p < 0.001$.

Main Finding Related to RQ3. As depicted in Fig. 3c, the analysis results indicate that a participant selected more targets when using the phone-tap modality instead of the air-tap modality. This result was expected as it directly correlates with RQ2. The faster a selection happens after look-up, the more likely to select more targets in a given period of time.

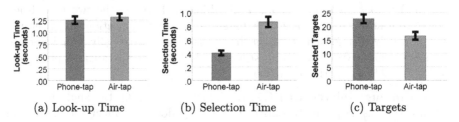

(a) Look-up Time   (b) Selection Time   (c) Targets

Fig. 3. Error bars showcasing the results regarding [RQ1-RQ3] for both modalities.

4.4   RQ4: User Perceptions on Ease of Task Completion, Physical and Mental Workload

To investigate RQ4, users were asked to opt either for the experimental or control modalities with regard to ease of task completion and physical and mental workload. The questionnaire was based on NASA-TLX and asked the participants to pick a value on a scale of 1–5, where 1 is selecting the experience of the phone-tap modality, while 5 is selecting the experience of the air-tap modality, and 3 indicates no preference over one modality. Table 1 summarizes the feedback gathered through the questionnaire.

Main Finding Related to RQ4. Most participants found no difference in the mental workload required for the two modalities but reported being more fatigued when using the air-tap. Participants also thought that they did better when using the phone-tap, an expected result given the ubiquity of the smartphone. Lastly, we'd like to note that while using the smartphone felt easier for most, they also felt that the air-tap provided a more immersive experience. In particular, several users agreed that "*The task was more fun and immersive when I used my hands instead of the phone.*"

Table 1. Questionnaire Results. Min and Max values are 1 and 5 respectively.

User Perception towards	Questionnaire Scale [1 to 5]	Average
Ease of Task Completion	phone-tap [1 2 3 4 5] air-tap	1.29 ± 0.55
Mental Workload	phone-tap [1 2 3 4 5] air-tap	3.33 ± 0.87
Physical Workload	phone-tap [1 2 3 4 5] air-tap	3.96 ± 0.91

5 Conclusion and Future Work

We designed and implemented a framework for facilitating cross-device interactions between a smartphone and a mixed reality head-mounted display. We subsequently used the framework to perform a comparative evaluation study that investigates user perceptions and performance between the native *air-tap* modality and the *phone-tap* modality.

Analysis of results revealed that participants selected significantly more 3D targets for the same time interval, and they were faster when using the *phone-tap* in contrast to the *air-tap*. This result was also confirmed by user feedback where the *phone-tap* was preferred with regard to ease of task completion. With this in mind, we can assume that designing different input modalities for the smartphone-MR system may benefit ease of use, especially when the native input is not particularly efficient and may cause fatigue. We also report that the *look-up* time was unaffected between the two modalities. This indicates that ease of navigation, i.e. head-movement or eye-gaze, is not particularly affected despite having to keep the hand inside the frame when using the *air-tap*. A final questionnaire revealed a subjective preference for the *phone-tap* regarding physical fatigue and efficiency, but a lack of immersion regarding user experience.

Our study underpins the added value of providing alternative means of user input in MR-HMD applications depending on the nature of the task and the purpose of a given MR-application. Adaptability and personalization aspects related to user input modalities in MR-contexts are a fruitful research direction, especially given the absence of comparative results on user experiments in this area. Our work aims to point to this direction.

As per future work, we aim to investigate more input modalities between the smartphone and an MR environment. We also aim to complement the framework to include other input modalities, such as EEG signal data. Subsequent investigations could involve ways to include the smartphone controller in security, educational and game-related applications.

Acknowledgment. This work has been financially supported by the Hellenic Foundation for Research & Innovation (HFRI) under the 2nd Call for proposals for H.F.R.I. Research Projects to Support Faculty Members and Researchers, under the project entitled Electroencephalography and Eye Gaze driven Framework for Intelligent and Real-Time Human Cognitive Modelling (CogniX) with Proposal ID 3849.

References

1. Mirror networking. https://mirror-networking.gitbook.io/docs/
2. Aguinis, H., Gottfredson, R.K., Joo, H.: Best-practice recommendations for defining, identifying, and handling outliers. Organ. Res. Methods **16**(2), 270–301 (2013)
3. Apple: Arkit. https://developer.apple.com/augmented-reality/arkit
4. Babic, T., Reiterer, H., Haller, M.: Pocket6: a 6dof controller based on a simple smartphone application. In: Proceedings of the 2018 ACM Symposium on Spatial User Interaction, pp. 2–10. SUI 2018, Association for Computing Machinery, New York, NY, USA (2018). https://doi.org/10.1145/3267782.3267785
5. Ban, Y., et al.: Augmented endurance: controlling fatigue while handling objects by affecting weight perception using augmented reality. In: Proceedings of the SIGCHI Conference on Human Factors in Computing Systems, pp. 69–78 (2013)
6. Bergé, L.P., Dubois, E., Raynal, M.: Design and evaluation of an "around the smartphone" technique for 3d manipulations on distant display. In: Proceedings of the 3rd ACM Symposium on Spatial User Interaction, pp. 69–78. SUI 2015, Association for Computing Machinery, New York, NY, USA (2015). https://doi.org/10.1145/2788940.2788941
7. Brudy, F., et al.: Cross-device taxonomy: survey, opportunities and challenges of interactions spanning across multiple devices, pp. 1–28. CHI 2019, Association for Computing Machinery, New York, NY, USA (2019). https://doi.org/10.1145/3290605.3300792
8. Büschel, W., Mitschick, A., Meyer, T., Dachselt, R.: Investigating smartphone-based pan and zoom in 3d data spaces in augmented reality. In: Proceedings of the 21st International Conference on Human-Computer Interaction with Mobile Devices and Services. MobileHCI 2019, Association for Computing Machinery, New York, NY, USA (2019). https://doi.org/10.1145/3338286.3340113
9. Google: Arcore. https://arvr.google.com/arcore
10. Hartmann, J., Gupta, A., Vogel, D.: Extend, push, pull: smartphone mediated interaction in spatial augmented reality via intuitive mode switching. In: Proceedings of the 2020 ACM Symposium on Spatial User Interaction. SUI 2020, Association for Computing Machinery, New York, NY, USA (2020). https://doi.org/10.1145/3385959.3418456
11. Kubo, Y., Takada, R., Shizuki, B., Takahashi, S.: Exploring context-aware user interfaces for smartphone-smartwatch cross-device interaction. Wearabl. Ubiquit. Technol. **1**(3), 1–21 (2017). https://doi.org/10.1145/3130934

12. Microsoft: Hololens 2 gestures for navigating a guide in dynamics 365 guides (2022). https://learn.microsoft.com/en-us/dynamics365/mixed-reality/guides/operator-gestures-hl2#gestures
13. Mohr, P., Tatzgern, M., Langlotz, T., Lang, A., Schmalstieg, D., Kalkofen, D.: Trackcap: enabling smartphones for 3d interaction on mobile head-mounted displays, pp. 1–11. CHI 2019, Association for Computing Machinery, New York, NY, USA (2019). https://doi.org/10.1145/3290605.3300815
14. NASA: Nasa task load index. https://hsi.arc.nasa.gov/groups/TLX/
15. Nath, A., Mukherjee, S.: Impact of mobile phone/smartphone: a pilot study on positive and negative effects. Int. J. Adv. Res. Comput. Sci. Manage. Stud. **3**, 294–302 (2015)
16. Nováek, T., Jirina, M.: Overview of controllers of user interface for virtual reality. Presence Teleoper. Virtual. Environ. **29**, 37–90 (2022). https://doi.org/10.1162/pres_a_00356
17. Paay, J., Raptis, D., Kjeldskov, J., Skov, M.B., Ruder, E.V., Lauridsen, B.M.: Investigating cross-device interaction between a handheld device and a large display. p. 6608–6619. CHI 2017, Association for Computing Machinery, New York, NY, USA (2017). https://doi.org/10.1145/3025453.3025724
18. Speicher, M., Hall, B.D., Nebeling, M.: What is mixed reality? In: Proceedings of the 2019 CHI Conference on Human Factors in Computing Systems, pp. 1–15. CHI 2019, Association for Computing Machinery, New York, NY, USA (2019). https://doi.org/10.1145/3290605.3300767
19. Unity: Unity's input system. https://docs.unity3d.com/Packages/com.unity.inputsystem@1.5/manual/index.html
20. Unlu, A.E., Xiao, R.: Pair: phone as an augmented immersive reality controller. In: Proceedings of the 27th ACM Symposium on Virtual Reality Software and Technology. VRST 2021, Association for Computing Machinery, New York, NY, USA (2021). https://doi.org/10.1145/3489849.3489878
21. Vinayak, Ramanujan, D., Piya, C., Ramani, K.: MobiSweep: exploring spatial design ideation using a smartphone as a hand-held reference plane. In: Proceedings of the TEI 2016: Tenth International Conference on Tangible, Embedded, and Embodied Interaction, pp. 12–20. TEI 2016, Association for Computing Machinery, New York, NY, USA (2016). https://doi.org/10.1145/2839462.2839490
22. Yan, Y., Yu, C., Yi, X., Shi, Y.: HeadGesture: hands-free input approach leveraging head movements for HMD devices. Proc. ACM Interact. Mob. Wearabl. Ubiquitous. Technol. **2**(4), 1–23 (2018). https://doi.org/10.1145/3287076
23. Zhu, F., Grossman, T.: Bishare: exploring bidirectional interactions between smartphones and head-mounted augmented reality. In: Proceedings of the 2020 CHI Conference on Human Factors in Computing Systems, pp. 1–14. CHI 2020, Association for Computing Machinery, New York, NY, USA (2020). https://doi.org/10.1145/3313831.3376233

Fitts' Throughput Vs Empirical Throughput: A Comparative Study

Khyati Priya[✉][iD] and Anirudha Joshi[iD]

IDC School of Design, IIT Bombay, Bombay, India
{khyatipriya,anirudha}@iitb.ac.in

Abstract. Every time a user taps on an element on a screen, she provides some "information". Classically, Fitts' law accounts for the speed accuracy trade-off in this operation, and Fitts' throughput provides the "rate of information transfer" from the human to the device. However, Fitts' throughput is a theoretical construct, and it is difficult to interpret it in the practical design of interfaces. Our motivation is to compare this theoretical rate of information transfer with the empirical values achieved in typical, realistic pointing tasks. To do so, we developed four smartphone-based interfaces - a 1D and a 2D interface for a typical Fitts' study and a 1D and a 2D interface for an empirical study. In the Fitts' study, participants touched the target bar or circle as quickly as possible. In the empirical study, participants typed seven 10-digit phone numbers ten times each. We conducted a systematic, within-subjects study with 20 participants and report descriptive statistics for the Fitts' throughput and the empirical throughput values. We also carried out statistical significance tests, the results of which are as follows. As we had expected, the Fitts' throughput for 1D task was significantly higher than the empirical throughput for the number typing task in 1D. Surprisingly, the difference was in the opposite direction for the 2D tasks. Further, we found that throughputs for both the 2D tasks were higher than their 1D counterparts, which too is an unusual result. We compare our values with those reported in key Fitts' law literature and propose potential explanations for these surprises, which need to be evaluated in future research.

Keywords: Fitts' law · Fitts' throughput · index of performance

1 Introduction

In 1954 Paul Fitts conducted a set of experiments to measure the rate of task performance when a user physically moved a stylus or any other object from its starting point to a target [8]. On the basis of his experiments, he formulated a relation of the hand movement time with the amplitude of the movement and the target width. The relation is known as Fitts' law. Today, this law accounts for the speed-accuracy trade-off that occurs when a user carries out a pointing task on an interface by moving her hand. The rate of "information transfer" from

© The Author(s), under exclusive license to Springer Nature Switzerland AG 2023
J. Abdelnour Nocera et al. (Eds.): INTERACT 2023, LNCS 14142, pp. 436–455, 2023.
https://doi.org/10.1007/978-3-031-42280-5_28

a human to a device that occurs in this process is known as Fitts' throughput. Fitts and Radford [9] interpreted this quantity as analogous to *"man's capacity for executing a particular class of motor responses"*. Fitts' throughput has been used as a single measure to evaluate human performance that accounts for both speed and accuracy. Users may choose to have different speed-accuracy trade-offs. Some users may be fast and reckless, and other users may be more careful. All the same, their Fitts' throughput is likely to be similar. Since 1954, many experiments on Fitts' law have been conducted, and they have led to more refined mathematical models of Fitts' law and Fitts' throughput [6, 19, 29].

These mathematical models have several limitations. First, it is unclear how one should interpret the values obtained from the model. Let's say a study reveals that the throughput value for interaction with a 2D touchscreen interface is 7 bps (bits per second). What does that mean, and can this information allow one to, for example, predict the time a user might take to input a number using a standard keypad on a phone? We are unable to use a given throughput value (such as 7bps) in predicting interaction with a realistic interface because we do not know how to interpret the Fitts' throughput of a realistic interface. This compels us to wonder whether Fitts' law models have external validity. Second, Fitts' law models are based on experiments done on interfaces in situations that are nowhere close to actual interfaces people interact with and their corresponding situations. Fitts' law studies are commonly done on custom-built abstract interfaces in which participants are asked to tap on bar(s) or circle(s) on a screen [20, 31]. In many ways, interfaces used for Fitts' law studies differ from actual interfaces used in day-to-day settings. In a Fitts' law study, the position of the entity to be selected is often randomised. In an actual interface, the positions of entities (buttons, display, etc.) are known and/or predictable. In a Fitts' law study, only a few entities may be present on the screen, and the entity to be selected is highlighted. In a day-to-day interface, several entities may be present on the screen at the same time and the user needs to search and select the appropriate or desired entity. Figure 1 illustrates these situations. In a day-to-day interface, the hand movement time may also get affected by the user's muscle memory, which may take months or years of experience to develop.

Due to these differences, we believe that the results from Fitts' law studies may not be applicable to real-life interfaces. Thus we designed an experiment to systematically compare Fitts' throughput with throughput values obtained in realistic situations. Our work is exploratory in nature; we have compared Fitts' throughout with only one realistic situation, and our method, as we will see, may not be applicable to realistic tasks involving non-discrete responses (for example, drawing with a pen). However, we hope that our work would open the gates for conducting more such studies in the future. In this paper, we present findings from a systematic, counterbalanced, within-subjects study with 20 users to compare Fitts' throughput with empirical throughput values that are obtained in realistic situations. For the study, we developed four smartphone-based interfaces — two of these (one in 1D and one in 2D) for a Fitts' study with serial tapping task and the other two (again, one in 1D and one in 2D) for

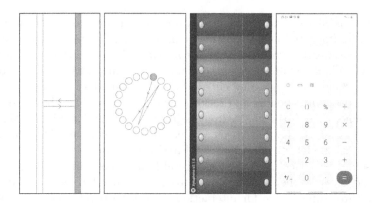

Fig. 1. (from left to right): (a) Typical interface for Fitts' 1D task (b) Typical interface for Fitts' 2D task (c) Example of realistic 1D interface (snapshot from a Xylophone app [2]) (d) Example of realistic 2D interface (snapshot of a calculator app)

a typical number typing task. The number typing task was contextualized for two situations. In the first situation, the researchers provided a 10-digit number and the participants memorized these on the spot before entry (an unknown number). In the second situation, the participant provided a 10-digit number that was already known to them.

Through this paper, we make the following contributions:

1. We propose a method to compare Fitts' throughput with empirical throughput, and a formula for calculating empirical throughput.
2. We reproduce a Fitts' law study to report Fitts' throughputs for 1D and 2D conditions on contemporary smartphones. We found a higher throughput in Fitts' 2D condition as compared to Fitts' 1D condition. This finding challenges several recent Fitts' law studies on smartphones.
3. We report empirical throughput values of 1D and 2D interfaces that simulate realistic interfaces. We compare these with corresponding Fitts' throughputs by the same participants in similar situations.
4. We compare our findings with those reported in the literature and provide potential explanations for some of the unusual data we obtained. Our main finding is that in real-life settings, people can achieve much higher throughputs than what is claimed by Fitts' law studies.

2   Background

2.1   Fitts' Throughput

Fitts conducted experiments to test if the basic concepts from information theory [26] such as the amount of information, noise, channel capacity, and rate of information transmission, could be extended to the human motor system [8]. Based on his study, he introduced the concept of Index of Performance (I_p)

to quantify the information output of the human motor system per unit time. According to Fitts, *"The average rate of information generated by a series of movements is the average information per movement divided by the time per movement"*. Mathematically,

$$I_p = \frac{ID_n}{MT} \tag{1}$$

where, ID_n= Index of Difficulty and MT=Average time per movement

The term ID_n encapsulates the *"minimum information required on the average for controlling or organizing each movement"* [8] and was originally calculated as

$$ID_n = log_2 \frac{2A_n}{W_n} \tag{2}$$

where, A_n= the distance between two targets and W_n= the width of the target.

Since then, the estimation for ID has undergone refinements. Crossman [6] suggested that the values of amplitude (A_n) and target width (W_n) be replaced with the values of "effective" amplitude (A_e) and "effective" target width (W_e). Effective Amplitude (A_e) is the mean of all movement amplitudes in a sequence of trials. Effective Width (W_e) is calculated as W_e= 4.133 × SD_x where SD_x is the standard deviation in the selection points along the axis joining the starting and the ending position. Mackenzie [19] modified the term within the logarithm to (A_e/W_e + 1). In Fitts' experiments, the data for both hits as well as ordinary misses are considered. This allows the Fitts' throughput to take errors into account. Only a few outliers where the touches are more than 20 mm from the target are removed as "unintended touches" [5]. Target widths are rarely over 10.4 mm (for example [5,20,31]). Thus, the formula for Index of Difficulty, as widely accepted today [11], is:

$$ID_e = log_2 \left(\frac{A_e}{W_e} + 1 \right) \tag{3}$$

Further, the term Index of Performance is now more commonly known as the Fitts' throughput(TP) [21]. Therefore,

$$TP = \frac{ID_e}{MT} \tag{4}$$

Traditionally, researchers calculate Fitts' throughput from a sequence of trials where they alter values of both A and W to obtain several combinations of $A{\times}W$, resulting in a range of ID_e values, for example [5,16]. Guiard [12] argues against doing so as this may introduce potential confounds and suggests a *Form × Scale* method – where either A or W is varied, but not both. We used Guiard's *Form × Scale* method for our Fitts' study and varied only the A values, keeping the W constant.

Over time, several methods of calculating the Fitts' throughput have evolved in literature. So that results from different studies can remain comparable, MacKenzie [20] suggested a "best-practice" method. MacKenzie suggests that the correct level of data aggregation for calculating the Fitts' throughput is a sequence of trials done in a single flow by a user. He also specifies the method to perform the calculation of the throughput. We have followed several suggestions from Mackenzie's paper for our study.

2.2 Fitts' Law and Realistic Interfaces

Several Fitts' law studies have been conducted, and many researchers have tried to include elements from realistic interfaces in their Fitts' law studies. For example, Murphy et al. [24] studied the effect of colour and contrast on movement times. While target colour did not affect the movement times, the contrast between the background and the target did; lower contrast led to slower movements. Pratt et al. [25] discovered that visual layout affected movement times – they found that the relative position of an element in a group of elements is important for Fitts' law. Lalanne [17] studied how the throughput of pointing tasks is affected by distractions on the interface. Teather et al. [28] studied the effect of target depth, background texture, highlight condition of the target (highlighted vs non-highlighted), and the presence of visual elements on pointing and selection tasks. They concluded that throughput remained unaffected in the last three conditions. Liao et al. [18] studied the target acquisition performance of users on interfaces with increased information complexity. In this study, the users were asked to rapidly click on the folder-icon shaped targets. The effect of the number of elements, colour of elements, and background clutter level on average movement time was studied. The authors concluded that the acquisition time increased on increasing the complexity level. All the studies mentioned here attempt to make the abstract interfaces (that are used in Fitts' law studies) more realistic, and use them to study Fitts'law. However, all of these studies are limited to comparing movement times of different interfaces. None of them evaluates the movement time or throughput of a user interaction with a realistic interface.

Bakaev et al. [4] derived a method to quantify the visual complexity of a user interface. The participants were asked to memorise the positions of coloured squares placed in a 5×5 or 6×6 grid. Then they were presented with an empty grid and asked to recreate the same graphical pattern by clicking on the squares of the grid. The authors expressed the index of difficulty in — what they termed as — *"spatial bits"*, and used this to calculate the throughput from the interactions with the abstract interface. During the experiment, the participants tried to accurately reproduce a given visual layout, but were not attempting a speed-accuracy trade-off. While this study attempted to quantify the participant's throughput, it did not systematically compare it with their Fitts' throughput.

Some researchers have conducted Fitts' law studies on interfaces people interact with. Van Zon et al. [33] experimented on three interfaces for flight decks. The first interface was a control panel with physical buttons. The second was a control display unit with a circular knob and other features. The third was a touch-based display. Participants were given instructions for interacting with each interface. The throughput for each interface was calculated based on Fitts' law equations. However, again, there was no attempt to compare these with traditional Fitts' throughput.

Evans et al. [7] studied pointing and clicking actions "in the wild" and compared them to lab-based Fitts' law studies. They ran an application in the background of a computer for a week to observe pointing and clicking actions of the mouse as well as text-entry speed through keyboard. In parallel, they also carried out a lab experiment of a Fitts' task and a text-entry task. The text entry speed and the throughput values of mouse-pointing tasks in the two settings were compared. However, the conditions in the wild and the lab were substantially different, so the throughput values may not be strictly comparable.

Another "in the wild" study was conducted by Henze et al. [13] by publishing a game in the Android market. In the game, the players have to tap on the circle which appears on their screen; tapping in less time results in more scores whereas tapping outside counts as a miss. On analysing the data obtained from 60,000+ devices, the researchers obtained an extremely high Fitts' throughput value of 25.01 bps. They conclude that *"the IP is unlikely high and the correlation is weak for all tested devices"* but do not discuss the reasons behind such high values. We interpret that the high Index of Performance values could have been because players often use two hands instead of one while interacting with a device. This study demonstrates the difficulty of conducting Fitts' law studies in the wild.

To the best of our knowledge, there have been no systematic studies to compare Fitts' throughput with empirical throughput (as we define it in the next section) under similar conditions.

2.3 Empirical Throughput

The well-known paper *"The magic number seven, plus or minus two"* by George Miller [23] puts forth the argument that humans can recall seven (plus or minus two) chunks of information. What is less known is that this work also discusses the concept of quantifying information that humans can deal with. Similarly, the Hick-Hyman law [14,15] quantifies the amount of information present in a user's response. A *bit* is defined as the amount of information required to decide between two alternatives. Therefore, specifying whether or not a person is taller than six feet requires the user to provide one bit of information. Similarly, specifying between four alternatives provides two bits, between eight provides three bits, and so on. In case of N equally likely alternatives, one must provide $\log_2 N$ bits of information. So, each time the user plays one note (out of eight possible notes) on the xylophone app shown in Fig. 1b she provides 3 bits of information. If a user plays two successive notes, she decides among $8 \times 8 = 64$ equally likely choices, providing $\log_2 64 = 6$ bits of information.

We define empirical throughput as:

$$Empirical\ throughput = \frac{Information\ in\ users'\ response\ (in\ bits)}{Time\ (in\ seconds)} \quad (5)$$

Humans constantly"provide" information as they go about their day-to-day activities, speak to other people, paint, sculpt, cook, drive a car, use a mouse etc. However, the number of bits of information output in many of these cases might not be easy to assess unambiguously, because information provided in these cases is analogue. On the other hand, activities such as playing a piano or typing a phone number are discrete, and the amount of information provided by the human can be unambiguously measured in bits. Hence, for this paper, we selected discrete tasks. To further simplify the task of estimating the information in the users' responses, we selected the discrete task of typing 10-digit phone numbers, as described in the next section.

3   Method

3.1   Interfaces

As mentioned above, we developed four smartphone interfaces: a 1D and a 2D interface to perform Fitts' law studies to calculate Fitts' throughput, and a 1D and a 2D number typing interface to calculate the empirical throughput. The interfaces were developed using Processing 3 software [3]. The experiment was conducted on a Samsung Galaxy M30s phone [1]. The display size of the phone was 147.5×68.06 mm. The screen resolution was 1080×2340 pixels and the pixel density was approximately 403 ppi. These interfaces collected the following data points: timestamp of the start and end of a touch, and x and y coordinates of the touch. These data points were used to determine whether the touch resulted in a hit or a miss, the distance of the touch point from the target's center, the time taken to reach the target, and the throughput value for a sequence of trials.

Figure 2a and b show our interfaces for the 1D and 2D conditions of the Fitts' law study (F-1D and F-2D respectively). Both conditions involved serial responses. F-1D replicated the traditional Fitts' 1D interface (Fig. 2a). For each trial, two bars were shown on the screen, out of which one was highlighted as the target (Fig. 2a). As soon as the highlighted bar was touched, the highlight moved to the other bar for the next trial. Thus, movements in F-1D app were back and forth (the characters A and B were not displayed in the interface and are shown in Fig. 2a only for demonstration). The width (W) of each bar was 6.81 mm. The amplitudes were measured from the centre of one bar to the other, and were in multiples of the width, ranging from 6.81 mm (1x) to 61.29 mm (9x). Thus, we had a constant width and 9 different amplitude values ($1W \times 9A$). The corresponding ID_n values varied between 1 and 3.32 bits. In this way, the ID_n values of the Fitts' task in the 1D condition (F-1D) were comparable with the 1D condition in the empirical task (N-1D), as described below.

For the 2D condition, instead of the conventional circular layout of targets like in [20] and Fig. 1b, we used a W-shaped arrangement (Fig. 2b). Five circles were shown on the screen, of which one was highlighted as the target. As soon as the highlighted circle was touched, the highlight moved to the next circle. The sequence of highlights was A-B-C-D-E-D-C-B-A (the characters A to

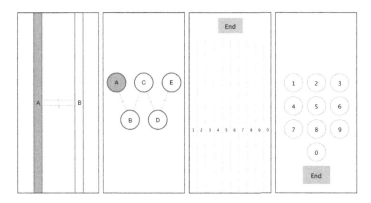

Fig. 2. Interfaces used for our study (from left to right): (a) Interface for Fitts' 1D task (F-1D) (b) Interface for Fitts' 2D task (F-2D) (c) Interface for entering phone numbers in 1D (N-1D) (d) Interface for entering phone numbers in 2D (N-2D)

E were not displayed in the interface, and are shown in Fig. 2b only for demonstration). Thus, movements in the F-2D interface were in a zigzag manner. This arrangement enabled us to include the higher amplitude values and make sure that the ID_n values were comparable between the 2D condition in the Fitts' task (F-2D) and the 2D condition in the empirical task (N-2D), as described below.

In the F-2D interface, the diameter (W) of each circle was 15.12 mm and was kept constant. The amplitudes (A) were measured from the centre of one circle to the next, and were 18.90, 26.74, 37.81, 42.28, 53.50, 56.72, and 59.80 mm respectively. These amplitude values correspond the A values of our number typing interface (note the distances between 1–2, 1–5, 1–3, 1–8, 1–9, 1–0, 2–0 in Fig. 2d). Thus, we had a constant width, and 7 different amplitude values ($1W \times 7A$). The corresponding ID_n values lie between 1.16 and 2.3 bits. Though our F-2D interface did not replicate the traditional layout, a user's interaction was the same as typical serial 2D Fitts' Law studies — the user tapped the highlighted circles one after the other as quickly and accurately as possible.

For our empirical study, we asked our users to input 10-digit phone numbers as a representative of day-to-day interactions. (Our participant group is familiar with 10-digit phone numbers. This enhances the external validity of our empirical study.) Fig. 2c and Fig. 2d show our interfaces for the 1D and 2D conditions of the empirical study (N-1D and N-2D respectively). The N-1D interface derives its design from virtual QWERTY keyboards (Fig. 3a). Strictly speaking, the input of the digits 1 to 0 on a QWERTY keyboard is a 2D task. Instead of square buttons, we used a row of vertical bars as targets (Fig. 2c). This design allowed us to present the users with a familiar QWERTY-keyboard-style layout and interaction while making it a 1-D task.

The 2D number typing interface (N-2D) replicated a typical smartphone number dialling app (Fig. 3b). The main change was that the horizontal and vertical distance between adjacent buttons was equal, unlike the interface shown

Fig. 3. (a) A number typing interface in a typical QWERTY keyboard on current smartphones, (b) A typical number dialling interface on current smartphones

in Fig. 3b. As mentioned above, we chose the exact same A and W values for both the Fitts' and empirical studies. Thus, the ID_n values in the interfaces for the empirical study varied between 1 and 3.32 bits for the N-1D interface, and between 1.16 to 2.3 bits for the N-2D interface.

The phone number entry task allowed us to easily measure the number of "empirical" bits transferred by the human accurately and unambiguously. A 10-digit number represents 33.21 bits of information. A 9-digit number represents 29.89 bits. And so on. While the information provided by the user was thus measurable, there could be some ambiguity about measuring the time taken, as it is not possible to determine the exact moment when the user started entering the number. To overcome this issue, we counted the time between the release timestamp of the first digit and the press timestamp of the last digit. Therefore, we ignored the information provided by the user when they pressed the first digit, effectively considering only the last 9 digits of the number to calculate the bits of information. This technique is common in text input studies [22].

3.2 Procedure

The participants were briefed about the study, the design of interfaces, and the task to be undertaken, at the start of the study. Practice sessions were NOT conducted. In case a participant was unable to understand a task, a brief demo of the task was given by the researcher. All participants were right-handed. They held the smartphone in their left hand and performed all the tasks using the index finger of their right hand. The participants sat on a chair while performing the task. The study lasted for 45 min to 75 min for each participant.

For the Fitts' tasks in 1D and 2D conditions (F-1D and F-2D), the participants were asked to select the highlights as quickly and accurately as possible. Errors comprised of touches landing outside the target. When a touch landed outside, the target briefly turned red to indicate a miss. The next target would get highlighted as soon as a tap, either a hit or a miss, was detected. When a participant made many consecutive errors, they were reminded to slow down to achieve higher accuracy. At the end of each sequence, the participants were shown the results of their performance, i.e. the total time taken to complete the sequence and the number of errors made.

A sequence in the 1D and 2D conditions of the Fitts' task consisted of 31 trials corresponding to one amplitude, yielding 30 data points and one Fitts' throughput value per amplitude per participant. As mentioned above, we had 9 amplitudes for the 1D condition of Fitt's task, leading to 9 throughput values per participant. Similarly we had 7 amplitudes for the 2D condition of the Fitts' task leading to 7 throughput values per participant. We took a mean of throughput values across amplitudes for each participant, and then a mean throughput values across participants for each condition (the mean of means method for throughput calculation [27]).

For the empirical tasks in 1D and 2D conditions (N-1D and N-2D), the participants were asked to enter seven phone numbers in each condition. Four of these were provided by the researcher (the unknown numbers). Participants typed the remaining three numbers of their choice, and from memory (the known numbers). (Originally, we had planned to ask the participants to type four known numbers. As several participants could not recall more than three phone numbers, we reduced this task to three known numbers.) The same seven numbers were used in both the N-1D and the N-2D conditions by a participant. We chose a combination of unknown numbers and known numbers because of the benefits each type of number offers. All participants were asked to type the same set of unknown numbers, thereby adding control and internal validity to the study. The known numbers simulated a realistic situation of recalling a number from memory and typing it, and thus contributed to the external validity of the study.

The unknown numbers we provided to the participants were 9126873045, 6749382501, 9702136485, and 8175342609. Together they cover all the 7 amplitude values at least once. These numbers also cover many of the amplitudes in many directions. For example, 4–0, 4–9, 3–8, 2–7, 1–6, all have same amplitudes but different directions. Overall, the selected four 10-digit numbers cover 36 of the 45 unique pairs of possible digits. The unknown numbers, in combination with the known numbers would have covered most, if not all pairs of digits. Each unknown number was provided to a participant on a piece of paper. The participant was allowed to take as much time as they wished to memorize the number. After the participant had memorized the number, the paper was taken away and the participant was asked to type the number as quickly and accurately as they could. If a participant forgot the number midway while typing, the data for that sequence was omitted, the piece of paper was provided again, and the sequence was re-initiated once the participant was ready.

For known numbers, participants were first asked to write down at least three 10-digit phone numbers they could recall. If a number had two or more repeating consecutive digits (e.g. 9912345678), such a number was not accepted. As far as possible, we tried to select numbers as they were written by the participant. In exceptional cases where a participant could not recall three 10-digit phone numbers that did not have any repeating consecutive digits, they were asked to modify a number they could recall by changing one of the digits.

After a target in an empirical task interface was tapped, it was briefly highlighted in grey colour to provide feedback of selection. When the touch landed outside a button, no feedback was given. This feedback mechanism is similar to the ones present on actual number typing interfaces. One sequence consisted of typing one 10-digit number. Each 10-digit number was typed 10 times in a row (10 sequences per number). If the participant missed one or more digits during a sequence, the data for that sequence was omitted, and the sequence was attempted again. At the end of each sequence, the total time taken to type a phone number and the errors made were displayed. The errors included touches landing outside the desired target, typing a wrong digit, and accidental extra touches (i.e. typing 11 digits instead of 10). For each sequence, the empirical throughput was calculated. Thus, we had 7 numbers (4 unknown + 3 known) × 10 digits per sequence × 10 sequences per number = 700 data points, and 7×10 = 70 empirical throughput values for each participant and each condition (1D and 2D).

The order of the conditions (N-1D, N-2D, F-1D and F-2D) was counterbalanced across participants. Within each condition for each participant, the order of the sequences was randomized.

We took several precautions to minimize sources of bias in the study. First, as already mentioned, we tried to neutralize the effect of memory on typing speed by allowing the participants as much time as they wanted to memorize a number. Second, if the participants showed signs of fatigue, they were given a small break during the study. Third, on-spot memorisation might affect the throughput value in studies like these. So, we also included the situation of typing known numbers. This allowed us to measure the throughputs in both the cases, recall from short-term memory as well as recall from long-term memory.

3.3   Participants

20 participants (10 female) were recruited for the study using a convenience sampling method on the university campus. The mean age of the participants was 24.7 years (SD = 2.3 years) and the ages ranged from 21 years to 29 years. All the participants were regular smartphone users.

Since the study was a within-subjects study, all the 20 participants did all four tasks. To justify the sample size, we conducted a power calculation of the experiment after the study had been conducted. The power of the experiment is 0.949 (well above the generally accepted 0.80 mark) at alpha=0.05.

4   Results

For the Fitts' tasks in 1D and 2D conditions (F-1D and F-2D), we first plotted ID_n vs MT and ID_e vs MT graphs (Fig. 4 and 5) to validate that Fitts' law was followed. As we can see, the R^2 values for ID_n vs MT in the 1D condition was

0.954 and in the 2D condition was 0.937. The corresponding R^2 values for ID_e vs MT were 0.933 and 0.836 respectively.

For the empirical tasks, we plotted attempt-wise empirical throughput values in 1D and 2D conditions for known numbers, unknown numbers and average (N-1D and N-2D) (Fig. 6). As each phone number is typed ten times, there were ten throughput values in each condition. As we can see, the practice effect leads to an increase in throughput values from the first attempt to the tenth one in both 1D and 2D conditions. Also, throughputs for known numbers are higher than for unknown numbers.

As mentioned above, in Fitts' law studies, the total time for a sequence is used to calculate the throughput while expecting 4% misses. The misses are accounted for through the effective width mechanism [11, 27]. For the throughput calculation, we considered the time taken to perform a sequence of trials, whether or not participants made errors. For the Fitts' task, the error rates in 1D and 2D conditions were 4.3% (95% CI from 3.62 to 4.7) and 1.94% (95% CI from 1.52 to 2.37) respectively. For the empirical tasks, the error rate in 1D condition was 2.33% (95% CI from 2.03 to 2.54) and in 2D condition was 0.93% (95% CI from 0.77 to 1.1).

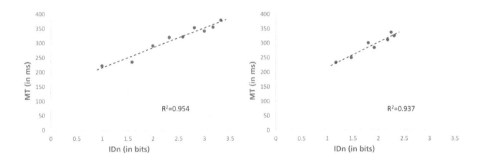

Fig. 4. IDn vs MT plots for the Fitts' 1D task (left) and the Fitts' 2D task (right)

We performed a 2×2 within subjects repeated measures ANOVA with throughput as the dependent variable and task (Fitts' or empirical) and dimensions (1D or 2D) as independent variables (N=20). In the first instance, when we ran the ANOVA and checked the Studentized residuals, we found that one of the users had t values of 3.58, 2.18, 1.72, and 2.44 for their four tasks. For N=20 (DF =19), the critical value for Student's t is 2.861 (p < .01, two tailed). Since 3.58 value was above the critical value, we considered this user as an outlier, omitted them and ran the same ANOVA again (N=19). This time, the highest studentized residual value was 2.19, so we proceeded with the ANOVA analysis.

Tests of within-subjects effects showed that the independent variable task (Fitts' vs empirical) was not significant (p=0.930) but the independent variable dimension (1D vs 2D) was significant (F(1,18) = 141.016, p<0.0005, $\eta_p^2 = 0.887$). We also found that there was a significant interaction effect between

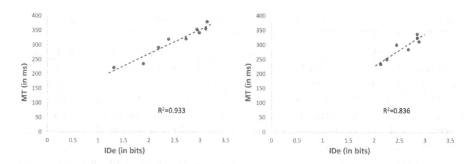

Fig. 5. IDe vs MT plots for the Fitts' 1D task (left) and the Fitts' 2D task (right)

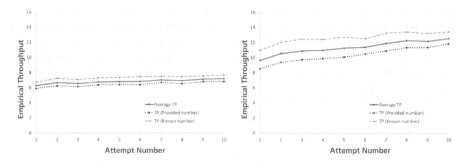

Fig. 6. Attempt-wise empirical throughput values in the (a) 1D condition (left) and (b) 2D (right) condition. Each plot also shows the empirical throughputs in unknown phone numbers (researcher provided) and known phone numbers (participant provided).

tasks and dimensions ($F(1, 18) = 38.744$, p<0.0005, $\eta_p^2 = 0.683$). We, therefore, analyzed the data to determine the simple main effects as suggested by [10], and looked at pairwise comparisons after applying the Bonferroni adjustment for multiple comparisons. For the Fitts' task, 1D throughput (8.162 bps, 95% CI from 7.516 to 8.808) was significantly lower (p=0.002) than 2D throughput (9.628 bps, 95% CI from 8.438 to 10.818). For the empirical tasks too, 1D throughput (6.707, 95% CI from 6.147 to 7.267) was significantly lower (p<0.0005) than 2D throughput (11.154 bps, 95% CI from 10.276 to 12.032). When looked at the other way, for 1D conditions, Fitts' throughput was significantly higher than empirical throughput (p<0.0005). On the other hand, for 2D conditions, Fitts' throughput was significantly lower than empirical throughput (p=0.018). (Fig. 7a)

We repeated the above ANOVA with a slight variation. Instead of considering throughputs of both the unknown and known numbers for the empirical task, we considered throughputs from only the unknown numbers. Once again, we found that while the independent variable task (Fitts' vs empirical(unknown)) had no significant effect (p=0.121), the independent variable dimension (1D vs 2D) did have a significant effect ($F(1, 18) = 113.602$, p<0.0005, $\eta_p^2 = 0.863$). There was

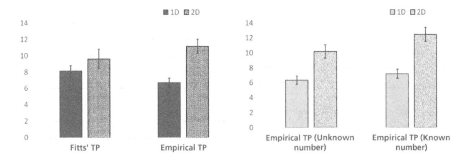

Fig. 7. (a) Fitts' throughput and empirical throughput values in 1D and 2D conditions, with 95% confidence intervals (left); (b) Empirical throughputs of unknown phone numbers (researcher provided) and known phone numbers (participant provided) in 1D and 2D conditions, with 95% confidence intervals (right)

Table 1. Task-wise and condition-wise throughputs in bits per second

Sl no	Interface	Mean (bps)	SD	95% CI from	95% CI to
1	Fitts' task in 1D	8.162	1.341	7.516	8.808
2	Fitts' task in 2D	9.628	2.469	8.438	10.818
3	Empirical task in 1D	6.707	1.162	6.147	7.267
4	Empirical task in 2D	11.154	1.822	10.276	12.032
5	Empirical task in 1D (unknown numbers)	6.350	1.132	5.804	6.895
6	Empirical task in 2D (unknown numbers)	10.167	1.850	9.275	11.059
7	Empirical task in 1D (known numbers)	7.183	1.280	6.566	7.800
8	Empirical task in 2D (known numbers)	12.470	1.961	11.525	13.415

also a significant interaction effect between task and dimension ($F(1, 18)=25.942$, $p<0.0005$, $\eta_p^2 = 0.590$). Analysis of pairwise comparison after applying Bonferroni adjustment showed that for typing unknown numbers on empirical tasks, the 1D throughput (6.350 bps, 95% CI from 5.804 to 6.895) was significantly lower ($p<0.0005$) than the 2D throughput (10.167 bps, 95% CI from 9.275 to 11.059). For 1D, throughput from the Fitts' task was significantly higher than throughput from the empirical task ($p<0.0005$) for unknown numbers. However, for 2D, the difference between the throughputs in Fitts' tasks and empirical tasks for unknown numbers was not significant ($p=0.357$).

We also studied the effect of the independent variable number type (known vs unknown) and dimension (1D vs 2D) on the empirical throughputs by performing two-way repeated measures ANOVA. We found that the effect of both the independent variables, type ($F(1,18) = 104.011$, $p<0.0005$, $\eta_p^2 = 0.852$) as well as dimension ($F(1,18) = 252.620$, $p<0.0005$, $\eta_p^2 = 0.933$), were significant. The interaction between type and dimension ($F(1,18) = 33.019$, $p<0.0005$, $\eta_p^2 = 0.647$) was also significant. The throughput from typing unknown numbers was

Table 2. Effect of independent variables on throughput values

Sl no	Dependent variable	Did task (Fitts'/Emp) have a significant effect?	Did dimension (1D/2D) have a significant effect?	Did task * dimension have a significant effect?
1	Fitts' and Empirical throughput in 1D and 2D	No (p=0.930)	Yes ($F(1,18)=$ 141.016, $p<0.0005$, $\eta_p^2=0.887$)	Yes ($F(1,18)=$ 38.744, $p<0.0005$, $\eta_p^2=0.683$)
2	Fitts' throughput in 1D and 2D and Empirical throughput of unknown numbers in 1D and 2D	No (p=0.121)	Yes (($F1,18)=$ 113.602, $p<0.0005$, $\eta_p^2 = 0.863$)	Yes ($F1,18)=$ 25.942, $p<0.0005$, $\eta_p^2 = 0.590$)
3	Empirical throughput of known and unknown numbers in 1D and 2D	Yes (($F(1,18)=$ 104.011, $p<0.0005$, $\eta_p^2 = 0.852$)	Yes (($F(1,18)=$ 252.620, $p<0.0005$, $\eta_p^2 = 0.933$)	Yes ($F(1,18)=$ 33.019, $p<0.0005$, $\eta_p^2 = 0.647$)

significantly lower ($p<0.0005$) than the throughput from typing known numbers in both the dimensions, 1D as well as 2D. For typing unknown numbers, the throughput was significantly higher ($p<0.0005$) in the 2D condition than in the 1D condition. For typing known numbers too, the 2D condition yielded a significantly higher ($p<0.0005$) throughput value than the 1D condition. The mean throughput values for entering known phone numbers were 7.183 (95% CI from 6.566 to 7.800) in 1D and 12.470 (95% CI from 11.525 to 13.415) in 2D (Fig. 7b). Table 1 and Table 2 summarises our results.

5 Discussion

Fitts' throughput has been considered to be the rate at which people can provide information to a digital device in a particular setting. However, this is mainly a theoretical construct. Surprisingly, and despite 70 years of Fitts' law research, there have been no attempts to systematically study how the Fitts' throughput compares with real-life interfaces. Our paper, although an exploratory work, is the first step in that direction. We compare Fitts' throughput with the rate at which the same people in a similar setting can provide information to a digital device in a realistic situation. For the 1D condition, the Fitts' throughput was 8.162 bps and the empirical throughput was 6.707 bps. For the 2D condition, the Fitts' throughput was 9.628 bps and the empirical throughput was 11.154 bps. To ensure that our settings are as similar to each other as possible, we had designed the studies to have identical amplitudes and the widths (and thereby the ID_n values) in each condition. Our first main finding is that in spite of this, the Fitts' throughput and the empirical throughput were significantly different from each other in both conditions.

The second main finding of our study is that people provide information to a digital device at a higher rate when they are familiar with the interface, and when they are familiar with the information they are providing. This by itself is hardly surprising. What was surprising was the rate of information transfer that our participants could achieve.

Ours was an exploratory study, and to the best of our knowledge, the first to systematically compare Fitts' throughput with empirical throughput. Hence we did not approach the study with a pre-defined hypothesis. Yet, we half expected that the abstract throughput that is traditionally reported in Fitts' law studies (such as MacKenzie's [20]) might represent a "theoretical maximum", and in reality people may be not be able to provide information at that rate in the empirical study. This expectation was aligned to Gori et al's view [11] that Fitts' law should be considered as *"a performance limit rather than a law of average performance"*. The findings of the throughput in the 1D condition are in line with this expectation. The Fitts' throughput in 1D condition was 8.162 bps, significantly higher than the empirical throughput in the 1D condition of 6.707 bps. However, this expectation did not hold in the 2D condition. The empirical throughput in 2D condition was 11.154 bps, significantly higher than the Fitts' throughout in the 2D condition of 9.628 bps. This is probably because the participants were only somewhat familiar with the QWERTY style 1D layout for the empirical study, while they were much more familiar with the 2D layout and had developed a muscle memory to use that interface, resulting in a higher throughput. Further, people could provide information at even higher rates of 12.470 when the numbers were known. When the numbers were unknown, the difference between Fitts' and empirical throughput was not significant, though the empirical throughput was still higher at 10.167 bps.

A third important finding is that empirical throughput values in both, the 1D condition and the 2D condition, kept increasing all the way till the 10th attempt (Fig. 6). This was not only true for unknown numbers, but also for known numbers. Hence we do not claim that our participants reached their peak performance in terms of throughput, hand movement speed and/or accuracy. Longer studies in future are needed before we can claim that.

Our study reproduced some results that are comparable to the literature, especially MacKenzie [20]. However, some of our findings vary from the literature. Here we analyse the similarities and differences and try to speculate the reasons. Our 1D interface in the Fitts' study was a close reproduction of the interface used by MacKenzie. For the 1D condition, MacKenzie reported Fitts' throughput of 7.52 bps, which is at the lower end of the 95% CI of our Fitts' throughput in 1D condition (8.162 bps, 95% CI from 7.516 to 8.808). The means of ages of participants in the two studies are comparable (24.7 vs 24.3 years). The slightly higher estimate in our study can be speculatively attributed to longer exposure to touchscreens that our participants have had by now in 2022 (compared to the exposure that participants may have had in 2015) and perhaps also to the better performance of contemporary touchscreens.

The biggest surprise lies in the 2D condition of the Fitts' task. MacKenzie [20] reported a Fitts' throughput of 6.39 bps in the 2D condition, which was lower than what they reported in their 1D condition, and which is much lower than what we report here (9.628 bps, 95% CI from 8.438 to 10.818). It is reasonable to argue that this big difference might have resulted from the different layout of the interfaces (circular in MacKenzie's case vs. zigzag in our case). We had selected the zigzag layout of the 2D interface to accommodate a larger range of amplitude values, and to retain comparability of ID_n values between the Fitts' task and the empirical task. We argue that a zigzag layout is better suited than the traditional circular layout for 2D Fitts' law studies involving serial responses on smartphones for two reasons.

We acknowledge that a circular layout allows for more angles of hand movements, and the angle of movement is known to have an effect on movement times, and correspondingly Fitts' throughput [30, 32]. However, a circular layout also limits the amplitudes to values smaller than the device width (to accommodate targets on both sides of the amplitude when the hand movement is horizontal). Since most smartphones are rectangular in shape, it is reasonable to assume that hand movements in the vertical direction would occur more often than in the horizontal direction. And for the same reason, larger amplitudes are common. Hence, for the sake of external validity, we argue that 2D Fitts' studies should accommodate larger amplitudes.

Secondly, a zigzag layout is perhaps more predictable than a circular layout, which made it easier for participants in our study to predict the next target. With a circular layout, after the user taps a target, the highlight moves to either the opposite target on the circle or to a target adjacent to the opposite target (as shown in Fig. 1b). The movement of highlights would thus have been less predictable for the participants and more time-consuming, which may have led to a lower throughput value. Given that Fitts' studies are supposed to model hand movement times and not the cognitive load or perception time, a more predictable layout arguably reports the throughput more accurately.

On the whole, based on our findings, we argue that Fitts' throughput values for the 2D condition reported in literature could have been underestimates. Human interaction with a touchscreen is naturally 2D, and we should not be surprised that people are able to achieve higher throughput in 2D conditions.

The empirical interface in the 1D condition resulted in the lowest throughput. This value may also be an underestimate, and in hindsight we consider the reasons. Our design choices could have led to an unintended difference between the 1D and 2D conditions of the empirical study. In the 2D condition of the empirical study, if the user tapped slightly outside the target, nothing happened, and the user could try again. However, there were no such blank spaces between targets in the 1D condition (just like there are none on a typical QWERTY keyboard). Tapping outside the target in the 1D condition of the empirical study automatically led to the selection of the adjacent target, which resulted in inputting wrong information. We observed that the participants were extra-cautious in the 1D condition of the empirical study, and this could have slowed them down and led to lower throughput. Similarly in the 1D condition of the Fitts' task, the immediate area surrounding the target was empty. Thus, we may say that densely packed targets can reduce the throughput. Future research could systematically explore the effects of varying the blank spaces around targets on empirical throughput.

We acknowledge some limitations of our studies. First, we tested only one of the conditions — typing a number on a realistic interface. Other discrete input tasks such as typing text or playing music may yield different throughput values. Second, we have not accounted for errors in the number entry task. In Fitts' studies, the throughput calculation using effective width (W_e) takes errors into account. In the number typing task, we got a 2.33% uncorrected error rate in 1D and 0.93% in 2D tasks, which we have no mechanism of accounting for in our comparisons. However, we feel that it might have an external validity - in real life too, people must be making comparable errors while typing numbers. Lastly, since our study was done on a limited number of participants and only 4 interfaces, we cannot strongly claim mathematical relationships between the dimensionality of the task and theoretical and empirical throughput values.

6   Conclusion

Through a within-subjects counter-balanced study, we reported throughput values for 1D and 2D conditions of a Fitts' study and an empirical study. While we found that in the 1D condition Fitts' throughput was higher than the empirical throughput, the empirical throughput in the 2D condition was higher than Fitts' throughput. The empirical throughput values kept rising with practice, and we may not have found the peak in our study. We compared our Fitts' throughput values with those reported in the literature and speculated the potential reasons for the similarities and differences. We argue that Fitts' throughput values reported in the literature may have been underestimates.

Interaction with digital interfaces is far from being a mindless job where a user merely selects a highlighted button on the screen. In actual interfaces, several factors such as information recall from memory, amount of information present on the screen, arrangement of the buttons, and practice effect are at play. Experiments on Fitts' law ignore all these other factors, thereby producing results that may not accurately predict a user's movements. Our experiments demonstrate that the throughput values obtained from Fitts' studies may not apply to the real interfaces that people interact with in day-to-day lives, and real interfaces could yield higher or lower throughput, depending on the conditions. While we found some answers, we may have stumbled upon more questions. Future research could learn from our experiences and answer some of them.

References

1. Samsung Galaxy M30s - Specs, Features and Price (2021). https://www.samsung.com/levant/microsite/galaxy-m/m30s/
2. Xylophone app by Role Playing Forums (2021). https://m.apkpure.com/xylophone/com.ape.apps.xylophone
3. Welcome to Processing! (2022). https://processing.org//

4. Bakaev, M., Razumnikova, O.: What makes a UI simple? difficulty and complexity in tasks engaging visual-spatial working memory. Future Internet **13**(1), 1–21 (2021). https://doi.org/10.3390/fi13010021

5. Bi, X., Li, Y., Zhai, S.: Ffitts law: Modeling finger touch with fitts' law, pp. 1363–1372 (2013). https://doi.org/10.1145/2470654.2466180

6. Crossman, E.: The information capacity of the human motor system in pursuit tracking. Q. J. Exp. Psychol. **12**(1), 1–16 (1960)

7. Evans, A.C., Wobbrock, J.O.: Taming wild behavior: the input observer for obtaining text entry and mouse pointing measures from everyday computer use, pp. 1947–1956 (2012). https://doi.org/10.1145/2207676.2208338

8. Fitts, P.M.: The information capacity of the human motor system in controlling the amplitude of movement. J. Exp. Psychol. **47**(6), 381–391 (1954). https://doi.org/10.1037/h0055392

9. Fitts, P., Radford, B.: Information capacity of discrete motor responses under different cognitive sets. J. Exp. Psychol. **71**(4), 475–482 (1966). https://doi.org/10.1037/h0022970

10. Gignac, G.: How2statsbook (Online Edition 1) (2022). http://www.how2statsbook.com/

11. Gori, J., Rioul, O., Guiard, Y.: Speed-accuracy tradeoff: a formal information-theoretic transmission scheme (Fitts). ACM Trans. Comput. Human Interact. **25**(5), 1–33 (2018). https://doi.org/10.1145/3231595

12. Guiard, Y.: The problem of consistency in the design of Fitts' law experiments: consider either target distance and width or movement form and scale, pp. 1809–1818 (2009). https://doi.org/10.1145/1518701.1518980

13. Henze, N., Boll, S.: It does not Fitts my data! Analysing large amounts of mobile touch data. In: Campos, P., Graham, N., Jorge, J., Nunes, N., Palanque, P., Winckler, M. (eds.) INTERACT 2011. LNCS, vol. 6949, pp. 564–567. Springer, Heidelberg (2011). https://doi.org/10.1007/978-3-642-23768-3_83

14. Hick, W.: On the rate of gain of information. Q. J. Exp. Psychol. **4**, 11–26 (1952)

15. Hyman, R.: Stimulus information as a determinant of reaction time. J. Exp. Psychol. **45**(3), 188–196 (1953). https://doi.org/10.1037/h0056940

16. Isokoski, P.: Variability of throughput in pointing device tests: button-up or button-down? vol. 189, pp. 68–77 (2006). https://doi.org/10.1145/1182475.1182483

17. Lalanne, D., Masson, A.: A Fitt of distraction: measuring the impact of distracters and multi-users on pointing efficiency, pp. 2125–2130 (2011). https://doi.org/10.1145/1979742.1979908

18. Liao, M.J., Wu, Y., Sheu, C.F.: Effects of perceptual complexity on older and younger adults target acquisition performance. Behav. Inf. Technol. **33**(6), 591–605 (2014). https://doi.org/10.1080/0144929X.2013.847974

19. MacKenzie, I.S.: Fitts' law as a performance model in human-computer interaction. Ph.D. dissertation, University of Totonto (1993)

20. Scott MacKenzie, I.: Fitts' throughput and the remarkable case of touch-based target selection. In: Kurosu, M. (ed.) HCI 2015. LNCS, vol. 9170, pp. 238–249. Springer, Cham (2015). https://doi.org/10.1007/978-3-319-20916-6_23

21. Mackenzie, I.: Fitts' law, vol. 1 (2017). https://doi.org/10.1002/9781118976005.ch17

22. Mackenzie, S.: A Note on Calculating Text Entry Speed (2002). http://www.yorku.ca/mack/RN-TextEntrySpeed.html

23. Miller, G.A.: The magical number seven, plus or minus two: some limits on our capacity for processing information. Psychol. Rev. **63**(2), 81–97 (1956). https://doi.org/10.1037/h0043158

24. Murphy, R.: The effect of target color and contrast on movement times in aimed movement tasks, pp. 2340–2344 (2006). https://doi.org/10.1177/154193120605002109
25. Pratt, J., Adam, J., Fischer, M.: Visual layout modulates Fitts's law: the importance of first and last positions. Psychon. Bull. Rev. **14**(2), 350–355 (2007). https://doi.org/10.3758/BF03194076
26. Shannon, C.: A mathematical theory of communication. Bell Syst. Techn. J. **27**(3), 379–423 (1948). https://doi.org/10.1002/j.1538-7305.1948.tb01338.x
27. Soukoreff, R., MacKenzie, I.: Towards a standard for pointing device evaluation, perspectives on 27 years of Fitts' law research in HCI. Int. J. Hum. Comput. Stud. **61**(6), 751–789 (2004). https://doi.org/10.1016/j.ijhcs.2004.09.001
28. Teather, R., Stuerzlinger, W.: Visual aids in 3d point selection experiments, pp. 127–136 (2014). https://doi.org/10.1145/2659766.2659770
29. Welford, A.T.: Fundamentals of skill (1968)
30. Whisenand, T., Emurian, H.: Effects of angle of approach on cursor movement with a mouse: consideration of Fitts' law. Comput. Hum. Behav. **12**(3), 481–495 (1996). https://doi.org/10.1016/0747-5632(96)00020-9
31. Wobbrock, J.O., Shinohara, K., Jansen, A.: The effects of task dimensionality, endpoint deviation, throughput calculation, and experiment design on pointing measures and models, pp. 1639–1648 (2011). https://doi.org/10.1145/1978942.1979181
32. Zhang, X., Zha, H., Feng, W.: Extending Fitts' law to account for the effects of movement direction on 2d pointing, pp. 3185–3194 (2012). https://doi.org/10.1145/2207676.2208737
33. van Zon, N., Borst, C., Pool, D., van Paassen, M.: Touchscreens for aircraft navigation tasks: comparing accuracy and throughput of three flight deck interfaces using Fitts' law. Hum. Factors **62**(6), 897–908 (2020). https://doi.org/10.1177/0018720819862146

Eye-Free, Gesture Interaction and Sign Language

Developing and Evaluating a Novel Gamified Virtual Learning Environment for ASL

Jindi Wang[1]([✉])(iD), Ioannis Ivrissimtzis[1](iD), Zhaoxing Li[1](iD), Yunzhan Zhou[1](iD), and Lei Shi[2](iD)

[1] Department of Computer Science, Durham University, Durham, UK
{jindi.wang,ioannis.ivrissimtzis,zhaoxing.li2,yunzhan.zhou}@durham.ac.uk
[2] Open Lab, School of Computing, Newcastle University, Newcastle upon Tyne, UK
lei.shi@newcastle.ac.uk

Abstract. The use of sign language is a highly effective way of communicating with individuals who experience hearing loss. Despite extensive research, many learners find traditional methods of learning sign language, such as web-based question-answer methods, to be unengaging. This has led to the development of new techniques, such as the use of virtual reality (VR) and gamification, which have shown promising results. In this paper, we describe a gamified immersive American Sign Language (ASL) learning environment that uses the latest VR technology to gradually guide learners from numeric to alphabetic ASL. Our hypothesis is that such an environment would be more engaging than traditional web-based methods. An initial user study showed that our system scored highly in some aspects, especially the hedonic factor of novelty. However, there is room for improvement, particularly in the pragmatic factor of dependability. Overall, our findings suggest that the use of VR and gamification can significantly improve engagement in ASL learning.

Keywords: Human Computer Interaction · ASL Learning · VR

1 Introduction

Sign language is a visual language that uses hand gestures and facial expressions to convey meaning. It is primarily used for communication with individuals who are deaf or hard of hearing or who experience difficulty speaking. Learning sign language is important for several reasons. Firstly, it enables better communication and social interaction with the hearing-loss community, thereby promoting inclusion and understanding. By learning sign language, one can break down communication barriers and establish meaningful connections with individuals who might otherwise feel excluded. Secondly, learning sign language has been shown to have numerous cognitive benefits, including enhancing cognitive development and language skills [4]. It is widely acknowledged that learning a second language has cognitive benefits, and the same is true for sign language. Finally,

J. Abdelnour Nocera et al. (Eds.): INTERACT 2023, LNCS 14142, pp. 459–468, 2023.
https://doi.org/10.1007/978-3-031-42280-5_29

for individuals who experience hearing or speech impairments, sign language can serve as a crucial mode of communication, allowing them to participate more fully in society. Despite the importance of learning sign language, traditional web-based methods of learning have not been able to generate much interest among learners, partly because of a lack of novelty. Therefore, there is a need for more engaging and innovative approaches to learning sign language that can increase user engagement and promote effective learning.

To improve the user experience of ASL learning, we developed a VR-based learning environment that incorporated a Whack-a-Mole type of game, inspired by the ASL game Sea Battle used by Bragg et al. for data collection [6]. We then conducted a user study, utilising a questionnaire proposed by Schrepp et al. [17], to evaluate the user experience of our system. To the best of our knowledge, there have been no previous user studies focused on the user experience of ASL learning from numeric to alphabetic in a gamified VR environment. Hence, our main research question was: *"Were users satisfied with the ASL learning experience from numeric to alphabetic in a gamified VR environment?"*. By conducting this user study, we aimed to gain insight into how users experienced our system and identify areas where improvements could be made. Ultimately, we hoped to demonstrate that incorporating gamification and VR technology into ASL learning can enhance user satisfaction and engagement. Our main contributions are as follows:

1. We successfully created an immersive virtual environment that supports ASL learning from numeric to alphabetic, incorporating a Whack-a-Mole type of game. Our system provides a unique and engaging approach to ASL learning, which we believe can enhance user satisfaction and engagement.
2. Our user study provided initial evidence that our approach has the potential to improve some aspects of user experience. These findings indicate that incorporating immersive elements and games into ASL education may be a promising direction for improving user satisfaction and learning outcomes.

2 Related Work

Sign Language Recognition: The recognition of sign language through deep learning and computer vision has been studied by various researchers. Bheda et al. [3] proposed a method that uses deep convolutional neural networks to recognize ASL gestures. Kim et al. [12] presented a novel approach that employs an object detection network for the region of interest (ROI) segmentation to pre-process input data for sign language recognition. Battistoni et al. [2] described a method that allows for monitoring the learning progress of ASL alphabet recognition through CNNs. Jiang et al. [11] proposed a transfer learning-based approach for identifying fingerspelling in Chinese Sign Language. Camgoz et al. [7] introduced a transformer-based architecture that jointly learns Continuous Sign Language Recognition and Translation. Zhang et al. [20] proposed a real-time on-device hand tracking pipeline called MediaPipe Hands for AR/VR applications. Goswami et al. [10] created a new dataset and trained a CNN-based model for recognizing hand gestures in ASL. Finally, Pallavi *et al.* [13] developed a deep learning model based on the YOLOv3 architecture, reporting high recognition rates for the ASL alphabet. These studies demonstrate the potential of deep learning and computer vision techniques in improving accessibility for individuals with hearing impairments.

Having reviewed the existing work on sign language recognition, we concluded that Mediapipe is the most suitable tool for the purposes of this paper, and thus, we used it for sign language recognition, benefiting from its highly accurate, real-time detection of hand landmark points. Moreover, as an open-source hand gesture detection framework from Google, it is well-documented and supported.

Sign Language Applications: The article discusses various research studies related to sign language applications. Bantupalli *et al.* [1] created a vision-based system to translate sign language into text to improve communication between signers and non-signers. Schnepp *et al.* [16] developed an animated sign language dictionary for caregivers to learn communication with residents who use sign language. Samonte [15] created an e-tutor system to assist instructors in teaching sign language. Economou *et al.* [9] designed a Serious Game to help adults learn sign language and bridge the communication gap between hearing-impaired and able-hearing people. Wang *et al.* [19] designed a sign language game with user-defined features and found that gamified sign language learning can improve the user's learning experience. These studies suggest that dictionary searches and gamification can improve the learning experience, and influenced the design choices for our system.

We developed a virtual reality system that offers an immersive and interactive learning experience for sign language. To improve the user experience, we incorporated a quiz and a small game into the system. Given the dearth of research in this area, we conducted user interviews using a questionnaire to evaluate users' satisfaction with ASL learning from numeric to alphabetic in the system. Our objectives were twofold: to thoroughly evaluate the performance of our system and to investigate users' experiences with it.

3   User Interface of VR Environment

This section provides an overview of the main components of our user interface (UI) and highlights the main features of our VR environment. The UI is comprised of four different modules designed to facilitate effective ASL learning.

1. The **Instructions** module, which consists of six basic steps, provides users with an overview of the ASL learning process and guides them through the initial stages of the programme.
2. The **Sign Language Dictionaries** module, which enables users to consult and search for the signs of numbers or letters. This module serves as a reference tool for users as they progress through the learning process.
3. The **Quiz** module, which contains question-answer quizzes that allow users to test their signing skills and self-assess their level of competence. This module

serves as a valuable feedback mechanism for users and encourages them to actively engage with the learning material.

4. The **Whack-a-Mole Game** module, which is to increase user motivation and engagement with the learning process. This module presents users with a fun and interactive way to practice their ASL skills, reinforcing their learning and providing a welcome break from more traditional learning methods.

Together, these four modules work in concert to provide users with a comprehensive and engaging VR-based ASL learning experience. By incorporating elements of gamification and interactivity into our VR environment, we hope to improve user satisfaction and facilitate more effective ASL learning outcomes.

We separated the scene of the immersive environment into two parts. Adopting the concept of a simple to complex learning process, the first part is for learning the numeric ASL, something that is considered a relatively easy task. The second part of the scene is for the more challenging task of learning the alphabetic ASL, excluding J and Z, which require dynamic gesturing.

Figure 1(a) shows the initial view of the user when entering the VR environment, which includes the **Instructions** and **Sign Language Dictionary** interfaces. Figure 1(b) shows the **Quiz** and **Whack-a-Mole Game** interfaces of numerical ASL learning, which are located to the left of the numerical ASL dictionary. Figure 1(c) shows the **Quiz** and **Whack-a-Mole Game** interfaces of alphabetic ASL learning, which are located to the right of the alphabetic ASL dictionary.

The scene was developed in Unity 2020.3.32f1, and user interaction was facilitated through eye tracking using HTC Vive Pro. After 3 s of fixed attention, users can click or select objects in the scene. An integrated camera was used to acquire images; openCV (version 3.4.2) [5] was used for image processing on a PC. Hand gestures were detected using Mediapipe, which extracted a feature vector of 21 points corresponding to landmarks on the detected hand. An MLP consisting of 3 fully connected layers was implemented in Python 3.6 [14] and Tensorflow 2.6.0 [8] for gesture recognition. The classifier was trained on a standard PC with an RTX3080 GPU, achieving recognition accuracy rates above 90%, deemed sufficient to ensure a smooth user experience in our study.

4   User Study Design

In order to evaluate the immersive environment design, we adopted the user survey scheme proposed by Schrepp *et al.* [17], which is commonly used to evaluate user experience in human-computer interaction systems. It consists of six evaluation factors, called *scales*: **Attractiveness, Efficiency, Perspicuity, Dependability, Stimulation, Novelty**. Each scale is further divided into four or six *items*, as shown in Table 1. We evaluated the proposed VR environment, on all scales and items, on a 7-point Likert scale ranging from −3 (fully agree with a negative term) to +3 (fully agree with a positive term), and studied the user feedback against the benchmark proposed in [18]. In that paper, the authors

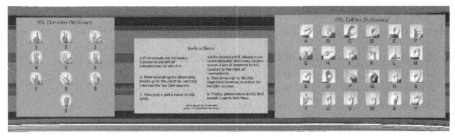

(a)

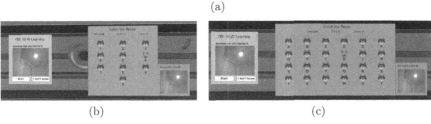

(b)   (c)

Fig. 1. The implemented immersive virtual environment. (a) **Left:** the numeric ASL sign language dictionary. **Centre:** Instructions interface. **Right:** the A-Y except for J sign language dictionary. (b) The numeric ASL learning quiz (left) and game (right). (c) The alphabetic ASL learning quiz (left) and game (right).

Table 1. Summary of the user experience questionnaire.

Attractiveness	Perspicuity
A1: annoying/enjoyable	**P1**: not understandable/understandable
A2: good/bad	**P2**: easy to learn/difficult to learn
A3: unlikable/pleasing	**P3**: complicated/easy
A4: unpleasant/pleasant	**P4**: clear/confusing
A5: attractive/unattractive	
A6: friendly/unfriendly	
Efficiency	**Dependability**
E1: fast/slow	**D1**: unpredictable/predictable
E2: inefficient/efficient	**D2**: obstructive/supportive
E3: impractical/practical	**D3**: secure/not secure
E4: organized/cluttered	**D4**: meets expectations/does not meet expectations
Stimulation	**Novelty**
S1: valuable/inferior	**N1**: creative/dull
S2: boring/exciting	**N2**: inventive/conventional
S3: not interesting/interesting	**N3**: usual/leading edge
S4: motivating/demotivating	**N4**: conservative/innovative

analysed a large database of questionnaire responses and derived the benchmark intervals shown in Table 2. These intervals correspond to the distribution:

- **Excellent**: In the range of the 10% best results.
- **Good**: 10% of results better, 75% of results worse.
- **Above average**: 25% of results better, 50% of results worse.
- **Below average**: 50% of results better, 25% of results worse.
- **Bad**: In the range of the 25% worst results.

Table 2. Benchmark intervals for the user experience scales.

	Attractiveness	Perspicuity	Efficiency	Dependability	Stimulation	Novelty
Excellent	≥1.75	≥1.78	≥1.90	≥1.65	≥1.55	≥1.40
Good	[1.52, 1.75)	[1.47, 1.78)	[1.56, 1.90)	[1.48, 1.65)	[1.31, 1.55)	[1.05, 1.40)
Above average	[1.17, 1.52)	[0.98, 1.47)	[1.08, 1.56)	[1.14, 1.48)	[0.99, 1.31)	[0.71, 1.05)
Below average	[0.70, 1.17)	[0.54, 0.98)	[0.64, 1.08)	[0.78, 1.14)	[0.50, 0.99)	[0.30, 0.71)
Bad	<0.70	<0.54	<0.64	<0.78	<0.50	<0.30

We conducted the user study obtaining feedback from 15 participants, 8 males and 7 females, aged between 19 and 21 years old, who had little or no prior experience with ASL or any other sign language. At the start of the session, participants had the freedom to explore the system and consult the Instructions module. Then, each participant followed a six stages learning process:

1. Learn numeric ASL for 3 min from corresponding dictionary module.
2. Improve numeric ASL comprehension for 3 min in numeric quiz module.
3. 30 s on numeric ASL game module.
4. Learn alphabetic ASL from corresponding dictionary module for 3 min.
5. Improve alphabetic ASL literacy for 3 min in alphabetic quiz module.
6. 30 s on alphabetic ASL game module.

5   Result Analysis

Figure 2 shows the average scores for the six scales, denoted by 'x', plotted over a colour code of the corresponding benchmark interval. For each scale, the minimum and the maximum of the average scores on its individual items are also shown. In Fig. 3, the box plots show the minimum, first quartile, median, third quartile, and maximum, for each individual item of each scale.

Attractiveness: The mean value of the user scores is 0.39 (SD = 1.24), placing it in the "Bad" category, indicating that their overall impression of the VR environment was not favourable, and the system requires further improvements. Notably, the average score for item **A5**, shown in Fig. 3(a), is slightly below 0, which suggests that the users did not find the system particularly appealing. This

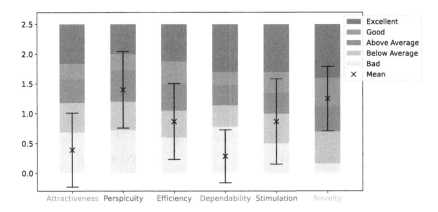

Fig. 2. Benchmark intervals for the six scales

may be because the learning environment relies on 2D user interfaces, whereas incorporating 3D elements may be more visually engaging for users. Therefore, we plan to integrate 3D user interfaces in future iterations of the ASL learning environment, aiming at enhancing its attractiveness.

Perspicuity: The average score is 1.40 (SD = 1.28), placing it in the "Above average" category, indicating that users perceive the VR environment as clear and understandable, facilitating their ASL learning experience. However, it seems that some of the users may have encountered some problems when using the environment, possibly due to their unfamiliarity with VR devices, and they may require some initial training.

Efficiency: In the "Below average" category, the average score is 0.87 (SD = 1.27). We note that, while the average score over the whole scale is slightly below average, analysis of individual item scores shows that our VR environment adequately fulfills some users' requirements. In particular, users found the system easy to use (as reflected by item **E1**) and believed that they could practice ASL effectively in the scenario (as reflected by item **E3**), see Fig. 3(c).

Dependability: In the "Bad" category, the average score is 0.28 (SD = 0.89). That means that the VR environment's dependability needs significant improvement. Despite the low overall average score, some users still believed that on individual items, particularly **D2** and **D4**, the system adequately fulfilled their requirements, see Fig. 3(d).

Stimulation: In the "Below average" category with an average score of 0.87 (SD = 1.43). Even though the score is slightly lower than average, the large variance indicates that some users find the learning environment stimulating. As shown in Fig. 3(e), the first quartile of all items is non-negative, indicating that a majority of users have a consistently favourable outlook regarding this scale.

Novelty: In the "Good" category with an average value of 1.25 (SD = 1.08). Again, the first quartile of all items is non-negative, see Fig. 3(f), indicating a

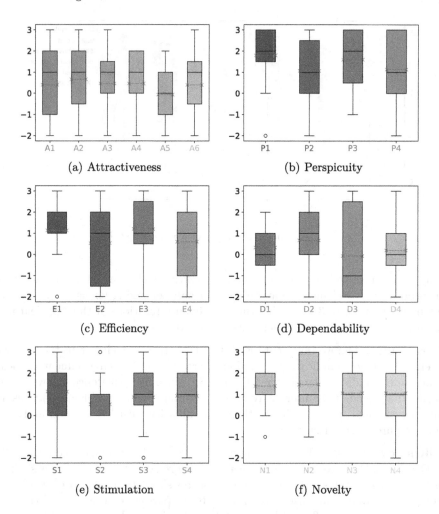

Fig. 3. Box-plots of the scores for each item of the six scales.

consistently favourable view from a majority of users. They perceive the VR environment as a novel and innovative way of learning ASL.

6   Conclusion

We have developed a VR system for learning numeric and alphabetic ASL and conducted a questionnaire-based user study to evaluate the user experience of learning ASL in the system. We found that to some extent it satisfied some user satisfaction factors, however, the system needs further development to enhance user experience, especially on the factors of attractiveness and dependability.

There are several limitations to our ASL learning system, which have been discussed for each scale of user experience separately. The identified shortcomings include a lack of animated hints; an interface that requires users to actively press a start button to commence an action; difficulty in moving around the VR scene; a relatively large number of incorrect judgments of correct signs, i.e., many false negatives; user expectations for a more creatively designed system; and an overall perception that the learning task was too easy. Additionally, the user study included 15 only participants, primarily between the ages of 19 and 21, and there was a complete lack of research on users in other age groups.

To address these limitations, we plan to revise the content, design, and implementation of the system as follows: add more interactive elements; implement automatic settings; create a follow-through user interface; develop a more robust sign recognition model; and include more sophisticated sign language learning material. We also plan to recruit a larger and more diverse group of participants for a follow-up user study.

References

1. Bantupalli, K., Xie, Y.: American sign language recognition using deep learning and computer vision. In: 2018 IEEE International Conference on Big Data (Big Data), pp. 4896–4899. IEEE (2018)
2. Battistoni, P., Di Gregorio, M., Sebillo, M., Vitiello, G.: AI at the edge for sign language learning support. In: 2019 IEEE International Conference on Humanized Computing and Communication (HCC), pp. 16–23. IEEE (2019)
3. Bheda, V., Radpour, D.: Using deep convolutional networks for gesture recognition in american sign language. arXiv preprint arXiv:1710.06836 (2017)
4. Bialystok, E., et al.: Bilingualism in Development: Language, Literacy, and Cognition. Cambridge University Press, Cambridge (2001)
5. Bradski, G., Kaehler, A.: OpenCV. Dr. Dobb's J. Softw. Tools **3**, 120 (2000)
6. Bragg, D., Caselli, N., Gallagher, J.W., Goldberg, M., Oka, C.J., Thies, W.: ASL sea battle: gamifying sign language data collection. In: Proceedings of the 2021 CHI Conference on Human Factors in Computing Systems, pp. 1–13 (2021)
7. Camgoz, N.C., Koller, O., Hadfield, S., Bowden, R.: Sign language transformers: Joint end-to-end sign language recognition and translation. In: Proceedings of the IEEE/CVF Conference on Computer Vision and Pattern Recognition, pp. 10023–10033 (2020)
8. Dillon, J.V., et al.: TensorFlow distributions. arXiv preprint arXiv:1711.10604 (2017)
9. Economou, D., Russi, M.G., Doumanis, I., Mentzelopoulos, M., Bouki, V., Ferguson, J.: Using serious games for learning British sign language combining video, enhanced interactivity, and VR technology. J. Univ. Comput. Sci. **26**(8), 996–1016 (2020)
10. Goswami, Tilottama, Javaji, Shashidhar Reddy: CNN model for American sign language recognition. In: Kumar, Amit, Mozar, Stefan (eds.) ICCCE 2020. LNEE, vol. 698, pp. 55–61. Springer, Singapore (2021). https://doi.org/10.1007/978-981-15-7961-5_6
11. Jiang, X., Hu, B., Chandra Satapathy, S., Wang, S.H., Zhang, Y.D.: Fingerspelling identification for Chinese sign language via AlexNet-based transfer learning and Adam optimizer. Sci. Program. **2020**, 1–13 (2020)

12. Kim, S., Ji, Y., Lee, K.B.: An effective sign language learning with object detection based ROI segmentation. In: 2018 Second IEEE International Conference on Robotic Computing (IRC), pp. 330–333. IEEE (2018)
13. Pallavi, P., Sarvamangala, D.: Recognition of sign language using deep neural network. Int. J. Adv. Res. Comput. Sci. **12**, 92–97 (2021)
14. Python, Why: Python. Python Releases for Windows 24 (2021)
15. Samonte, M.J.C.: An assistive technology using FSL, speech recognition, gamification and online handwritten character recognition in learning statistics for students with hearing and speech impairment. In: Proceedings of the 2020 the 6th International Conference on Frontiers of Educational Technologies, pp. 92–97 (2020)
16. Schnepp, J., Wolfe, R., Brionez, G., Baowidan, S., Johnson, R., McDonald, J.: Human-centered design for a sign language learning application. In: Proceedings of the 13th ACM International Conference on PErvasive Technologies Related to Assistive Environments, pp. 1–5 (2020)
17. Schrepp, M., Hinderks, A., Thomaschewski, J.: Applying the user experience questionnaire (UEQ) in different evaluation scenarios. In: Marcus, A. (ed.) DUXU 2014. LNCS, vol. 8517, pp. 383–392. Springer, Cham (2014). https://doi.org/10.1007/978-3-319-07668-3_37
18. Schrepp, M., Thomaschewski, J., Hinderks, A.: Construction of a benchmark for the user experience questionnaire (UEQ). Int. J. Interact. Multimed. Artif. Intell. **4**(4), 40–44 (2017)
19. Wang, J., Ivrissimtzis, I., Li, Z., Zhou, Y., Shi, L.: User-defined hand gesture interface to improve user experience of learning American sign language. In: Frasson, C., Mylonas, P., Troussas, C. (eds.) ITS 2023. LNCS, vol. 13891, pp. 479–490. Springer, Cham (2023). https://doi.org/10.1007/978-3-031-32883-1_43
20. Zhang, F., et al.: MediaPipe hands: on-device real-time hand tracking. arXiv preprint arXiv:2006.10214 (2020)

Effects of Moving Speed and Phone Location on Eyes-Free Gesture Input with Mobile Devices

Milad Jamalzadeh[1]([⊠]), Yosra Rekik[2], Laurent Grisoni[1], Radu-Daniel Vatavu[3], Gualtiero Volpe[4], and Alexandru Dancu[3]

[1] Lille University, Lille, France
milad.jamalzadeh@univ-lille.fr
[2] Université Polytechnique Hauts-de-France, Valenciennes, France
[3] MintViz Lab, Stefan cel Mare University, Suceava, Romania
[4] University of Genoa, Genoa, Italy

Abstract. Using smartphones while moving is challenging and can be dangerous. Eyes-free input gestures can provide a means to use smartphones without the need for visual attention from users. In this study, we investigated the effect of different moving speeds (standing, walking, or jogging) and different locations (phone held freely in the hand, or phone placed inside a shoulder bag) on eyes-free input gestures with smartphone. Our results from 12 male participants showed gesture's entering duration is not affected by moving speed or phone location, however, other features of gesture, such as length, height, width, area, and phone orientation, are mostly affected by moving speed or phone location. So, eyes-free gestures' features vary significantly as the user's environmental factors, such as moving speed or phone location, change and should be considered by designers.

Keywords: Eyes-free gestures · user's moving speed · phone's location · gesture features · phone movements · mobile device

1 Introduction

Unlike desktop computers, which are typically used in a fixed and stable environment (*e.g.*, a typical setting would be the user seated), small screen devices like smartphones can be used in different environments, including indoors, outdoors, and so on [25]. Meanwhile, gesture input is mainstream on mobile device and a large majority of interaction with the touchscreen requires the visual attention of the user. However, a visual focus is not always possible or may be dangerous, *e.g.*, while walking or jogging. Gesture input can provide a modality to implement the interaction without the need to look at the smartphones [20]. In the literature, many empirical studies investigated the effect of different contextual factors on changes in user performance due to context, with varying findings.

In particular, interaction with touch surfaces in different mobility conditions is well studied in the literature, including note-taking when sitting [9], text entry when walking [6], wearable touch surfaces while standing [10], and web searching on a treadmill [14]. Different gestures based interaction techniques have been also proposed. For example, Kubo et al. [16] introduced B2B-Swipe for eyes-free gesture from a bezel to a bezel on rectangular touchscreens, in particular for smartwatches. Negulescu et al. [17] studied the cognitive demands of an eyes-free tap, swipe, or move on a smartphone in distracted scenarios. Tinwala et al. [22] introduced an eyes-free text entry technique on touchscreens using graffiti strokes. However, to the best of our knowledge, no previous study have investigated the effect of mobility and smartphone location on eyes-free gesture production.

In this work, we investigate the effect of user's moving speed and phone location on the articulation characteristics of gesture input. We run an experiment with 12 male participants to study the effect of three moving speeds (standing, walking and jogging) and two phone locations (the phone is hold freely alongside the body and in a shoulder bag) on gestures. Our findings indicate that the environmental factors (moving speed, and phone location) can significantly change gestures entered by participants. For example, the more is the user moving speed the more the gesture is bigger, faster and the more the phone move. While, holding the phone in a shoulder bag, have the inverse effect. Our findings also revealed that gesture production time was not affected by any of the variables.

2 Experiment

We conducted an experiment to evaluate the effect of the user's moving speed and phone location on eyes-free gesture articulation on a mobile device.

2.1 Participants

Since the average walking and jogging speeds between genders are different and the same speed can cause different mental and physical loads for different genders [7], we only conducted experiments with twelve male participants to avoid increasing the number of independent variables in the analysis. Participants' ages were between 20 and 34 years ($mean = 26.8$, $sd = 4.3$). All participants were right-handed, without any known mobility impairment, and had been using smartphones for several years.

2.2 Gesture Set

The gesture set used in this study had 20 gestures in it. These gestures were selected from previous works (*e.g.*, [2,4,26]) and were composed of operands, letters, mark segments, rationally invariant and mnemonic gestures (see Fig. 1).

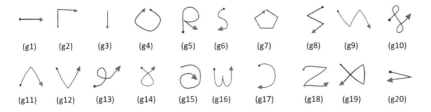

Fig. 1. Gesture set.

2.3 Apparatus

We collected stroke gestures using our custom software on a Samsung Galaxy S7 smartphone running Android 6.0.1. The smartphone was attached to a 1.5-m cellphone lanyard to ensure it didn't fall. The smartphone's screen size is 5.65″ × 2.78″ with a display resolution of 1440 × 2560 pixels and a pixel density of 227 pixels per cm. The smartphone's screen was mirrored onto a Samsung Galaxy Tab 7 tablet in front of participants while they were standing, walking, or jogging on a FreeMotion Reflex T11.8 treadmill. The dimensions of the shoulder bag used in the experiments were 20 cm × 20 cm × 5 cm.

2.4 Design

The experiment used a 3 × 2 within-subject design with two factors: *moving speed* and *smartphone location*. We followed [15] and chose to control the moving speed during the experiment. As in [15], the rationale for fixing the walking speed is that first, we assume that users will be unable to slow down or stop walking to use their mobile device, and second, by doing so, impaired walking effects are maximized as users can not slow down if the task becomes difficult. *Moving speed* covers three conditions: (1) standing at 0 km/h, (2) walking at 4.6 km/h, and (3) jogging at 8 km/h. The moving speed values are defined through preliminary experiments with two participants. We chose speeds that are different and fast enough that they have the potential to cause an effect while still being comfortable for participants to hold and use their smartphones. The participants in the preliminary experiment reported high frustration and difficulty conducting experiments at high speeds, such as 10 km/h. We therefore did not consider a running condition. *Phone location* describes how the phone is held by the dominant hand and covers two conditions: (1) free where the phone is hold freely alongside the body (see Fig. 2a) and (2) bag where the phone is hold inside a shoulder bag (see Fig. 2b).

2.5 Task and Procedure

During the experiment, participants stand on a treadmill in a gym. Participants were then asked to hold the phone with their dominant hand and use the thumb of their dominant hand to draw gestures on the screen without looking at the

(a) Smartphone is held freely in the hand.

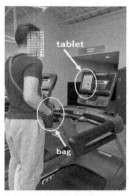

(b) Smartphone used in the bag.

Fig. 2. Phone location during experiment: a) freely b) in the bag.

phone. In the free condition, participants were asked to hold the phone alongside their body (see Fig. 2a). In the bag condition, participants were asked to hold the phone inside a shoulder bag (see Fig. 2b). A preview of the gesture they had to draw was shown on a tablet placed in front of them on the treadmill. Since all the gestures in this experiment were single strokes, as soon as they lifted their finger from the touchscreen next gesture appeared. In case of any false entry, participants always had the option to use the back button of the phone to return to previous gestures.

In the experiment phase, two phone location conditions were randomly presented to the participants. For each phone location, the three moving speed conditions were also randomly presented. Each participant in total performed 600 gestures (=2 *phone locations* × 3 *moving speeds* × 20 gesture types × 5 repetitions). For each moving speed and phone location condition the gestures were presented to participant in a random order. The experiment took 30 min on average to complete.

3   Results

Our results include gesture features and smartphone directional movements. We also analyzed the qualitative observations. All analyses used a two-way ANOVA. Tukey post-hoc tests were used post-hoc when significant effects were found. Only significant effects and interactions are reported.

3.1   Gesture Features

We selected six geometric features: (a) gesture length, (b) gesture height, (c) gesture width, (d) gesture area, (e) gesture duration, and (f) gesture speed. These features have been employed in the gesture recognition and analysis literature [1,3,19,21,23] in order to characterize how stroke-gestures are produced by users.

Gesture Length. Gesture length is the cumulative path distance from the first touch event registered to the last. We found significant main effects of *speed moving* ($F_{2,22} = 27.232$, $p < .0001$) and *phone location* ($F_{1,11} = 10.659$, $p = .008$) on *gesture length*. The jogging (*mean* $= 10.63$ cm, $sd = 4.53$ cm) led participants entering gestures with the longest lengths then walking (*mean* $= 10.20$ cm, $sd = 4.63$ cm) and standing (*mean* $= 9.67$ cm, $sd = 4.55$ cm). Post-hoc test confirms differences between all pairs ($p < .05$). Holding phone freely (*mean* $= 10.52$ cm, $sd = 4.53$ cm) led also to gestures with significantly longer lengths than when holding it in a bag (*mean* $= 9.85$ cm, $sd = 4.45$ cm)($p < .05$).

Gesture Height. Gesture height is the height of the bounding box that contains the gesture ($max_y - min_y$). We found significant main effects of *moving speed* ($F_{2,22} = 6.444$, $p = .006$) and *phone location* ($F_{1,11} = 23.963$, $p = .0005$) on *gesture height*. Post-hoc tests show that standing (*mean* $= 3.70$ cm, $sd = 1.77$ cm) determined participants to produce gestures with significantly smaller heights than both walking (*mean* $= 3.83$ cm, $sd = 1.74$ cm) and jogging (*mean* $= 3.87$ cm, $sd = 1.64$ cm))($p < .05$). Holding phone freely (*mean* $= 3.97$ cm, $sd = 1.64$ cm) led to gestures with significantly higher heights than holding phone in a bag (*mean* $= 3.65$ cm, $sd = 1.68$ cm)($p < .05$).

Gesture Width. Gesture width is the width of the bounding box that contains the gesture ($max_x - min_x$). We found significant main effects of *moving speed* ($F_{2,22} = 18.615$, $p < .0001$) on *gesture width*. Larger widths than both walking (*mean* $= 3.15$ cm, $sd = 1.16$ cm) and standing (*mean* $= 3.06$ cm, $sd = 1.20$ cm)($p < .05$).

Gesture Area. Gesture area is the surface area of the bounding box containing the gesture (height $\times$ width). We found significant main effects of *moving speed* ($F_{2,22} = 7.415$, $p = .004$) and *phone location* ($F_{1,11} = 11.823$, $p = .006$) on *gesture area*. Post-hoc tests show that jogging (*mean* $= 13.32$ cm^2, $sd = 8.86$ cm^2) led to gestures with significantly larger area than both walking (*mean* $= 12.99$ cm^2, $sd = 9.52$ cm^2)and standing (*mean* $= 12.33$ cm^2, $sd = 9.58$ cm^2)($p < .05$). Holding phone freely (*mean* $= 13.76$ cm^2, $sd = 8.86$ cm^2) produced gestures with significantly larger area than when smartphone was in a bag (*mean* $= 12.05$ cm^2, $sd = 8.89$ cm^2)($p < .05$).

Gesture Duration. Gesture duration is the time elapsed while entering the gesture, *i.e.*, the timestamp of the last touch event registered for the gesture minus the timestamp of the first touch event. We found no significant main effects on *gesture duration* nor interaction between moving and grasping ($p > 0.057$).

Gesture Speed. Gesture speed is the average speed registered over all the touch events belonging to a gesture (length/duration). We found significant

Fig. 3. Axes and orientations of the smartphone.

main effects of *moving speed* ($F_{2,22} = 15.966$, $p < .0001$) and *phone location* ($F_{1,11} = 13.596$, $p = 0.004$) on *gesture speed*. Post-hoc tests show that the jogging ($mean = 12.40\,\mathrm{cm/s}$, $sd = 3.99\,\mathrm{cm/s}$) determined participant to produce significantly faster gestures than both walking ($mean = 10.84\,\mathrm{cm/s}$, $sd = 3.52\,\mathrm{cm/s}$) and standing ($mean = 10.81\,\mathrm{cm/s}$, $sd = 3.55\,\mathrm{cm/s}$)($p < .05$). Holding phone freely ($mean = 12.25\,\mathrm{cm/s}$, $sd = 3.99\,\mathrm{cm/s}$) led to significantly faster gestures than holding phone in the bag ($mean = 10.45\,\mathrm{cm/s}$, $sd = 3.63\,\mathrm{cm/s}$)($p < .05$).

3.2   Mobile Directional Movement

Previous work showed that hand usage and body postures affect smartphone movement as users' perception of the smartphone device could be boosted [11]. It is therefore important to understand how eyes-free interaction may influence the tilt and rotation of the smartphone during gesture production. We then consider the same dependent variables than in [11] to characterise the phone's movement: Alpha (z-axis), Beta (x-axis) and Gamma (y-axis) using the inbuilt accelerometer and gyroscope (see Fig. 3). For each of the directional axes, we captured the total deviation made around this axis, computed as the difference between the largest and the smallest value.

Alpha Deviation – Deviation Around z Axis. There were significant main effects of *moving speed* ($F_{2,22} = 107.146$, $p < .0001$) and *phone location* ($F_{1,11} = 7.038$, $p = 0.023$) on *alpha*. Post-hoc test show that during jogging ($mean = 14.34°$, $sd = 9.14°$) participants held smartphone with significantly larger deviation around z axis than both during walking ($mean = 9.19°$, $sd = 7.06°$) and standing ($mean = 4.91°$, $sd = 5.20°$), and walking had larger deviation around z axis compared to standing. We also found that the deviation of the phone around the z axis while holding it freely ($mean = 11.47°$, $sd = 9.14°$) is significantly larger than when it is held in a bag ($mean = 7.83°$, $sd = 7.39°$)($p < .05$).

Beta Deviation – Deviation Around x Axis. There was significant main effect of *moving speed* ($F_{2,22} = 68.322$, $p < .0001$) on *beta*. Post-hoc test show that during jogging ($mean = 22.75°, sd = 11.59°$) participants held smartphone with significantly higher deviation around x axis than during walking ($mean = 16.32°, sd = 9.90°$) and standing ($mean = 6.43°, sd = 6.18°$), and walking had larger deviation around x axis compared to standing ($p < .05$).

Gamma Deviation – Deviation Around y Axis. There was a significant main effects of *moving speed* ($F_{2,22} = 93.213$, $p < .0001$) on *gamma* with *moving speed* × *phone location* ($F_{2,22} = 8.538$, $p < .002$) interaction. Post-hoc tests show, when standing (respectively, walking), holding the smartphone freely ($mean = 5.60°, sd = 4.36°$) (respectively, $mean = 9.39°, sd = 6.65°$) implies larger deviation around y axis than when holding the phone in a bag ($mean = 2.65°, sd = 3.07°$) (respectively, $mean = 6.442°, sd = 4.728°$)($p < .05$). However, when user runs the gamma deviation is significantly larger when the smartphone is placed in a bag ($mean = 12.10°, sd = 7.52°$) compared to when it's hold freely ($mean = 10.56°, sd = 3.07°$)($p < .05$).

3.3 Qualitative Findings

During the experiments, some participants reported that when they were jogging they felt like they want to draw gestures faster. Some participant found some gestures were more complex and need more focus to draw which can be challenging to draw in a real time scenario, where they need to also remember the gesture shape. In particular, our participants found letter shaped gestures with curves and corners more complex to draw than the remainder gestures shapes. Jogging at 8 km/h was physically difficult for some participants and they had to take breaks in between.

4   Discussion and Future Work

Our key finding is that the faster the moving speed, the longer, larger, and faster stroke gestures are produced. Inversely, when holding the phone in a bag, the produced gestures are slower, shorter, and smaller than when holding the phone freely. We also found no significant interaction ($p > .05$), suggesting that these findings are consistent across respectively, different phone locations and moving speeds. Consequently, for walking and jogging, as well as for holding the phone in a bag, recognizers that rely on geometric and kinematic gesture descriptors, such as [21] (p. 335) should be used with precaution.

Importantly, it was interesting that our results showed that gesture production time was not affected by moving speed nor by phone location. In particular, moving faster or holding the phone freely led to faster gestures without requiring less time to draw the gesture but instead longer gestures which caused the gesture entering speed to increase. This result was expected due to findings from motor control theory that proved a dependency between writing speed and path length [24]. This finding advocates that long gestures as convenient shortcuts for different users moving speeds as people compensate the extra gesture length with increased gesture speed.

When it comes to the orientation of the smartphone a similar trend was observed. Generally, the higher moving speed participant had the more deviation in the angles alpha and beta were observed. These findings can be explained by the fact that the more the user body moves, the more the phone will move. Consequently, designers should take into account this additional phone movement when considering motion gestures in their design for walking contexts [17].

However an opposite effect (*i.e.*, less phone movements) was observed when the phone is hold in a bag compared to holding the phone freely in particular for alpha deviation as well as when standing or walking for gamma deviation. These findings can be explained by the fact that when the phone is in a shoulder bag, there is less space to manipulate the phone which implies a phone more stable.

Our findings also indicate that gestures shapes (*e.g.*, letters) with complex geometries (*i.e.*, with a mixture of curves and lines) were more complex to draw. Thus, we recommend designers to avoid using such gesture shapes for moving contexts. And if needed they should be designed so that they are easy to articulate such that learning and memorization are facilitated.

Like any study, our study presents limitations. For example, in our study participants were younger than the population average, were right-handed, and all are men. Undoubtedly, elder people, children, left-handed or woman participants would behave differently. Participants were instructed to use a single-handed grip to generate the gestures on the touchscreen device. Additionally, as other phone locations exist with other dimensions like holding the phone in the pocket or inside other types/sizes of bags, and as the features of the produced gesture might change depending on the available space to hold the phone. These factors limits the overall generalizability of our findings for others interaction involving different hand grips [11] or body postures [12]. Also, only one phone was used in the experiments. Other phone sizes or form factors may produce different results or observations. These issues are worthy of investigation, but are beyond the scope of the current work. Moreover, the number of participants in our study was only 13 which is enough for a pilot study but more number of participants can be recruited in future.

Future work will also consider more challenging scenarios where participants are encumbered (*e.g.*, holding objects such as shopping bags [18]) or had to focus their attention on some other primary task that could be cognitively or/and visually demanding (*e.g.*, writing a text [5,13], performing a saturation attention task [13] or driving [8]). Finally, future work will investigate the effect of adding haptic feedback during eyes-free gesture production.

Acknowledgements. This project has received funding from the European Union's Horizon 2020 research and innovation program under the Marie Skłodowska-Curie grant agreement No 860114. Alexandru Dancu acknowledges support from project no. PN-III-P4-ID-PCE-2020-0434 (PCE29/2021), within PNCDI III.

References

1. Anthony, L., Brown, Q., Nias, J., Tate, B.: Examining the need for visual feedback during gesture interaction on mobile touchscreen devices for kids. In: Proceedings of the 12th International Conference on Interaction Design and Children, IDC 2013, pp. 157–164. Association for Computing Machinery, New York (2013). https://doi.org/10.1145/2485760.2485775

2. Appert, C., Zhai, S.: Using strokes as command shortcuts: cognitive benefits and toolkit support. In: Proceedings of the SIGCHI Conference on Human Factors in Computing Systems, CHI 2009, pp. 2289–2298. ACM, New York (2009). https://doi.org/10.1145/1518701.1519052

3. Blagojevic, R., Chang, S.H.H., Plimmer, B.: The power of automatic feature selection: Rubine on steroids. In: Proceedings of the Seventh Sketch-Based Interfaces and Modeling Symposium, pp. 79–86. Eurographics Association, Goslar, DEU (2010)

4. Bragdon, A., Nelson, E., Li, Y., Hinckley, K.: Experimental analysis of touch-screen gesture designs in mobile environments. In: Proceedings of the SIGCHI Conference on Human Factors in Computing Systems, pp. 403–412 (2011). https://doi.org/10.1145/1978942.1979000

5. Chen, Q., Perrault, S.T., Roy, Q., Wyse, L.: Effect of temporality, physical activity and cognitive load on spatiotemporal vibrotactile pattern recognition. In: Proceedings of the 2018 International Conference on Advanced Visual Interfaces, AVI 2018, Association for Computing Machinery, New York (2018). https://doi.org/10.1145/3206505.3206511

6. Clawson, J., Starner, T., Kohlsdorf, D., Quigley, D.P., Gilliland, S.: Texting while walking: an evaluation of mini-qwerty text input while on-the-go. In: Proceedings of the 16th International Conference on Human-Computer Interaction with Mobile Devices & Services, pp. 339–348 (2014). https://doi.org/10.1145/2628363.2628408

7. Coast, J.R., Blevins, J.S., Wilson, B.A.: Do gender differences in running performance disappear with distance? Can. J. Appl. Physiol. **29**(2), 139–145 (2004)

8. Cockburn, A., Woolley, D., Thai, K.T.P., Clucas, D., Hoermann, S., Gutwin, C.: Reducing the attentional demands of in-vehicle touchscreens with stencil overlays. In: Proceedings of the 10th International Conference on Automotive User Interfaces and Interactive Vehicular Applications - AutomotiveUI 2018, pp. 33–42. ACM Press (2018)

9. Dai, L., Sears, A., Goldman, R.: Shifting the focus from accuracy to recallability: a study of informal note-taking on mobile information technologies. ACM Trans. Comput.-Hum. Interact. (TOCHI) **16**(1), 1–46 (2009)

10. Dobbelstein, D., Winkler, C., Haas, G., Rukzio, E.: PocketThumb: a wearable dual-sided touch interface for cursor-based control of smart-eyewear. Proc. ACM Interact. Mob. Wearable Ubiquitous Technol. **1**(2), 1–17 (2017)

11. Eardley, R., Roudaut, A., Gill, S., Thompson, S.J.: Understanding grip shifts: how form factors impact hand movements on mobile phones, pp. 4680–4691. ACM, New York (2017)

12. Eardley, R., Roudaut, A., Gill, S., Thompson, S.J.: Investigating How Smartphone Movement is Affected by Body Posture, pp. 1–8. ACM, New York (2018)

13. Guettaf, A., Rekik, Y., Grisoni, L.: Effect of attention saturating and cognitive load on tactile texture recognition for mobile surface. In: Ardito, C., et al. (eds.) INTERACT 2021, Part IV. LNCS, vol. 12935, pp. 557–579. Springer, Cham (2021). https://doi.org/10.1007/978-3-030-85610-6_31

14. Harvey, M., Pointon, M.: Searching on the go: the effects of fragmented attention on mobile web search tasks. In: Proceedings of the 40th International ACM SIGIR Conference on Research and Development in Information Retrieval, pp. 155–164 (2017)

15. Kane, S.K., Wobbrock, J.O., Smith, I.E.: Getting off the treadmill: evaluating walking user interfaces for mobile devices in public spaces. In: Proceedings of the 10th International Conference on Human Computer Interaction with Mobile Devices and Services, pp. 109–118. ACM, New York (2008)

16. Kubo, Y., Shizuki, B., Tanaka, J.: B2B-swipe: swipe gesture for rectangular smartwatches from a bezel to a bezel. In: Proceedings of the 2016 CHI Conference on Human Factors in Computing Systems, pp. 3852–3856 (2016)

17. Negulescu, M., Ruiz, J., Li, Y., Lank, E.: Tap, swipe, or move: attentional demands for distracted smartphone input. In: Proceedings of the International Working Conference on Advanced Visual Interfaces, AVI 2012, pp. 173–180. ACM, New York (2012)

18. Ng, A., Williamson, J., Brewster, S.: The effects of encumbrance and mobility on touch-based gesture interactions for mobile phones. In: Proceedings of the 17th International Conference on Human-Computer Interaction with Mobile Devices and Services, MobileHCI 2015, pp. 536–546. Association for Computing Machinery, New York (2015). https://doi.org/10.1145/2785830.2785853

19. Rekik, Y., Vatavu, R.D., Grisoni, L.: Understanding users' perceived difficulty of multi-touch gesture articulation. In: Proceedings of the 16th International Conference on Multimodal Interaction, pp. 232–239. ACM, New York (2014)

20. Roudaut, A., Rau, A., Sterz, C., Plauth, M., Lopes, P., Baudisch, P.: Gesture output: eyes-free output using a force feedback touch surface, pp. 2547–2556. ACM, New York (2013)

21. Rubine, D.: Specifying gestures by example. In: Proceedings of the 18th Annual Conference on Computer Graphics and Interactive Techniques, SIGGRAPH 1991, pp. 329–337. ACM, New York (1991)

22. Tinwala, H., MacKenzie, I.S.: Eyes-free text entry on a touchscreen phone. In: 2009 IEEE Toronto International Conference Science and Technology for Humanity (TIC-STH), pp. 83–88 (2009)

23. Vatavu, R.-D., Vogel, D., Casiez, G., Grisoni, L.: Estimating the perceived difficulty of pen gestures. In: Campos, P., Graham, N., Jorge, J., Nunes, N., Palanque, P., Winckler, M. (eds.) INTERACT 2011. LNCS, vol. 6947, pp. 89–106. Springer, Heidelberg (2011). https://doi.org/10.1007/978-3-642-23771-3_9

24. Viviani, P., Terzuolo, C.: 32 space-time invariance in learned motor skills. In: Stelmach, G.E., Requin, J. (eds.) Tutorials in Motor Behavior, Advances in Psychology, vol. 1, pp. 525–533. North-Holland (1980)

25. Wobbrock, J.O.: Situationally aware mobile devices for overcoming situational impairments. In: Proceedings of the ACM SIGCHI Symposium on Engineering Interactive Computing Systems, EICS 2019. ACM, New York (2019)

26. Wobbrock, J.O., Wilson, A.D., Li, Y.: Gestures without libraries, toolkits or training: a $1 recognizer for user interface prototypes. In: Proceedings of the 20th Annual ACM Symposium on User Interface Software and Technology, UIST 2007, pp. 159–168. ACM, New York (2007)

Hap2Gest: An Eyes-Free Interaction Concept with Smartphones Using Gestures and Haptic Feedback

Milad Jamalzadeh[1]([✉]), Yosra Rekik[2], Alexandru Dancu[3], and Laurent Grisoni[1]

[1] Lille University, Lille, France
milad.jamalzadeh@univ-lille.fr
[2] Université Polytechnique Hauts-de-France, Valenciennes, France
[3] MintViz Lab, Stefan cel Mare University, Suceava, Romania

Abstract. Smartphones are used in different contexts, including scenarios where visual and auditory modalities are limited (e.g., walking or driving). In this context, we introduce a new interaction concept, called *Hap2Gest*, that can give commands and retrieve information, both eyes-free. First, it uses a gesture as input for command invocation, and then output information is retrieved using haptic feedback perceived through an output gesture drawn by the user. We conducted an elicitation study with 12 participants to determine users' preferences for the aforementioned gestures and the vibration patterns for 25 referents. Our findings indicate that users tend to use the same gesture for input and output, and there is a clear relationship between the type of gestures and vibration patterns users suggest and the type of output information. We show that the gesture's speed profile agreement rate is significantly higher than the gesture's shape agreement rate, and it can be used by the recognizer when the gesture shape agreement rate is low. Finally, we present a complete set of user-defined gestures and vibration patterns and address the gesture recognition problem.

Keywords: Hap2Gest concept · Eyes-free interaction · Haptic · Gesture input · Gesture output · Elicitation study

1 Introduction

Smartphones have become a necessity for many people throughout the world and offer a wide range of functions through their touchscreens. Touchscreen displays are the primary input modality supported by smartphones. A typical way of operating a smartphone is to first reach it and then operate it while looking at its display. This can draw the user's visual focus to the device, which is not desirable if the visual attention is needed elsewhere. For instance, checking directions on

Supplementary Information The online version contains supplementary material available at https://doi.org/10.1007/978-3-031-42280-5_31.

J. Abdelnour Nocera et al. (Eds.): INTERACT 2023, LNCS 14142, pp. 479–500, 2023.
https://doi.org/10.1007/978-3-031-42280-5_31

Fig. 1. *Hap2Gest* concept and context: (left) eyes-free context of use example, (center) command invocation by drawing the input gesture, and then (right) drawing the output gesture and receiving the haptic feedback that corresponds to the output information through this gesture.

a navigation app while driving should cause the minimum distraction and be efficient to perform. Leaving users' visual attention free to perform additional tasks is one of the fundamental motivations for eyes-free interaction [5]. Several eyes-free interaction techniques have been developed that use gestures (*e.g.*, [23]) or voice (*e.g.*, [9]) as input, along with various forms of output feedback (*e.g.*, audio [12] and/or tactile output [28]).

Both gestures and haptic feedback have been used intensively in many studies. Gesture interaction can offer a control interface that eliminates the need for reaching towards a device. Furthermore, haptic feedback can free up even more visual attention for other tasks. For instance, haptic feedback seems effective as a substitute for visual and audio feedback and tends to be quickly perceived when the user is engaged in another primary task [6–8,10,11,26,29]. However, technological means for creating tactile feedback remain very limited and not as developed as display technology. Most smartphones on the market are only equipped with a simple vibration motor to provide haptic feedback. Designing an interaction concept that can be achieved by a simple vibration motor will make that concept accessible to more people.

In this work, we introduce Hap2Gest, a novel interaction concept based on surface gestures and vibration motors, that permits command invocation and information recovery, both eyes-free. First, the user draws an eyes-free input gesture to ask the system to invoke a command, then the user draws an eyes-free output gesture through which the vibration patterns that constitute the output information are felt by the user (Fig. 1). In the last fifteen years, in particular for input gesture, an impressive body of work has been published on elicitation studies: the design of intuitive gesture commands that are reflective of end-user behavior for controlling all kinds of interactive devices, applications, and systems. In this context, we conducted an elicitation study to determine user preferences for input gestures, output gestures, and the vibration patterns for interacting eyes-free with smartphones for the design of *Hap2Gest*. Unlike earlier elicitation studies, we studied user-defined gestures when haptic feedback is available to provide feedback, using a simple vibration motor, in the absence of visual cues.

To the best of our knowledge, this is the first study that investigates the elicitation gestures for eyes-free interaction with a smartphone in the presence of haptic feedback. The results of this study not only show which gestures users prefer for eyes-free interaction with smartphones but also show how they prefer to receive haptic feedback. We also report agreement rates in terms of gesture's shape, gesture's speed profile, and vibration pattern. Our understanding of agreement for user-defined gestures and user-defined vibration patterns allows the creation of more natural sets of user gestures and user vibration patterns. We finally discuss the implications of this research for the design of *Hap2Gest*, in particular, and more generally for eyes-free interaction on smartphones in twofold: (i) from the perspective of gesture design and recognition, and (ii) from the perspective of haptic design. We hope our results will prove useful to designers and practitioners interested on eyes-free gestures and haptic designs.

2 Related Work

Methodologies that involves users as part of the design process have gained popularity since the work of Wobbrock et al. [39]. They created a set of user-defined gestures for touchscreens by showing participants the outcome of an action and asking them to make a gesture that would produce that action. After collecting the designs of all participants, experimenters quantified the degree of consensus among gestures proposed by participants using an agreement score. The gestures with the highest agreement rates were selected as the most appropriate for each action. Since then, the elicitation methodology has been widely used to create gestures for freehand TV control [18] and smart glasses [34], unmanned aerial vehicles [24], handheld objects [30], deformable displays [32], and blind people [13].

Besides the user preference for input gestures, several studies have recently adopted the elicitation methodology for user preferences for haptic outputs. Haptics have commonly been used as feedback or notifications. Lawrence et al. [3] studied the user preferences for mid-air haptic sensation to match gestures used for interacting with an augmented reality menu environment. Kim et al. [15] conducted an elicitation study on haptic patterns for social touch, generated by a haptic display called SwarmHaptics. Wei et al. [38] conducted a similar experiment for mediated social touch on touchscreens. In our work, users have to define the gestures and vibration patterns in order to give a command to the smartphone and then retrieve information, both eyes-free.

Researchers have proposed several new solutions in recent years to provide haptic feedback to touchscreens [1,16,27,37,40]. Vibrotactile actuators are the simplest and most common way to add haptic feedback to touchscreens. Zhao et al. [40] created the illusion of a moving tactile stimulus on a tablet by attaching several vibrators to the tablet. Variable friction displays are another way to provide haptic feedback on a touchscreen [1,16,27,37]. The haptic feedback on touchscreens can also be achieved by using intermediate parts. Roudault et al. [28] built two prototypes that could move the finger on the screen to reproduce a given gesture, like a letter or a symbol, without the need to look at it. Our proposed concept makes use of the smartphone's vibration motor instead.

Vibrotactile messages can be used to transfer non-visual information by different vibration patterns by changing the frequency, intensity, and duration of vibration [4,6]. A recent review presents a comprehensive overview [14] of hands-free devices for transmitting speech and language with the tactile modality distinguishing between tactual language units and tactual words by encoding speech units and signal, phonemes, letters, and morse code. An inspiring work that aimed to find out the achievable throughput of the skin, the bandwidth of vibrotactile communication, is that of Novich et. al [22] who showed that vibrotactile patterns encoded in both the spatial and temporal dimension using a haptic vest exceed performance of spatially encoded patterns. Zhao et. al [41] showed how users were able to remember 20 haptic words under 30 min of training using 6 actuators on the forearm, while Tan et. al [31] succeeded in the acquisition of 500 words after 10 d of training.

On the application level, Marino et al. [17] developed WhatsHap, which helped two participants to have a conversation by mapping speech to tactile feedback on the arms. Wei et al. [38] applied mediated touch gestures in an instant messaging application as haptic icons. In this work, we introduce a new interaction concept called *Hap2Gest* that permits the users to have an eyes-free dialog with their smartphone devices while engaged in another primary task.

3   Hap2Gest Interaction Concept

On modern mobile phones, gestures are commonly used as input. When it's combined with haptic feedback, it enables richer output (alongside the richness of multi-touch input), *i.e.*, a richer interactive experience (*e.g.*, [28]). Gestures and haptic feedback have been used in the context of eyes-free interaction. For instance, when the user is performing a primary task (*e.g.*, walking down the street [7,10,21] or working [7,11]) and does not wish to be disturbed from an attention point of view but in the mean time wishes to check for new mails, text messages, or calls on the cellphone without looking at it.

In this context, we introduce *Hap2Gest*, a new eyes-free interaction concept that uses gestures both as the input modality and as part of the output modality, combined with haptic feedback. First, the user draws an eyes-free gesture on the touchscreen of the smartphone to give a command to the phone (input). Then, the user draws a second eyes-free gesture, the same or different from the first one, and can feel one or multiple vibrations on different parts of the gesture (Fig. 1). The vibration pattern they feel-the number and locations of vibrations-through the output gesture are the vocabulary of this interaction concept for output. The output modality uses a combination of tactile and kinesthetic senses. The vibration created by the vibration motor of a smartphone creates the tactile sense, and the finger speed and position create the kinesthetic sense. Thus, Hap2Gest would enable a less obtrusive way to retrieve information from user' phone, *i.e.*, without looking at the display or turning on his phone.

Our interaction design is similar to Roudaut et al., [28] as we both use gestures to give commands to the smartphone (input) and retrieve information with gestures and haptic feedback (output), in an eyes-free configuration. However, in their work, the output gesture is created by a force feedback system that moves the finger. Consequently, the haptic feedback is used to guide the user to draw the output gesture, while the output gesture constitutes the main output information. For example, if the drawn output gesture is "8", the user understand that he received eight new messages. However, in our work, the output gesture is a predefined gesture drawn by the user, and the haptic feedback is created using the vibration motor at some points throughout the output gesture. Thus, the vibration patterns (their number and locations) constitute the main output information.

4   User Study

(a) The experiment setup   (b) The eyes-free setup

Fig. 2. The experiment setup. The participant manipulates the smartphone while their hands are inside a box to maintain eyes-free interaction. The user interface of the experiment was displayed on a monitor in front of participants.

We conducted an elicitation study to determine users' preferences for the design of *Hap2Gest*: (i) eyes-free input gestures for command invocation on a smartphone in the absence of visual cues, (ii) eyes-free output gestures for receiving the output information, and (iii) vibration patterns to get eyes-free output information through the output gesture.

The main premises underlying this research are that (i) a good gesture-set needs to be easy to use and remember by the user, and (ii) vibration patterns need to be easy to understand, remember, and recognize by the user. Consequently, to support these main premises, we asked our participants to design gestures that are easier to remember and to come up with vibration patterns that take less time and effort to understand. In addition, in order to avoid compromising the system in differentiating between the different commands, we asked participants to try their best to avoid having exactly the same gestures for different commands.

Table 1. The five interaction scenarios and the different referents considered in each scenario.

A. Scenario in presence of auditory feedback

R1. Accept call	R2. Reject call

B. Scenario with a yes/no response

R3. Is it a call from my favorite contacts?	R4. Do I have any missed calls?
R5. Is my phone silent?	R6. Do I have new messages?
R7. Do I have new messages from a favorite contact?	R8. Do I have new notifications?
R9. Do I have a notification from Instagram?	R10. Do I have a notification from Facebook?
R11. Do I have a notification from Twitter?	R12. Do I have a notification from WhatsApp?
R13. Accept the call and tell me if it's from a favorite contact.	R14. Reject the call and tell me if it's from a favorite contact
R15. Mute my phone with success feedback.	R16. Unmute my phone with success feedback

C. Scenario with categorical responses

R17. Which application do I have a notification from (Instagram or Facebook)?	R18. Which application do I have a notification from (Instagram, Facebook, or Twitter)?
R19. Which application do I have a notification from (Instagram, Facebook, Twitter, or WhatsApp)?	R20. Which application do I have a notification from (Instagram, Facebook, Twitter, WhatsApp, or Telegram)?
R21. How is the weather today? (sunny, cloudy, rainy, or snow)	R22. Which day of the week is it? (Monday, Tuesday, Wednesday, Thursday, Friday, Saturday, or Sunday)
R23. Which month is it? (January, February, March, April, May, June, July, August, September, October, November, or December)	

D. Scenario with numerical responses

R24. How many new notifications do I have? (0, 1, 2, 3, 4, or 5)

E. Scenario for time range

R25. At which time today do I have a meeting?

Similarly to previous gesture elicitation studies [20, 25, 39], we do not want participants to focus on recognizer issues for the defined gesture set. Consequently, we do not provide participants with recognition feedback during gesture production. We also asked participants to ignore recognition issues by considering the smartphone to be able to understand and recognize any gesture they might wish to perform. In addition, for vibration patterns, as we want to identify user preferences, we do not want participants to focus on tactile rendering issues. Consequently, no haptic feedback was provided to our participants during the task. We also encouraged participants to ignore haptic feedback issues by considering the smartphone to be able to render any vibration pattern they might wish to have.

4.1   Participants

12 participants (three females, and nine males) volunteered to take part in our experiment. Participants' ages were between 20 and 32 years ($mean = 22.9$, $SD = 3.7$). All participants were right-handed and had used smartphones for several years and were familiar with the vibration motors of smartphones.

4.2   Scenarios and Referents

We wanted to create a list of common smartphone commands that users frequently use when visual cues are not available. Moreover, we wanted to cover different types of data that can be provided to users: binary data, categorical data, numerical data, range, or assisted with auditory feedback. For this purpose, we considered five interaction scenarios in which users frequently need to execute such commands on the smartphone. Each scenario contains between one and 14 referents. Overall, the experiment included 25 referents. The list of the five interaction scenarios and associated referents are available in Table 1.

4.3   Procedure

First, participants watched a video, available as supplementary material, which explained our proposed interaction concept and the instructions for the experiment. The video served as *priming* [19] since it contained contexts of use and examples so that participants would think more generally about the proposed gestures. Written instructions were then handed out as printed forms, with 25 referents and possible responses for each referent. Participants were then asked to draw the gesture and vibration patterns for each interaction scenario on the paper forms. The participants were asked to pay attention to the following points while giving their answers:

- The participants will draw the gesture with one finger. They are allowed to hold the phone with the same hand or with the other hand.
- Try their best to avoid having the same gesture for different commands.
- Design gestures that are easier to remember.
- Come up with vibration patterns that take less time and effort to understand.

After finishing their designs on paper, participants moved to the next step in the experiment. In this step, participants were asked to enter the solutions they had just designed on paper to a smartphone in eyes-free configuration. For this purpose, the participants held the smartphone in a box to avoid having any visual cues. Five participants manipulated the phone with only one hand and the rest manipulated the phone with the dominant hand and hold it with other hand. Then, the papers on which they designed their solutions were given to them, and they were asked to copy their solutions from paper to smartphone one by one. An android application was developed to capture participants' responses in an eyes-free configuration. The screen of the smartphone was mirrored on a display in front of participants to guide them during the experiment and maintain the eyes-free interaction with the smartphone itself, as shown in Fig. 2. At the top of the screen, the interaction scenario and the answers were displayed one after another. The participants had to first draw the gesture for giving command, and then they had to specify vibration points one by one by drawing the gesture from the beginning to the point they wished to get the vibration. No visual cue was shown on the display about the touch point or gesture path, to ensure eyes-free condition. At the bottom of the screen, there was a green sliding button, which was used to approve the response by swiping right or return to previous steps by swiping left. A paper strap was glued on top of this virtual button, so participants could feel its position without seeing the phone. The average duration of the experiment for each participant was 50 min.

4.4   Apparatus

For the second stage of the study, we used a Samsung Galaxy S6 smartphone running Android 6.0.1. The phone's dimensions were 5.65 "× 2.78". Display resolution was 1440×2560 pixels. We developed our application using Java to record the participants' gestures and vibration patterns. Users' hands were videotaped using a Microsoft LifeCAM Studio webcam. One author observed each session and took detailed notes.

5   Results

Our results include the agreemate rate measures, user-defined gestures set, and the user-defined vibration patterns set.

5.1   Agreement Rate Measure

To evaluate the degree of consensus among our participants, we used AGATe (AGreement Analysis Toolkit) software [35] for calculating an agreement rate for each referent. An agreement rate, $AR(r)$, quantifies the magnitude of agreement among the gestures elicited from participants, where:

$$AR(r) = \frac{|P|}{|P| - 1} \sum_{P_i \subseteq P} (|\frac{P_i}{P_t}|)^2 - \frac{1}{|P| - 1} \tag{1}$$

In Eq. 1, P is the set of all proposals for referent r, $|P|$ is the size of the set, and P_i is the subsets of identical proposals from P. The range for $AR(r)$ is $[0, 1]$. In our study, we used the formula above to calculate two agreement rates: (1) the gesture's shape agreement rate and (2) the gesture's speed profile agreement rate.

The gesture's shape agreement rate is the same as the agreement rate in previous elicitation studies. In this study, participants propose two gestures for each referent (an input gesture and an output gesture). We assumed two designs were identical if they had identical input gestures and identical output gestures.

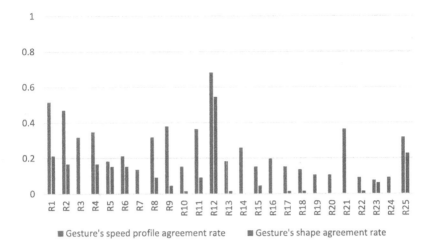

Fig. 3. The gesture's shape agreement rates and the gesture's speed profile agreement rates are shown for all scenarios.

After gathering all participants' proposals, authors created a codebook [36] to evaluate the similarity of proposals. We considered two gestures identical if they were made from equal number of strokes and the deviation between stroke angles were less than 45°C, even if two gestures had differences between their absolute position on the screen, their overall shape size, or strokes' lengths. Consequently, we calculate one gesture agreement rate for each design. However, in 96 percent of the designs, participants proposed the same gesture for input and output. Chance agreement [33,36] was not considered and corrected since the user elicitation study was not conducted with a fixed set of nominal categories out of which participants chose their proposals.

In order to calculate gestures speed agreement rate, we derived the speed profile of gestures by taking the derivative of finger displacement with respect to time. The speed profile of all participants for each referent is available in supplementary materials. Then, we used the same formula above on the speed profile. The codebook used for evaluating the similarity of speed profiles were different than the one used for shape agreement rate. First, the peaks and lows in the speed profile was detected. Then, the speed profile was translated to series of peaks and lows, with the same order as they appear on time axis. Two speed profiles were considered identical if they had same number of lows and peaks in same order. To the best of our knowledge, we are the first gesture elicitation study that measures the speed profile agreement rate. The gesture set proposed by participants encouraged us to look at the agreement rate on the speed profile. We observed that the gesture shape proposed by participants for some referents had relatively low agreement, but the agreement rate among the speed profile of the same referent was significantly higher. So, it's more likely to find consensus by using gesture speed profile rather than gesture shape. Figure 3 shows the gesture agreement rates and speed profile agreement rates for all 25 referents.

A paired-samples t-test was conducted to compare the gesture agreement rate and speed profile agreement rate of the 25 referents. There was a significant difference between the gesture's shape agreement rates ($mean = .081, SD = .122$) and gesture's speed profile agreement rates ($mean = 0.252, SD = 0.153$); $t(24) = 8.545, p < 0.00001$. The gesture's shape agreement rate is, in particular, low. Thus, to better understand the cause of this low rate and, in particular, if it depends on the scenario or not, we decided to calculate the gesture's shape agreement rate by scenario. We also calculate the speed agreement rate for each scenario in order to determine if the gesture's speed profile agreement rate compensates for the gesture's shape agreement rate in cases where the latter is low.

Finally, the vibration pattern agreement rate VAR is calculated for each referent using the formula below:

$$VAR(r) = \frac{|V|}{|V| - 1} \sum_{V_i \subseteq P} (|\frac{V_i}{V_t}|)^2 - \frac{1}{|V| - 1} \tag{2}$$

where P is the set of all proposal vibration patterns for referent r, $|P|$ is the size of the set, and P_i is the subsets of identical vibration patterns from P. The range for VAR is $[0, 1]$. The criteria used to consider two vibration patterns identical for each scenario is explained in the next section.

5.2   User-defined Eyes-Free Gestures and Vibration Patterns Sets

In the following, we present, for each scenario, the most used input gestures, output gestures, and vibration patterns, along with the agreement rates for gesture's shapes, gesture's speed profiles, and vibration patterns.

Interaction Scenarios in the Presence of Auditory Feedback. The most common gesture suggested for accepting a call was a straight line drawn from left to right by seven participants, and for rejecting a call, a straight line drawn from right to left by six participants. The mean agreement rates for gesture shape and gesture speed profile are 0.190 and 0.493, respectively.

For accepting or rejecting call scenarios where auditory feedback is available, 75 percent of participants preferred not to have any haptic feedback for either of the referents. The rest of the participants all preferred to have a single vibration at the end of the output gestures, which were identical to the input gestures, for both referents. The vibration agreement rates for both accept and reject call referents were 0.591.

Interaction Scenarios with Yes/no Response. In this scenario, for eight of the referents the most agreed gestures were gestures with shape of a letter from referent. For instance "N" shaped gesture for "Do I have new notifications?" referent and "M" shaped gesture for "Do I have new messages?" referent. All

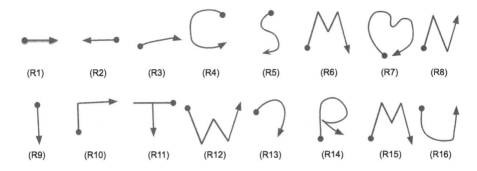

Fig. 4. The most suggested gestures referents R1 to R16. The filled circle shows the start point of the gesture. The arrow shows the ending point of the gesture.

participants suggested same gesture for input and output for every single referent. For this scenario, the mean agreement rate for gesture shape and gesture speed profile were 0.094 and 0.277, respectively. Figure 4 shows the most suggested gestures for yes/no feedback scenario referents.

The vibration patterns participants suggested can be categorized by three parameters. First, the number of locations on gestures where vibration is present. Figure 5a shows that the users suggested between zero and two vibration points for these interaction scenarios. 96 percent of users preferred to have a vibration at a single point for yes response and only four percent preferred to have vibrations at two points on a gesture for yes responses. For no response, most participants, 63 percent, again preferred to have vibration at one point on the gesture. However, contrary to the yes responses, 37 percent proposed not having any vibration for the no response.

Second, the vibration patterns can be categorized based on the number of vibrations proposed by participants. Figure 5b shows that participants suggested between zero and two vibrations for this interaction scenario. Most participants, 77 percent for yes responses and 64 percent for no responses, suggested one vibration on the gesture for the feedback. However, the rest of the participants proposed no vibration for no response and two vibrations for a yes response.

Third, the vibration patterns can be grouped based on the position of the vibrations. Figure 5c shows the distribution of vibrations on gestures by categorizing them into three groups: at the beginning of the gesture, at the end of the gesture, and in between. Our results show that most participants prefer to have a vibration at the end of gesture for yes response. However, for no response, the vibration is preferred both at the beginning and at the end of gesture.

Using the three criteria stated above for considering the vibration patterns identical, we calculated the vibration agreement rate for all 14 referents. Results indicate the mean vibration pattern agreement rate for "yes" answer was $(mean = 0.263, SD = 0.082)$ and the mean vibration pattern agreement for "no" answer was $(mean = 0.242, SD = 0.046), t(13) = 3.802, p = 0.001$. Though most participants used similar vibration patterns for different referents of this

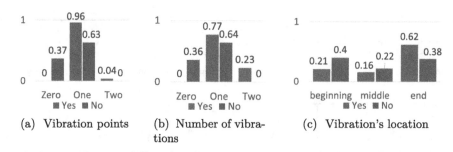

Fig. 5. The vibration patterns suggested by users for yes/no response scenarios. Figure (a) shows on how many points participants prefer to have vibration for each response. Figure (b) shows the number of vibrations they prefer to have for each response. Figure (c) shows where on the gesture they preferred to have the vibrations for each response.

scenario, no participant applied the same vibration pattern to every single referent of this scenario. The most suggested haptic feedback was one vibration at the beginning of the gesture for "no" response and one vibration at the end of the gesture for "yes" response.

Interaction Scenario for Categorical Responses. This interaction scenario includes seven referents. Four of these referents were analogues, R17 to R20, in the sense that the question asked was the same but the number of possible answers was different. In all these four referents, the question was "Which application do I have notification from" and the possible response was one application from two, three, four, or five applications. The most popular design was suggested by three participants. They differentiated the referents by adding an extra stroke to the end of the previous referent to increase the number of possible answers. Though the gesture shape they used was different, the speed profiles of those gestures were similar. For this set of designs, participants always assigned the vibration to the corners of the gestures. Figure 6 shows the most popular design for referents R17 to R20. Two participants used same gesture four all these analogues referents and assigned different vibration points for each referent. They always assigned the vibration to the same location for the same application in all referents. Two participants used the first letters of the applications for gestures. The next most common suggested gesture shape was drawing the letter from each possible response as both the input and the output gesture and feeling the vibration at the end of the corresponding letter, depending on the response. For instance, when the possible answers was "Instagram" or "Facebook", they drew "IF" for this referent. When the possible answers was "Instagram", or "Facebook", or "Twitter", or "WhatsApp" they drew "IFTW". Referents R21, R22, and R23 were unrelated questions with four, seven, and 12 possible responses. For referents R21 and R22 with four and seven possible responses, respectively, 70 percent of participants proposed gestures with clear corners and assigned the vibrations to the corners of the gesture. However, for referent R23, with 12

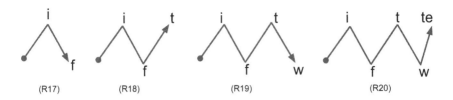

Fig. 6. The most suggested gestures for referents R17 to R20. The filled circle shows the beginning of the gesture. The arrow shows the ending point of the gesture. The red letters show the vibration point for each response."i" for Instagram, "f" for Facebook, "t" for Twitter, "w" for WhatsApp, and "te" for Telegram. (Color figure online)

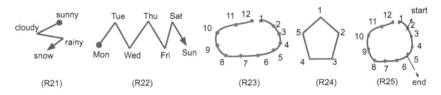

Fig. 7. The most suggested gestures for referents R21 to R25. (R23) numbers 1 to 12, represent the vibrations for month from January to December, respectively.(R24) shows participants suggest no vibration for number zero feedback and one vibration on the corners of the pentagon. (R25) The design suggested by half of the participants for a time range. They suggested feeling a vibration at the beginning of the time range (i.e. at 2 o'clock in the figure) and one at the end (i.e. at 5 o'clock in the figure) while they were drawing a circle.

possible responses this percentage was 25 percent. Figure 7 shows the most suggested referents for these three referents.

This interaction scenario included referents with two to twelve possible responses. Our results show that the users prefer to have gestures with clear corners, such as zigzag patterns or geometric shapes such as rectangles, or hexagons, and assign the vibration to the corners of these shapes. The gesture shape agreement rate and gesture speed profile agreement rate were 0.015 and 0.147. The vibration agreement rate for this scenario was 0.056 ± 0.061.

Interaction Scenario for Numerical Responses from 0 to 5. For numerical responses, 75 percent of participants preferred gestures with clear corners, similar to categorical responses. The most suggested gesture for this referent was a pentagon, as shown in Fig. 7. However, some other designs were also suggested, like having vibration at different places in a straight line (for the "1" response vibration at the beginning of a straight line and for the "5" at the end of the straight line) or varying the number of vibrations (one vibration for the response "1" and five vibrations for the response "5"). In this case, the participant suggested a gesture shaped like the letter "N" as input gesture, and no gesture as the output gesture. The gesture's shape agreement rate was 0.000 and gesture's speed profile agreement rate was 0.091. The vibration agreement rate for this scenario was 0.106.

Interaction Scenario for Time Range. For this scenario, we had one referent that asks at what time range do I have a meeting today. For this referent, unlike other referents, participants didn't have access to possible responses when they designed their gestures on the paper. We asked them to devise a solution that covers all possible time spans. 50 percent of participants suggested a circular shape gesture, which corresponds to a clock, and they proposed to have one vibration at the beginning of the time range and one at the end. This design was the most popular one (an illustration is shown in Fig. 7). The other participants suggested a similar idea but for shapes other than circles such as triangles. The gesture's shape agreement rate and gesture's speed profile agreement rate were both 0.439. The vibration agreement rate for this scenario was 0.439.

6   Discussion and Future Work

In our study, the overall average agreement rate for the gesture's shape was very low ($mean = 0.081, SD = 0.122$). The five scenarios in this study can be listed in descending order based on gesture shape agreement rate as follows: 1) scenario for time range ($mean = 0.227$), 2) scenario in presence of the auditory feedback ($mean = 0.190$), 3) scenario with yes/no responses ($mean = 0.094$), 4) scenario with categorical responses ($mean = 0.015$), and 5) scenario for numerical responses ($mean = 0.000$). The time range scenario has the highest agreement rate, though based on our participants' feedback, it was the most challenging scenario to design. However, at the end, half of the participants suggested the same design. Their design was based on a simple illustration of a clock's hours on a circle. The second scenario with the highest agreement rate was for accept and reject call referents. The gestures suggested by users are very similar to gestures used on many smartphones to accept and reject calls when visual cues are available. For the yes/no response scenario, though the gesture's shape agreement rate was low, the most popular design was to use a letter from the scenario. Among the other scenarios, the categorical and numerical responses scenarios had the lowest rate of agreement for gesture's shape. This can be due to the fact that they were difficult to illustrate with a simple, widely accepted gesture, and the required haptic feedback was more complicated. However, for these two scenarios, the mean agreement rate of gesture's speed profile were higher, 0.147 and 0.091, respectively. This findings suggests that for such scenarios, the gesture speed is more important to users than the gesture shape.

Based on our findings, in the following, we discuss the implications of our results for the design of the *Hap2Gest* concept in terms of gesture design, gesture recognition, and haptic design.

6.1   Gesture Design and Recognition Implications

From our study, we recommend designers and researchers to **use the same gesture for input and output** to increase learnability and memorability. It also simplifies recognition. In our study, although we allowed participants to use different gestures for input and output, our user-designed sets emerged with 96 percent of the same gesture for input and output. This can be due to the fact that using the same gesture for input and output requires less memory effort for participants. Though participants decided this without considering the recognition problem, it is beneficial to the recognizer too. Since the two gestures drawn by users for input and output are quite similar to each other, the recognizer has a reference to compare the output gesture with. For instance, if a user wants to draw a circle as the gesture, it is a very challenging task to detect online where on the circle the touch point is, especially at the initial stages. But when the input gesture is already recorded, the recognizer can easily detect the position on the circle by comparing the incomplete output gesture with the input gesture, if there is not a significant difference between the input and output gestures.

Although we recommend the designers use the same gesture for input and output in most cases, we don't recommend it when the gesture is too long. Drawing two long gestures can be slow and exhausting. To solve this issue, we recommend excluding the output gesture and providing the information with only vibrotactile messages at the end of the input gesture, or using a shorter input gesture. For instance, for referent R22 and R23, where there were 7 and 12 possible responses, respectively, some participants used a short letter as the input gesture (*i.e.*, letter "Z" as input gesture and a longer zigzag as output gesture for referent R22).

Our findings show there is a clear relation between the type of gestures and vibration patterns users suggest and the type of output information. First, **stroke gestures with geometric patterns (like rectangle, zigzag, polygon, etc.) should be preferred over alphabetic gestures for commands that can provide the user with many output information,** like in the scenario with categorical responses. What is important in this case is that the number of strokes that make up the output gesture is significant to the participants: **the more strokes the gesture contains, the more corners there are, and the more output information the output gesture can provide the user.** However, when the size of output information is so large, drawing so many strokes can be exhausting. To resolve this problem, some participants suggested assigning multiple vibrations to a line or a curve, and not only on corners. In this way, the gesture becomes shorter and easier to draw. The agreement between the shapes of the geometries for such a referent, R23, was very low, but the majority of participants spread the vibrations on straight lines. However, the most popular design was spreading the 12 vibrations over a circle. Though this was the most popular suggestion, it doesn't show that it would work. Further experiments are required to determine if participants can accurately locate these 12 points on a circle while drawing gestures. If the circular gestures can't have high accuracy, then the other design suggested by users can be used instead. Some participants, for example, proposed spreading the 12 points across a geometry with four edges, with three vibration points on each edge. The corners available in this geometry may result in higher accuracy for locating the vibration points.

In contrast, **alphabetic gestures are interesting to use when considering commands that provide the user with a binary response, like those in the scenario with a yes or no response.** In this case, the letter that corresponds to the first letter of the name of the application is a good choice for the input and output gestures. For example, to check if the user has received a message, the letter "M" can be used. This finding is correlated with the work of Roudaut et al. [28], where letters are used as output gesture accompanied with haptic feedback to notify the user that he received a message. Successive letter shapes can also be used, for example, in the case where the user wants to have different notifications from different applications.

For challenging scenarios like the time range, we recommend using gestures, which are simple illustrations of an object or act related to the scenario. For example, our participants used a circle to illustrate a clock's hours. However, a commonly accepted illustration of every scenario is not possible. For instance, there is no common visual representation of months or weeks accepted by the public. Finally, **for scenarios where gestures are famously already used on smartphones, like to accept and reject calls, we recommend using these familiar gesture shapes.**

As Wobbrock et al. [39] we advocate gesture reuse to increase learnability and memorability. Our user-designed set emerged with reusable gestures for analogous operations. Interestingly, in order to exclude ambiguity between different referents, in addition to relying on the target of the gesture as observed by Wobbrock et al. [39], our participants rely on the location of the haptic feedback for the output information. Two participants used the same gesture for all four referents, which were asking which application they have notifications from. They just added new vibration locations to each additional application while keeping the same gesture for the four referents. **For the categorical and numerical response scenarios, the recognizer should be focused more on the speed profile and not on the geometry of the gesture,** as there is more agreement between the speed profiles. For example, for a majority of categorical referents, users draw a gesture with clear corners, such as a polygon or zigzag, and assign the vibration to the corners of the gesture. Although the gestures mean shape agreement rates for categorical and numerical scenarios were not high (0.015 and 0.000, respectively), the gestures mean speed profile agreement rates were significantly higher (0.147 and 0.091, respectively). This shows that the gestures participants suggested were quite different, but the speed pattern was much more similar. In this case, the speed profile of these gestures is formed from consecutive bumps where, at the corners of the geometry, the corresponding speed is close to zero, at the bottom of bumps in the speed profile, and that's where most users prefer to have the vibrations.

6.2   Haptic Design Implications

Designers and Researchers should Privilege Positioning the Output Vibration on the Corner of the Output Gesture. For example, in the first scenario, accept and reject call, all the participants who decided to have haptic feedback chose to have it at the end of the gesture. In the second scenario, yes/no responses, 89 percent of participants assigned vibrations at the beginning, end, or in between but on the corners. In the third scenario, categorical responses, the preference of participants was for having gestures with clear corners and assigning the vibration to the corners. However, it was a function of the number of possible responses. The percentage of participants who decided to have shapes with clear corners such as a zigzag pattern increased from 50 percent to 75 percent when the number of responses increased from 2 to 6. However, for the number of responses greater than 6, this percentage was less, *i.e.*, 33 percent for 12 possible responses. For the numerical response scenario, there was also a high tendency to assign vibration to corners, 75 percent. These results show that participants find it easy to feel the vibration on corners and tend to focus on the speed pattern of the finger rather than the geometry of the gesture.

The number of successively perceived vibrations could be used to provide users with numerical output information. While this solution was not the most suggested, it is still an interesting way to receive the output information. After drawing the input gesture, the user will simply remain stationary and count the number of perceived separate vibrations. This method was suggested by one user for referents R22, R23, and R24. Referent R24's output is intrinsically a number. However, the outputs of referents R22 and R23 can have an order and can be numerated by the users, *i.e.*, one corresponds to the first month of the year and 12 corresponds to the last month of the year. Consequently, it is interesting to study in future work from both cognitive and precision points of view, for numerical output information, if it is better to perceive different vibrations through the gesture, each of which corresponds to a different number, or to stay stationary after drawing the input gesture while perceiving many successive vibrations (at the same location) such that their number corresponds to the output information.

When Auditory Feedback is Available, Haptic Feedback can be Excluded. For example, for accepting or rejecting call referents, most participants preferred not to have haptic feedback. However, as our study was made without a primary task, this implication can depend on the context of the interaction. For example, in [2], authors found that, after training with visual and auditory feedback, the use of haptic feedback permits users to reduce their attention to the touchscreen.

6.3   Limitations

Like any study, our study presents limitations. In this study, participants were younger than the population average, were right-handed, and were all students at the university. Undoubtedly, older people, children, or left-handed people would behave differently. Moreover, the number of participants we recruited can be increased to draw more robust conclusions and derive a gesture set that is more generalizable. These issues are worthy of investigation, but are beyond the scope of the current work.

Unlike previous gesture elicitation studies on touchscreens, our study introduced the haptic channel to the equation. However, participants designed their solution without trying the haptic part. It's possible some of the solutions participants designed may not be accurate or achievable in practice. We tried to minimize this problem by warning the participants in the instruction to try their best to come up with simple vibration patterns that are easier to remember and understand. Moreover, the solutions suggested by participants may not be necessarily the best solution in practice. In future, we plan to conduct psychophysical experiments on the solutions suggested by participants to evaluate them, in terms of accuracy, speed, and memory effort.

7   Conclusion

The nature of the haptic actuators used in smartphones makes the transmission of high-dimensional data difficult as they are limited to patterns such as intensity, duration, and frequency. In this work, we add one other dimension, kinesthetic perception of the finger, to human interaction with smartphones through haptic channel. We introduced *Hap2Gest*, a two-stage gesture-based, eyes-free interaction concept that leverages tactile and kinesthetic senses to retrieve information from a smartphone. We conducted the first elicitation study in the literature where gestures on touchscreens are selected not only by the task but also by considering the tactile channel for retrieving information. The results show that in more than 96 percent of the cases, participants prefer to have the same gesture for input and output, which is good news for designers as it makes recognition easier and online recognition possible. Our findings also show that there is a clear relationship between the type of gestures and vibration patterns suggested by users and the type of output information. Moreover, we showed that the gesture's speed profile agreement rate is significantly higher than the gesture's shape agreement rate, and it can be used by the recognizer when the gesture shape agreement rate is low. Finally, we highlight the implications of our work on the paradigm of gesture interaction design, gesture recognition, and haptic design. We hope that our results will prove useful to gesture and haptic interface designers, assisting them toward improved gesture and haptic designs that consider users' behavior and preferences.

Acknowledgements. This project has received funding from the European Union's Horizon 2020 research and innovation program under the Marie Skłodowska-Curie grant agreement No. 860114.

References

1. Bau, O., Poupyrev, I., Israr, A., Harrison, C.: Teslatouch: electrovibration for touch surfaces. In: Proceedings of the 23nd Annual ACM Symposium on User Interface Software and Technology, UIST 2010, pp. 283–292. Association for Computing Machinery, New York, NY, USA (2010). https://doi.org/10.1145/1866029.1866074
2. Bernard, C., Monnoyer, J., Ystad, S., Wiertlewski, M.: Eyes-off your fingers: gradual surface haptic feedback improves eyes-free touchscreen interaction. In: Proceedings of the 2022 CHI Conference on Human Factors in Computing Systems. CHI 2022, Association for Computing Machinery, New York, NY, USA (2022). https://doi.org/10.1145/3491102.3501872
3. Van den Bogaert, L., Geerts, D.: User-defined mid-air haptic sensations for interacting with an AR menu environment. In: Nisky, I., Hartcher-O'Brien, J., Wiertlewski, M., Smeets, J. (eds.) EuroHaptics 2020. LNCS, vol. 12272, pp. 25–32. Springer, Cham (2020). https://doi.org/10.1007/978-3-030-58147-3_3
4. Brewster, S., Brown, L.M.: Tactons: structured tactile messages for non-visual information display. In: Proceedings of the Fifth Conference on Australasian User Interface, AUIC 2004, vol. 28. pp. 15–23. Australian Computer Society Inc, AUS (2004)
5. Brewster, S., Lumsden, J., Bell, M., Hall, M., Tasker, S.: Multimodal 'eyes-free' interaction techniques for wearable devices. In: Proceedings of the SIGCHI Conference on Human Factors in Computing Systems, CHI 2003, pp. 473–480. Association for Computing Machinery, New York, NY, USA (2003). https://doi.org/10.1145/642611.642694
6. Cauchard, J.R., Cheng, J.L., Pietrzak, T., Landay, J.A.: Activibe: design and evaluation of vibrations for progress monitoring. In: Proceedings of the 2016 CHI Conference on Human Factors in Computing Systems, CHI 2016, pp. 3261–3271. Association for Computing Machinery, New York, NY, USA (2016). https://doi.org/10.1145/2858036.2858046
7. Chen, Q., Perrault, S.T., Roy, Q., Wyse, L.: Effect of temporality, physical activity and cognitive load on spatiotemporal vibrotactile pattern recognition. In: Proceedings of the 2018 International Conference on Advanced Visual Interfaces, AVI 2018, Association for Computing Machinery, New York, NY, USA (2018). https://doi.org/10.1145/3206505.3206511
8. Cockburn, A., Woolley, D., Thai, K.T.P., Clucas, D., Hoermann, S., Gutwin, C.: Reducing the attentional demands of in-vehicle touchscreens with stencil overlays. In: Proceedings of the 10th International Conference on Automotive User Interfaces and Interactive Vehicular Applications, pp. 33–42. AutomotiveUI 2018, Association for Computing Machinery, New York, NY, USA (2018). https://doi.org/10.1145/3239060.3239061
9. Ghosh, D., Liu, C., Zhao, S., Hara, K.: Commanding and re-dictation: developing eyes-free voice-based interaction for editing dictated text. ACM Trans. Comput.-Hum. Interact. (TOCHI) 27(4), 1–31 (2020)
10. Guettaf, A., Rekik, Y., Grisoni, L.: Effect of physical challenging activity on tactile texture recognition for mobile surface. Proc. ACM Hum.-Comput. Interact. 4(ISS) (2020). https://doi.org/10.1145/3427318
11. Guettaf, A., Rekik, Y., Grisoni, L.: Effect of attention saturating and cognitive load on tactile texture recognition for mobile surface. In: Ardito, C., et al. (eds.) INTERACT 2021, Part IV. LNCS, vol. 12935, pp. 557–579. Springer, Cham (2021). https://doi.org/10.1007/978-3-030-85610-6_31

12. Kajastila, R., Lokki, T.: Eyes-free interaction with free-hand gestures and auditory menus. Int. J. Hum.-Comput. Stud. **71**(5), 627–640 (2013)
13. Kane, S.K., Wobbrock, J.O., Ladner, R.E.: Usable gestures for blind people: Understanding preference and performance. In: Proceedings of the SIGCHI Conference on Human Factors in Computing Systems, CHI 2011, pp. 413–422. Association for Computing Machinery, New York, NY, USA (2011). https://doi.org/10.1145/1978942.1979001
14. Kappers, A.M., Plaisier, M.A.: Hands-free devices for displaying speech and language in the tactile modality—methods and approaches. IEEE Trans. Haptics **14**(3), 465–478 (2021)
15. Kim, L.H., Follmer, S.: Swarmhaptics: haptic display with swarm robots. In: Proceedings of the 2019 CHI Conference on Human Factors in Computing Systems, CHI 2019, pp. 1–13. Association for Computing Machinery, New York, NY, USA (2019). https://doi.org/10.1145/3290605.3300918
16. Levesque, V., et al.: Enhancing physicality in touch interaction with programmable friction. In: Proceedings of the SIGCHI Conference on Human Factors in Computing Systems, CHI 2011, pp. 2481–2490. Association for Computing Machinery, New York, NY, USA (2011). https://doi.org/10.1145/1978942.1979306
17. Marino, D., de Vargas, M.F., Weill-Duflos, A., Cooperstock, J.R.: Conversing using whatshap: a phoneme based vibrotactile messaging platform. In: 2021 IEEE World Haptics Conference (WHC), pp. 943–948 (2021). https://doi.org/10.1109/WHC49131.2021.9517186
18. Morris, M.R.: Web on the wall: insights from a multimodal interaction elicitation study. In: Proceedings of the 2012 ACM International Conference on Interactive Tabletops and Surfaces, ITS 2012, pp. 95–104. Association for Computing Machinery, New York, NY, USA (2012). https://doi.org/10.1145/2396636.2396651
19. Morris, M.R., et al.: Reducing legacy bias in gesture elicitation studies. Interactions **21**(3), 40–45 (2014)
20. Nacenta, M.A., Kamber, Y., Qiang, Y., Kristensson, P.O.: Memorability of pre-designed and user-defined gesture sets. In: Proceedings of the SIGCHI Conference on Human Factors in Computing Systems, CHI 2013, pp. 1099–1108. Association for Computing Machinery, New York, NY, USA (2013). https://doi.org/10.1145/2470654.2466142
21. Negulescu, M., Ruiz, J., Li, Y., Lank, E.: Tap, swipe, or move: attentional demands for distracted smartphone input. In: Proceedings of the International Working Conference on Advanced Visual Interfaces, AVI 2012, pp. 173–180. ACM, New York, NY, USA (2012). https://doi.org/10.1145/2254556.2254589
22. Novich, S.D., Eagleman, D.M.: Using space and time to encode vibrotactile information: toward an estimate of the skin's achievable throughput. Exp. Brain Rese. **233**(10), 2777–2788 (2015)
23. Perrault, S.T., Lecolinet, E., Eagan, J., Guiard, Y.: Watchit: simple gestures and eyes-free interaction for wristwatches and bracelets. In: Proceedings of the SIGCHI Conference on Human Factors in Computing Systems, CHI 2013, pp. 1451–1460. Association for Computing Machinery, New York, NY, USA (2013). https://doi.org/10.1145/2470654.2466192
24. Peshkova, E., Hitz, M., Ahlström, D.: Exploring user-defined gestures and voice commands to control an unmanned aerial vehicle. In: Poppe, R., Meyer, J.-J., Veltkamp, R., Dastani, M. (eds.) INTETAIN 2016 2016. LNICST, vol. 178, pp. 47–62. Springer, Cham (2017). https://doi.org/10.1007/978-3-319-49616-0_5

25. Piumsomboon, T., Clark, A., Billinghurst, M., Cockburn, A.: User-defined gestures for augmented reality. In: CHI 2013 Extended Abstracts on Human Factors in Computing Systems, CHI EA 2013, pp. 955–960. Association for Computing Machinery, New York, NY, USA (2013). https://doi.org/10.1145/2468356.2468527
26. Rekik, Y., Lank, E., Guettaf, A., Grisoni, L.: Multi-channel tactile feedback based on user finger speed. In: Proceedings of the ACM on Human-Computer Interaction, vol. 5(ISS) November 2021. https://doi.org/10.1145/3488549
27. Rekik, Y., Vezzoli, E., Grisoni, L., Giraud, F.: Localized haptic texture: a rendering technique based on taxels for high density tactile feedback. In: Proceedings of the 2017 CHI Conference on Human Factors in Computing Systems, CHI 2017, pp. 5006–5015. ACM, New York, NY, USA (2017). https://doi.org/10.1145/3025453.3026010
28. Roudaut, A., Rau, A., Sterz, C., Plauth, M., Lopes, P., Baudisch, P.: Gesture output: eyes-free output using a force feedback touch surface. In: Proceedings of the SIGCHI Conference on Human Factors in Computing Systems, CHI 2013, pp. 2547–2556. Association for Computing Machinery, New York, NY, USA (2013). https://doi.org/10.1145/2470654.2481352
29. Scott, J., Gray, R.: A comparison of tactile, visual, and auditory warnings for rear-end collision prevention in simulated driving. Hum. Factors **50**(2), 264–275 (2008)
30. Sharma, A., Roo, J.S., Steimle, J.: Grasping microgestures: eliciting single-hand microgestures for handheld objects. In: Proceedings of the 2019 CHI Conference on Human Factors in Computing Systems, CHI 2019, pp. 1–13. Association for Computing Machinery, New York, NY, USA (2019). https://doi.org/10.1145/3290605.3300632
31. Tan, H.Z., et al.: Acquisition of 500 English words through a tactile phonemic sleeve (taps). IEEE Trans. Haptics **13**(4), 745–760 (2020)
32. Troiano, G.M., Pedersen, E.W., Hornbæk, K.: User-defined gestures for elastic, deformable displays. In: Proceedings of the 2014 International Working Conference on Advanced Visual Interfaces, AVI 2014, pp. 1–8. Association for Computing Machinery, New York, NY, USA (2014). https://doi.org/10.1145/2598153.2598184
33. Tsandilas, T.: Fallacies of agreement: a critical review of consensus assessment methods for gesture elicitation. ACM Trans. Comput.-Hum. Interact. (TOCHI) **25**(3), 1–49 (2018)
34. Tung, Y.C., et al.: User-defined game input for smart glasses in public space. In: Proceedings of the 33rd Annual ACM Conference on Human Factors in Computing Systems, CHI 2015, pp. 3327–3336. Association for Computing Machinery, New York, NY, USA (2015). https://doi.org/10.1145/2702123.2702214
35. Vatavu, R.D., Wobbrock, J.O.: Formalizing agreement analysis for elicitation studies: new measures, significance test, and toolkit. In: Proceedings of the 33rd Annual ACM Conference on Human Factors in Computing Systems, CHI 2015, pp. 1325–1334. Association for Computing Machinery, New York, NY, USA (2015). https://doi.org/10.1145/2702123.2702223
36. Vatavu, R.D., Wobbrock, J.O.: Clarifying agreement calculations and analysis for end-user elicitation studies. ACM Trans. Comput.-Hum. Interact. (TOCHI) **29**(1), 1–70 (2022)
37. Vezzoli, E., Sednaoui, T., Amberg, M., Giraud, F., Lemaire-Semail, B.: Texture rendering strategies with a high fidelity - capacitive visual-haptic friction control device. In: Bello, F., Kajimoto, H., Visell, Y. (eds.) EuroHaptics 2016. LNCS, vol. 9774, pp. 251–260. Springer, Cham (2016). https://doi.org/10.1007/978-3-319-42321-0_23

38. Wei, Q., Li, M., Hu, J., Feijs, L.: Creating mediated touch gestures with vibrotactile stimuli for smart phones. In: Proceedings of the Fourteenth International Conference on Tangible, Embedded, and Embodied Interaction, TEI 2020, pp. 519–526. Association for Computing Machinery, New York, NY, USA (2020). https://doi.org/10.1145/3374920.3374981

39. Wobbrock, J.O., Morris, M.R., Wilson, A.D.: User-defined gestures for surface computing. In: Proceedings of the SIGCHI Conference on Human Factors in Computing Systems, CHI 2009, pp. 1083–1092. Association for Computing Machinery, New York, NY, USA (2009). https://doi.org/10.1145/1518701.1518866

40. Zhao, S., Israr, A., Klatzky, R.: Intermanual apparent tactile motion on handheld tablets. In: 2015 IEEE World Haptics Conference (WHC), pp. 241–247 (2015). https://doi.org/10.1109/WHC.2015.7177720

41. Zhao, S., Israr, A., Lau, F., Abnousi, F.: Coding tactile symbols for phonemic communication. In: Proceedings of the 2018 CHI Conference on Human Factors in Computing Systems, pp. 1–13 (2018)

User-Centered Evaluation of Different Configurations of a Touchless Gestural Interface for Interactive Displays

Vito Gentile[1], Habiba Farzand[2], Simona Bonaccorso[3], Davide Rocchesso[3], Alessio Malizia[4], Mohamed Khamis[2], and Salvatore Sorce[5(✉)]

[1] synbrAIn srl, Milano, Italy
[2] University of Glasgow, Glasgow, UK
[3] Università degli Studi di Palermo, Palermo, Italy
[4] Università degli Studi di Pisa, Pisa, Italy
[5] Università degli Studi di Enna "Kore", Enna, Italy
salvatore.sorce@unikore.it

Abstract. Approaches for improving the user experience when interacting with touchless displays have been proposed, such as using activation gestures and representing users as avatars in real-time. However, the novelty of such approaches may hinder users' natural interaction behavior bringing challenges such as ease of use. In this paper, we investigate how the presence of avatars and their configurations, the usage of activation gestures, and the arrangement of interactive tiles in a touchless visual interface impact users' experience, usability and task performance. We also compare users' willingness to promote the interaction setup, perceived task difficulty, and time consumed to perform four different tasks in each configuration. We found that using a squared arrangement of elements, adopting activation gestures to trigger actions, and showing a moving avatar, resulted in the highest perceived usability and user experience, also reducing errors, task completion time, and perceived task difficulty. Our findings support the design of interactive displays to ensure high usability and user experience.

Keywords: Touchless Gestural Interfaces · Public Displays · Interface Evaluation

1 Introduction

Hands-free interaction with displays is becoming more and more pervasive. Interactive displays are being deployed at various public places such as airports, train stations, and alike [9]. While they are being adopted at a fast speed, novel interaction styles have also been proposed such as using avatars to represent the user and facilitate interaction [13] (Fig. 1). However, these novel methods bring along user experience and usability challenges.

Avatars and activation gestures have been studied in many contexts in terms of perceived cognitive load [13] or their effectiveness in communicating touchless

J. Abdelnour Nocera et al. (Eds.): INTERACT 2023, LNCS 14142, pp. 501–520, 2023.
https://doi.org/10.1007/978-3-031-42280-5_32

Fig. 1. Interactive displays are now commonly used in various contexts such as airports, train stations, and much more. The figure shows an example of interacting with a display in the presence of an avatar.

interactivity [29]. Prior work focused on exploring perceived cognitive load with the presence and absence of avatars and activation gestures [13]. It was found that the use of avatars may reduce perceived cognitive load by increasing performance and reducing user efforts. However, usability and user experience are yet to be explored with respect to the presence of activation gestures and avatars. Exploring user experience and usability is crucial because, without prime usability and user experience, users are more likely to make errors and not utilize the system to its full features. Usability and user experience are the two important factors for determining user acceptance and appreciation of a system.

In this paper, we explore how user experience and usability are impacted by the presence, use, and behavior of the avatar, by the presence of activation gestures, and by the layout of the visual interface (i.e. squared and middle of the screen arrangement of icons). We report comparative results from a within-subject study with 19 participants.

Our results show that usability was perceived as highest in a squared layout with a moving avatar and activation gestures. User experience was optimum when using a squared layout with a fixed avatar and a required activation gesture and in a squared layout with an activation gesture but without an avatar.

Contribution Statement: In the context of touchless gesture interaction with displays, this study investigates the impact of the avatar presence, the usage of activation gestures, and the visual interface layout on usability and user experience.

2   Related Work

In this section, we present previous work around interactive displays, interaction media and paradigms, and evaluation of user experience and usability.

2.1   Interactive and Public Displays

Many of today's public displays are interactive. Examples include ticket vending machines, ATMs, and info stands in malls and airports. While the predominant interaction modality used on these devices is touch, more displays today support touchless interaction. Touchless interaction can come in several forms. Some displays are gaze-enabled [20], allowing users to interact using their eye movements. Several works proposed leveraging personal mobile devices to interact with displays [31]. Closer to our work, displays can also support interaction using mid-air gestures [11,36]. Researchers have also proposed techniques that combine gaze and mid-air gestures. For example, in their implementation of Pocket Transfers [23] Mäkelä et al. deployed a display where users can transfer content from the display to their phones by gazing at items on the screen and using mid-air gestures to indicate which items they wish to transfer.

Our work focuses on interaction using mid-air gestures. This interaction modality is more common for large displays and has been argued to be particularly useful for public displays as they allow hygienic interactions that do not require touching the display. Its playful nature also contributes to extending interaction durations [2]. There are also downsides to interaction using gestures. For example, they often require the use of user representations to communicate interactivity [2,18]. Also to distinguish natural body movements from interactions, the system needs to either teach its users very specific gestures [1,35] or require the use of activation gestures to trigger the interaction [26]. The presented study investigates the impact of multiple configurations on usability and user experience, including configurations that involve an avatar to represent users and activation gestures.

2.2   Evaluating and Supporting Interaction

Bystanders often miss or ignore interactive public displays thinking they are advertisements [9]. This can also be due to passersby being overwhelmed by the amount of information on the screen or when the interactive features are not noticeable or unintuitive. This results in a phenomenon referred to as interaction blindness [4,29]. Apart from this, even after users have noticed that the system is interactive, they still encounter difficulty in understanding how to interact with it. This problem, known as affordance blindness, is due to the novel and uncommon media that is often used to interact. This is particularly true for public displays for which common mouse/keyboard or even touch-screens are not often feasible due to being deployed in public places. Therefore, these unique circumstances necessitate innovative interaction paradigms that cater to distinct user behaviors and require specialized study methods. In this section, we will describe said evaluation methods and users' behaviors in the context of public displays.

Evaluation Methods for Public Displays. Observational studies, surveys, and experiments all have their place in evaluating user experience and systems usability in general. Still, their effectiveness can be significantly enhanced when combined into a mixed-method approach. The complexity and variety of interactions with public displays necessitate this diverse approach to capture the full range of user behaviors and experiences [4]. Observational studies are widely used in the field of public display research. They involve researchers closely observing and recording the behavior of individuals or groups interacting with the display. For instance, a researcher might note the time a person interacts with a display or the number of errors during the interaction [6]. Sometimes observation in the real world might be so difficult or expensive that it requires the use of models or simulations [24]. Surveys, either self-administered or interviewer-led, are another common method for evaluating public displays. These may be used to gather subjective information on user perceptions and experiences, such as satisfaction, understanding, and intention to interact again. Müller et al. [30] used a survey method in conjunction with video observation to assess whether and why people pay attention to public displays. Of course one could use custom questionnaires. Still, to allow for comparisons and thus reliable evaluations, there are some well-known questionnaires or surveys whose scores can be measured and then compared with established thresholds. Among them, particularly in the context of public displays, researchers often use NASA Task Load Index (NASA-TLX) [15], System Usability Scale (SUS) [7], User Experience Questionnaire (UEQ) [22], and Net Promoter Score (NPS) [37], which are widely used tools for evaluating various aspects of human interaction with technology. They each serve a specific purpose: NASA-TLX for perceived workload, SUS for overall usability, UEQ for user experience, and NPS for customer satisfaction and loyalty. These all contribute to evaluating usability and user experience in a comprehensive, objective, and unbiased way. Experimental designs are employed when researchers seek to establish causal relationships. This involves manipulating one or more variables (independent variables) and measuring their effect on other variables (dependent variables). For example, an experiment could manipulate the content of a public display to determine its impact on user engagement, such as in [34].

Display and Interaction Blindness. A major contributor to interaction blindness is display blindness [25]. If passersby cannot see or notice the display, they will not consider interacting with it. Dalton et al. [8] studied display blindness in an eye-tracking study to find that passersby often look at displays. However, the study could not conclude whether passersby actually notice the displays, as people may gaze at a target without paying attention to it [19]. Display blindness was tackled by using a stimulus that attracts attention to the display [27] such as curiosity-provoking artifacts [16], or an animatronic hand [17].

More commonly, avatars and silhouettes that mirror passersby's behavior were found to be effective in tackling display blindness [18].

Even if display blindness is overcome, passersby may never realize that the display they noticed is interactive [29]. Many similar approaches were deployed to address interaction blindness. For example, in Looking Glass [29], passersby's movements were mirrored on displays and combined with call-to-action labels to explain to users how to interact. Once users start interacting with a display, the honeypot effect results in attracting other passersby to the display [6,24].

Activation Gestures. Representing users using silhouettes and avatars helps overcome display and interaction blindness. A byproduct of representing users using silhouettes and avatars is that their arms and hands are visible on the screen; this makes interaction using mid-air gestures easier to communicate and to give feedback on. However, a drawback of touchless gestural interaction is that it lacks an equivalent of a "mouse click". As a result, the system needs a mechanism by which users can indicate whether they are simply pointing, or activating. One way to address this is by requiring users to move their hands on top of the desired target and "dwell" on it i.e., keep the hand steady on the target for a short period, typically in seconds [38]. An alternative approach is to require an activation gesture. For example, Yoo et al. [38] compared point-and-dwell to activation gestures such as push and grab-and-pull to find that the former is more accurate while push was preferred for selection and grab-and-pull was preferred for navigation. Gentile et al. [14] found that activation gestures may discourage users from continuing to interact and also that they may require a steep learning curve compared to point-and-dwell.

2.3 Research Gap

In summary, previous work on interactive displays shows that deploying avatars that mirror user movements has a positive impact on display and interaction blindness and that requiring activation gestures is sometimes necessary to avoid unintentional selections. Our work studies the impact of the presence of an avatar, its configuration, the layout of the screen, and the configuration of activation gestures on usability and user experience.

3 User Study

In this study, we aim to understand how usability and user experience are affected by the layout of the visual interface and by the presence and behavior of an avatar that is displayed in the middle of the screen. We also explore the use and impact of activation gestures on the above-mentioned factors. To this end, we used different metrics, including task difficulty, task completion time, number of errors, and well-known questionnaires to evaluate perceived usability and user experience as discussed in the previous Section.

3.1   Apparatus

The system used for our study consisted of a 65" projected display placed at eye level, showing the interface being tested. The projector was driven by a computer, to which a Kinect for Xbox One was connected. The Kinect was placed below the screen, and gathered information on users' body gestures, using the Microsoft Kinect SDK v2. The study was conducted in the lab at our institute.

Visual Interface Layout (L). We selected two interface layouts: (1) square (SQ) and (2) middle (MID). In the square layout, the icons were arranged in a square style along the edges of the interface (see Fig. 2B and 2D), whereas, in the middle layout, the icons were arranged all over the interface, including the middle part of it (see Fig. 2A and 2C). The interface layouts were chosen based on previous work [13].

Activation Gesture (AG). In our interfaces, we used the "two hands icon" for interactive tile selection purposes as shown in Fig. 2. The hand icons moved along with the hands of the users. For the purposes of our study, we tried two different solutions for interactive tile activation: (1) no activation gesture: in this case, the users can trigger the interaction events just by driving the hand icons and keeping them on top of the available tile-shaped components (i.e., point and dwell). (2) With an activation gesture: in this case, the user must execute a gesture that, if executed when a cursor (hand icon) overlays an interactive tile, triggers the corresponding event. We used a "push-to-press" gesture, which emulates a mid-air pushing action in accordance with Microsoft's Human Interface Guidelines (HIG) [26].

Avatar Design (AV). Avatars have been intensively studied for their use in interactive displays [28, 29, 35]. An avatar is a user representation on the interface that mimics the user's movements. We adopted an avatar design from prior work by Gentile et al. [13]. In our study, we experimented with three possible solutions for the user's avatar: (1) avatar present and fixed (FIX) in the middle of the screen (see Fig. 2C and D); (2) avatar present and moves on the x-axis (MV), mirroring the user's body position in front of the display (see Fig. 2E); (3) avatar absent (NO) (see Fig. 2A and B). In both MV and FX, the avatar was always mimicking the user's arm movements.

3.2   Study Design

Our study was designed as a repeated measures experiment with three independent variables: IV1) visual interface layout (L), which had two conditions: a) *square* (SQ) and b) *middle* (MID); IV2) Activation Gesture (AG), which had two conditions: a) *absent* and b) *present*; and finally IV3) Avatar design (AV), which had three conditions: a) *present and fixed* in the middle of the screen

(FIX), b) *present and movable* on the x-axis (MV), and c) *absent* (NO). Note that in IV3a and IV3b, the avatar mimicked the user's arm movements.

While the total number of conditions was $2\,L \times 2\,AG \times 3\,AV = 12$, we discarded the two conditions that had an avatar present (one condition had the moving avatar whereas one had the fixed avatar), a middle-positioned layout, and did not feature an activation gesture. These two conditions were excluded because a) they are subject to involuntary activations of tiles which are located at the bottom of the interface, and b) they were reported to be disliked by users in prior work [14]. The tested conditions in this study are summarized in Table 1.

The dependent variables of interest for our study, and the methods and metrics used to evaluate them, were:

- **perceived usability**, evaluated using the System Usability Scale (SUS) questionnaire [7], which provides a score ranging from 1 to 100;
- **user experience**, evaluated using the User Experience Questionnaire (UEQ) [22] and the Net Promoter Score (NPS) [37];
- **task difficulty**, evaluated using the Single Ease Question (SEQ) [33] which provides a 7-point rating scale to assess how difficult users find a task, where 1 = "very difficult" and 7 = "very easy";
- **task completion time**, evaluated counting the time in seconds elapsed from the moment each task was started by the participant until successful completion;
- **error rates**, evaluated counting the number of times users perform an error. We counted an error whenever the user did any of the following:
  - activated the wrong interactive tile;
  - tried to activate a non-interactive tile;
  - assessed that they have finished the task when they actually had to continue;
  - asked for help;
- **two-handed interactions**, evaluated counting the number of times the user:
  - switched from using one arm to another arm;
  - used both arms simultaneously.

3.3 Procedure

We welcomed participants with an information sheet that provided details of the study. The participants were then presented with a consent form. Upon receiving the participants' consent, they were presented with the display and were provided with a training session of five minutes. This was to ensure adequate interaction and familiarity with the display. During the training session, the experimenter debriefed participants about the available features and interactive tiles. After the training session, the participants were asked to perform the following tasks by driving the Avatar's hands (in cases where an avatar was present) or the hand-shaped cursor (in cases where there was no avatar): (1) find specific news, (2) access university information, (3) find the timetable for a specific class, and

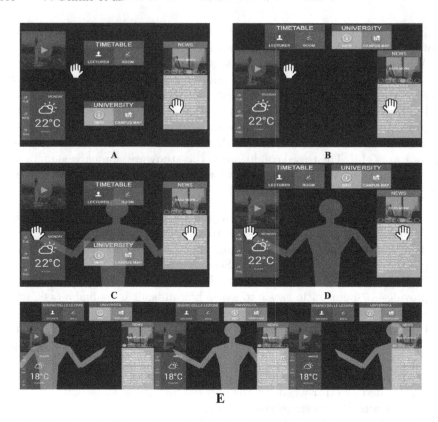

Fig. 2. The investigated configurations of a Touchless Gestural Interface: avatar absence (A, B) vs. presence (C, D, E); squared (B, D) vs. middle (A, C) tile layout; fixed (C, D) vs. moving (E) avatar.

Table 1. The table shows the conditions investigated in this paper.

Condition ID	L (Layout)	AV (Activation Avatar)	AG (Activation Gesture)
CN1	Square	with moving avatar	with activation gesture
CN2		with moving avatar	without activation gesture
CN3		with fixed avatar	with activation gesture
CN4		with fixed avatar	without activation gesture
CN5		without avatar	with activation gesture
CN6		without avatar	without activation gesture
CN7	Middle	with moving avatar	with activation gesture
CN8		with fixed avatar	with activation gesture
CN9		without avatar	with activation gesture
CN10		without avatar	without activation gesture

(4) play a video. All the visual components that allow the above-mentioned tasks were accessible from the main page of the interface.

Participants were instructed to perform the tasks as fast as they can and as accurately as possible. We used a within-group setup i.e., all participants experienced all the conditions. In each condition, participants were required to perform all four tasks. The order of the conditions was counterbalanced to reduce the biases and to level out any learning effects. After the completion of each task, participants were presented with a questionnaire comprising the System Usability Scale (SUS), the User Experience Questionnaire (UEQ), the Net Promoter Score, and the Single Ease Question (SEQ). During the study, the experimenter manually took notes of errors made, time consumed to perform each task, and if participants used one or both hands for interaction. After the completion of all tasks, participants were presented with an exit questionnaire asking questions about the different conditions such as preference for the layout, avatar preference, and use of activation gestures for selecting the interactive tiles. The followed procedure is visualized in Fig. 3.

Our institute has no ethics board, therefore we followed the best practices and ethics guidelines when conducting our study. The participants were briefed before and after the study, were made aware they can withdraw anytime, had to read an information sheet and sign a consent form before participating, and were made aware that their data was stored securely to protect sensitive information.

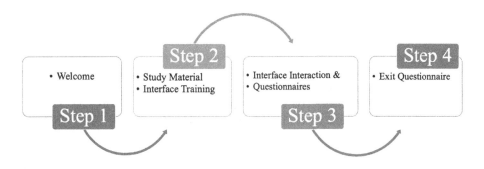

Fig. 3. The figure shows the followed procedure in our study.

3.4   Participants

We recruited $N = 19$ participants ($M = 7$, Female $= 12$; self-identified) through word of mouth and snowball sampling. This number of participants was found to be appropriate in consideration of the number of participants in similar studies such as [5,12,29]. Participants were on average 30.89 years old ($SD = 12.90$). Sixteen participants were right-handed and three participants reported to be equally good with left and right-handedness. None of the participants had issues that could limit their movements. A few participants ($N = 3$) reported having used a similar gesture-based interaction system before such as in training sessions for disabled children, on PlayStation, and in museums. Whereas, the majority of the participants (N = 16) had no prior experience.

3.5   Data Analysis

We use participant IDs to refer to participants, such as P2 throughout the data collection and reporting to ensure anonymity. Where necessary, we use participants' quotes to support the results of the study but they cannot be traced back to the participants' identities. We ran one-way repeated measures ANOVA and used Bonferroni correction to correct for multiple comparisons in post-hoc tests. The results of the standardized questionnaires (i.e., SUS, UEQ and NPS and SEQ) were analyzed using the corresponding standard analysis for each. Qualitative responses were analyzed using open coding to translate them into meaningful snippets.

3.6   Limitations and Future Work

Although our study was carefully designed, like all studies it has some limitations. We acknowledge the following limitations. This study was conducted in a controlled lab environment. While in-the-lab studies impact ecological validity, they also allow controlling numerous confounding variables such as distraction caused by the presence of bystanders that may impact users' task performance, which is commonplace in public display interactions [12]. Second, this study was conducted at our academic institute where there are many computer science students who are knowledgeable about technology. However, the users' experience may vary as their knowledge and technology experience change.

Third, we acknowledge that the small number of left-handed participants (N = 3) may have impacted the results. Further, the effect of habituation was absent from the user study as the only way the habituation effect would have been possible would have been during the training session where the repeated aspect of the interaction from one setup to another was the task set. However, the participants were only knowledgeable of what the tiles do but not how to interact with them as this is the only information we provided about them in the training session. Another way habituation could have happened can be due to repeating the task. Even though the task was the same, the way it was carried out by the participants was different in every condition. Thus, we expect there is little to no effect of habituation. We counterbalanced the conditions to avoid learning effect.

Lastly, the sample size chosen for this study is appropriate in line with guidelines for usability studies [3,10,32], however, we realise this sample size may appear low from some perspectives therefore, we acknowledge and propose that future studies with more diversity and large sample size should be conducted.

4   Results

The main goal of this study was to evaluate the impact of the avatar presence, the usage of activation gestures, and of the visual interface layout on perceived usability and user experience, task difficulty, task completion time, and use of two-handed interactions. To this end, we evaluated the dependent variables in ten different conditions corresponding to the ten relevant combinations of the independent variables, as described in the previous section. In this section, we present the findings gathered from $N = 19$ participants, which are detailed in the following subsections and summarized in Tables 2 and 3.

4.1   Usability

System Usability Scale (SUS). The System Usability Scale (SUS) [7] is a standard metric for evaluating usability. We used it to check for usability for all conditions. The perceived usability was the highest in CN1 i.e., square arrangement with a moving avatar and an activation gesture, among all conditions and CN8 i.e., middle arrangement with a fixed avatar and with an activation gesture, received the lowest SUS score.

A Friedman test for the SUS scores revealed significant differences ($\chi^2(9)$ = 107.920, $p < 0.0005$). Pairwise comparisons revealed significant differences between CN8 and CN7 ($p = 0.005$), CN8 and CN9 ($p = 0.003$), CN8 and CN10 ($p = 0.002$), CN8 and CN6 ($p = 0.002$), CN8 and CN4 ($p < 0.0005$), CN8 and CN3 ($p < 0.0005$), CN8 and CN5 ($p < 0.0005$), CN8 and CN1 ($p = 0.0005$), CN2 and CN1 ($p < 0.0005$), CN7 and CN1 ($p < 0.0005$), CN9 and CN1 ($p < 0.0005$), CN10 and CN1 ($p < 0.0005$), CN6 and CN1 ($p < 0.0005$), CN4 and CN1 ($p = 0.001$), CN3 and CN1 ($p = 0.001$), and CN5 and CN1 ($p = 0.033$).

Task Difficulty and Duration. After each condition, participants were asked to rate their perceived difficulty of the interaction on a scale from 1 to 7 where 1 represented the least difficulty and 7 represented the highest difficulty. We then checked for significant differences in task difficulty of each task in each condition. A Friedman test was run (with a Bonferroni correction for multiple comparisons where appropriate) to determine if there are significant differences between the task difficulty in each condition. No significant differences were found for all tasks' perceived difficulty across all conditions. Next, we checked which task took longer to perform in each condition. Significant differences were only found for Task 3 ($\chi^2(9) = 26.505$, $p = 0.002$). Pairwise comparisons revealed significant differences between CN10 and CN2 ($p = 0.003$) and CN10 and CN3 ($p = 0.027$).

4.2   User Experience and Willingness to Promote the Interface

The user experience was recorded using the short version of the User Experience Questionnaire [22]. It assesses user experience on two aspects; pragmatic and hedonic quality. Values between -0.8 and 0.8 represent a neutral evaluation whereas values greater than 0.8 represent a positive evaluation and values less than -0.8 represent a negative evaluation. The range of the scales is between -3 ("horribly bad") and $+3$ ("extremely good"). Overall, CN3 and CN5 provided the best user experience both with a score of 0.618.

Next, we measured participants' willingness to promote the interface system through Net Promoter Score (NPS) [37]. NPS is a frequently used market research metric that assesses how likely users are to promote a product or a service. Participants rated their likelihood of promoting the interaction on a scale of one to ten. We then calculated the NPS score using the dedicated score calculation method [37]. CN5 received the highest NPS score (47.37) while CN10 received the lowest NPS score (−57.89). The results of UEQ, NPS, and SUS scores for all conditions are summarized in Table 2, where: Layout L can be square (SQ) or middle (MID); Avatar AV can be movable (MV), fixed (FIX), or absent (NO); Activation Gesture AG can be present (Y) or absent (N).

Table 2. The Table shows User Experience Questionnaire (UEQ), Net Promoter Score (NPS), and System Usability Score (SUS) for the conditions investigated in the study.

CONDITIONS				RESULTS				
				UEQ			NPS	SUS
	L	AV	AG	Pragmatic Quality	Hedonic Quality	Overall		
CN1	SQ	MV	Y	0.434	0.618	0.526	42.11	91.45
CN2			N	0.33	0.47	0.428	5.26	33.74
CN3		FIX	Y	0.5	0.74	0.618	31.58	37.95
CN4			N	0.54	0.5	0.519	21.05	36.47
CN5		NO	Y	0.51	0.72	0.618	47.37	38.32
CN6			N	0.49	0.55	0.52	5.26	36.84
CN7	MID	MV	Y	0.38	0.63	0.507	31.58	36.63
CN8		FIX		0.32	0.54	0.428	21.05	28.11
CN9		NO		0.43	0.68	0.559	31.58	37.42
CN10			N	0.41	0.5	0.454	−57.89	36.26

4.3   Overall Evaluation

To evaluate the layout design, use of avatars and activation gestures, we asked participants to rate their experience of each on a scale of 1 to 10 where 1 represented the least rating and 10 represented the highest rating. We also asked participants to provide reasoning for their choice. In this section, we report the descriptive and statistical analysis of the ratings and results of the inductive coding of the qualitative insights. To analyse the qualitative data, one researcher went through the data and assigned codes. Then, the second researcher revisited the qualitative data and assigned codes. The two researchers then discussed the disagreements and finalized the codes. This iterative refinement of the coding process ensured the validity of the results. In the following results, we report the frequency of codes appearing in the dataset to give the readers an impression of how many times each category appeared.

Table 3. The Table shows the participants' perceived average task difficulty, time consumed to perform each task, and errors made in each condition while performing tasks.

Conditions			Task Difficulty				Task Duration				Errors Committed			
L	AV	AG	Task 1	Task 2	Task 3	Task 4	Task 1	Task 2	Task 3	Task 4	Task 1	Task 2	Task 3	Task 4
CN1	SQ	MV	Y	6.63	6.68	6.63	6.79	10.68	8.58	13.21	7	0	0.11	0.32	0
CN2			N	6.79	6.68	5.58	6.42	6.89	7.05	13.68	5.74	0.11	0.21	1.11	0
CN3		FIX	Y	6.85	6.8	6.8	6.7	7.58	7.05	11.79	5.89	0.1	0.1	0.45	0.05
CN4			N	6.95	6.84	6.32	6.89	7.95	5.58	11.58	5.26	0.11	0	0.42	0
CN5		NO	Y	6.89	7	6.79	6.89	7.84	5.95	11.05	5.21	0.11	0.05	0.21	0.05
CN6			N	6.63	6.47	6.32	6.89	6.74	6.68	12.21	4.79	0.26	0.32	0.68	0
CN7	MID	MV	Y	6.74	6.53	6.84	6.89	7	6.47	10.58	5.68	0.16	0.26	0.05	0.05
CN8		FIX		6.89	6.21	6.63	6.84	7	6	9.32	6	0.21	0.05	0.11	0.11
CN9		NO		6.53	6.53	6.53	6.74	6.63	6.42	12.05	5.84	0.32	0.16	0.32	0
CN10			N	6.68	6.84	6.84	6.84	5.42	4.89	8.79	4.79	0.16	0.11	0.21	0

Layout (L): Square layout received a mean rating of 8.89 out of 10 (Min $=6$, Max $=10$, SD $=1.37$) for participants' experience while the middle layout received a mean rating of 7.89 out of 10 (Min $=1$, Max $=10$, SD $=2.30$). Nine participants preferred the square layout whereas ten participants preferred the middle layout. An exact sign test was run to uncover significant differences between the ratings of the two layouts but no significant differences were found ($p=1.000$).

The qualitative insights reveal that the square layout was preferred mainly for two reasons; the arrangement of icons (6), ease of selection (2), and visual appearance (1). The arrangement of icons gave freedom of movement to the participants. Other reasons included the fact that information is easier to reach with hands and the possibility to freely move hands without activating the central icons. One participant mentioned "...*comfortable arrangement of windows*" (P1) as the reason for preferring the square layout. Participants did not prefer the middle layout because it offered less freedom of movement, and close placement of the icons, and some participants even found it "..*confusing..*" (P16). On the contrary, the middle layout was preferred mainly for four reasons; the arrangement of icons (2), visual appearance (4), and ease of selection (5). Less empty space, the centre positioning of the interface, and the orderly position of icons were the reasons to opt for the middle layout.

Avatar (AV): Participants rated their experience of interaction without the avatar present with a mean of 8.15 out of 10 (Min $=4$, Max $=10$, SD $=1.92$) and a mean of 8.36 out of 10 for interaction with the avatar present (Min $=5$, Max $=10$, SD $=1.53$). A Wilcoxon signed-rank test did not reveal significant differences ($z=0.516$, $p=606$). Avatar was not preferred by participants (N $=9$) due to visual cumbersome (4), inconvenience (1) and because participants felt that its presence was unnecessary (1) and it made the view complicated to deal with (1). However, some participants (N $=10$) preferred to have an avatar with a predilection towards having the avatar mobile (N $=8$) as compared to a fixed position (N $=2$). The mobile positioning of the avatar was liked by participants because it bought convenience (5), better engagement (1), and design (1). Participants were able to move around better and mirror themselves in the avatar. The mobile state of the avatar made it easier reach to icons and facilitated movement. It was also seen as letting the users be more involved in the interaction and being able to understand the interaction through the avatar. The fixed position of the avatar was favoured as participants felt that the accuracy of the hands was better (1) and due to convenience (1).

Activation Gestures (AG): The experience with activation gestures (AG) was rated a mean of 8.84 out of 10 (Min $=4$, Max $=10$, SD $=1.46$). An exact sign test revealed significant differences ($p=0.035$). Participants were inclined towards preferring activation gestures (N $=15$). This was mainly because of four reasons; controlled interaction (6), accuracy (3), ease of use (3), and fewer chances of error (1). Participants voiced that activation gestures appeared as

"..safer in use" (P1). Participants felt that they could safely move around the screen without activating unneeded functions. On the contrary, some participants (N = 4) also felt that the greater ease that is provided by activation gestures is not really needed (1), could result in system failure because sometimes the system did not recognize the activation gesture (1), and that the system is faster (1) and simpler without AG (1).

One-Handed vs Two-Handed Interaction: All participants (N = 19) reported having used and preferred both hands for interaction. Participants felt that the use of both hands was convenient (6), and allowed free (6) and fast movement (3). Participants also mentioned that use of both hands was a source of comfort while interacting (3) and therefore was necessary (1). Participants also voiced that using two hands while interacting made them pay more attention to the task.

Lastly, we asked participants what they perceive are the advantages of using one-handed interaction. The participants voiced that using one hand for interaction is easy (1) and gives greater freedom (1). It also leaves the other hand to perform some other task (2) such as holding a jacket. Further, they also mentioned that single-handed interaction could assist people with disabilities (1). For two-handed interaction, participants mentioned that using two hands appears more naturalistic (2) and focused (1). Use of two hands was perceived as providing faster interaction (6), free movement (5), convenient (1), ease of selection (1), and giving more opportunities to interact (1).

5   Discussion

Our study revealed how usability and user experience are influenced by modifications in the interface style i.e. one and two-dimensional and with avatar and activation gestures. Based on our findings, we present the following general observations and key takeaways.

5.1   General Observations

Prior work [13] evaluated whether and how the presence of an Avatar that replays the user's movements may decrease the perceived cognitive workload during interactions. In this paper, we focus on the user experience and usability. From the users' perspective, usability and user experience are highest in the square interface layout. On the other hand, middle-layout has the lowest usability. Considering the design perspective, the arrangement of icons on the layout should be placed carefully as users look for "neatness" in design and "freedom of movement". The avatars can support the users' communication with the touchless display if they are in a mobile position. The activation gestures further facilitate the selection process, assisting in making fewer mistakes and making the user more involved.

The use of two hands was highly favoured by participants as it makes the interaction a lot easier than one-handed interaction. On the contrary, in a study by Walter et al. [36], 80% of users only used their right hand to perform the interaction while they were given the option of both hands. However, participants in our study favoured using two hands. This was especially the case for complex tasks such as using a map. One of the reasons our results differ from those of Walter et al. [36] could be because people usually carry something such as a bag or a jacket in public places and therefore prefer to use one hand for the interaction. However, the use of two hands is perceived to make interaction easier and quicker. Second, Walter et al. [36] state that a possible reason their study participants preferred using one hand was that they were asked to register a gesture, and thus the participants continued to use the same hand used for registration believing this was the only way to interact. We expect the reason we had a different result is that our participants were free to use one or both hands. Considering the results of our study, it can be implied that simple tasks requiring only a few interactions could be designed for one-handed interaction as they give the freedom to the other hand to perform other tasks. This is also beneficial from the perspective of designing accessible interaction as voiced by the participants of our study.

On the other hand, some participants found that the use of two hands is problematic when carrying other objects. This was also reported in prior work on two-handed interaction using mid-air gestures with public displays [21]. This suggests that interactive displays deployed in public spaces should provide users with the option of interacting using one hand.

5.2   Key Takeaways

Based on the findings of our user study, we pen down the following key takeaways.

Usability is perceived as highest in a square layout with moving avatar and activation gestures. Participants in our study were slightly inclined towards the square layout as opposed to the middle layout. This was so because the square layout allowed participants to move freely with an easier reach to icons. The moving avatar helped the participants in mirroring themselves in the interface making the interaction closer to real. It is likely that this supported participants in reaching farther targets e.g., to activate a target on the left, the user could not only extend their arm but also move to the left to reach the target. The activation gestures assisted in giving a sense of confirmation of the selection of icons to the participants which in turn was perceived as helping in making fewer interaction errors.

User experience is optimum in a square layout with activation gestures irrespective of whether the avatar was moving or fixed. The User Experience Questionnaire focuses on two aspects; pragmatic (i.e., efficiency, dependability, and perspicuity) and hedonic quality (i.e., stimulation and novelty). Square layout with activation gestures outperformed in both qualities, hedonic and pragmatic. The state of the avatar did not impact the user experience as the user experience was found to be optimum with the moving and fixed state of the avatar. On the contrary, activation gestures influenced the user experience. All conditions with activation gestures received higher user experience questionnaire scores as compared to conditions without activation gestures.

A square layout with activation gestures only appears most likely to be promoted. Because activation gestures were perceived as helpful in making selections, the conditions with activation gestures were found to be more promoted by participants. Huge differences were found in the NPS score between the presence and absence of activation gestures. This shows that the design elements that assist in making and confirming selections are likely to be more promoted and appreciated by users. Activation gestures are one such example. This is in line with previous work that compared point-and-dwell to grab-and-pull, to find that the former is more suitable for selections whereas the latter is more suitable for navigation [38]. A possible explanation of this result in our study could also be attributed to legacy bias; that is, users are more accustomed to separating the tasks of pointing and activating, and may thus prefer activation gestures compared to selection by dwelling at targets.

Use of two-handed interaction facilitates the touchless interaction with the display. Interaction with displays is not just about a few selections but sometimes it can also be as complex as navigating a map. In complex scenarios, the use of two-handed interaction is favored by users. The use of two-handed interaction not only makes the interaction easier but also facilitates it by increasing the time required to perform the task. As mentioned earlier, it is important to allow users to also use one hand especially if the display is deployed in a public space, as users of public displays may have an occupied hand.

6 Conclusion

To make displays more interactive, numerous efforts have been made such as introducing avatars to represent the user, finding new ways for triggering interactive items, and identifying general rules for optimal visual layout arrangements. While such innovations are impressive, they have a risk of impacting the user experience and usability of the system. Without optimum user experience and usability, users are less likely to use the system. For this reason, we investigated two possible layouts, and the use of avatars and activation gestures, and evaluated their impact on usability and user experience in visual interfaces for interactive displays. We found that the square layout is preferred more than the middle layout, showing higher usability and better user experience. We also found that the presence of a moving avatar had a positive impact on the perceived usability of the interface. As far as the usage of an activation gesture is concerned, we found that using one has a positive impact on both perceived usability, the user experience, and general appreciation. The results and findings of our study are summed up as key takeaways which could be a quick and useful reference list for the design of future interactive displays.

Acknowledgements. This work was partly supported by the EPSRC (EP/V008870/1), and the PETRAS National Centre of Excellence for IoT Systems Cybersecurity, which is also funded by the EPSRC (EP/S035362/1).

References

1. Ackad, C., Clayphan, A., Tomitsch, M., Kay, J.: An in-the-wild study of learning mid-air gestures to browse hierarchical information at a large interactive public display. In: Proceedings of the 2015 ACM International Joint Conference on Pervasive and Ubiquitous Computing, UbiComp 2015, pp. 1227–1238. Association for Computing Machinery, New York (2015). https://doi.org/10.1145/2750858.2807532
2. Ackad, C., Tomitsch, M., Kay, J.: Skeletons and silhouettes: comparing user representations at a gesture-based large display. In: Proceedings of the 2016 CHI Conference on Human Factors in Computing Systems, CHI 2016, pp. 2343–2347. Association for Computing Machinery, New York (2016). https://doi.org/10.1145/2858036.2858427
3. Alroobaea, R., Mayhew, P.J.: How many participants are really enough for usability studies? In: 2014 Science and Information Conference, pp. 48–56. IEEE (2014). https://doi.org/10.1109/SAI.2014.6918171
4. Alt, F., Schneegaß, S., Schmidt, A., Müller, J., Memarovic, N.: How to evaluate public displays. In: Proceedings of the 2012 International Symposium on Pervasive Displays, PerDis 2012. Association for Computing Machinery, New York (2012). https://doi.org/10.1145/2307798.2307815
5. Alt, F., Shirazi, A.S., Kubitza, T., Schmidt, A.: Interaction techniques for creating and exchanging content with public displays. In: Proceedings of the SIGCHI Conference on Human Factors in Computing Systems, pp. 1709–1718 (2013). https://doi.org/10.1145/2470654.2466226
6. Brignull, H., Rogers, Y.: Enticing people to interact with large public displays in public spaces. In: INTERACT 2003-9th IFIP TC13 International Conference on Human-Computer Interaction, vol. 3, pp. 17–24 (2003)
7. Brooke, J., et al.: SUS-a quick and dirty usability scale. In: Usability Evaluation in Industry, vol. 189, no. 194, pp. 4–7 (1996)
8. Dalton, N.S., Collins, E., Marshall, P.: Display blindness? Looking again at the visibility of situated displays using eye-tracking. In: Proceedings of the 33rd Annual ACM Conference on Human Factors in Computing Systems, CHI 2015, pp. 3889–3898. Association for Computing Machinery, New York (2015). https://doi.org/10.1145/2702123.2702150
9. Davies, N., Clinch, S., Alt, F.: Pervasive displays: understanding the future of digital signage. Synth. Lect. Mob. Pervasive Comput. **8**(1), 1–128 (2014). https://doi.org/10.1007/978-3-031-02484-9
10. Francik, E.: Five, ten, or twenty-five - how many test participants? (2015). https://www.humanfactors.com/newsletters/how_many_test_participants.asp. Accessed 09 May 2023
11. Gentile, V., Khamis, M., Milazzo, F., Sorce, S., Malizia, A., Alt, F.: Predicting mid-air gestural interaction with public displays based on audience behaviour. Int. J. Hum.-Comput. Stud. **144**, 102497 (2020). https://doi.org/10.1016/j.ijhcs.2020.102497. http://www.sciencedirect.com/science/article/pii/S1071581920300999
12. Gentile, V., Khamis, M., Sorce, S., Alt, F.: They are looking at me! Understanding how audience presence impacts on public display users. In: Proceedings of the 6th

ACM International Symposium on Pervasive Displays, pp. 1–7 (2017). https://doi.org/10.1145/3078810.3078822

13. Gentile, V., Sorce, S., Malizia, A., Milazzo, F., Gentile, A.: Investigating how user avatar in touchless interfaces affects perceived cognitive load and two-handed interactions. In: Proceedings of the 6th ACM International Symposium on Pervasive Displays, pp. 1–7 (2017). https://doi.org/10.1145/3078810.3078831

14. Gentile, V., Sorce, S., Malizia, A., Pirrello, D., Gentile, A.: Touchless interfaces for public displays: can we deliver interface designers from introducing artificial push button gestures? In: Proceedings of the International Working Conference on Advanced Visual Interfaces, pp. 40–43 (2016). https://doi.org/10.1145/2909132.2909282

15. Hart, S.G.: Nasa-task load index (NASA-TLX); 20 years later. In: Proceedings of the Human Factors and Ergonomics Society Annual Meeting, vol. 50, pp. 904–908. Sage Publications, Los Angeles (2006). https://doi.org/10.1177/154193120605000909

16. Houben, S., Weichel, C.: Overcoming interaction blindness through curiosity objects. In: CHI 2013 Extended Abstracts on Human Factors in Computing Systems, CHI EA 2013, pp. 1539–1544. Association for Computing Machinery, New York (2013). https://doi.org/10.1145/2468356.2468631

17. Ju, W., Sirkin, D.: Animate objects: how physical motion encourages public interaction. In: Ploug, T., Hasle, P., Oinas-Kukkonen, H. (eds.) PERSUASIVE 2010. LNCS, vol. 6137, pp. 40–51. Springer, Heidelberg (2010). https://doi.org/10.1007/978-3-642-13226-1_6

18. Khamis, M., Becker, C., Bulling, A., Alt, F.: Which one is me? Identifying oneself on public displays. In: Proceedings of the 36th Annual ACM Conference on Human Factors in Computing Systems, CHI 2018. ACM, New York (2018). https://doi.org/10.1145/3152832.3157813

19. Khamis, M., Bulling, A., Alt, F.: Tackling challenges of interactive public displays using gaze. In: Adjunct Proceedings of the 2015 ACM International Joint Conference on Pervasive and Ubiquitous Computing. ACM (2015). https://doi.org/10.1145/2800835.2807951

20. Khamis, M., Klimczak, A., Reiss, M., Alt, F., Bulling, A.: Eyescout: active eye tracking for position and movement independent gaze interaction with large public displays. In: Proceedings of the 30th Annual ACM Symposium on User Interface Software & Technology, UIST 2017. ACM, New York (2017). https://doi.org/10.1145/3126594.3126630

21. Khamis, M., et al.: Cueauth: comparing touch, mid-air gestures, and gaze for cue-based authentication on situated displays. Proc. ACM Interact. Mob. Wearable Ubiquitous Technol. 2(4) (2018). https://doi.org/10.1145/3287052

22. Laugwitz, B., Held, T., Schrepp, M.: Construction and evaluation of a user experience questionnaire. In: Holzinger, A. (ed.) USAB 2008. LNCS, vol. 5298, pp. 63–76. Springer, Heidelberg (2008). https://doi.org/10.1007/978-3-540-89350-9_6

23. Mäkelä, V., Khamis, M., Mecke, L., James, J., Turunen, M., Alt, F.: Pocket transfers: interaction techniques for transferring content from situated displays to mobile devices. In: Proceedings of the 36th Annual ACM Conference on Human Factors in Computing Systems, CHI 2018. ACM, New York (2018). https://doi.org/10.1145/3173574.3173709

24. Mäkelä, V., et al.: Virtual field studies: conducting studies on public displays in virtual reality. In: Proceedings of the 2020 CHI Conference on Human Factors in Computing Systems, CHI 2020, pp. 1–15. Association for Computing Machinery, New York (2020). https://doi.org/10.1145/3313831.3376796

25. Memarovic, N., Clinch, S., Alt, F.: Understanding display blindness in future display deployments. In: Proceedings of the 4th International Symposium on Pervasive Displays, PerDis 2015, pp. 7–14. Association for Computing Machinery, New York (2015). https://doi.org/10.1145/2757710.2757719

26. Microsoft: Microsoft human interface guidelines (2014). https://download. microsoft.com/download/6/7/6/676611b4-1982-47a4-a42e-4cf84e1095a8/ kinecthig.2.0.pdf. Accessed 31 Jan 2023

27. Müller, J., Alt, F., Michelis, D., Schmidt, A.: Requirements and design space for interactive public displays. In: Proceedings of the 18th ACM International Conference on Multimedia, MM 2010, pp. 1285–1294. Association for Computing Machinery, New York (2010). https://doi.org/10.1145/1873951.1874203

28. Müller, J., Bailly, G., Bossuyt, T., Hillgren, N.: Mirrortouch: combining touch and mid-air gestures for public displays. In: Proceedings of the 16th International Conference on Human-Computer Interaction with Mobile Devices & Services, pp. 319–328 (2014). https://doi.org/10.1145/2628363.2628379

29. Müller, J., Walter, R., Bailly, G., Nischt, M., Alt, F.: Looking glass: a field study on noticing interactivity of a shop window. In: Proceedings of the SIGCHI Conference on Human Factors in Computing Systems, pp. 297–306 (2012). https://doi.org/ 10.1145/2207676.2207718

30. Müller, J., et al.: Display blindness: the effect of expectations on attention towards digital signage. In: Tokuda, H., Beigl, M., Friday, A., Brush, A.J.B., Tobe, Y. (eds.) Pervasive 2009. LNCS, vol. 5538, pp. 1–8. Springer, Heidelberg (2009). https://doi. org/10.1007/978-3-642-01516-8_1

31. Ng, P.C., She, J., Jeon, K.E., Baldauf, M.: When smart devices interact with pervasive screens: a survey. ACM Trans. Multimedia Comput. Commun. Appl. 13(4), 1–23 (2017). https://doi.org/10.1145/3115933

32. Nielsen, J., Landauer, T.K.: A mathematical model of the finding of usability problems. In: Proceedings of the INTERACT 1993 and CHI 1993 Conference on Human Factors in Computing Systems, pp. 206–213 (1993). https://doi.org/10. 1145/169059.169166

33. Sauro, J.: If you could only ask one question, use this one (2010). https:// measuringu.com/single-question/. Accessed 31 Jan 2023

34. Vom Lehn, D., Heath, C.: Displacing the object: mobile technologies and interpretive resources. Arch. Museum Inform. 2 (2003)

35. Walter, R., Bailly, G., Müller, J.: Strikeapose: revealing mid-air gestures on public displays. In: Proceedings of the SIGCHI Conference on Human Factors in Computing Systems, pp. 841–850 (2013). https://doi.org/10.1145/2470654.2470774

36. Walter, R., Bailly, G., Valkanova, N., Müller, J.: Cuenesics: using mid-air gestures to select items on interactive public displays. In: Proceedings of the 16th International Conference on Human-Computer Interaction with Mobile Devices & Services, pp. 299–308 (2014). https://doi.org/10.1145/2628363.2628368

37. Wikipedia, The Free Encyclopedia: Net promoter score (2022). https://en. wikipedia.org/wiki/Net_promoter_score. Accessed 08 Jan 2023

38. Yoo, S., Parker, C., Kay, J., Tomitsch, M.: To dwell or not to dwell: an evaluation of mid-air gestures for large information displays. In: Proceedings of the Annual Meeting of the Australian Special Interest Group for Computer Human Interaction, OzCHI 2015, pp. 187–191. Association for Computing Machinery, New York (2015). https://doi.org/10.1145/2838739.2838819

Haptic Interaction

Assignment of a Vibration to a Graphical Object Induced by Resonant Frequency

Marco Kurzweg[1(✉)], Simon Linke[2], Yannick Weiss[3], Maximilian Letter[1], Albrecht Schmidt[3], and Katrin Wolf[1]

[1] Berlin University of Applied Science and Technologies (BHT), Berlin, Germany
marco.kurzweg@beuth-hochschule.de
[2] Hamburg University of Applied Sciences (HAW), Hamburg, Germany
[3] LMU Munich, Munich, Germany

Abstract. This work aims to provide tactile feedback when touching elements on everyday surfaces using their resonant frequencies. We used a remote speaker to bring a thin wooden surface into vibration for providing haptic feedback when a small graphical fly glued on the board was touched. Participants assigned the vibration to the fly instead of the board it was glued on. We systematically explored when that assignment illusion works best. The results indicate that additional sound, as well as vibration, lasting as long as the touch, are essential factors for having an assignment of the haptic feedback to the touched graphical object. With this approach, we contribute to ubiquitous and calm computing by showing that resonant frequency can provide vibrotactile feedback for images on thin everyday surfaces using only a minimum of hardware.

Keywords: Assignment · Illusion · Haptic Feedback · Resonant Frequency

1 Introduction

Nowadays, touch is the dominant way to interact with computers. Haptic feedback, given during touch interaction, for example, when pressing a button, increases users' performance [5].

In the case of interacting with smartphones, tablets, or game controllers, small embedded vibration motors provide users with haptic feedback. Designing haptic feedback for augmented environments and everywhere displays [33] in comparison is challenging. Following Weiser, who envisioned that future technology should be calm and interwoven into everyday materials [44], raises the question of how future smart environments and objects, including required haptic feedback, might look and feel.

Supplementary Information The online version contains supplementary material available at https://doi.org/10.1007/978-3-031-42280-5_33.

© The Author(s), under exclusive license to Springer Nature Switzerland AG 2023
J. Abdelnour Nocera et al. (Eds.): INTERACT 2023, LNCS 14142, pp. 523–545, 2023.
https://doi.org/10.1007/978-3-031-42280-5_33

Research on haptic feedback explored a wide range of technologies, such as vibrotactile actuators [3,18,23], peltier elements [14,32], and electrotactile devices [50]. In addition, the interaction of the visual and the aural sense has been explored [41,52] as well as how audio itself can influence haptic experiences to create haptic sensations [42,43]. While everyday materials and surfaces are promising candidates for future interaction [17], it remains unclear how to provide haptic feedback when interacting with them.

We are inspired by a physical phenomenon called Eigen- or resonant frequency, which can be used to bring, for example, wooden boards into vibration using sound from an external speaker somewhere in the room [28]. Creating haptic feedback for interactions with surfaces in our environment via audio has the advantage of using existing objects, as surfaces can be found everywhere, and speakers are present in most households. Another advantage of using resonant frequency through a speaker is that the speaker does not have to be attached to the surface to stimulate it. Instead, it can be placed anywhere in the environment. Therefore, one speaker could energize different surfaces and create haptic feedback to various images presented at them. This makes the approach scalable to create haptic feedback for several objects of different sizes presented on various surfaces with one sound source. It has to be kept in mind that the use of speakers results in hearable sounds, which might disturb the illusion. However, this effect could be eliminated with speakers able to play infrasound frequencies.

But how can we facilitate vibrating boards for interface design? Imagine a keyboard drawn on a thin wooden board, and a camera or attached capacitive sensors detect when and where the board is touched. If the touched board vibrates using resonant frequency and a user assigns that vibration to the key they press, we could use the board's vibration as haptic feedback when interacting with smart materials and surfaces without thinking about how to embed space-consuming technology into them.

In this work, we introduce the idea of using resonant frequency for haptic feedback when interacting with everyday surfaces. We further examine a proof-of-concept evaluation and show that vibration can be associated with graphical objects on a surface that vibrates when touched. Moreover, such vibration is associated with the graphical objects and is not assigned to the entire surface. As an example, in this work, the image of a fly is placed on a surface, leading to the image being perceived as a fly while the fly undergoes an embodiment process (in this work referred to as fly-embodiment). As a surface, a wooden board was excited by its resonant frequency, which was examined in a technical evaluation. Furthermore, we empirically explore the impact of additional auditive feedback on the perceived fly-embodiment of the touched graphical object. Finally, we look at the effects of feedback duration and timing on the fly-embodiment.

2   Related Work

This paper investigated whether sound can be used to activate haptic feedback for user interfaces. Therefore, we have reviewed (1) work on vibrotactile feedback,

(2) research on how audio can create haptic feedback, and (3) how resonant frequency can be used for haptic feedback creation.

2.1 Vibrotactile Feedback

A commonly popular method to induce haptic sensations is using vibrotactile feedback. This is known from devices using small vibrators to create haptic sensations, like VR controllers, smartphones, or other touch displays, but also for illusionary haptic feedback like phantom sensations (e.g., Funnel illusion [7], Saltation [13], and Stimulus-Onset-Asynchrony (SOA) [6]).

Several works investigated if haptic feedback can be felt anywhere between the hands out of the body [3,23,38]. Berger et al. took advantage of virtual environments and used vibrations of VR controllers to create haptic sensations [3]. In their study, participants had to hold a virtual object in their hands, which could be seen in the virtual scene as a wooden stick. Participants perceived an illusory sense of touch in the space between their hands, induced by several strength vibrations of the controllers. Kim et al. investigated phantom sensations between the participants' hands using a mobile device [23]. They fixed vibrotactile actuators in a row at the back of a mobile device. Depending on active actuators, a resulting phantom sensation should be located. Participants had to figure out the location of this resulting vibration on the mobile device screen. They showed that the phantom sensations were perceived between the hands in a 2D space at different locations depending on which actuators were used. Seo et al. used a mockup of a mobile device made of acrylic resin and fixed a vibrotactile actuator on each end [38]. By varying the frequency of each actuator, a resulting haptic sensation should be felt on the mockup somewhere between the hands. In a study, they elicited that participants perceived haptic sensations at different locations depending on the frequency of each of the two actuators.

Other researchers also investigated phantom sensations felt in the space between hands but without additional devices, like smartphones, mockups, or controllers. Instead, they fixed the vibrotactile actuators directly at the users' fingertips [26,27,30]. Lee et al. fixed one vibrotactile actuator on the fingertips of each index finger [27]. Participants had to judge the position of the phantom sensation (with the help of an augmented ruler) between their fingertips. The results showed that the phantom sensation was localized differently depending on the frequency of each actuator. In a separate study, Lee et al. investigated the same haptic sensation. This time the vibrotactile actuators were fixed at the index finger and thumb of the same hand while participants performed a pinch gesture [26]. In their experiment, they were able to elicit that a phantom sensation is felt between the fingers, with no physical object connected to the participants' bodies, using different stimulation methods of the actuators.

Further, other works investigated haptic sensations felt on the own body using vibrations [18,21]. Israr et al. investigated different patterns and amounts of vibrotactile actuators placed on various parts of the body [18]. They aimed to explore if different movement patterns can be felt on the skin. Their results showed participants felt varying movement sensations using a large grid of vibro-tactile actuators. Kim et al. placed actuators on opposite sides of body zones, like the back of the hand and palm or back and front of the upper body [21]. They showed that haptic sensations could be felt if tactile stimulation was performed through body parts. Further, they presented that the frequency of the actuators is important, and duration and direction are less crucial. Bau et al. used electrovibrations when people moved fingers across a touch surface [2]. In four different experiments, they investigated the potential of these electrovibrations to induce tactile feedback. They found electrovibration can be used for various tactile sensations, like the perception of textures, or for different interactions, like dragging or the alignment of an object.

Another research interest is investigating the movement of felt haptic sensations from one hand to another induced by vibrotactile actuators [34,35,54]. Therefore, different devices for creating vibrational feedback were used. Pittera et al. made a custom vibrotactile device for each hand and investigated how the moving vibrations are perceived [35]. In their experiment, they varied the frequency and duration of the stimulation. They showed that illusionary movement was perceived while holding separate objects with non-contiguous parts of the body. In another study, Pittera et al. used ultrasound speakers to stimulate the palm of participants' hands with vibrational feedback [34]. They showed that illusionary movement is also perceived by using midair technology. Zhao et al. used a tablet with fixed vibrotactile actuators on each end [54]. A moving sensation was created by activating the actuators with different asynchronous stimuli over different durations. This sensation was supported through a moving graphical illustration. They presented that the graphical representation enhances the perceived haptic feedback.

While most related works used actuators and devices directly attached to the users or placed in their hands, we used sound to create the vibration. Further, the speaker is not directly attached to the user or the surface.

2.2 Haptic Feedback Using Audio

Our approach relies on the assignment of the haptic feedback using sound. Hence, we looked at related work investigating haptic sensations with additional sound.

Cho et al. investigated the sound of a pencil writing on paper in combination with vibrotactile feedback [9]. The sound, as well as the vibrotactile feedback, was coupled with the writing speed and pressure. They elicited that users perceived the haptic sensation of writing on a sheet of paper when writing with a pen on a tablet screen. The effect was most intense for the combination of audio and tactile feedback, compared to one modality alone. Etzi et al. created haptic sensations of pleasantness and roughness of materials by using the sound of paper and sandpaper combined with the visual sense by presenting images of different surfaces. [12]. While participants explored the same surface within the study, they perceived sounds and saw images of different materials. These sounds let the participants feel different pleasantness and roughness of the same material.

Won et al. examined how the perceived tactile intensity can be changed by auditory feedback [51]. In a study, they were able to show that the presence of audio influenced the perceived tactile intensity. Besides, the frequency of the auditory feedback was not significant and did not have to coincide with the tactile feedback. The perceived duration of haptic feedback was researched by Villanueva et al. by investigating interference of audio and touch [43]. Both auditory and tactile stimuli were used as distractors to the other modality. They found incongruent conditions influenced each other modality in terms of duration perception by decreasing performance. Further, congruent auditory feedback did not enhance tactile perception performance. Lai et al. elicited if audio feedback can influence the perceived physicality when applying force with a finger on a rigid surface [25]. Therefore, in an experiment, participants had to press on the same rigid surface while perceiving various auditory feedback in each condition. The auditory feedback was based on real-world material, object, or phenomenon. The results indicated that audio, as an interaction channel, enriched the perceived physicality when pressing a rigid surface.

When audio is used to create haptic sensations, it is usually done by using material or other real-world sounds. In contrast, we used a special frequency to stimulate a real-world surface and bring it into vibration, but we did not use hearable sounds.

2.3 Haptic Feedback Using Resonant Frequency

As we use resonant frequency of an object to create haptic feedback, we also looked at research on the resonant frequency to create haptic sensations.

Using resonant frequency to improve haptic sensations is a conventional method to increase the perceived haptic feedback on a maximum value for linear resonant actuators or piezoelectric actuators [39,53]. Silva et al. investigated different technologies to create haptic feedback [39]. They found the linear resonant actuator operating with a voice coil to drive the mass as energy efficient and powerful when operating at resonant frequency. The actuator requires little power to reach the resonant frequency, is small, and can provide powerful vibrations and haptic sensations. Yeh et al. used piezoelectric actuators to create a working abstraction of a haptic feedback system where users can feel the stiffness of an object [53]. They investigated the setup number and stimulation possibilities of the piezoelectric actuator. They showed that the piezoelectric actuator yields better efficiency if it has a resonant frequency.

Further, research on the resonant frequency investigated the use of speakers to create haptic sensations [46,47]. Wi et al. used resonant frequency to prototype a haptic feedback assistive device for visually-impaired drivers [46]. They created a haptic device with pins of different diameters and lengths and resonant frequencies ordered in a square layout. They were connected to the voice coil of a speaker. The results showed slight differences in the pins' structure were enough to stimulate specific pins with a resonant frequency, which resulted in a high-resolution haptic display. Withana et al. researched if audio can create haptic sensations in the own body by using the resonant frequency [47]. They used a

Fig. 1. Left: Wooden board with the graphical representation of a fly. **Right**: Rear of the wooden board with copper tape at the same position as the fly and copper wire connected to an Arduino, detecting resistance change when the fly is touched.

custom chair on which four acoustic actuators were placed under the seat. These actuators played sounds with different frequencies. Participants had to judge where inside the body they perceived haptic sensations. They found that they can provide haptic sensations to multiple body parts via just one contact point.

Previous works that investigated resonant frequency used different actuators, like piezoelectric or linear resonant actuators, and attached them to objects or surfaces. Our approach differs from these by not attaching a speaker to a certain object or surface but using a speaker placed anywhere in the room. Thus, we can use one single speaker to add vibrotactile feedback for different surfaces or objects remotely.

2.4   Summary

Due to space, weight, and other limitations, not every object can be equipped with hardware, such as a vibrotactile motor. One alternative solution for this might be using haptic illusions, which can, for example, be created through a sound source. Existing works utilizing audio to create haptic illusions investigated the phantom sensations of a localization or a movement. While these works investigated if the feedback can be perceived at another location than it is produced, it remains unclear how to understand such haptic illusions or what mental models they create. A first step towards understanding the interpretation of sound-induced haptic feedback could be if it will be assigned to the entire vibrating surface or to a graphical representation placed on the surface.

3   Concept and Prototyping

Calm Computing: Aiming to contribute to calm computing, we explore if sound can be used to create haptic feedback and, in particular, if such haptic feedback could be assigned to a graphical object. The term calm computing was introduced by Weiser [45]. Calm technology should stay out of the focus when it is not needed but has to be there with all powers and opportunities when the user wants to interact with it. Hence, we turned a wooden board into a touch interface that provides vibrotactile feedback while using minimal technology. We merely used three components: (1) a wooden board, which is a common material and used for furniture, doors, floors, and device cases, (2) a speaker, in our case, an off-the-shelf Bluetooth box, while speakers can also be found in phones, TVs or media systems, and (3) a copper tape, which can make surfaces touch-sensitive when being part of an electrical circuit with a capacitance measuring unit. The copper tape can even be attached to the rear of a wooden board and still allow for touch detection. This retains the touch and feel of the wooden board, and the technology will stay out of sight but is able to create haptic sensations; see Fig. 1. Therefore, our work contributes to the basic idea of calm computing.

Resonant Frequency: The phenomenon we rely on to bring a surface into vibration is described as resonance frequencies. Resonance frequencies are the frequencies with which an object, in our case, a wooden board, vibrates when it is stimulated, e.g., through a hammer hit or, for our planned interface, through sound. The benefit of using a hammer instead of sound during the technical evaluation to identify the resonance frequency for our interface is that the hammer excites a struck board with all possible resonance frequencies. We used a hammer to determine the most practical of these frequencies and later recreated this resonant frequency using sound. This resonant frequency, when played, stimulates the entire board so that the vibration can be felt wherever the board is touched. The resonance frequencies of a board depend on the size, thickness, and material of the board. We tested four wooden boards, all made out of chip wood of different thicknesses, 1 mm, 3 mm, 6 mm, and 10 mm, all having the same size (26 cm × 53.5 cm). The four boards were struck ten times with an impulse hammer (Dytran 5800SL) by hand in the center of the board. Each time, the impulse response of the board was recorded at a different position close to the board's edges using a piezoelectric sensor. Then, the average of the ten recorded signals was calculated to analyze the frequency-dependent mobility of the board, see Fig. 2. Mobility refers to the relative velocity with which the board vibrates after being hit with the hammer [36]. This is given in decibels relative to full scale ($dBFS$), which can be a maximum of zero decibels [1].

Selection of the Board: Figure 2 shows the averaged frequency measures of the thinnest board, which was selected later for our apparatus. The thinnest board was selected as it is more likely to vibrate when excited with low-frequency signals, see Fig. 2, left. High mobility is of interest to us because it will create a well-perceivable haptic sensation. With commercially available speakers as we used in this study, this approach has the drawback of producing unwanted hearable sounds. An alternative would be the use of infrasound resonant frequency. Since off-the-shelf speakers do not allow this, our goal was to reach a resonant frequency as low as possible. Therefore, we used the thinnest wooden board; as the resonance frequency increases with board thickness, more energy is needed to excite it.

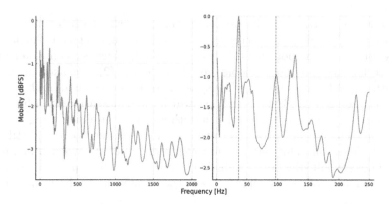

Fig. 2. Mean mobility per frequency triggered through 10 hammer strikes on the thinnest wooden board of 1 mm thickness and 26 cm × 53.5 cm size. The left diagram shows that mobility decreases with increasing frequency. An enlarged presentation of the most promising lowest frequencies on the right shows that the main resonant frequency at 35 Hz would be most suitable for our apparatus, as the board here vibrates with the highest intensity. As the highest excursion of the measured resonant frequency at 35 Hz can hardly be radiated by most of today's commercially available speakers, the next-higher resonant frequency at 96 Hz was chosen for our apparatus. Although the peak value for the resonant frequency 130 Hz was higher than the peak value for 96 Hz, we chose the latter because it was the lowest resonant frequency with a high excursion that the speaker could reproduce.

Latency: We connected an Arduino that detects touch and gives acoustic feedback in the form of playing the resonant frequency at that moment. As latency of different feedback modalities informing about the same action affects user experience [19], we had to determine the exact latency of the system precisely. Therefore, we measured the round trip latency of the analog-digital and digital-analog conversion of the used computer, which was 91 ms. As this is a comparable high delay, we added an external audio interface to the existing system and reached a round trip latency of 33 ms. Combined with the minor latency of the Arduino (2 ms), the overall latency was 35 ms. Even though this latency might be an issue in certain musical and rhythmic tasks, it is suitable for most multimedia applications [19,24]. Nevertheless, this is still a critical value that can only be reached with dedicated hardware. As this can not be assumed in all real-world scenarios, we decided to investigate the possible impact of a delay, too.

Noise-Cancelling Headphones: The speaker is placed underneath the wooden board to play the resonance frequency. However, while it could be placed anywhere in the room, the closeness of the speaker to the board allowed for lower sound volume. Despite this, some sound was still audible, possibly disturbing the illusion. To isolate the stimuli during the empirical evaluation, participants listened to white noise via noise-canceling headphones.

4   Empirical Evaluation

A user study was conducted to explore if vibrotactile feedback could be assigned to a passive graphical object displayed on a wooden board vibrating with a resonant frequency. Further, the goal was to understand how such an illusion would work best.

4.1   Experiment Design

It is commonly accepted that coherent and consistent multimodal feedback increases realism [48]. Moreover, the latency of vibrotactile feedback influences the haptic experience and perception of an object's attributes [19].

Independent Variables: We chose feedback modality and feedback latency as our independent variables. Our controlled experiment had a $2 \times 3 \times 2$ within-subjects design with the independent variables MODALITIES (touch only (T) and touch plus audio (TA)), LATENCY (direct (35 ms latency), smallLatency (100 ms latency), and largeLatency (200 ms)), and DURATION (3 s (which was also the touch duration) and 0.5 s). The three-second touch duration was chosen in alignment with the work of Wolf et al. [50] and the 0.5 s touch duration was chosen related to the work of Schönauer et al. [37].

Dependent Variables: Our dependent variables were SIMULTANEITY JUDG-MENT (as a test to measure if the feedback latency was perceived), FLY-EMBODIMENT (to measure to what extent the graphical image—using a fly picture as an example—would be perceived as realistic fly), FLY-EMBODIMENT INFLUENCING PARAMETERS (to identify the reasons for an increased fly-embodiment), and QUALITATIVE FEEDBACK (to possibly better understand our quantitative and qualitative results).

4.2   Measurements

To measure the SIMULTANEITY JUDGMENT, we followed the design of Kaaresoja et al. [19] and asked the following question for each condition: *"Was the received feedback simultaneously to the touch interaction?"* Participants could answer Yes or No.

For the FLY-EMBODIMENT, a standardized embodiment questionnaire [31] was taken as a reference to measure under what conditions the fly image might be more or less perceived as a real fly. This questionnaire was chosen as it contains questions related to multisensory feedback and some questions directly asked for the assignment of feedback, both important for this work. As these questions relate to different subscales within the questionnaire and the questionnaire itself is designed to compute a final score [31], all questions were kept for our study. Nevertheless, we slightly adjusted the questions to the physical context of this study. To maintain the meaningfulness of the questionnaire, we replaced the phrase *my body* with *a real fly* or *my finger*, and the phrase *virtual body* with *a graphical fly*. To stay consistent with the initial embodiment questionnaire's

Fig. 3. This figure shows the study setup, once like the participants saw it during the study with a covered speaker (left) and once, the setup without the covered speaker (right).

rating, we had to negate the first question to be consistent for later analysis. The altered questionnaire can be found in the appendix. All questions were answered using a 7-item Likert scale.

Afterward, to investigate FLY-EMBODIMENT INFLUENCING PARAMETERS, we asked semi-structured questions about reasons for creating or breaking the fly-embodiment illusion:

- What helped to create the illusion that it was a real fly?
- What broke the illusion that it was a real fly?

4.3 Apparatus

For our apparatus, we used a Razer Blade 15 Laptop and an external Behringer UMC22 sound card. Via the audio software Waveform, we played the sounds (resonant frequency of the wooden board and sound of a fly), created latencies (between the sounds and for the start of playing the sounds), and generated the white noise for masking the sound of the resonant frequency.

Through noise-canceling headphones (Sony WH-1000XM4), we covered frequencies not masked by the white noise. Both methods, also in combination, are commonly used to mask sounds and frequencies [16,20,22,29]. We used both to make sure all external sounds were masked.

A LATENCY of 35 ms was chosen as the value for the *direct* MODALITY as it is the internal latency of the hardware and the minimum latency possible with our technical setup. With a value under 50 ms, it is still perceived as synchronous for auditory feedback, and no latency should be recognized [19]. 100 ms was chosen as the value for the *smallLatency* condition because it is not perceived as synchronous regarding Kaaresoja et al. [19], but still in the cognitive range of the human processor model [8]. 200 ms was chosen as the value for *largeLatency* as we doubled the previous value of 100 ms to have a value that should be perceived as latency regarding Kaaresoja and the human processor model [8,19].

The selected wooden board was sufficiently thin (1 mm) that even sound with lower volume provided adequate vibration The board was placed on four small wooden cubes, damped with felt pieces on the bottom to ensure its vibrational behavior remained unaffected. The board was placed on two cardboard boxes, hiding the speaker underneath it; see Fig. 3.

On top of the board, a sticker with the appearance of a fly was placed at the point where the participants had to touch the board to receive the haptic feedback. A graphical representation of a fly was chosen as an object where people could anticipate a reaction the moment it is touched. When interacting with a real fly (e.g., capturing or covering it), we expect to feel an object's vibration and hear a fly's sound. While another graphical object that produces feedback by touching it could alternatively be used, a representation of an object that creates feedback before touching it would break that metaphor (i.e., a smartphone).

To detect when the fly is touched while at the same time having a "natural" look of the everyday life surface and no additional hardware on the participants' fingers, we used an Arduino UNO and the "CapacitiveSensor library". The copper tape as an electrical conductor was mounted on the rear of the wooden board. When adjusting the size of the conductive area, the contact is recognized when the fly is touched but not at other parts of the wooden board. This should raise the illusion that the origin of the haptic feedback is at that exact point.

The speaker (JBL Charge 4) was directly placed under the wooden board with a distance of 3 cm and could not be seen because, in front, it was covered by black fabric. While the white noise and the sound of the fly were played via the headphones, the speaker was used to excite the board with its resonant frequency. The sound signal was not restricted to a pure sine wave to perceive a strong vibration at low volumes. Instead, a sawtooth wave was used, which also excited the plate with higher frequencies due to the upper partials. To match the partials to the plate, they are weighted with the related mobility (shown in Fig. 2) according to their frequency. To ensure that all participants' time of touch is the same over each condition, we had a second LED light behind the wooden board that lighted up when the fly was touched, see Fig. 3. After three seconds, the light went out, and the exploration time was over.

4.4   Participants, Task, and Procedure

We recruited 24 participants (9 female, 15 male) with an age range from 23 to 53 years and an average of 31,79 years (SD = 8,26). The experiment was conducted as a lab study. First, the participants were welcomed and asked to agree to a consent form. They were informed that participation in the study was voluntary and that taking a break was possible. After filling in a demographic questionnaire, participants started with the study. Our 12 conditions were counter-balanced using a Latin square design [4]. In each condition, the participants wore noise-canceling headphones and touched the graphical fly with their right index finger, which let them perceive feedback according to the experimental conditions. This procedure could be repeated as often as the participants wanted. No time limitation was given. The participants were also allowed to explore other areas of the wooden board where no feedback was provided. After each condition, participants filled in the questionnaire on a dedicated computer and answered the semi-structured questions. Finally, we showed all participants the setup, how the haptic feedback was created, and where it was present. Then we recorded the general statements about the interface.

5 Results

We first analyzed our quantitative data to learn if LATENCY, DURATION, or SOUND affected the FLY-EMBODIMENT (assignment of the haptic feedback). Further, we analyzed if there were any interaction effects between our independent variables. We then evaluated the qualitative data to gain a better understanding of the quantitative results.

5.1 Quantitative Results

In our quantitative analyses, we used the aligned rank transformation (ART) to perform an ANOVA with our non-parametric results [10,49]. The ART also allows performing post-hoc analysis with pairwise comparisons.

Simultaneity. To explore if the latency between touching the graphical object and the perceived haptic feedback is relevant for an assignment of feedback, we began the questionnaire with a simultaneity judgment, see Sect. 4.2.

The results showed that in 245 out of 288 cases (85 percent), the haptic feedback was perceived simultaneously to the point of touching the fly, independent of the present latency. Looking at the different latencies individually, most often, feedback was perceived simultaneously for a latency of 100 ms (87 out of 96 cases) and least often for 200 ms (75 out of 96 cases). For 35 ms, it was perceived as simultaneous in 83 out of 96 cases.

Assignment of Haptic Feedback. In line with the results of the simultaneity judgment, we could not find any statistically significant results for LATENCY, performing an ANOVA on the fly-embodiment questionnaire scores [31]. On the opposite, the ANOVA revealed statistically significant differences for the two remaining variables, DURATION ($F_{(1,253)} = 63.2, p < .001$) and SOUND ($F_{(1,253)} = 27.86, p < .001$).

Post-hoc pairwise comparison revealed a better assignment of the feedback to the graphical object if the perceived feedback is as long as the touch, compared to a short impulse ($p < .001$) and a better fly-embodiment for additional sound (related to the touched object) compared to no sound ($p < .001$), see Fig. 4.

Further, the results showed an interaction effect between DURATION × SOUND ($F_{(1,253)} = 9.08, p = .003$). Post-hoc pairwise comparison revealed a statistically significant better assignment of the feedback for a long duration with additional sound (3 s, sound) compared to an impulse without additional sound (0.5 s, none) ($p < .001$), compared to an impulse with additional sound (0.5 s, sound) ($p < .001$), and compared to a long duration without additional sound (3s, none)

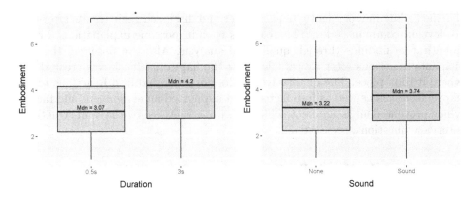

Fig. 4. Box plots showing significant differences for the assignment of the haptic feedback to the graphical object based on the score of the fly-embodiment questionnaire. **Left**: Box plot of the fly-embodiment score for DURATION. **Right**: Box plot of the fly-embodiment score for SOUND.

$(p < .001)$, see Fig. 5. Also, a significantly better assignment for a long duration without additional sound (3s, none) compared to an impulse without additional sound (0.5 s, none) $(p = .001)$ could be measured, see Fig. 5.

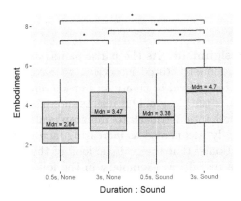

Fig. 5. The box plot shows the assignment of the feedback to the graphical object based on the fly-embodiment questionnaire score. The figure presents significant differences in the interaction effects of DURATION and SOUND.

5.2   Qualitative Results

The qualitative data were coded using Grounded Theory [40]. Axial and selective coding was applied by building categories according to the questions that asked for positive or negative perceived aspects of a system [40]. Two researchers did the coding independently of each other and discussed their results afterward to develop common codes. The goal was to gain possible explanations for the quantitative findings through qualitative analysis. Also, we observed the participants' reactions after we revealed how the haptic feedback was created and where it took place. The qualitative results are separated into Reactions to the haptic feedback as well as into factors that supported an assignment and factors which prevented an assignment, which was pre-structured by the semi-structured interview questions, see Sect. 4.2.

Reactions to the Haptic Feedback. After the last condition for every participant, we revealed the setup and functionality of the prototype to the participants and recorded their reactions. We aimed to get insights if the illusion worked as intended and if the haptic feedback matched the functionality of the setup. Most participants were surprised and mentioned that they had not expected such a setup (18 out of 24 participants). Many of them stated that they did not expect the whole wooden board to vibrate (13 out of 18 participants): (*"I would have never believed that the whole board is vibrating. It did not feel like a "real" fly, but also definitely felt like the feedback just directly came from the fly"*, P.16) In addition, some participants mentioned that they were surprised that the feedback was created by a speaker (5 out of 18 participants): (*"I never thought that feedback is produced by a speaker. I believed there was an actuator connected at the other side of the board producing the feedback, as the feedback was very strong"*, P.24)

Supporting an Assignment. As the participants were not forced to answer the questions of the semi-structured interview, we have a total number of 216 answers for reasons that helped to create an illusion and a total of 122 answers as reasons for a break of the illusion. Our results showed three factors supporting the assignment of the haptic feedback to the graphical fly. First, the graphical representation of the fly was named as increasing factor 23 out of 216 answers. All participants mentioned that the realistic look of the sticker helped to think they were touching a real fly, as exemplary in the following statements: (*"The image creates a perception that is in line with known experience and gives a connection to a real fly"*, P.10) and (*"The realistic image of the fly"*, P.15)

Further, the sound of the fly was named in 80 out of 216 answers as a supporting factor to create an illusion of touching a real fly. The participants mentioned it was helpful that there was a sound of a fly at all, sounding like a flying fly (66 out of 80 times). Also, some participants noticed that the sound has many variations and seems to come from the fly spatially (14 out of 80 times): (*"The sound helps to perceive it like a representation of a fly"*, P.2), (*"Variations in the sound of the fly"*, P.23), (*"The fly was moving as long as it touched the fly. Thus I noticed the sound was coming from the image of the fly a little more"*, P.9), and (*"The sounds created the illusion as if a fly had flown away from the place I touched and, after a short time, sat down again somewhere"*, P.10),

At last, participants stated the felt vibration at their fingertips reminded them of touching a fly and helped to create good illusional feedback in 113 out of 216 answers. This stemmed from the fact that there just was a vibration (87 out of 113 times), that the vibrations, just like the sound, were felt as they had variations (3 out of 113 times), and the feedback was common to known experiences (19 out of 113 times). Further, the vibration slightly created a feeling of touching a three-dimensional object (4 out of 113 times): ("*The vibration helped me to create the illusion*", P.3), ("*The vibrations felt similar to that when touching a fly. The frequency of vibrations was well chosen*", P.9), and ("*The vibration on the finger felt 3D. The light buzzing made it realistic*", P.14),

Preventing an Assignment. In line with the factors for creating the illusion of touching a real fly, we also found three factors preventing the participants from assigning the haptic feedback to the graphical object. One of the three factors mentioned by the participants here (21 out of 122 answers) is sound, similar to previously stated points. Besides participants noticing completely missing sound as the breaking point of the illusion (12 out of 21 cases), they also mentioned the short sound to be too monotone (9 out of 21 cases): ("*There was no sound*", P.7) and ("*The sound was too short: It was too monotone*", P.11),

In addition, the participants were disappointed by the felt vibrations (mentioned before as a supporting factor) when it was just a short impulse (16 out of 40 times) and complained about the unnatural feeling of the vibrations when the feedback just had a short DURATION (24 out of 40 times): ("*The intensity of the vibration was very weak*", P.4) and ("*The abrupt stop of the motion. A real fly would continue to move since I touched it slightly and not too hard*", P.3).

As a final reason for breaking the illusion, the non-existing shape of the graphical object was given in half of the answers (61 out of 122 answers). It was answered that the haptic (three-dimensional shape) of the object is missing (50 out of 61 times) and the feeling of touching a board is higher than touching a fly (11 out of 61 times): ("*The feeling of touching the board was higher than touching the fly*", P.1) and ("*The fly had no haptic or real body*", P.17).

5.3   Summary

In summary, our qualitative results reflect and substantiate the quantitative findings. Our results show that haptic feedback created through an audio source would be assigned to a graphical object when touching the latter. When doing so, participants perceived the graphical object as the source of the felt feedback and not the surface that was actually vibrating. We found sound and perceived haptic feedback as important factors for having an assignment of the feedback to the graphical object, as well as preventing such an assignment. A short impulse of haptic feedback is perceived differently from a long duration in terms of intensity, naturality, and expectations compared to real-life experience. Further, not only the duration of the sound is important, but also if there is sound at all. The assignment of feedback to a graphical object requires the appearance of suitable sound, or the assignment will not be made. In addition, the qualitative results indicate a good visual representation to be important. The illusion of touching a three-dimensional shape could increase the perceived haptic feedback and the feeling of touching a real fly, as it further matches our expectations.

6   Discussion

We investigated which factors are important to assign haptic feedback created on an everyday life object to a graphical object and if consequently the graphical object is perceived as the source of the haptic feedback. Further, we looked at the limitations of our design and the current technology and how these could be solved by future research or improved hardware.

6.1   Assignment of Haptic Feedback

Overall, our findings indicate that the graphical object (in this case, the graphical representation of the fly) was perceived as the source of the haptic feedback. This was further supported by the participants' reactions after revealing the setup and telling them about the prototype's functionality. This is in line with the answers to question 13 of the questionnaire (*"It seemed as if I felt the motion of a real fly in the location where I touched the graphical fly"*), where the overall median is 5.0. The conditions, with additional sound and a feedback duration as long as the touch, have a median of 6.0. This supports our concept that speakers can provide haptic feedback for graphical objects on surfaces that vibrate in resonance frequency through a sound played by the speakers. In the following, we discuss in more detail factors that are important to create such an assignment illusion, the mental modal that this illusion relies on, and limitations of the current prototype that should be considered and addressed for future work.

Mental Model. As mentioned before, several factors (sound, duration of the haptic and auditive feedback, look & feel of the embodied object) influence the assignment of the haptic feedback to the graphical object. All these aspects have in common that users can build the mental modal of a real fly being touched. Through the multimodal feedback - the seen graphical fly, which they also feel through resonant frequency, and hear through sound feedback when touching the graphical object - users' expectations when touching a real fly are fulfilled. Hence, to a certain extent, they believe the illusion of touching a fly. Multisensory perception and the human ability to integrate information from different senses into one unified illusionary concept is possible if all senses coherently and consistently fulfill humans' expectations or the information of one sense is overwritten with expected information that fits the information of another sense [11].

Important Factors. Several questions of the fly-embodiment questionnaire target the kind of assignment by asking for the source of the feedback, see Sect. 4.2.

Therefore, fly-embodiment-increasing factors have been identified that influence the assignment level of the perceived haptic feedback.

For assigning the haptic feedback to the graphical object, we identified different factors to be important. The duration of the vibration feedback has to be perceived over the entire touch duration. The sound a user perceives when touching the graphics must be played when and as long the graphical object is touched. The look of the graphical object determines the mental model built by the user and the expectation of any other feedback when touching the image. If the image had a corresponding elevated shape, the fly-embodiment could become stronger. The factors of sound and duration of the haptic feedback were also relevant for the level of perceived haptic feedback, as shown in quantitative results. The importance of a realistic look and felt shape was identified through the answers of the semi-structured interview, see Sect. 5.2.

While previous work used resonant frequency to create haptic feedback through speakers directly mounted on a specific object [46] or for haptic feedback provided on different body parts [47], we used remote speakers to serve as haptic feedback devices. In addition, we investigated if images could serve as a mental model to create illusionary objects to which the feedback can be assigned. Previous work used capacitive touch and investigated haptic sensations when touching a flat surface [2]. While the work of Bau et al. used a touch screen and investigated the perception of textures, this approach is about the assignment of haptic feedback when touching a graphical object placed on an everyday life surface, like a table. Thus, analog materials could be used as an interface and provide realistic touch experiences useful in ubiquitous computing.

In summary, the discussed factors were identified to influence the level of fly-embodiment, which represents the assignment of the feedback coming from the graphical image (and neither from the speakers nor from the entire vibrating board). Our results indicate that a higher level of the fly-embodiment will more likely result in an assignment of the haptic feedback to the graphical object and vice versa.

Limitations and Future Work. One limitation of our setup is that there always will be a specific latency between the point of touch and the creation of the haptic feedback. In our study, we measured the round trip latency of the AD and DA conversion of the used computer, audio interface, and microcontroller. We reached a latency of 35 ms, which should be recognized as no latency regarding the human processor model and other related work [8,19]. With other hardware and additional devices, the latency might be higher. Within our study, we used latencies up to 200 ms, which still were perceived as synchronous. Therefore, the effect can be recreated at home with simple hardware and devices which are not computationally powerful computers.

Another limiting factor might be the creation and use of sound frequencies to let the surface vibrate. While using a single audio source to create haptic feedback on different real-life objects is an advantage, the frequency needed to achieve that also brings disadvantages. A disadvantage is that the frequency to let real-life objects vibrate mostly is in a range that the users will hear, and the sound would be annoying and might disturb the illusion. This disadvantage probably will not be an issue in noisy environments, but when silence is appreciated. While we could determine the heard frequency by using noise-canceling headphones and white noise, as we did in the study setup, this might neither be practical nor comfortable in later applications. Alternatively, future research could further look into how to utilize infrasound frequencies for this use case.

The sound used as resonant frequency could be modified by filtering and deleting certain frequencies that are not needed [15]. Depending on the targeted surface, the resonant frequency might be very high. Thus, it should be investigated in the future, until which point this solution will work.

Future research might investigate if the assignment of the feedback will also work for multiple objects placed on the same physical object. This would be of interest because the feedback induced through resonance frequency is coupled to the surface and, therefore, the same for all objects that are placed on it, even though these could differ in size and look. For this case, a ubiquitous solution for a practical implementation has to be found. It would not be a ubiquitous approach to have multiple sensors detecting capacitive touch beneath the surface.

For this work, a speaker activated a single surface. In the scenario of using a single speaker to stimulate an arbitrary amount of surfaces in an environment, it has to be researched how feasible and scalable such an approach is. This includes evaluating which materials can be addressed, what frequencies can be supported, or what distances can be reached.

7   Conclusion

This work aimed at exploring if and under what conditions touch feedback can be assigned to a graphical object illustrated on an everyday surface using resonant frequency. A user study showed that haptic feedback induced through resonant frequency is assigned to a passive graphical object if (1) the duration of the feedback lasts as long as the touch and (2) additional auditive feedback is provided. On the contrary, the feedback assignment (fly-embodiment) fails if (1) the duration of the feedback is shorter than the touch on the graphical object and (2) no additional sound is played when the graphical object is touched.

Qualitative results suggested additional factors that might influence an assignment of feedback to the graphical object: (1) The realism of the graphical representation of the object seems to support the assignment. Therefore, a realistic design of the graphical object is recommended, and (2) the fly-embodiment of the graphical object could be enriched when touching an elevated shape.

It can be stated that it is important to fulfill users' expectations about the touched object in order to cause an assignment of feedback towards that object. Overall, we showed that vibrotactile feedback for images applied on surfaces can be provided due to resonant frequencies of the corresponding surfaces. This was achieved for surfaces of rather thin thickness (1 mm) using only a minimum of hardware. Thus, we not only contribute to the research domain of haptics and multimodal feedback but also to ubiquitous computing as our approach can be considered to be interwoven into everyday material and, therefore, is what Weiser called "calm".

Acknowledgement. This project is funded by the Deutsche Forschungsgemeinschaft (DFG, German Research Foundation)–425869442 and is part of Priority Program SPP2199 Scalable Interaction Paradigms for Pervasive Computing Environments.

A   Appendix

The questions from the original embodiment questionnaire [31] were slightly adjusted for our study as follows:

1. I did not believe it was a real fly.
2. It felt as if the graphical fly was slightly becoming real.
3. It felt as if the movements of the graphical fly were influencing my tactile perception.
4. It felt as if the graphical fly was turning into a real fly.
5. At some point, it felt as if a real fly was starting to move simultaneously with the graphical fly.
6. It felt as if there was one more fly in the room from when I came in.
7. It felt as if the fly had changed.
8. I felt a motion at my fingertip when I touched the fly.
9. It felt as if the fly's body could be affected by my touch.
10. It felt as if the graphical fly was a real fly.
11. At some point, it felt that the graphical fly resembled a real fly in terms of shape, color, and motion.
12. I felt that a real fly was located where I saw the graphical fly.
13. It seemed as if the felt motion came from the fly.
14. It seemed as if I felt the motion of a real fly in the location where I touched the graphical fly.
15. It seemed as if the motions I felt were caused by the movement of the graphical fly.
16. It seemed as if my finger was touching a real fly.

References

1. AES standard method for digital audio engineering - measurement of digital audio equipment (1991). https://www.aes.org/publications/standards/search.cfm?docID=21. Accessed 25 Jan 2023
2. Bau, O., Poupyrev, I., Israr, A., Harrison, C.: Teslatouch: electrovibration for touch surfaces. In: UIST 2010. Association for Computing Machinery, New York (2010). https://doi.org/10.1145/1866029.1866074
3. Berger, C.C., Gonzalez-Franco, M.: Expanding the sense of touch outside the body. In: SAP 2018. Association for Computing Machinery, New York (2018). https://doi.org/10.1145/3225153.3225172

4. Bradley, J.V.: Complete counterbalancing of immediate sequential effects in a Latin square design. J. Am. Stat. Assoc. **53**(282), 525–528 (1958)
5. Brewster, S., Chohan, F., Brown, L.: Tactile feedback for mobile interactions. In: CHI 2007. Association for Computing Machinery, New York (2007). https://doi.org/10.1145/1240624.1240649
6. Burtt, H.E.: Tactual illusions of movement. J. Exp. Psychol. **2**, 371–385 (1917). https://doi.org/10.1037/h0074614
7. v. Békésy, G.: Funneling in the nervous system and its role in loudness and sensation intensity on the skin. J. Acoust. Soc. Am. **30**(5), 399–412 (1958). https://doi.org/10.1121/1.1909626
8. Card, S., Moran, T., Newell, A.: The model human processor - an engineering model of human performance. In: Handbook of Perception and Human Performance, vol. 2, no. 45–1, pp. 1–35 (1986)
9. Cho, Y., Bianchi, A., Marquardt, N., Bianchi-Berthouze, N.: Realpen: providing realism in handwriting tasks on touch surfaces using auditory-tactile feedback. In: Proceedings of the 29th Annual Symposium on User Interface Software and Technology, UIST 2016, pp. 195–205. Association for Computing Machinery, New York (2016). https://doi.org/10.1145/2984511.2984550
10. Elkin, L.A., Kay, M., Higgins, J.J., Wobbrock, J.O.: An aligned rank transform procedure for multifactor contrast tests. In: The 34th Annual ACM Symposium on User Interface Software and Technology, UIST 2021, pp. 754–768. Association for Computing Machinery, New York (2021). https://doi.org/10.1145/3472749.3474784
11. Ernst, M.: Putting together the puzzle of multisensory perception. In: University of Glasgow: Seminar Series in Psychology (2006)
12. Etzi, R., Ferrise, F., Bordegoni, M., Zampini, M., Gallace, A.: The effect of visual and auditory information on the perception of pleasantness and roughness of virtual surfaces. Multisensory Res. **31**(6), 501–522 (2018)
13. Geldard, F.A., Sherrick, C.E.: The cutaneous "rabbit": a perceptual illusion. Science **178**(4057), 178–179 (1972)
14. Gongora, D., Peiris, R.L., Minamizawa, K.: Towards intermanual apparent motion of thermal pulses. In: Adjunct Publication of the 30th Annual ACM Symposium on User Interface Software and Technology, UIST 2017, pp. 143–145. Association for Computing Machinery, New York (2017). https://doi.org/10.1145/3131785.3131814
15. Gyeltshen, S.: High pass filter designation and it report (2012)
16. Heo, S., Lee, J., Wigdor, D.: Pseudobend: producing haptic illusions of stretching, bending, and twisting using grain vibrations. In: Proceedings of the 32nd Annual ACM Symposium on User Interface Software and Technology, UIST 2019, pp. 803–813. Association for Computing Machinery, New York (2019). https://doi.org/10.1145/3332165.3347941
17. Ishii, H., Lakatos, D., Bonanni, L., Labrune, J.B.: Radical atoms: beyond tangible bits, toward transformable materials. Interactions **19**(1), 38–51 (2012). https://doi.org/10.1145/2065327.2065337
18. Israr, A., Poupyrev, I.: Tactile Brush: Drawing on Skin with a Tactile Grid Display, pp. 2019–2028. Association for Computing Machinery, New York (2011). https://doi.org/10.1145/1978942.1979235
19. Kaaresoja, T., Brewster, S., Lantz, V.: Towards the temporally perfect virtual button: touch-feedback simultaneity and perceived quality in mobile touchscreen press interactions. ACM Trans. Appl. Percept. **11**(2) (2014). https://doi.org/10.1145/2611387

20. Katzakis, N., et al.: Stylo and handifact: modulating haptic perception through visualizations for posture training in augmented reality. In: Proceedings of the 5th Symposium on Spatial User Interaction, SUI 2017, pp. 58–67. Association for Computing Machinery, New York (2017). https://doi.org/10.1145/3131277.3132181
21. Kim, J., Oh, S., Park, C., Choi, S.: Body-Penetrating Tactile Phantom Sensations, pp. 1–13. Association for Computing Machinery, New York (2020). https://doi.org/10.1145/3313831.3376619
22. Kim, S., Lee, G.: Haptic feedback design for a virtual button along force-displacement curves. In: Proceedings of the 26th Annual ACM Symposium on User Interface Software and Technology, UIST 2013, pp. 91–96. Association for Computing Machinery, New York (2013). https://doi.org/10.1145/2501988.2502041
23. Kim, Y., Lee, J., Kim, G.J.: Extending "out of the body" tactile phantom sensations to 2D and applying it to mobile interaction. Personal Ubiquitous Comput. **19**(8), 1295–1311 (2015). https://doi.org/10.1007/s00779-015-0894-4
24. Lago, N.P., Kon, F.: The quest for low latency. In: ICMC (2004)
25. Lai, C.H., Niinimäki, M., Tahiroglu, K., Kildal, J., Ahmaniemi, T.: Perceived physicality in audio-enhanced force input. In: Proceedings of the 13th International Conference on Multimodal Interfaces, ICMI 2011, pp. 287–294. Association for Computing Machinery, New York (2011). https://doi.org/10.1145/2070481.2070533
26. Lee, J., Kim, Y., Jounghyun Kim, G.: Rich pinch: perception of object movement with tactile illusion. IEEE Trans. Haptics **9**(1), 80–89 (2016). https://doi.org/10.1109/TOH.2015.2475271
27. Lee, J., Kim, Y., Kim, G.: Funneling and Saltation Effects for Tactile Interaction with Virtual Objects, pp. 3141–3148. Association for Computing Machinery, New York (2012). https://doi.org/10.1145/2207676.2208729
28. Longo, R., Delaunay, T., Laux, D., El Mouridi, M., Arnould, O., Le Clezio, E.: Wood elastic characterization from a single sample by resonant ultrasound spectroscopy. Ultrasonics **52**(8), 971–974 (2012)
29. Nunez, C.M., Williams, S.R., Okamura, A.M., Culbertson, H.: Understanding continuous and pleasant linear sensations on the forearm from a sequential discrete lateral skin-slip haptic device. IEEE Trans. Haptics **12**(4), 414–427 (2019). https://doi.org/10.1109/TOH.2019.2941190
30. Patel, P., Ray, R.K., Manivannan, M.: Power law based "out of body" tactile funneling for mobile haptics. IEEE Trans. Haptics **12**(3), 307–318 (2019). https://doi.org/10.1109/TOH.2019.2933822
31. Peck, T.C., Gonzalez-Franco, M.: Avatar embodiment. A standardized questionnaire. Front. Virtual Reality **1**, 44 (2021)
32. Peng, W., Peiris, R.L., Minamizawa, K.: Exploring of simulating passing through feeling on the wrist: using thermal feedback. In: Adjunct Publication of the 30th Annual ACM Symposium on User Interface Software and Technology, UIST 2017, pp. 187–188. Association for Computing Machinery, New York (2017). https://doi.org/10.1145/3131785.3131819
33. Pinhanez, C.: The everywhere displays projector: a device to create ubiquitous graphical interfaces. In: Abowd, G.D., Brumitt, B., Shafer, S. (eds.) UbiComp 2001. LNCS, vol. 2201, pp. 315–331. Springer, Heidelberg (2001). https://doi.org/10.1007/3-540-45427-6_27
34. Pittera, D., Ablart, D., Obrist, M.: Creating an illusion of movement between the hands using mid-air touch. IEEE Trans. Haptics **12**(4), 615–623 (2019). https://doi.org/10.1109/TOH.2019.2897303

35. Pittera, D., Obrist, M., Israr, A.: Hand-to-hand: an intermanual illusion of movement. In: Proceedings of the 19th ACM International Conference on Multimodal Interaction, ICMI 2017, pp. 73–81. Association for Computing Machinery, New York (2017). https://doi.org/10.1145/3136755.3136777

36. Rossing, T.D.: Modal analysis. In: Rossing, T.D. (ed.) Springer Handbook of Acoustics, pp. 1165–1177. Springer, New York (2014). https://doi.org/10.1007/978-1-4939-0755-7_28

37. Schönauer, C., Mossel, A., Zaiti, I.-A., Vatavu, R.-D.: Touch, movement and vibration: user perception of vibrotactile feedback for touch and mid-air gestures. In: Abascal, J., Barbosa, S., Fetter, M., Gross, T., Palanque, P., Winckler, M. (eds.) INTERACT 2015. LNCS, vol. 9299, pp. 165–172. Springer, Cham (2015). https://doi.org/10.1007/978-3-319-22723-8_14

38. Seo, J., Choi, S.: Perceptual analysis of vibrotactile flows on a mobile device. IEEE Trans. Haptics 6(4), 522–527 (2013). https://doi.org/10.1109/TOH.2013.24

39. Silva, B., Costelha, H., Bento, L.C., Barata, M., Assuncao, P.A.A.: Subjective evaluation of haptic feedback technologies for interactive multimedia. In: IEEE EUROCON 2019-18th International Conference on Smart Technologies, pp. 1–6 (2019). https://doi.org/10.1109/EUROCON.2019.8861847

40. Strauss, A., Corbin, J.M.: Grounded Theory in Practice. Sage, Thousand Oaks (1997)

41. Turchet, L., Marchal, M., Lécuyer, A., Nordahl, R., Serafin, S.: Influence of auditory and visual feedback for perceiving walking over bumps and holes in desktop VR. In: Proceedings of the 17th ACM Symposium on Virtual Reality Software and Technology, VRST 2010, pp. 139–142. Association for Computing Machinery, New York (2010). https://doi.org/10.1145/1889863.1889893

42. Turchet, L., Serafin, S., Cesari, P.: Walking pace affected by interactive sounds simulating stepping on different terrains. ACM Trans. Appl. Percept. 10(4) (2013). https://doi.org/10.1145/2536764.2536770

43. Villanueva, L., Zampini, M.: Reciprocal interference between audition and touch in the perception of duration. Multisensory Res. 31(5), 351–371 (2018)

44. Weiser, M.: The computer for the 21st century. Sci. Am. 265(3), 94–105 (1991)

45. Weiser, M., Brown, J.S.: Designing calm technology. PowerGrid J. 1(1), 75–85 (1996)

46. Wi, D., Sodemann, A., Chicci, R.: Vibratory haptic feedback assistive device for visually-impaired drivers. In: 2017 IEEE SmartWorld, Ubiquitous Intelligence & Computing, Advanced & Trusted Computed, Scalable Computing & Communications, Cloud & Big Data Computing, Internet of People and Smart City Innovation (SmartWorld/SCALCOM/UIC/ATC/CBDCom/IOP/SCI), pp. 1–5. IEEE (2017)

47. Withana, A., Koyama, S., Saakes, D., Minamizawa, K., Inami, M., Nanayakkara, S.: Rippletouch: initial exploration of a wave resonant based full body haptic interface. In: Proceedings of the 6th Augmented Human International Conference, AH 2015, pp. 61–68. Association for Computing Machinery, New York (2015). https://doi.org/10.1145/2735711.2735790

48. Witmer, B.G., Singer, M.J.: Measuring presence in virtual environments: a presence questionnaire. Presence 7(3), 225–240 (1998)

49. Wobbrock, J.O., Findlater, L., Gergle, D., Higgins, J.J.: The aligned rank transform for nonparametric factorial analyses using only anova procedures. In: Proceedings of the SIGCHI Conference on Human Factors in Computing Systems, CHI 2011, pp. 143–146. Association for Computing Machinery, New York (2011). https://doi.org/10.1145/1978942.1978963

50. Wolf, K., Bäder, T.: Illusion of surface changes induced by tactile and visual touch feedback. In: Proceedings of the 33rd Annual ACM Conference Extended Abstracts on Human Factors in Computing Systems, CHI EA 2015, pp. 1355–1360. Association for Computing Machinery, New York (2015). https://doi.org/10.1145/2702613.2732703
51. Won, H.I., Altinsoy, M.E.: Effect of auditory feedback on tactile intensity perception in a touchscreen application. IEEE Trans. Haptics 13(2), 343–353 (2020). https://doi.org/10.1109/TOH.2019.2947553
52. Yamada, T., Shibata, F., Kimura, A.: Analysis of the R-V dynamics illusion behavior in terms of auditory stimulation. In: Proceedings of the 24th ACM Symposium on Virtual Reality Software and Technology, VRST 2018. Association for Computing Machinery, New York (2018). https://doi.org/10.1145/3281505.3281595
53. Yeh, C.H., et al.: Application of piezoelectric actuator to simplified haptic feedback system. Sens. Actuators, A 303, 111820 (2020)
54. Zhao, S., Israr, A., Fenner, M., Klatzky, R.L.: Intermanual apparent tactile motion and its extension to 3d interactions. IEEE Trans. Haptics 10(4), 555–566 (2017). https://doi.org/10.1109/TOH.2017.2678502

GuidingBand: A Precise Tactile Hand Guidance System to Aid Visual Perception

Atish Waghwase[✉] and Anirudha Joshi

IDC School of Design, IIT Bombay, Mumbai 400076, India
atish.w@iitb.ac.in
www.idc.iitb.ac.in

Abstract. Computerised guidance systems can help alleviate tedious everyday tasks such as identifying a desired object in a collection of similar objects. Such guidance systems can prove useful as microinteractions if they are made accessible as a consumer wearable that delivers tactile feedback. We designed a wrist-wearable tactile guidance system called GuidingBand that provides vibrational cues to help the user pick visual targets out of an array. We conducted two studies to evaluate it. The studies involve presenting visual targets to users on a screen and giving them visual search tasks. In study 1, we identified the error rate of our guidance system. We presented users ($N = 20$) with arrays of identical, square targets to pick from, progressively reduced the target sizes and evaluated error rates for each size. Notably, we observed a 4% error rate at a target size of 10 mm. In study 2, we compared the error rate of the guidance system with and without the help of human visual perception in a visual search task. We constructed a task that involved showing users an array of rectangles varying only in length and asked them to identify the correct target which was previously shown to them. Users ($N = 13$) had fewer errors when they tried to identify targets with tactile guidance alone, followed by guidance and perception combined and perception alone. It was surprising that instead of improving the precision of the users' performance, their visual perception in fact deteriorated it.

Keywords: Vibrotactile · Spatial Guidance · Precise · Hand-tracking · Wearable · Human-Computer Interaction

1 Introduction

Locating a specific object in a set of visually similar objects can quickly become time-consuming and tedious as the number of objects increases. Common scenarios include finding a book in a library, a medicine in a warehouse, a specific connection on a large control panel or a screw of a particular thread size in a hardware store. These tasks can require a person to find the target by carefully inspecting each item in the set in order to differentiate them using their visual perceptual abilities. For example, all editions of a magazine often look similar

© The Author(s), under exclusive license to Springer Nature Switzerland AG 2023
J. Abdelnour Nocera et al. (Eds.): INTERACT 2023, LNCS 14142, pp. 546–562, 2023.
https://doi.org/10.1007/978-3-031-42280-5_34

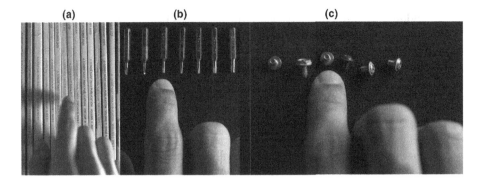

Fig. 1. Examples of scenarios that require careful visual inspection to differentiate between objects - (a) Picking a magazine out of a set of magazines on a shelf, (b) Picking the correct size of screwdriver bit, (c) Identifying a screw of particular thread size and length among a collection of screws.

on the spine and might require pulling out of the shelf to identify the specific edition the user is looking for. Similarly, small screws in hardware stores have minute differences in size which might be imperceptible without comparison or trial and error (Fig. 1).

With an increasing number of objects or with decreasing variation between the objects, it can get harder to rely on the precision of visual perception [9]. The visual search may become a tedious task of serially analysing each object in the set [18]. Such search and selection tasks can be alleviated by using the help of computerised guidance systems that can locate the target and the user (or the user's hand or finger) in space and communicate the relative location of the target to the user.

While there are many modes of communicating information to the user, tactile modes have the unique ability to be private and non-disruptive of the user's visual engagement with the environment. They are suitable for dexterous tasks if applied directly to the hand due to the natural stimulus-response behaviour of humans. The equipment necessary to deliver tactile stimuli can also be quite small, which makes it a viable choice for wearable devices such as smartwatches.

For any guidance system, there will be a limit to the tracking precision with which the user's finger can be guided till the target, beyond which the error rate should increase. However, once they know an approximate location, humans can use their perception to distinguish between potential discrete alternatives. With the help of this, the users may be able to achieve lower error rates even for targets smaller than the limit of the guidance system. Conversely, as previously mentioned, relying solely on visual perception can be overwhelming at larger set sizes. Our aim is to study this interplay of limiting cases of tactile guidance (machine) and visual perception (human).

In this paper, we present a low-cost system to locate the user's finger and guide the user to the target in a unidimensional array of objects. To evaluate the system, we conducted two studies. In study 1, we tried to evaluate the precision of our guidance system and identified error rates as a function of the width of the target. In study 2, we compared the error rates of the users in locating targets based on their perception alone, guidance alone, and a combination of perception and guidance. Through this paper, we make the following contributions:

- We present a novel tactile hand guidance system which makes use of relatively cheap hardware (especially as compared to literature)
- We present a study that estimates the error rate of this guidance system at various target sizes
- We present a study that estimates the effect of using visual perception to aid target selection on error rate while using the guidance system.

2 Background

Visual Perception: The limits of absolute judgement in visual perceptual tasks have been studied for a long time. Eriksen and Hake [4] have found that the capacity for visually judging the sizes of squares is 2.2 bits, or about 5 different sizes, under a wide range of experimental conditions. The well-known George Miller [14] compiled the findings of diverse experiments that point to the following conclusion - in unidimensionally varying stimuli, we have a capacity for absolute judgement to be 7 items (± 2) beyond which we cannot reliably tell the stimuli apart. It is concluded that it is the multidimensional variation in objects that lets us recognise and distinguish hundreds of objects. It has also been verified by Luck & Vogel [11] in visual tasks. In fact, they found the set size to be around 4 objects for orientation and colour. Therefore, visually inspecting unidimensionally varying objects should start getting erroneous around a set size of 7. Lehtinen et al. [9] have demonstrated that the performance of users using a vibrotactile spatial guidance device in a visual search task remained almost indifferent as the researchers increased the set size. However, they used an array of identical distractors with a unique, visually distinct target, whereas we want to study the performance in visual search tasks where each item is distinct and slightly varying, since we believe that is more representative of real-life scenarios.

Guidance Systems: A guidance system may have at least three components – it needs to locate the target, it needs to locate the user's finger with respect to the target, and it needs to communicate with the user to guide the user's finger to the target. Locating a target is beyond the scope of this paper. We assume that the spatial location of the target is already known to the system (either previously known, or detected through embedded sensors, or a user interface, for example). In this paper, we focus on locating the user's finger with respect to the target, and on communicating with the user to guide his/her finger to the target.

A hand-guidance system is not an entirely new concept. Günther et al. [6] developed a glove that provides vibrotactile stimulus to the hand to guide it in 3D space. Günther et al. evaluated the performance of the guidance system in terms of time taken to acquire a target, but they did not investigate its spatial precision. Similarly, Lehtinen et al. [9] used tactile cueing to guide users to a target in an array of distractors, but used time to evaluate the performance. We could not find any prior work that quantifies the precision of tactile guidance in terms of distance.

For the purpose of this paper, we define the precision of a guidance system as "the smallest distance that a guidance system can distinctly resolve". Correspondingly, we define the error rate of a guidance system as "the percentage of failed attempts compared to the total number of attempts of target selection".

Locating the User's Finger: In recent times, locating the user's finger has become very accessible even with low-cost devices. Meta Quest 2 [13], a budget VR headset, includes full hand tracking that uses purely optical tracking. Open source tools like OpenCV [15] use AI-based object recognition that can be processed in real-time for optical tracking of any given object. Hand tracking can be deployed using low-cost hardware such as an Android phone or a webcam using AI and machine learning through Google's open-source MediaPipe [5] machine learning pipeline. This enables tracking individual finger segments with reasonably low noise and usable coordinates in the camera's FOV.

Communicating with the User: There are various modes of communicating the direction of the target and the distance from the user's fingertip to the target: audio, visual, tactile, etc. In this paper, we focus on tactile communication. A common way to communicate tactile information is to use tactors to convey information through vibrations. For example, vibrational cues have been used to assist visually impaired persons in navigation [19]. Vibrations also have been used to provide directional cues to improve performance in physical activities like rowing [16], improving standing balance [2], gait rehabilitation [12], improving touch sensation in stroke victims [3], and improving the bowing technique in novice violinists [10]. More specifically, directional information cues have been shown to reliably be conveyed through tactile stimulation to the wrist [7]. Wrist-worn 2D vibrotactile guidance has been demonstrated to be useful in search and rescue scenarios in human-robot collaboration [1] and for speeding up visual search tasks [9].

To guide a user's finger to a target, two parameters need to be communicated to them - distance and direction. A variety of vibrotactile patterns can be used to communicate information to the user, often referred to as metaphors. Two such metaphors commonly used to communicate direction in current literature are Pull and Push metaphors. On a given tactile display, the Pull metaphor activates the tactor closest to the target and gives the sensation that the hand is being 'pulled' toward it, whereas the Push metaphor activates the tactor farthest from the target. Günther et al. [6] found that the Pull metaphor yields better performance and fewer errors than the Push metaphor.

In order to encode distance, Günther et al. [6] used frequency modulation. That means the frequency of tactile pulses increases as the target gets closer. Lehtinen et al. [9] used amplitude modulation to communicate distance such that the amplitude of vibration decreases as the target gets closer. Lee & Starner [8] state that humans are better at distinguishing pulsating vibration actuation than continuous.

3   Design of GuidingBand

We designed a one-dimensional finger guidance system called "GuidingBand". In this section, we first describe the wrist-worn hardware used in GuidingBand to provide tactile guidance feedback to the user. Next, we describe how Guiding-Band tracks the user's finger. Lastly, we describe the intended interaction that the user has with GuidingBand.

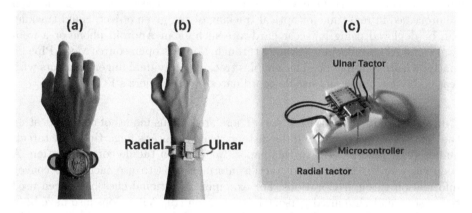

Fig. 2. (a) The intended design of our tactile system (b) The GuidingBand prototype with a Seeeduino Xiao microcontroller, two tactors and two rubber bands, worn on the wrist indicating radial and ulnar sides (c) The prototype by itself

Tactile Guidance Hardware. Most smartwatches and smart bands available in the market today come with one tactor, which can only deliver 1 bit of information at a time (either on or off). This one bit of information is quite useful to attract the attention of the user and is enough for notifications and alerts. However, even with amplitude or frequency modulation, it cannot convey directional information without using complicated codes. Directional feedback in a one-dimensional guidance system would need at least two bits of information at a time (for example, left-on/left-off, right-on/right-off) in order to intuitively convey direction. We designed GuidingBand to resemble a smartwatch (Fig. 2, (a)) with two tactors, one on either side of the wrist - the additional cost of which is 30 INR (0.37 USD at the time of writing) per tactor - that can communicate two bits of information simultaneously. For the scope of this study, we built the prototype to guide in only one dimension. In the future, we can develop the system further to guide in 2 or 3 dimensions. This can be achieved, for example, by adding more tactors or an interaction that makes the user rotate their wrist to switch the axis/plane of guidance.

Our prototype Fig. 2, (b) (c) consists of two wrist-mounted tactors - one on the radial side (i.e. towards the body) and the other on the ulnar side (i.e. away from the body) - and a Seeeduino Xiao microcontroller [21]. This microcontroller was chosen because of its small size (21 mm × 18 mm), which allows the prototype to have a smartwatch-like form factor. The tactors are flat 7 mm ERM coin motors operating between 1.2 V and 3.3 V. The three components are held together using two rubber bands that go around the wrist that allow for exact placement of the tactors on the radial and ulnar sides. Although our prototype was tethered to a laptop for communication and power, it can also be made wireless by adding a small battery and using a microcontroller capable of wireless communication like the ESP32-C3 variant of the Xiao [20] (which was unavailable at the time).

Positioning System. Hand tracking was done using a single overhead Logitech C270 webcam with Google's MediaPipe Hands tracking tool. The video feed (Fig. 3) was processed at 640 × 480 pixels at 30 fps while tracking the distal segment (fingertip) of the index finger, giving a maximum of 640 discrete possible targets along the x-axis. In our studies (described below) we used a 24-in. (61 cm) 1080p panel to display the targets. For example, in study 1, the targets were identical squares along the x-axis without any gap (Fig. 5). At the time of calibration, two dots were displayed on either side of the array. The software drew two movable calibration points on the video feed from the camera that were aligned with two dots on either side of the object array. The positioning system then used a mathematical model to take 'n' as an input and set the target on the nth square from the left.

Interaction. As mentioned earlier, Günther et al. [6] found that the Pull metaphor yields better performance and fewer errors than the Push metaphor, so we decided to incorporate the Pull metaphor to cue direction (which means the left tactor is active if the target is to the left, and the right tactor is active if the target is to the right). The use of two tactors allowed us to easily and intuitively give directional feedback to the users.

There are several ways to provide distance feedback to users. As mentioned, Lee & Starner [8] had found that humans are better at distinguishing pulsating vibrations than continuous vibrations. However, that was in the context of recognising discrete alerts with tactile displays. A hand guidance system such as ours requires users to continuously reposition their fingers while getting vibrotactile feedback from the tactors. In our early trials, we discovered that modulating the frequency of pulses to communicate distance information is inherently slow due to the delay between pulses. Hence to encode distance we decided to incorporate amplitude modulation. As shown in Fig. 4, in our design, the amplitude of vibration increases as the distance to the target increases, and the amplitude

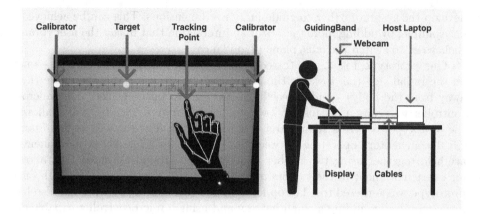

Fig. 3. (Left) The video feed from our hand tracking system (Right) The complete setup

decreases as the finger gets closer to the target (an 'elastic' pull metaphor). More specifically, the amplitude is the highest (operating at 3.3 V) at the calibration point farthest from the target and is the minimum (operating at 1.2 V) at the target. When the finger is exactly on the target point, both the tactors beep continuously (100 ms on and 100 ms off) to give 'confirmatory clicks' to the user.

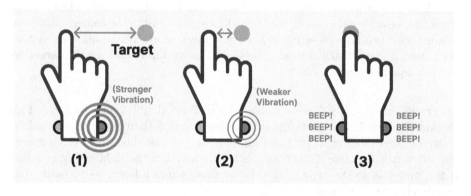

Fig. 4. The Pull metaphor with amplitude modulation and confirmatory clicks. In (1), when the finger is far from the target, the tactor in the direction of the target vibrates with higher amplitude. As the finger comes nearer the target (2), the amplitude decreases. When the finger is on the target (3), both tactors beep to give confirmatory clicks.

4   Evaluation

We conducted two studies to evaluate this tactile guidance system - one to measure the error rate over varying target sizes and another to evaluate its error rate compared to purely visual-perception-based target selection.

4.1   Study 1: Target Width v/s Error Rate

For any hand guidance system, guiding the user to larger targets is easier, but it gets increasingly difficult as the targets get smaller. The goal of this study was to evaluate the error rate of the tactile guidance system at different target widths. We presented the participants an array of numbered identical squares (Fig. 5), one of which was the target (unknown to the user).

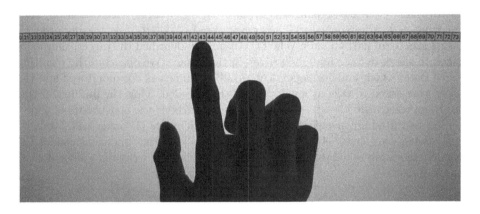

Fig. 5. The width of 6 mm targets compared to a human finger

We determined the sizes of squares by the harmonic progression $f(x) = cx/n$ where x is the side of the square and c is a constant. This gave us fewer large targets and many smaller targets, allowing us to determine the precision of the guidance system better. Our hand tracking system tracks the fingertip of the index finger, so we used 15 mm as the approximate width of the tip of a human index finger as the base value, with 1 term greater than and 3 terms smaller than 15 mm as the sizes for the target squares. That gave us $c = 3$ and 5 target sizes, with the series being 30 mm, 15 mm, 10 mm, 7.5 mm, and 6 mm. In each condition, the potential targets were arranged in a horizontal line covering almost the whole width of the screen (Fig. 5). Thus in the 6mm condition, the screen (width = approximately 520 mm) could display 80 squares. In the 30 mm condition, the same screen could display 16 squares. In real-life scenarios, the minimum size of 6mm corresponds to objects such as spines of magazines on a shelf, or a set of Allen keys, drill bits, small electronic components, etc. in a box. The maximum target size of 30 mm corresponds to university textbooks on a bookshelf, or nuts and bolts in an assembly line.

When the participant walked in, we first took informed consent. Next, to familiarise the participant with GuidingBand, we gave them a practice task, in which we presented them a target array and explained how to use the system. After that, we asked users to locate targets with the help of our guidance system, starting with 30 mm targets. The squares were numbered, and the participant was asked to call out the number of the square that they thought was the target after they had identified it. The participants were allowed to take as much time as they desired.

Thus, this was a within-subject study with 5 conditions of target sizes (30 mm, 15 mm, 10 mm, 7.5 mm, and 6 mm), which was our independent variable. The user was asked to identify a random target (unknown to the user at first) from an array of squares, with the help of GuidingBand (Fig. 5). There were 5 arrays, each with identical squares of the given size, numbered from 1 to n (where n is the maximum possible number of squares) in ascending order from left to right. Each participant was given 5 trials per target size condition, thus resulting in 25 trials per user. The arrays were presented in decreasing order of target size to all participants. When the user had identified the target, they were asked to speak out the number written in the square. We observed the resulting Error Rate, which was our dependent variable. Time was not monitored and the users were asked to take as much time as they needed. Thus the findings of this study represent the lowest error rates possible without the constraints of time.

We recruited a convenient sample of 20 participants (17 male and 3 female, one left-handed) aged between 20 to 32 years. To keep the conditions consistent, participants were asked to wear the device on their right wrist regardless of their handedness.

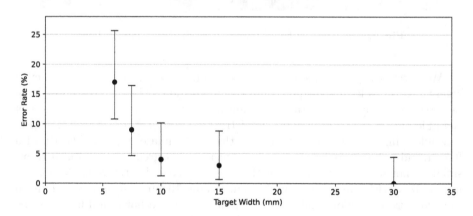

Fig. 6. Error rates and 95% confidence intervals with respect to the target widths. As expected, lower target widths had higher error rates.

Results. For each target width, we had (20 users × 5 attempts per user =) 100 attempts, each of which could either be successful or could fail. Thus, the error rate at a particular target width was calculated as (number of failures at that target width)/100. We calculated adjusted Wald confidence intervals for binomial proportions at each target width as shown in Fig. 6. We also identified how much the users were deviating from the intended target, and in which direction. Figure 6 and Table 1 summarise the result for each width. As expected, error rate increases with decreasing target size. At 30 mm target size, we recorded no errors in the 100 trials. Even at 10mm target size, the error rate was a reasonable 4%. However, error rate rose to 9% by 7.5mm, which might be reasonable depending on the use case. For the smallest targets that we used i.e. 6mm, the error rate was an unusable 17%.

We also recorded the deviations in case of errors. For example, if the target was square number 33, but the user said it was 34, this represented a deviation of 1, and in the right direction. All deviations were at the most one square. As we can see in Table 1, most deviations were on the right side. Whether this was a result of the right-handedness of the user, or whether there was a bias in the system is not clear, and will need systematic investigation in the future.

Table 1. Error rates, 95% confidence intervals for error rates and deviation from the target in the left and right directions from Study 1.

Width	Error Rate	CI (Lower)	CI (Upper)	Left Dev	Right Dev
6 mm	17%	10.80%	25.65%	1%	16%
7.5 mm	9%	4.62%	16.42%	2%	7%
10 mm	4%	1.24%	10.16%	0%	4%
15 mm	3%	0.65%	8.83%	1%	2%
30 mm	0%	0.00%	4.44%	0%	0%

4.2   Study 2: Perception vs Tactile Guidance

Consider a visual search task in which the user is looking for a specific object in a set of similar objects that are distinguishable from each other by a specific feature (e.g. a screw of a specific length in a box of screws of different lengths). Currently, humans perform such visual search tasks purely using their visual perception abilities. To locate the intended object, the user will need to compare each candidate object with the intended object by close inspection. The task is easy for a small set size. But as the set size increases, the search task becomes harder and more time-consuming. A hand guidance system such as the one presented in this paper can help people locate objects. However, a guidance system could be error-prone, as we saw in the last section. In spite of the errors, though, a hand guidance system could still be useful as it can narrow down the area of search. Humans need not rely completely on the guidance system alone, or visual perception alone, but can use them in combination.

The goal of this study was to investigate this interplay of limiting cases of tactile guidance and visual perception. In this study, our independent variable Mode had three conditions - perception alone, guidance alone and guidance and perception combined. Our hypothesis for study 2 is that 'guidance and perception combined' will be the most precise among the three modes, while perception alone will be the least precise (Fig. 7).

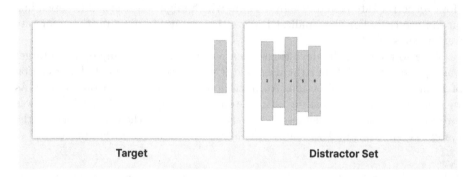

Target   **Distractor Set**

Fig. 7. In study 2, we first showed the participant a stimulus rectangle of 30 mm width and a certain length (left) and was asked to memorise the same. Then we showed the participant a distractor set of rectangles, all of the same width but different lengths (right). Only one rectangle in the distractor set matched the length of the stimulus. All rectangles were numbered. The user was asked to recognise the rectangle that matched the length of the stimulus.

In this study, the participants were shown a stimulus rectangle of a certain size and they were required to pick an identical rectangle from an array of rectangles of varying sizes. We first displayed a stimulus (a solid grey rectangle 30 mm wide and of a certain length) near the top-right side of the screen for 2 s. Next, we displayed a set of rectangles, all of the same width (30 mm) but different lengths (ranging from 65 mm to 255 mm with increments of 20 mm). Only one rectangle in the set had the same length as that of the stimulus. The rectangles were numbered in ascending order from left to right regardless of their length. The user was asked to recognise the number of the rectangle that matched the length of the stimulus. The distractor set was vertically centre-aligned and shown on the left side of the screen. This was done to prevent visual overlap between the stimulus and distractor set. The distractor set as a whole was also misaligned with the stimulus to prevent the user from using visual alignment cues. The distractor set size had n=9 levels, with the number of rectangles in the set in each level given by (n+1). The width of all rectangles in the stimulus and the distractor set was kept constant at 30 mm (the largest width used in study 1), as we did not want to bottleneck the performance of the guidance system by using small targets.

We told participants that each attempt would be timed. We did this to give a sense of urgency to the participants, thus simulating a realistic scenario of searching for something. The screen displayed the word 'Ready?' before starting each attempt. In the perception-alone condition and in the guidance and perception combined condition, the participants were shown the stimulus for 2 s, followed by a blank screen for 1 s, followed by the distractor set. For the guidance-alone condition, no stimulus was shown; there was a delay for 1 s after the word 'Ready?' followed by the distractor set. In all three conditions, the timer started when the distractor set was revealed and stopped when the participants announced the number corresponding to their selected rectangle.

Thus, this was a within-subject study with Set Size as the first independent variable with 9 conditions (2 to 10 rectangles) and Mode as the second independent variable with 3 conditions (perception alone, guidance alone and guidance and perception combined). The order of the three Mode conditions was randomised between subjects. Originally, we wanted to analyse both error rate and time taken as dependent variables. However, during analysis, we discovered that our manual time recording method had errors. Hence we choose to not report the time-related data in this paper.

We conducted Study 2 with 13 participants out of the 20 participants of Study 1 (10 male and 3 female, aged 20 to 32). Study 2 was conducted immediately after Study 1, so participants were already well familiar with the tactile guidance system.

Results. We had 13 participants × 9 sets per condition × 3 modes, leading to 351 trials. Table 2 and Fig. 8 summarise our findings from Study 2. As expected, the perception alone condition had highest error rates (38.46%, CI from 29.64% to 47.27%). Somewhat surprisingly, the guidance alone condition had the lower error rates (1.68%, CI 0.00% to 3.96%), even compared to the guidance and perception combined condition (5.04%, CI from 1.11% to 8.97%). Contrary to our expectations, the visual perception of users seems to worsen the precision of the guidance system instead of improving it. We must mention that since the sample completion rates in our conditions are greater than 90%, we used the Laplace method to report error rates in the guidance alone condition and in the combined condition, as recommended by Sauro and Lewis [17]. In this method, we add one success and one failure while reporting the error rate percentages.

We performed a Chi-square test to determine whether the proportion of errors was significantly different between the conditions. The test revealed $\chi^2(2, N=351) = 81.487$, p < 0.00001, indicating that error rate differs by mode of guidance. Pairwise comparisons showed that only the perception alone condition differed from the other two significantly (ps < 0.00005). Guidance alone and the combined conditions were not significantly different from each other.

Figure 8 also shows how error rates changed for set sizes. To find the effect of set size, we carried out separate simple linear regressions for each mode using set size as our independent variable and error rate as the dependent variable. The error rates for guidance alone and combined condition

Table 2. Error rates and 95% confidence intervals for error rates from Study 2. Values of Combined and Guidance Alone were calculated using the Laplace method [17] and are marked using *

Mode	Failures	Successes	Error Rate	CI (Lower)	CI (Upper)
Guidance Alone	1	116	1.68%*	0.00%*	3.96%*
Combined	5	112	5.04%*	1.11%*	8.97%*
Perception Alone	45	72	38.46%	29.64%	47.27%

for each distractor set were adjusted using the Laplace method. None of the regressions returned significant models. We found that guidance alone (F = 0.1338, p = 0.7254), combined (F = 1.16, p = 0.3173) and perception alone (F = 0.3717, p = 0.5614), all seem to be unaffected by set size.

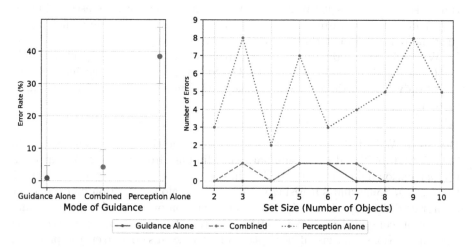

Fig. 8. (Left) Error rates of guidance modes for each set size (Right) Overall error Rates of each mode of guidance. Lower the error rate, higher the precision.

5   Discussion and Future Work

We developed a hand guidance system called GuidingBand that can guide the user's hand to an intended target. We conducted two studies to assess the precision of GuidingBand. While our studies gave several useful results, since these were our first studies with this system, they were also somewhat exploratory and threw up several questions that can only be answered through additional research.

From the first study, we report the error rates of GuidingBand for various target widths. We found zero errors at a target width of 30 mm, which suggests that this apparatus is fit for implementation in cases where the spacing between the centre points of objects is greater than 30 mm. This can be useful for distinguishing between medicines in a warehouse, switches on a wall switchboard, or thicker books in a library. Even at 10mm target width, we recorded an acceptable 4% error rate, which implies this system can distinguish between smaller connections or switches on a control panel or medicines in a warehouse or shelf or switches on a switchboard. However, it might be impractical for objects smaller than 7.5mm such as magazines on a shelf or soldering points on a circuit board unless additional error correction mechanisms are available.

Notably, when the users were off-target, the deviation from the target was never more than one square. Surprisingly, a large majority of the deviations were towards the right direction. It is not clear if this is a systematic bias in our implementation, or if it was related to the use of the right hand of the participant as a control variable, and needs to be systematically investigated in future research.

In our second study, we evaluated the error rates while using visual perception abilities to locate known targets in various set sizes, with and without the GuidingBand. We had initially hypothesised that using visual perception combined with tactile guidance by GuidingBand would have the least error rate because users would get a double advantage of guidance and perception. However, Study 2 results showed that the guidance alone condition was more precise with only 1 error out of 117 compared to 5 errors in the combined condition. While the differences were not significant, this finding is still unexpected. Even if the system guides the human hand to the appropriate target, the visual perception of the user makes them choose another target. This finding needs to be reproduced in future research and investigated systematically.

We did not observe any effect of set size on error rates in any of the modes. This may well have been the case because, perhaps, our range of set sizes (2 to 10) was too small, and within the range of capacity of human absolute judgement of 7 items (± 2). It may be possible to detect such an effect at larger set sizes (like 50, 100 or 500), and needs to be investigated in future work. We also observed that the error rates did not vary uniformly with set size, and had large random spikes (Fig. 8). It could well be the case that some specific arrangements of distractors were more visually confusing than others, and the spikes could be eliminated by randomising the choices and arrangements of distractors across participants in future studies. It would be interesting to also see the effect of targets with widths smaller than 30 mm for Study 2, to estimate the effect of target size on error rate across different set sizes.

The error rate is dependent on the accuracy of the hand-tracking system. Since our system was not tracking the targets themselves - but was using a mathematical model to estimate the location of the target, and we were using a relatively lower-resolution webcam, there were rounding errors in our tracking abilities. It may be possible to improve the precision of the estimated location of the target by using higher resolution cameras, better calibration and/or better tracking of the targets. Since we could not reliably measure time in this study, we can gain deeper insights by studying the time taken to find the target in future studies. Also, the guidance target was a point and did not cover the entire visual area of the target. That means that even if the finger was visually inside the target, the user needed to move their finger to the exact centre of the target to trigger the confirmatory clicks. Giving confirmatory clicks in a larger area of the target could improve the user's performance, however, using the entire area of the target could result in confusion with the neighbouring targets at the edges. Therefore, the optimal area for confirmatory clicks may be calculated considering the target size and finger width. Lastly, even though the GuidingBand is currently limited to guiding along one axis at a time, an option to change the axes could be added in future.

Based on these results, we believe that GuidingBand demonstrates the precision and potential of tactile guidance systems for real-world scenarios. Apart from aiding the visual perception of sighted users, it could prove useful to users with low vision by narrowing their area of search. It can also prove useful as a guidance system in scenarios where the target is obscured from the user. Its non-intrusive nature and discreet form factor make it feasible to implement along with other guidance methods. It can provide confirmatory feedback to visual guidance to improve the user experience.

6   Conclusion

We demonstrated that even a low-cost positioning and tactile communication system can guide the user's hand to a target with reasonable precision. We intentionally created a prototype with a smartwatch-like form factor to validate the usefulness of the tactile guidance interactions for wrist wearable devices. After comparing the error rate with the size of the targets, we can conclude that tactile communication is a precise means of guidance for objects as small as the width of a human finger. We found that visual perception was more error-prone in identifying targets. Contrary to our initial hypothesis, using visual perception in combination with guidance did not improve the precision, but in fact deteriorated it (though not significantly). Our study informs the design decisions in creating interactions for wearable devices in hand guidance systems, and we can conclude that our work demonstrates a feasible way to add tactile guidance to them.

References

1. Aggravi, M., Salvietti, G., Prattichizzo, D.: Haptic wrist guidance using vibrations for human-robot teams. In: 2016 25th IEEE International Symposium on Robot and Human Interactive Communication (RO-MAN). IEEE (2016). http://dx.doi.org/10.1109/roman.2016.7745098
2. Ballardini, G., Florio, V., Canessa, A., Carlini, G., Morasso, P., Casadio, M.: Vibrotactile feedback for improving standing balance. Front. Bioeng. Biotechnol. **8**, 94 (2020). https://doi.org/10.3389/fbioe.2020.00094

3. Enders, L.R., Hur, P., Johnson, M.J., Seo, N.: Remote vibrotactile noise improves light touch sensation in stroke survivors' fingertips via stochastic resonance. J. Neuroeng. Rehabil. 10(1), 105 (2013). https://doi.org/10.1186/1743-0003-10-105
4. Eriksen, C.W., Hake, H.W.: Absolute judgments as a function of stimulus range and number of stimulus and response categories. J. Exp. Psychol. 49(5), 323 (1955)
5. Google: Mediapipe hands. https://google.github.io/mediapipe/solutions/hands.html
6. Günther, S., Müller, F., Funk, M., Kirchner, J., Dezfuli, N., Mühlhäuser, M.: Tactileglove. In: Proceedings of the 11th PErvasive Technologies Related to Assistive Environments Conference. ACM, New York (2018). http://dx.doi.org/10.1145/3197768.3197785
7. Jin, Y.S., Chun, H.Y., Kim, E.T., Kang, S.: VT-ware: a wearable tactile device for upper extremity motion guidance. In: The 23rd IEEE International Symposium on Robot and Human Interactive Communication. IEEE (2014). http://dx.doi.org/10.1109/roman.2014.6926275
8. Lee, S.C., Starner, T.: Buzzwear: alert perception in wearable tactile displays on the wrist. In: Proceedings of the SIGCHI Conference on Human Factors in Computing Systems, CHI 2010, , pp. 433–442. Association for Computing Machinery, New York (2010). https://doi.org/10.1145/1753326.1753392
9. Lehtinen, V., Oulasvirta, A., Salovaara, A., Nurmi, P.: Dynamic tactile guidance for visual search tasks. In: Proceedings of the 25th Annual ACM Symposium on User Interface Software and Technology - UIST 2012. ACM Press, New York (2012). http://dx.doi.org/10.1145/2380116.2380173
10. van der Linden, J.: Good vibrations: guiding body movements with vibrotactile feedback (2009). http://oro.open.ac.uk/19251/
11. Luck, S.J., Vogel, E.K.: The capacity of visual working memory for features and conjunctions. Nature 390(6657), 279–281 (1997). https://doi.org/10.1038/36846
12. Ma, C.Z.H., Zheng, Y.P., Lee, W.C.C.: Changes in gait and plantar foot loading upon using vibrotactile wearable biofeedback system in patients with stroke. Top. Stroke Rehabil. 25(1), 20–27 (2017). https://doi.org/10.1080/10749357.2017.1380339
13. Meta: Getting started with hand tracking on meta quest headsets (2022). http://www.meta.com/help/quest/articles/headsets-and-accessories/controllers-and-hand-tracking/hand-tracking-quest-2/
14. Miller, G.A.: The Magical Number Seven, Plus-or-Minus Two or Some Limits on Our Capacity for Processing Information, pp. 175–202. University of California Press (1966). http://dx.doi.org/10.1525/9780520318267-011
15. OpenCV: Opencv modules. https://docs.opencv.org/4.x/index.html
16. Ruffaldi, E., Filippeschi, A., Frisoli, A., Sandoval, O., Avizzano, C.A., Bergamasco, M.: Vibrotactile perception assessment for a rowing training system. In: World Haptics 2009 - Third Joint EuroHaptics Conference and Symposium on Haptic Interfaces for Virtual Environment and Teleoperator Systems. IEEE (2009). http://dx.doi.org/10.1109/whc.2009.4810849
17. Sauro, J., Lewis, J.R.: How precise are our estimates? Confidence intervals. In: Sauro, J., Lewis, J.R. (eds.) Quantifying the User Experience, 2nd edin, pp. 19–38. Morgan Kaufmann, Boston (2016). https://doi.org/10.1016/B978-0-12-802308-2.00003-5. https://www.sciencedirect.com/science/article/pii/B9780128023082000035
18. Wolfe, J.M., Võ, M.L.H., Evans, K.K., Greene, M.R.: Visual search in scenes involves selective and nonselective pathways. Trends Cogn. Sci. 15(2), 77–84 (2011). https://doi.org/10.1016/j.tics.2010.12.001. Feb

19. Yelamarthi, K., DeJong, B.P., Laubhan, K.: A kinect based vibrotactile feedback system to assist the visually impaired. In: 2014 IEEE 57th International Midwest Symposium on Circuits and Systems (MWSCAS). IEEE (2014). http://dx.doi.org/10.1109/mwscas.2014.6908495
20. Zuo, B.: Getting started with seeed studio XIAO ESP32C3. https://wiki.seeedstudio.com/XIAO_ESP32C3_Getting_Started/
21. Zuo, B.: Getting started with seeed studio XIAO SAMD21. https://wiki.seeedstudio.com/Seeeduino-XIAO/

Mid-air Haptic Cursor for Physical Objects

Miroslav Macík[1](✉)[iD] and Meinhardt Branig[2][iD]

[1] FEE, Czech Technical University in Prague, Prague, Czech Republic
macikmir@fel.cvut.cz
[2] TU Dresden, Dresden, Germany
meinhardt.branig@tu-dresden.de

Abstract. We investigate whether mid-air tactile stimuli generated using ultrasonic arrays can be used as a haptic cursor for physical objects. We combined an ultrasonic array and an interactive haptic map into one setup. Evaluation with 15 participants showed that the method is efficient for guiding user hands to physical objects – miniatures of room equipment. The average error rate was 14.4 %, and the best participant achieved a 5.1 % error rate. Our in-depth analysis provided insights into issues of the method, like signal reflections and user-induced interference of problems with distinguishing physical objects that are too close.

Keywords: Ultrasonic stimulation · haptic maps · haptic guidance

1 Introduction

Ultrasonic mid-air tactile stimulation recently attracted the attention of researchers as it can provide distinctive haptic feedback in a precisely specified location in the three-dimensional (3D) space.

Previous research showed that interactive haptic maps efficiently create mental maps for people with visual impairment (VI) [3,6]. Low-abstraction haptic maps comprising miniatures of real-world objects are usable even for older adults with VI [11]. Guiding users toward a specific location in the map space requires complex interaction methods such as hand tracking and voice output. Some methods even require special gloves that can interfere with touch sensitivity. Especially for older adults with VI, these methods can be inefficient and frustrate some users.

In this paper, we focus on the research question of whether ultrasonic mid-air stimulation (haptic cursor) in combination with a map comprising physical objects – miniatures of room equipment – can guide the user's attention toward particular objects. Furthermore, we want to measure the objective (time to react, accuracy) and subjective (comfort, ease of use) properties of the proposed method.

2 Related Work

Ultrasonic tactile stimulation has been investigated for a long time, e.g., Dalecki et al. [4] investigated the force of acoustic radiation to determine the threshold

J. Abdelnour Nocera et al. (Eds.): INTERACT 2023, LNCS 14142, pp. 563–572, 2023.
https://doi.org/10.1007/978-3-031-42280-5_35

for tactile perception in a human finger and the upper forearm. They found that the maximum tactile sensitivity of the fingers occurs at 200 Hz. Further development showed that mid-air tactile stimuli could be actuated in a 3D position by ultrasonic tactile stimulation based on phase-arrayed ultrasound speakers [7,10]. These devices can generate non-contact mid-air ultrasound tactile stimuli that can be sensed by various parts of human skin or even lips; however, providing stimuli to palms and fingers is the most common approach. To our knowledge, no method focused on marking a specific location in 3D space by localized tactile stimuli in combination with physical objects.

Marzo et al. in [12] present an open-source system for mid-air ultrasound interaction based on Arduino Mega. In [16], Suzuki et al. presented a scalable mid-air ultrasound haptic display. Their solution allows connecting multiple modules (similar to the module depicted in Fig. 1 via Ethernet. It allows individual control of the phase and amplitude of each of the connected transducers. The authors achieved a synchronization accuracy of $0.1\mu s$, and the phase and amplitude can be specified using the 8 bits resolution. This allows for covering larger portions of 3D space.

Hajas et al. [5] investigated the perception of 2D shapes rendered mid-air using ultrasonic arrays. They conducted two experiments to measure accuracy and confidence. The authors evaluated two methods for displaying 2D geometric shapes in mid-air – static and dynamic. The static method relies on the presentation of a full outline in mid-air, while the dynamic method relies on a haptic pointer (focal point) moving along the perimeter of the shapes. The results show that the participants identified dynamic shapes more accurately and with greater confidence. Moreover, the authors suggest that a short pause in the movement of the haptic pointer in corners of polygons can drastically improve shape recognition accuracy. Alakhawand et al. [1] propose a method to test mid-air haptics with a biomimetic tactile sensor. Their approach allows for producing detailed visitations of mid-air sensations in 2D and 3D space.

Voudouris et al. [18] state that the perception of tactile stimuli presented on a moving hand is systematically suppressed, which could be attributed to the limited capacity of the brain to process task-irrelevant sensory information. The authors investigated whether humans can enhance relevant tactile signals in parallel movement when performing a goal-directed reach movement. The experiments carried out suggest that the participants were able to flexibly modulate tactile sensitivity by suppressing movement-irrelevant signals and enhancing movement-relevant signals in parallel when performing target-reaching tasks. Bensmaia et al. [2] investigate the effects of extended suprathreshold vibratory stimulation on the sensitivity of three types of neural afferents (slowly adapting type 1, rapidly adapting, and Pacinian). The results indicate that prolonged suprathreshold stimulation can result in substantial desensitization of all types of neural afferents. Juravle and Spence [9] investigated sensory suppression in complex motor tasks such as juggling. The experiment required participants to detect gaps in the continuous signal provided by different modalities (haptic, auditory). The authors stated that the participants were significantly

Fig. 1. Interactive tactile map integrated Ultrahaptics® mid-air ultrasonic array (left), Experiment setup (right).

less sensitive to detecting a gap in tactile stimulation while juggling. The results demonstrate movement-related tactile sensory suppression related to the decision component in tactile suppression.

Rakkolainen and Raisamo [14] surveyed possible advantages, problems, and applications of mid-air ultrasonic haptic feedback. They state that most methods use frequencies of 200 Hz to trigger Lamellar corpuscles that are dense in the palm and are associated with sensing vibrations and pressure. However, other mechanoreceptors can be used, such as Meissner corpuscles on the face or Merkel cell disks, and Ruffini corpuscles on the human upper body. In [8], Jingu et al. proposed a tactile notification system called *LipNotif*. It provides mid-air ultrasound tactile notifications that can be sensed using lips.

In [13], Paneva et al. investigated the possibilities of using mid-air haptics for conveying Braille. The researchers tested three tactile stimulation methods: aligned temporally (constant), not aligned temporally (point-by-point), and combination (row-by-row). They reached the highest average accuracy of 88 % using the point-by-point method. Suzuki et al. in [15] investigate whether human subjects can move a hand along a path produced by ultrasound without visual information. The path is presented by switching ultrasound focal points in a way the users perceive it as a line. Users can move their hand to the target position by tracing this line. The experiment showed that the participants were able to trace the trajectory of a curved line with an average deviation of less than 40 mm.

The current research showed that ultrasonic tactile stimulation could provide salient sensations in specific locations in 3D space. However, an application as a haptic cursor for physical objects would be a novel application.

3   Interactive Modular Tactile Map with Mid-Air Haptics

The design of an interactive modular haptic map of rooms and related interaction methods is primarily focused on older adults with vision impairments. In detail, the original design was described in [11]. The experiments showed that the participants used audio labels to identify objects on the map and a potential need for guidance toward particular objects in more complex interaction scenarios. This paper focuses on an interaction method that uses mid-air tactile stimulation as a haptic cursor for passive physical objects.

We follow the *come as you are* design constraint [17], so the users are not required to use any specific equipment attached to their body to use the method. Figure 1 shows the integration of the Ultrahaptics Stratos Explore® ultrasonic array with our interactive haptic map. Unlike typical setups, the ultrasonic array was mounted perpendicularly to the haptic map. Therefore, the mid-air tactile sensations are detectable primarily by the fingers rather than by the palm surface.

Our setup involved seven physical objects – miniatures of room equipment. The tactile sensations (haptic cursors) associated with each of the objects were prepared in advance. For all the haptic cursors, the focal point generated by the ultrasonic array created a virtual square with a leg of $30mm$. The only difference was the x, y offset and height of the haptic cursors that were set experimentally to appear directly above objects on the haptic map.

4   Experiment

Participants. We recruited 15 participants (P1-P15, five female, age $MEAN = 28.7$, $SD = 6.5$, $MIN = 21$, $MAX = 41$). All participants, except one, were right-handed. One participant reported a scar on the left thumb that could influence sensitivity in this area. One participant is challenged with color blindness and has bad vision in his left eye (he uses only his right eye).

Procedure. After a short ice-breaking session, participants received a consent form related to data collection, processing, and anonymization, followed by a brief introduction to the experiment. The setup of the experiment is depicted in Fig. 1. Each participant was instructed that the experiment involved physical objects and mid-air sensations (haptic cursor) that they would feel through the skin of their hands/fingers as a little vibration. The haptic cursors will be placed above one of the physical objects. Their task is to locate the object where the haptic cursor is most noticeable and press it toward the underlying board. Then the haptic cursor will move above another object.

The total number of unique physical objects marked by a mid-air haptic cursor was seven. The experiment consisted of two phases – learning and measurement. In the learning phase, participants were exposed to 49 different locations of the haptic cursor and received confirmation whether they selected the correct object. In the measurement phase, there were 98 attempts. To mitigate the

Table 1. Measurement phase - confusion matrix [%]

	0 (t.)	1 (ch.)	2 (a.)	3 (d.)	4 (w.)	5 (b.)	6 (t).
0 (table)	95.7	14.8	1.0	2.4	0.5	1.4	0.0
1 (chair)	3.3	84.3	0.5	0.5	1.4	6.2	0.5
2 (armchair)	0.0	0.0	87.6	5.2	0.5	2.4	9.0
3 (drawer)	0.0	0.0	7.6	87.6	2.4	0.5	5.2
4 (wardrobe)	0.5	0.0	1.4	3.3	84.3	0.5	13.3
5 (bed)	0.0	1.0	0.0	0.0	1.4	89.0	1.4
6 (trashbin)	0.5	0.0	1.9	1.0	9.5	0.0	70.5

learning effect, the order of objects/haptic cursors was determined using Latin squares (7×7) iterated in a zig-zag manner to counterbalance the learning effect. The Latin squares were randomly generated for each phase of the experiment. For the measurement phase, the same Latin square was iterated twice.

Interaction with a haptic cursor is detectable by touch is also audible. As a countermeasure, the participants received headphones. Using the headphones, white noise was played and participants received feedback when they pressed an object. In the learning phase, the feedback was *"Correct"* or *"Not correct"*, followed by the statement *"Find the next item, please."*

Participants were asked to find and press the object marked by the haptic cursor. We also told them: *"Be as fast and as precise as possible; precision is the priority."* Participants received no specific guidance on the strategy they should use for their exploration process.

Measures. In each session, we recorded information about which object had been marked by a haptic cursor and which was selected by the participant. We also measured the time between object selections. This allowed us to construct confusion matrices and compute speed-related and error-rate-related statistics. During each session, we collected observational data on participant behavior and strategy. After the measurement session, we collected data about the self-reported subjective experience during the experiment and subjective assessment on a five-level Likert scale (haptic cursors were comfortable, and the experience during interaction on the level of individual objects – easily noticeable, strong, distinguishable with others).

Results. All participants were able to complete both test phases (learning and measurement). Table 1 shows the confusion matrix of the measurement phase. The average false negative rate (FNR) was 23.0 % ($SD = 7.2$ %) for the learning phase, dropping to 14.4 % ($SD = 7.7$ %) in the measurement phase. As shown in Table 2, the highest FNR of 29.5 % ($SD = 18.5$ %) was recorded for the trash bin object (frequently confused with the nearby wardrobe). The lowest FNR of 4.3 % ($SD = 8.0$ %) was achieved for the table object in the measurement phase.

Table 2. Times and error rates per class

Class	Learning phase			Measurement phase		
	Avg. time [s]	FNR [%]	FPR [%]	Avg. time [s]	FNR [%]	FPR [%]
0 (table)	6.61	18.1	34.3	6.14	4.3	20.0
1 (chair)	7.25	22.9	30.5	6.16	15.7	12.4
2 (armchair)	7.17	17.1	29.5	5.71	12.4	17.1
3 (drawer)	6.20	30.5	7.6	5.61	12.4	15.7
4 (wardrobe)	6.98	17.1	34.3	6.14	15.7	19.0
5 (bed)	7.19	20.0	9.5	5.41	11.0	3.8
6 (trashbin)	7.36	35.2	15.2	5.62	29.5	12.9
AVERAGE	6.97	23.0	23.0	5.83	14.4	14.4
SD	0.42	7.2	11.8	0.31	7.7	5.5

As shown in Table 2, the average time between object confirmation was $6.97\,s, SD = 0.42$ for the learning phase and $5.83\,s, SD = 0.31$ in the measurement phase.

We performed a one-way single-factor ANOVA for attempt groups and normalized reaction times ($t_{norm} = t_{abs}/t_{avg}$), where t_{abs} is the actual value in seconds and t_{avg} is the average time of a participant in a particular experiment phase). It revealed that there was a statistically significant difference in t_{norm} between at least two groups ($F(6,98) = 6.53, p < 0.001$) in the learning phase. Tukey's post-hoc test for multiple comparisons revealed that the mean value of normalized time was significantly different between the attempt group 1–7 ($M = 1.29, SD = 1.12$) and the groups 22–28 ($M = 0.95, SD = 0.10, q = 5.86$), 29–35 ($M = 0.93, SD = 0.2, q = 6.19$), 36–42 ($M = 0.92, SD = 0.15, q = 6.34$), 43–49 ($M = 0.82, SD = 0.20, q = 7.97$)). A one-way ANOVA revealed that there were no statistically significant differences between the attempt groups in t_{norm} in the measurement phase ($F(13,196) = 0.78, p = 0.67$) and between the attempt groups and the number of errors in both the learning phase ($F(6,98) = 0.82, p = 0.54$) and the measurement phase ($F(13,196) = 0.51, p = 0.91$)).

A one-way ANOVA for object types and t_{norm} revealed that there was no statistically significant difference between object types in the learning phase ($F(6,98) = 1.78, p = 0.11$)) and the measurement phase ($F(6,98) = 2.14, p = 0.056$)). It revealed that there was not a statistically significant difference between object types and the number of errors in the learning phase ($F(6,98) = 0.82, p = 0.055$)), but revealed a statistically significant difference in the measurement phase ($F(6,98) = 3.87, p = 0.002$)). Tukey's post-hoc test for multiple comparisons revealed that the mean value of normalized time was significantly different between the attempt group ($p = 0.05, q_{crit} = 4.31$): table ($M = 0.60, SD = 1.12$) and chair ($M = 2.20, SD = 2.18$), ($q = 4.34$), table ($M = 0.60, SD = 1.12$) and wardrobe ($M = 2.20, SD = 2.18$), ($q = 4.34$), table ($M = 0.60, SD = 1.12$) and trash bin ($M = 4.13, SD = 2.59$),

$(q = 9.58)$, chair $(M = 2.20, SD = 2.18)$ and trash bin $(M = 4.13, SD = 2.59)$, $(q = 5.12)$, armchair $(M = 1.73, SD = 2.15)$ and trash bin $(M = 4.13, SD = 2.59)$, $(q = 6.51)$, drawer $(M = 1.73, SD = 2.34)$ and trash bin $(M = 4.13, SD = 2.59)$, $(q = 6.51)$, and bed $(M = 1.53, SD = 1.96)$ and trash bin $(M = 4.13, SD = 2.59)$, $(q = 7.05)$.

Figure 2 shows the results of the subjective assessment of the haptic cursor. The majority of 87 % participants agreed that the interaction using the mid-air haptic cursor was comfortable. The following questions focused on individual objects: the bed was assessed as the most noticeable object, the haptic cursor associated with the table as the strongest, and the bed with drawer was assessed as the most easily distinguishable from other objects. On the contrary, the trash can was assessed as the least noticeable, strong, and distinguishable object.

Observations. Among the study group, we observed that 8 individuals opted to use both hands for exploration, with *two* of these participants demonstrating a noticeable preference for their dominant hand. Conversely, the remaining 7 participants engaged in the task by exclusively using their dominant hand.

During the study, 7 participants reported experiencing symptoms of fatigue, ranging from tingling sensations in their fingers to numbness after a certain period of time. These sensations were perceived with varying intensity among the individuals. In some cases, the impact of fatigue was minimal, allowing participants to continue with little disruption. In more severe cases, participants who had previously used both hands used only one hand as they progressed, switching hands, rubbing their fingers or taking short breaks to relieve discomfort. The other 8 participants did not experience such symptoms.

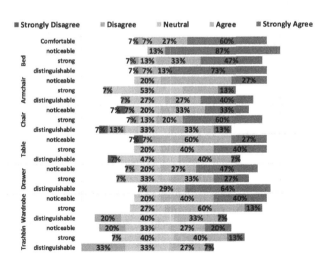

Fig. 2. Subjective assessment of haptic cursor sensations related to objects on the Likert scale.

Most of the participants (9) described the sensation of a haptic cursor as a stream of air. *Two* even described it as having different temperatures. All participants indicated that they experienced additional/false haptic cursors during the task, which increased the overall difficulty. However, they adapted their strategy by selecting the object where the haptic cursor was the strongest. These additional points perceived as haptic cursors can be explained by secondary focal points of the ultrasonic array.

5   Discussion

The experiment positively answered our research question – a combination of mid-air ultrasonic haptics and the physical environment is plausible. After a short learning period, participants were able to distinguish which object was marked by a haptic cursor with high accuracy. However, the combination of ultrasonic mid-air haptics and physical map, as depicted in Fig. 1, also involves specific issues. Most importantly, the haptic cursor is still present, but significantly less strong and noticeable for objects shielded from the ultrasonic array (trash bin) by other objects (wardrobe). We also observed that shielding the intended haptic cursor by participants' hand(s) is possible, most often for those who chose the bi-manual exploration strategy.

6   Conclusion and Future Work

The fusion of a map comprising physical objects and mid-air haptics in a role of haptic cursor is an efficient method for guidance toward the objects. Users will more easily match their hand's 3D position with small-scale 3D objects positioned on a flat (2D) surface. An experiment with 15 participants showed that the average FNR was 14.4 %, $SD = 7.7$ %. Considering that the experiment purposely involved edge cases of objects shielded by other objects, the accuracy could be considerably better for well-tuned setups.

Although the proposed method requires a non-standard orientation of the ultrasonic array, the results show that it is still very efficient in conveying information. This opens new possibilities for combining ultrasonic mid-air haptics with physical objects. In this paper, we focus on a low-abstraction (skeuomorphic) interactive haptic map. Still, any use case involving a haptic cursor marking a specific area in the 3D space could be considered. The community can use it to guide users towards a particular spot or, in contrast, to convey information about places where the presence of fingers is not wanted. In this way, it could be used to improve learning to play musical instruments like the piano.

A more detailed investigation of other objectives, such as response times and subjective outcomes, is out of the scope of this format. Evaluation with older adults with vision impairments is the subject of imminent future work. We also plan to evaluate the method in other use cases involving different types of topographical maps. A comparative study focused on other guidance methods involving haptic interaction will provide more insights into the application of these methods for particular use cases.

Acknowledgments. This research has been supported by research the project RCI (reg. no. CZ.02.1.01/0.0/0.0/16_019/0000765) supported by EU.

References

1. Alakhawand, N., Frier, W., Freud, K.M.A., Georgiou, O., Lepora, N.F.: Sensing ultrasonic mid-air haptics with a biomimetic tactile fingertip. In: Nisky, I., Hartcher-O'Brien, J., Wiertlewski, M., Smeets, J. (eds.) EuroHaptics 2020. LNCS, vol. 12272, pp. 362–370. Springer, Cham (2020). https://doi.org/10.1007/978-3-030-58147-3_40
2. Bensmaia, S.J., Leung, Y.Y., Hsiao, S.S., Johnson, K.O.: Vibratory adaptation of cutaneous mechanoreceptive afferents. J. Neurophysiol. **94**(5), 3023–3036 (2005). https://doi.org/10.1152/jn.00002.2005
3. Brock, A.M., Truillet, P., Oriola, B., Picard, D., Jouffrais, C.: Interactivity improves usability of geographic maps for visually impaired people. Hum.-Comput. Interact. **30**(2), 156–194 (2015). https://doi.org/10.1080/07370024.2014.924412
4. Dalecki, D., Child, S.Z., Raeman, C.H., Carstensen, E.L.: Tactile perception of ultrasound. J. Acoust. Soc. Am. **97**(5), 3165–3170 (1995). https://doi.org/10.1121/1.411877
5. Hajas, D., Pittera, D., Nasce, A., Georgiou, O., Obrist, M.: Mid-air haptic rendering of 2D geometric shapes with a dynamic tactile pointer. IEEE Trans. Haptics **13**(4), 806–817 (2020). https://doi.org/10.1109/TOH.2020.2966445
6. Holloway, L., Marriott, K., Butler, M.: Accessible maps for the blind: comparing 3D printed models with tactile graphics. In: Proceedings of the 2018 CHI Conference on Human Factors in Computing Systems. p. 198. ACM (2018). https://doi.org/10.1145/3173574.3173772
7. Hoshi, T., Takahashi, M., Iwamoto, T., Shinoda, H.: Noncontact tactile display based on radiation pressure of airborne ultrasound. IEEE Trans. Haptics **3**(3), 155–165 (2010). https://doi.org/10.1109/TOH.2010.4
8. Jingu, A., Kamigaki, T., Fujiwara, M., Makino, Y., Shinoda, H.: LipNotif: use of lips as a non-contact tactile notification interface based on ultrasonic tactile presentation. In: The 34th Annual ACM Symposium on User Interface Software and Technology, pp. 13–23 (2021). https://doi.org/10.1145/3472749.3474732
9. Juravle, G., Spence, C.: Juggling reveals a decisional component to tactile suppression. Exp. Brain Res. **213**, 87–97 (2011). https://doi.org/10.1007/s00221-011-2780-2
10. Korres, G., Eid, M.: Haptogram: ultrasonic point-cloud tactile stimulation. IEEE Access **4**, 7758–7769 (2016). https://doi.org/10.1109/ACCESS.2016.2608835
11. Macik, M., Ivanic, T., Treml, L.: Interactive modular tactile maps of rooms for older adults with vision impairments. In: Ardito, C., et al. (eds.) INTERACT 2021. LNCS, vol. 12932, pp. 321–330. Springer, Cham (2021). https://doi.org/10.1007/978-3-030-85623-6_20
12. Marzo, A., Corkett, T., Drinkwater, B.W.: Ultraino: an open phased-array system for narrowband airborne ultrasound transmission. IEEE Trans. Ultrason. Ferroelectr. Freq. Control **65**(1), 102–111 (2017). https://doi.org/10.1109/TUFFC.2017.2769399
13. Paneva, V., Seinfeld, S., Kraiczi, M., Müller, J.: HaptiRead: reading braille as mid-air haptic information. In: Proceedings of the 2020 ACM Designing Interactive Systems Conference, pp. 13–20 (2020). https://doi.org/10.1145/3357236.3395515

14. Rakkolainen, I., Sand, A., Raisamo, R.: A survey of mid-air ultrasonic tactile feedback. In: 2019 IEEE International Symposium on Multimedia (ISM), pp. 94–944. IEEE (2019). https://doi.org/10.1109/ISM46123.2019.00022

15. Suzuki, S., Fujiwara, M., Makino, Y., Shinoda, H.: Midair hand guidance by an ultrasound virtual handrail. In: 2019 IEEE World Haptics Conference (WHC), pp. 271–276. IEEE (2019). https://doi.org/10.1109/WHC.2019.8816123

16. Suzuki, S., Inoue, S., Fujiwara, M., Makino, Y., Shinoda, H.: Autd3: Scalable airborne ultrasound tactile display. IEEE Trans. Haptics **14**(4), 740–749 (2021). https://doi.org/10.1109/TOH.2021.3069976

17. Triesch, J., Von Der Malsburg, C.: Robotic gesture recognition by cue combination. In: Dassow, J., Kruse, R. (eds.) Informatik'98: Informatik zwischen Bild und Sprache 28. Jahrestagung der Gesellschaft für Informatik Magdeburg, 21–25 September 1998, pp. 223–232. Springer, Berlin, Heidelberg (1998). https://doi.org/10.1007/978-3-642-72283-7_22

18. Voudouris, D., Fiehler, K.: Enhancement and suppression of tactile signals during reaching. J. Exp. Psychol. Hum. Percept. Perform. **43**(6), 1238 (2017). https://doi.org/10.1037/xhp0000373

Stress Embodied: Developing Multi-sensory Experiences for VR Police Training

Jakob Carl Uhl[1,2]([envelope]) [ORCID], Georg Regal[1,2] [ORCID], Michael Gafert[1] [ORCID], Markus Murtinger[1,2] [ORCID], and Manfred Tscheligi[1,2] [ORCID]

[1] AIT Austrian Institute of Technology, Vienna, Austria
jakob.uhl@ait.ac.at
[2] PLUS University of Salzburg, Salzburg, Austria

Abstract. VR applications primarily rely on audio-visual stimuli, limiting the sense of immersion. Multi-sensory stimuli show promise in enhancing presence, realistic behavior, and overall experience. Existing approaches are either stationary or wearable, and movement-intensive. Multi-user VR police training requires a mobile device for intensive multi-sensory stimuli. This paper presents the design and development of a mobile platform for multi-sensory feedback, introducing heat, wind, mist, and pain to improve immersion. Preliminary evaluations indicate promising effects on stress in VR. The paper concludes with lessons learned for designing multi-sensory experiences in police VR training.

Keywords: Virtual Reality · Multi-Sensory · VR Training

1 Introduction

In recent years, Virtual Reality (VR) has expanded to new application areas such as occupational skill training [16,22] or collaborative work [18]. In training, realism is a central requirement to achieve goals, because it helps to create an authentic and immersive experience that closely mirrors real-world situations.

Currently, VR realism is mainly achieved through audio-visual stimuli, but humans experience the world through multiple senses. For example, police work relies on multi-sensory information to perceive hazards. Enriching a virtual environment (VE) with contextual cues like heat, wind, haptics, or olfaction [14] has shown positive effects on presence, task performance, and Quality of Experience (QoE), particularly in training environments [5,26] and high load conditions [13]. Existing multi-sensory VR applications and devices are often limited to a single modality, stationary, or cumbersome to set up. Mobile solutions that provide intense multi-sensory stimuli are needed for applications like police training.

In this paper, we present the design, development, and formative evaluation of a novel mobile Multi-Sensory Platform (MSP) prototype for evoking intense multi-sensory experiences in various training environments, aiming to answer the following research questions:

Supplementary Information The online version contains supplementary material available at https://doi.org/10.1007/978-3-031-42280-5_36.

J. Abdelnour Nocera et al. (Eds.): INTERACT 2023, LNCS 14142, pp. 573–583, 2023.
https://doi.org/10.1007/978-3-031-42280-5_36

- **RQ1:** Does the proposed implementation of a multi-sensory device enable mobile and intense multi-sensory stimuli to research its effect on trainees?
- **RQ2:** Does the augmentation of stressful elements in a VR training scenario for police officers impact the perceived stress and presence of trainees?

2   Related Work

2.1   Effects of Multi-sensory VR

Melo et al. [14] found that 84% of literature reported positive effects of multi-sensory VR on presence, performance, and learning efficiency. However, incongruent stimuli can negatively impact the experience [1]. Dinh et al. [6] concluded that more sensory cues in VR increase the sense of presence. High-fidelity simulations with tactile or olfactory stimuli enhance presence ratings and physiological correlates [19]. Munyan et al. [15] report similar findings, with [5] noting improved experiences in virtual training environments. Conversely, Jones et al. [10] found no significant increase with olfactory stimuli, and [13] observed positive effects only in high load conditions.

Various sensory modalities have been explored in VR. Shaw et al. [24] used infrared heaters in VR fire evacuation training, resulting in greater urgency, perceived pressure, and adaptive behavior. Giraldo et al. [7] observed increased presence and wind direction accuracy. [12] simulated a typhoon using wind and moisture, while [11] reported improved task performance with wind and floor vibrations. Haptics has shown promising growth, with touch in VR increasing e.g. immersion [8] and learning [2]. Body ownership illusion also improves with haptic stimulation [3]. Pain stimulation in VR is scarce, with most studies focusing on pain alleviation [25]. However, in high-risk situations, pain presence may impact behavior and caution, potentially leading to more realistic training experiences.

2.2   Stress Experiences in VR

VR training can realistically simulate dangerous situations [16], and stress is an important factor influencing the training experience. Most multi-sensory VR research though focuses on stress relief. For example, [20] introduced olfactory cues in a biodiversity virtual environment, reducing stress and heart rate. A similar stress reduction was observed by [9] using congruent olfactory stimuli in an urban green space simulation.

Few multi-sensory VR applications aim to elicit stress. [4] created a stressful decision-making environment for aerial firefighter training, but found no significant differences between multi-sensory and normal VR groups. Viciana-Abad et al. [27] investigated presence and stress in VR training, suggesting a correlation between the two measurements. Environmental stressors in training can enhance immersive environments [17], and we hypothesize that more realistic multi-sensory cues will lead to higher experienced stress and presence.

The literature review of related work illustrates, that little research has been done investigating the effects of multi-sensory VR on stress and presence in the context of police training. By aiming to closing this gap in this work, our contribution therefore is:

- The MSP concept and prototype.
- An investigation of the research gap regarding the effects of multi-sensory stressors on stress and presence in VR for training.
- Lessons learned and recommendations for multi-sensory VR police training.

3   The Mobile Multi-sensory Platform

In a series of six co-creation workshops (Total N = 60 police officers, trainers, or officials) cf. [blank for review], we gathered requirements for a virtual reality training application from police officers. These workshops took place in six European cities with respective officers and trainers as participants.

Three primary needs emerged from all workshops: *realistic graphics, sensory elements*, and *different scenarios*. Additionally, three workshops highlighted the need for varying weather conditions, as they often impact police actions through impaired sight or slippery ground due to rain. Mentioned sensory elements included smell (e.g., smoke or blood), heat (fire), or wind (weather conditions), representing potentially dangerous environmental cues influencing behavior and stress response.

To explore the relationship between multi-sensory environmental cues, stress, and presence, we constructed a physical prototype of a mobile platform, allowing any combination of sensory modalities to be applied as appropriate in a given VR scenario. A literature review identified haptic feedback, heat, cold, and wind as the most prevalent modalities in VR. We combined these with moisture and light pain sensations.

3.1   Platform Design

The design requirements for the technical implementation of the platform included mobility, intensity, and monitoring. The platform needed to be movable to different spots in the space during and between scenarios to ensure flexibility in various training contexts. The stimuli had to be intense enough to be noticeable from a distance, allowing for a more immersive experience. Additionally, a method for monitoring the platform's position within the virtual environment was required to guarantee proper alignment and integration of the multi-sensory stimuli.

Frame: We used steel tubes and fire-proof wood to create a sturdy 150cm * 40cm * 40cm (height, width, and length) frame with three levels and a front panel with cavities for multi-sensory modules. Four omnidirectional wheels ensure mobility, and diagonal steel tubes serve as a handle, anticipating the considerable weight of the parts.

Control Module, Interface, and Monitor: A Raspberry Pi 3 with a 7" touchscreen display and a modular interface is placed on the top level. The interface includes sliders and trigger buttons for controlling the intensity and activation of five modalities (heat, wind, moisture, vibration, pain). A tablet displays a live stream of the VR view, allowing for better monitoring (Fig. 1).

Fig. 1. From left to right: a) The multi-sensory platform prototype with front facing heat, wind and moisture modules; b) the Pavlok shock-band for inducing light pain, c) the interface enabling dynamic change of intensity of each multi-sensory stimuli and d) the MSP in use at a field trial.

Power Source: A mobile power supply by Jackery (518 Wh, 1 kW peak output) powers the modules and control unit, ensuring the MSP's wireless operation. This power supply is placed on the bottom level of the platform, and is spatially separated from the gas tank next to it by a fire-proof board.

Heat Module: A gas-powered Einhell 300 NIRO hot air generator was chosen due to its high intensity (30 kW output performance) compared to electric heaters (which have shown to be of little intensity) producing noticeable heat up to 5 m away.

Wind Module: The 124W Vacmaster Air Fan generates high-velocity wind, selected for its intensity and narrow output area. The fan's intensity levels are controllable by the Raspberry Pi controller.

Mist Module: A water pump directs water from a tank through metallic nozzles, creating a fine mist. The control unit adjusts water dispersion for intensity control, allowing for moisture and cooling effects.

Pain/Vibration Module: The wearable Pavlok 2 device was chosen for its ability to deliver electric shocks and vibrations, controllable via Bluetooth from the interface.

Integration in VR: The MSP prototype is calibrated with the VR environment by marking corresponding physical locations for multi-sensory stimuli. Experimenters monitor VR on a tablet and administer stimuli as needed, ensuring accurate and timely stimulus delivery.

4 Formative Evaluation

To gather first insights into whether multi-modal enhancement of environmental cues in police VR training can have an effect on stress and the sense of presence, we conducted an formative evaluation. We performed this evaluation during the first of 5 field trials of the developed VR training system. This "in-the-wild" approach to designing and evaluating multi-sensory experiences for VR police training was chosen to get feedback from the actual training context and to infer further design goals for the MSP.

4.1 Methods

Participants The participants were police trainers, who were taking part voluntarily to experience the developed VR training. In total, 33 police trainers took part in the training grouped into teams of 3 or 4. The field trials were mainly an event for the police to train with the system (i.e. our study being 'in-the-wild'), the police trainers chose which scenarios would be trained: 15 trainees (all male) trained scenario 1 and 18 trainees (16 male, 2 female) trained scenario 2.

Scenarios: In a large-scale 30×30 meter indoor sports hall, the multi-user VR setup featured two scenarios with the same environment but different weather: dark sky with fast-moving clouds in scenario 1, and bright sunshine in scenario 2. Trainees began outside a hotel in a city tasked with removing an unruly person, role-played by an actor, who wouldn't harm trainees, and aimed for a peaceful resolution through communication.

Study Design: As two scenarios were trained by different groups, we opted for a 2×1 between-subjects design, with training groups being randomly assigned to either the control group (VR) or the treatment group (VR + MSP). As out come variables we looked at subjective stress and presence ratings.

Multi-sensory Enhancement: We administered wind and heat as environmental cues with the MSP for multi-sensory groups in the starting area outside the hotel in both scenarios. In scenario 1, cold wind matched the dark clouds and bad weather, while in scenario 2, warm wind corresponded to the clear sky and good weather. An operator moved the MSP alongside trainees at a 5-meter distance until they entered (see Fig. 2c). Heat and wind were chosen, as the trained scenarios did not include cues requiring either mist or pain feedback.

Measurements: For presence, we used the i-group presence questionnaire (IPQ) [21], with the sub scales *Involvement, Spatial Presence, Realism* and *General Presence*. All items were answered on a 6-point Likert scale. The IPQ was administered once after the teams finished their respective training session.

To explore the stress evoking capabilities of multi-sensory enhancement of environmental cues, we included a visual analog scale (VAS) for subjective stress for both scenarios, allowing for continuous indication of the amount of stress between the two poles "not at all stressed" - 0 and "extremely stressed" - 100.

4.2 Results

Stress. Subjective Stress was assessed for each scenario independently on the VAS. For Scenario 1, the subjective stress was rated higher in the VR + Wind group (M = 26.6, SD = 16.6) than in the VR only group (M = 13.3, SD = 7.8).

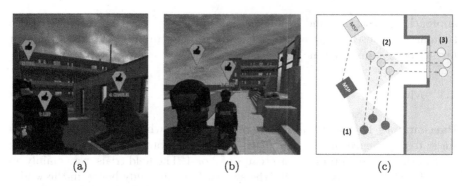

Fig. 2. Screenshot of a) bad weather in scenario 1 and b) good weather in scenario 2. A schematic of the procedure of adding the multi-sensory stimuli (c). Participants start in either cold or warm wind (1) and proceeded to the entrance (2) with the MSP following in the same distance. Once inside (3), the MSP was turned off.

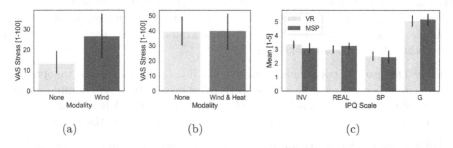

Fig. 3. Barplots of (a) subjective Stress (VAS) for scenario 1 (bad weather) and (b) scenario 2 (good weather), as well as overall presence ratings for both groups (c).

A following t-test resulted in a significant p-value of p = 0.037. Contrasting, in scenario 2, subjective Stress was rated as slightly lower in the VR + Wind (M = 40.0, SD = 17.5) than in the VR only group (M = 39.5, SD = 16.9). This difference was not significant (p = 0.948). The subjective stress results are visualized in Fig. 3a and 3b.

Presence. Presence ratings were homogeneous between the groups, with neutral ratings for involvement, and realism, and slightly lower ratings for spatial presence. The general presence factor was rated positive to very positive, with the VR + MSP group at a mean of 5.1 (SD = 0.9) and the VR group at 5.2 (SD = 0.8). No significant differences could be found between the two groups.

4.3   Design Implications from the Formative Evaluation:

The formative evaluation served as a proof of concept. The MSP could be moved in the training space to deliver different sensory experiences in a high intensity.

Further, the ratings of stress and presence formed our hypotheses for future studies. There seems to be a difference at least in perceived stress when stressful elements of the virtual environment were enhanced (i.e., the bad weather), and no difference when neutral elements were enhanced (i.e., the good weather). Sensory enhancement of high risk training scenarios therefore promised a heightening of the intensity of the training. For a future iteration of our MSP prototype, we will incorporate four main learnings:

Wizard of Oz Elements: The MSP prototype relied on manual control for stimulus timing and location, which posed challenges for time-sensitive stimuli like pain. While ambient stimuli like wind and smell worked well, a fully-realized system should automate these elements for improved realism. However, the method was sufficient for evaluation purposes.

Mobility: MSP mobility was limited in the controlled evaluation due to the gym hall floor's elasticity and friction with the device's wheels. Future developments should consider various training contexts to ensure mobility, which is essential for applying multi-sensory stimuli in different environments.

Safety: Participant safety was a concern, as they couldn't see the MSP in the virtual environment. Even for an automated version of the platform, reacting quickly to users' movements would be a challenge. Designing virtual environments that position multi-sensory elements in safe locations, or using an automated version of the platform, could mitigate this issue. Current stationary multi-sensory VR implementations already use this approach.

Noise Levels: The gas-powered heater used for intensity produced noise that distracted some participants, even with noise-cancellation headphones. Additionally, the noise could be stressful for trainers who were not wearing headphones. Future devices should consider alternative methods, like electrical heaters, to reduce noise while maintaining mobility and power efficiency in various settings.

5 Discussion

RQ1: Enablement of Multi-sensory Research for VR Training. The formative evaluation as well as the controlled evaluation has shown, that the MSP prototype was adequate for conducting research on multi-sensory VR in a large-scale VR training for police. In general, all modules worked as intended and the two modalities used during the experiment (heat and wind) could be operated without issues. Nevertheless, some limitations became evident.

For one, the mobility of the MSP depended on the characteristics of the floor, which made it more difficult to use in the controlled user-study. This further ties into the issue of trainee safety, as they would not see the MSP during their training in VR, which demanded careful attention of the experimenters to move the MSP according to the trainees movements. As the MSP could deliver the multi-sensory stimuli from afar (approx. 5 m), this was not a severe limitation, but has to be considered in future iterations of a mobile multi-sensory platform.

Further, a central challenge for future work in this area will be the heat module. The gas-powered solution achieved the desired intensity at a low energy cost, but was experienced as noisy when turned on, which impacts the overall experience of trainees during the training. For future versions of such a device electric heaters should be reconsidered, given adequate battery power.

RQ2: Impact of Multi-sensory Stressors on Stress and Presence. The results from the formative evaluation were twofold: For one, we observed that augmenting a potential stressor (i.e. the bad weather) with a congruent multi-sensory stimuli led to higher ratings of stress by the participants, and the augmentation of a neutral stressor (i.e. the good weather) led to similar ratings between the VR and the VR + MSP groups. However, we did not find any differences in presence ratings between the two conditions. This further highlights, that there is an interplay between the type of stimuli and the context in which it is placed. When implementing multi-sensory stressors in VR, this interplay must be considered, to achieve the wanted effects.

The findings suggest, that the multi-sensory enhancement of environmental cues can increase perceived stress when the environmental cue is one that poses a challenge in reality. The notion, that contextual variables like the weather influence decisions in such a situation, can be observed in this multi-sensory setting. Materializing stressors in VR training, therefore, appears to be of value, as it uncovers layers of threat in the environment, that would not be visible otherwise. Future work is needed to investigate this relationship and its moderators in more detail. On the other hand, we found no differences in presence ratings in the formative evaluation, which is in line with some existing research [23], Presence could though be a moderator of the effect of multi-sensory stimuli on stress: Similarly to [27], it might be that the association between stress and presence might only be present for sub groups of participants, who usually do not immerse themselves much into a virtual environment.

5.1 Future Development

In future work, the full capabilities of the MSP including all sensory modalities will be investigated, as this was out of scope of this work due to the available training scenarios. Also, we plan to develop a Unity SDK to enable automatic triggering of different modalities and integrate omnidirectional robotic wheels for the MSP's automatic movement to desired locations. We also aim to create an "experience designer" application for managing and crafting multi-sensory presets. Additionally, further investigation of the relationship between stress and presence is needed, taking inter-individual differences into account. If increased stress through multi-sensory stimuli results in higher presence for typically less immersed individuals, it could be a valuable addition to VR training.

6   Conclusion

This paper introduced the design, development, and evaluation of a mobile multi-sensory platform (MSP) for enhancing immersion in police VR training. The MSP deliveres intense stimuli, such as heat, wind, mist and pain, resulting in higher stress ratings. However, presence ratings were not significantly different between conditions. The findings emphasize the need to consider the interplay between stimuli and context in VR training. Future research should further examine the relationships between multi-sensory stimuli, stress, and presence. Ultimately, the MSP prototype demonstrates potential for creating more realistic and engaging training environments for police and other high-stress professions.

Acknowledgements. This work was supported by the European Commission's Horizon 2020 Research and Innovation Programme (Grant number: 833572) and by the industrial PhD program of the austrian research promotion agency (FFG) under grant agreement No FO999887876.

References

1. Bessa, M., Melo, M., De Sousa, A.A., Vasconcelos-Raposo, J.: The effects of body position on reflexive motor acts and the sense of presence in virtual environments. Comput. Graph. **71**, 35–41 (2018)
2. Bouhelal, A., Badiani, S., AlAraimi, B., Patel, H., Patel, B.: Laparoscopic training in virtual reality (VR): haptic vs. none haptic. Int. J. Surg. **8**(11), 704 (2013)
3. Caola, B., Montalti, M., Zanini, A., Leadbetter, A., Martini, M.: The bodily illusion in adverse conditions: virtual arm ownership during visuomotor mismatch. Perception **47**(5), 477–491 (2018)
4. Clifford, R.M., Jung, S., Hoermann, S., Billinghurst, M., Lindeman, R.W.: Creating a stressful decision making environment for aerial firefighter training in virtual reality. In: 2019 IEEE Conference on Virtual Reality and 3D User Interfaces (VR), pp. 181–189. IEEE (2019)
5. Cooper, N., Millela, F., Cant, I., White, M.D., Meyer, G.: Transfer of training-virtual reality training with augmented multisensory cues improves user experience during training and task performance in the real world. PLoS ONE **16**(3), e0248225 (2021)
6. Dinh, H.Q., Walker, N., Hodges, L.F., Song, C., Kobayashi, A.: Evaluating the importance of multi-sensory input on memory and the sense of presence in virtual environments. In: Proceedings IEEE Virtual Reality (Cat. No. 99CB36316), pp. 222–228. IEEE (1999)
7. Giraldo, G., Servières, M., Moreau, G.: Perception of multisensory wind representation in virtual reality. In: 2020 IEEE International Symposium on Mixed and Augmented Reality (ISMAR), pp. 45–53. IEEE (2020)
8. Gomes, G.D., Flynn, R., Murray, N.: A QoE evaluation of an immersive virtual reality autonomous driving experience. In: 2020 Twelfth International Conference on Quality of Multimedia Experience (QoMEX), pp. 1–4. IEEE (2020)
9. Hedblom, M., et al.: Reduction of physiological stress by urban green space in a multisensory virtual experiment. Sci. Rep. **9**(1), 1–11 (2019)

10. Jones, L., Bowers, C.A., Washburn, D., Cortes, A., Satya, R.V.: The effect of olfaction on immersion into virtual environments. In: Human Performance, Situation Awareness and Automation: Issues and Considerations for the 21st Century, pp. 282–285 (2004)
11. Jung, S., Wood, A.L., Hoermann, S., Abhayawardhana, P.L., Lindeman, R.W.: The impact of multi-sensory stimuli on confidence levels for perceptual-cognitive tasks in VR. In: 2020 IEEE Conference on Virtual Reality and 3D User Interfaces (VR), pp. 463–472. IEEE (2020)
12. Ke, P., Keng, K.N., Jiang, S., Cai, S., Rong, Z., Zhu, K.: Embodied weather: promoting public understanding of extreme weather through immersive multi-sensory virtual reality. In: The 17th International Conference on Virtual-Reality Continuum and its Applications in Industry, pp. 1–2 (2019)
13. Marucci, M., et al.: The impact of multisensory integration and perceptual load in virtual reality settings on performance, workload and presence. Sci. Rep. 11(1), 1–15 (2021)
14. Melo, M., Gonçalves, G., Monteiro, P., Coelho, H., Vasconcelos-Raposo, J., Bessa, M.: Do multisensory stimuli benefit the virtual reality experience? A systematic review. IEEE Trans. Vis. Comput. Graph. 28, 1428–1442 (2020)
15. Munyan, B.G., III., Neer, S.M., Beidel, D.C., Jentsch, F.: Olfactory stimuli increase presence in virtual environments. PLoS ONE 11(6), e0157568 (2016)
16. Murtinger, M., Jaspaert, E., Schrom-Feiertag, H., Egger-Lampl, S.: CBRNe training in virtual environments: SWOT analysis & practical guidelines. Int. J. Saf. Secur. Eng. 11(4), 295–303 (2021)
17. Nguyen, Q., Jaspaert, E., Murtinger, M., Schrom-Feiertag, H., Egger-Lampl, S., Tscheligi, M.: Stress out: translating real-world stressors into audio-visual stress cues in VR for police training. In: Ardito, C., et al. (eds.) INTERACT 2021. LNCS, vol. 12933, pp. 551–561. Springer, Cham (2021). https://doi.org/10.1007/978-3-030-85616-8_32
18. Pedersen, G., Koumaditis, K.: Virtual reality (VR) in the computer supported cooperative work (CSCW) domain: a mapping and a pre-study on functionality and immersion. In: Chen, J.Y.C., Fragomeni, G. (eds.) HCII 2020. LNCS, vol. 12191, pp. 136–153. Springer, Cham (2020). https://doi.org/10.1007/978-3-030-49698-2_10
19. Ranasinghe, N., et al.: Season Traveller: multisensory narration for enhancing the virtual reality experience. In: Proceedings of the 2018 CHI Conference on Human Factors in Computing Systems, pp. 1–13 (2018)
20. Schebella, M.F., Weber, D., Schultz, L., Weinstein, P.: The nature of reality: Human stress recovery during exposure to biodiverse, multisensory virtual environments. Int. J. Environ. Res. Public Health 17(1), 56 (2020)
21. Schubert, T., Friedmann, F., Regenbrecht, H.: The experience of presence: factor analytic insights. Presence: Teleoperators Virtual Environ. 10(3), 266–281 (2001)
22. Schwarz, S., Regal, G., Kempf, M., Schatz, R.: Learning success in immersive virtual reality training environments: practical evidence from automotive assembly. In: Proceedings of the 11th Nordic Conference on Human-Computer Interaction: Shaping Experiences, Shaping Society, pp. 1–11. ACM (2020)
23. Servotte, J.C., et al.: Virtual reality experience: immersion, sense of presence, and cybersickness. Clin. Simul. Nurs. 38, 35–43 (2020)
24. Shaw, E., Roper, T., Nilsson, T., Lawson, G., Cobb, S.V., Miller, D.: The heat is on: exploring user behaviour in a multisensory virtual environment for fire evacuation. In: Proceedings of the 2019 CHI Conference on Human Factors in Computing Systems, pp. 1–13 (2019)

25. Solcà, M., et al.: Enhancing analgesic spinal cord stimulation for chronic pain with personalized immersive virtual reality. Pain **162**(6), 1641–1649 (2021)
26. Uhl, J.C., Schrom-Feiertag, H., Regal, G., Gallhuber, K., Tscheligi, M.: Tangible immersive trauma simulation: is mixed reality the next level of medical skills training? In: Proceedings of the 2023 CHI Conference on Human Factors in Computing Systems. CHI '23, Association for Computing Machinery, New York (2023). https://doi.org/10.1145/3544548.3581292
27. Viciana-Abad, R., Reyes-Lecuona, A., García-Berdonés, C., Díaz-Estrella, A., Castillo-Carrión, S.: The importance of significant information in presence and stress within a virtual reality experience. Annu. Rev. Cyberther. Telemed. **2**, 111–118 (2004)

Healthcare Applications
and Self-Monitoring

Co-designing an eHealth Solution to Support Fibromyalgia Self-Management

Pedro Albuquerque Santos[1,2] ⓘ, Rui Neves Madeira[1,2](✉) ⓘ, Hugo Ferreira[1] ⓘ, and Carmen Caeiro[3] ⓘ

[1] Sustain.RD, ESTSetúbal, Instituto Politécnico de Setúbal, Setúbal, Portugal
pedro.albuquerque@estsetubal.ips.pt, hugo.ferreira20@estudantes.ips.pt
[2] NOVA LINCS, NOVA School of Science and Technology, NOVA University of Lisbon, Lisbon, Portugal
rui.madeira@estsetubal.ips.pt
[3] CIIAS, School of Health, Instituto Politécnico de Setúbal, Setúbal, Portugal
carmen.caeiro@ess.ips.pt

Abstract. Fibromyalgia is a rheumatic condition that causes a wide range of symptoms, such as pain, fatigue, attention and concentration deficit, and sleep disorders. Guidelines recommend a combination of pharmacological and non-pharmacological approaches, such as physiotherapy, emphasizing the relevance of the latter as first-line therapy. Usually, patients have difficulties in self-managing their condition. We designed an eHealth solution based on a mobile application that allows people with fibromyalgia to self-manage their condition and perform hybrid sessions with physiotherapists. The solution was created by applying a co-design process, where patients and physiotherapists were involved from start to finish, following the design thinking methodology. The paper also includes a preliminary user study with expected positive and encouraging results due to the co-design process.

Keywords: fibromyalgia · physiotherapy · ehealth · self-management · co-design · design thinking · mobile app · human-computer interaction

1 Introduction and Background

Fibromyalgia (FM) is a rheumatological condition characterized by widespread pain that may be migratory and can fluctuate in intensity over time. Fatigue, sleep disturbances, and cognitive dysfunction (including concentration and memory deficits) are common FM symptoms [10]. It can also be associated with musculoskeletal issues, cardiovascular problems, gastrointestinal disorders, and psychological symptoms, such as depression and anxiety [12].

Patients with this condition report several limitations in daily activities, including at work, which can lead to a high level of absenteeism. Therefore,

J. Abdelnour Nocera et al. (Eds.): INTERACT 2023, LNCS 14142, pp. 587–597, 2023.
https://doi.org/10.1007/978-3-031-42280-5_37

FM can have a significant impact on society, families, and the economy. Moreover, not all healthcare systems are able to provide sufficient care for patients with chronic diseases, and the COVID-19 pandemic has only made the situation worse by reducing non-urgent consultations. This scenario can be exacerbated for people who live far from healthcare facilities or have a lower socioeconomic status, showing more difficulty in receiving proper treatment, which can have consequences regarding the identification, monitoring, and treatment of several health conditions, including those associated with chronic pain, such as FM [6].

There is a need to implement strategies that expand beyond the limitation of the current healthcare systems. The recommendation for treating patients with FM is to use non-pharmacological approaches first [17], such as exercise and symptom self-management education [13]. Self-management interventions have been identified as a priority area for healthcare services because they empower people to take an active role in managing their health and conditions [8]. Supported self-management involves collaboration between the individual and their healthcare professional, and it has been shown to lead to positive outcomes such as reduced pain and improved self-efficacy [14]. Telerehabilitation is an increasingly popular and effective intervention model for supporting vulnerable groups, and studies show that it is an acceptable, safe and effective approach that facilitates contact and adherence to the intervention [17]. However, there is no telerehabilitation solution for people diagnosed with FM focused on the condition's self-management.

ProFibro does not exactly implement a telerehabilitation approach, but it is a free mobile app that promotes self-care as a complement to physiotherapy for managing FM [20]. The authors involved expert physiotherapists in the app's development, but we could not find the involvement of people with FM in the design process. An interesting solution is a Web-based and mobile app to support physical activity in individuals with rheumatoid arthritis called tRAppen [18]. In this case, it was employed a co-design strategy with people diagnosed with the condition, clinical physiotherapists and researchers, an officer from the Swedish Rheumatism Association (SRA), and a designer. The resulting solution was based on two preliminary frameworks, "My self-monitoring" and "My peer group". The former has the goal of providing a way to plan, set goals and record physical activity (PA) and progress. The latter consists of building a small community for positive feedback and support from peers. Moreover, Rosser and Eccleston conducted a review of mobile apps for pain management [19], finding that out of 111 apps, only seven were related to specific long-term conditions such as FM, arthritis, and degenerative disc disease. The majority of the apps did not involve healthcare professionals in their development, and there was limited information about the origin and validity of the content. Moreover, they were only designed to provide information or allow users to track pain levels and medications.

In order to develop a solution that meets the needs of people with FM, we followed a design thinking methodology to involve them in the design of the solution. The participation of the physiotherapists that will configure, communicate with, and monitor the progress of the people with FM was also a key part of the design of the solution. The paper presents the design process, an overview of the proposed solution, and a preliminary user study with potential end users.

2   The Co-Design Process

In order to co-create an eHealth solution for people with FM, the team followed the design thinking methodology, which involves five phases [4]. These phases were adapted to the project's context and involved conducting workshops with different stakeholders, including people with FM, representatives of associations, but also physiotherapists, psychologists and a rheumatologist, which has broadened the spectrum of healthcare professionals involved in the process.

In the Empathize phase, the team conducted a focus group study to identify critical points in the development of the solution. These included integrating exercise into daily routines, ensuring privacy and family integration, overcoming technological barriers, addressing fears of incorrect exercise, maintaining motivation and adherence to remote sessions, establishing effective communication between the physiotherapist and the patient, addressing difficulties of initial evaluation and the lack of therapeutic touch, and personalizing interventions for each participant.

Following the initial assessment, a series of workshops (Fig. 1) were organized to guide the design process. These workshops were divided into two types, one for individuals with FM and another for physiotherapists. Moreover, health researchers also attended the final workshop.

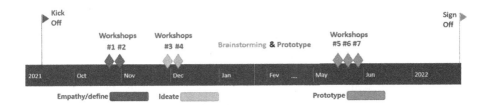

Fig. 1. Overview of the workshops timeline

Two workshops with ten participants each were held to conduct the *Empathize* and *Define* phases. The goal was to build trust and encourage participants to share their needs and problems. Two additional workshops were held in November and December 2021 in the *Ideate* phase, involving the same group of people who participated in the previous workshops. Hypothetical scenarios about individuals diagnosed with FM were created for each workshop to encourage productive discussions and generate relevant and meaningful ideas. The research team provided questions related to the scenario to guide the discussions towards addressing concerns previously identified.

In the first two workshops, participants discussed the challenges of providing physiotherapy interventions in an online format. They talked about the importance of an initial onsite meeting between physiotherapist and patient to nurture the therapeutic relationship, building and nurturing the online group dynamic, and crucial moments to foster group dynamics. Participants proposed strategies to ensure that individual needs are met, such as effective initial assessment and the use of an initial onsite session. They also discussed ways to increase confidence in the safety and efficacy of online interventions, such as continuous communication through various channels and the physiotherapist's ability to demonstrate proper exercise technique. The challenges of maintaining patient motivation and trust in the online format can be addressed through the use of sensors, video calls, and verbal feedback during exercises.

Workshop 3 discussed technological solutions for FM patients, with participants exploring various aspects such as customization, use of reminders, and point systems available. In Workshop 4, strategies for integrating physical exercise into daily routines and promoting motivation for patients were discussed. The questions focused on making adherence easier, with suggestions for flexible scheduling and session formats, and the inclusion of a buddy system, group challenges, and a reward system. A chat feature for direct communication between patients and therapists was also suggested. Finally, the advantages and disadvantages of a mobile or desktop web application were discussed.

In internal brainstorming sessions prior to the last three workshops, the team conceptualized the solution and prioritized different components for it based on the needs of patients and therapists. For physiotherapists, communication, management and holding sessions were identified as important components, with community and sensor-based functionalities having a lower priority. For patients, sessions and communication modules were the most important, followed by the user profile, with motivation and community having a lower priority. The team decided to initially implement the solution as a mobile app for patients, with the possibility of later expanding it to support physiotherapists' needs, either through a web application or a mobile app.

The research team developed initial interactive non-functional prototypes using *Figma* based on the findings from the previous workshops. These prototypes were presented in Workshops 5, 6, and 7 to people with FM and physiotherapists for feedback on usability, information presented, and user experience. Feedback included suggestions to simplify the way exercises were presented, add functionality like start, stop, and finish buttons for autonomous sessions, and filter by exercise type. Participants also suggested adding an option to hide/show information on the group challenge detail screen and presenting only the average pain over time in the patient's profile.

3 Proposed Solution

This section presents the prototype that resulted from the co-design process. The *Dashboard* (Fig. 2a) is the first screen shown to users upon registration or authentication. It includes a gamification component with a bar that increases as people perform their sessions of the current month, giving access to information about the next session, group challenges, exercises, and additional information.

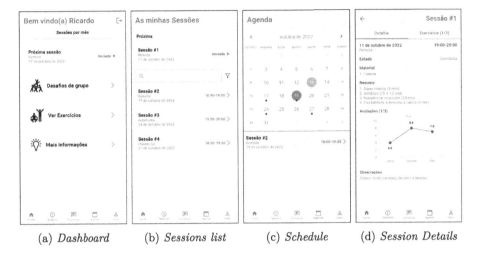

(a) *Dashboard*   (b) *Sessions list*   (c) *Schedule*   (d) *Session Details*

Fig. 2. *Dashboard, Sessions* and *Schedule* user interfaces

The sessions screen allows users to view upcoming sessions, with the option to search and filter by text, session type, and date range. The next session is highlighted and it shows the sessions that occur in the next two weeks (Fig. 2b). Another way to visualize the sessions set is through a calendar that allows users to have an easy overview (schedule) of their sessions in each month (Fig. 2c). The information is simplified in both of these screens. Clicking on a session will open a details screen that displays additional information, such as the equipment needed, summary, status, evaluations, observations, and exercises that are part of the session (Fig. 2d). The evaluations consist of tracking pain, heart rate, and fatigue in three phases of the session (beginning, middle, and end), and data is presented in line charts. Physiotherapists can add notes in the session details interface for sessions. Similarly, patients can add observations about autonomous sessions. The user can also view the exercises associated with a session by selecting the respective tab at the top of the screen (see Fig. 3a). This section shows exercises that have been performed as part of a physiotherapy session, or that the patient should do as part of an autonomous session. It contains a textual explanation and a video tutorial for each exercise along with information about sets, repetitions, and rest time.

The remote sessions are managed by the physiotherapist, who starts the session and changes the status to *In Progress* in the application. A video call is launched within the app when the session is clicked. Once the session is finished, the physiotherapist updates the status to *Finished*. In the case of onsite sessions, the app will only register the session information and will not play an active role during the session (it only has status *Scheduled* and *Finished*).

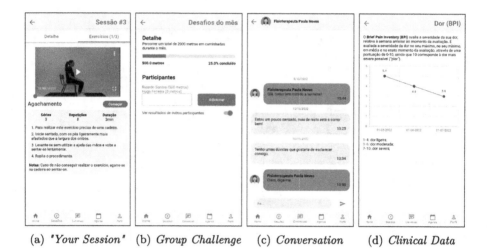

(a) *"Your Session"*   (b) *Group Challenge*   (c) *Conversation*   (d) *Clinical Data*

Fig. 3. User interfaces related to sessions

The physiotherapist can create groups of patients to participate in challenges. This is an initial feature that aims to motivate users and provide a sense of community. Currently, the challenges consist of the group members walking a certain number of meters to reach a goal. The patient will be able to see the challenges that have been completed by the groups they belong to, as well as the list of ongoing challenges with information about the total meters to cover, a progress bar, and the number of participants. By clicking on the challenge, the patient can see more information such as its description, percentage completion, and a list of participants and their contributions (see Fig. 3b). The latter can be toggled on/off depending on whether the patient likes to see the progress of others or not (e.g., they feel motivated by seeing others progress, or unmotivated by not being able to keep up). Patients can also register the distance they walked during a walk and the information will be automatically updated.

The conversations screen lists all chats in which the patient is involved, including private chats with the physiotherapist and group challenge chats. It works similarly to other messaging applications, such as *WhatsApp*. The patient can open a chat and send messages in real-time, which updates automatically on all devices that have the chat open (see Fig. 3c). It promotes a sense of community among patients. The chat feature is intended to make it easier for patients to ask questions, get feedback and support from their therapists, but also to stay connected with other patients.

The mobile app also allows physiotherapists to track patients' progress over time through the use of questionnaires that measure indicators, such as quality of sleep, pain, fatigue, health status, and functional capacity. The results are displayed as line charts on the health data screen within the patient's profile, which includes a color-coded legend (green for positive, yellow for average, and red for negative results) to explain the results (see Fig. 3d). The result value is also color-matched to the legend for better understanding. The currently supported questionnaires include: Fibromyalgia Impact Questionnaire Revised (FIQr) [2], Fatigue Assessment Scale (FAS) [16], Brief Pain Inventory (BPI) [7] and Pittsburgh Sleep Quality Index (PSQI) [5].

4   Preliminary User Study

The application's usability and user experience are major concerns. It should be easy to use and intuitive to avoid frustration. These preliminary tests were included in the Test phase, being conducted to identify points for improvement.

4.1   Participants and Protocol

The preliminary study had seven participants who were all women with a mean age of 51.29 ($s = 7.18$, median $= 52$). They had been diagnosed with FM between 2 and 17 years prior ($\bar{x} = 5.86$, $s = 5.15$, median $= 5$).

The tests consisted of five scenarios where a situation and a goal were given to participants that needed to perform tasks through the app's main functionalities: **Scenario 1** - recording a hypothetical number of walked meters, as part of a group challenge set by her physiotherapist with a goal of walking 2000 m in a month; **Scenario 2** - having doubts about an exercise and contacting the physiotherapist through the app by sending a message; **Scenario 3** - joining a simulated remote session scheduled for the day of the test; **Scenario 4** - following the instructions about a self-directed session proposed by the physiotherapist; **Scenario 5** - reviewing the results of questionnaires completed during previous sessions, trying to understand if the results were positive or negative.

The evaluation of the application included a questionnaire for participants to provide feedback on its usability, including their sense of clarity, ease of use, and understanding of the various functionalities. The questionnaire is divided into several sections, including demographic information, FM diagnosis and treatment, experience with technology, and relevance of the app's functionalities. The questionnaire also included questions from the System Usability Scale (SUS) [3], European Portuguese [15], using a seven-point Likert scale instead of the usual five-point Likert scale, since it is more likely to reflect a respondent's true subjective evaluation of a usability questionnaire item [9].

Objective measures (time to complete the task, task completion, etc.) were not included in this preliminary study, as it would be our first assessment with this target audience, who, already being observed, would not be so comfortable, besides during the test they would be communicating with the researcher in an informal interview setting. It was more important to have the participants comfortably talking to the team in order to discover some important points, since we were still in the last phase of the co-design process. Therefore, they were not solely focused on completing tasks having in mind the best performance.

The complete evaluation took around one hour and was conducted individually with the support of team members from technology and physiotherapy.

4.2   Results and Discussion

The scenarios performed by participants helped them understand the app. Participants found the application to be easy to use and intuitive, and the results of the Likert scale questions in the questionnaire were positive. As can be seen in Table 1, the average scores for all questions were close to the highest possible value of 7, indicating a high level of agreement among the participants. The low standard deviation suggests that there was little variation in the scores, indicating consistency in the participants' evaluations. The results suggest that the functionalities were relevant and appropriate to tackle the intended problem.

Table 1. Domain-specific questions for each participant (P1-P7).

Questions	P1	P2	P3	P4	P5	P6	P7	$\bar{x}$	s	M
Q1: I consider that the current implementation of the group challenges is adequate to promote motivation to exercise	6	7	7	7	7	6	7	6.71	0.49	7
Q2: I consider that the current implementation of the chat is adequate to promote a close contact with the physiotherapist	7	7	7	7	7	6	7	6.86	0.38	7
Q3: I consider the current video call interface adequate to support remote sessions	7	7	7	7	7	6	7	6.86	0.38	7
Q4: I consider that the options provided to perform autonomous sessions are adequate	7	7	7	7	7	6	7	6.86	0.38	7
Q5: I consider that the current health indicator information implementation is adequate to support disease self-management	6	7	7	7	7	6	7	6.71	0.49	7
Q6: I consider the information on health indicators relevant	7	7	7	7	7	6	7	6.86	0.38	7

Despite the positive results, some difficulties were observed in the understanding of certain functionalities, such as difficulty in understanding how to enter values in the group challenges and navigating the conversation and autonomous session features. To improve this, suggestions were made to add explanatory text and arrows to indicate appropriate actions, respectively. Some participants also had difficulties realizing that, in order to send a message to the therapist, they first needed to open the conversation instead of typing a message in the field to search through conversations.

Regarding SUS, the results were also very positive. The score result for the application was 97.38 on the SUS Scale, meaning the results can be interpreted as being in the 96th to 100th percentile range [11]. This score is within the range of a *Best Imaginable* usability rating and an *A* grade [1]. Even if we consider the lower bound of the Student's t distribution 95% confidence interval of [94.19, 100], this rating will still hold.

It is important to note that the sample size for the user testing was relatively small since the process of recruiting participants is complex, depending on the availability of people to spend an hour and expose their condition. It is a very sensitive process and, moreover, we needed to find people that did not participate in the design. Therefore, this preliminary evaluation is a work-in-progress that served as a means to gauge the progress of the project and to determine if the direction of the development was aligned with the needs of the intended users. We are aware the results should not be considered representative of the population at large. Nevertheless, despite most of them having little trouble starting to explore the app, there were some participants that were not as comfortable given that they were not very proficient in using smartphones.

5   Conclusion and Future Work

The primary goal of this research was to study, design, and implement a digital solution that would assist individuals diagnosed with FM in managing their symptoms on a daily basis, but also facilitate telerehabilitation with their physiotherapists. The use of design thinking ensured the final product was user-centered, meeting the users' needs, thus contributing to the so positive results of the preliminary study.

Before continuing with further development, more usability tests should be performed, thus having a larger number of participants in order to have more reliable results and paying more attention to objective measures and observation metrics, such as time to complete a task, mistakes made or requests for help. Afterwards, effectiveness tests will be conducted in the wild for a 12-week period, with participants using the app as part of their daily lives under a physiotherapy program.

References

1. Bangor, A., Kortum, P., Miller, J.: Determining what individual SUS scores mean: adding an adjective rating scale. J. Usability Studies **4**, 114–123 (2009)
2. Bennett, R.M., Friend, R., Jones, K.D., Ward, R., Han, B.K., Ross, R.L.: The revised fibromyalgia impact questionnaire (FIQR): validation and psychometric properties. Arthritis Res. Ther. **11**(4), R120 (2009)

3. Brooke, J.: Sus - a quick and dirty usability scale. In: Jordan, P.W., Thomas, B., McClelland, I.L., Weerdmeester, B. (eds.) Usability Evaluation in Industry, chap. 21, pp. 189–194. CRC Press, 1st edn. (1996)
4. Brown, T.: Change by Design: How Design Thinking Transforms Organizations and Inspires Innovation. Harper Collins, New York (2009)
5. Buysse, D.J., Reynolds, C.F., Monk, T.H., Berman, S.R., Kupfer, D.J.: The pittsburgh sleep quality index: a new instrument for psychiatric practice and research. Psychiatry Research **28**(2), 193–213 (1989) https://doi.org/10.1016/0165-1781(89)90047-4, www.sciencedirect.com/science/article/pii/0165178189900474
6. Clauw, D.J.: Fibromyalgia: an overview. Am. J. Med. **122**, S3–S13 (2009). https://doi.org/10.1016/J.AMJMED.2009.09.006
7. Cleeland, C.S., Ryan, K.M.: Pain assessment: global use of the brief pain inventory. Ann. Acad. Med. Singapore **23**(2), 129–138 (1994)
8. DE SILVA, D.: evidence: helping people help themselves: a review of the evidence considering whether it is worthwhile to support self-management (2011). www.scie-socialcareonline.org.uk/evidence-helping-people-help-themselves-a-review-of-the-evidence-considering-whether-it-is-worthwhile-to-support-self-management/r/a11G000000182gLIAQ
9. Finstad, K.: Response interpolation and scale sensitivity: evidence against 5-point scales. J. Usability Stud. **5**(3), 104–110 (2010)
10. Häuser, W., et al.: Fibromyalgia. Nat. Rev. Dis. Primers **2015** 1:1 1, 1–16 (2015). https://doi.org/10.1038/nrdp.2015.22, www.nature.com/articles/nrdp201522
11. Lewis, J.R., Sauro, J.: Item benchmarks for the system usability scale. J. Usability Stud. **13**, 158–167 (2018)
12. LP, Q.: Worldwide epidemiology of fibromyalgia. Curr. Pain Headache Rep. **17** (2013). https://doi.org/10.1007/S11916-013-0356-5, www.pubmed.ncbi.nlm.nih.gov/23801009/
13. Macfarlane, G.J., et al.: Eular revised recommendations for the management of fibromyalgia. Ann. Rheum. Dis. **76**, 318–328 (2017). https://doi.org/10.1136/ANNRHEUMDIS-2016-209724, www.pubmed.ncbi.nlm.nih.gov/27377815/
14. Mann, E.G., LeFort, S., VanDenKerkhof, E.G.: Self-management interventions for chronic pain. Pain Manage. **3**(3), 211–222 (2013) https://doi.org/10.2217/pmt.13.9
15. Martins, A.I., Rosa, A.F., Queirós, A., Silva, A., Rocha, N.P.: European Portuguese validation of the system usability scale (SUS). Procedia Comput. Sci. **67**, 293–300 (2015). https://doi.org/10.1016/j.procs.2015.09.273, www.sciencedirect.com/science/article/pii/S1877050915031191, proceedings of the 6th International Conference on Software Development and Technologies for Enhancing Accessibility and Fighting Info-exclusion
16. Michielsen, H.J., De Vries, J., Van Heck, G.L.: Psychometric qualities of a brief self-rated fatigue measure: the fatigue assessment scale. J. Psychosom. Res. **54**(4), 345–352 (2003) https://doi.org/10.1016/S0022-3999(02)00392-6, www.sciencedirect.com/science/article/pii/S0022399902003926
17. Plow, M., Golding, M.: Using mhealth technology in a self-management intervention to promote physical activity among adults with chronic disabling conditions: Randomized controlled trial. JMIR Mhealth Uhealth **5**(12), e185 (2017). www.mhealth.jmir.org/2017/12/e1855, e6394 (2017). https://doi.org/10.2196/MHEALTH.6394, www.mhealth.jmir.org/2017/12/e185

18. Revenäs, Å., Opava, C.H., Martin, C., Demmelmaier, I., Keller, C., Åsenlöf, P.: Development of a web-based and mobile app to support physical activity in individuals with rheumatoid arthritis: results from the second step of a co-design process. JMIR Res. Protoc. **4**(1), e22 (2015). https://doi.org/10.2196/resprot.3795, https://doi.org/10.2196/resprot.3795
19. Rosser, B.A., Eccleston, C.: Smartphone applications for pain management. J. Telemedicine Telecare **17**(6), 308–312 (2011) https://doi.org/10.1258/jtt.2011.101102
20. Yuan, S.L.K., Marques, A.P.: Development of profibro - a mobile application to promote self-care in patients with fibromyalgia. Physiotherapy **104**(3), 311–317 (2018) https://doi.org/10.1016/j.physio.2018.04.005, www.sciencedirect.com/science/article/pii/S0031940618300762

Designing Remote Patient Monitoring Technologies for Post-operative Home Cancer Recovery: The Role of Reassurance

Constantinos Timinis[1]([✉]) [ID], Jeremy Opie[2,3] [ID], Simon Watt[3],
Pramit Khetrapal[3,4,5], John Kelly[1], Manolis Mavrikis[1], Yvonne Rogers[2] [ID],
and Ivana Drobnjak[1] [ID]

[1] Centre for Medical Image Computing and Department of Computer Science,
University College London, London, UK
constantinos.timinis.17@ucl.ac.uk
[2] University College London Interaction Centre, University College London, London,
UK
[3] Wellcome/EPSRC Centre for Interventional and Surgical Sciences, University
College London, London, UK
[4] Division of Surgery, University College London, London, UK
[5] Department of Urology, Royal Free Hospital, London, UK

Abstract. While cancer patients are recovering in hospital after major surgery, they are continually monitored by clinical teams. However, once discharged, they spend their remaining recovery isolated at home with minimal contact with the clinical team. The first 30 days upon returning home after surgery are identified to be a critical and challenging period for patients not only emotionally, practically, and mentally, but also poses a real danger of further complications, readmission, and potentially surgical related death. Remote Patient Monitoring (RPM) systems are extremely promising, allowing clinicians to care for and support patients remotely, however, although these technologies are mature, the level of adoption by the patients is still very low. To address this challenge, we focus on identifying and understanding the patients' concerns and requirements when adopting a novel RPM technology. We conducted a series of iterative Patient Public Involvement workshops following a user-centred approach. We explored various scenarios based on prototypes and facilitated reflective discussions with cancer patients to identify existing barriers preventing them from adopting RPM technologies. The work-shops revealed a wide range of concerns expressed by participants, cate-gorised in five themes. However, lack of reassurance was identified as the central theme during the 30-day post-operative post-discharge period. In conclusion, reassurance proves to be central in engaging patients and making RPM technologies fit for purpose, potentially leading to elevated levels of adoption and improvement on health outcomes and quality of life.

© The Author(s), under exclusive license to Springer Nature Switzerland AG 2023
J. Abdelnour Nocera et al. (Eds.): INTERACT 2023, LNCS 14142, pp. 598–619, 2023.
https://doi.org/10.1007/978-3-031-42280-5_38

Keywords: remote patient monitoring · user-centred design · reassurance

1   Introduction

Cancer, despite the huge amount of research already conducted, remains one of the leading illnesses people currently face, with over 19 million new cases and 10 million deaths globally in 2020 [51]. Living with cancer is a major challenge [12] and the cancer trajectory along with its different events and phases, needs at each phase, and ways to address these needs have been the subject of research for a long time [14,42]. One of the key events in this trajectory is surgery, as more than half of cancer patients are having at least one during their cancer journey [33]. After surgery, the recovery of patients happens in two phases: in the hospital where monitoring is continuous with both devices and clinical teams, and after hospital discharge where monitoring is minimal.

The post-operative post-discharge (POPD) period is particularly critical for cancer patients undergone major surgeries since as many as 27% of patients are re-admitted with serious complications [36]. Over 90% of these cases arise within the first 30 days post-operative, which is also when most surgical related deaths occur [24,56]. It is also the time when patients are left on their own after a period where others were responsible for looking after them [49]. At the same time, patients need to manage unprecedented conditions and incidents including surgery complications, following specific rehabilitation instructions, and monitoring their progress [27]. On top of this, patients still need to live with the disease, attend doctor appointments and treatments, and take their medication. As a result, more than any other period of the cancer journey, patients experience feelings of fear, anxiety, and uncertainty. It is this period of the 30-day POPD period that this research focuses on (see Fig. 1), a period in which reassuring patients becomes crucial [50].

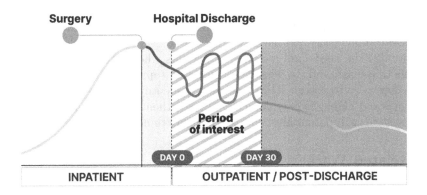

Fig. 1. The *Acute Care & Treatment* phase as identified by Hayes et al. [14], highlighting the period of interest of this study along with other major events.

Remote Patient Monitoring (RPM) technologies have a strong potential to address the challenges outlined above [22,43] whilst reassuring patients effectively. RPM is a healthcare delivery model that uses technological advances to monitor patients outside of a traditional care setting [55]. RPM can collect a variety of patient data, including vital signs, symptoms, and medical history through smart watches, wearable sensors, and mobile phones [39]. This data is shared with health care professionals (HCPs) and can be analysed to inform treatment decisions in a timely and informed fashion. Simultaneously, through portals, patient dashboards, and remote consultations, RPM enables patients to track their disease progress and acquire support and guidance [23,44]. These attributes are particularly important in the POPD period which carries some of the highest risks, thus early action can prevent life-threatening situations [31].

Despite their numerous advantages, the spread of RPM technologies into healthcare and hospitals remains low, which is somewhat surprising given the range of advances commercially available [2,17]. This spread depends on each individual's decision to use technology, defined as *adoption*, and on the collective adoption process of groups of individuals using technology over time, defined as *diffusion* [30]. The low adoption rate by patients is attributed, but not limited, to data protection, privacy, safety, reliability, and accuracy [37]. Another factor affecting the adoption of such systems is the challenging design process [22,54], attempting to satisfy a diverse range of needs from varying end-users simultaneously [32]; the two primary groups being patients and the clinical teams. Both groups need to engage with the technology, while patients are also expected to comply with the given advice. In this study, we will refer to *engagement* as the time spent interacting with the employed technology, and *compliance* as following the instructions or advice given.

In this work, we focus on identifying and understanding the patients' concerns and requirements of adopting a novel RPM technology during the 30-day POPD period. A user-centred process built on a Patient Public Involvement (PPI) approach was used to understand how to increase patients' motivation and willingness to adopt RMP technology [47]. We accomplish this according to the five-stage process proposed by Bowen et al. [4] and conducting three iterative online PPI workshops with cancer patients. The goal of the workshops was to investigate and identify: (1) the post-discharge recovery journey of post-operative patients, (2) the needs and concerns of patients when returning home and the barriers that exist, and (3) what features would support patients in their recovery if they were to use an RPM system. We identify cancer patients' concerns in themes and highlight reassurance as the key theme, which if addressed by an RPM system, will potentially motivate patients to adopt such technologies.

2   Related Work

2.1   Cancer Journey Phases and Needs

Cancer patients go through different cancer journeys attributed to their age, cancer type, stage of cancer, and treatment plan [7]. Despite this, there are commonalities between patients' cancer journeys described in five main phases: *Screening & Diagnosis, Initial Information-Seeking, Acute Care & Treatment, No Evidence of Disease*, and *Chronic Disease & Disease Management* [14]. While research has been conducted to identify and meet patient needs [18], these studies group all five stages of the cancer journey together rather than exploring their individual requirements [34]. Considering the challenges of each different phase can inform the focus which designers should have in designing health technologies, and patients to benefit the maximum [19]. Since we are expecting patients to adopt technologies, so must the technologies be designed according to each phase's needs.

Within HCI the *Acute Care & Treatment* phase has gained a considerable amount of attention due to the major events of surgery taking place; specifically the post-operative post-discharge (POPD) period. Only patients who undergo surgery experience the post-operative period, which is full of challenges including unexpected complications and feelings of anxiety and uncertainty as the result of the surgery [19]. The post-operative period becomes even more challenging when combined with the post-discharge period. Sanger et al. [45] mentions that improper care of wound monitoring during this period can affect both clinical outcomes and quality of life of patients, while Saunders et al. [46] links poorer outcomes with untimely communication between patients and health care professionals (HCPs). However, existing research either concentrates on a specific type of cancer [1], on specific domains of needs like access to information [20,25,26] and psycho-social support [48], or is limited to the interactions patients made during their hospital visits [42]. Therefore, there is a need to re-evaluate cancer patient concerns specifically during the 30-day POPD period and suggest approaches which can practically be applied to treat these concerns.

2.2 Reassurance in Healthcare

One approach that has been examined to treat patients' concerns is to consider the role of reassurance. This is defined by Linton et al. [29] as *"a set of behaviours carried out by practitioners, which aims to reduce concerns in patients"*. Reassurance is emerging as important to address in the contexts of non-specific conditions, like lower back pain [53], mainly in the occurrence of acute episodes [16] and during interactions between patients and HCPs [15,16]. The importance that reassurance has for cancer patients has already been demonstrated [52], but existing studies are limited to follow-up consultations [50] or tracking of symptoms [1].

Pincus et al. [41] addressed the need for reassurance during the particular phase of initial information-seeking and suggests reassurance as the main factor to improve patient outcomes by providing clear explanations and information during consultations. However, effectively reassuring patients in phases where uncertainty is present, like the acute treatment phase, is still unexplored. In addition, despite the measures used by Holt et al. [16], which solely rely on the patient's input, comprehensive and reliable measures of reassurance are still needed [41]. Such measures will enable the evaluation of reassurance's impact on patient outcomes, recalling information, compliance with advice, symptoms resolution, and well-being. In sum, reassurance is currently poorly understood when applied to clinical practice [9,16]. Our research seeks to address this in the context of when patients return home after surgery for cancer.

2.3 Supporting Cancer Patients When at Home

Monitoring patients allows HCPs to detect whether the patient is recovering as expected and predict future complications and potential re-admissions [3]. Recent advances related to eHealth and mHealth (e.g., telehealth, electronic health records, web and mobile platforms) use health data provided by patients to facilitate self-monitoring in a range of conditions [38]. Remote Patient Monitoring (RPM) enable patients to control their disease progress and acquire support and guidance [31] by tracking symptoms, monitoring vital signs and receiving remote consultations through portals and dashboards [40]. These attributes are particularly important in the POPD period which entails some of the highest risks since RPMs can enable early intervention from clinicians to prevent deterioration and life-threatening situations [31]. Overall, RPMs are shown to have the capability of improving clinical outcomes, reduce healthcare costs, and empower patients to take control of their health [40].

Despite the development of RPMs for self-monitoring of chronic diseases, the lack of adopting such technologies remains unknown. People stop using self-tracking technologies, referred to as *abandonment*, mainly due to a mismatch between users' hopes and expectations and device capabilities [8] or technology not fitting in their lives nor supporting their goals [10]. Lazar et al. [28] classifies abandonment into three main categories: (1) devices not fitting with participants' conceptions of themselves, (2) acquired data not useful, and (3) devices needing effort and maintenance. While recommendations to avoid abandonment [11] and influence adoption have already been made [11], currently there is no research that has identified the reasoning behind why the uptake and adoption of mHealth technology, specifically for cancer patients, is so low.

3 Methods

The aim of this study is to identify and understand the needs of cancer patients in using a Remote Patient Monitoring (RPM) system. Designing such novel technologies for users with different characteristics and perspectives is challenging and requires different concerns and expectations to be taken into account [54]. To achieve this, we relied on the first three of the five-stage approach developed by Bowen et al. [4] consisting of (i) understanding and sharing experiences, (ii) exploring blue-sky ideas, (iii) selecting and developing blue-sky concepts, (iv) converging to practical proposals, and (v) prototyping and evaluating. These stages were adopted through three iterative Patient Public Involvement (PPI) workshops, as illustrated in Fig. 2. The methodology of the study relies on an

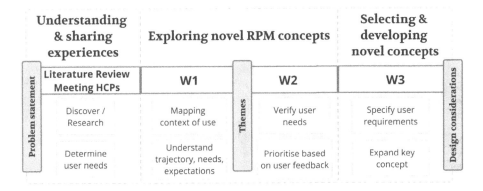

Fig. 2. The first three stages of Bowen et al. [4] approach used to inform our iterative, user-centred design process consisting of three PPI workshops.

iterative user-centred process where the findings of each workshop informed the design of each subsequent workshop [13].

The theoretical framework of the '*Understanding and sharing experiences*' stage was used to define the agenda and aim of workshop one (W1). The goal of W1 was to understand the patients' experiences and get their views on how remote monitoring could be facilitated throughout their cancer journey; thus, allowing us to identify and classify cancer patients' needs in terms of specific themes. These themes informed the design of the prototypes used in W2 and W3. In W2 participants verified the identified themes and discussed which theme they think as the most important when using RPMs. In W3 we explored user requirements focusing on the key theme identified by the previous two workshops. Throughout the workshops we adopted a sharing, suggesting, and exploring methodology [5] through discussing lived experiences, using case scenarios to promote discussion, and interacting with a prototype.

3.1 Participants

The participants recruited for the workshops were found through advertising via online events, university networks, and referrals from health care professionals (HCPs). Sampling criteria were developed collectively by the research team and the HCPs to ensure adequate sampling in terms of gender, age, cancer type and stage, and treatment type, with all participants having had surgery at some point in their cancer journey. Eight accepted our invitation and made it to the first workshop, with their characteristics detailed in Table 1. All eight participants were able to join the second workshop, whilst only six were able to attend the third. All participants were recovered or recovering cancer patients, thus, for some participation was more difficult than others and subject to unexpected incidents, e.g., feeling ill or exhausted from undergoing treatment.

Once the participants were recruited they each received a participant information sheet detailing the project and how their data would be obtained and

Table 1. The information of the PPI workshops' participants.

Patient ID	Sex	Age Group	Cancer Type	Cancer Stage	Treatment(s) Type
P1	F	70-75	Breast	-	Surgery, Chemotherapy, Radiotherapy, Hormonal Therapy
P2	F	65-70	Colon	-	Surgery, Chemotherapy
P3	M	65-70	Bowel	III/IV	Surgery
P4	M	51-55	Lung	IV	Surgery, Chemotherapy
P5	M	55-60	Bowel	IV	Surgery, Chemotherapy, Radiotherapy, Drug treatment
P6	F	45-50	Breast	-	Surgery, Radiotherapy, Drug treatment
P7	F	61-65	Breast	-	Surgery, Radiotherapy, Drug treatment
P8	M	65-70	Bowel	III	Surgery, Radiotherapy, Drug treatment

stored. Prior to each workshop participants' consent was acquired before any data collection in both written and oral form, as part of our ethical clearance #UCLIC/1819/008/RogersProgrammeEthic. Each workshop lasted for approximately 2.5 h with participants being compensated for their time with a cash voucher. Participants were also free to withdraw at any time without providing a reason. To reduce the strain on participants, and to allow time for reflection and iteration from the research team on prototypes, the workshops were held every 5 months, with the first in September 2021, and the last in June 2022. Owing to the COVID-19 pandemic, the workshops were conducted remotely.

During the workshops, all of the discussions were video recorded, transcribed, anonymised, and analysed using NVivo, a tool used to interpret qualitative data. The data was analysed using thematic analysis and systematically categorised into themes and sub-themes [6]. Thematic analysis is a commonly used method for analysing and reporting themes within qualitative data by becoming familiar with the data; generating initial codes; searching for themes; reviewing themes; defining and naming themes; and producing a report [6].

3.2 Workshops

Workshop One (W1). Participants received a short introduction to the background of the research, followed by a general discussion to set the scene and establish expectations and understanding around the key concept. Group discussion explored the idea of "remote monitoring of well-being". Then, participants were divided into two smaller groups, with a mix in terms of background based on their profile. The breakout groups covered several aspects of remote monitoring including: benefits, opportunities, requirements, practicalities, concerns, and motivation. Specific questions served as a catalyst for initiating discussion. To conclude, participants were shown screenshots of an early prototype, designed by the HCPs' team prior to the workshops without any input from patients. While exploring the prototypes participants were asked two specific questions that were intended to prompt focused discussion and encourage them to broadly comment on their preferences looking for an initial understanding of whether there is consensus (or not). The questions examined: (a) whether patients would prefer being in control of the information they provide or letting clinicians ask the questions that are important to them, and (b) whether patients would prefer the welcome screen of the app to be task-oriented or information-oriented.

Workshop Two (W2). To initiate W2 we explored the concept of "Nice-to-have" vs. "Need-to-have", a widely used concept in user experience (UX) to describe and categorise end-users' requirements [35]. This concept provides insights regarding the importance of the identified requirements, while at the same time evoking end-users to think about the difference between critical and non-critical requirements. As the workshop was online, we used Menti, which is an audience engagement platform that supports live and instant polls, quizzes, and informative Q&As, thus allowing participants to interact with the data easily without requiring any registration on their end. Menti also enabled a real-time visual representation of the results according to each patient's vote, allowing participants to provide their input while not creating bias. To prioritise the sub-themes and determine which themes are most important to participants we ran a dot-voting activity. This was achieved using Miro, another online platform where participants could place votes on the sub-themes. Each participant was granted three votes, which they could place on any of the sub-themes they deemed most important, and participants had the ability to place more than one dot on the same sub-theme if they deemed it more important than other sub-themes. The second part of the workshop involved discussing and gathering feedback on the top two sub-themes according to the dot-voting activity. Since the two sub-themes were not known in advance of W2, the research team had to prepare a prototype app to showcase examples for each sub-theme. The two top sub-themes were presented by case scenarios alongside prototype app displays to initiate discussion and promote further understanding of how RPM could support each sub-theme.

Workshop Three (W3). The third workshop focused on the key theme as identified in W1 and W2 and its relationship to RPMs during the 30-day post-operative post-discharge period. To begin, a review of W1 and W2 was given, explaining how the conclusions drawn from these workshops inspired the next, resulting in setting the scene for W3. Following this, a group discussion covered four questions relating to the identified key theme. To complete W3, suggested features relating to the key theme which identified in W1 and W2 were presented to the participants, introduced by five case scenarios, see Table 2. These scenarios were based on the concerns of the participants gathered in prior workshops and based on lived experiences, allowing participants to explore new features whilst giving feedback for each scenario. Additionally, we investigated possible overlaps with other identified themes in relation to the key theme to ensure that we have prioritised the correct theme.

Table 2. The five case scenarios used to introduce the prototype for each of the suggested features during W3.

Case scenario	Description
1	You need to be able to interpret your progress: (1) Set and follow specific & achievable goals, (2) Understand how you are doing by comparing among patients with similar characteristics, (3) Receive informed feedback on each different day and adapt goals accordingly
2	You had your latest interaction with your healthcare team two weeks ago: (1) You don't remember part of the given instructions, (2) You need to recall what was mentioned, (3) You want to share with a family member who could not make it to the appointment
3	You get back home after your latest interaction, but not everything is clear: (1) You want to know more regarding a term, (2) You need to trust information you find, (3) You want to get this information through different mediums, (4) You need to translate this information
4	In the 30 days after surgery and hospital discharge you have several things to remember: (1) Medications uptake, (2) Attend appointments, (3) Keep track of your progress, (4) Keep up with monitoring tasks
5	You need to talk with your healthcare team about something that troubles you: (1) You can't find the point of contact you were given, (2) You need to know when someone is available, (3) You need to know your healthcare team is aware you are trying to contact them

4   Results

This section presents the findings of our iterative design process based on the three Patient Public Involvement (PPI) workshops. The findings include the themes identified through the thematic analysis, how the key theme was selected, promotes further understanding of the key theme and suggests design considerations on how the key theme can drive the development of Remote Patient Monitoring (RPM) technology.

4.1   Themes and Sub-themes

The thematic analysis of the data obtained in W1 identified five themes and 13 supporting sub-themes (see Table 3), which describe the needs of patients that should be satisfied in the implementation of RPM technology.

Table 3. The identified five themes along with its sub-themes.

Themes	Sub-themes
Reassurance	- Progress Indicators
	- Comparison (with other patients)
	- Informed feedback/advice - Guidance based on data
Access to information	- Effortless/Reliable/Targeted
	- Translatable
Personalisation	- Cancer type & stage/Treatment type & status
	- Control/Track of ongoing events
	- Reminders
Communication	- Out-of-office hours contact
	- Talk with the right person
Data use	- In charge of **who** is accessing & **how** is used
	- Efficient use/Coordination among various doctors
	- Responsiveness/Real-time monitoring

4.2 Prioritising Sub-themes

Participants undertook a theme prioritising task during W2 aiming to resonate which of the sub-themes identified during W1 were the most important. The only theme with two of its sub-themes voted was '*Reassurance*', indicative of its importance. In addition, participants were repeatedly raising the theme of '*Reassurance*' while discussing the other themes, even though it was not mentioned directly. The indicative overlapping between reassurance as noted during the analysis of W2, led the research team to revise the data obtained from W1. This was corroborated by a statement from P8 during W1 "*So if your app doesn't cover the reassurance piece, it can be functionally very rich, maybe over rich, but I think that's an issue*". At the time reassurance was identified as an individual theme amongst others, but upon reflection and in conjunction with the results from W2, we decided that reassurance held a critical role in the adoption of RPM technology. Therefore, we identified reassurance as a concept arising during the discussions of both, W1 and W2, and collectively interwoven throughout the other four themes (Personalisation, Access to information, Communication, Data use). Thus, a new arrangement of the themes was proposed, illustrated in Fig. 3, with reassurance highlighted as the key theme. To investigate further how the participants' needs might be met in regards to reassurance, a potential prototype of an mHealth app was designed and demonstrated to participants, gauging their feedback on how well it could address their needs, see Fig. 4.

Fig. 3. The connection which the workshops revealed between the '*Reassurance*' theme and the other four themes.

4.3   Reassurance: The Key Theme

The discussion during the first part of W3 was framed by four questions aimed to offer insights into understanding the key theme. The results for each of the four questions are given in the following sub-sections.

What Does Reassurance Mean for Patients? Reassurance, as defined by the participants, is connected with: (1) confidence, when things do not turn out as expected (*"The first line of reassurance is to give people back confidence if they are feeling certain symptoms"* - P4, W3), (2) understanding the unknown and building knowledge (*"So what you need to provide is a form of being informed and being reassured that this is normal or not for where you are in your journey at the moment"* - P8, W3), (3) effective communication and timely support (*"I don't want to ring 999 if it's not a 999 situation, but how, as a patient, am I supposed to know that?"* - P8, W3) and (4) using the deployed technology efficiently (*"Having this sensor feeding information back provided we know that is going to be monitored, I think that would have given me a really good sort of reassurance in a lot of ways"* - P2, W3).

What Does Reassurance Mean for Patients During the Post-operative Post-discharge Period? Building on the previous views, participants were asked to think about reassurance in the specific context of the POPD period. In this specific context, participants related reassurance with the uncertainty of having someone looking after them, which occurs when they leave the hospital (*"[..]You know someone is there to look after you. That's the reassurance you need when you leave that environment"* - P8, W3).

Is Reassurance More Important at Any (other) Period of Your Cancer Journey? When discussing reassurance it became apparent that the most critical time patients require reassurance is after being discharged from the hospital. This was emphasised by P1 who stated *"I think the scary time came when I was discharged."* and P8 adding that *"The time when I was the most concerned and needed reassurance it was when I was left on my own, so certainly on hospital discharge."*. The previous statements were followed by P2 adding *"With infections and stuff picked up during surgery, post-surgery is when you need reassurance."*

How Can It Be Practically Applied? Can You Visualise It? Participants were asked to recall cases when they successfully received reassurance as well as cases when they did not receive the reassurance they were seeking. P2 stated *"I would like rather than an app, to contact another person - this is more important to me"*, underlining the importance of communication in receiving reassurance. Additionally, P4 visualised reassurance in the form of a feature which can monitor vital signs in real-time and provide guidance to the patient *"Particularly to give you all the indicators you need to know. If your temperature goes up or you're feeling unwell, 'hey, you know, this is normal'. If this is included in the app, the patient might feel reassured at the time and would be very beneficial"*. Following a comment from a member of the research team, participants discussed whether reassurance could be provided by people other rather than HCPs, such as previous patients. P2 stated *"I was a community champion on the Bell Cancer Forum for six years and I was able to give a lot of reassurance to a lot of people because I had been there"*, with P5 having a similar opinion *"Forums mean a lot to me and have been really helpful"*.

4.4 Features to Support Reassurance

To investigate further the views of participants on specific features relating to reassurance, the last part of W3 incorporated discussion based on case scenarios (Table 2). Each of the following subsections describes a specific solution given to satisfy the reassurance needs, expressed either directly or indirectly, according to the presented case scenarios.

Direct Reassurance. Direct reassurance relates to all features that are satisfying reassurance directly and not as part of other themes. Participants expressed the need to know and interpret their progress. This was complemented by the need to know how good patients were doing compared to other patients with the same conditions (*"I like being part of this data collection, you can compare* *yourself with others like you, people like me*" - P1, W1). To address this we introduced the feature of '*Hub*' (Fig. 4a). The '*Hub*' feature demonstrates the progress of passively (e.g. vital signs, steps) or actively (e.g. surveys) collected data, and if desired patients can enable an average indication and population progress, thus allowing patients to compare themselves with patients with the same characteristics. Additionally, honest feedback ("*You don't always want positive comments. Honest comments are the most helpful*" - P8, W2), was collectively described by participants as a way to help them interpret what they were seeing in the progress charts and collectively agreed that should be expressed with encouragement and positivity ("*Even if we have failings, highlight the shortcoming, but balance it with encouragement and positivity*" - P5, W2), whilst avoiding repetitive messages ("*Receiving the same message day after day, it's a bit like Amazon recommendations: you may have bought it a night ago, but they're still recommending it to you*" - P8, W2).

Reassurance as the Result of Access to Information. Participants expressed the need to recall important information communicated during their interactions with HCPs. When discussing this scenario participants were raising reassurance as the reference point to discussions they had with HCPs, with P3 stating that "*[..] doctors being recorded when they give a diagnosis or an opinion, this is reassurance that has to be given*". To address this need, we suggested '*Recording*' a feature which supports voice recording and that could easily be activated by either the HCP or the patient, see Fig. 4b. The feature was designed to support a function entitled '*Library*', serving as an archive of recordings, allowing filtering by date and HCP for easier and more convenient access to data.

Another concept discussed by participants was the extent of which clinical terminology is used during their interactions with HCPs and the subsequent lack of interpreting such terminology by accessing reliable sources ("*[..] there are links if I want to dive further, [..] my question is what would make that reliable?*" - P8, W2). Thus, this is a common place where potential misinterpretation between what the clinicians are instructing and what patients interpret, happens. P4 stated that "*I wonder why you are collecting certain information. People don't always understand [..], but if you explain to them, then they improve their health literacy and it can be both educational and motivating*", expressing the importance of understanding the information they receive from HCPs and linked it directly with health literacy. To address these needs we introduced a function to auto-transcribe recording (Fig. 4c), highlight clinical terms and link with resources approved by HCPs, providing patients with the reassurance that they can interpret information effectively and with reliability.

Participants also reached a consensus that more options for interpreting relevant information ("*A cartoon or something more expressive would be more appreciated than textual form.* - P1, W3") are indicative of increased levels of reassurance; especially relevant to those with English as an additional language ("*It would be helpful to have some images particularly for people whose English is not*

(a)   (b)   (c)   (d)

Fig. 4. (a) '*Hub*' - Collated progress from wearable & survey data. (b) '*Recording*' - Voice recording, note-taking, and "action" flags. (c) '*Transcription*' - Auto-transcribe, highlighting clinical terms with reliable links. (d) '*Calendar*' - Appointments, medication reminders, daily tasks, and '*Passive mode*'.

their first language - P1, W3"). To satisfy this we proposed a feature that makes the relevant information available in multiple forms including text, visual, audio, audio-visual and discussion (forums). We also suggested that the transcriptions are auto-translated into the patient's native language.

Reassurance as the Result of Personalisation. During the 30-day POPD period patients are required to continue taking their medication, attending appointments, and keeping track of their progress. P4 stated *"[..] create a positive influence for a cancer patient to have some control back in their life. And if an app can provide that, I think that's great"*, with P6 adding *"I know it's difficult because everybody is different and not everybody will experience the same things at the same time"*, emphasising the different perceptions regarding how patients would like to track their progress. P8 suggested reminders stating *"It's about that time, is it? Time to take your tablets. That's a useful reminder [..]"*. Participants emphasised the meaning of personalising reminders and notifications according to the ongoing events or tasks, or according to a particular day. '*Calendar*' is a feature developed to assist patients to organise their upcoming events (Fig. 4d) classified in categories. Actions required by the patient are also linked, e.g., scheduling a blood test. The '*Calendar*' feature allows personalising reminders and notifications (e.g., time of the day, muted, etc.), setting personal goals, and scheduling notifications with associated tasks.

Participants expressed their willingness to be prompted according to their daily tasks and monitoring instructions. However, due to patients' continual changes in conditions, ongoing treatments, and needs for medication, sometimes completing such tasks is not feasible. On such days patients do not want to complete tasks, do not want to receive notifications, and do not even want to get out of bed as clearly indicated by P2 *"When I had my surgery and I came home I was fine. I could cope with filling in a survey more or less every day, but when I was going through chemo, the last thing I would want to do was fill in the survey because I was ill. Some days I didn't want to get out of bed. I didn't want to do other things"*. Considering this we proposed a function called '*Passive mode*' (Fig. 4d), which allows patients to manually toggle this function and silent tasks and notifications resulting from the app. From the HCP's perspective, we know that this creates a gap in data, however, it offers insights about the underlying reasons why this gap occurred, e.g., the patient did not feel capable at that time. These underlying reasons can become more insightful for HCPs if combined with the information included in the '*Calendar*', e.g., a scheduled treatment, creating patterns which HCPs can identify. HCPs could then follow up on these cases by reaching out to patients to identify specific needs, thus, providing qualitative data to explain gaps identified in quantitative data.

Reassurance as the Result of Communication. Participants expressed the need to know that someone is available when they need them most. These concerns arise in cases when their point of contact is on vacation, during out-of-office hours, or when phone lines are busy and staffing resources are limited. P2 stated *"Things happen, but I don't know whether anybody is aware of it. Chatting online is fine when you know people, but sometimes if there's a voice at the end of the line, they can give you far more reassurance than someone chatting to you online can"*. P3 agreed saying *"Coaching and support are crucial. Links to people like Macmillan or Cancer Research, whoever deals specifically with the type of cancer that people have been suffering from"*.

To rectify this we proposed a chatbot informed by: (1) collected patient data from wearable devices and manual input, (e.g., surveys, questionnaires), (2) data captured by other functions of the app, (e.g., automatic transcription of recordings) and (3) geographical data, (e.g., local weather). The chatbot is intended to provide reassurance for patients when human contact is not feasible. Some participants agreed that chatbots could be helpful and address the issue of the unavailability of HCPs, such as P3 who stated that *"Research indicates that the automated diagnosis programs and routines are just as good as an actual human. Maybe the chatbots could be very useful. You know they could actually be very accurate indeed and address the problem of availability of humans"*. Others thought they could not adequately substitute a HCP such as P8 who stated that *"My experience with chatbots has not been great, it's like an interactive version of FAQ. The answer you get doesn't relate to the question you asked, so it's not going to be a personalised thing anyway"*. In sum, participants were not against the idea, but all were highlighting their shortcomings.

Reassurance as the Result of Data Use. Patients want to be reassured regarding who is able to access their data, for example, P2 stating *"It's one thing I hadn't thought about: who has access to this data?"*. P6 then mentioned the issue of the efficient use of data stating *"[..] that data being collected is brilliant. But if it's going to sit for ages before somebody accesses it and does something with it then you could have a really sharp period of decline and deterioration before it's acted upon"*. Another common issue is the coordination between the various doctors a patient is attending. This was raised by P5 - *"A disconnection between my clinician for IBS and the urologist it was the reason of becoming stage four"*. Thus, when patients become either sceptical regarding providing their data or unsure whether the employed technology can be of any help, their assurance in using the app is lost.

To address these concerns we proposed the *'Share'* function, designed to allow patients to be in control of their files and documents and who has access to them (Figs. 4c and 4d). To provide patients with the reassurance that HCPs have reviewed their data, we introduced the *'Delivery receipt'* function, so patients can view who has accessed what information and when.

5   Discussion

Our research has shown how it is possible to identify the requirements for a Remote Patient Monitoring (RPM) tool, that has the potential to improve adoption and compliance, through a series of Patient Public Involvement (PPI) workshops. This paper has focused on the concerns of cancer patients who have undergone major surgery while in the 30-day period rehabilitating at home. Our main finding identified by participants was the need for reassurance during this period. This work extends on existing studies of designing technologies for cancer patients and contributes to the body of knowledge in this area by exploring how reassurance is perceived by patients and how can be improved during self-monitoring of their health and general well-being.

The workshops revealed a high level of willingness and satisfaction from patients in using mHealth technology for self-monitoring. However, we found this contradictory given the low level of adoption of these technologies. The qualitative methodological approach we undertook, allowed us to reveal what the current technology lacks despite being over-rich in terms of features. First, we approached the *Acute Care & Treatment* phase, identified by Hayes et al. [14], independently from the rest of the cancer journey, as patients' needs change based on which phase they are in [19]. Second, coupling an mHealth app with a wearable sensor proved to be intriguing for patients and allowed us to explore additional dimensions of needs already identified in the literature [20,25,26]. This perspective enabled us to observe the prevalent role of uncertainty as the result of rehabilitating in the remote setting after major surgery, together with magnified concerns, fears and worries. Thus, more than any other period of the cancer journey, treating such feelings should become the priority of any health technology. Our research identifies the emerging need for reassurance specifically in the 30-day post-operative post-discharge (POPD) period and suggests tangible solutions which are capable of providing direct or indirect reassurance to patients through RPM technology.

Reassurance in healthcare is still poorly supported [9,16]. In this research we were able to identify key instances of reassurance that patients seek during the 30-day POPD period; specifically, when unforeseen symptoms occur, patients are unable to track their own progress, and when they are unable to recall or interpret information exchanged with HCPs. Pincus et al. [41] highlight that reassurance can be improved by providing clear explanations and information, but when patients are recovering at home, access to this information is not as easy to obtain. We relied on three core concepts to address these concerns that provide the necessary reassurance to patients. First, we provide patients with guidance on what they should expect based on their current stage of recovery through personalised and data-informed feedback. Second, we allow patients to view and interact with this data whilst tracking their progress against average patient data. Third, we allow patients to capture and review previous discussions with HCPs, while interpreting and recalling this information through reliable sources.

These design ideas can impact reassurance, potentially inspire engagement, and improve adoption and compliance. In addition, previous work has suggested that customisation, mobility, balance of information, and privacy are key to improving adoption [21]. However, we argue that in the phase of *Acute Care & Treatment*, patients are more likely to adopt and comply with technology if they know their data is being reviewed and be reassured they can reach the correct person when in need. Such tasks put a great deal of pressure on clinicians, mainly because of the workload and the number of patients in the clinician's care. As the workshops revealed, patients understand these struggles while also not wanting to be a burden or seeking assistance when it is not a real emergency. However, such judgements are built on each individual's level of health literacy and understanding of the technology's capabilities. Although our proposed app cannot fully replace the presence of clinical teams, it can mitigate the fears, concerns, worries, and uncertainty patients may harbour. Providing this certain level of reassurance could significantly reduce the burden on hospitals and prevent potential re-admissions. To achieve this, we propose applying machine learning on real-time data to determine whether a clinical intervention is needed coupled with chatbots to facilitate continuous reassurance based on available data (e.g., appointments, treatments, given advice).

A strength of our research is the iterative approach of three PPI workshops in which the outcome of each workshop informed the agenda and the aims of the subsequent workshop. Participants could reflect on the findings of the previous workshops by enriching their views and recalling specific personal experiences. At the same time, the research team could confirm the theoretical framework used to initiate the workshops, verify the findings of each previous workshop, and highlight key findings. However, the group setting of the workshops proved to be challenging, primarily due to the varying levels of PPI experience across the group, limiting any technical input from more experienced participants. In addition, the virtual activities did not engage the participants as much as the in-person workshops would have and required additional time. Despite the challenges, this setting allowed us to recruit participants that we otherwise would not have been able to as travelling to venues was no longer a burden. To understand how our proposed app can be effectively applied to clinical practice, we will need to deploy the app within the remote setting and gather feedback from both patients and healthcare providers. It is also important to evaluate the long-term effectiveness, scalability, and potential limitations of the app through usability testing studies and large-scale clinical trials. Additionally, determining whether reassurance has a measurable impact on adoption and compliance, including establishing comprehensive and reliable measures of reassurance, specifically in the context of RPM, are also potential areas of future investigation.

6 Conclusion

The majority of cancer patients go through the post-operative post-discharge period which involves additional challenges compared to the rest of the cancer journey. In this study, participants confirmed the special and additional needs which occur as a result of surgery and confirmed the period where they are left on their own post-surgery as one of the most critical. Participants identified reassurance as central to their recovery and that it should be incorporated within Remote Patient Monitoring (RPM) technologies. Through our design recommendations, we anticipate this can improve adoption and compliance of RPM technology during this specific period. Finally, these recommendations are capable of enhancing the care provided to cancer patients, improving health outcomes and expanding into the acute care for other chronic diseases, specifically those that involve a major surgery.

Acknowledgements. This work was supported by the Engineering and Physical Sciences Research Council (EPSRC) [EP/N509577/1]; the Computer Science Department in University College London (UCL); and the Wellcome/EPSRC Centre for Interventional and Surgical Sciences (WEISS) [203145Z/16/Z]. We also acknowledge The Urology Foundation and the Champniss Foundation for funding the application development and the clinical trial. Finally, we would like to thank all participants for their valuable and insightful input.

References

1. Ancker, J.S., Stabile, C., Carter, J.: Informing, reassuring, or alarming? Balancing patient needs in the development of a postsurgical symptom reporting system in cancer. In: AMIA Annual Symposium Proceedings 2018, pp. 166–174 (2018)
2. Baig, M.M., GholamHosseini, H., Moqeem, A.A., Mirza, F., Lindén, M.: A systematic review of wearable patient monitoring systems - current challenges and opportunities for clinical adoption. J. Med. Syst. **41**(7), 115 (2017). https://doi.org/10.1007/s10916-017-0760-1

3. Bartoli, L., Zanaboni, P., Masella, C., Ursini, N.: Systematic review of telemedicine services for patients affected by chronic obstructive pulmonary disease (COPD). Telemed. J. e-Health **15**(9), 877–883 (2009)

4. Bowen, S., Mcseveny, K., Lockley, E., Dearden, A.: How was it for you?: experiences of participatory design in the UK health service. CoDesign **9**, 230–246 (2013). https://doi.org/10.1080/15710882.2013.846384

5. Brandt, E., Binder, T., Sanders, E.: Tools and techniques: ways to engage telling, making and enacting, pp. 145–181 (2012)

6. Braun, V., Clarke, V.: Using thematic analysis in psychology. Qual. Res. Psychol. **3**(2), 77–101 (2006)

7. Chou, Y.H., Chia-Rong Hsieh, V., Chen, X., Huang, T.Y., Shieh, S.H.: Unmet supportive care needs of survival patients with breast cancer in different cancer stages and treatment phases. Taiwan. J. Obstet. Gynecol. **59**(2), 231–236 (2020). https://doi.org/10.1016/j.tjog.2020.01.010

8. Clawson, J., Pater, J.A., Miller, A.D., Mynatt, E.D., Mamykina, L.: No longer wearing: investigating the abandonment of personal health-tracking technologies on craigslist. In: Proceedings of the 2015 ACM International Joint Conference on Pervasive and Ubiquitous Computing, pp. 647–658 (2015)

9. Coia, P., Morely, S.: Medical reassurance and patients' responses. J. Psychosom. Res. **45**(5), 377–386 (1998)

10. Epstein, D.A., Caraway, M., Johnston, C., Ping, A., Fogarty, J., Munson, S.A.: Beyond abandonment to next steps: understanding and designing for life after personal informatics tool use. In: Proceedings of the 2016 CHI Conference on Human Factors in Computing Systems, pp. 1109–1113 (2016)

11. Epstein, D.A., Kang, J.H., Pina, L.R., Fogarty, J., Munson, S.A.: Reconsidering the device in the drawer: lapses as a design opportunity in personal informatics. In: Proceedings of the 2016 ACM International Joint Conference on Pervasive and Ubiquitous Computing, pp. 829–840 (2016)

12. Fransson, P.: Fatigue in prostate cancer patients treated with external beam radiotherapy: a prospective 5-year long-term patient-reported evaluation. J. Cancer Res. Ther. **6**(4), 516–520 (2010)

13. Gregory, J.: Scandinavian approaches to participatory design. Int. J. Eng. Educ. **19**, 62–74 (2003)

14. Hayes, G., Abowd, G., Davis, J., Blount, M., Ebling, M., Mynatt, E.: Opportunities for Pervasive Computing in Chronic Cancer Care (2008)

15. Holt, N., Mansell, G., Hill, J.C., Pincus, T.: Testing a model of consultation-based reassurance and back pain outcomes with psychological risk as moderator: a prospective cohort study. Clin. J. Pain **34**(4), 339 (2018)

16. Holt, N., Pincus, T.: Developing and testing a measure of consultation-based reassurance for people with low back pain in primary care: a cross-sectional study. BMC Musculoskelet. Disord. **17**, 277 (2016)

17. Iyanna, S., Kaur, P., Ractham, P., Talwar, S., Islam, A.K.M.N.: Digital transformation of healthcare sector. What is impeding adoption and continued usage of technology-driven innovations by end-users? J. Bus. Res. **153**, 150–161 (2022). https://doi.org/10.1016/j.jbusres.2022.08.007

18. Jacobs, M.L., Clawson, J., Mynatt, E.D.: Articulating a patient-centered design space for cancer journeys. EAI Endorsed Trans. Pervasive Health Technol. **3**(9), e5 (2017)

19. Jacobs, M., Clawson, J., Mynatt, E.D.: A cancer journey framework: guiding the design of holistic health technology. In: Proceedings of the 10th EAI International Conference on Pervasive Computing Technologies for Healthcare, pp. 114–121 (2016)
20. Jacobs, M., Johnson, J., Mynatt, E.D.: MyPath: investigating breast cancer patients' use of personalized health information. Proc. ACM Hum.-Comput. Interact. **2**(CSCW), 1–21 (2018)
21. Jacobs, M.L., Clawson, J., Mynatt, E.D.: My journey compass: a preliminary investigation of a mobile tool for cancer patients. In: Proceedings of the SIGCHI Conference on Human Factors in Computing Systems, pp. 663–672 (2014)
22. Jeddi, Z., Bohr, A.: Remote patient monitoring using artificial intelligence. In: Bohr, A., Memarzadeh, K. (eds.) Artificial Intelligence in Healthcare, pp. 203–234. Academic Press (2020)
23. Kakria, P., Tripathi, N.K., Kitipawang, P.: A real-time health monitoring system for remote cardiac patients using smartphone and wearable sensors. Int. J. Telemed. Appl. **2015**, 373474 (2015)
24. Khetrapal, P., et al.: Measuring patient compliance with remote monitoring following discharge from hospital after major surgery (DREAMPath): protocol for a prospective observational study. JMIR Res. Protoc. **11**(4), e30638 (2022). https://doi.org/10.2196/30638
25. Klasnja, P., Hartzler, A., Powell, C., Pratt, W.: Supporting cancer patients' unanchored health information management with mobile technology. In: AMIA Annual Symposium Proceedings. AMIA Symposium 2011, pp. 732–741 (2011)
26. Klasnja, P., Hartzler, A.C., Unruh, K.T., Pratt, W.: Blowing in the wind: unanchored patient information work during cancer care. In: Proceedings of the SIGCHI Conference on Human Factors in Computing Systems, pp. 193–202 (2010)
27. de Kok, M.: Patients' opinions on quality of care before and after implementation of a short stay programme following breast cancer surgery. Breast **19**(5), 404–409 (2010)
28. Lazar, A., Koehler, C., Tanenbaum, T.J., Nguyen, D.H.: Why we use and abandon smart devices. In: Proceedings of the 2015 ACM International Joint Conference on Pervasive and Ubiquitous Computing, pp. 635–646 (2015)
29. Linton, S.J., McCracken, L.M., Vlaeyen, J.W.: Reassurance: help or hinder in the treatment of pain. PAIN **134**(1), 5–8 (2008)
30. Liu, L., Miguel-Cruz, A.: Technology adoption and diffusion in healthcare at onset of COVID-19 and beyond. Healthc. Manage. Forum **35**(3), 161–167 (2022). https://doi.org/10.1177/08404704211058842
31. Malasinghe, L.P., Ramzan, N., Dahal, K.: Remote patient monitoring: a comprehensive study. J. Ambient. Intell. Humaniz. Comput. **10**(1), 57–76 (2019). https://doi.org/10.1007/s12652-017-0598-x
32. McCurdie, T., et al.: mHealth consumer apps: the case for user-centered design. Biomed. Instrum. Technol. Suppl. 49–56 (2012). https://doi.org/10.2345/0899-8205-46.s2.49
33. Miller, K.D., et al.: Cancer treatment and survivorship statistics, 2022. CA: Cancer J. Clin. **72**(5), 409–436 (2022). https://doi.org/10.3322/caac.21731
34. Mistry, A., Wilson, S., Priestman, T., Damery, S., Haque, M.: How do the information needs of cancer patients differ at different stages of the cancer journey? A cross-sectional survey. JRSM Short Rep. **1**(4), 30 (2010). https://doi.org/10.1258/shorts.2010.010032

35. Momeni, K., Martinsuo, M.: Remote monitoring in industrial services: need-to-have instead of nice-to-have. J. Bus. Ind. Mark. **33**(6), 792–803 (2018). https://doi.org/10.1108/JBIM-10-2015-0187

36. Montero, A.J., et al.: Reducing unplanned medical oncology readmissions by improving outpatient care transitions: a process improvement project at the cleveland clinic. J. Oncol. Pract. **12**(5), e594–e602 (2016). https://doi.org/10.1200/JOP.2015.007880

37. Philip, N.Y., Rodrigues, J.J.P.C., Wang, H., Fong, S.J., Chen, J.: Internet of things for in-home health monitoring systems: current advances, challenges and future directions. IEEE J. Sel. Areas Commun. **39**(2), 300–310 (2021). https://doi.org/10.1109/JSAC.2020.3042421

38. Owen, T., Pearson, J., Thimbleby, H., Buchanan, G.: ConCap: designing to empower individual reflection on chronic conditions using mobile apps. In: Proceedings of the 17th International Conference on Human-Computer Interaction with Mobile Devices and Services, pp. 105–114 (2015). https://doi.org/10.1145/2785830.2785881

39. Paradiso, R., Loriga, G., Taccini, N., Gemignani, A., Ghelarducci, B.: WEALTHY, a wearable health-care system: new frontier on etextile. J. Telecommun. Inf. Technol. **4**, 105–113 (2005)

40. Patel, R.A., Klasnja, P., Hartzler, A., Unruh, K.T., Pratt, W.: Probing the benefits of real-time tracking during cancer care. In: AMIA Annual Symposium proceedings. AMIA Symposium 2012, pp. 1340–1349 (2012). Place: United States

41. Pincus, T., et al.: Cognitive and affective reassurance and patient outcomes in primary care: a systematic review. Pain **154**(11), 2407–2416 (2013)

42. Rooeintan, M., Khademi, M., Toulabi, T., Nabavi, F.H., Gorji, M.: Explaining postdischarge care needs of cancer patients: a qualitative study. Indian J. Palliat. Care **25**(1), 110–118 (2019)

43. Sabesan, S., Sankar, R.: Improving long-term management of epilepsy using a wearable multimodal seizure detection system. Epilepsy Behav. **46**, 56–57 (2015). https://doi.org/10.1016/j.yebeh.2015.02.057

44. Sanfilippo, F., Pettersen, K.: A sensor fusion wearable health-monitoring system with haptic feedback. In: 11th International Conference on Innovations in Information Technology (IIT), Dubai, United Arab Emirates, pp. 262–266 (2015). https://doi.org/10.1109/INNOVATIONS.2015.7381551

45. Sanger, P., Hartzler, A., Lober, W., Evans, H.: Provider Needs Assessment for mPOWEr: a Mobile tool for Post-Operative Wound Evaluation (2013)

46. Saunders, R.S., et al.: Outpatient follow-up versus 30-day readmission among general and vascular surgery patients: a case for redesigning transitional care. Surgery **156**(4), 949–956 (2014). https://doi.org/10.1016/j.surg.2014.06.041

47. Schnall, R., et al.: A user-centered model for designing consumer mobile health (mHealth) applications (apps). J. Biomed. Inform. **60**, 243–51 (2016). https://doi.org/10.1016/j.jbi.2016.02.002

48. Skeels, M.M., Unruh, K.T., Powell, C., Pratt, W.: Catalyzing social support for breast cancer patients. In: Proceedings of the SIGCHI Conference on Human Factors in Computing Systems, pp. 173–182 (2010). https://doi.org/10.1145/1753326.1753353

49. Sklenarova, H., et al.: When do we need to care about the caregiver? Supportive care needs, anxiety, and depression among informal caregivers of patients with cancer and cancer survivors. Cancer **121**(9), 1513–9 (2015). https://doi.org/10.1002/cncr.29223

50. Stark, D., Kiely, M., Smith, A., Morley, S., Selby, P., House, A.: Reassurance and the anxious cancer patient. Br. J. Cancer **91**(5), 893–899 (2004). https://doi.org/10.1038/sj.bjc.6602077

51. Sung, H., et al.: Global cancer statistics 2020: GLOBOCAN estimates of incidence and mortality worldwide for 36 cancers in 185 countries. CA Cancer J. Clin. **71**(3), 209–249 (2021). https://doi.org/10.3322/caac.21660

52. Tamburini, M., et al.: Cancer patients' needs during hospitalisation: a quantitative and qualitative study. BMC Cancer **3**(1), 12 (2003). https://doi.org/10.1186/1471-2407-3-12

53. Traeger, A.C., O'Hagan, E.T., Cashin, A., McAuley, J.H.: Reassurance for patients with non-specific conditions - a user's guide. Braz. J. Phys. Ther. **21**(1), 1–6 (2017). https://doi.org/10.1016/j.bjpt.2016.12.007

54. Vaajakallio, K., Mattelmäki, T.: Collaborative design exploration: envisioning future practices with make tools. In: Proceedings of the 2007 Conference on Designing Pleasurable Products and Interfaces, DPPI 2007, pp. 223–238 (2007). https://doi.org/10.1145/1314161.1314182

55. Vegesna, A., Tran, M., Angelaccio, M., Arcona, S.: Remote patient monitoring via non-invasive digital technologies: a systematic review. Telemed. e-Health **23**(1), 3–17 (2017). https://doi.org/10.1089/tmj.2016.0051

56. Yu, P., Chang, D.C., Osen, H.B., Talamini, M.A.: NSQIP reveals significant incidence of death following discharge. J. Surg. Res. **170**(2), e217–e224 (2011). https://doi.org/10.1016/j.jss.2011.05.040

SELFI: Evaluation of Techniques to Reduce Self-report Fatigue by Using Facial Expression of Emotion

Salma Mandi[1]($\boxtimes$), Surjya Ghosh[2], Pradipta De[3], and Bivas Mitra[1]

[1] Indian Institute of Technology Kharagpur, Kharagpur, India
salmamandi@kgpian.iitkgp.ac.in, bivas@cse.iitkgp.ac.in
[2] BITS Pilani, Goa, India
surjyag@goa.bits-pilani.ac.in
[3] Microsoft Corporation, Redmond, USA
prade@microsoft.com

Abstract. This paper presents the SELFI framework which uses information from a range of indirect measures to reduce the burden on users of context-sensitive apps in the need to self-report their mental state. In this framework, we implement multiple combinations of facial emotion recognition tools (Amazon Rekognition, Google Vision, Microsoft Face), and feature reduction approaches to demonstrate the versatility of the framework in facial expression based emotion estimation. The evaluation of the framework involving 20 participants in a 28-week in-the-wild study reveals that the proposed framework can estimate emotion accurately using facial image (83% and 81% macro-F1 for valence and arousal, respectively), with an average reduction of 10% self-report burden. Moreover, we propose a solution to detect the performance drop of the model developed by *SELFI*, during runtime without the use of ground truth emotion, and we achieve accuracy improvements of 14%.

Keywords: Experience Sampling Method (ESM) · Emotion prediction · Self-report burden · Facial image processing

1 Introduction

In recent years, context-sensitive mobile applications have become pervasive due to the penetration of smartphones in our daily life [6,24,29,34]. These context-aware applications dynamically adjust their behaviors depending on the present context (say, the current mental state of the user, the current computational and physical environment etc.), so that the user can focus on their current activity. The core of context-sensitive applications is to accurately detect the context (such as location of use, collection of nearby people, emotion of the user, schedules for the day, etc.) and adapt applications according to the changes in context [8,9,15]. Context-sensitive applications typically deploy supervised machine learning models, which are trained by correlating data collected from

© The Author(s), under exclusive license to Springer Nature Switzerland AG 2023
J. Abdelnour Nocera et al. (Eds.): INTERACT 2023, LNCS 14142, pp. 620–640, 2023.
https://doi.org/10.1007/978-3-031-42280-5_39

various sensors with the reported context information [17,19,41]. The availability of diverse sensors facilitates the development of context-sensitive applications, however, collecting the ground truth context information is still a challenge.

Importantly, state-of-the-art context-sensitive applications mostly rely on manual efforts of users to collect self-reported context information [18,22,30]. For instance, consider a music recommendation system, which is capable of dynamically recommending music that adapts to the emotion of an individual. In order to develop such applications, researchers typically rely on manually collected emotion self-reports as ground truth context information relying on the Experience Sampling Methods [5,21]. However, as manual self-reporting is a burden and time-consuming for users, collecting context information from a long-term study is challenging as participants may respond arbitrarily, or drop out [26,27]. Therefore, efficient strategies to reduce the self-report burden while collecting the context information is essential to develop an effective context-sensitive application. In this paper, we aim to facilitate the users of the emotion aware context-sensitive applications, hence, we propose a mechanism to reduce the *human in the loop* while collecting ground truth emotion self-reports.

One promising approach for reducing the *human in the loop* in emotion self-report collection is to use the *alternative information sources* for inferring emotion, based on initial self-reports provided by the participant. Those inferred emotions will be subsequently considered as the ground truth self-reports (in place of directly asking the participants) to train the supervised models. A diverse set of indirect measures (physiological data, speech, facial expression, posts in Online Social Networks) is already known to carry a signature of human emotion [10,23,43,48]. For example, passively sensed heart rate data or skin conductance data using a wearable device can be used as an alternative information source to infer a user's emotion instead of asking for self-report labels [3,35]. Similarly, inferred emotion from the voice clips can be used as a substitute of emotion self-report [12]. Another promising alternative is to capture the facial image in place of directly collecting emotion self-report from the user, and subsequently infer the emotion label from the facial expression, which may work as a substitute of self-reported labels.

However, the applicability of these alternative sources of information to infer users' emotion labels poses a number of challenges. First of all, the performance and suitability of various alternative information sources widely vary depending on the context and the participants involved in the study. Notably, the reduction in self-reports leads to poor model training, which may significantly drop the emotion prediction performance of the model. Hence, a flexible toolbox is essential to conveniently explore the role of multiple alternative information sources and investigate their impact on reducing the self-report burden, with a tradeoff with emotion prediction performance. The lack of such a toolbox creates a major bottleneck to examining the potential of various alternative sources of information in reducing the self-report burden. Second, recent advances in machine learning algorithms allow the extraction of a large set of features from these alternative information sources. However, identifying the most relevant features, which are effective in reducing the self-report burden for developing the emotion prediction model, is a challenge. Deep learning models [39] may facilitate the automation of feature extraction, however, the scarcity of data from large scale field trials with users restricts the applicability of deep learning models. Third, the performance of the developed emotion prediction model may degrade over time, as the model gets obsolete due to the change in the context, environment, and behavioral pattern of the users. Hence, one needs to assess the quality of the estimates of users' emotional states on runtime and automatically *adapt* the framework, once it detects any degradation in the performance. Therefore, the development of an *adaptive framework*, which allows one to (i) explore various alternative sources of information, and (ii) to identify the relevant features from this sources of information, may facilitate the developers of the context-sensitive applications to reduce the burden of the participating users. This paper takes one step towards this direction.

In this paper, we propose *SELFI*, a framework which relies on alternative sources of information, to reduce the self-report burden of the users of emotion aware context-sensitive applications. In particular, we use facial expression as the alternative source of information for emotion estimation, since (i) facial expression is considered as a strong indicator of human emotion [19], (ii) images are easy to capture in a seamless manner, and (iii) a number of facial image recognition tools (Amazon Rekognition [46], Google Vision [2], and Microsoft Azure [1]) are commercially available. The framework consists of two major building blocks. The first building block (termed as *Facial image processing block*) takes the facial images (captured using a smartphone) as input and extracts a set of features. The second block (termed as *feature reduction tool*) takes the large feature set as input and decomposes it by adopting any suitable feature reduction method. Once the feature set is reduced, the correspondence between the facial image and the self-reports is established by training a machine learning model for inferring the emotion based on the facial image. The proposed framework provides flexibility to explore any information source (various facial image recognition tools, in this case) and any feature decomposition method (to select relevant features) for emotion estimation.

In order to evaluate the proposed framework, we have developed an Android application for capturing facial images and emotion self-reports. We conducted a 28-week field study of the framework with 20 participants, who recorded their facial expressions and instantaneous emotions throughout the day. The emotion self-report collection was guided by the Circumplex model of emotion, which suggests every emotion is a combination of valence and arousal [33]. Our experimental results demonstrate that the proposed framework estimates the valence and arousal with an average F1-score of 83% and 81% respectively, based on the facial images as an alternative information source. Side by side, *SELFI* reduces the volume of required self-reports up to 10% (on average).

2   Background and Data Collection Apparatus

In this section, first we discuss the various ways of representing emotion. Next, we describe the development of the data collection application and procedure.

2.1   Emotion Representation

Emotions are intense feelings caused by a specific event [11] persist for a short duration, whereas moods, in contrast, are feelings less intense than emotions that often do not depend on contextual stimuli [45] last longer than emotions. Notably, unlike moods, emotions tend to be more clearly revealed with facial expressions [16], which motivates us to rely on facial images as an alternative source of information for emotion estimation. In this paper, we followed the Circumplex model that presents emotion in a 2-dimensional plane (see Fig. 1). The x-axis called valence refers to the positive (pleasant) and negative (unpleasant) degree of emotion, while the y-axis called arousal refers to the degree to which an emotion is associated with high (activation) or low energy (deactivation). Thus any emotion can be described using valence and arousal dimensions mapped in one of the 4 quadrants. For instance, the emotion *happy* is high valence and high arousal state located in the 1st quadrant. We notice that four dominant emotions *happy, angry, sad,* and *relaxed* from four different quadrants of the Circumplex model are pretty discriminative Fig. 1. In the following, we develop an app (see Fig. 2) to collect valence and arousal states as emotion self-reports, directly from the users.

Fig. 1. Circumplex Emotion Model [28].

Fig. 2. Data collection UI.

2.2   UI Development and Self-report Collection

We have developed a smartphone based Android application[1] to collect the data from the participants. This application enables us to collect two specific information, (a) self-reported emotion labels, and (b) facial images of the participants. Since capturing facial images may raise privacy concerns, we take utmost care to capture and process the facial images. The application checks the phone status (lock or unlock) at 2 h intervals to probe a notification to record the data. If the screen is locked at the time of triggering the notification, the notification is held back and issued once the participant unlocks the phone. The interval value is chosen based on a study presented by Schmidt et al [36]. In response to the

---

[1] In https://anonymous.4open.science/r/Image_collection_Upload_Dropbox-0565/ we provide the implementation of the data collection apparatus.

notification, the data collection UI records emotion labels and facial images of the participant. The process is illustrated in Fig. 3. The data collection UI consists of two modules, *self-report collection module* and *Facial Image collection module*.

(a) Self-report Collection Module: This module collects the valence and arousal state from participants in the form of two questions (shown in Fig. 2). Participants are asked to select the suitable radio button to record their perceived emotion state and press the "Record data" to record the self-report. Notably, participants are also allowed to skip self-reporting by selecting the 'No Response' option, which is set as default. Once the participant responds to the notification, the notification probing time, emotion reporting time, and reported emotion states are saved in a file.

(b) Facial Image Collection Module: We have implemented the facial image collection component, which is embedded within the data collection UI. The responsibility of this module is to capture the facial images of the user at the moment of recording the emotion self-report, in a *privacy preserving* manner. The module triggers automatic collection of the facial image of the participant within one second of the probe notification. It captures three images in succession to record at least one image with the full frontal face. We record the date and time of the captured image, which facilitates us to map it with its corresponding emotion self-report.

The participants are instructed as part of the self-report collection to ensure that a selfie is captured. If the participant does not provide the self-report, then the photo is marked "No response". To ensure privacy, this application provides an *image review button* to review the images at any time before it is uploaded. Participants can select and delete the images with the delete button if they do not want to upload a specific image. If the participant deletes *all photos* captured with an emotion self-report, then the corresponding self-report label is also removed. This is important to note that participants can audit and remove pictures from phone storage, but capturing a photo is not allowed on their own.

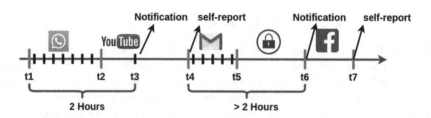

Fig. 3. Schematic showing the process of a participant recording self-report emotion label. For example, in the time interval between t_1 and t_3, the participant is engaged with different apps (Whatsapp, Youtube). A notification is received at t_3 as 2 h are passed and it is answered at t_4. Similarly, more than 2 h is elapsed from the last reported emotion and notification received at t_6 since the phone was locked.

3 Pilot Study

We conducted a pilot study to demonstrate the limitations of the facial image based emotion recognition tools. We have taken approval from the Institute Ethical Committee of IIT Kharagpur[2] to collect facial images and emotion self-reports from the participants.

3.1 Study Focus Group

We conducted a survey among 33 participants to judiciously select the volunteers, who are active with their smartphone engagements. We asked the participants to fill out a questionnaire through a Google form[3] to collect information regarding their daily smartphone usage, such as average duration of phone usage, types of applications usage and their duration, time of the day with peak usage of the phone, etc. Based on the collected data, we recruited 5 participants (2 males, 3 females; aged 17 to 35 years) from different job backgrounds (3 students, 1 teacher, and businessman), who are highly active with their smartphone usage, which ensures the collection of sufficient volume of data in a limited time period.

3.2 Study Protocol

We instructed the participants to install the app on their devices to use it for 3 weeks. First, we familiarize the participants with the basic definition of emotion and apprise them about the functionality of the app. We instructed the participants to respond to the notification received to record their emotion self-report, whenever they strongly felt some emotion. After the pilot study, on average we have collected 100 emotion labels (on average 5 self-reports per day) and 165 facial images from each participant. We paid a token honorarium to all the volunteers.

3.3 Challenges of Using Facial Images

(a) **Limitations of Commercial Image Processing Tools:** First, we demonstrate the limitations of the state of the art facial image processing tools such as Amazon Rekognition [46], Google Vision [2], and Microsoft Azure [1] to predict emotion from the collected facial images. These tools return a set of discrete emotions from the facial images, along with their respective confidence scores. We consider the emotion with the highest confidence score as the predicted emotion. We map the predicted emotion of each participant in the *valence* and *arousal* scale of the Circumplex model. In Fig. 4a, we compare this predicted emotion with the ground truth emotion label. We observe that, on average, the

---

[2] The IRB approval number IIT/SRIC/SAO/2017.
[3] We advised the participants to rely on the *Digital Wellbeing and Parental Control* tool to respond to the smartphone usage related questionnaire.

prediction accuracy is 63% and 48% for valence and arousal, respectively, which demonstrates the limitations of the aforementioned pre-trained tools.

It has been shown in the literature that specific facial landmarks are responsible for expressing a particular emotion [13]. For example, points in the cheek and lip region express emotion *happy*; on the contrary, the eyebrow and lip corner mainly reveal emotion *sad*. Therefore we focus on two individual landmarks, say the right eyebrow and the mouth position, to investigate if they are capable to correctly discriminate the (high and low) valance states. We extract the 2D landmark features (right eyebrow, mouth position) from the facial images using commercial image processing tools. Next, we apply k-means clustering (with $k = 2$) to cluster all the images in two classes based on those extracted landmark features. In Fig. 4b, we present a scatter plot, where the coordinate of each point represents the 2D landmark features obtained from the facial image, the color of the point (brown or green) represents the predicted valance state (high or low), and the shape of the point (star or disk) represents the ground truth emotion label collected from the participants. We observe that albeit the facial landmark features exhibit some potential to classify the high and low valance states, however, their accuracy does not cross 50% (for both right eyebrow and mouth position features), revealing the limitations of the *individual* landmark features.

The aforementioned experiments point to the necessity of developing a *personalized* toolbox, as we cannot directly rely on the generalized pre-trained tools for automatic emotion recognition. Albeit these commercial tools provide a large set of facial landmark features to represent a facial expression, however, *individually* those landmark features do not exhibit elegance in classifying the valance states.

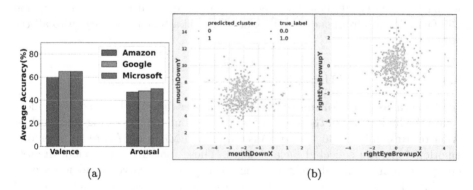

(a)   (b)

Fig. 4. (a) Performance of three facial image processing tools for emotion prediction, (b) Scatter plot showing the role of the facial landmark features (mouth down, right eyebrow) in classifying the emotion label. The coordinate of each point represents the landmark features, the color of the point (brown or green) represents the k-means based valance state (high or low), and the shape of the point (star or disk) represents the ground truth emotion label. (Color figure online)

(b) Variation of Facial Features over Time: We consider the data collected from a specific user U_1 and extract features from facial images using different image analysis tools. We split the data (both emotion labels and the features) into fixed size time windows. We take the data segment of the first window and calculate the biserial correlation [20] between every facial feature and ground truth emotion labels. In Fig. 5a, we show the top correlated feature in the second, fifth, and seventh time windows. Interestingly, we observe that the top correlated facial feature "PosePitch" in the second window drops in the fifth and seventh time window, whereas the other facial feature "upperJawlineLeftY" and "PoseYaw" appears at the top in the fifth and seventh time windows, respectively. This observation indicates that facial features, which are highly correlated with self-reported emotion in one time window, may exhibit low correlation in the subsequent time windows. Further, we compute the cross-correlation between the top correlated feature (PoseRoll) of one time window, with the top correlated feature (PosePitch) of the subsequent window. Figure 5b depicts that the cross-correlation between the pair of top features in two subsequent windows is pretty low, which points to the significant changes of facial features across various time windows. This study shows that the critical facial features, which may play a key role in developing emotion estimation models, vary across different time windows. Hence, one time development and training of the emotion estimation model may not suffice, as the model may get obsolete over time.

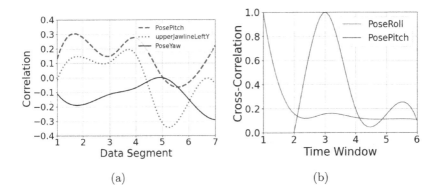

(a)   (b)

Fig. 5. (a) Correlation score for the top correlated feature in one time window decreases gradually in the subsequent time window, (b) Cross-correlation score between the top correlated feature from different time window reduces with the higher time window indicates the changes of the top correlated feature.

4   Methodology

In this section, first we illustrate the problem addressed in this paper, followed by the implementation of the proposed framework *SELFI*.

4.1   Problem Statement

Consider a scenario where we wish to predict the emotion label $e_{(n+1)}$ of a user at time instance $(n+1)$, from the past n self-reported emotion labels. This predicted emotion label $e_{(n+1)}$ will be later considered as $(n+1)^{th}$ self-report of the user. Here the emotion label e_i represents the (high or low) valence and arousal state of the user at time instance i. Multiple models [47] have been proposed in the literature to estimate the emotion $e_{(n+1)}$ from the past n labels, incurring the burden of self-report fatigue n. The objective of this paper is to develop a framework $SELFI$, which only collects initial self-report emotion labels $n' < n$ directly from the users, and relies on the facial image $f_{(n+1)}$ collected at time instance $(n+1)$ (as alternative information), to correctly estimate the emotion label $e_{(n+1)}$ at time instance $(n+1)$. Hence, the proposed framework $SELFI$ aims to reduce the self-report burden by $(n - n')$ with correctly estimating the emotion labels for the time period $(n - n')$.

4.2   Development of $SELFI$

The overview of the proposed framework $SELFI^4$ is presented in Fig. 6. This framework relies on two different input blocks. In the first block, (a) **Emotion self-report processing**, we collect the past self-reported emotion labels (e_i, $i \in [1, n']$), provided by the user and subsequently compute the handcrafted features (i) Influence and (ii) Emotion Sequence Length. The second block (b) **Facial image processing**, we implement this block in two steps, (i) first, we fed the facial image $f_{(n+1)}$ collected at time instance $(n+1)$ to the image analysis tool (say, Amazon Rekognition [46], Google Vision [2], and Microsoft Azure [1]), which extracts all facial landmarks as facial features. (ii) In the second step, those features are fed to the feature reduction tool (say, Kernel Principal Component Analysis ($KPCA$) and Kernel Discriminant Analysis (KDA), which reduces the dimension of features. Finally, we use the extracted (a) self-reported features and (b) facial features to develop a machine learning model, which predicts the emotion label $e_{(n+1)}$ at time instance $(n+1)$. In this section, we describe in detail the various building blocks of $SELFI$. We develop two separate prediction models for $SELFI$; one to estimate the valence state and another one to estimate the arousal state of the user.

Emotion Self-report Processing: We compute the following two self-report features from the past n' emotion labels e_i (say, valence) $\in \{1, 0\}$ collected from the user.

(a) Influence (F_{e_i})*:* This feature measures the influence of the current self-report emotion e_i on the next self-report $e_{(i+1)}$, where $e_i, e_{(i+1)} \in \{1, 0\}$. In order to compute *Influence*, first we define a 2×2 state-transition matrix P, where each

---

[4] In https://anonymous.4open.science/r/SELFI-77A3/ we provide the implementation of the SELFI framework, with a toy dataset.

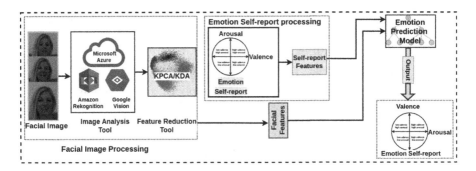

Fig. 6. The overall architecture of the emotion estimation framework *SELFI*.

element of $P = \{p_{ij}\}$, $\forall i, j \in \{1, 0\}$ denotes the state transition probability from emotion label e_i to label e_j, where e_i, $e_j \in \{1, 0\}$. Moreover, a current emotion label e_i has an impact on the next state based on the time elapsed between the current self-report e_i and the next self-report $e_{(i+1)}$. We define $\tau_{e_{(i+1)}}$ as a normalized elapsed time since last observed self-report $e_{(i+1)}$. Hence, the feature *Influence* F_{e_i} is designed to capture the influence of a current self-report state e_i on the next self-report $e_{(i+1)}$ as $F_{e_{(i+1)}} = p_{e_i e_{(i+1)}} \times (1 - \tau_{e_{(i+1)}})$, where $p_{e_i e_{(i+1)}}$ indicates the probability of the next emotion state determined as $e_{(i+1)}$ based on the current self-report e_i and $(1 - \tau_{e_{(i+1)}})$ indicates a weight of the current emotion state to the next emotion state in terms of the elapsed time.

(b) Emotion Sequence Length (L_{e_i})**:** This feature captures the typical sequence length of a specific emotion self-report label e_i, reflecting once a user reports an emotion label e_i, how many times in a row, the user repeats the same emotion at-a-stretch.

Facial Image Processing: We implement this block following two steps.

(a) Facial Feature Extraction: We rely on the various facial image analysis tools (such as, Amazon Rekognition [46], Google Vision [2], and Microsoft Azure [1] etc.) to extract features from facial images. The basic principle of those tools is to first detect the faces in the image and return a bounding box demarcating the face in the image. Next, it identifies the various facial landmarks, such as the position of the eyebrow, pupil, mouth, nose, chin, etc as attributes (e.g., leftEyeBrowLeft, rightPupil, mouthUp, noseLeft, chinBottom, etc.). These tools provide the location of each landmark attribute on the face in terms of two or three dimension coordinates. Apart from landmarks, those tools also return some other attributes from the images, such as age range, gender, image quality, as well as some binary attributes such as the presence of beard on the face, the presence of eyeglasses, etc. However, in our model construction, we only consider the extracted facial landmarks and their respective attribute coordinates as the facial features. Precisely, *Amazon Rekognition*, *Microsoft Azure* and *Google Vision* provide us 60, 54 and 96 facial features, respectively from each facial image. We

stress on the fact that in the development of $SELFI$, one may feel free to choose any commercially available facial image analysis tools to implement the *Facial image processing* block for extracting the facial features.

(b) Feature Reduction: Since facial image analysis tools extract a large number of facial features from images, it is necessary to apply feature reduction to maintain a sufficient density of the samples per feature. This reduces the risk of model overfitting, developed based on facial features. This issue is specifically critical in our context, as we aim to collect fewer self-report emotion labels from each user, limiting the volume of available data samples. We implement two specific feature reduction techniques such as (i) Kernel Principal Component Analysis $(KPCA)$ [37] considers the correlation between independent features and (ii) Kernel Discriminant Analysis (KDA) [32] considers the correlation between independent and dependent features, both of which are set to return a *single facial feature* after reduction. We implement $KPCA$ with Gaussian Radial Basis Function (RBF) kernel [31], select *arpack* as eigensolver, and set one as the number of principal components to be returned. In KDA, we implement the same kernel function as used for $KPCA$. We stress on the fact that in the implementation of *Facial image processing* block, one may feel free to (i) choose a suitable feature reduction method and (ii) decide the dimension of the reduced features.

Emotion Prediction Model: Using the aforesaid (i) self-report features, computed from the past n' collected emotion labels and (ii) facial features, computed from the facial image captured for all time instance n', we train a Random Forest (RF) model to predict the emotion $e_{(n'+1)}$ at time instance $(n'+1)$. We develop two personalized models for each user to predict valence and arousal separately; each model implements a two state classifier to predict the state (high, low) of the emotion (valence and arousal). We implement 50 decision trees for the RF model, with no specific value chosen for the tree's maximum depth (hence depth is unlimited). This is important to note that state-of-the-art packages, such as ATOM [25], H2O [14], can be utilized to implement this block, enabling flexibility to explore the suitable ML models.

Estimating Emotion at Time $(n+1)$ from Initial n' Self-reports: From the collected initial n' self-reports and the captured facial image $f_{(n'+1)}$ at time instance $(n'+1)$, $SELFI$ predicts the emotion label $e_{(n'+1)}$ for time instance $(n'+1)$. The predicted emotion label $e_{(n'+1)}$ works as a substitute of the self-report for time instance $(n'+1)$. Extending this principle, $SELFI$ relies on the past n self-reports and the facial image $f_{(n+1)}$ at time instance $(n+1)$, to estimate the emotion label $e_{(n+1)}$ at time instance $(n+1)$. Here we obtain the past n self-reports as the (i) initial n' self-reports, collected directly from the users, and (ii) the remaining $(n-n')$ emotion labels recursively predicted by the model, thus reducing the self-report burden by $(n-n')$.

4.3   Retraining and Runtime Adaptation of *SELFI*

The developed model may get stale over a period of time, due to the changes in the feature pattern, which may result in a drop in accuracy in the estimated emotion labels. During runtime, we first check if retraining is needed after a certain time interval, and if it is needed, we record the ground truth emotion self-reports directly from the users and retrain the model. Initially, we train the model with a n number of data samples collected over the first few days, where the value of n is decided based on the study in the development phase. On these training samples, we calculate the K-L divergence score [7] T_k between the features labeled as high and low valance (arousal) states. Next, in the running phase, we fix the time instances at which the model estimates the emotion labels in a sequence. After each prediction phase, we calculate the K-L divergence score P_H between the features predicted as high valance (arousal) state in the prediction phase and the features labeled as high valance (arousal) state in the training data. Likewise, a similar score P_L is calculated for features with low valance (arousal) states. Subsequently, we take an average of P_L and P_H, denoted as P_{avg}, which indicates, on average, the deviation between the test and the training data distribution. Finally, we compare P_{avg} against T_k, where higher P_{avg} indicates the misclassification in valance (arousal) estimation and subsequently calls for retraining the model with the new self-reported emotion labels, directly collected from the users.

5   Experimental Setup

In this section, we describe the field study procedure including the collected dataset, and explain the experiment procedure in detail.

5.1   Field Study

Survey Focus Group: Initially, we recruited 33 participants (24 Female, 9 Male) aged between 17 to 60 years from different work backgrounds (such as office executive, student, teacher, nurse, businessman, retired person, etc.) via an offline snowball recruiting method [38] maintaining work background, age, gender wise diversity. In addition, our participants were chosen from a diverse range of cities such as tier-II cities (3), tier-I urban agglomeration (7), urban agglomeration (18), and metropolitan cities (5), etc. We asked participants to install the app (described in Sect. 2) on their smartphones, allow the app to access the smartphone camera, and instructed them to use it for 28 weeks to record their emotion states. We notice that the participants use a variety of Android-based smartphones (such as Samsung, Redmi, Realme, Oppo, etc.) with different configurations. During the study, we came across several challenges such as participants leaving the study in the middle (four participants), the data collection app stopped working due to some issues with their phone model (six participants), certain participants recording data rarely (three participants recorded less than 100 emotion labels), etc. Finally, we collected data from 20 participants (12 female, 8 male).

Instruction to the Focus Group: Once the participants installed the app on their devices, we advised them to engage normally with their phones. We have taken consent from the participants for capturing the facial images using the app and asked them to fill up a registration form recording their name, age, gender, occupation, and demographic information. We apprise the participants that sometimes they may receive a notification to record their emotion self-report, once they unlock their phone. Participants are instructed to respond to the notification *only if* they feel a strong emotion at that moment (otherwise they may skip the notification). We also advised participants to record *No response* label if they do not wish to record the emotion self-report. Moreover, we informed the participants that they can review the recorded images anytime using the *image review button*. This makes sure that we capture emotion, not mood.

Field Study Dataset: On average, we have collected 350 emotion labels and 600 facial images from each participant. Next, we preprocess the collected data as follows, (a) First, we manually remove all the images with no facial impression (for example, participants with face masks, blank images) and the images which are difficult to visualize (say, too dark or too bright images). (b) We remove the entries with *No response* labels, as they do not reveal any emotion. Finally, after data preprocessing, on average we obtain 310 emotion labels and 500 facial images from each participant, on which we conduct the evaluation experiments. Valence and Arousal in both datasets, we maintain a 60:40 ratio between high and low class.

5.2   Evaluation Procedure

We evaluate the framework using the nested cross-validation method [44], as the traditional cross-validation approach is not suitable due to the presence of temporal dependency in time series data. In every fold (or iteration) of this cross-validation approach, the temporal dependency is maintained i.e., the training portion does not include data from the future segment. In each iteration, we use 80% of data (first 60% for training and next 20% for testing). In the first iteration, an initial 60% is used for training, and the next 20% is used for testing, while in the second iteration, we discard the initial 20%, use the next 60% for training, and the last 20% for testing. This approach ensures that at every fold, we perform the training and testing on an equal amount of data and at the same time, future data is not used for training. In order to evaluate $SELFI$, we measure the macro f1-score from every iteration and compute the average values of two iterations to obtain the performance metric.

5.3   Baseline Algorithms

We implement the following baseline algorithms to evaluate the performance of $SELFI$.

(a) Feature Based Emotion Model (FBEM): We implement a variation of *SELFI* as *FBEM*, which aims to estimate the emotion label $e_{(n+1)}$ of a user at time instance $(n + 1)$, *only* relying on the 'Facial image processing' block of the *SELFI* framework (and ignoring the past emotion self-reports). We apply the image analysis tools of the facial image processing block to obtain the features from the facial image $f_{(n+1)}$ captured at time instance $(n + 1)$. Subsequently, we compute the correlation between each facial feature and the self-reported emotion label, and select the top two features with the highest correlation. Finally, we build the emotion prediction model based on these top facial features to predict the emotion label $e_{(n+1)}$.

(b) Self-reported Emotion Model (SREM): We implement a variation of *SELFI* as *SREM*, which aims to estimate the emotion label $e_{(n+1)}$ of a user at time instance $(n + 1)$, *only* relying on self-report emotion labels in the past n time instances [42]. Precisely, by implementing this *SREM*, we conducted an ablation study of *SELFI*, dropping the 'Facial image processing' block from the framework pipeline.

(c) Past-Current Data Based Emotion Model (PCDEM): We implement another variation of *SELFI* as *PCDEM*, which aims to estimate the emotion label $e_{(n+1)}$ of a user at time instance $(n + 1)$, relying on all the collected self-report emotion labels in the past n time instances and the facial image collected at time instance n and $(n + 1)$, both [40]. We develop this baseline to jointly observe the influence of the current and the previous facial image on the prediction of emotion labels for the current instance.

6   Evaluation of *SELFI* Framework

In this section, we evaluate the emotion prediction performance and reduction in the self-report burden of *SELFI*. We demonstrate the versatility of the *SELFI* framework across various image analysis toolkits.

6.1   Emotion Prediction Performance

In Table 1, we evaluate and compare the performance of *SELFI* framework with baseline algorithms, in the light of correctly estimating the emotion label $e_{(n+1)}$ at time instance $(n + 1)$. In this evaluation, for all the algorithms, we have collected the *identical volume* of self-report emotion labels directly from the participants in the past n time instances to train the respective models.

Valence Estimation: In Table 1, we observe that for all the model variants, *SELFI* framework consistently outperforms the baseline algorithms in the valence dimension. The macro F1-score of *SELFI* and the *SREM* algorithm is 83% and 77%, respectively, which justifies the utility of the 'Facial image processing' block of *SELFI*. Poor performance of *FBEM* demonstrates the important role played by the past emotion self-reports of the *SELFI* framework. On the other hand, the baseline model $PCDEM$ exhibits marginally inferior performance compared to $SELFI$, since the collected facial image at the previous time instance introduces noise in the model performance. Among all the variants of $SELFI$, we obtain the best performance for the {*Microsoft Azure and KPCA*} combination (macro F1: 83%). Nevertheless, for the other two facial emotion recognition toolkit (Amazon, Google) and feature reduction technique (*KPCA*, *KDA*) combination also, the $SELFI$ exhibit a decent performance (macro F1) ranging from 80% to 82%.

Table 1. Reporting F1-score (%) of valence and arousal for information source Facial Image. We report F1-score for different features for 3 image analysis tools (*Amazon, Google, Microsoft*) across all baselines and $SELFI$ framework. We highlight the highest accuracy score achieved by model $SELFI$.

	Facial Image					
Features	Amazon		Google		Microsoft	
Emotion Class	Valence	Arousal	Valence	Arousal	Valence	Arousal
FBEM	60	54	60	57	62	60
SREM	77	77	77	77	77	77
PCDEM	80	79	80	77	81	80
KPCA SELFI	**82**	80	**82**	80	**83**	**81**
KDA SELFI	81	79	80	77	81	78

Arousal Estimation: In the arousal dimension too, Table 1 demonstrates that $SELFI$ outperforms the baseline algorithm for all the variants. $SELFI$ achieves the mean F1-score of 80% for Amazon, Google and Microsoft toolkit (with both *KPCA* and *KDA* based model), whereas baseline models *FBEM*, *SREM* and *PCDEM* achieve the mean F1-score of 57%, 77% and 80% respectively. Notably, among all the $SELFI$ variants, the combination {*Microsoft Azure and KPCA*} returns the best arousal detection performance (macro F1: 81%).

In summary, $SELFI$ framework outperforms all the baseline algorithms across all model variants and emotion dimensions (valence, arousal). Since $SREM$ baseline model performs a little better compared to the $FBEM$, in the rest of the paper we compare the performance of $SELFI$ with the $SREM$ model only. Notably, the combination of Microsoft Azure toolkit and $KPCA$ in the case of facial image exhibits superior performance for the $SELFI$ framework. The improvement in emotion prediction performance of $SELFI$ opens up the possibility of reducing the self-report burden, which we explore in detail in the following section.

6.2 Reduction in Self-report Burden

In this section, we measure the volume of emotion self-reports required to train the $SELFI$ framework, which can achieve the identical emotion prediction performance as the baseline model *SREM* (see Fig. 7). In this experiment, we implement the *SELFI* framework with various image processing tools (Amazon Rekognition, Google Vision, and Microsoft Azure) and the *KPCA* feature reduction technique (since it exhibits the best performance). In Fig. 7a and Fig. 7b, the x-axis represents the model performance in terms of F1-score (%) and the y-axis represents the volume (%) of emotion self-report labels required to achieve that respective emotion prediction performance (for both valence and arousal). Overall, we observe that *SELFI* requires fewer volume of self-report labels compared to the baseline algorithm, to achieve a similar emotion prediction performance. Precisely, in the case of valence, *SELFI* reduces the self-report burden by 10% for Microsoft Azure and by 6% for Amazon and Google Vision toolkits, compared to the baseline algorithm. Similarly, in the case of arousal, *SELFI* reduces the self-report burden by 8% for Amazon Rekognition, and by 6% for Google Vision and Microsoft Azure.

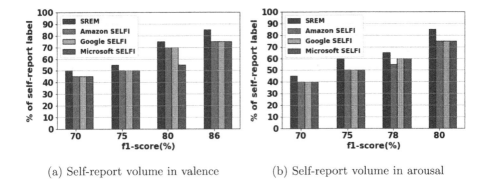

(a) Self-report volume in valence   (b) Self-report volume in arousal

Fig. 7. *SELFI* reduces the self-report burden.

6.3 Versatility of the *SELFI* Framework

In Fig. 8, we demonstrate the versatility of the *SELFI* framework, which allows one to plug and play with various image analysis tools (Amazon Rekognition, Google Vision, and Microsoft Azure) to implement the framework. This is comforting for us to observe that, for a majority of participants, the *SELFI* framework outperforms the baseline model *SREM* across all the facial image analysis tools. This emphasizes the role of facial expression as an alternative information source to supplement the past self-reported emotion labels to improve the prediction performance, which in turn, paves the way to reduce the self-report burden. User centric close inspection reveals that *Microsoft Azure* based *SELFI* framework achieves the best performance across all the image analysis tools, where 9 participants outperformed the *Baseline*. We observe that for 6 participants, the performance of *SELFI* framework remains same as the *Baseline* algorithm, indicating that facial features do not provide any additional benefit for those participants. This performance is followed by *Amazon Rekognition* and *Google*

Vision toolkit, which exhibits superior performance for 8 participants and 7 participants, respectively. In a nutshell, *Microsoft Azure* exhibits 4% performance improvement over the *SREM* model, closely followed by *Amazon Rekognition* model, which exhibits 3% improvement.

Finally, we identify 5 participants, whose performance drops compared to the *SREM* model across all the facial image analysis tools. Delving deep, we observe that *permutation importance* [4] (depicting feature importance) of facial features is negative for all these 5 participants, indicating that facial features play a detrimental role in predicting the emotion for those participants. Manual inspection of images reveals that indeed the facial expression of those participants *visibly* does not reflect their self-reported emotion, resulting in a drop in the model performance.

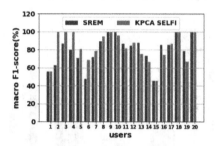 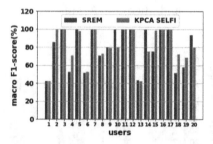

(a) Microsoft valence performance   (b) Microsoft arousal performance

Fig. 8. User-centric emotion estimation performance of the best model of *SELFI* framework.

This observation opens up the possibility to identify the *pertinent* users apriori, for whom the *SELFI* framework is most suitable. Before applying *SELFI*, one may calculate point biserial correlation [20] between the facial features and self-reported emotion label for each user. If the facial features correlate well with the emotion self-reports, then we consider that user as *pertinent*, hence applying the *SELFI* framework only on the *pertinent* users. Since computing correlations from numerous facial features, obtained from the facial analysis tools, may be expensive, we use the *feature reduction* step (sec Sect. 4) to select the most relevant features to compute the correlations. While applying *SELFI* only on the *pertinent* users (15 participants in our dataset), we observe on average an appreciable 8% and 12% performance improvement over baselines, for valence and arousal respectively. However, the reduction in the self-report burden remains almost identical to Sec VI-C, on average 10% and 8% for valence and arousal respectively.

6.4   Runtime Evaluation

In this section, we evaluate the runtime performance of the model developed using *SELFI* with and without applying the retraining point detection method.

We take 50% and 5% of the size of the whole dataset as the training and prediction window size since it is observed that this window size is enough to have almost balanced data. Given these settings, the number of prediction phases becomes 10.

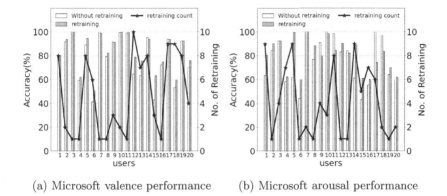

(a) Microsoft valence performance   (b) Microsoft arousal performance

Fig. 9. User-wise runtime emotion estimation performance with and without retraining detection method and count of retraining instances.

We summarize the best results in Fig. 9, showing two bars for each user that indicate accuracy with and without retraining. In the facial image based *SELFI* model, we achieve the best performance for *Microsoft Azure* and *KPCA* for both the case valence and arousal. It is observed that the model accuracy improved significantly for applying retraining point detection for 12 users. On average, we achieve a 14% accuracy increment over 5 retraining instances for valence and arousal.

7   Conclusion and Discussion

The major contribution of this paper is to provide a generic platform, where one can explore various alternative information sources to train supervised models for emotion prediction, with *reduced self-report burden*. Our experiments have shown that *SELFI* framework exhibits 4% performance improvement in emotion prediction (with 83% & 81% macro-F1 in valence and arousal, respectively), compared to the baseline model *SREM*, which solely relies on the past emotion self-reports. This manifests the role of facial expression as an alternative information source, to replace the self-reported emotions directly collected from the participants. Evidently, *SELFI* facilitates us to achieve 10% reduction in self-report burden, compared to the *Baseline* algorithm.

Importantly, the elegance of *SELFI* comes from its flexibility, which allows one to plug in various image analysis tools (say, Amazon Rekognition, Google Vision, and Microsoft Azure) and feature reduction techniques (say, *KPCA*,

KDA etc.) to develop the framework. Considering the (un)reliability of facial expression as an indicator of emotion, one may suitably explore the plausibility of various other mediums (such as audio, video, IMU sensors etc.) as the alternative source of information. Moreover, in order to assess the potential benefit of *SELFI in practice*, one may develop context-sensitive applications, which solely rely on the emotions estimated from *SELFI* to train the supervised models (in place of directly collecting labels from the users). The performance of those context-sensitive applications will essentially manifest the effectiveness of *SELFI* to reduce the self-report burden in practice.

References

1. Face API - facial recognition software — Microsoft Azure (2021). http://azure. microsoft.com/en-in/overview/what-is-azure/. Accessed 29 Dec 2021
2. Vision API - image content analysis — Google Cloud (2021). http://cloud.google. com/vision/. Accessed 29 Dec 2021
3. Agrafioti, F., Hatzinakos, D., Anderson, A.K.: ECG pattern analysis for emotion detection. IEEE Trans. Affect. Comput. **3**(1), 102–115 (2011)
4. Altmann, A., Toloşi, L., Sander, O., Lengauer, T.: Permutation importance: a corrected feature importance measure. Bioinformatics **26**(10), 1340–1347 (2010)
5. Arshad, R., Baig, M.A., Tariq, M., Shahid, S.: Acceptability of persuasive prompts to induce behavioral change in people suffering from depression. In: Lamas, D., Loizides, F., Nacke, L., Petrie, H., Winckler, M., Zaphiris, P. (eds.) INTERACT 2019. LNCS, vol. 11749, pp. 120–139. Springer, Cham (2019). https://doi.org/10. 1007/978-3-030-29390-1_7
6. Asim, Y., Azam, M.A., Ehatisham-ul Haq, M., Naeem, U., Khalid, A.: Context-aware human activity recognition (CAHAR) in-the-wild using smartphone accelerometer. IEEE Sens. J. **20**(8), 4361–4371 (2020)
7. Bouhlel, N., Dziri, A.: Kullback-Leibler divergence between multivariate generalized gaussian distributions. IEEE Signal Process. Lett. **26**(7), 1021–1025 (2019). https://doi.org/10.1109/LSP.2019.2915000
8. Cao, L., Wang, Y., Zhang, B., Jin, Q., Vasilakos, A.V.: GCHAR: an efficient group-based context-aware human activity recognition on smartphone. J. Parallel Distrib. Comput. **118**, 67–80 (2018)
9. Chitkara, S., Gothoskar, N., Harish, S., Hong, J.I., Agarwal, Y.: Does this app really need my location? Context-aware privacy management for smartphones. Proc. ACM Interact. Mob. Wearable Ubiquit. Technol. **1**(3), 1–22 (2017)
10. Diamantini, C., Mircoli, A., Potena, D., Storti, E.: Automatic annotation of corpora for emotion recognition through facial expressions analysis. In: 2020 25th International Conference on Pattern Recognition (ICPR), pp. 5650–5657. IEEE (2021)
11. Frijda, N.H.: Moods, emotion episodes, and emotions (1993)
12. Furey, E., Blue, J.: Alexa, emotions, privacy and GDPR. In: Proceedings of the 32nd International BCS Human Computer Interaction Conference, vol. 32, pp. 1–5 (2018)
13. Gund, M., Bharadwaj, A.R., Nwogu, I.: Interpretable emotion classification using temporal convolutional models. In: 2020 25th International Conference on Pattern Recognition (ICPR), pp. 6367–6374. IEEE (2021)

14. H2O.ai: H2O: Scalable Machine Learning Platform, version 3.30.0.6 (2020). http://github.com/h2oai/h2o-3

15. Huang, Y.N., Zhao, S., Rivera, M.L., Hong, J.I., Kraut, R.E.: Predicting well-being using short ecological momentary audio recordings. In: Extended Abstracts of the 2021 CHI Conference on Human Factors in Computing Systems, pp. 1–7 (2021)

16. Hume, D.: Emotions and moods. Organizational behavior (258–297) (2012)

17. Khalil, R.A., Jones, E., Babar, M.I., Jan, T., Zafar, M.H., Alhussain, T.: Speech emotion recognition using deep learning techniques: a review. IEEE Access 7, 117327–117345 (2019)

18. Khwaja, M., Matic, A.: Personality is revealed during weekends: towards data minimisation for smartphone based personality classification. In: Lamas, D., Loizides, F., Nacke, L., Petrie, H., Winckler, M., Zaphiris, P. (eds.) INTERACT 2019. LNCS, vol. 11748, pp. 551–560. Springer, Cham (2019). https://doi.org/10.1007/978-3-030-29387-1_32

19. Ko, B.C.: A brief review of facial emotion recognition based on visual information. Sensors 18(2), 401 (2018)

20. Kornbrot, D.: Point biserial correlation. Wiley StatsRef: Statistics Reference Online (2014)

21. Larson, R., Csikszentmihalyi, M.: The experience sampling method. In: Flow and the Foundations of Positive Psychology, pp. 21–34. Springer, Dordrecht (2014). https://doi.org/10.1007/978-94-017-9088-8_2

22. Lim, J., et al.: Assessing sleep quality using mobile EMAs: opportunities, practical consideration, and challenges. IEEE Access 10, 2063–2076 (2022)

23. Liu, W., Zhang, L., Tao, D., Cheng, J.: Reinforcement online learning for emotion prediction by using physiological signals. Pattern Recognit. Lett. 107, 123–130 (2018). https://doi.org/10.1016/j.patrec.2017.06.004. www.sciencedirect.com/science/article/pii/S0167865517302003

24. Mandi, S., Ghosh, S., De, P., Mitra, B.: Emotion detection from smartphone keyboard interactions: role of temporal vs spectral features. In: Proceedings of the 37th ACM/SIGAPP Symposium on Applied Computing, pp. 677–680 (2022)

25. Mavs: ATOM: A Python package for fast exploration of machine learning pipelines (2019). aTOM version 2.0.3. www.tvdboom.github.io/ATOM/

26. Mehrotra, A., Vermeulen, J., Pejovic, V., Musolesi, M.: Ask, but don't interrupt: the case for interruptibility-aware mobile experience sampling. In: Adjunct Proceedings of the 2015 ACM International Joint Conference on Pervasive and Ubiquitous Computing and Proceedings of the 2015 ACM International Symposium on Wearable Computers, pp. 723–732 (2015)

27. Pejovic, V., Musolesi, M.: Interruptme: designing intelligent prompting mechanisms for pervasive applications. In: Proceedings of the 2014 ACM International Joint Conference on Pervasive and Ubiquitous Computing, pp. 897–908 (2014)

28. Posner, J., Russell, J.A., Peterson, B.S.: The circumplex model of affect: an integrative approach to affective neuroscience, cognitive development, and psychopathology. Dev. Psychopathol. 17(3), 715–734 (2005)

29. Qi, W., Su, H., Aliverti, A.: A smartphone-based adaptive recognition and real-time monitoring system for human activities. IEEE Trans. Hum.-Mach. Syst. 50(5), 414–423 (2020)

30. Rabbi, M., Li, K., Yan, H.Y., Hall, K., Klasnja, P., Murphy, S.: ReVibe: a context-assisted evening recall approach to improve self-report adherence. Proc. ACM Interact. Mob. Wearable Ubiquit. Technol. 3(4), 1–27 (2019)

31. Rasmussen, C.E.: Gaussian processes in machine learning. In: Bousquet, O., von Luxburg, U., Rätsch, G. (eds.) ML -2003. LNCS (LNAI), vol. 3176, pp. 63–71. Springer, Heidelberg (2004). https://doi.org/10.1007/978-3-540-28650-9_4

32. Roth, V., Steinhage, V.: Nonlinear discriminant analysis using kernel functions. In: NIPS, vol. 12, pp. 568–574 (1999)

33. Russell, J.A.: A circumplex model of affect. J. Pers. Soc. Psychol. **39**(6), 1161–1178 (1980)

34. Sarker, I.H., Abushark, Y.B., Khan, A.I.: Contextpca: predicting context-aware smartphone apps usage based on machine learning techniques. Symmetry **12**(4), 499 (2020)

35. Schmidt, P., Reiss, A., Dürichen, R., Laerhoven, K.V.: Wearable-based affect recognition-a review. Sensors **19**(19), 4079 (2019)

36. Schmidt, P., Reiss, A., Dürichen, R., Van Laerhoven, K.: Labelling affective states "in the wild" practical guidelines and lessons learned. In: Proceedings of the 2018 ACM International Joint Conference and 2018 International Symposium on Pervasive and Ubiquitous Computing and Wearable Computers, pp. 654–659 (2018)

37. Schölkopf, B., Smola, A., Müller, K.-R.: Kernel principal component analysis. In: Gerstner, W., Germond, A., Hasler, M., Nicoud, J.-D. (eds.) ICANN 1997. LNCS, vol. 1327, pp. 583–588. Springer, Heidelberg (1997). https://doi.org/10.1007/BFb0020217

38. Sedgwick, P.: Snowball sampling. BMJ **347** (2013)

39. Sepas-Moghaddam, A., Etemad, A., Correia, P.L., Pereira, F.: A deep framework for facial emotion recognition using light field images. In: 2019 8th International Conference on Affective Computing and Intelligent Interaction (ACII), pp. 1–7 (2019). https://doi.org/10.1109/ACII.2019.8925445

40. Shahriar, S., Kim, Y.: Audio-visual emotion forecasting: characterizing and predicting future emotion using deep learning. In: 2019 14th IEEE International Conference on Automatic Face & Gesture Recognition (FG 2019), pp. 1–7. IEEE (2019)

41. Shu, L., et al.: A review of emotion recognition using physiological signals. Sensors **18**(7), 2074 (2018)

42. Suhara, Y., Xu, Y., Pentland, A.: Deepmood: forecasting depressed mood based on self-reported histories via recurrent neural networks. In: Proceedings of the 26th International Conference on World Wide Web, pp. 715–724 (2017)

43. Tashtoush, Y.M., Orabi, D.A.A.A.: Tweets emotion prediction by using fuzzy logic system. In: 2019 Sixth International Conference on Social Networks Analysis, Management and Security (SNAMS), pp. 83–90. IEEE (2019)

44. Varma, S., Simon, R.: Bias in error estimation when using cross-validation for model selection. BMC Bioinform. **7**(1), 1–8 (2006)

45. Weiss, H.M., Cropanzano, R.: Affective events theory. Res. Organ. Behav. **18**(1), 1–74 (1996)

46. Wikipedia contributors: Amazon rekognition – Wikipedia, the free encyclopedia (2021). www.en.wikipedia.org/w/index.php?title=Amazon_Rekognition&oldid=1024901190. Accessed 29 Dec 2021

47. Zhang, X., Li, W., Chen, X., Lu, S.: Moodexplorer: towards compound emotion detection via smartphone sensing. Proc. ACM Interact. Mob. Wearable Ubiquit. Technol. **1**(4), 1–30 (2018)

48. Zhang, Z., Wu, B., Schuller, B.: Attention-augmented end-to-end multi-task learning for emotion prediction from speech. In: ICASSP 2019–2019 IEEE International Conference on Acoustics, Speech and Signal Processing (ICASSP), pp. 6705–6709. IEEE (2019)

Usability and Clinical Evaluation of a Wearable TENS Device for Pain Management in Patients with Osteoarthritis of the Knee

Fatma Layas[1]([✉]) [iD], Billy Woods[2]([✉]) [iD], and Sean Jenkins[1]([✉]) [iD]

[1] Assistive Technologies Innovation Centre, University of Wales Trinity Saint David, Swansea SA1 8PH, UK
{f.layas,sean.jenkins}@uwtsd.ac.uk
[2] Hywel Dda University Health Board, TriTech Institute, Swansea SA14 9TD, UK
billy.wood@wales.nhs.uk

Abstract. An evaluation of the usability and clinical benefits of a Transcutaneous Electrical Nerve Stimulation (TENS) device offered as an adjunct to standard care for thirty patients with Osteoarthritis (OA) of the knee was carried out. A four-stage approach was adopted for this evaluation using a mix of surveys, semi-structured interviews, user diaries, and patient reported outcome measures (PROMS) collected over a three-month period. The findings of the study demonstrate that a combined approach generates a richer picture of patient experience while using a TENS device to manage pain at home. The study also points to how such an approach, that captures insights into the user's experience alongside PROMS can explain the differences between patients who adopt and benefit from these devices and those who do not.

Keywords: Evaluation Methods · Usability Evaluation · Transcutaneous Electrical Nerve Stimulation (TENS)

1 Introduction

Osteoarthritis (OA) of the knee is characterised by damage that causes the joint to become painful and stiff. This typically also causes a reduced range of motion which leads to the joint locking or giving way and muscle weakness [1]. The global prevalence of knee OA is estimated to be 16% in individuals over 15 and 22.9% in individuals aged 40 and over [2]. OA can decrease quality of life and as result increase the use of the health care system [3]. Nonsurgical solutions can be used to treat and manage OA symptoms, however, when symptoms become severe and difficult to manage there are surgical solutions available [4]. Total knee arthroplasty (TKA) is one of the most commonly undertaken and cost-effective musculoskeletal surgical procedures [5].

An index score on the EuroQol five-dimension (EQ-5D) of <0 defines a state 'worse than death' (WTD) [6]. A study to compare TKA waiting list data from ten UK centres (in 2020) against retrospective pre-Covid waiting lists (from 2014 to 2017), showed that 2020 had significantly worse EQ-5D scores and higher rates of patients in a state

J. Abdelnour Nocera et al. (Eds.): INTERACT 2023, LNCS 14142, pp. 641–649, 2023.
https://doi.org/10.1007/978-3-031-42280-5_40

WTD. 80% of this 2020 group felt their quality of life had deteriorated whilst waiting for surgery [7]. Pharmacological solutions for managing pain often come with side effects associated with long term use such as addiction or organ damage, non-pharmacologic solutions utilising technology for pain relief avoid many of these side effects [8].

Transcutaneous Electrical Nerve Stimulation (TENS) is used clinically in a range of scenarios for the reduction, or relief of pain. TENS is a non-invasive modality that is easy to apply with relatively few contraindications. The mechanism behind TENS is that a small electrical impulse is delivered at varying amplitudes and frequencies through the skin using conductive adhesive electrodes. The sensation felt varies between user but most report a 'tingling' sensation as the nerves below the electrode sites receive the electrical impulses [9]. TENS is an intervention that activates selective peripheral nerve fibres to elicit physiological neuromodulation. This translates as an ability to 'block' pain signals in some individuals. While TENS is a recommended treatment in 8 out of 10 guidelines for the management of knee OA [10], a systematic review [11] on physical therapy interventions for patient with knee OA reported a "moderate-quality evidence" on pain relief using TENS. However, a meta-analysis [12] showed a significant decrease in pain for patients with knee OA using TENS. By its very nature TENS offers a relatively temporary pain relief measure [8]. It can help reducing pain intensity during walking and subsequently increases walking function [13]. Previous studies [12–14] showed that the frequency, intensity and continuous use of TENS devices are factors that influence how effective they can be in alleviating pain.

This combined usability and clinical evaluation study presents an opportunity to test a TENS device with patients who are currently awaiting TKA in a real-world clinical setting to help inform a TENS device company's future development of the product and provide insights that may inform new product development opportunities.

2   Evaluation Method

The main goals of this evaluation study were to assess (1) potential clinical benefits; (2) to assess usability and acceptability; (3) and to understand how clinical outcome data relates to user experience for this TENS device. The TENS device used (See Fig. 1) is wearable, battery powered with a rechargeable USB port that has six treatment modes, each with variable intensity. Authors of this paper are independent evaluators, and have no affiliation with the company supplying the device.

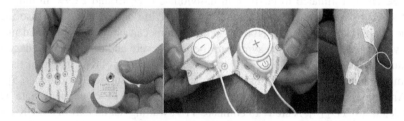

Fig. 1. The TENS device

2.1 Design

This mixed-methods study of patients awaiting TKA, examines the clinical benefits and usability of the TENS device to provide insights that may inform new product development opportunities, and to help better understand how this device could help these patients. A 4-stage research design was adopted. The data collection period in this evaluation was 3 months.

2.2 Participants

A total of 30 patients took part in the study. Participants age range was 51 to 79 years old, with a mean age of 66.8 (SD = 8.1) years old.

Of the 30 participants, 8 participants were excluded because they either submitted incomplete data sets (4 participants) or had early knee surgery (4 participants), which would have introduced bias into the results. This meant a total of 22 (73%) participants completed stage 1 usability survey and 22 (73%) participants completed the clinical outcome survey. However, of the 22 participants who took part in stage 1 only 20 (67%) participants agreed to take part in stage 2 interviews, and of those 14 (47%) patients took part in the series of interviews. A total of 19 (63%) participants completed stage 3 user diaries, this means that at least 4 weeks of data was collected. Finally, 20 (67%) patients took part in the final series of interviews.

2.3 Procedure

Participants were recruited through an NHS, TKA waiting list under clinical guidance of an orthopaedic surgical consultant. The patients were pre-screened by NHS staff, and those deemed suitable were invited to participate. Patients who wanted to take part were invited for an initial consultation. During this consultation, the following aspects were discussed: the aims and rationale of the evaluation, the nature of the evaluation and patients' involvement; patients contact with primary care and their medication relating to their pain; and how to use the TENS device at home. Each patient was given the device and a study folder which contained a consent form and participants' information sheet; a copy of stage 1 surveys; four first class paid envelops to return completed surveys (one for each survey); 12 copies of the user diary (one for each week).

Participants who agreed took part in the follow up interviews, were invited between week 4 and 6 of the trial to do the interview over the phone or via Microsoft Teams.

2.4 Materials

Stage 1 Surveys: This stage consisted of two surveys, as follows:

(1) A usability survey consisting of four main sections (to be completed once): Some demographic questions; Questions around their lifestyle; First impression of the device before first use; and first impression of the device after first use.

(2) A clinical outcomes survey consisting of three main PROMS (Baseline was collected in the initial consultation and then to be completed by participants at the end of each month of the trial): Numerical Rating Scale (NRS), a 10-point Likert scale (0 = No pain at all, and 10 = Worst pain imaginable); EQ-5D-5L, a multi attribute general health questionnaire that can be used to assess a patient's health related quality of life; and KOOS-PS, a self-report questionnaire measures the physical function of the knee. These PROMS are in line with international value-based health recommendations [15].

Stage 2 Interim Interviews: A structured interview followed, comprising of 18 questions. This included questions about: User experience interacting with the device; Look and feel of the device; How helpful the device has been in reducing pain and preforming daily activities; Meeting expectations and satisfaction after long term use; Recommending the device to others; and how different the experience of using this device has been to any other device they might have used previously.

Stage 3 User Diary: The user diary collected data about participants' interaction with the device each week. This included four main sections as follows: Knee pain rating; Use of the device (Frequency of use, mode and intensity level used); Marking the locations of where the device was used on the knee; and Overall experience and satisfaction while using the device.

Stage 4 Final Round of Interviews: A structured interview followed, comprising of 10 questions. This included questions about: Design changes to the device; The device ease of use, how beneficial the device was, and the overall satisfaction of the device; Use of the device (When, where, frequency of use, what would help to use it more); Meeting expectations after long term use; Attitude toward electrical stimulation; and thoughts on whether or not the knee surgery is the only solution that will help with their knee pain.

3 Results

In **stage 1**, the usability survey, participants were asked to rate their overall first impression of the device's packaging (0 = Not pleasing, 10 = Very pleasing). Participants gave a rating mean of 8.7 (SD = 1.5). Results of a one-sample Wilcoxon signed rank test showed that ratings were significantly higher than the neutral midpoint ($W = 3.9$, $p < .001$). The most frequently mentioned reason for participants' ratings were that the device is compact, and small. Participants were asked to rate their experience of unpacking the device (0 = Very difficult, 10 = Very easy). Participants gave a rating mean of 8.1 (SD = 2.2). Ratings were significantly higher than the neutral midpoint ($W = 3.6$, $p < .001$). Most participants have found the device easy to unpack. Only one participant found it difficult to unpack. Participants were asked to rate their overall first impression of the device itself (0 = Not pleasing, 10 = Very pleasing). Participants gave a rating mean of 9.0 (SD = 1.1). Ratings were significantly higher than the neutral midpoint ($W = 4.0$, $p < .001$). Again, participants here commented on how small the device is. Participants also thought the device will be easy to use. Based on their overall first impressions participants were asked to rate their expectations on how the device will help them manage the pain (0 = Very low expectations, 10 = Very high expectations). Participants gave a rating mean of 6.4 (SD = 2.1). Ratings were significantly higher than the neutral midpoint (W = 2.4, p < .05). While the ratings were significantly higher than the neutral, participants' comments were divided between some being hopeful that the device will help them manage the pain, others being more sceptical.

Participants were asked to rate their experience of using the device for the first time (0 = Very difficult, 10 = Very easy). Participants gave a rating mean of 8.4(SD = 1.6). Ratings were significantly higher than the neutral midpoint (W = 4.0, p < .001). Generally, participants experience using the device for the first time was positive. Participants found the device comfortable and easy to use. What participants liked the most about the device was the ease and simplicity of use and the size of the device. Only one participant commented about the charging process being the least favourite thing about the device.

In **stage 2,** 19 of the study participants were interviewed to investigate patients' experiences and perception after long term use. Overall participants had a positive experience using the device. Participants noted that the device was easy to use; simple and user friendly; did not require any physical or mental effort to use it; and was easy and quick to learn how to use it. In addition, all participants were happy with the actual size of the device, its weight, appearance, and the overall quality. All participants thought charging was easy, with many noting that the device hardly needs recharging and that it charges very quickly. Only one participant had an issue with the charging port. Two participants had an issue with the controller bleeping. Participants were asked how they feel now compared to before they started using the device. Overall, 8 participants thought the device helped them manage their knee pain. Some participants said that they were sleeping better (particularly those who used it in the evening); were not using painkillers as much; and a few noticed that there was less swelling around the knee. However, 5 participants did not notice any difference between now and before starting using the device. A few participants thought this could be due to the nature or the severity of their pain. Two participants noted that the pain relief is very temporary after using the device. Participants were asked to describe how helpful the device has been in reducing the pain. Interestingly, 12 participants thought that they noted a general reduction in pain. However, of those, two participants thought that the effectiveness of the device reduced after the first month of use. Only two participants did not notice any reduction in pain. Nonetheless, when participants were asked if the device has helped with walking, only 6 participants reported a noticeable effect. Three participants were not sure if the device had helped with walking, and 5 participants did not notice any effect. Similarly, when participants were asked whether the device had helped them to perform their day-to-day tasks more easily, only 5 participants noticed any changes. Most participants felt that the device had not helped with completing the tasks more easily or more quickly. Overall, participants thought the device had meet their expectations of managing the Pain. Only two participants thought that the device had not achieved everything they expected it to do. Four participants thought the device had not been beneficial for them while waiting for the surgery. All the other participants thought the device has been beneficial for them while waiting for the surgery. Participants perception after long term use, is that the device was pleasant to use (unless the intensity level was set too high); they felt comfortable and confident in using the device; and they felt safe in using the device. What participants liked the most about the device was the ease of use (11 Participants); the compact size (9 Participants); simple to use (6 Participants); discreet (4 Participants); good quality (2 Participants); portability (2 Participants); light weight (2 Participants); ease of storage (2 Participants); holding charge (2 Participants); and ease of charging (1 Participant). All participants said that they would recommend the device to friends and family members who might need it. Six participants said that they have already recommended the device for others to use.

In **stage 3** of the study, participants who completed less than 4 weeks of their user diary sheets were excluded from the analysis. Generally, participants were happy about the device, and they thought the device was easy to use; compact; simple to use; user friendly; comfortable; easy to store; charges well; soothing; relaxing; light weight; not time consuming. Interestingly, 4 of the participants who completed the 12-week diaries, noted that the device easily became part of their daily routines. However, five participants reported that they did not use the device as much during the holiday season (during Christmas), as they kept forgetting to use the device because they were busy with guests. One participant, commented on how it is difficult to hear the beeps to change between different moods or intensities. Two participants, noted that it was challenging for them to know what mode and intensity level they should use, as well as, how long the electrodes should be on their knee. Lastly, in regards of pain reduction, 4 participants noted a temporary relief. 11 participants noted no real difference during the trial. However, even though participants said that the device did not reduce the pain some of them noted that the device helped in other ways, for example, knee is not so stiff; walking with less of a limp; help with the bruises; colour of the knee is better; better circulation; help with the knee and ankle swelling; sleep better; and less cramp. Five participants thought the device did help reduce pain. Participants were asked to indicate where they were placing the electrodes for each use. Figure 2 shows the most frequent pad placement.

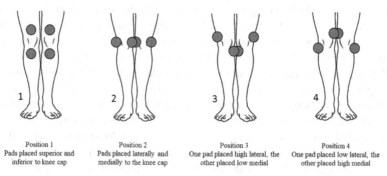

Position 1	Position 2	Position 3	Position 4
Pads placed superior and inferior to knee cap	Pads placed laterally and medially to the knee cap	One pad placed high lateral, the other placed low medial	One pad placed low lateral, the other placed high medial

Fig. 2. Pad placement diagram for both left and right leg

In **stage 4,** the final round of interviews, participants were asked what they would change about the device and why. Participants thoughts on this question were consistent with their thoughts during previous stages. Most participants said that they would not change anything about the device. Only two participants commented on how they initially found the charging port a bit fiddly. Another two participants noted that the device beeps were quite loud, and that visual cue would help them keep track of the settings. Based on their long-term use participants were asked to rate the ease of use of the device (0 = difficult to use, 10 = very easy to use). Participants gave a rating mean of 8.8 (SD = 1.4). Ratings were significantly higher than the neutral midpoint (W = 3.9, $p < .001$).

Participants were also asked to rate how beneficial the device was while waiting for the surgery (0 = not at all beneficial, 10 = very beneficial). Participants gave a rating mean of 4.2 (SD = 3.4). Ratings were not significantly different to the neutral midpoint (W = $-1.1, p > .05$). Lastly, participants were asked to rate how satisfied they are with the device (0 = not at all satisfied, 10 = very satisfied). Participants gave a rating mean of 7 (SD = 2.3). Ratings were significantly different to the neutral midpoint (W = $-2.4, p < .05$). On average participants used the device once or twice a day throughout the trial. Participants were asked what would have helped them to use the device more often. 8 participants said that they would have used it more often if it was effective, and 4 participants said that being busy with work lead to less frequency of use. Participants were also asked if they think this kind of technology can be beneficial to patients who are suffering with OA knee pain. On 5-point Likert scale, participants gave a rating mean of 4.4 (SD = 0.9). Ratings were significantly different to the neutral midpoint (W = 3.5, $p < .001$). They were also asked if they think that knee replacement is the only real solution to the pain associated with OA. On 5-point Likert scale, participants gave a rating mean of 4.1 (SD = 0.9). Ratings were significantly different to the neutral midpoint (W = 3.3, $p < .001$).

To assess any potential clinical benefits of the device a series of Wilcoxon Signed Rank tests were conducted for all three clinical measures (Pain NRS, EQ-5D and KOOS-PS). For the whole group of participants, the results indicated that there was no significant difference in pain NRS score (W = $101.5, p > .1$); there was an increase of KOOS-PS scores (W = $153.0, p < .05$) indicating a decrease in knee function; and EQ-5D scores indicated a worsening quality of life (W = $57.5, p < .05$). However, when splitting participants into two groups (11 participants in each) based on the frequency of use as per the user diary, participants in the 'least' use group had a worsening of KOOS-PS scores (W = $52, p < .01$), whereas participants in the 'most' use group did not (W = $25, p > .0.5$). There was no significant difference in pain NRS and EQ-5D scores in the split groups. Improved sleep, reduced swelling and more confidence in daily activities were positive factors reported by participants in the 'most' group during the study, but not the 'least' group.

Pearson's coefficient tests were conducted to understand how clinical outcome data relates to the device's usability and user experience data. Results showed a positive correlation between change in EQ-5D score and the final device satisfaction score ($r = 0.48, p < .05$). EQ-5D score also positively correlated with the device's benefit score ($r = 0.5, p < .05$). There was a negative correlation between early device satisfaction score and change in pain NRS scores ($r = -0.6, p < .05$). This indicates that participants who gave a higher rating on the early satisfaction question were also more likely to report a reduction in pain at the end of the study. In addition, change in pain NRS score negatively correlated with the total number of uses ($r = -0.46, p < .05$). This indicates that more frequent device use has a relationship with the reduction in pain scores and overall benefits felt by the participants. Early and final satisfaction scores were positively correlated with the device benefit score ($r = 0.92, p < .0001$) and ($r = 0.71, p < .0001$) respectively. No correlation was found between KOOS-PS scores and any of the clinical outcomes or the usability and user experience data.

4   Discussion and Conclusions

This study sought to examine the clinical befits and usability of a TENS Device. A 4-stage research design was adopted, and a total of 30 patients with orthopaedic knee pain took part in the study.

Overall, the results of the study showed that there were no significant design issues or difficulties encountered during the use of the device. The devices' form factor and usability were good. However, in term of the effectiveness of the device in managing pain, participants' comments were not consistent. For example, only 8 participants thought the device has helped them managing the pain, but 12 participants thought that they noted a general reduction in pain. of those, only 6 participants reported a noticeable effect in walking and only 5 participants reported a noticeable effect in preforming day-to-day tasks. Nonetheless, when participants were asked if they would recommend the device to a friend or a family member who might need it, they all said yes. In fact, some of them had already recommended the device to others. In addition, their rating on how satisfied they were with the device were positively above the midpoint of the scale. Whereas their ratings on how beneficial the device was for them while waiting for the surgery were neutral. There was no change in pain scores from baseline to end of the trial, whereas there was a significant decrease in quality of life and knee function difficulty scores. On this basis it could be concluded that, overall, this group of patients are degenerating whilst waiting for surgery and the device is ineffective.

However, by splitting the cohort by 'most' and 'least' total device uses; the 'least' use group had a worsening of KOOS-PS scores whereas the 'most' group did not. Improved sleep, reduced swelling and more confidence in daily activities were only reported by participants in the 'most' group. Without the user feedback collected as part of the usability evaluation we would not have observed the variance in use across the cohort. As result we would not have been able to split the group in this way and would have not gained the insight as to why there was a difference in the 'most' and 'least' groups with KOOS-PS group scores. The physiological response from a TENS device could not have altered the underlying osteoarthritis of the knee, but increased exercise may have helped the participants knee function scores [13]. While monitoring of pain, EQ-5D and KOOS-PS for patient outcomes in osteoarthritis of the knee is recommended by ICHOM [15], this study has provided some evidence that monitoring activity levels and sleep may give more insights into the potential benefits of TENS devices for osteoarthritis.

Finally, there are some limitations with this study arising from the relatively small sample size and the lack of a control group, so the findings need to be treated very cautiously.

References

1. Sharma, L.: Osteoarthritis of the knee. N. Engl. J. Med. **384**(1), 51–59 (2021)
2. Cui, A., Li, H., Wang, D., Zhong, J., Chen, Y., Lu, H.: Global, regional prevalence, incidence and risk factors of knee osteoarthritis in population-based studies. EClinicalMedicine. **1**(29), 100587 (2020)
3. Rosemann, T., Grol, R., Herman, K., Wensing, M., Szecsenyi, J.: Association between obesity, quality of life, physical activity and health service utilization in primary care patients with osteoarthritis. Int. J. Behav. Nutr. Phys. Act. **5**(1), 1–8 (2008)
4. Lützner, J., Kasten, P., Günther, K.P., Kirschner, S.: Surgical options for patients with osteoarthritis of the knee. Nat. Rev. Rheumatol. **5**(6), 309–316 (2009)
5. Price, A.J., et al.: Knee replacement. The Lancet. **392**(10158), 1672–1682 (2018)
6. Scott, C.H., MacDonald, D.J., Howie, C.R.: 'Worse than death' and waiting for a joint arthroplasty. Bone Joint J. **101**(8), 941–950 (2019)
7. Clement, N.D., Scott, C.E., Murray, J.R., Howie, C.R., Deehan, D.J.: IMPACT-Restart Collaboration. The number of patients "worse than death" while waiting for a hip or knee arthroplasty has nearly doubled during the COVID-19 pandemic: A UK nationwide survey. Bone Joint J. **103**(4), 672–80 (2021)
8. Johnson, M.I.: Resolving long-standing uncertainty about the clinical efficacy of transcutaneous electrical nerve stimulation (TENS) to relieve pain: a comprehensive review of factors influencing outcome. Medicina **57**(4), 378 (2021)
9. Sluka, K.A., Walsh, D.: Transcutaneous electrical nerve stimulation: basic science mechanisms and clinical effectiveness. J. Pain **4**(3), 109–121 (2003)
10. Zhang, W., et al.: OARSI recommendations for the management of hip and knee osteoarthritis, Part II: OARSI evidence-based, expert consensus guidelines. Osteoarthr. Cartil. **16**(2), 137–162 (2008)
11. Jamtvedt, G., et al.: Physical therapy interventions for patients with osteoarthritis of the knee: an overview of systematic reviews. Phys. Ther. **88**(1), 123–136 (2008)
12. Bjordal, J.M., Johnson, M.I., Ljunggreen, A.E.: Transcutaneous electrical nerve stimulation (TENS) can reduce postoperative analgesic consumption. A meta-analysis with assessment of optimal treatment parameters for postoperative pain. Eur. J. Pain **7**(2), 181–188 (2003)
13. Rakel, B., Frantz, R.: Effectiveness of transcutaneous electrical nerve stimulation on postoperative pain with movement. J. Pain **4**(8), 455–464 (2003)
14. Li, L., Au, W.M., Li, Y., Wan, K.M., Wan, S.H., Wong, K.S.: Design of intelligent garment with transcutaneous electrical nerve stimulation function based on the intarsia knitting technique. Text. Res. J. **80**(3), 279–286 (2010)
15. International consortium for health outcomes measurement (ICHOM): Hip & Knee Osteoarthritis; Patient-Centred Outcome Measures. Version 4.0.0 (2022). Accessed Jan 2022

Author Index

A

Abdelrahman, Yomna 359
Abdrabou, Yasmeen 359
Ahmed, Faizan 416
Ajayi, Opeyemi Dele 369
Albuquerque Santos, Pedro 587
Alese, Boniface Kayode 369
Alkhathlan, Mallak 224
Alt, Florian 359
Aromaa, Susanna 297
Asbeck, Marco 359
Ashok, Ashwin 349
Avouris, Nikolaos 426

B

Bailly, Charles 3
Bates, Matthew 317
Belloum, Rafik 349
Beltrão, Gabriela 379
Bhatnagar, Tigmanshu 67
Blanchard-Dauphin, Anne 155
Bødker, Susanne 275
Bonaccorso, Simona 501
Branig, Meinhardt 563
Bressa, Nathalie 275
Buffa, Michel 101

C

Caeiro, Carmen 587
Cairns, Paul 89
Castet, Julien 3
Cook, Glenda 165
Correia, Nuno 307

D

Dancu, Alexandru 469, 479
de Almeida Souza, Maurício Ronny 135
de Oliveira, Káthia Marçal 155, 349
De, Pradipta 620
Degbelo, Auriol 416
DeHaven, Triskal 89

Delcroix, Véronique 155
Diab, Isam 176
Drobnjak, Ivana 598

E

Eriksson, Eva 275

F

Farzand, Habiba 501
Fasae, Kemi 369
Ferreira, Hugo 587
Ferreira, Simone Bacellar Leal 135
Fidas, Christos 426
Freire, André Pimenta 135
Frier, William 43

G

Gafert, Michael 573
Gentile, Vito 501
Ghosh, Surjya 620
Goncalves, Jorge 20
González, Álvaro 176
Greenfield, Julia 155
Grisoni, Laurent 469, 479
Guo, Hanyu 123

H

Hassib, Mariam 359
Heikkilä, Päivi 297
Holloway, Catherine 67
Holmquist, Lars Erik 165

I

Inal, Yavuz 111, 339
Ivrissimtzis, Ioannis 459

J

Jain, Mohit 201
Jamalzadeh, Milad 469, 479
Jenkins, Sean 641

Johansen, Stine S. 247
Joshi, Anirudha 436, 546

K

Kelly, John 598
Kerr, Oliver 317
Khamis, Mohamed 501
Khetrapal, Pramit 598
Kjeldskov, Jesper 247
Klokmose, Clemens N. 275
Kolski, Christophe 155
Kumar, Pratyush 201
Kurzweg, Marco 391, 523

L

Lamas, David 379
Lammi, Hanna 297
Layas, Fatma 641
Lepreux, Sophie 155
Letter, Maximilian 391, 523
Li, Zhaoxing 459
Lin, Weiyue 123
Linke, Simon 523
Liu, Yuhan 123
Lochrie, Mark 317
Luo, Yalan 123

M

Macík, Miroslav 563
Maffra, Sergio Alvares 43
Malizia, Alessio 501
Mandi, Salma 620
Marquardt, Nicolai 67
Mateus, Delvani Antônio 135
Mavrikis, Manolis 598
May, Lloyd 101
Miodownik, Mark 67
Mitra, Bivas 620
Muralidhar, Deepa 349
Murtinger, Markus 573

N

Nave, Carla 307
Neate, Timothy 43
Neves Madeira, Rui 587
Nicholson, James 369
Nie, Xiaomei 123
Nielsen, Peter Axel 247
Nunes, Francisco 307

O

Opie, Jeremy 598

P

Papadoulis, Georgios 426
Peeters, Dennis 416
Pfeuffer, Ken 359
Poddar, Roshni 201
Pometti, Lucas 3
Power, Christopher 89
Priya, Khyati 436

Q

Qian, Xiang 123

R

Rakovic, Ivana 339
Ranasinghe, Champika 416
Rao, P. V. Madhusudhan 67
Regal, Georg 573
Rekik, Yosra 469, 479
Rivero-Espinosa, Jesica 176
Rocchesso, Davide 501
Rogers, Yvonne 598
Romão, Teresa 307
Rundensteiner, Elke A. 224

S

Salai, Ana-Maria 165
Schmidt, Albrecht 523
Shi, Lei 459
Sim, Gavin 317
Sintoris, Christos 426
Sorce, Salvatore 501
Sousa, Sonia 379
Sridhar, Advaith 201
Stec, Kashmiri 247
Suárez-Figueroa, Mari Carmen 176

T

Timinis, Constantinos 598
Tlachac, M. L. 224
Torkildsby, Anne Britt 111
Tscheligi, Manfred 573

U

Uhl, Jakob Carl 573
Upadhyay, Vikas 67

V
Vatavu, Radu-Daniel   469
Vidal-Mazuy, Antoine   101
Volpe, Gualtiero   469

W
Waghwase, Atish   546
Wang, Jindi   459
Watt, Simon   598
Weiss, Yannick   523
Wilson, Stephanie   43
Winckler, Marco   101

Wolf, Katrin   391, 523
Woods, Billy   641
Wu, Zhiqing   20

Y
You, Zihao   43
Yu, Difeng   20

Z
Zhou, Yunzhan   459
Zubair, Misbahu S.   317

Printed in the United States
by Baker & Taylor Publisher Services